PRISON SCHOOL

AKIRA HI

7

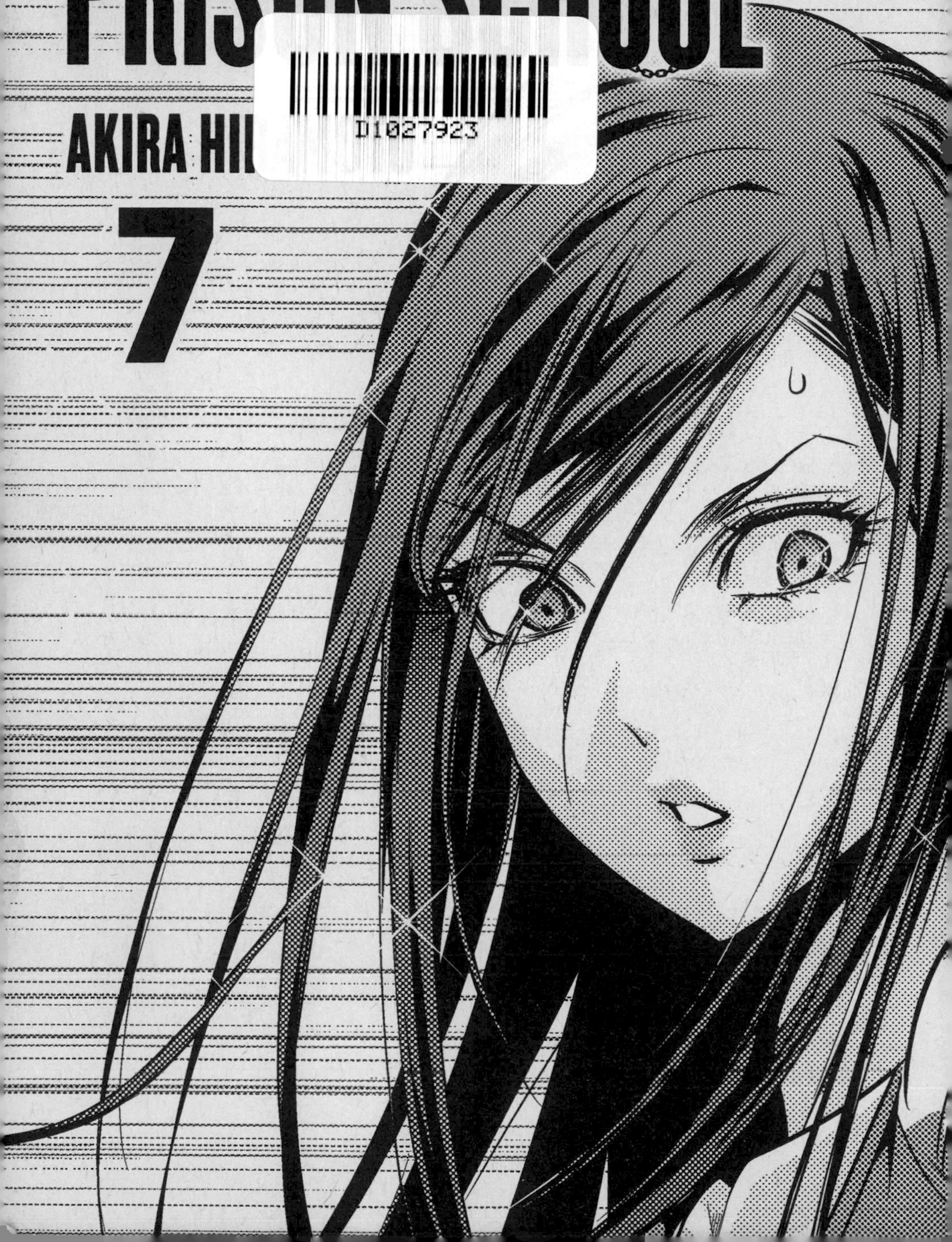

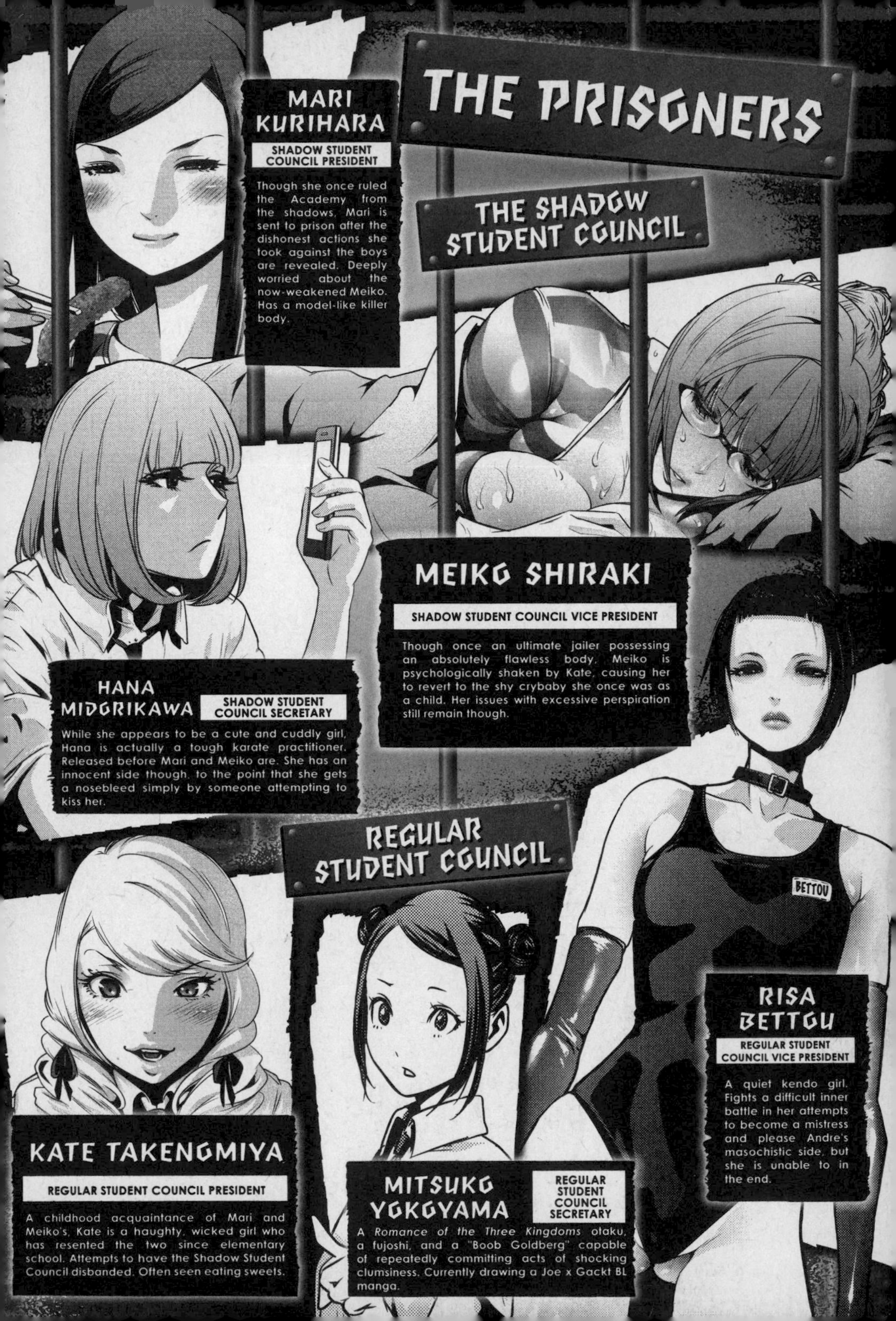
THE PRISONERS
THE SHADOW STUDENT COUNCIL
MARI KURIHARA
SHADOW STUDENT COUNCIL PRESIDENT
Though she once ruled the Academy from the shadows, Mari is sent to prison after the dishonest actions she took against the boys are revealed. Deeply worried about the now-weakened Meiko. Has a model-like killer body.
MEIKO SHIRAKI
SHADOW STUDENT COUNCIL VICE PRESIDENT
Though once an ultimate jailer possessing an absolutely flawless body, Meiko is psychologically shaken by Kate, causing her to revert to the shy crybaby she once was as a child. Her issues with excessive perspiration still remain though.
HANA MIDORIKAWA
SHADOW STUDENT COUNCIL SECRETARY
While she appears to be a cute and cuddly girl, Hana is actually a tough karate practitioner. Released before Mari and Meiko are. She has an innocent side though, to the point that she gets a nosebleed simply by someone attempting to kiss her.
REGULAR STUDENT COUNCIL
BETTOU
KATE TAKENOMIYA
REGULAR STUDENT COUNCIL PRESIDENT
A childhood acquaintance of Mari and Meiko's, Kate is a haughty, wicked girl who has resented the two since elementary school. Attempts to have the Shadow Student Council disbanded. Often seen eating sweets.
MITSUKO YOKOYAMA
REGULAR STUDENT COUNCIL SECRETARY
A *Romance of the Three Kingdoms* otaku, a fujoshi, and a "Boob Goldberg" capable of repeatedly committing acts of shocking clumsiness. Currently drawing a Joe x Gackt BL manga.
RISA BETTOU
REGULAR STUDENT COUNCIL VICE PRESIDENT
A quiet kendo girl. Fights a difficult inner battle in her attempts to become a mistress and please Andre's masochistic side, but she is unable to in the end.

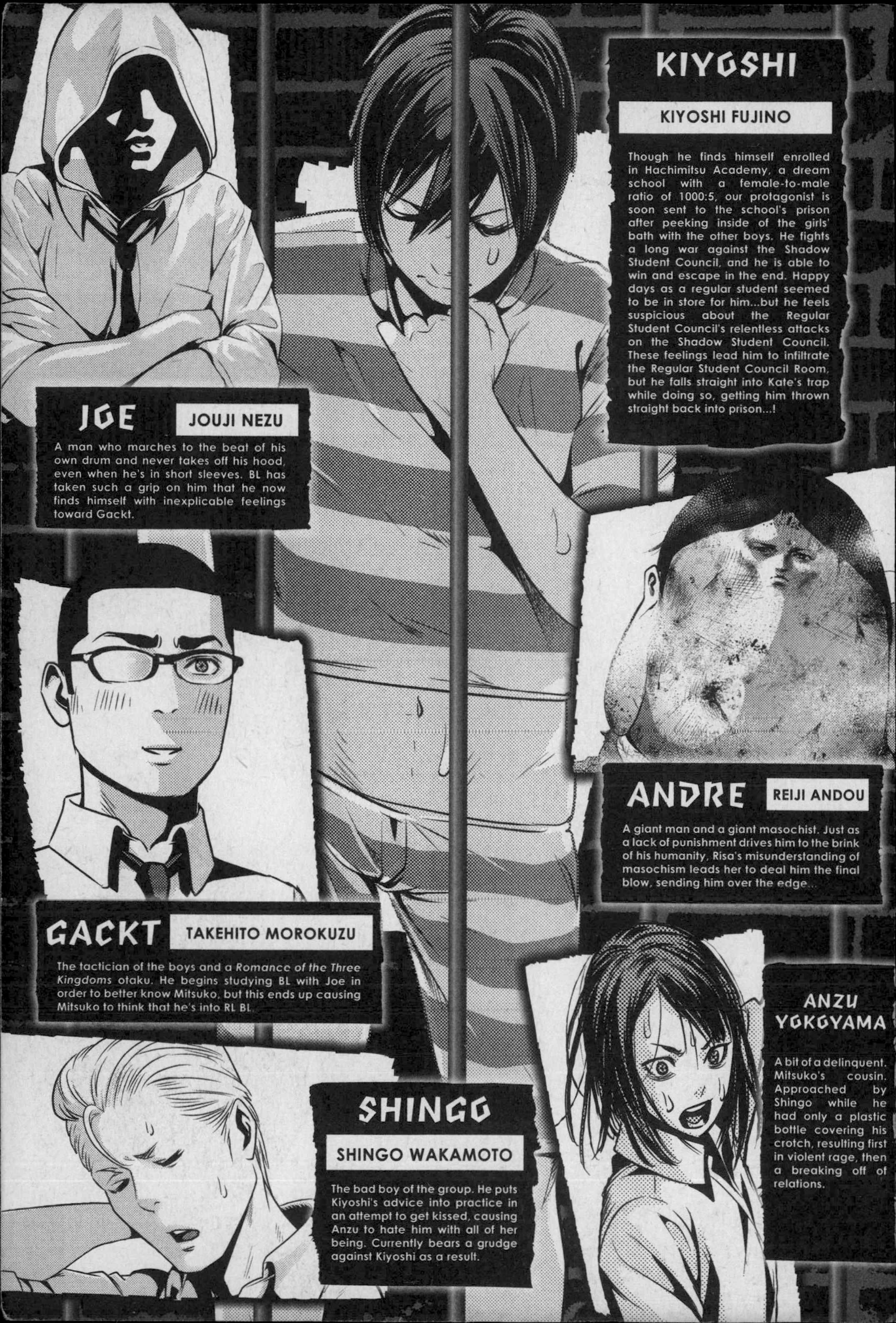
KIYOSHI
KIYOSHI FUJINO
Though he finds himself enrolled in Hachimitsu Academy, a dream school with a female-to-male ratio of 1000:5, our protagonist is soon sent to the school's prison after peeking inside of the girls' bath with the other boys. He fights a long war against the Shadow Student Council, and he is able to win and escape in the end. Happy days as a regular student seemed to be in store for him...but he feels suspicious about the Regular Student Council's relentless attacks on the Shadow Student Council. These feelings lead him to infiltrate the Regular Student Council Room, but he falls straight into Kate's trap while doing so, getting him thrown straight back into prison...!
JOE
JOUJI NEZU
A man who marches to the beat of his own drum and never takes off his hood, even when he's in short sleeves. BL has taken such a grip on him that he now finds himself with inexplicable feelings toward Gackt.
ANDRE
REIJI ANDOU
A giant man and a giant masochist. Just as a lack of punishment drives him to the brink of his humanity, Risa's misunderstanding of masochism leads her to deal him the final blow, sending him over the edge...
GACKT
TAKEHITO MOROKUZU
The tactician of the boys and a *Romance of the Three Kingdoms* otaku. He begins studying BL with Joe in order to better know Mitsuko, but this ends up causing Mitsuko to think that he's into RL BL.
ANZU YOKOYAMA
A bit of a delinquent. Mitsuko's cousin. Approached by Shingo while he had only a plastic bottle covering his crotch, resulting first in violent rage, then a breaking off of relations.
SHINGO
SHINGO WAKAMOTO
The bad boy of the group. He puts Kiyoshi's advice into practice in an attempt to get kissed, causing Anzu to hate him with all of her being. Currently bears a grudge against Kiyoshi as a result.

CONTENTS

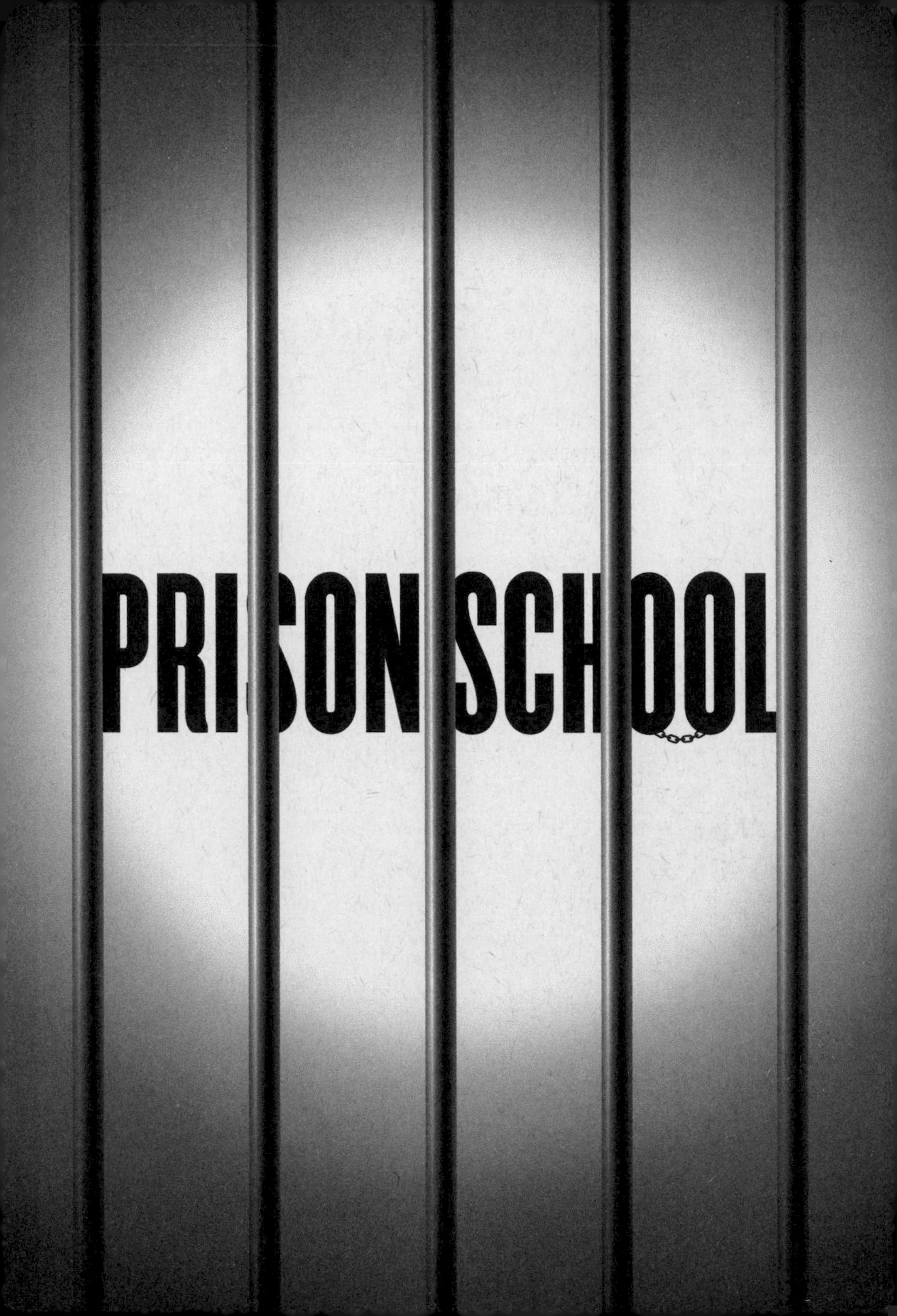
PRISON SCHOOL

CHAPTER 119: HIGH AND LOW

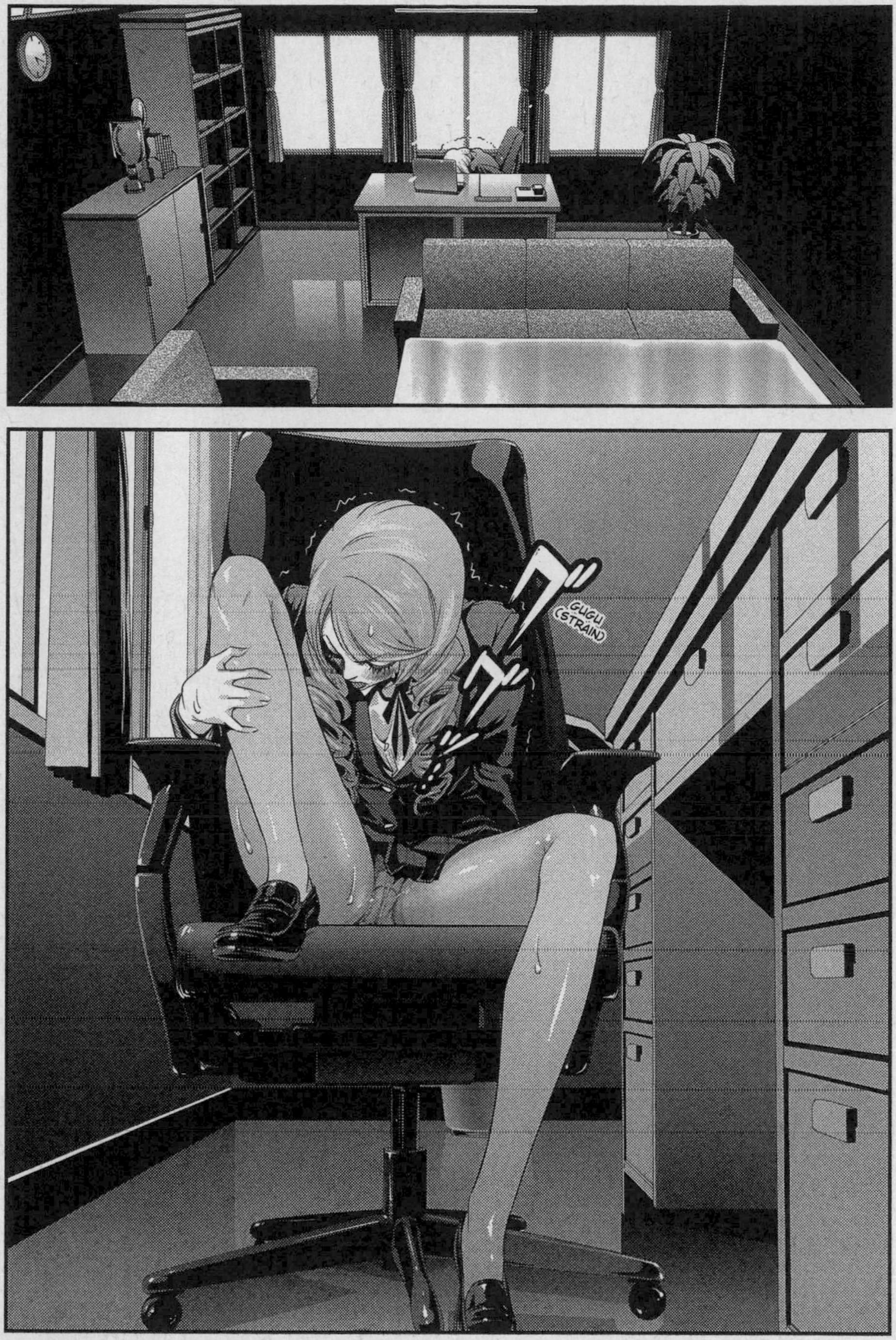
GUGU (STRAIN)

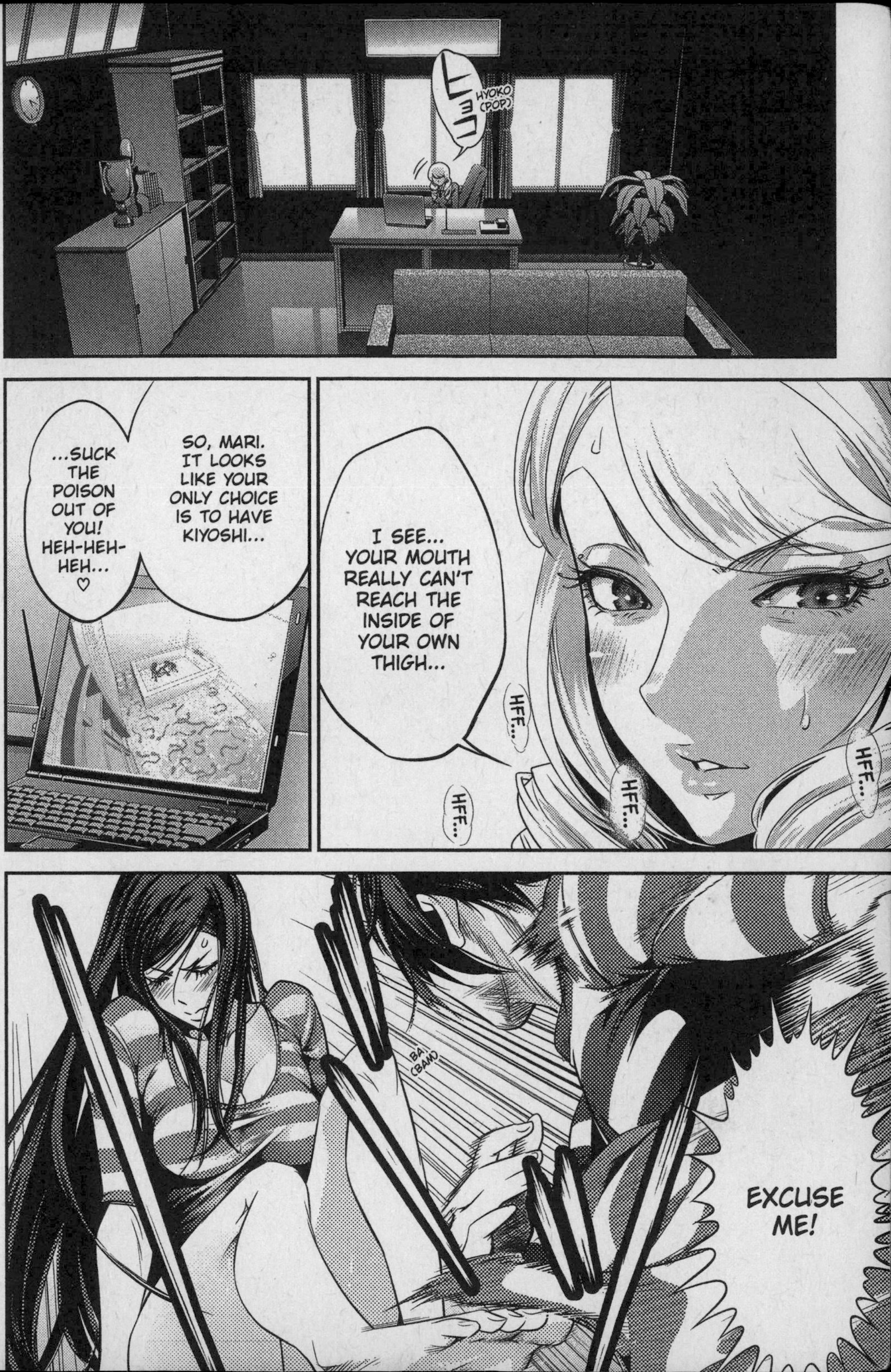
HYOKO (POP)
I SEE... YOUR MOUTH REALLY CAN'T REACH THE INSIDE OF YOUR OWN THIGH...
HFF...
HFF...
HFF...
HFF...
SO, MARI. IT LOOKS LIKE YOUR ONLY CHOICE IS TO HAVE KIYOSHI...
...SUCK THE POISON OUT OF YOU! HEH-HEH-HEH... ♡
EXCUSE ME!
BA (BAM)

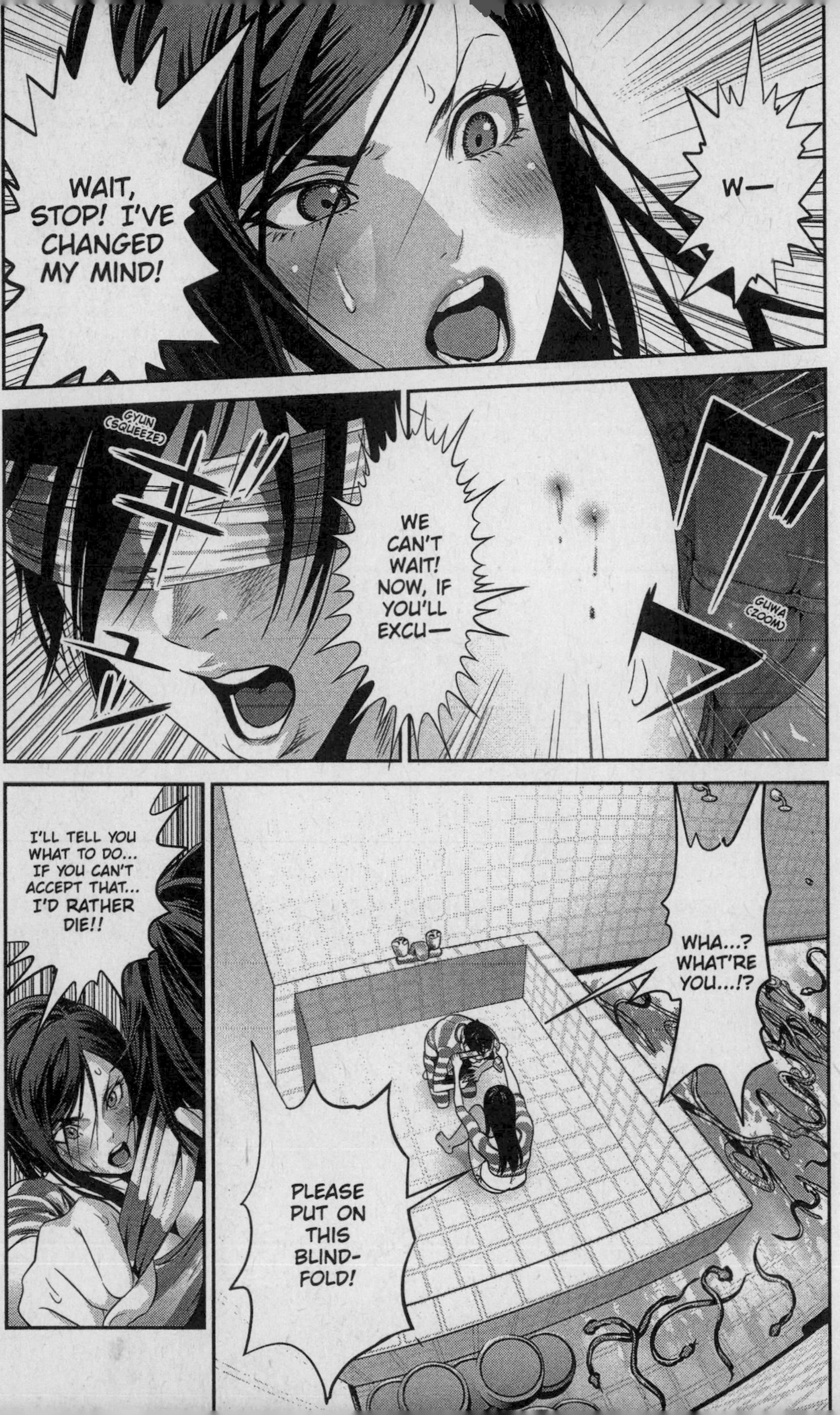
W—
WAIT, STOP! I'VE CHANGED MY MIND!
GUWA (ZOOM)
WE CAN'T WAIT! NOW, IF YOU'LL EXCU—
GYUN (SQUEEZE)
WHA...? WHAT'RE YOU...!?
PLEASE PUT ON THIS BLIND-FOLD!
I'LL TELL YOU WHAT TO DO... IF YOU CAN'T ACCEPT THAT... I'D RATHER DIE!!

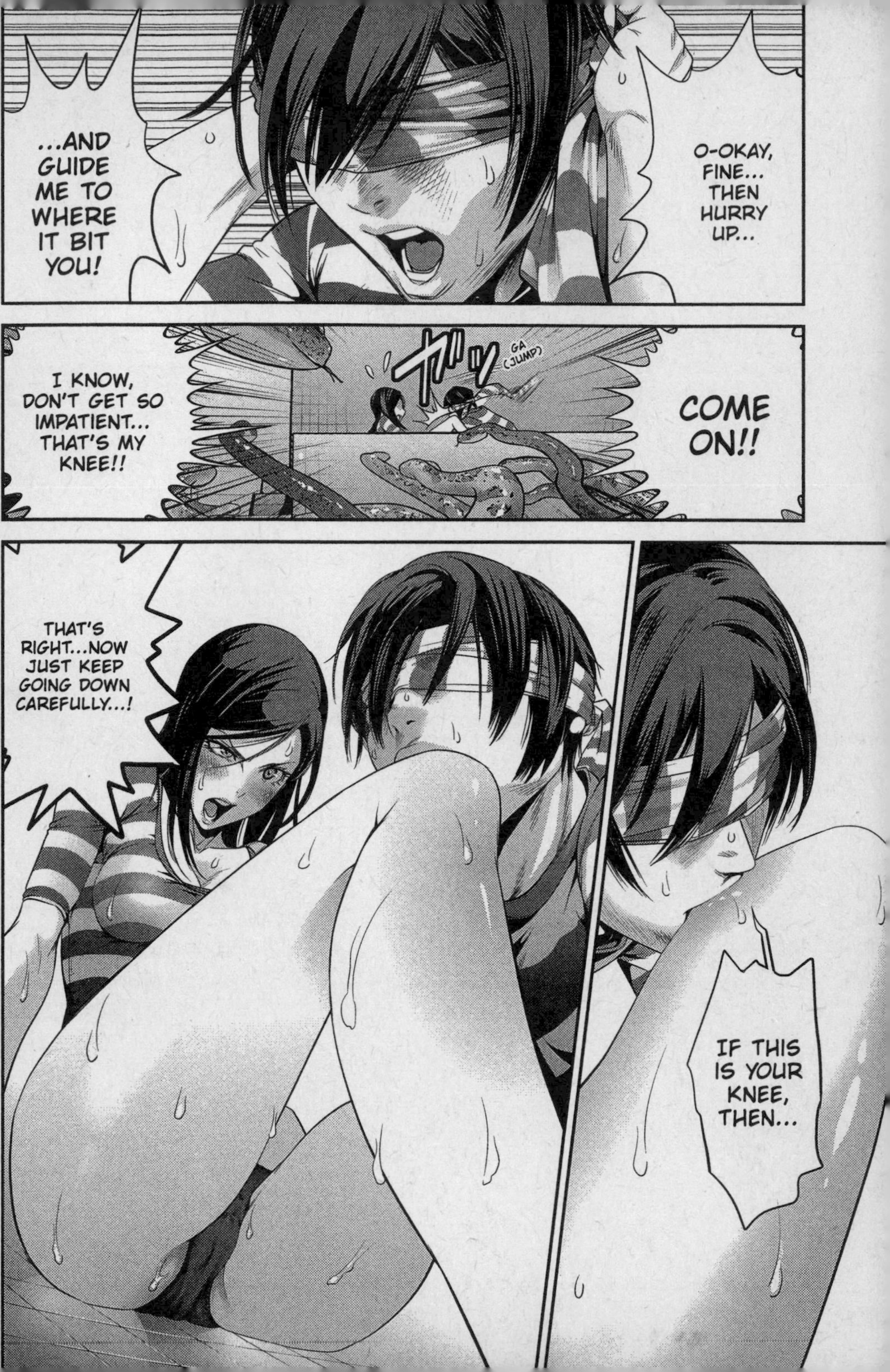
O-OKAY, FINE... THEN HURRY UP...
...AND GUIDE ME TO WHERE IT BIT YOU!
COME ON!!
GA (JUMP)
I KNOW, DON'T GET SO IMPATIENT... THAT'S MY KNEE!!
IF THIS IS YOUR KNEE, THEN...
THAT'S RIGHT...NOW JUST KEEP GOING DOWN CAREFULLY...!

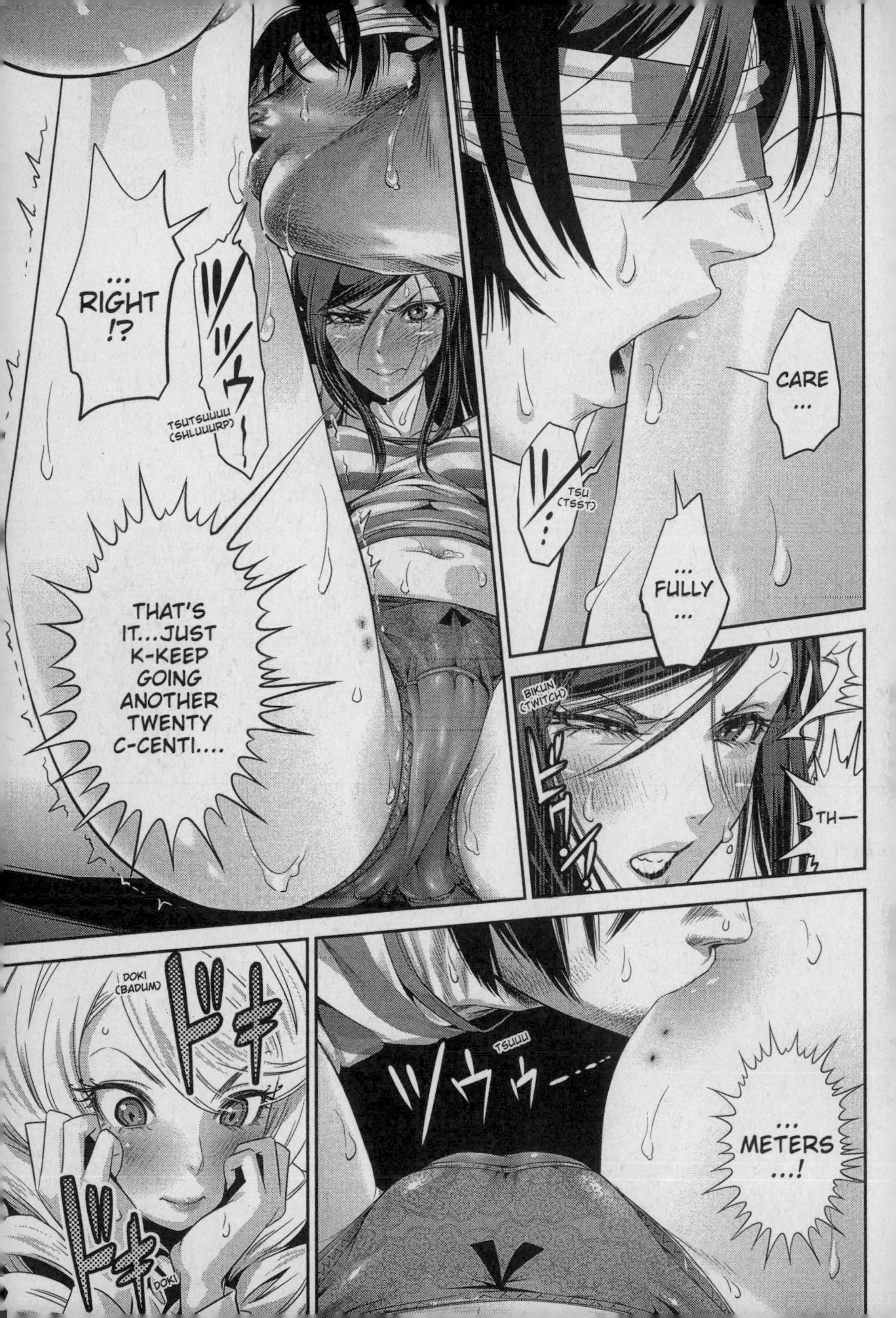
CARE ...
TSU (TSST)
... FULLY ...
... RIGHT !?
TSUTSUUUU (SHLUUURP)
THAT'S IT...JUST K-KEEP GOING ANOTHER TWENTY C-CENTI....
BIKUN (TWITCH)
TH—
TSUUU
... METERS ...!
DOKI (BADUM)
ドキ
ドキ
DOKI

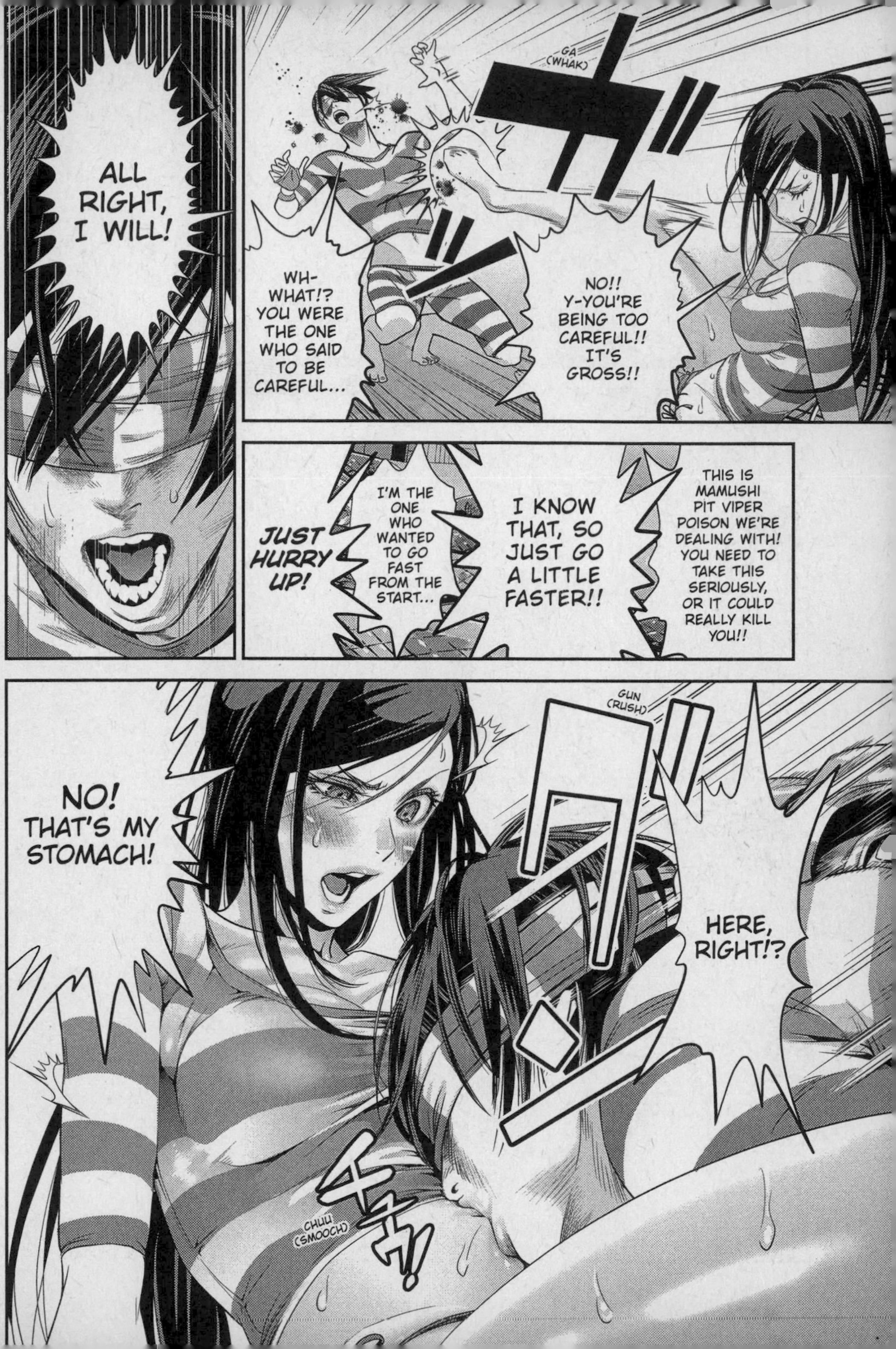
GA (WHAK)
NO!! Y-YOU'RE BEING TOO CAREFUL!! IT'S GROSS!!
WH-WHAT!? YOU WERE THE ONE WHO SAID TO BE CAREFUL...
THIS IS MAMUSHI PIT VIPER POISON WE'RE DEALING WITH! YOU NEED TO TAKE THIS SERIOUSLY, OR IT COULD REALLY KILL YOU!!
I KNOW THAT, SO JUST GO A LITTLE FASTER!!
I'M THE ONE WHO WANTED TO GO FAST FROM THE START...
JUST HURRY UP!
ALL RIGHT, I WILL!
GUN (RUSH)
HERE, RIGHT!?
NO! THAT'S MY STOMACH!
CHUU (SMOOCH)

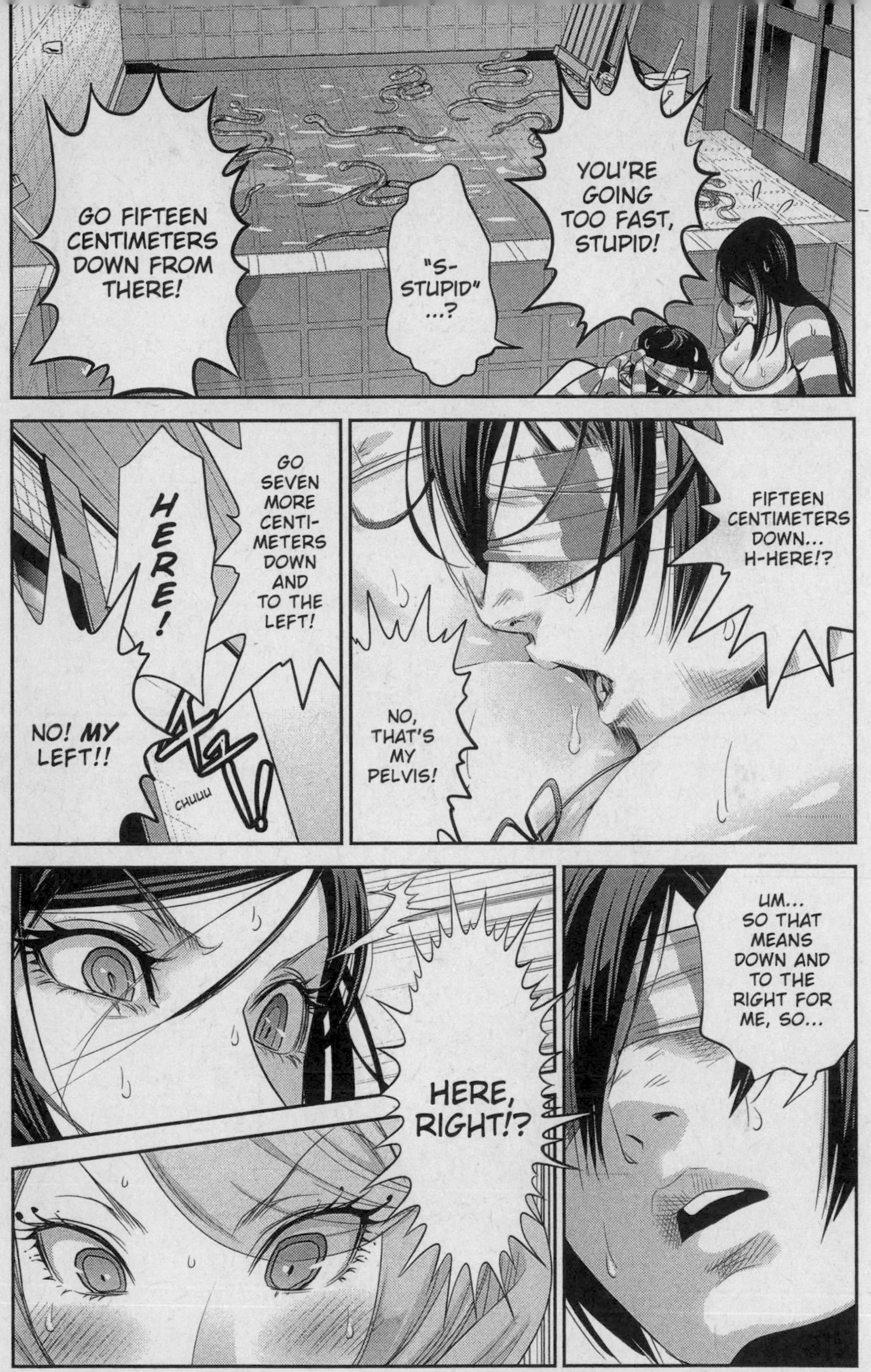
YOU'RE GOING TOO FAST, STUPID!
"S-STUPID" ...?
GO FIFTEEN CENTIMETERS DOWN FROM THERE!
FIFTEEN CENTIMETERS DOWN... H-HERE!?
NO, THAT'S MY PELVIS!
GO SEVEN MORE CENTI-METERS DOWN AND TO THE LEFT!
HERE!
CHUUU
NO! MY LEFT!!
UM... SO THAT MEANS DOWN AND TO THE RIGHT FOR ME, SO...
HERE, RIGHT!?

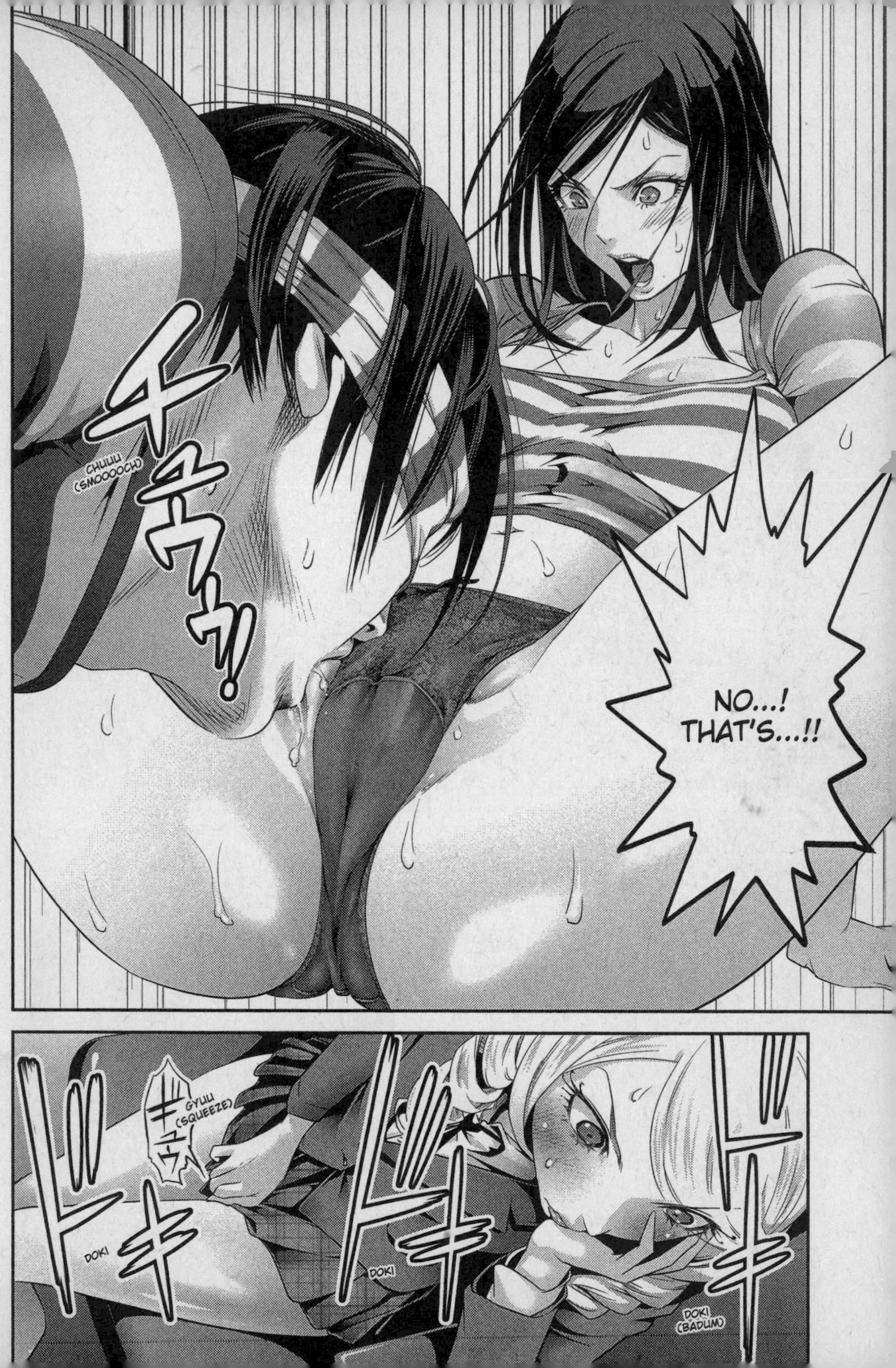
NO...! THAT'S...!!
CHUUU (SMOOOOCH)
DOKI (BADUM)
DOKI
GYUU (SQUEEZE)
DOKI

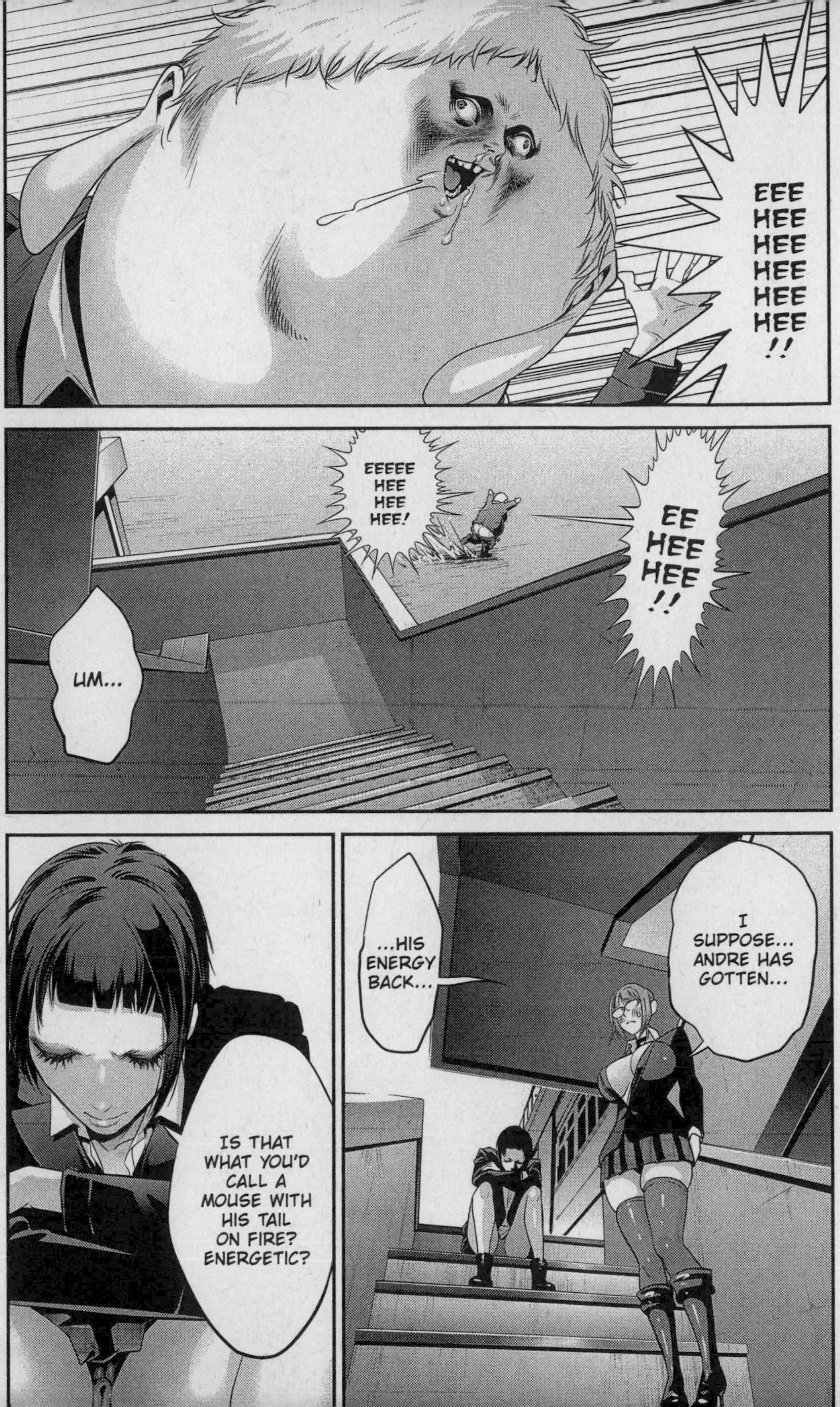
EEE HEE HEE HEE HEE HEE!!
EEEEE HEE HEE HEE!
EE HEE HEE!!
UM...
I SUPPOSE... ANDRE HAS GOTTEN...
...HIS ENERGY BACK...
IS THAT WHAT YOU'D CALL A MOUSE WITH HIS TAIL ON FIRE? ENERGETIC?

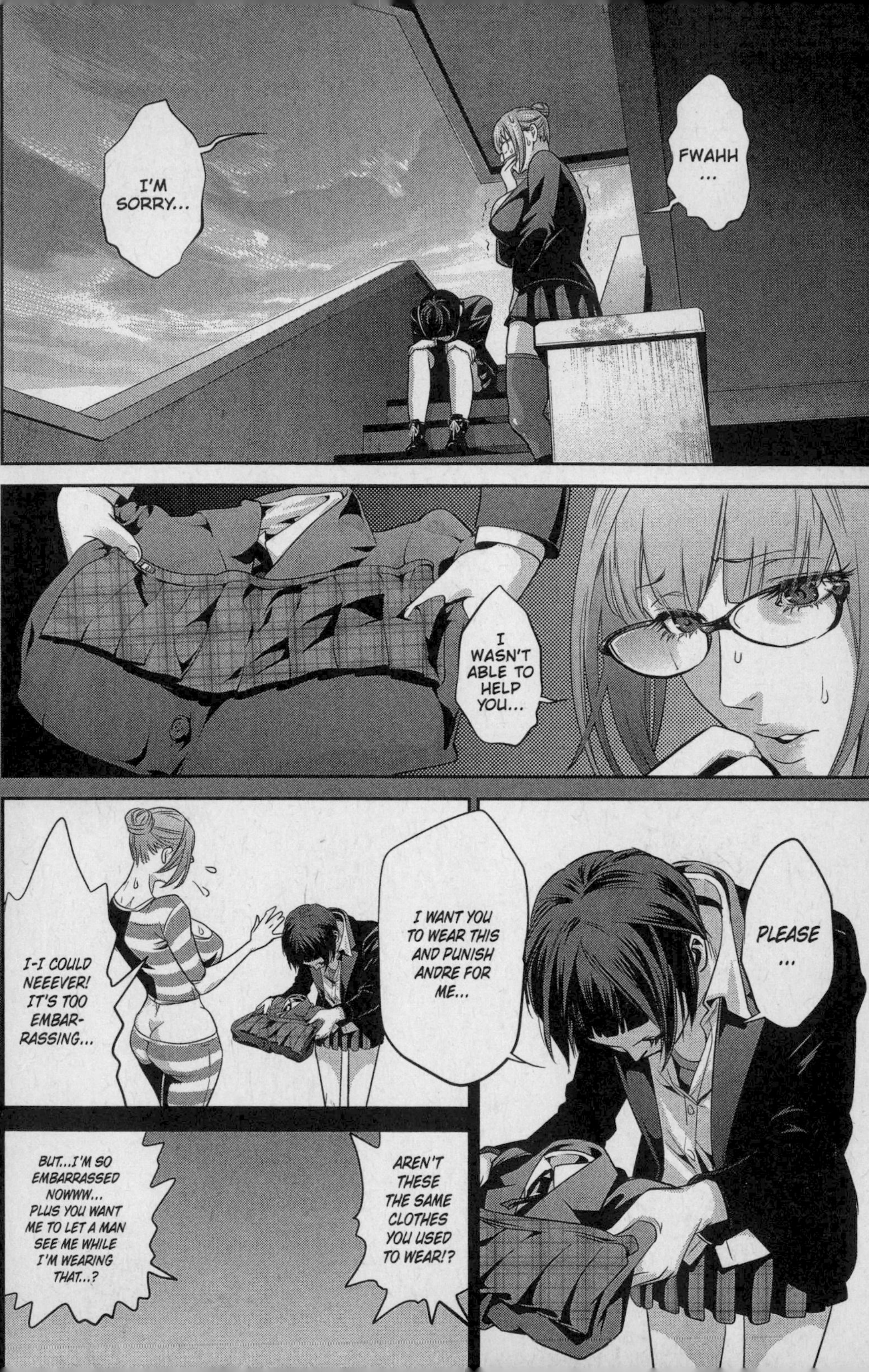
FWAHH ...
I'M SORRY...
I WASN'T ABLE TO HELP YOU...
PLEASE ...
I WANT YOU TO WEAR THIS AND PUNISH ANDRE FOR ME...
I-I COULD NEEEVER! IT'S TOO EMBAR-RASSING...
AREN'T THESE THE SAME CLOTHES YOU USED TO WEAR!?
BUT...I'M SO EMBARRASSED NOWWW... PLUS YOU WANT ME TO LET A MAN SEE ME WHILE I'M WEARING THAT...?

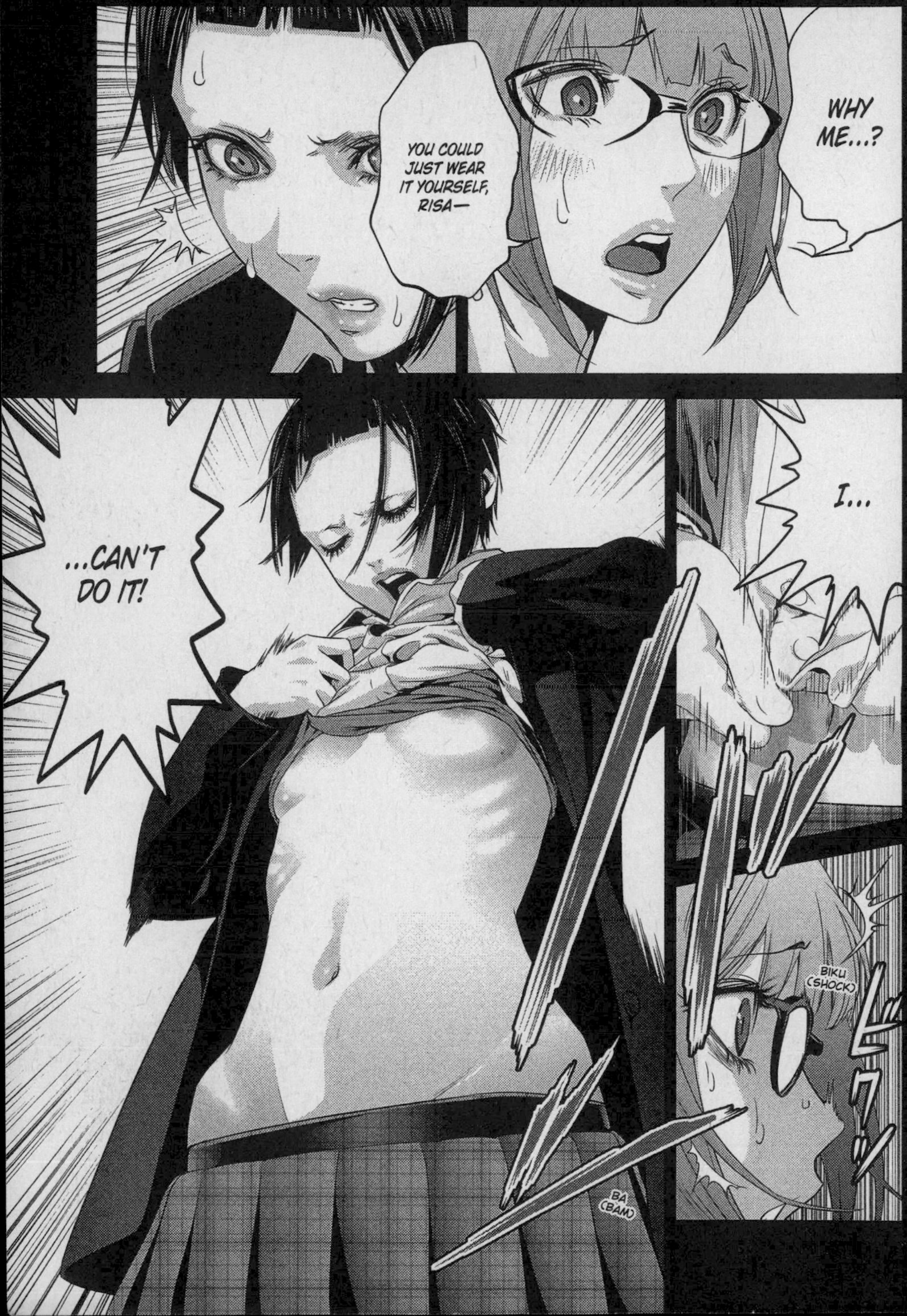
WHY ME...?
YOU COULD JUST WEAR IT YOURSELF, RISA—
I...
...CAN'T DO IT!
BIKU (SHOCK)
BA (BAM)

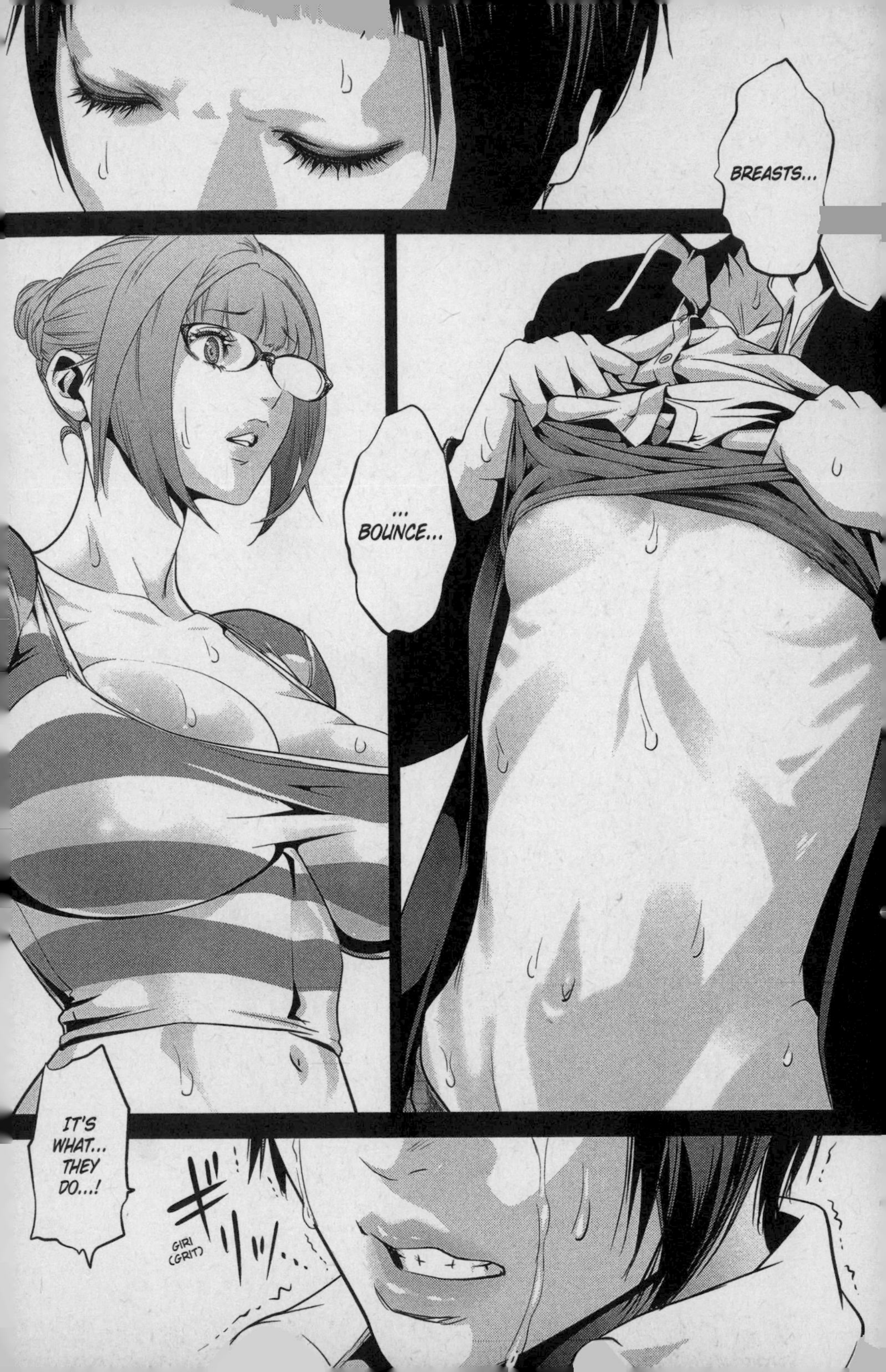
BREASTS...
... BOUNCE...
IT'S WHAT... THEY DO...!
GIRI (GRIT)

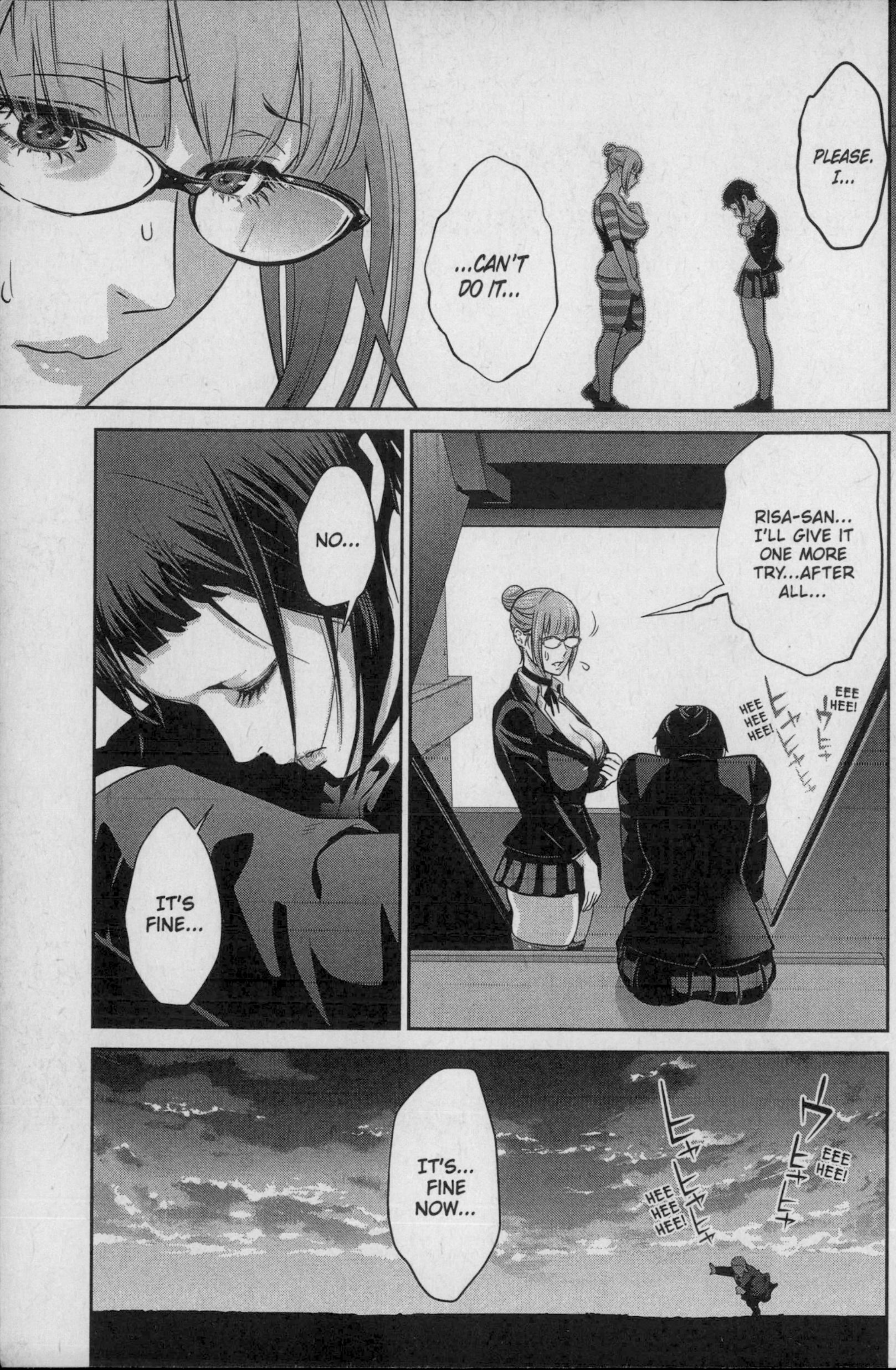
PLEASE. I...
...CAN'T DO IT...
RISA-SAN... I'LL GIVE IT ONE MORE TRY...AFTER ALL...
EEE HEE!
HEE HEE HEE!
NO...
IT'S FINE...
EEE HEE!
HEE HEE HEE!
IT'S... FINE NOW...

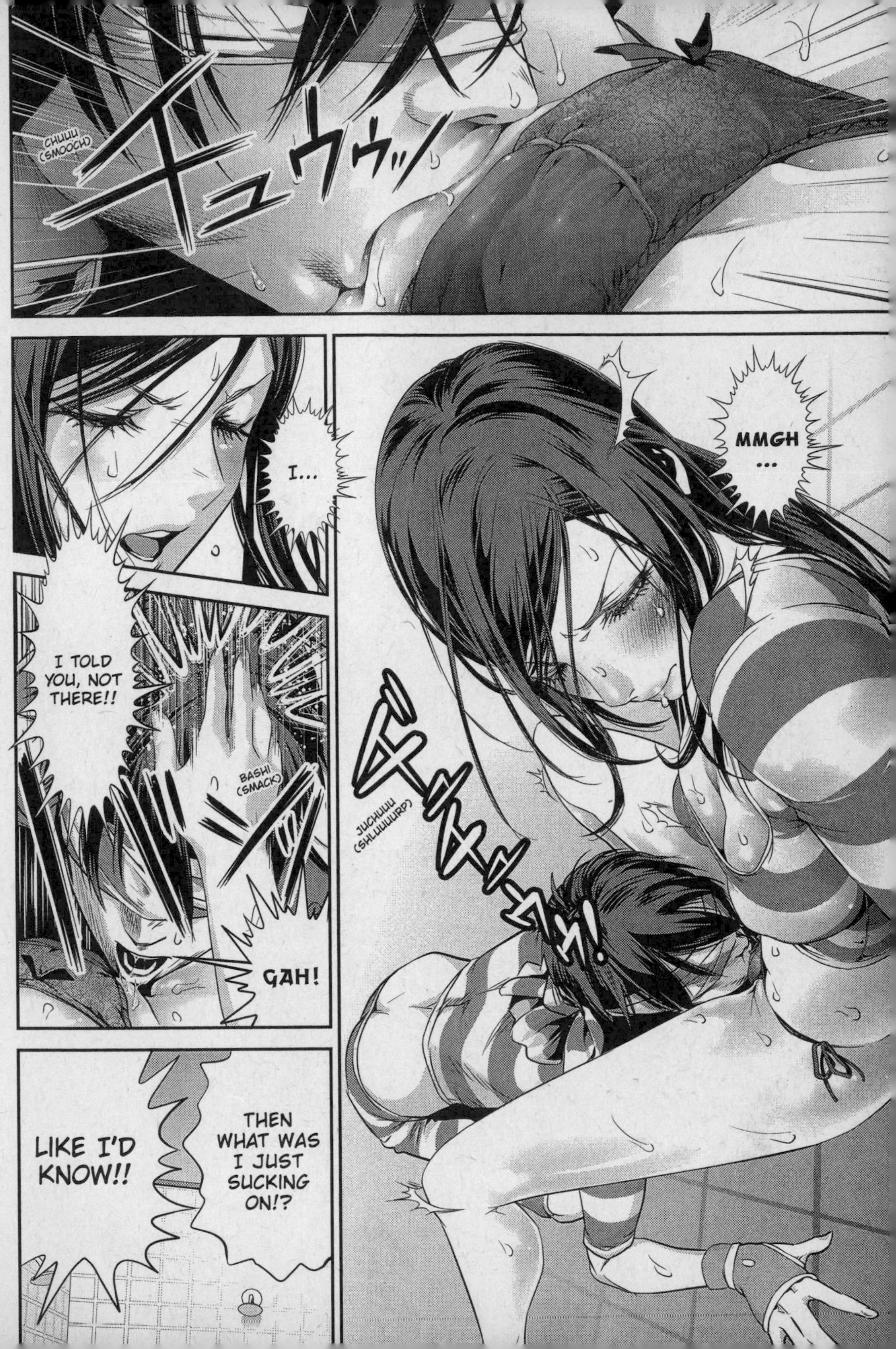
CHUUU (SMOOCH)
MMGH ...
JUCHUUU (SHLUUUURP)
I...
I TOLD YOU, NOT THERE!!
BASHI (SMACK)
GAH!
THEN WHAT WAS I JUST SUCKING ON!?
LIKE I'D KNOW!!

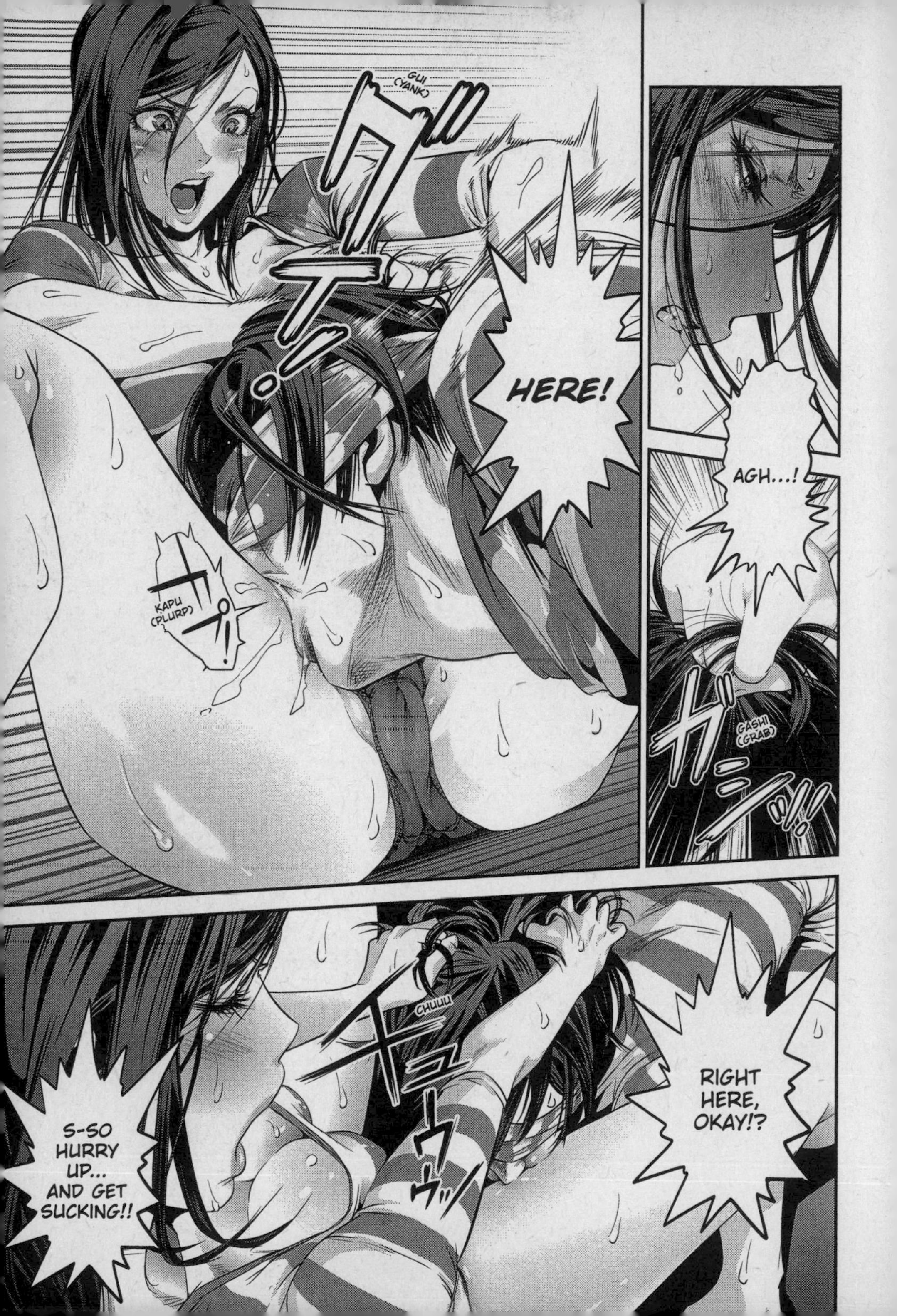
AGH...!
GASHI (GRAB)
GUI (YANK)
HERE!
KAPU (PLURP)
RIGHT HERE, OKAY!?
CHUUU
S-SO HURRY UP... AND GET SUCKING!!

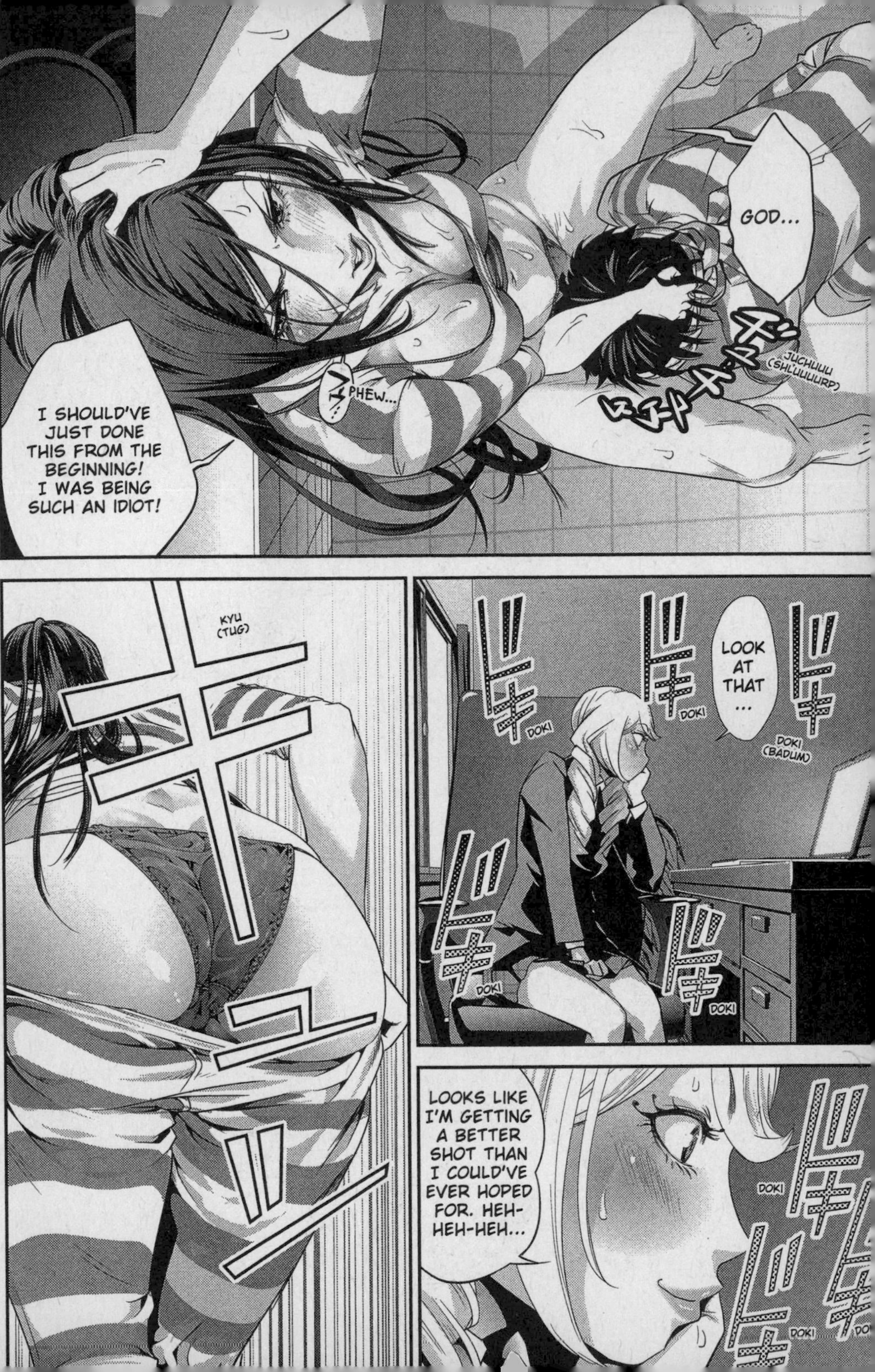
GOD...
JUCHUUU (SHLUUUURP)
PHEW...
I SHOULD'VE JUST DONE THIS FROM THE BEGINNING! I WAS BEING SUCH AN IDIOT!
LOOK AT THAT ...
DOKI
DOKI (BADUM)
DOKI
DOKI
DOKI
KYU (TUG)
LOOKS LIKE I'M GETTING A BETTER SHOT THAN I COULD'VE EVER HOPED FOR. HEH-HEH-HEH...
DOKI
DOKI

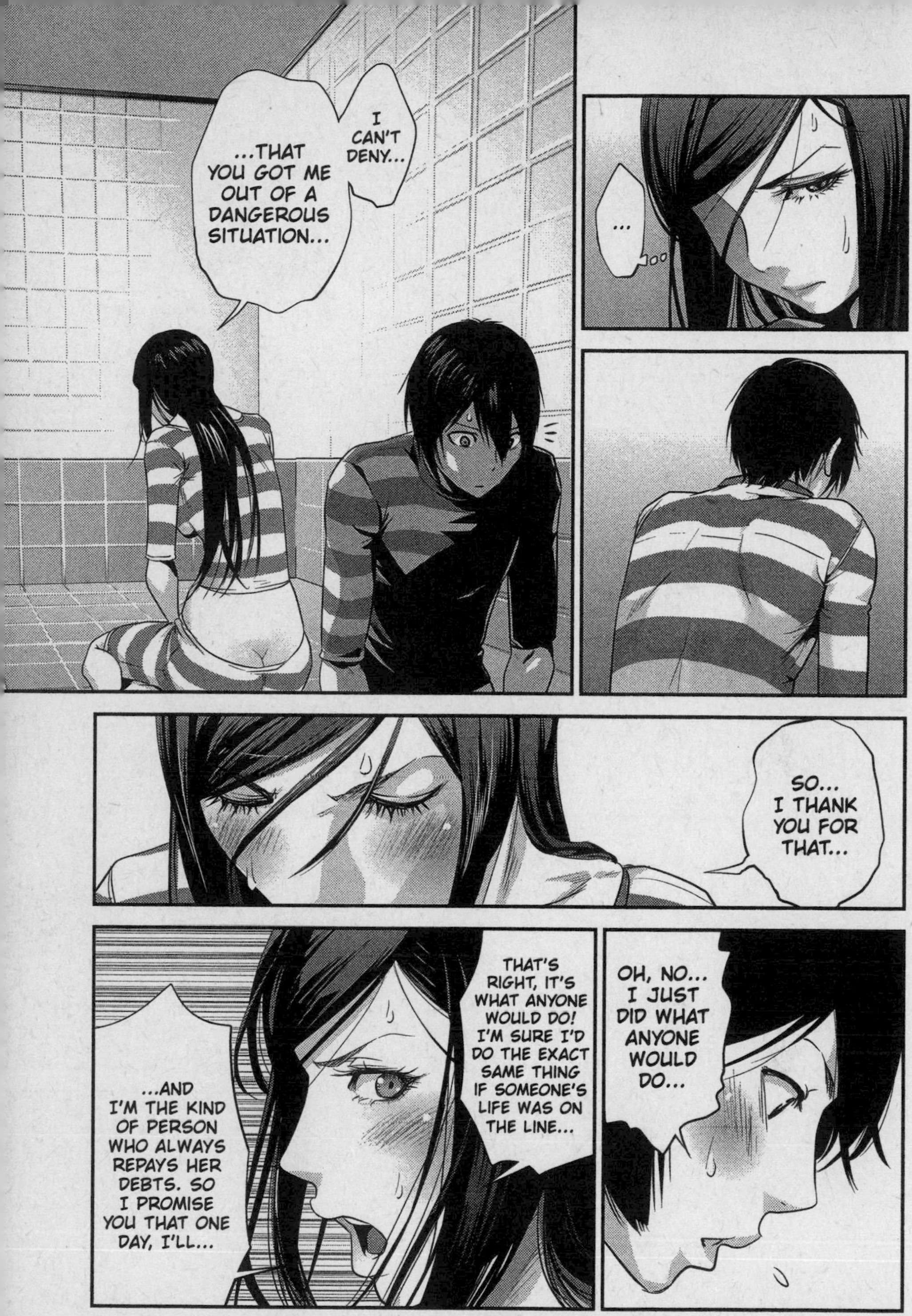

I CAN'T DENY...
...THAT YOU GOT ME OUT OF A DANGEROUS SITUATION...
...
SO... I THANK YOU FOR THAT...
OH, NO... I JUST DID WHAT ANYONE WOULD DO...
THAT'S RIGHT, IT'S WHAT ANYONE WOULD DO! I'M SURE I'D DO THE EXACT SAME THING IF SOMEONE'S LIFE WAS ON THE LINE...
...AND I'M THE KIND OF PERSON WHO ALWAYS REPAYS HER DEBTS. SO I PROMISE YOU THAT ONE DAY, I'LL...

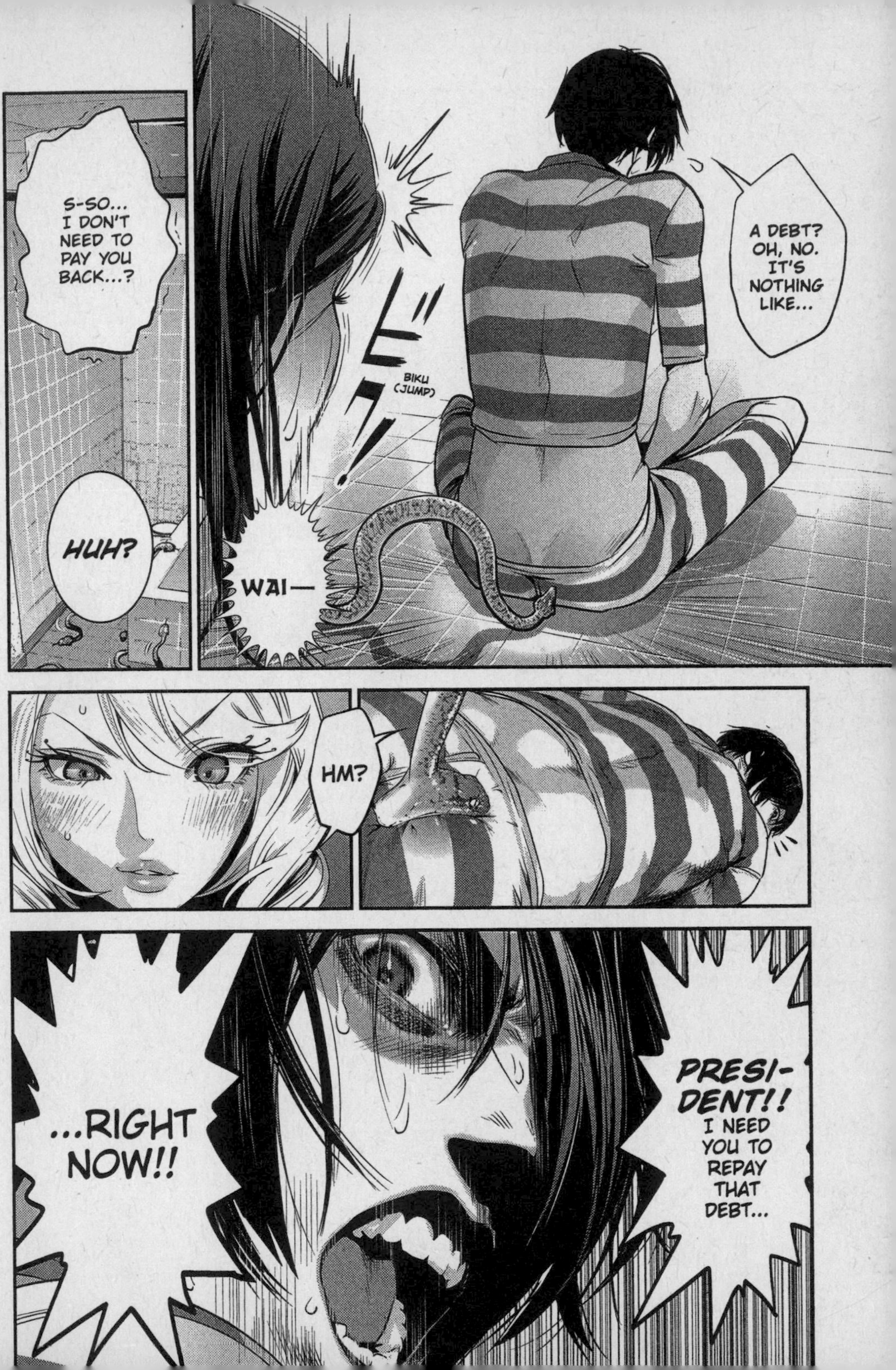
A DEBT? OH, NO. IT'S NOTHING LIKE...
BIKU (JUMP)
WAI—
S-SO... I DON'T NEED TO PAY YOU BACK...?
HUH?
HM?
PRESI- DENT!! I NEED YOU TO REPAY THAT DEBT...
...RIGHT NOW!!

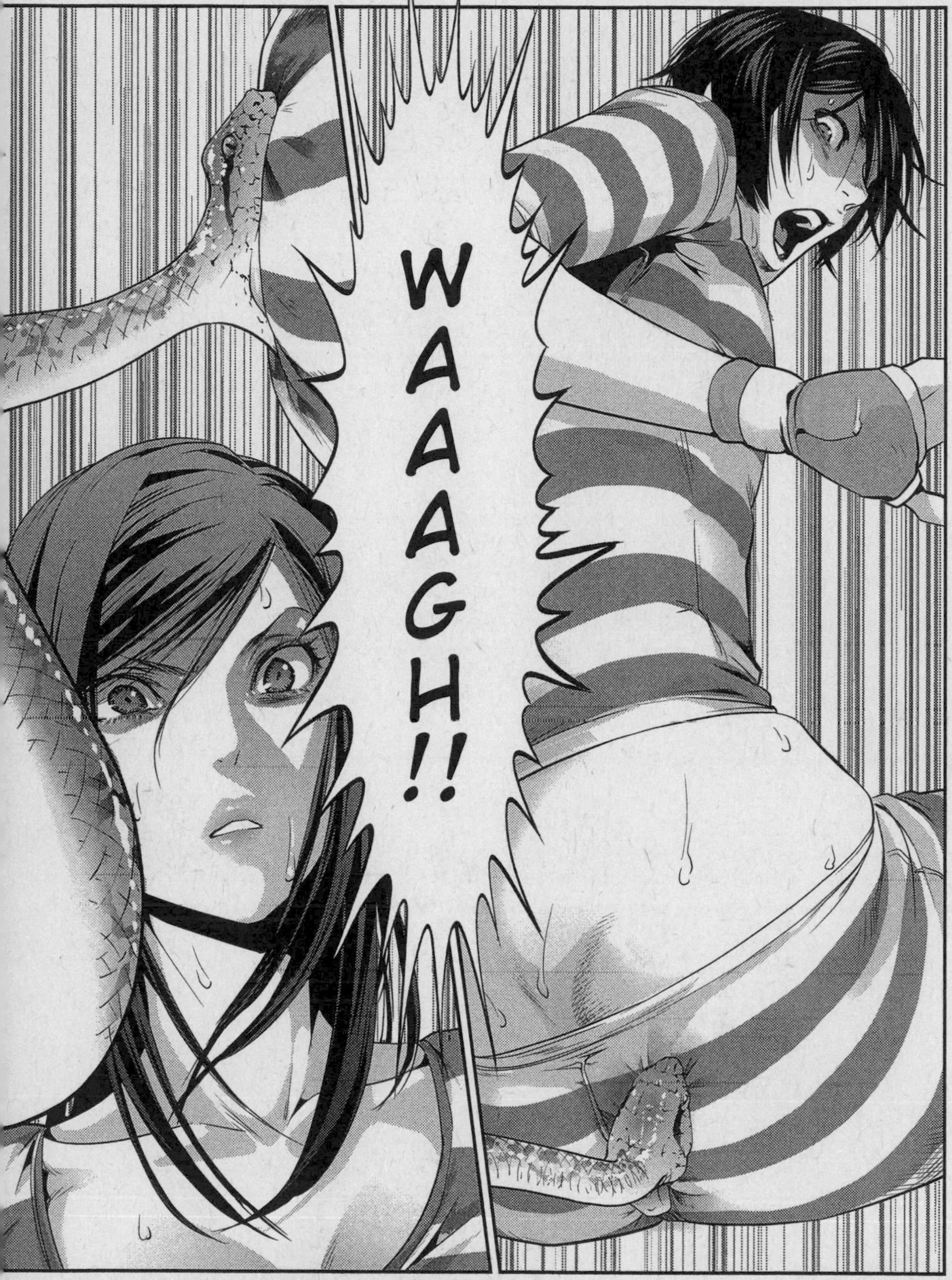
WAAAGH!!

CHAPTER 126: KISS-ASS

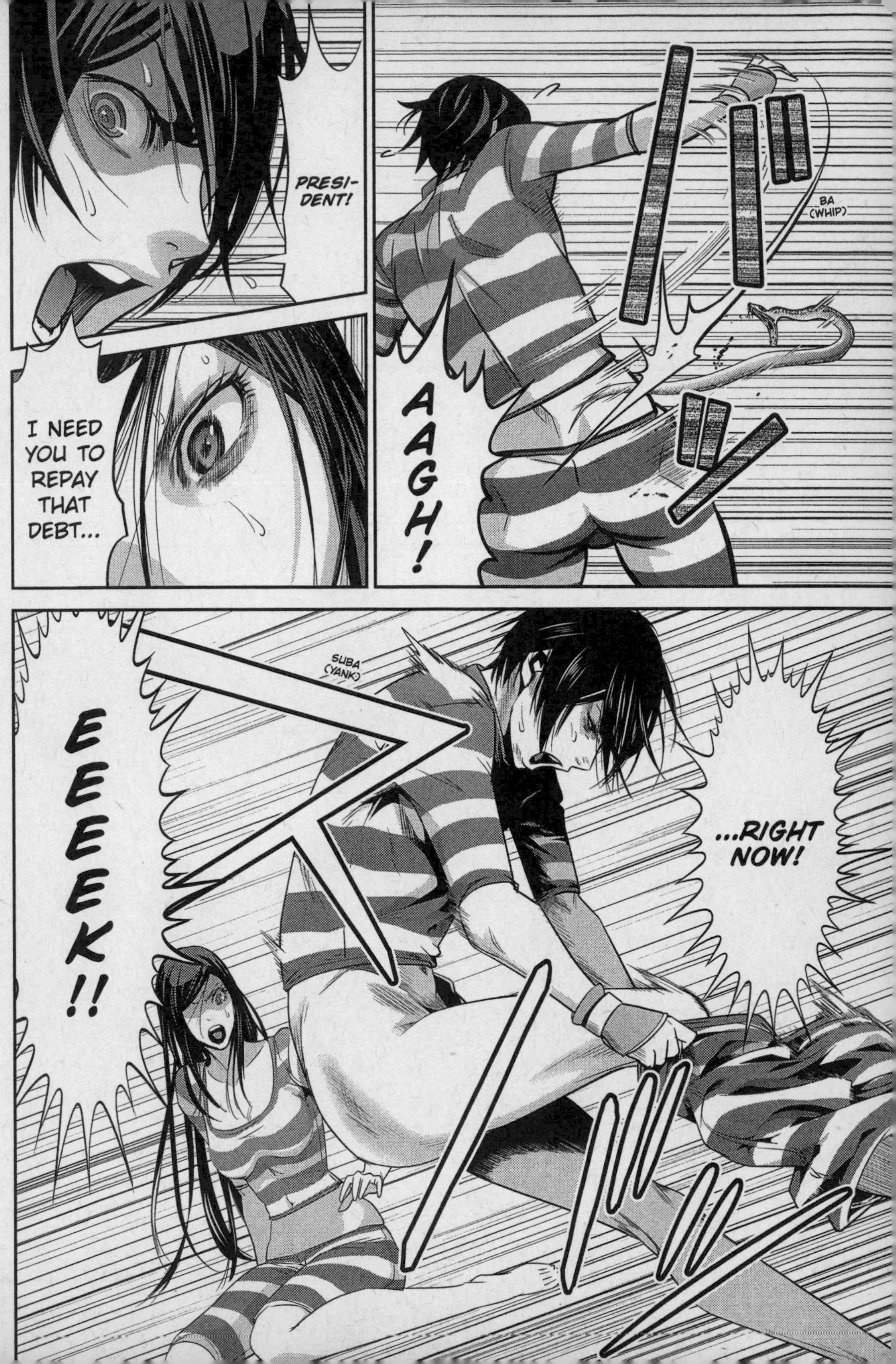
BA (WHIP)
AAGH!
PRESI-DENT!
I NEED YOU TO REPAY THAT DEBT...
...RIGHT NOW!
SUBA (YANK)
EEEEK!!

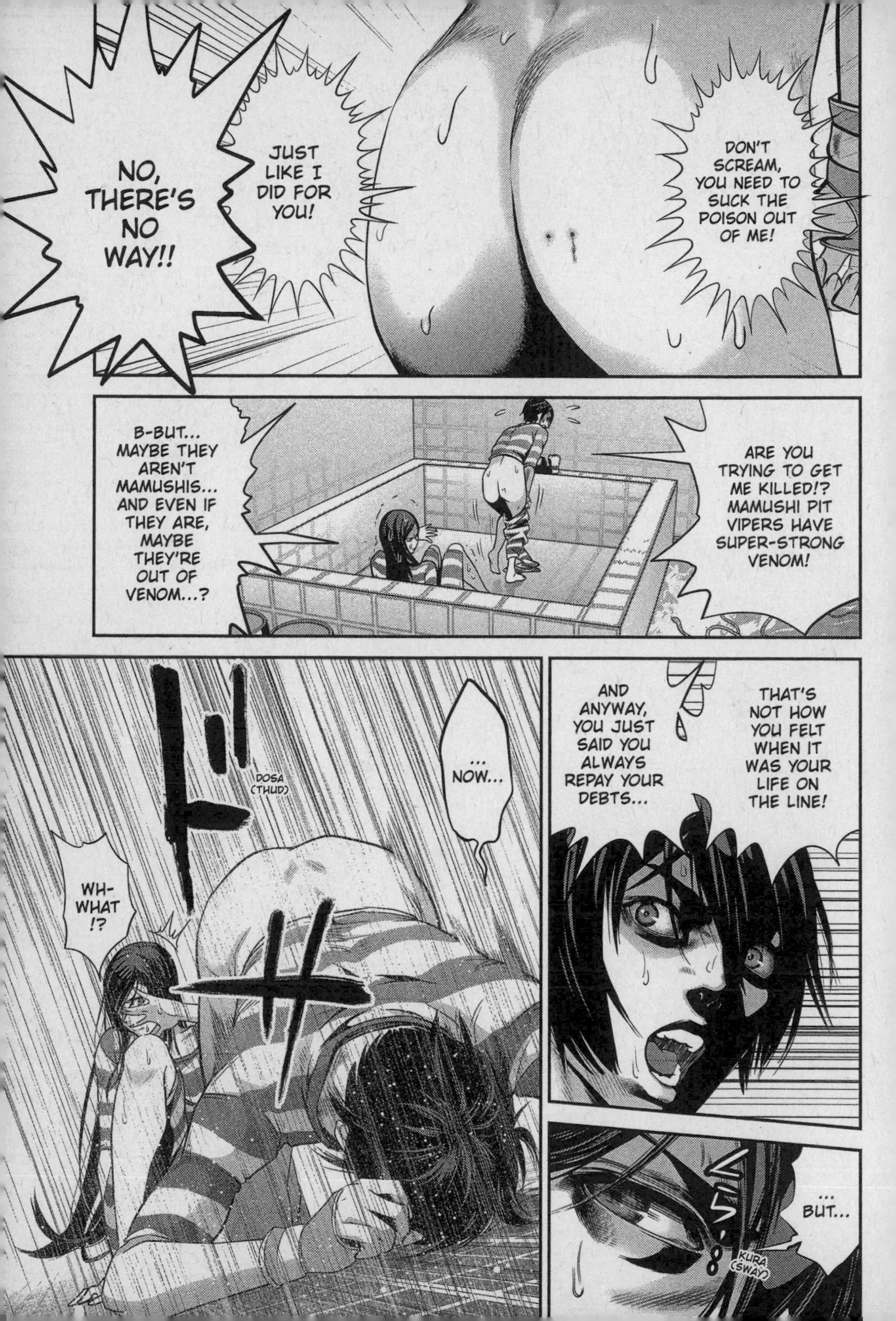
DON'T SCREAM, YOU NEED TO SUCK THE POISON OUT OF ME!
JUST LIKE I DID FOR YOU!
NO, THERE'S NO WAY!!
ARE YOU TRYING TO GET ME KILLED!? MAMUSHI PIT VIPERS HAVE SUPER-STRONG VENOM!
B-BUT... MAYBE THEY AREN'T MAMUSHIS... AND EVEN IF THEY ARE, MAYBE THEY'RE OUT OF VENOM...?
THAT'S NOT HOW YOU FELT WHEN IT WAS YOUR LIFE ON THE LINE!
AND ANYWAY, YOU JUST SAID YOU ALWAYS REPAY YOUR DEBTS...
... BUT...
KURA (SWAY)
... NOW...
DOSA (THUD)
WH-WHAT!?

UURGH... I THINK THE POISON...IS GETTING INTO MY BLOOD-STREAM...

HFF...

HFF...

HFF...

HFF...

HFF...

HFF...

I DON'T WANT... TO DIE HERE...

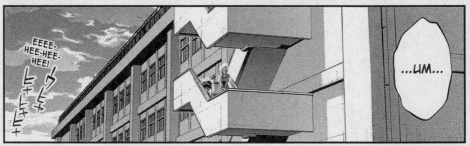

EEEE-HEE-HEE-HEE!

ヒヒヒヒ！
ヒヒヒ

...UM...

NO... IT'S FINE.

YOU WAIT HERE.

I OUGHT TO HEAD BACK SOON... I WAS IN THE MIDDLE OF CLEANING THE BATH...

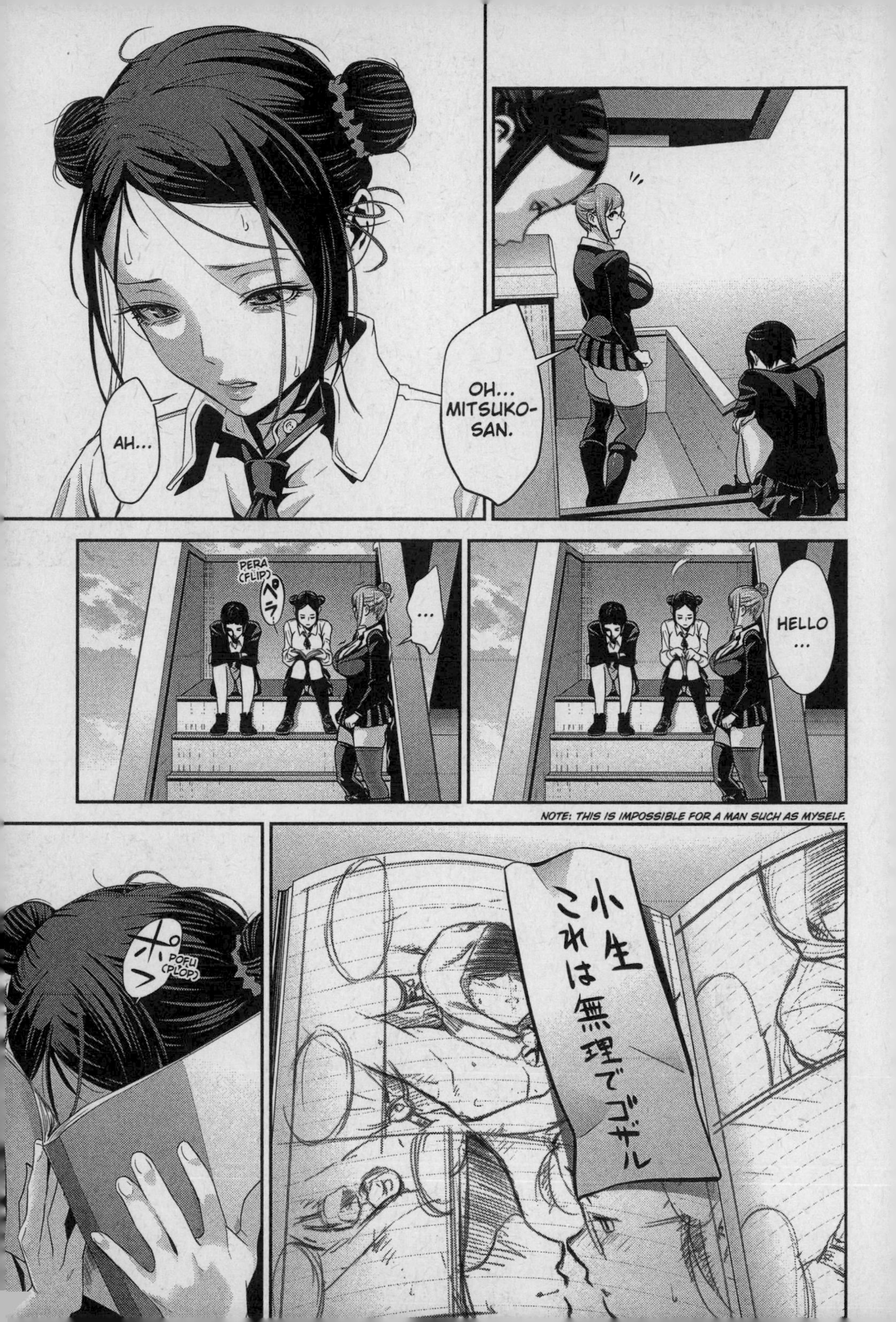
OH... MITSUKO-SAN.
AH...
HELLO ...
...
PERA (FLIP) ペラ
NOTE: THIS IS IMPOSSIBLE FOR A MAN SUCH AS MYSELF.
小生これは無理でゴザル
ポフ POFU (PLOP)

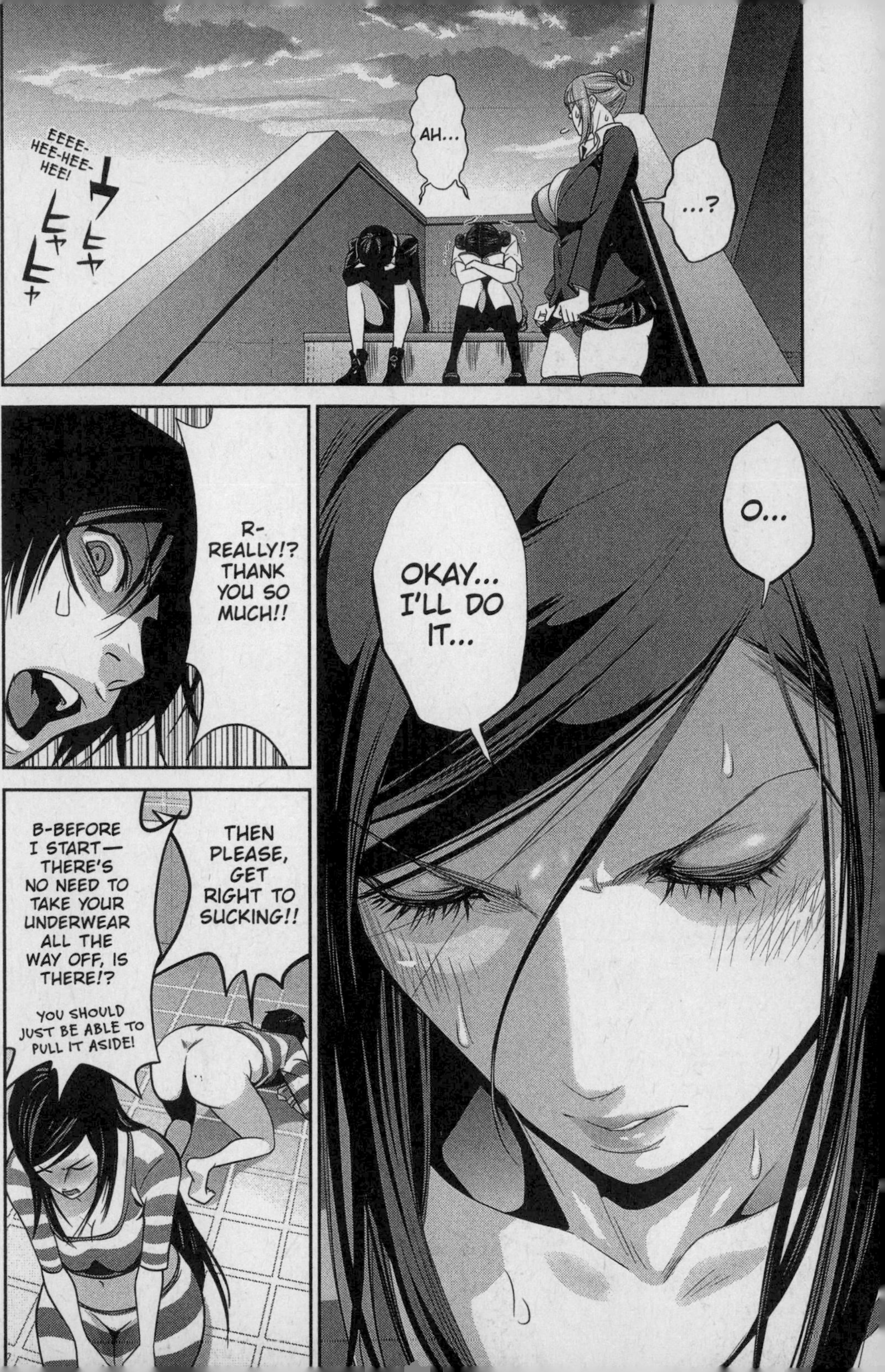
...?
AH...
EEEE-HEE-HEE-HEE!
O...
OKAY... I'LL DO IT...
R-REALLY!? THANK YOU SO MUCH!!
THEN PLEASE, GET RIGHT TO SUCKING!!
B-BEFORE I START— THERE'S NO NEED TO TAKE YOUR UNDERWEAR ALL THE WAY OFF, IS THERE!?
YOU SHOULD JUST BE ABLE TO PULL IT ASIDE!

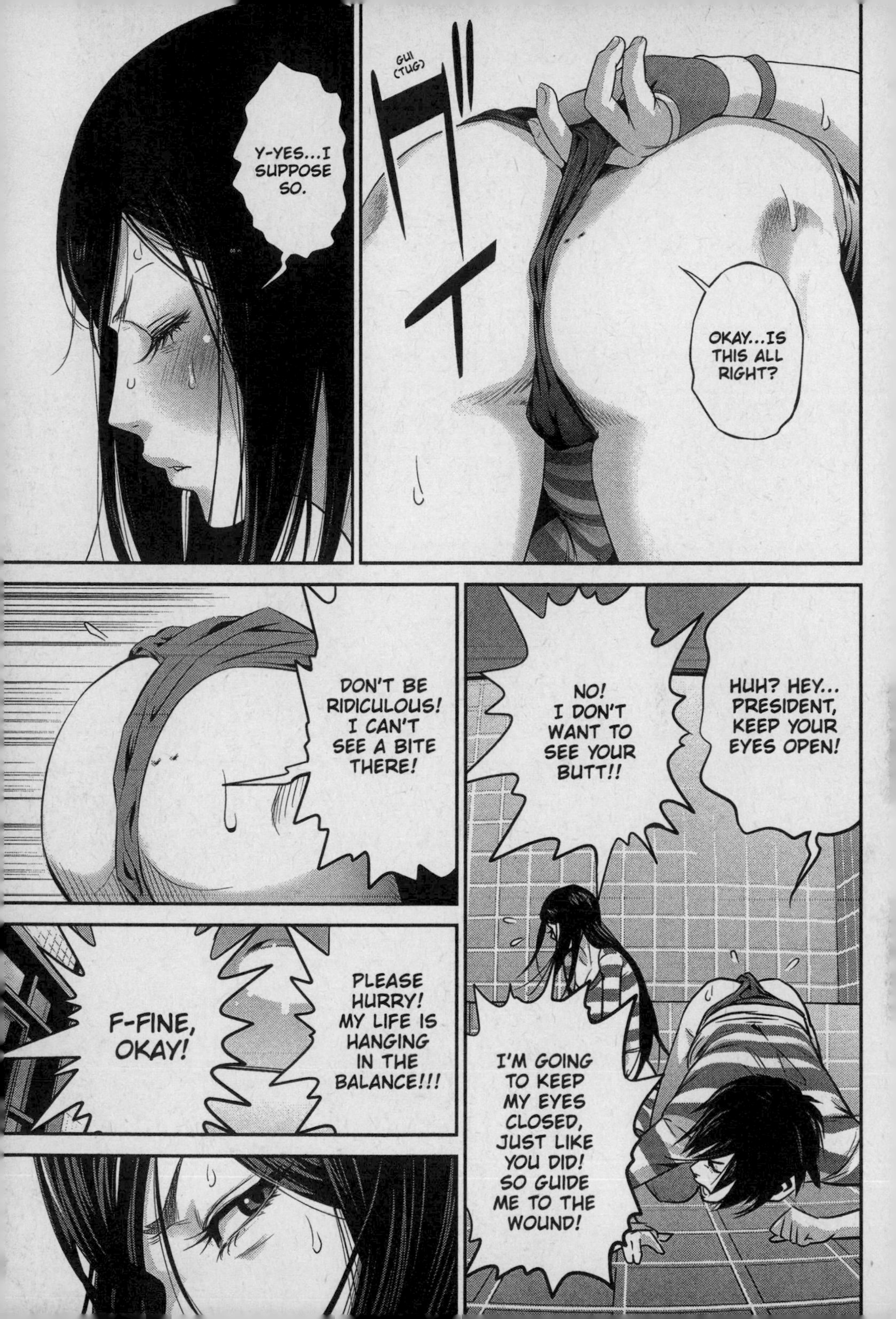
GUI (TUG)
OKAY...IS THIS ALL RIGHT?
Y-YES...I SUPPOSE SO.
HUH? HEY... PRESIDENT, KEEP YOUR EYES OPEN!
NO! I DON'T WANT TO SEE YOUR BUTT!!
I'M GOING TO KEEP MY EYES CLOSED, JUST LIKE YOU DID! SO GUIDE ME TO THE WOUND!
DON'T BE RIDICULOUS! I CAN'T SEE A BITE THERE!
PLEASE HURRY! MY LIFE IS HANGING IN THE BALANCE!!!
F-FINE, OKAY!

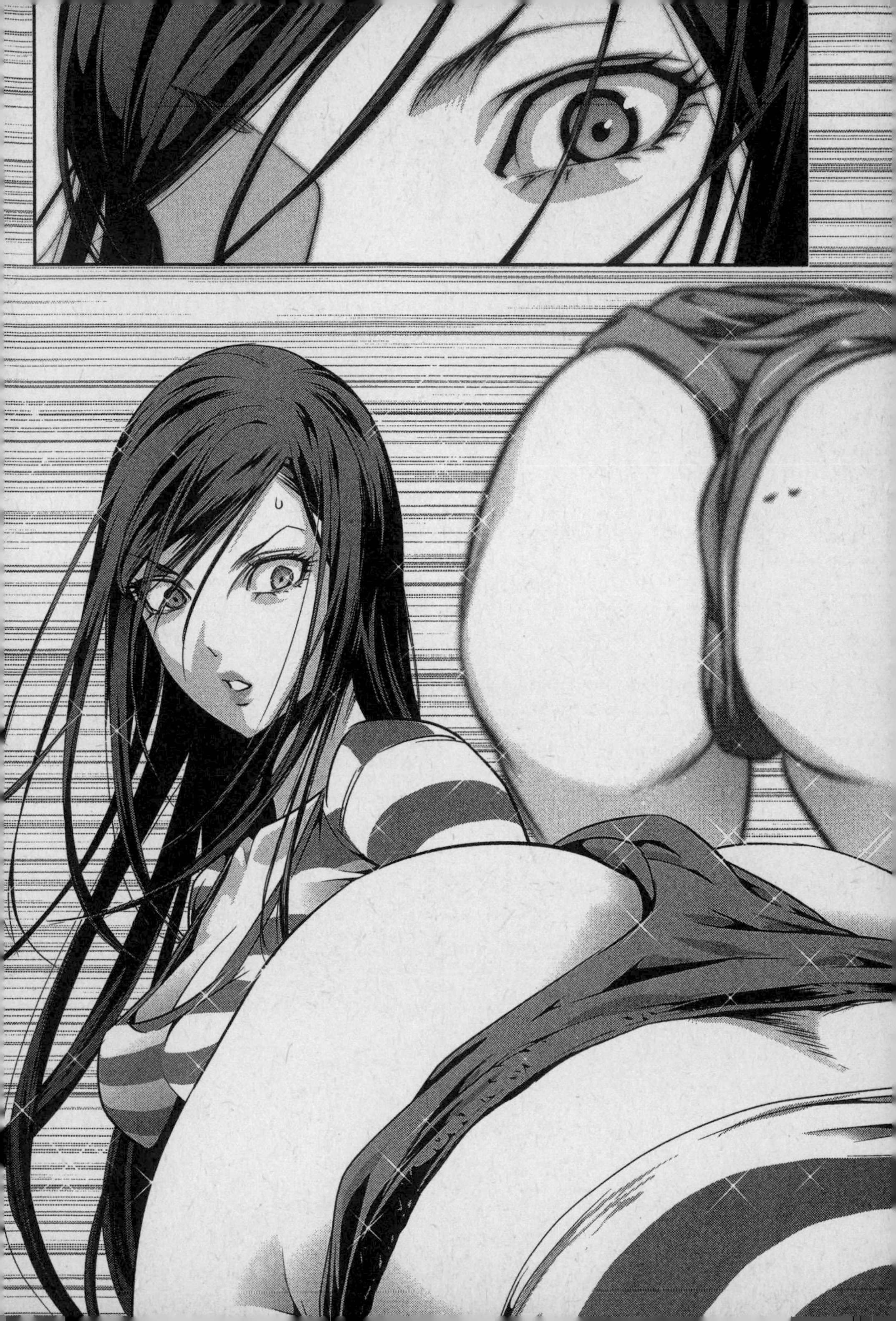

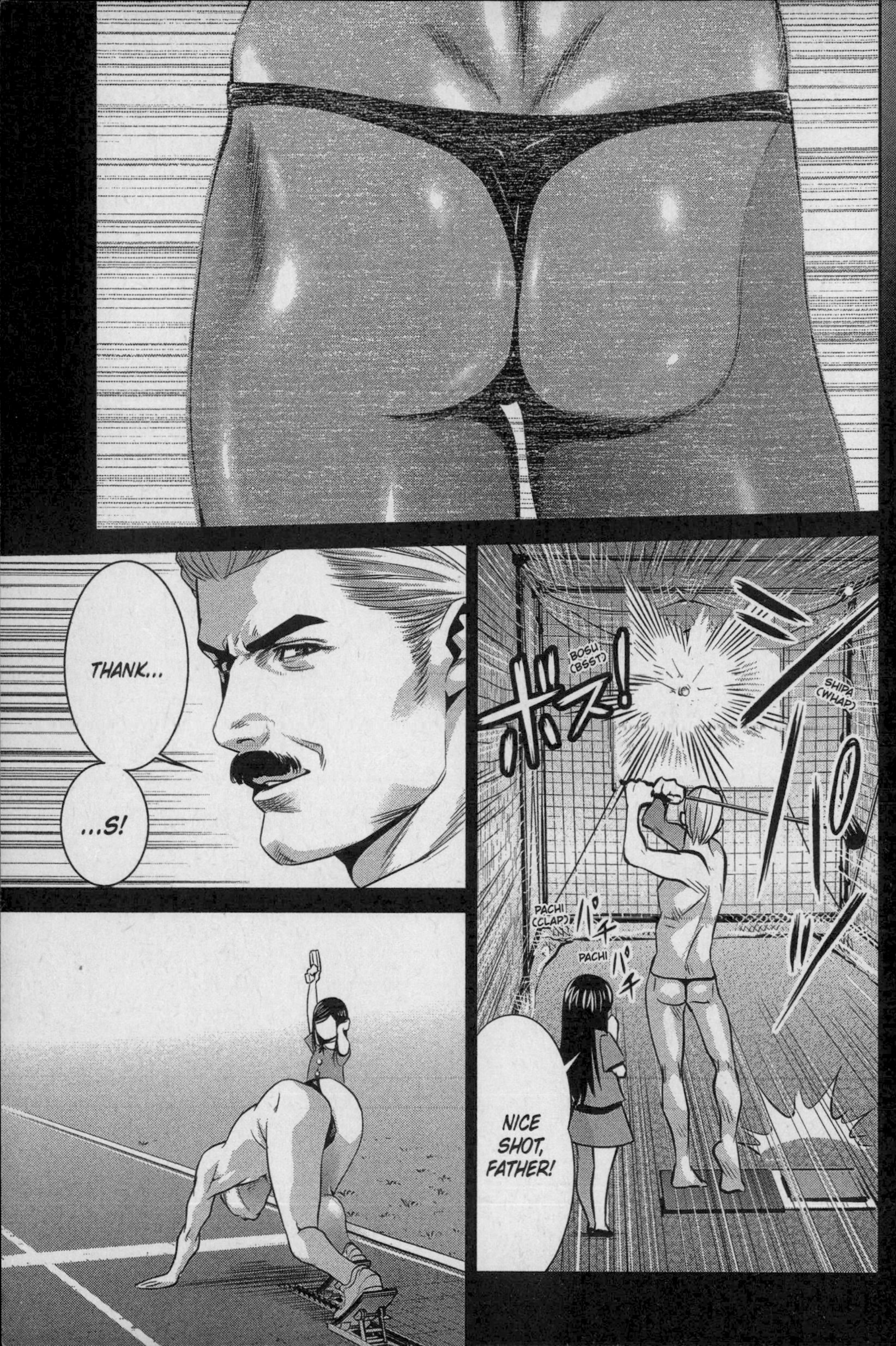

BOSU (BSST)
ボス!
SHIPA (WHAP)
PACHI (CLAP)
パチ
PACHI
パチ
NICE SHOT, FATHER!
THANK...
...S!

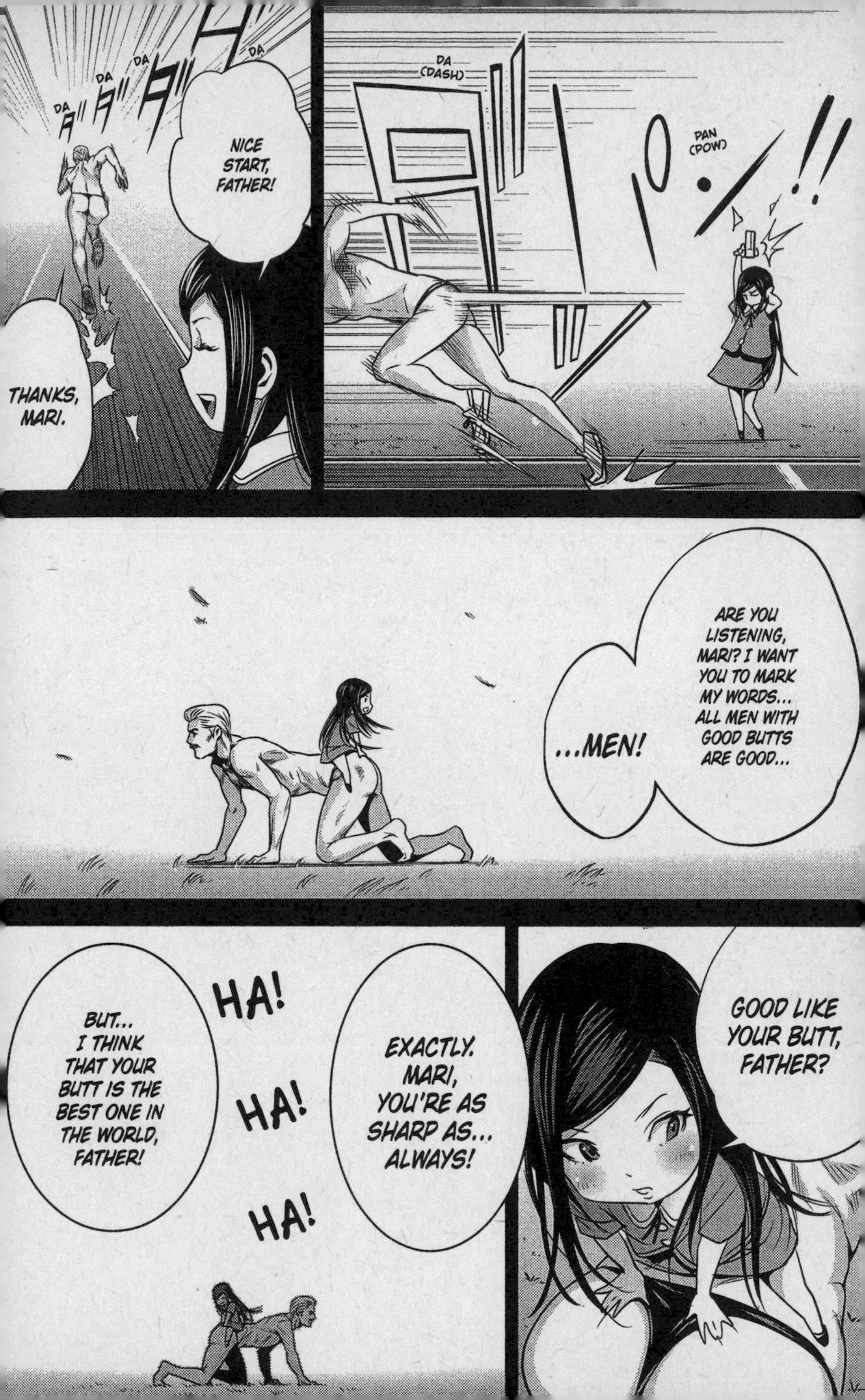

DA (DASH)
PAN (POW)
DA
DA
DA
DA
NICE START, FATHER!
THANKS, MARI.
ARE YOU LISTENING, MARI? I WANT YOU TO MARK MY WORDS... ALL MEN WITH GOOD BUTTS ARE GOOD...
...MEN!
GOOD LIKE YOUR BUTT, FATHER?
EXACTLY. MARI, YOU'RE AS SHARP AS... ALWAYS!
HA!
HA!
HA!
BUT... I THINK THAT YOUR BUTT IS THE BEST ONE IN THE WORLD, FATHER!

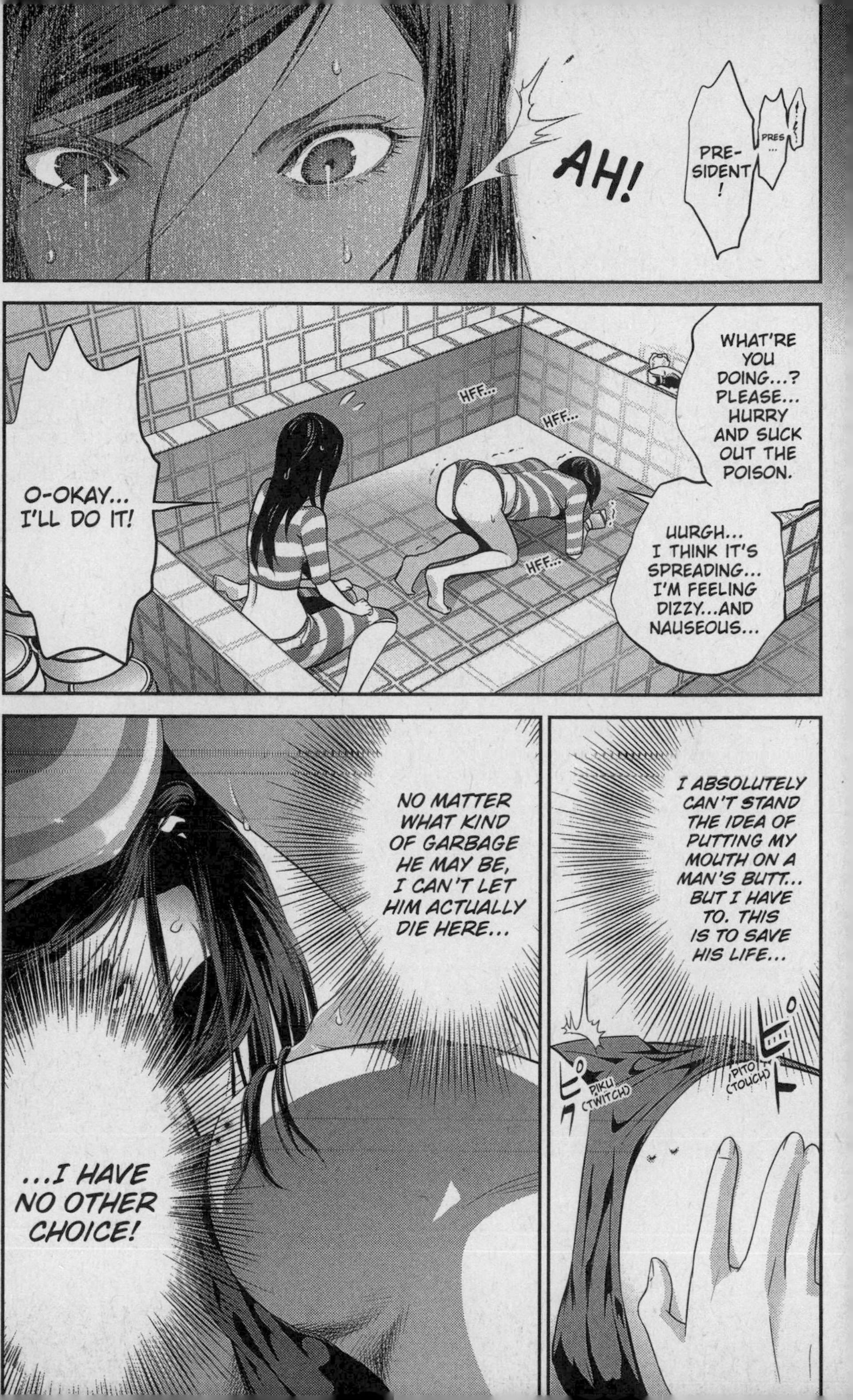
PRES...
PRE-SIDENT!
AH!
WHAT'RE YOU DOING...? PLEASE... HURRY AND SUCK OUT THE POISON.
UURGH... I THINK IT'S SPREADING... I'M FEELING DIZZY...AND NAUSEOUS...
HFF...
HFF...
HFF...
O-OKAY... I'LL DO IT!
I ABSOLUTELY CAN'T STAND THE IDEA OF PUTTING MY MOUTH ON A MAN'S BUTT... BUT I HAVE TO. THIS IS TO SAVE HIS LIFE...
PITO (TOUCH)
PIKU (TWITCH)
NO MATTER WHAT KIND OF GARBAGE HE MAY BE, I CAN'T LET HIM ACTUALLY DIE HERE...
...I HAVE NO OTHER CHOICE!

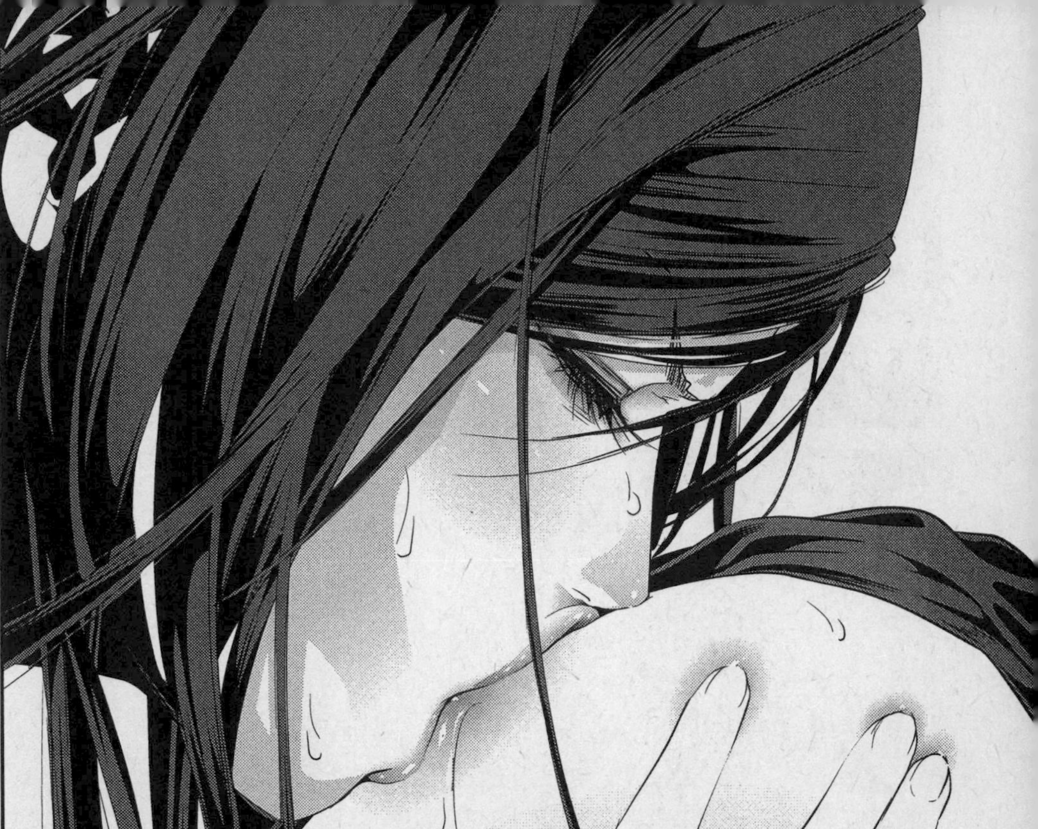

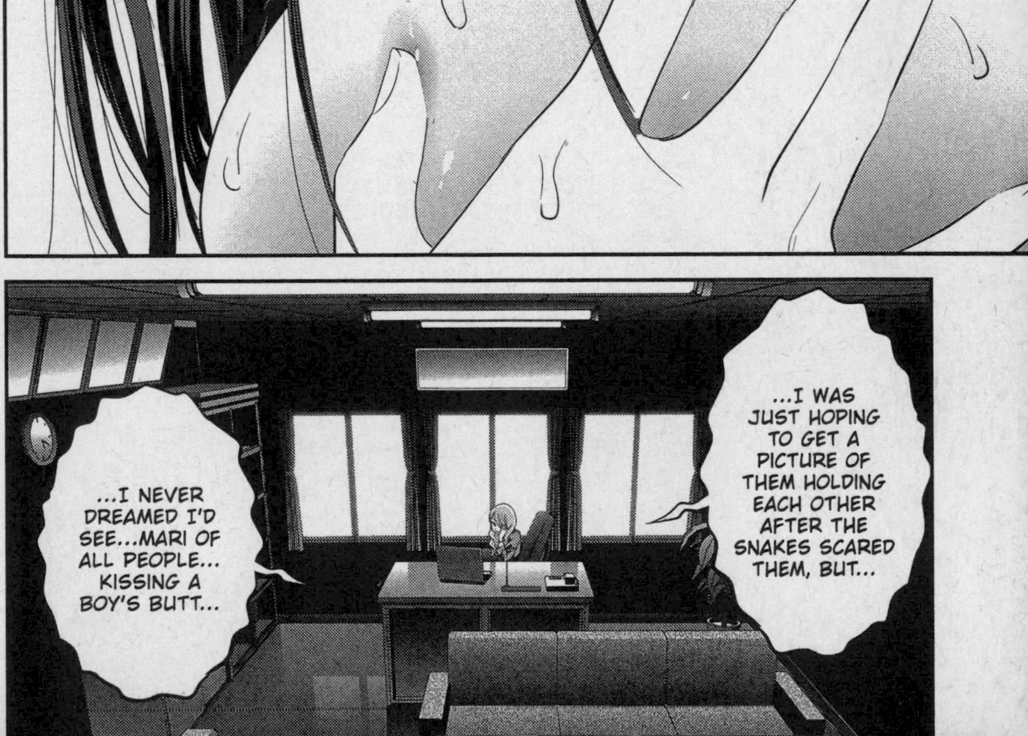
...I WAS JUST HOPING TO GET A PICTURE OF THEM HOLDING EACH OTHER AFTER THE SNAKES SCARED THEM, BUT...
...I NEVER DREAMED I'D SEE...MARI OF ALL PEOPLE... KISSING A BOY'S BUTT...

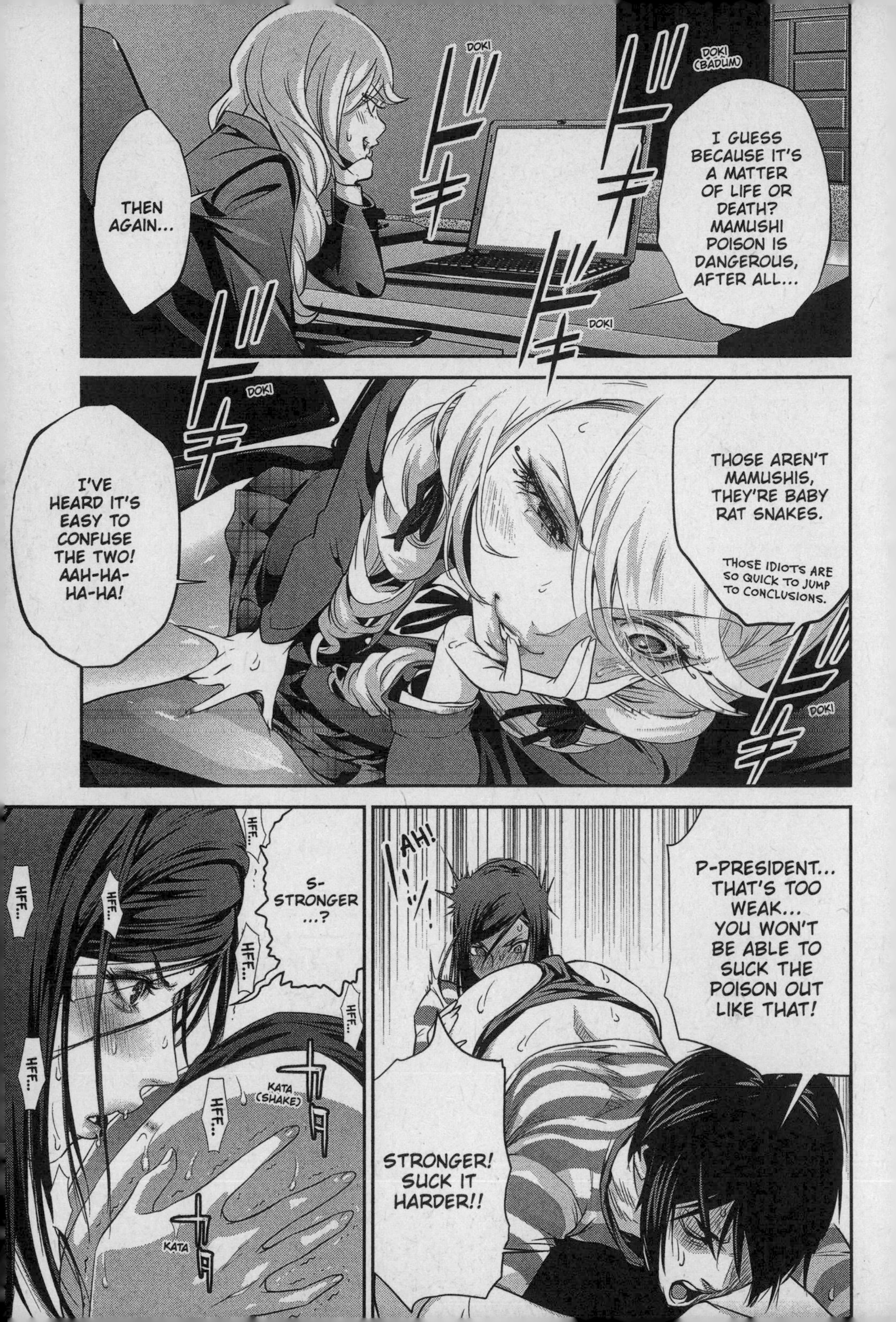
DOKI
DOKI (BADUM)
I GUESS BECAUSE IT'S A MATTER OF LIFE OR DEATH? MAMUSHI POISON IS DANGEROUS, AFTER ALL...
DOKI
THEN AGAIN...
DOKI
THOSE AREN'T MAMUSHIS, THEY'RE BABY RAT SNAKES.
THOSE IDIOTS ARE SO QUICK TO JUMP TO CONCLUSIONS.
DOKI
I'VE HEARD IT'S EASY TO CONFUSE THE TWO! AAH-HA-HA-HA!
P-PRESIDENT... THAT'S TOO WEAK... YOU WON'T BE ABLE TO SUCK THE POISON OUT LIKE THAT!
AH!
STRONGER! SUCK IT HARDER!!
HFF...
S-STRONGER...?
HFF...
HFF...
HFF...
HFF...
HFF...
KATA (SHAKE)
HFF...
KATA

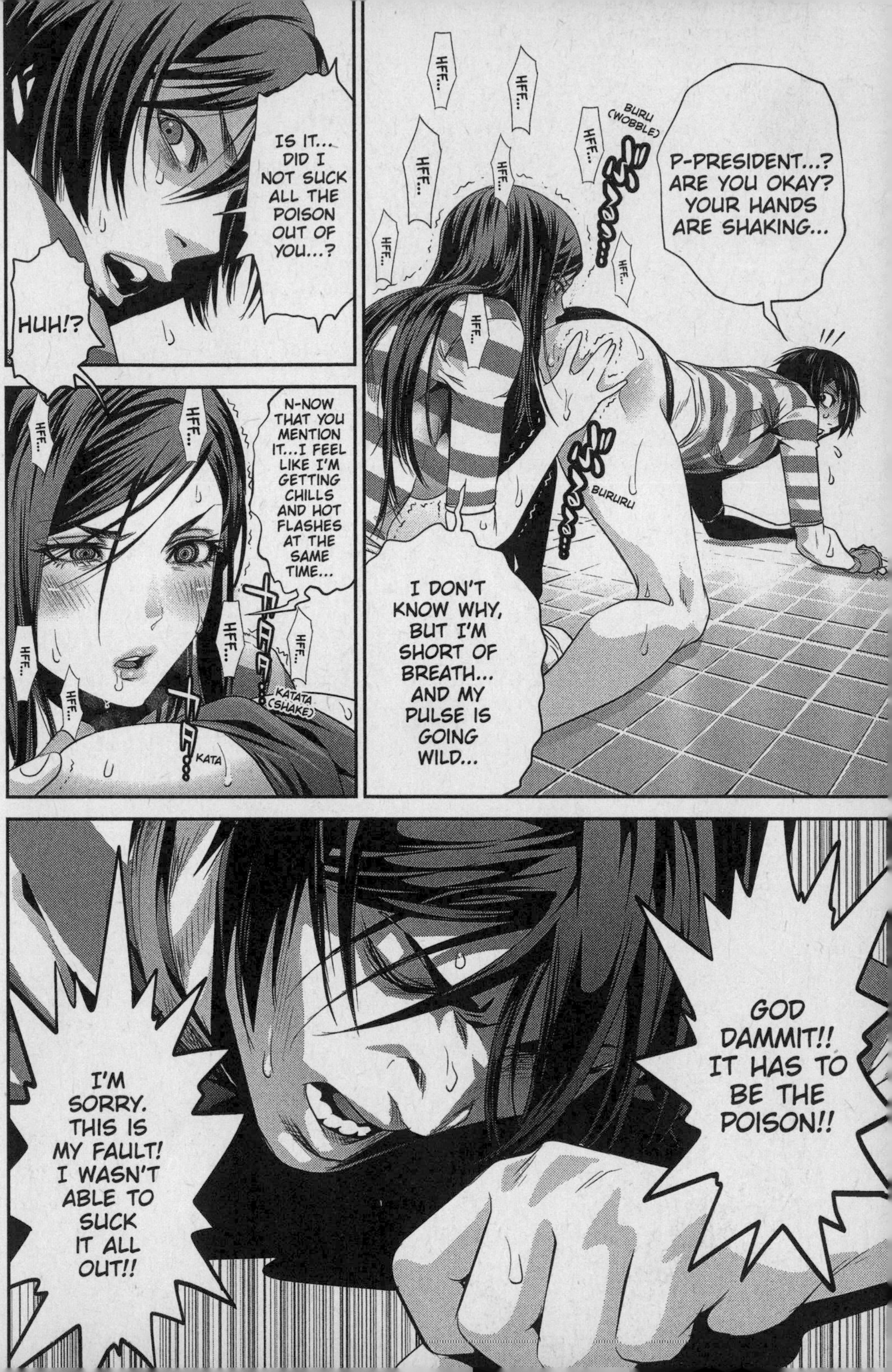
P-PRESIDENT...? ARE YOU OKAY? YOUR HANDS ARE SHAKING...
BURU (WOBBLE)
HFF...
HFF...
HFF...
HFF...
HFF...
HFF...
HFF...
HFF...
BURURU
I DON'T KNOW WHY, BUT I'M SHORT OF BREATH... AND MY PULSE IS GOING WILD...
IS IT... DID I NOT SUCK ALL THE POISON OUT OF YOU...?
HUH!?
N-NOW THAT YOU MENTION IT...I FEEL LIKE I'M GETTING CHILLS AND HOT FLASHES AT THE SAME TIME...
HFF...
HFF...
HFF...
HFF...
HFF...
KATATA (SHAKE)
KATA
GOD DAMMIT!! IT HAS TO BE THE POISON!!
I'M SORRY. THIS IS MY FAULT! I WASN'T ABLE TO SUCK IT ALL OUT!!

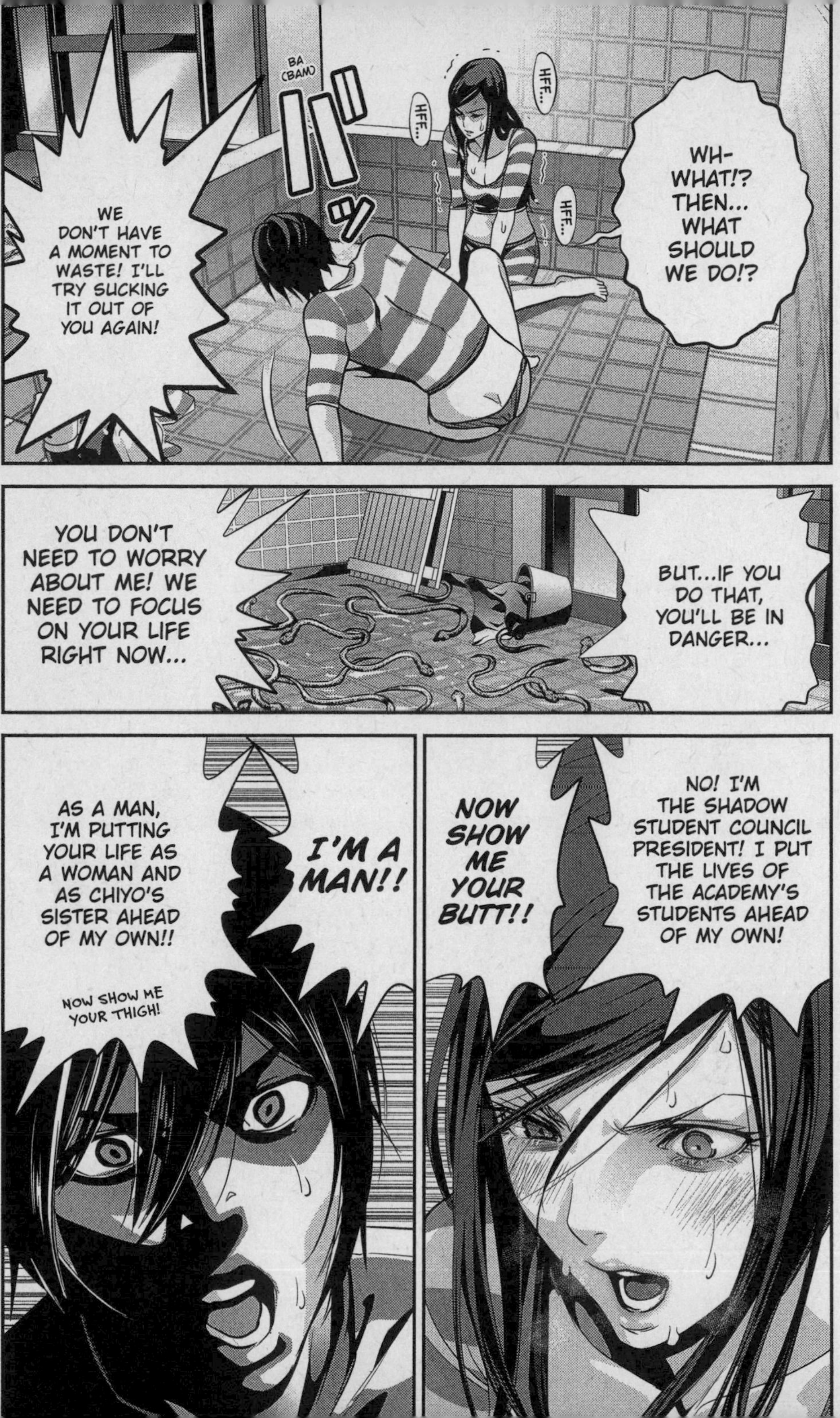
HFF...
HFF...
HFF...
WH-WHAT!? THEN... WHAT SHOULD WE DO!?
BA (BAM)
WE DON'T HAVE A MOMENT TO WASTE! I'LL TRY SUCKING IT OUT OF YOU AGAIN!
BUT...IF YOU DO THAT, YOU'LL BE IN DANGER...
YOU DON'T NEED TO WORRY ABOUT ME! WE NEED TO FOCUS ON YOUR LIFE RIGHT NOW...
NO! I'M THE SHADOW STUDENT COUNCIL PRESIDENT! I PUT THE LIVES OF THE ACADEMY'S STUDENTS AHEAD OF MY OWN!
NOW SHOW ME YOUR BUTT!!
AS A MAN, I'M PUTTING YOUR LIFE AS A WOMAN AND AS CHIYO'S SISTER AHEAD OF MY OWN!!
I'M A MAN!!
NOW SHOW ME YOUR THIGH!

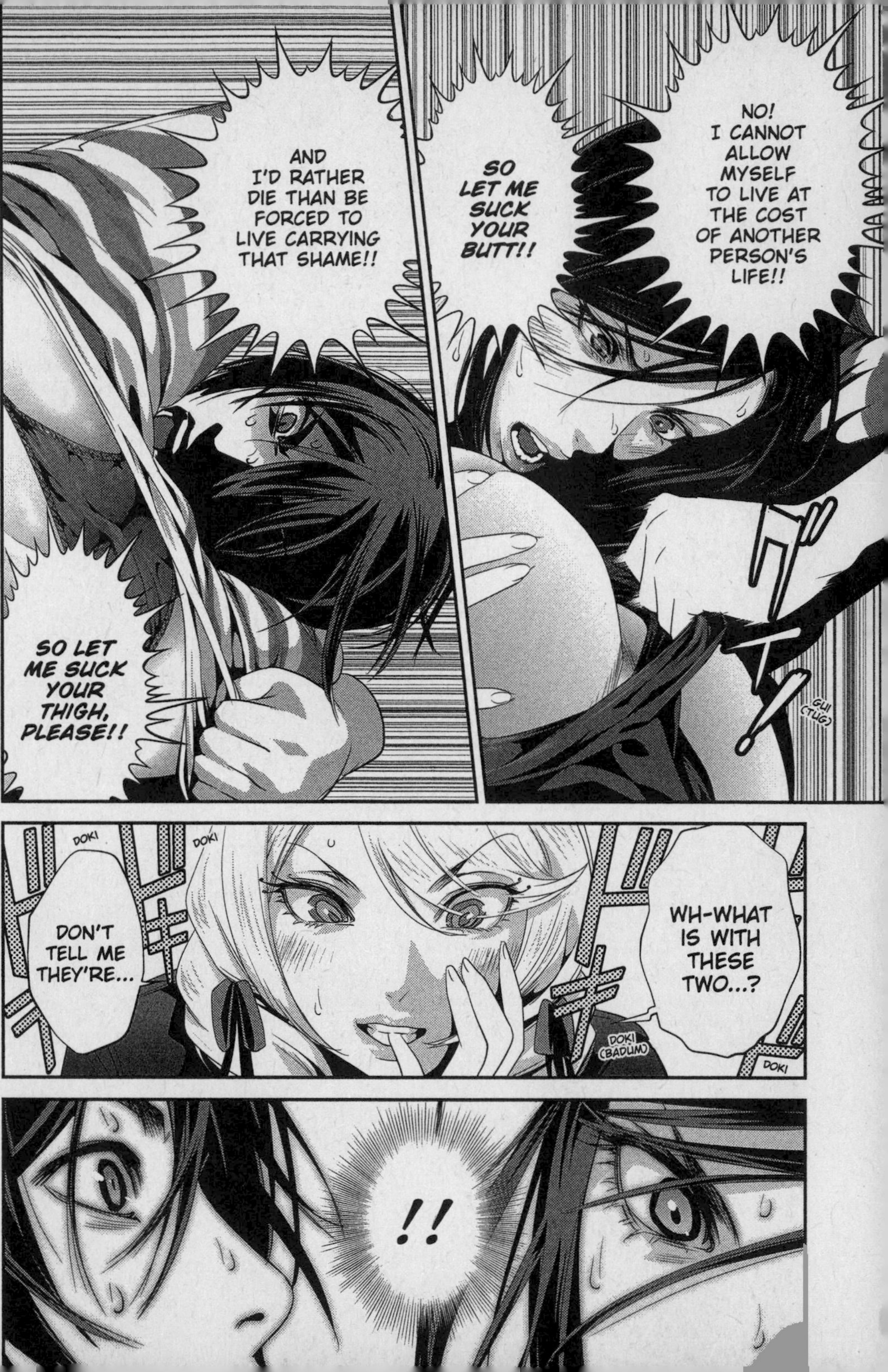
NO! I CANNOT ALLOW MYSELF TO LIVE AT THE COST OF ANOTHER PERSON'S LIFE!!
SO LET ME SUCK YOUR BUTT!!
GUI (TUG)
AND I'D RATHER DIE THAN BE FORCED TO LIVE CARRYING THAT SHAME!!
SO LET ME SUCK YOUR THIGH, PLEASE!!
WH-WHAT IS WITH THESE TWO...?
DOKI
DOKI (BADUM)
DON'T TELL ME THEY'RE...
DOKI
DOKI
!!

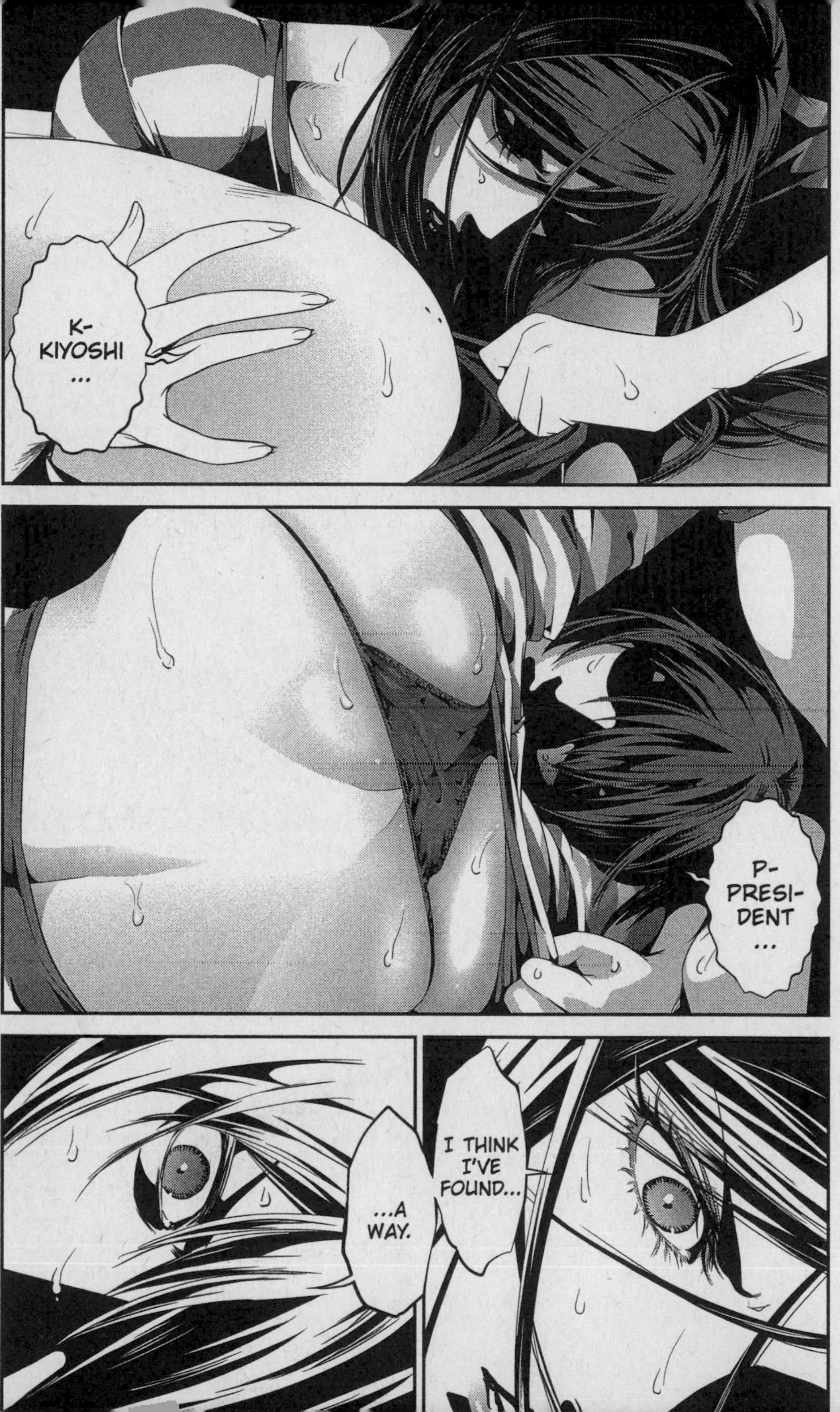
K-KIYOSHI...
P-PRESIDENT...
I THINK I'VE FOUND...
...A WAY.

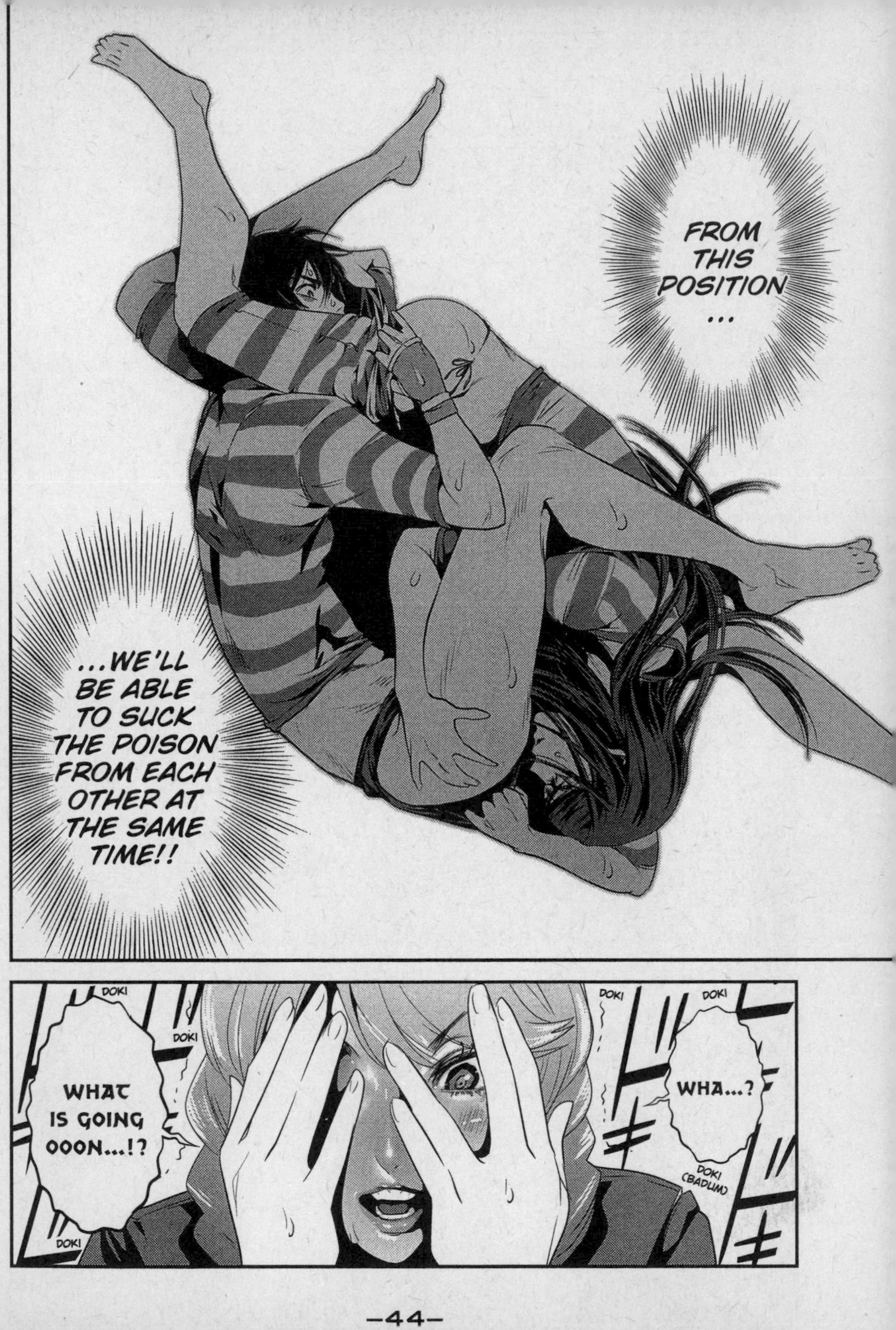
FROM THIS POSITION ...
...WE'LL BE ABLE TO SUCK THE POISON FROM EACH OTHER AT THE SAME TIME!!
DOKI
DOKI
WHA...?
DOKI (BADUM)
DOKI
DOKI
WHAT IS GOING OOON...!?
DOKI

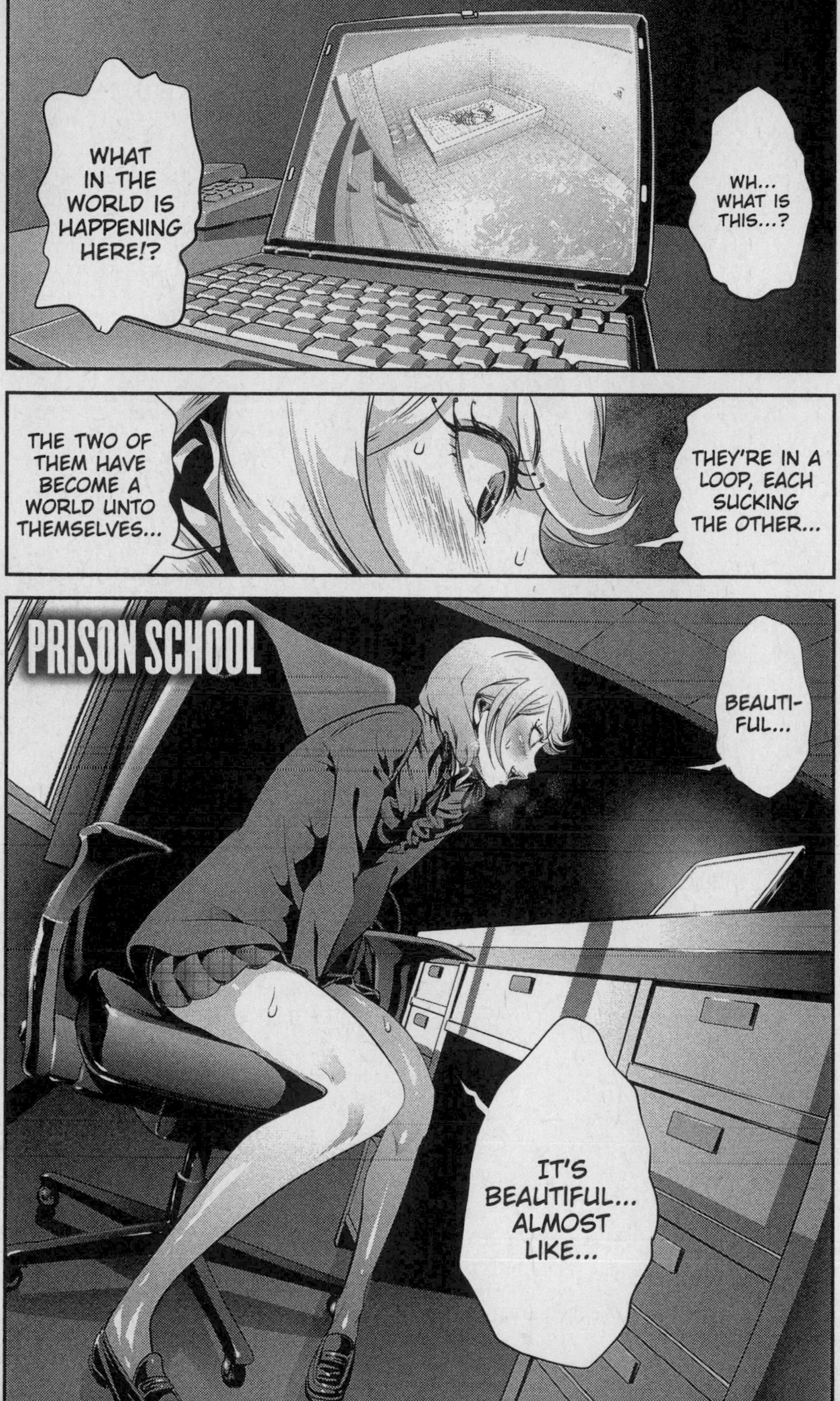
WH... WHAT IS THIS...?
WHAT IN THE WORLD IS HAPPENING HERE!?
THEY'RE IN A LOOP, EACH SUCKING THE OTHER...
THE TWO OF THEM HAVE BECOME A WORLD UNTO THEMSELVES...
PRISON SCHOOL
BEAUTIFUL...
IT'S BEAUTIFUL... ALMOST LIKE...

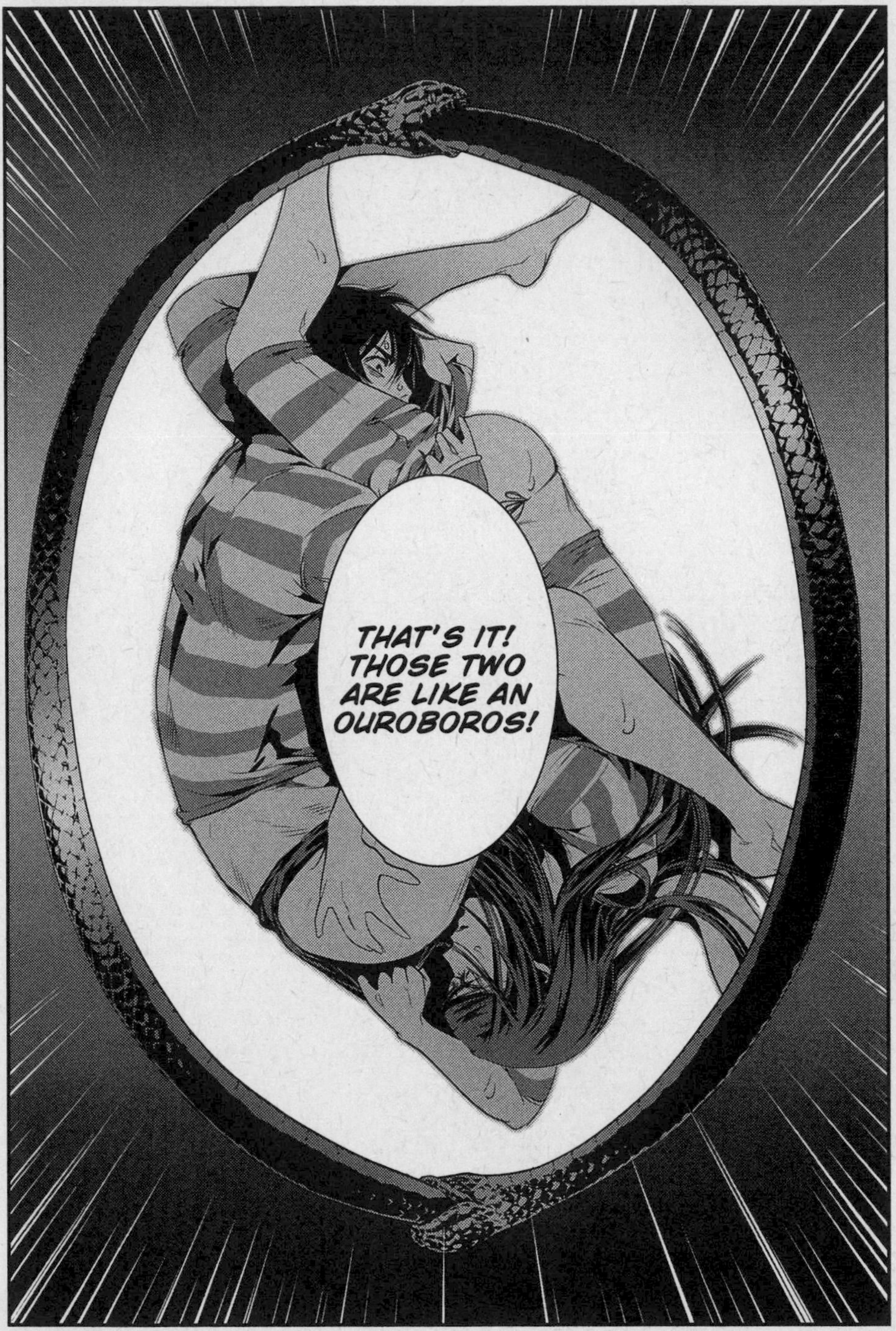
THAT'S IT! THOSE TWO ARE LIKE AN OUROBOROS!

CHAPTER 121: ENTRAPMENT

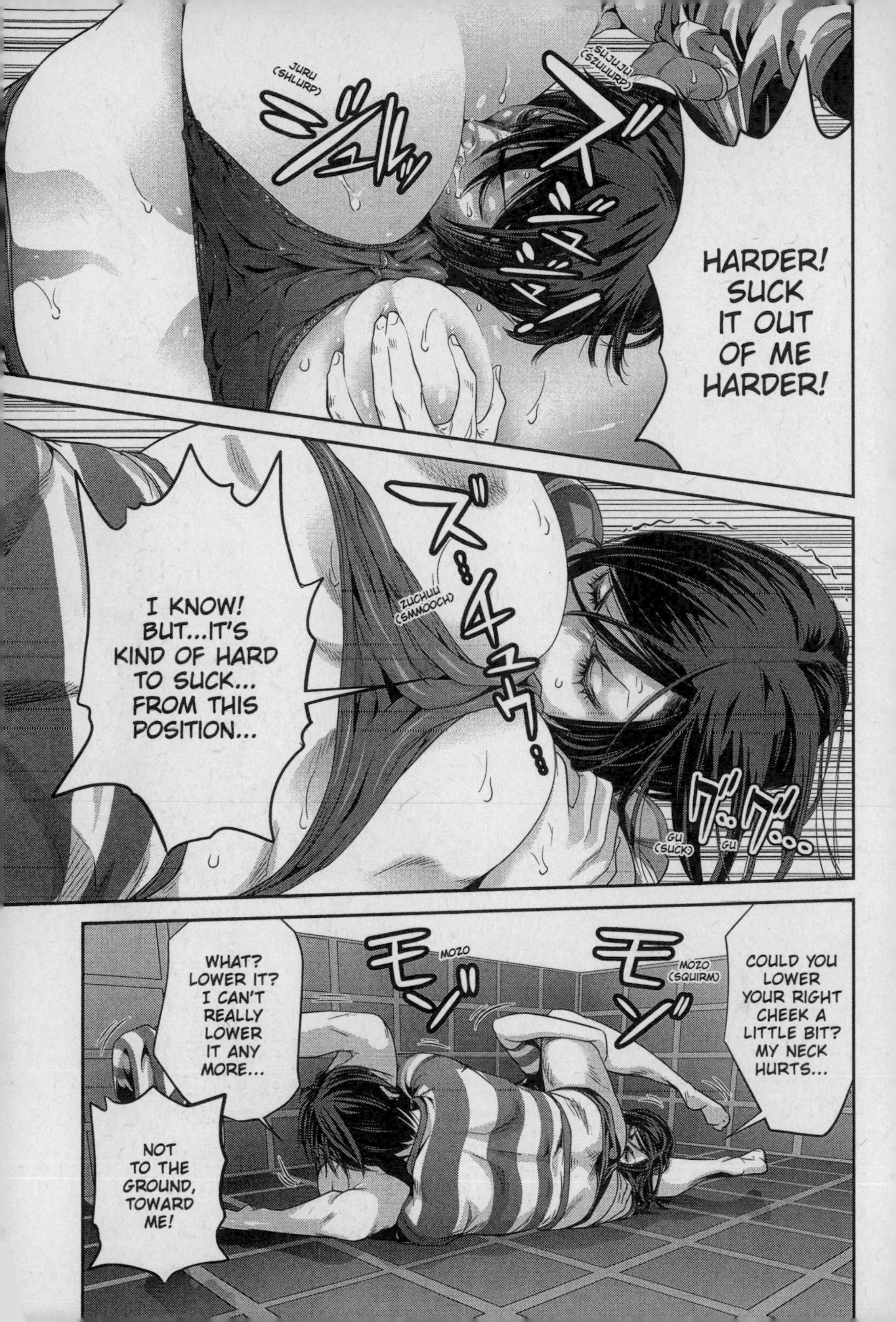
SUJUJU (SZUUURP)
JURU (SHLURP)
HARDER! SUCK IT OUT OF ME HARDER!
ZUCHUU (SMMOOCH)
I KNOW! BUT...IT'S KIND OF HARD TO SUCK... FROM THIS POSITION...
GU GU (SUCK)
COULD YOU LOWER YOUR RIGHT CHEEK A LITTLE BIT? MY NECK HURTS...
MOZO (SQUIRM)
MOZO
WHAT? LOWER IT? I CAN'T REALLY LOWER IT ANY MORE...
NOT TO THE GROUND, TOWARD ME!

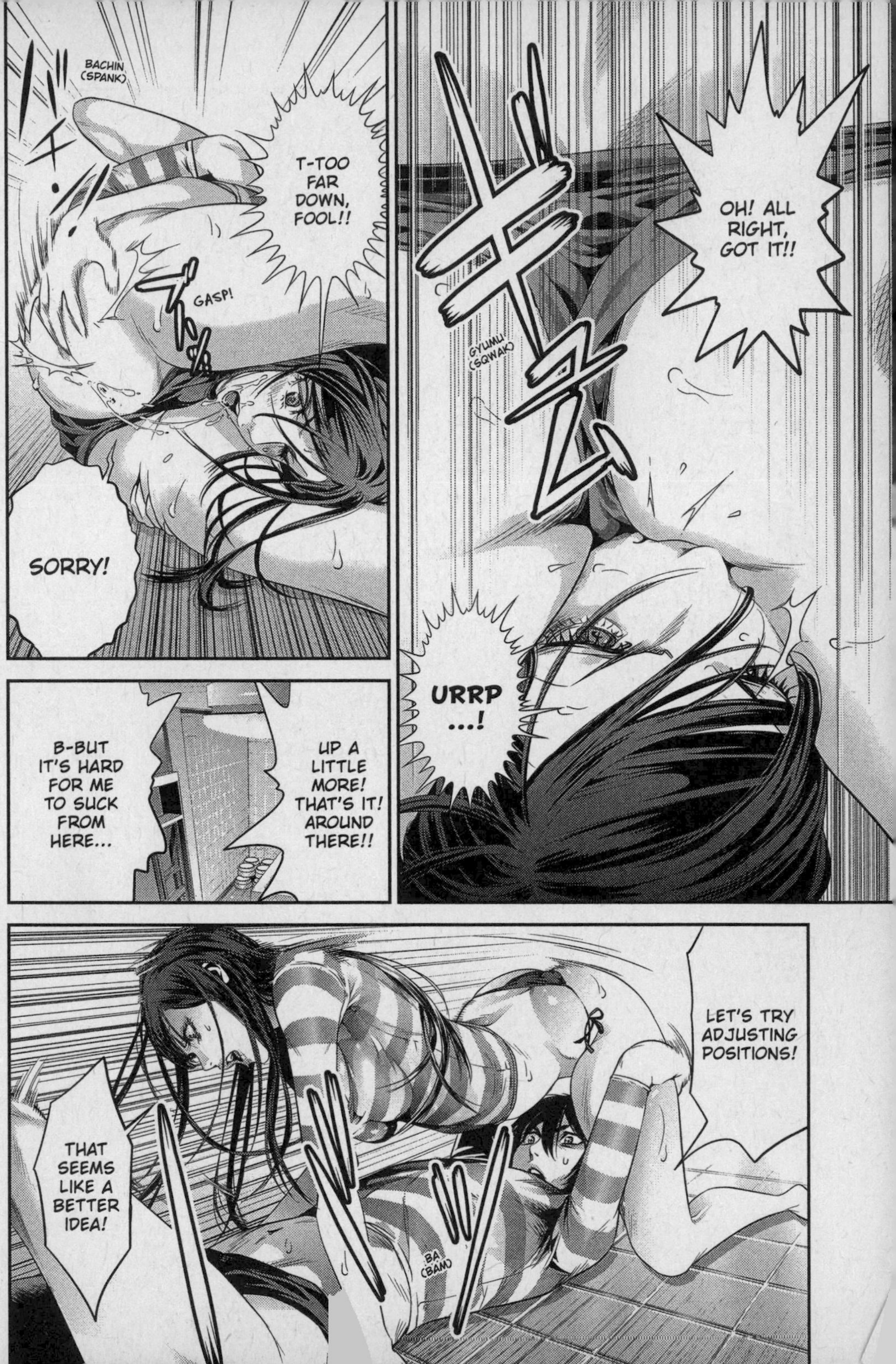
OH! ALL RIGHT, GOT IT!!
GYUMU (SQWAK)
URRP ...!
BACHIN (SPANK)
T-TOO FAR DOWN, FOOL!!
GASP!
SORRY!
UP A LITTLE MORE! THAT'S IT! AROUND THERE!!
B-BUT IT'S HARD FOR ME TO SUCK FROM HERE...
LET'S TRY ADJUSTING POSITIONS!
THAT SEEMS LIKE A BETTER IDEA!
BA (BAM)

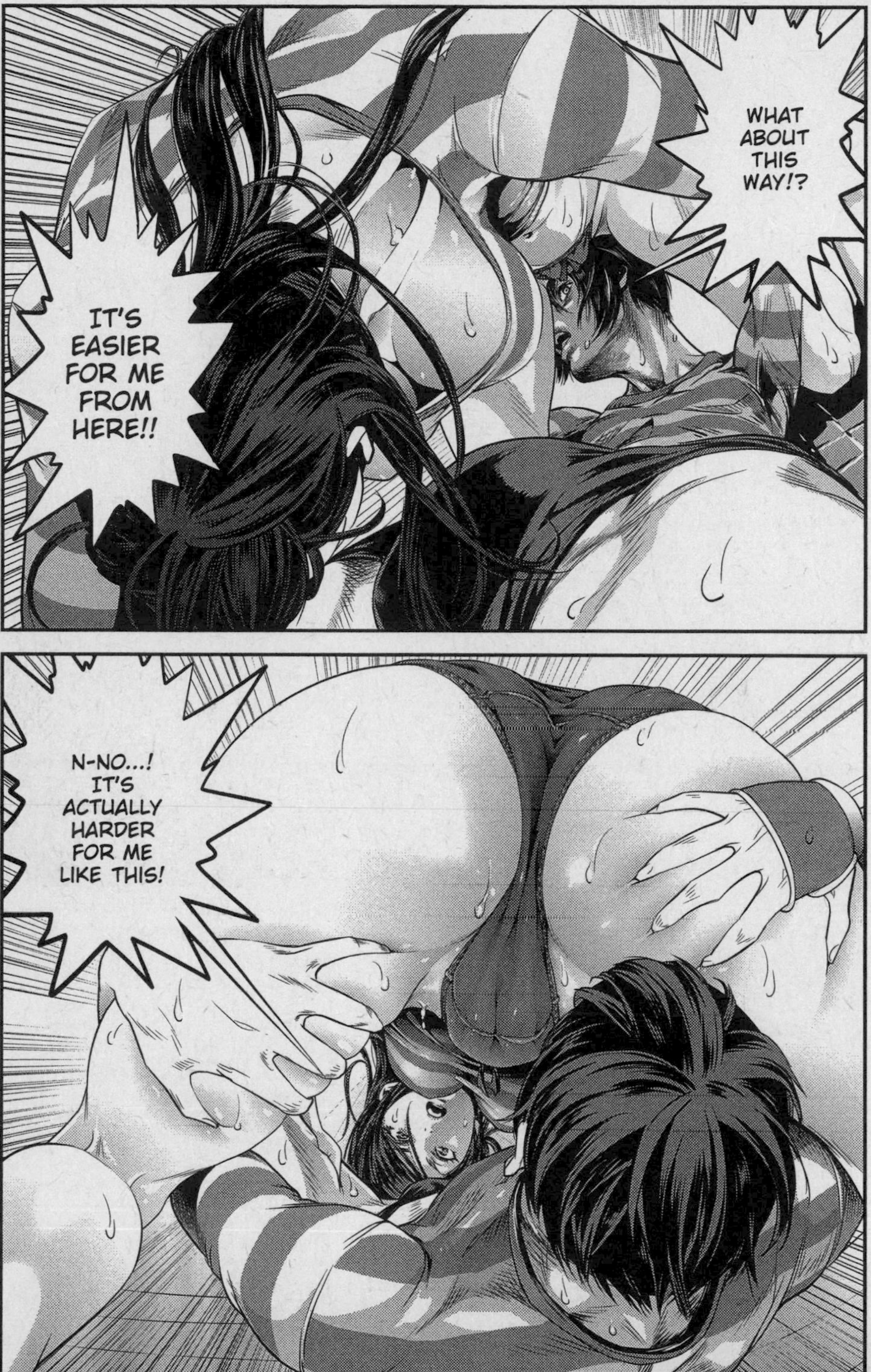
WHAT ABOUT THIS WAY!?
IT'S EASIER FOR ME FROM HERE!!
N-NO...! IT'S ACTUALLY HARDER FOR ME LIKE THIS!

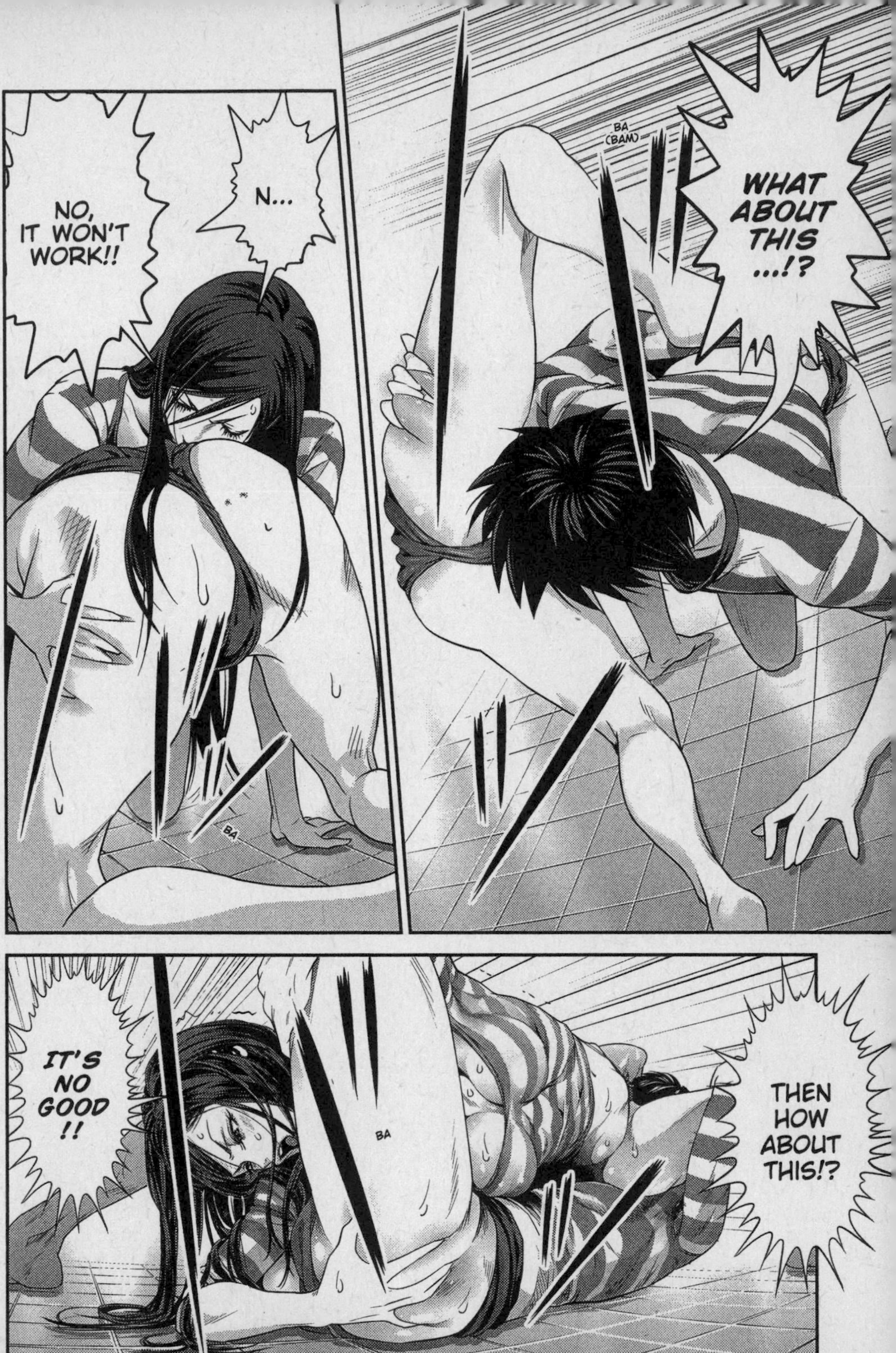
BA
(BAM)
WHAT ABOUT THIS ...!?
N...
NO, IT WON'T WORK!!
BA
THEN HOW ABOUT THIS!?
BA
IT'S NO GOOD !!

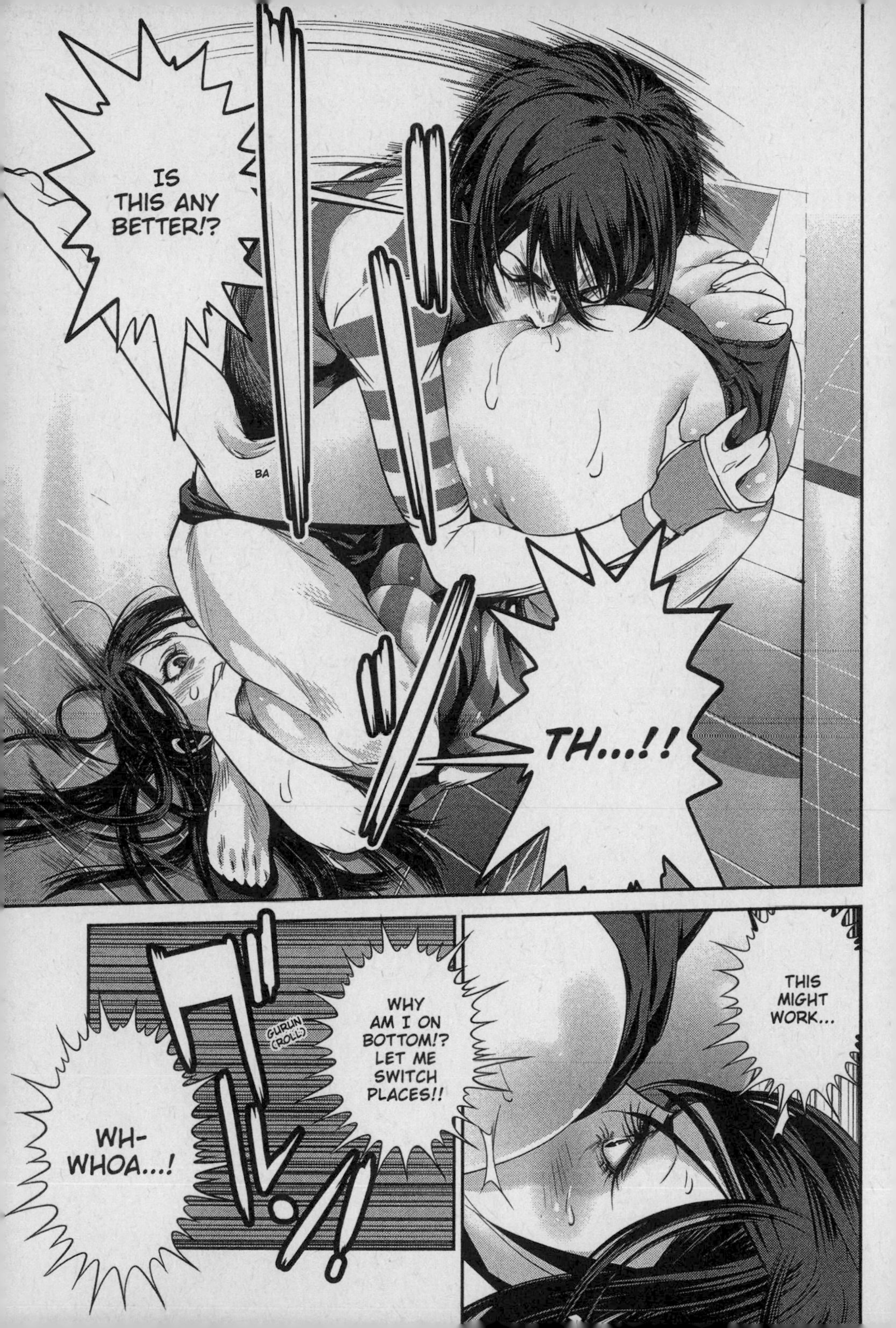
IS THIS ANY BETTER!?
BA
TH...!!
THIS MIGHT WORK...
WHY AM I ON BOTTOM!? LET ME SWITCH PLACES!!
GURUN (ROLL)
WH- WHOA...!

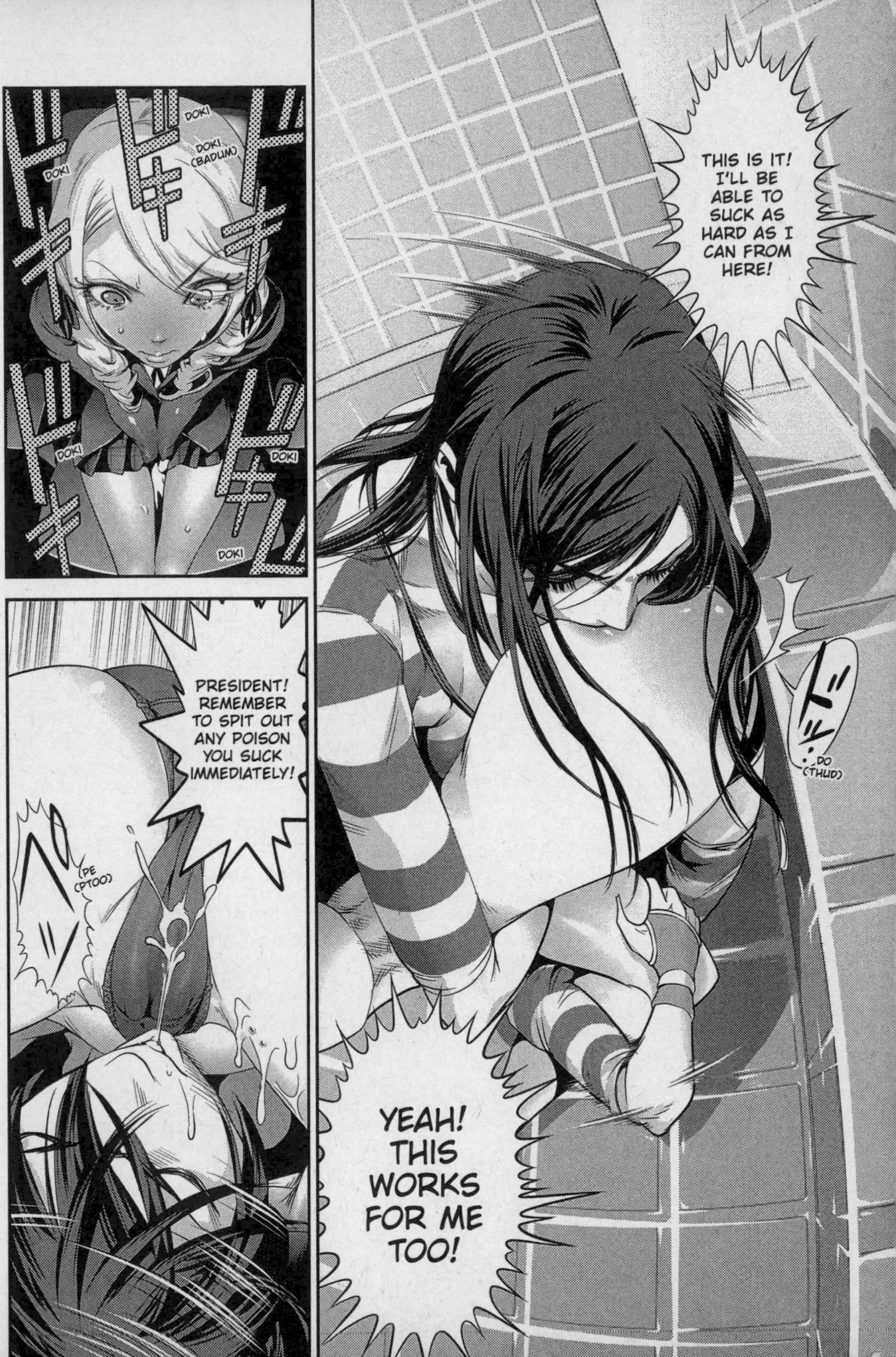
THIS IS IT! I'LL BE ABLE TO SUCK AS HARD AS I CAN FROM HERE!
DO (THUD)
YEAH! THIS WORKS FOR ME TOO!
DOKI
DOKI (BADUM)
DOKI
DOKI
DOKI
DOKI
PRESIDENT! REMEMBER TO SPIT OUT ANY POISON YOU SUCK IMMEDIATELY!
PE (PTOO)

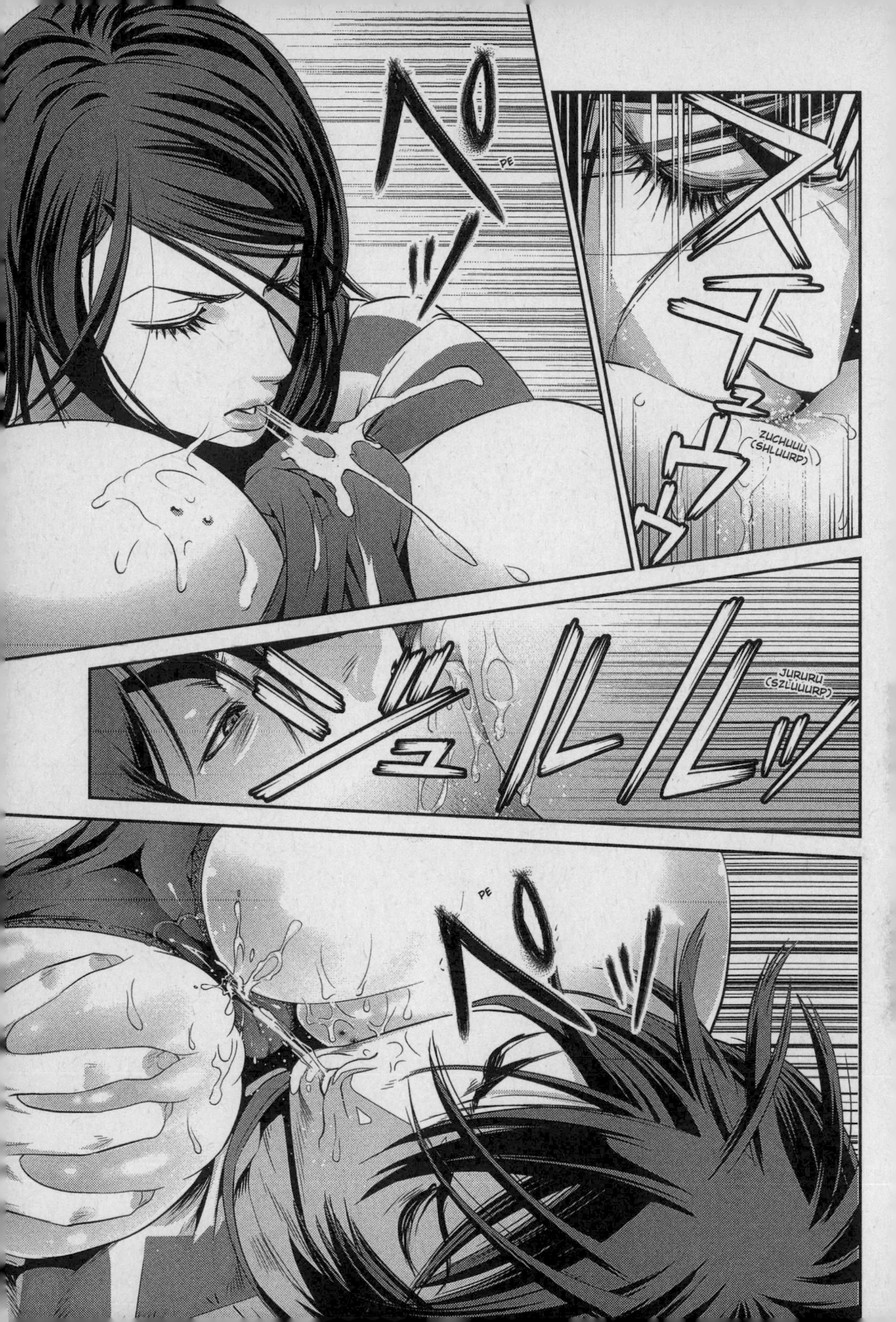
ZUCHUUU (SHLUURP)
PE
JURURU (SZLUUURP)
PE

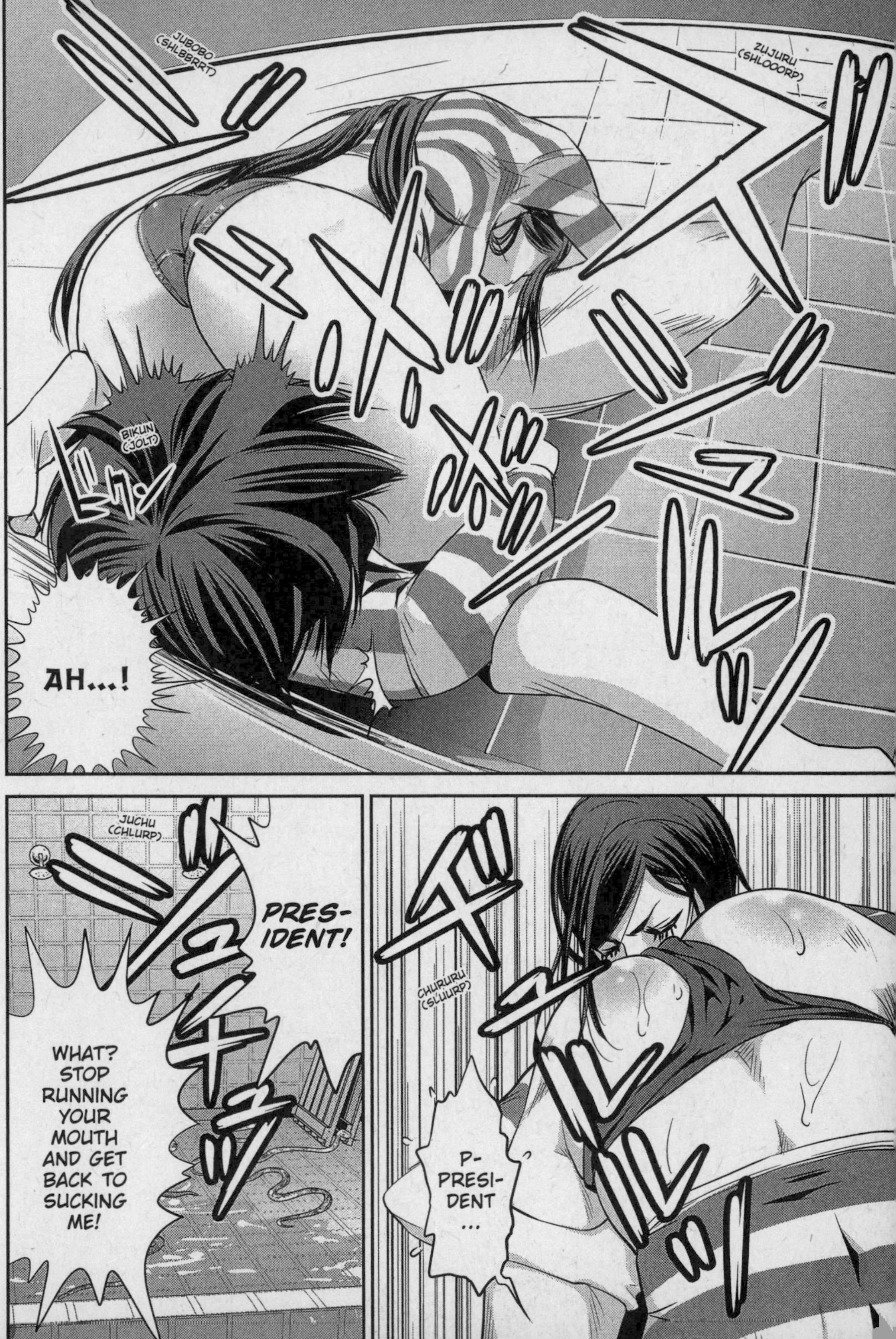
ZUJURU (SHLOOORP)
JUBOBO (SHLBBRRT)
BIKUN (JOLT)
AH...!
CHURURU (SLUURP)
P-PRESIDENT...
JUCHU (CHLURP)
PRESIDENT!
WHAT? STOP RUNNING YOUR MOUTH AND GET BACK TO SUCKING ME!

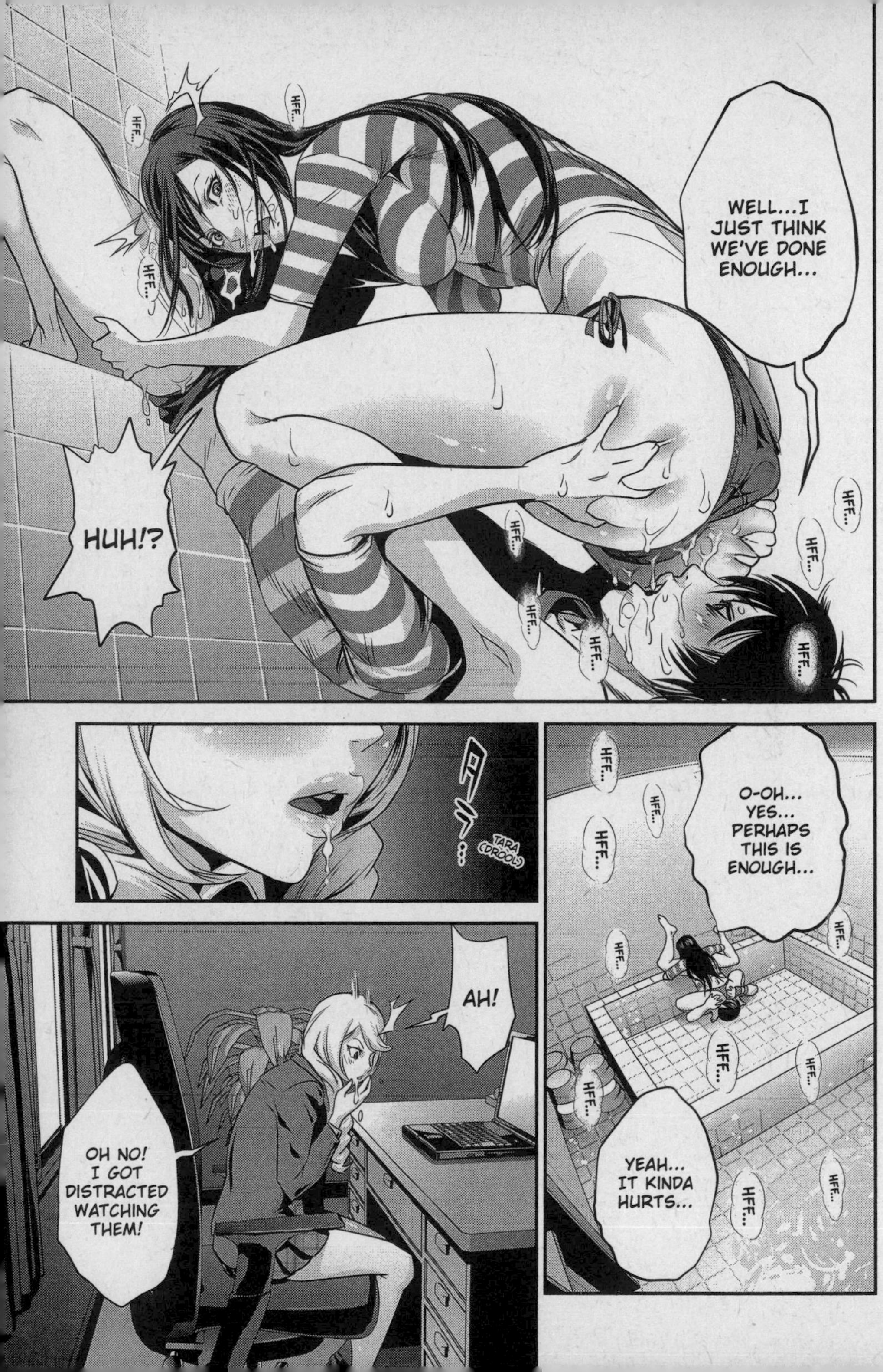
WELL...I JUST THINK WE'VE DONE ENOUGH...
HFF...
HFF...
HFF...
HFF...
HFF...
HFF...
HFF...
HFF...
HUH!?
O-OH... YES... PERHAPS THIS IS ENOUGH...
HFF...
HFF...
HFF...
YEAH... IT KINDA HURTS...
HFF...
HFF...
HFF...
HFF...
HFF...
HFF...
TARA (DROOL)
AH!
OH NO! I GOT DISTRACTED WATCHING THEM!

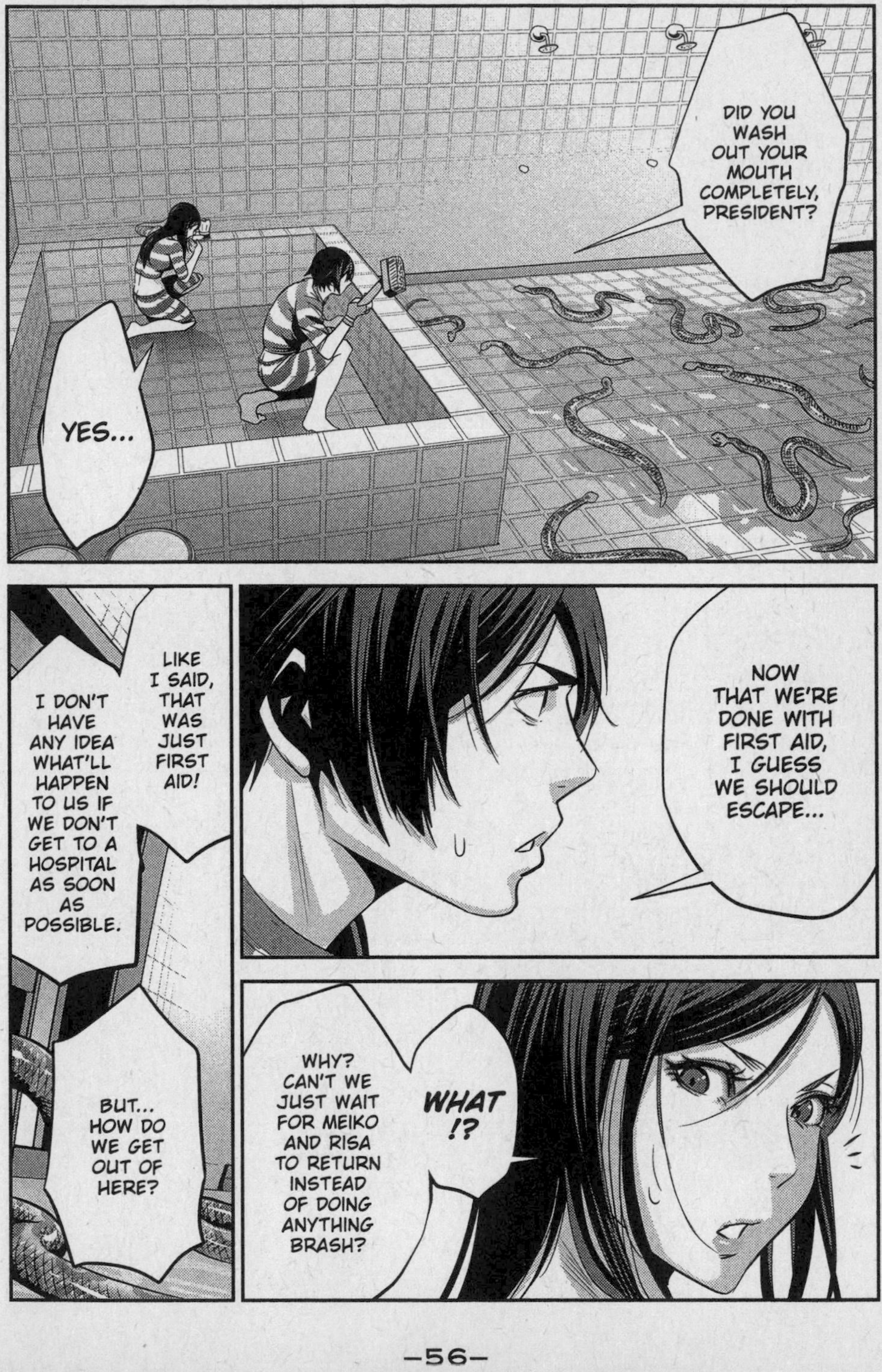
DID YOU WASH OUT YOUR MOUTH COMPLETELY, PRESIDENT?
YES...
NOW THAT WE'RE DONE WITH FIRST AID, I GUESS WE SHOULD ESCAPE...
WHAT!?
WHY? CAN'T WE JUST WAIT FOR MEIKO AND RISA TO RETURN INSTEAD OF DOING ANYTHING BRASH?
LIKE I SAID, THAT WAS JUST FIRST AID!
I DON'T HAVE ANY IDEA WHAT'LL HAPPEN TO US IF WE DON'T GET TO A HOSPITAL AS SOON AS POSSIBLE.
BUT... HOW DO WE GET OUT OF HERE?

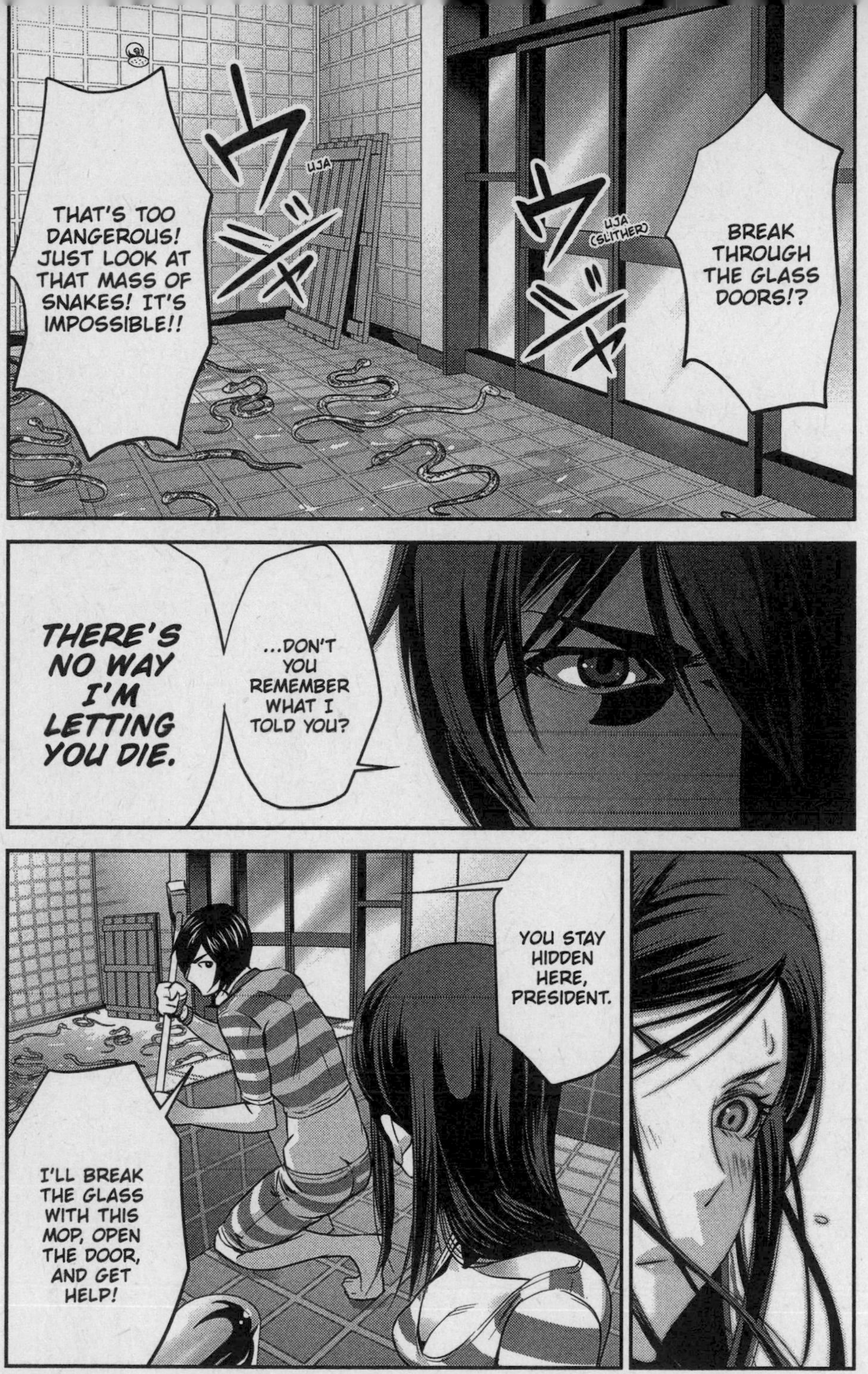
UJA (SLITHER)
BREAK THROUGH THE GLASS DOORS!?
UJA
THAT'S TOO DANGEROUS! JUST LOOK AT THAT MASS OF SNAKES! IT'S IMPOSSIBLE!!
...DON'T YOU REMEMBER WHAT I TOLD YOU?
THERE'S NO WAY I'M LETTING YOU DIE.
YOU STAY HIDDEN HERE, PRESIDENT.
I'LL BREAK THE GLASS WITH THIS MOP, OPEN THE DOOR, AND GET HELP!

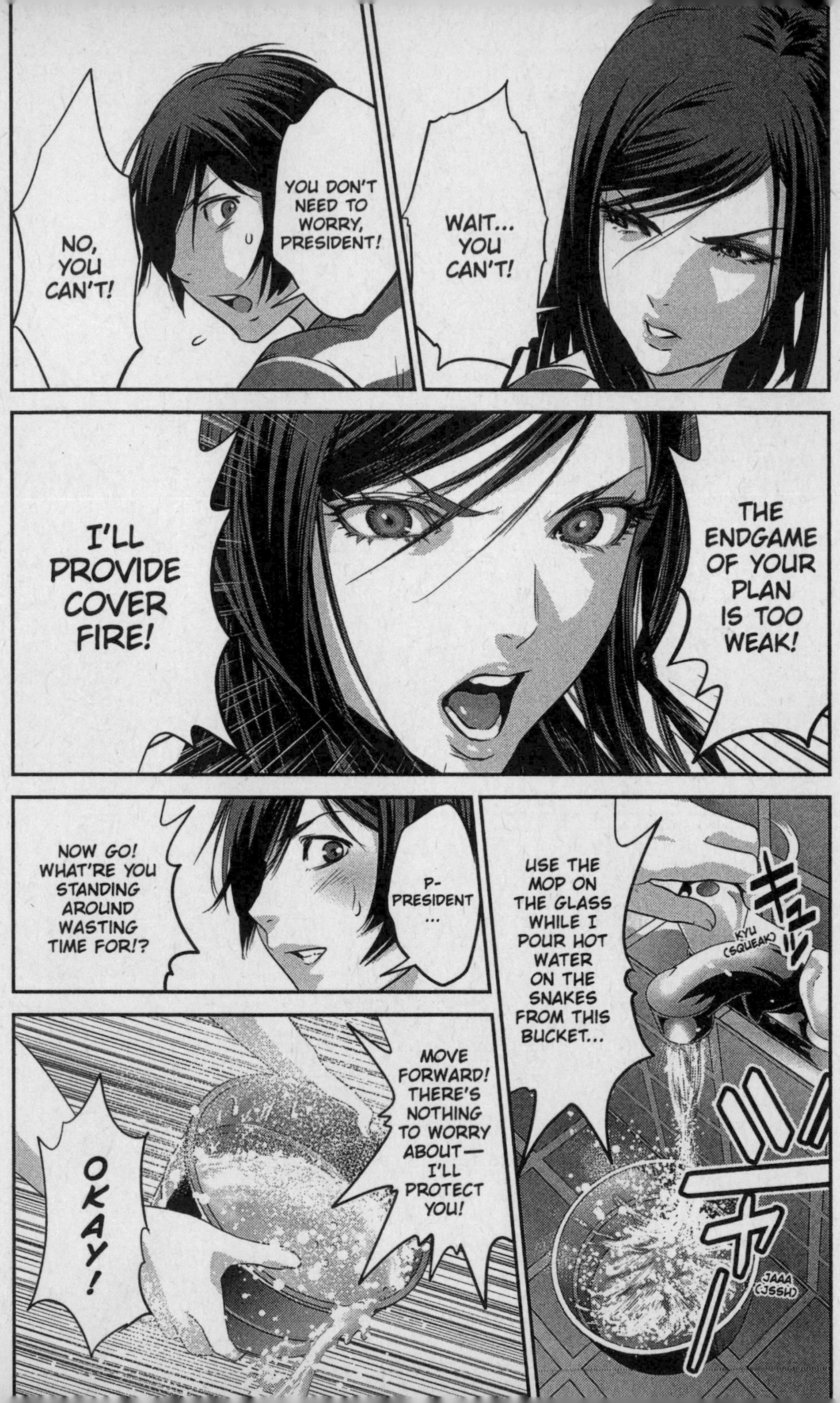
WAIT... YOU CAN'T!
YOU DON'T NEED TO WORRY, PRESIDENT!
NO, YOU CAN'T!
THE ENDGAME OF YOUR PLAN IS TOO WEAK!
I'LL PROVIDE COVER FIRE!
USE THE MOP ON THE GLASS WHILE I POUR HOT WATER ON THE SNAKES FROM THIS BUCKET...
KYU (SQUEAK)
P-PRESIDENT...
NOW GO! WHAT'RE YOU STANDING AROUND WASTING TIME FOR!?
JAAA (JSSH)
MOVE FORWARD! THERE'S NOTHING TO WORRY ABOUT—I'LL PROTECT YOU!
OKAY!

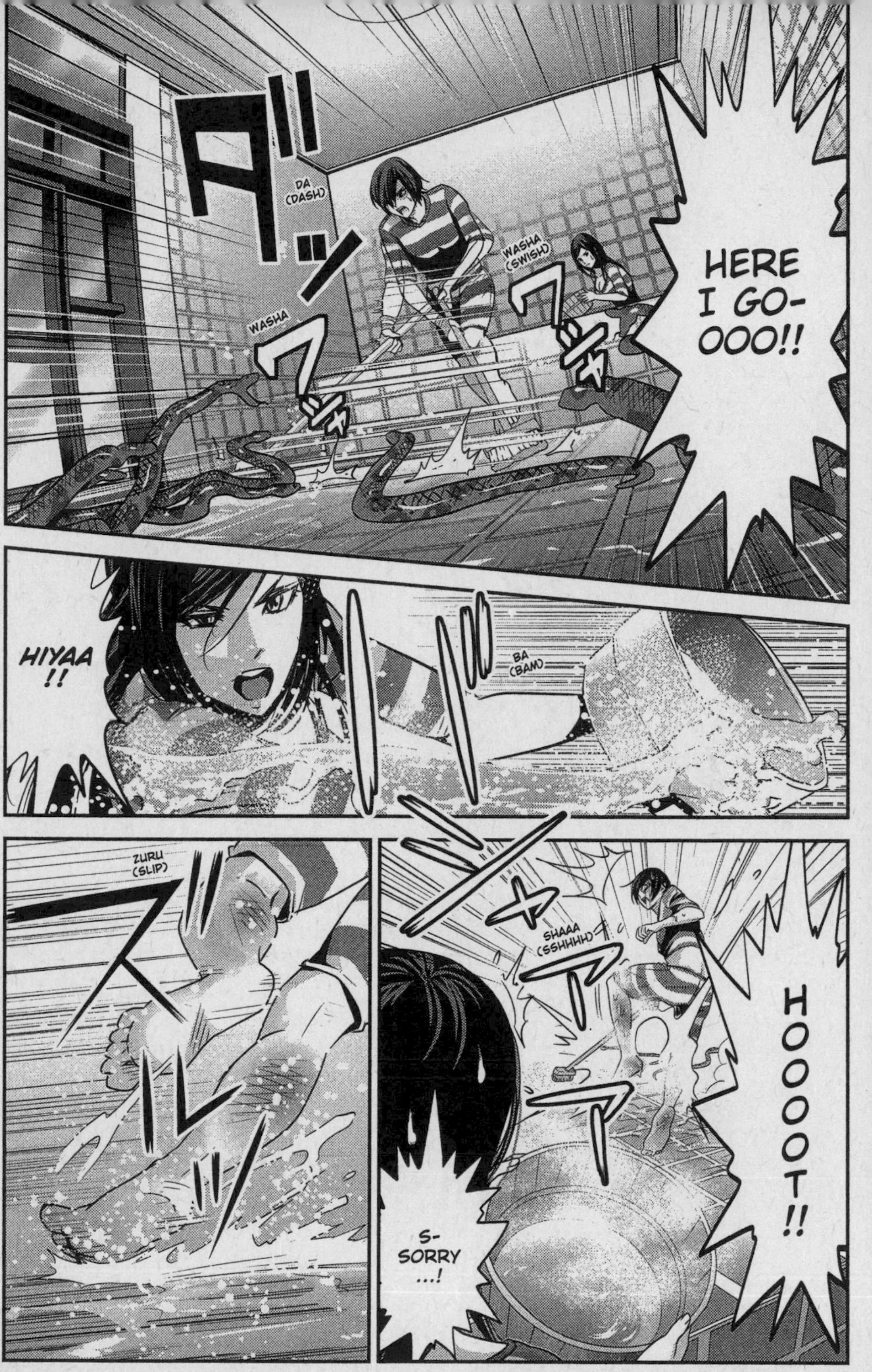
HERE I GO-OOO!!
DA (DASH)
WASHA (SWISH)
WASHA
HIYAA !!
BA (BAM)
SHAAA (SSHHHH)
HOOOOT!!
ZURU (SLIP)
S-SORRY ...!

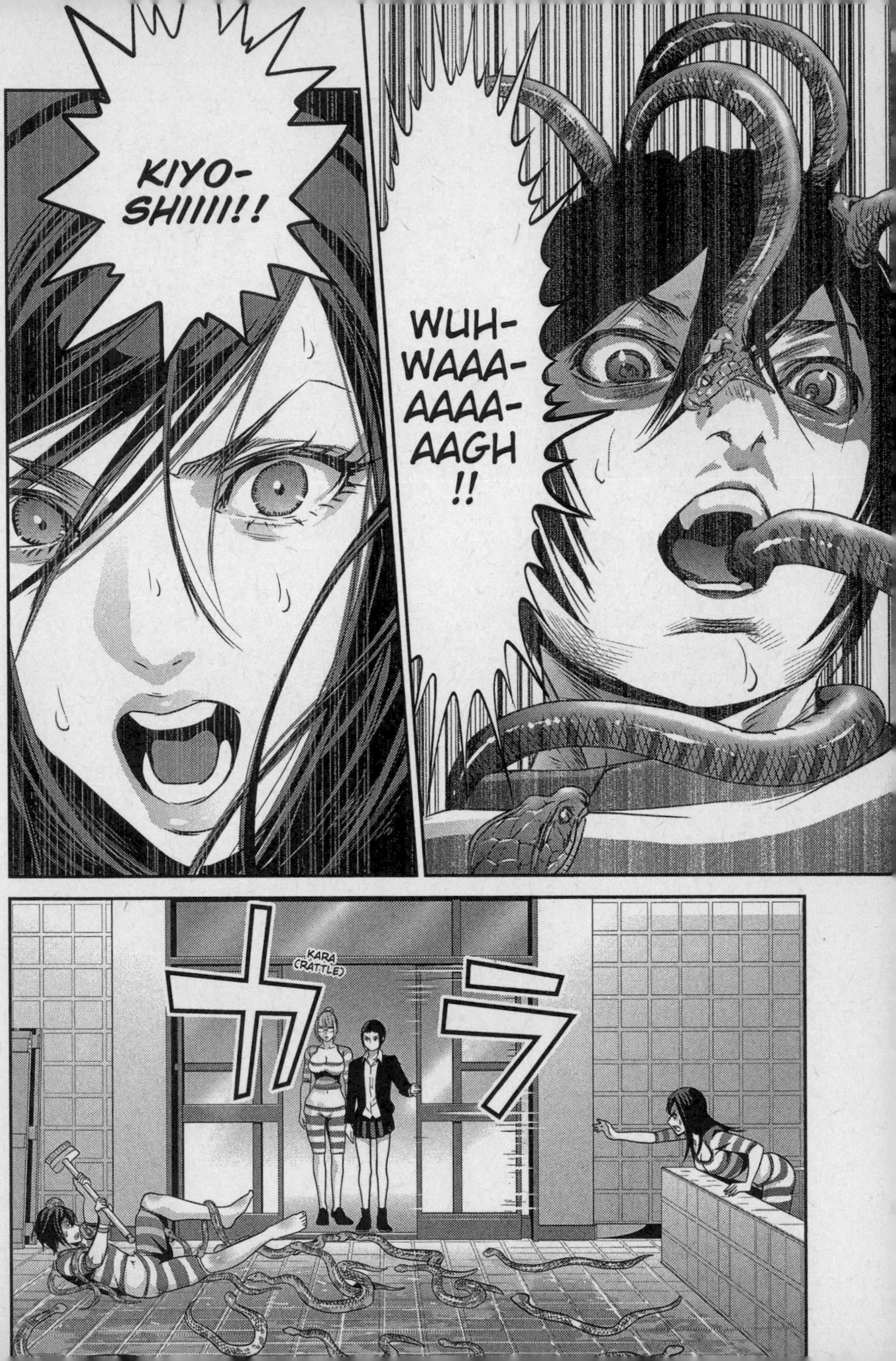
WUH-WAAA-AAAA-AAGH!!
KIYO-SHIIIII!!
KARA (RATTLE)
カラ

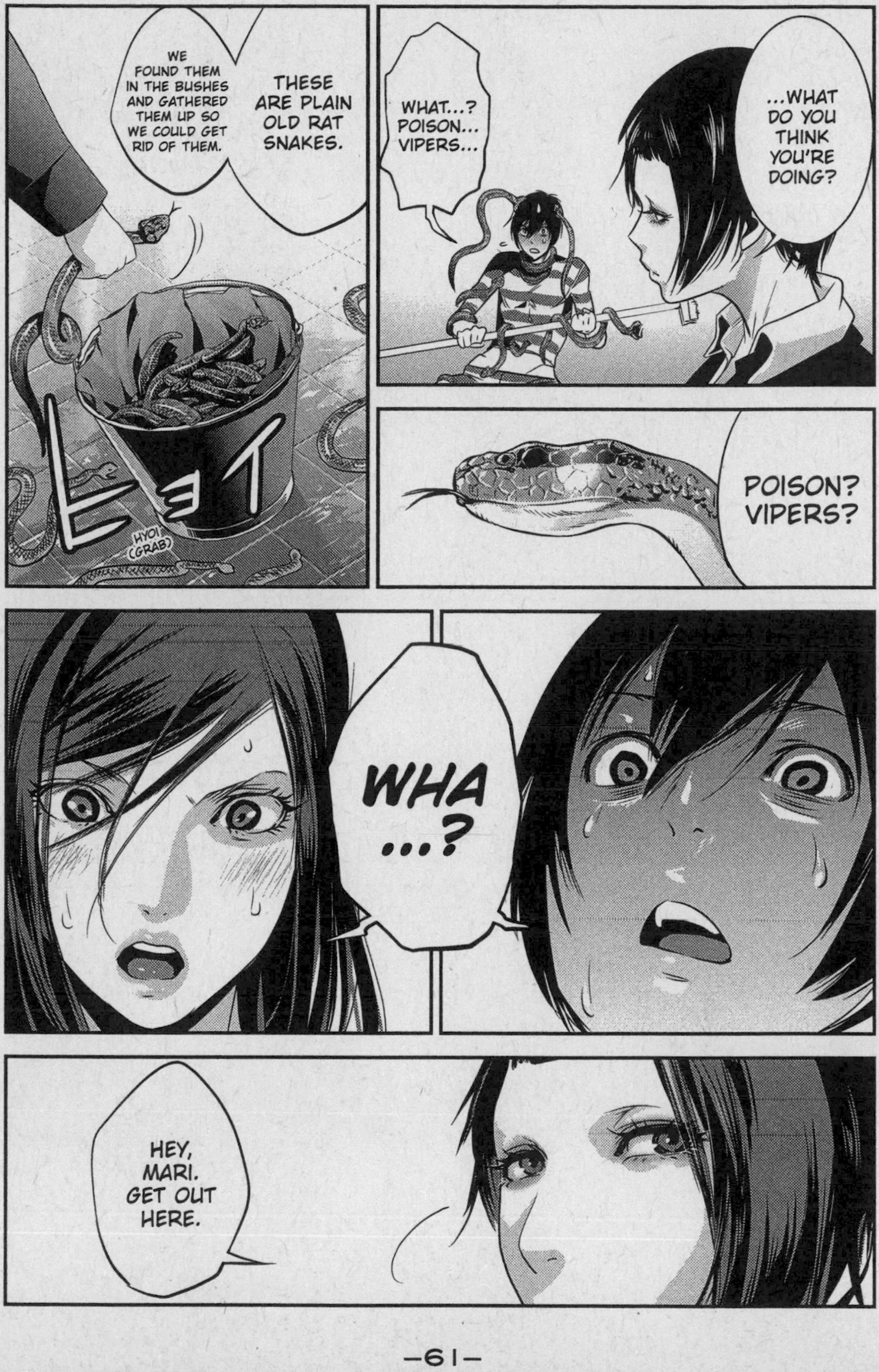
...WHAT DO YOU THINK YOU'RE DOING?
WHAT...? POISON... VIPERS...
THESE ARE PLAIN OLD RAT SNAKES.
WE FOUND THEM IN THE BUSHES AND GATHERED THEM UP SO WE COULD GET RID OF THEM.
HYOI (GRAB)
POISON? VIPERS?
WHA ...?
HEY, MARI. GET OUT HERE.

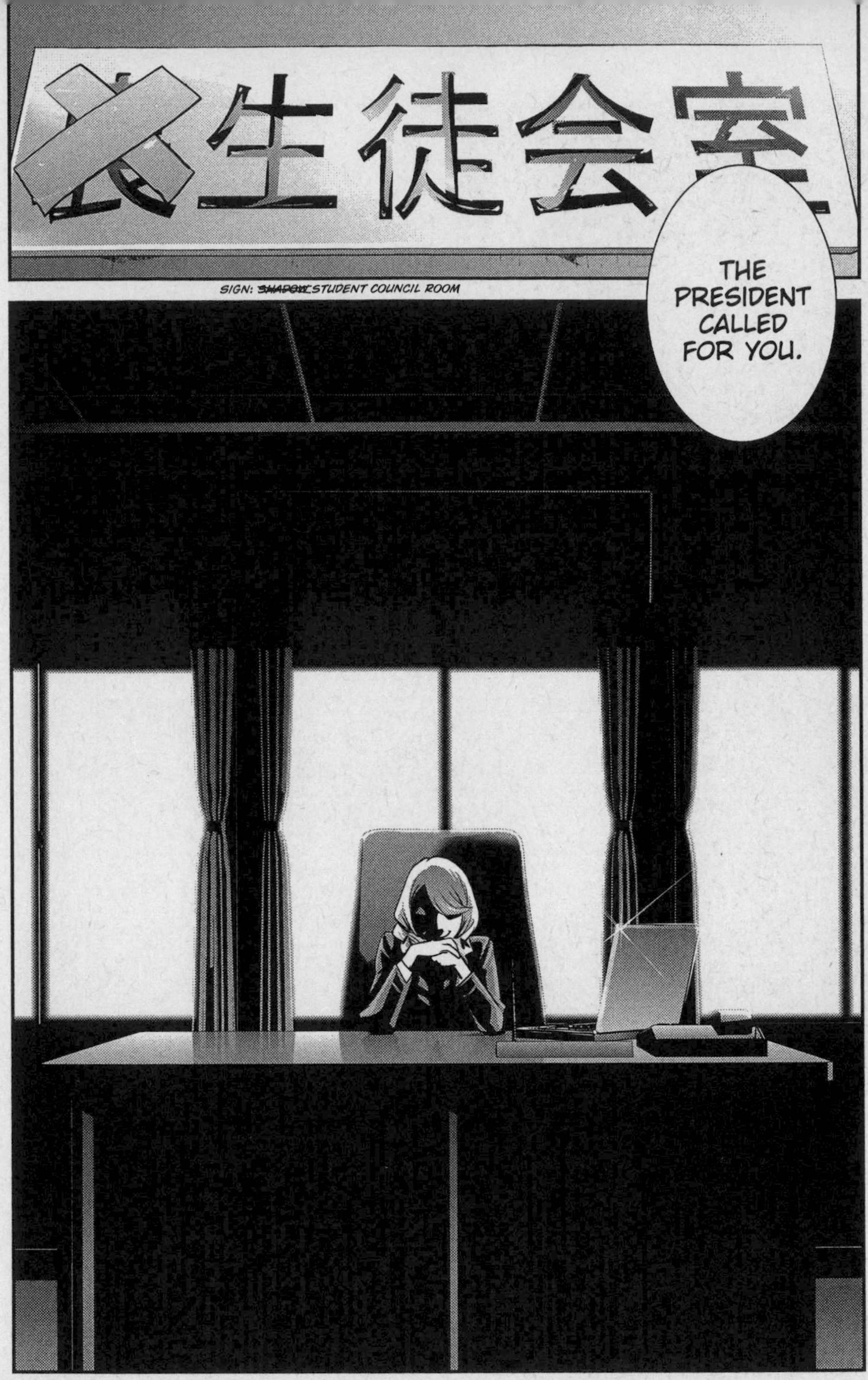
生徒会室
SIGN: ~~SHADOW~~ STUDENT COUNCIL ROOM
THE PRESIDENT CALLED FOR YOU.

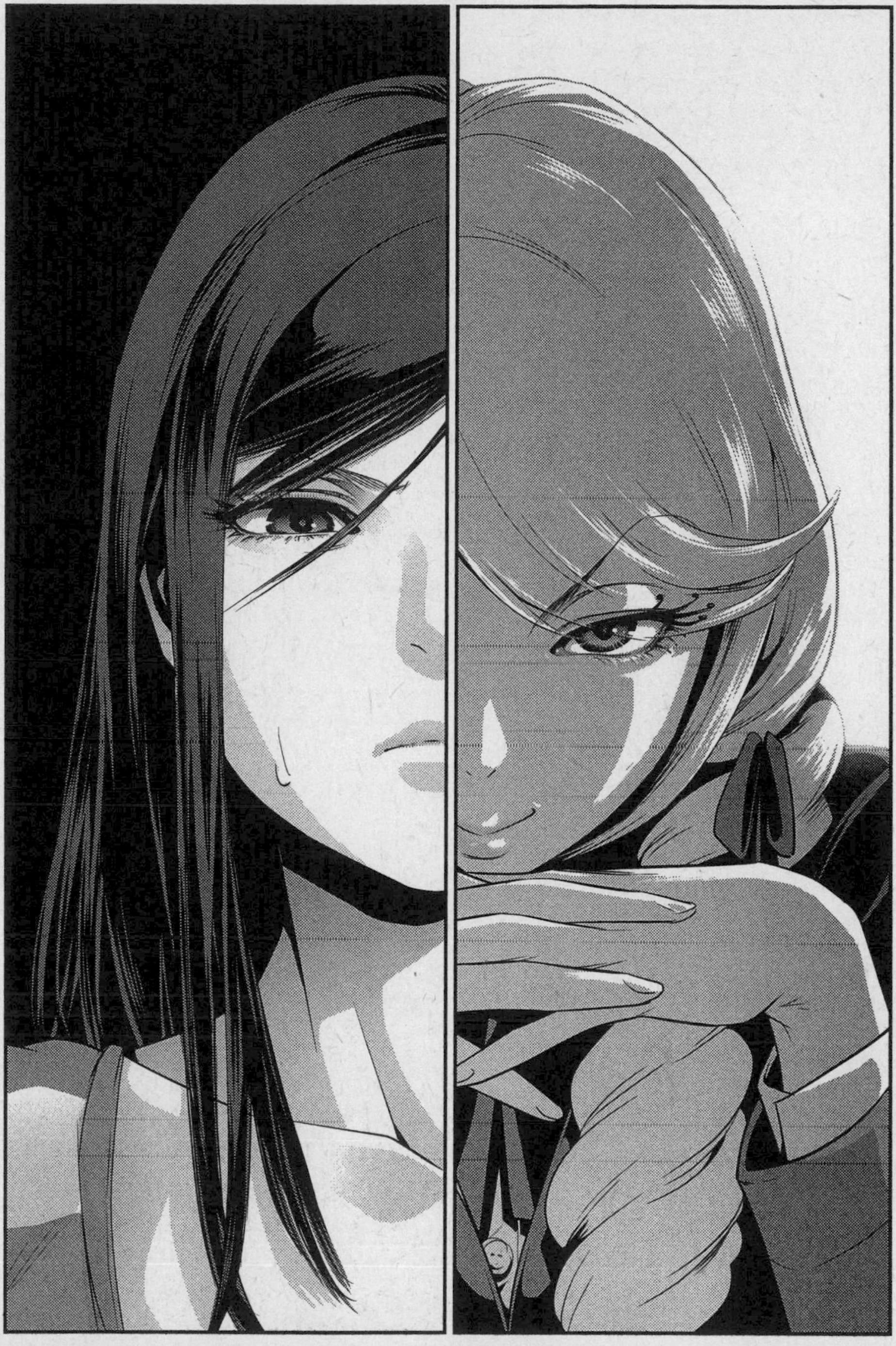

CHAPTER 122: THE BAD SLEEP WELL

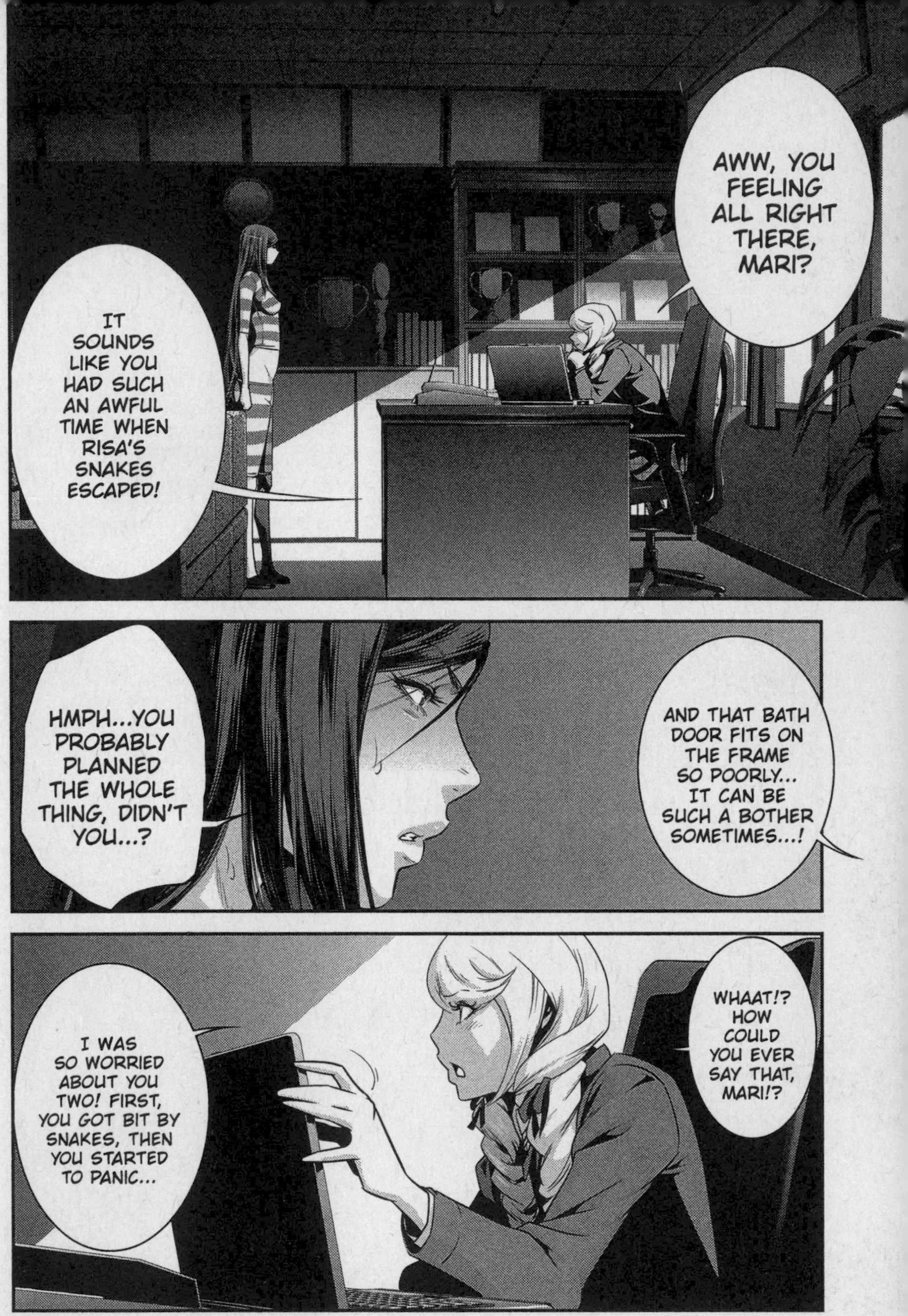
AWW, YOU FEELING ALL RIGHT THERE, MARI?
IT SOUNDS LIKE YOU HAD SUCH AN AWFUL TIME WHEN RISA'S SNAKES ESCAPED!
AND THAT BATH DOOR FITS ON THE FRAME SO POORLY... IT CAN BE SUCH A BOTHER SOMETIMES...!
HMPH...YOU PROBABLY PLANNED THE WHOLE THING, DIDN'T YOU...?
WHAAT!? HOW COULD YOU EVER SAY THAT, MARI!?
I WAS SO WORRIED ABOUT YOU TWO! FIRST, YOU GOT BIT BY SNAKES, THEN YOU STARTED TO PANIC...

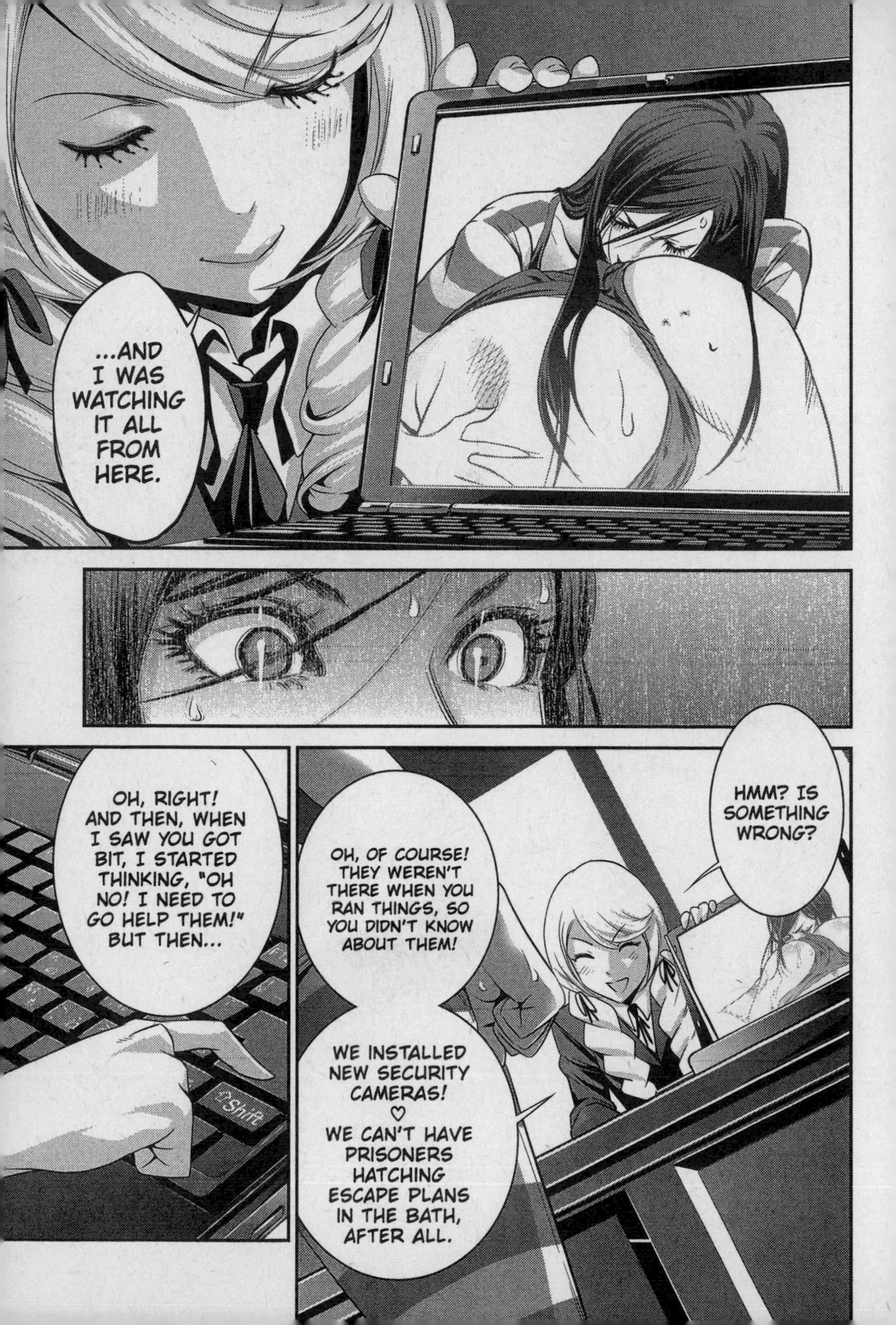
...AND I WAS WATCHING IT ALL FROM HERE.
HMM? IS SOMETHING WRONG?
OH, OF COURSE! THEY WEREN'T THERE WHEN YOU RAN THINGS, SO YOU DIDN'T KNOW ABOUT THEM!
WE INSTALLED NEW SECURITY CAMERAS! ♡ WE CAN'T HAVE PRISONERS HATCHING ESCAPE PLANS IN THE BATH, AFTER ALL.
OH, RIGHT! AND THEN, WHEN I SAW YOU GOT BIT, I STARTED THINKING, "OH NO! I NEED TO GO HELP THEM!" BUT THEN...
Shift

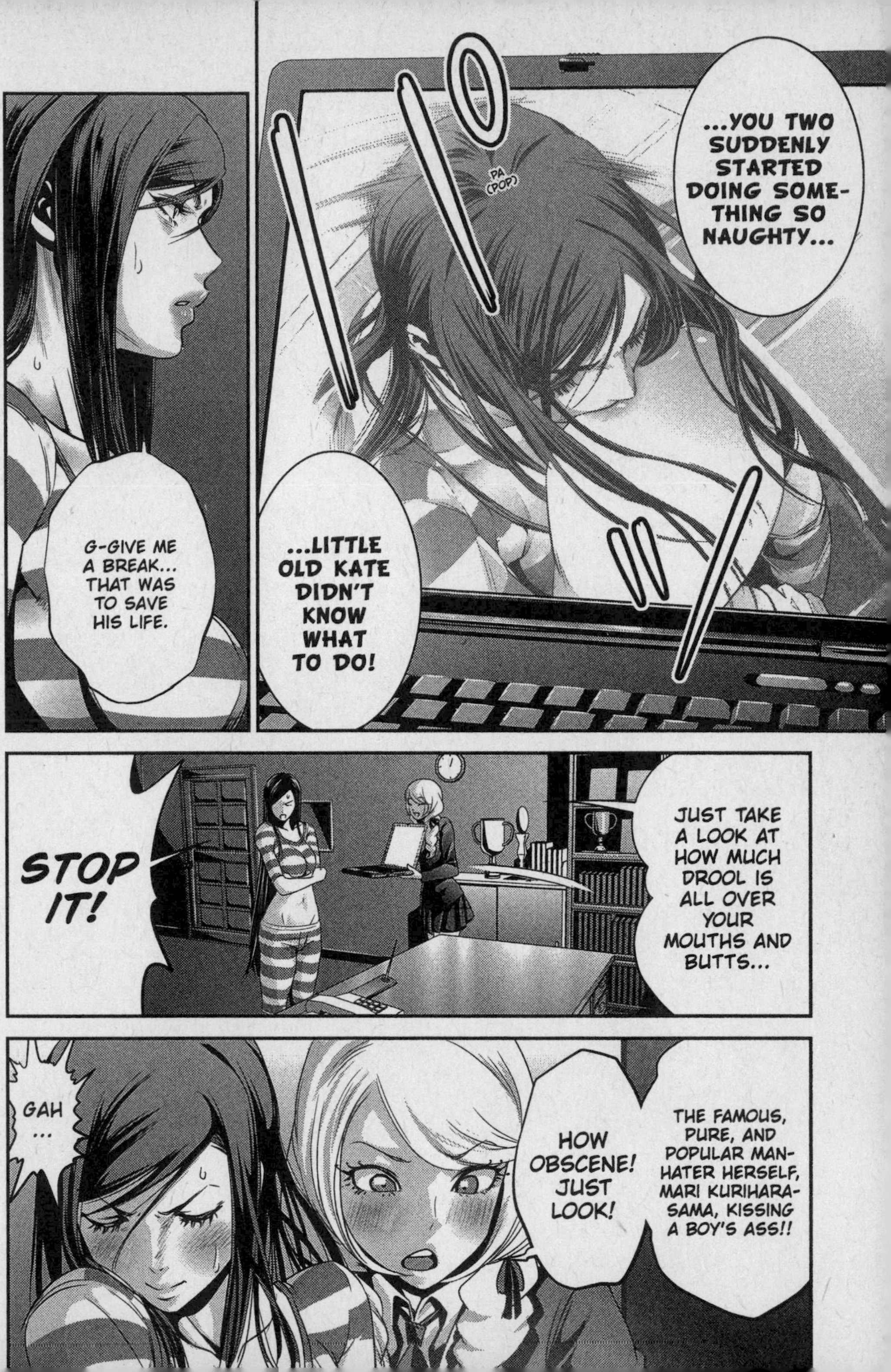
...YOU TWO SUDDENLY STARTED DOING SOME-THING SO NAUGHTY...
PA (POP)
...LITTLE OLD KATE DIDN'T KNOW WHAT TO DO!
G-GIVE ME A BREAK... THAT WAS TO SAVE HIS LIFE.
JUST TAKE A LOOK AT HOW MUCH DROOL IS ALL OVER YOUR MOUTHS AND BUTTS...
STOP IT!
THE FAMOUS, PURE, AND POPULAR MAN-HATER HERSELF, MARI KURIHARA-SAMA, KISSING A BOY'S ASS!!
HOW OBSCENE! JUST LOOK!
GAH ...

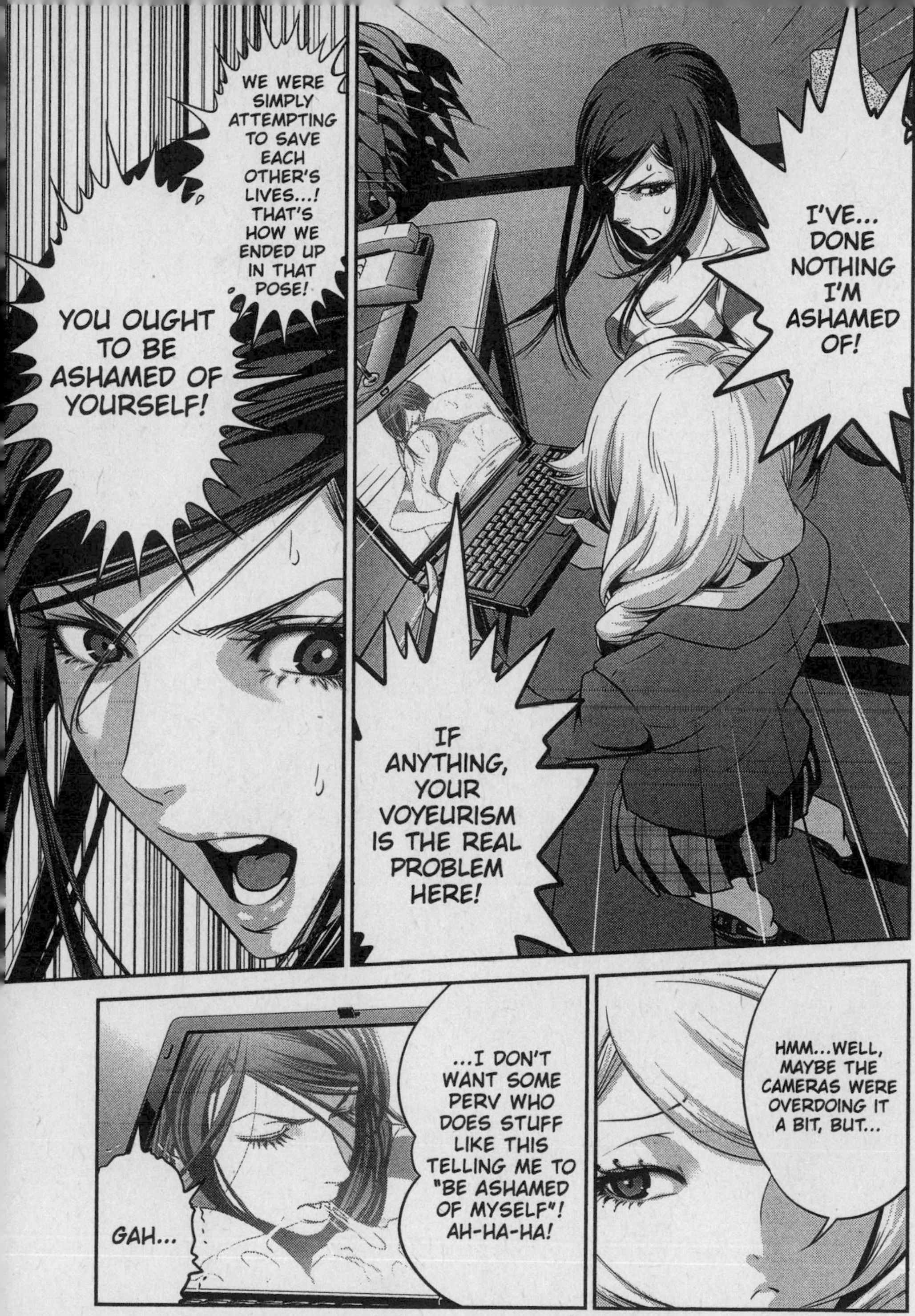
YOU OUGHT TO BE ASHAMED OF YOURSELF!
WE WERE SIMPLY ATTEMPTING TO SAVE EACH OTHER'S LIVES...! THAT'S HOW WE ENDED UP IN THAT POSE!
I'VE... DONE NOTHING I'M ASHAMED OF!
IF ANYTHING, YOUR VOYEURISM IS THE REAL PROBLEM HERE!
HMM...WELL, MAYBE THE CAMERAS WERE OVERDOING IT A BIT, BUT...
...I DON'T WANT SOME PERV WHO DOES STUFF LIKE THIS TELLING ME TO "BE ASHAMED OF MYSELF"! AH-HA-HA!
GAH...

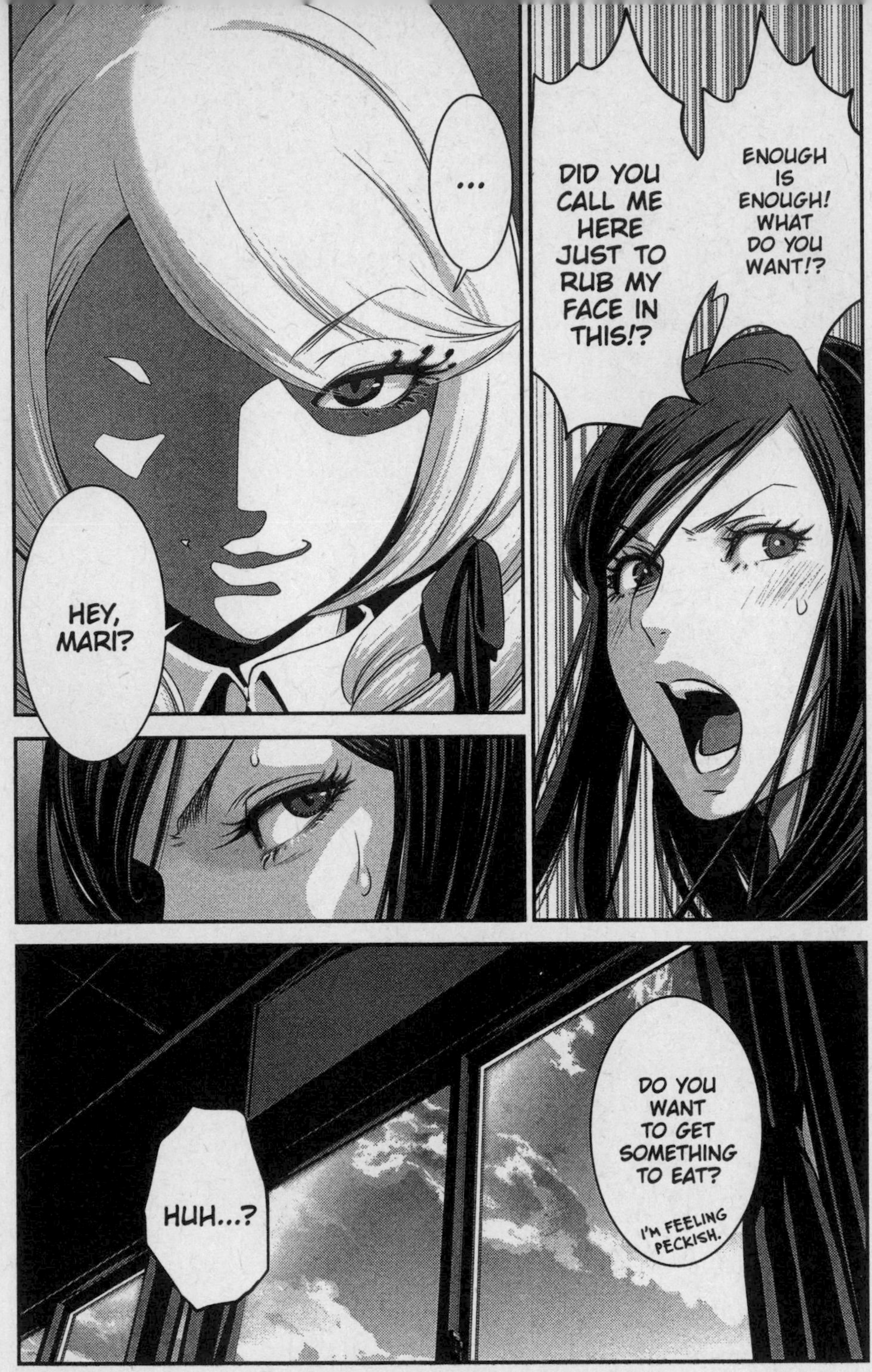
ENOUGH IS ENOUGH! WHAT DO YOU WANT!?
DID YOU CALL ME HERE JUST TO RUB MY FACE IN THIS!?
...
HEY, MARI?
DO YOU WANT TO GET SOMETHING TO EAT?
I'M FEELING PECKISH.
HUH...?

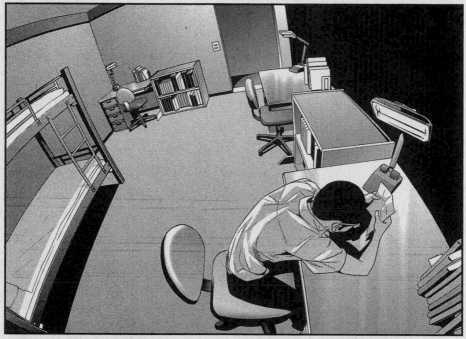

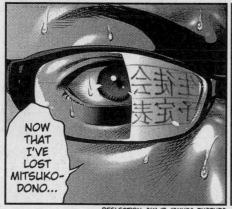

NOW THAT I'VE LOST MITSUKO-DONO...

KASA (RUSTLE)

REFLECTION: STUDENT COUNCIL PLANS

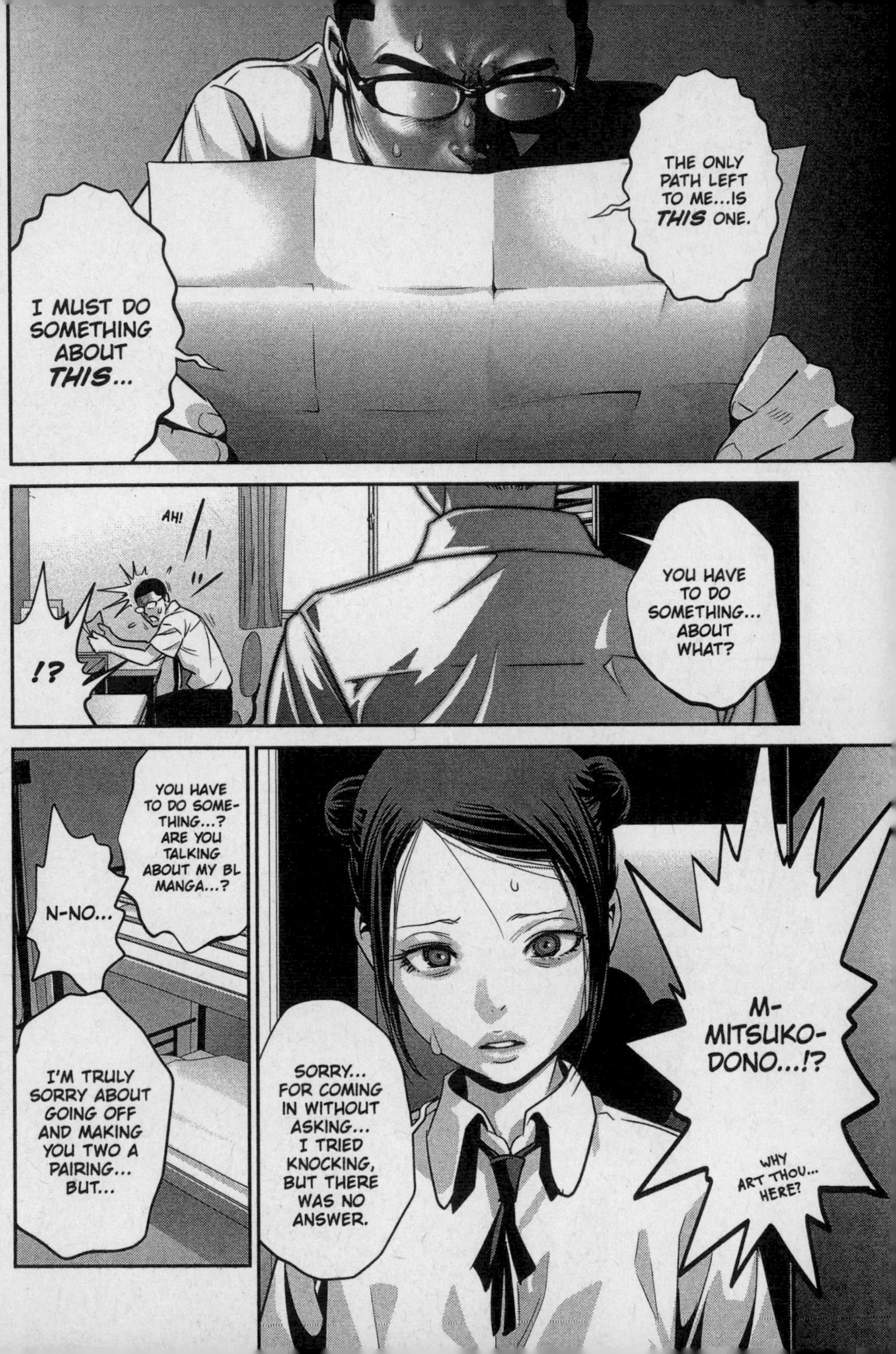
THE ONLY PATH LEFT TO ME...IS THIS ONE.
I MUST DO SOMETHING ABOUT THIS...
YOU HAVE TO DO SOMETHING... ABOUT WHAT?
AH!
!?
M-MITSUKO-DONO...!?
WHY ART THOU... HERE?
SORRY... FOR COMING IN WITHOUT ASKING... I TRIED KNOCKING, BUT THERE WAS NO ANSWER.
YOU HAVE TO DO SOME-THING...? ARE YOU TALKING ABOUT MY BL MANGA...?
N-NO...
I'M TRULY SORRY ABOUT GOING OFF AND MAKING YOU TWO A PAIRING... BUT...

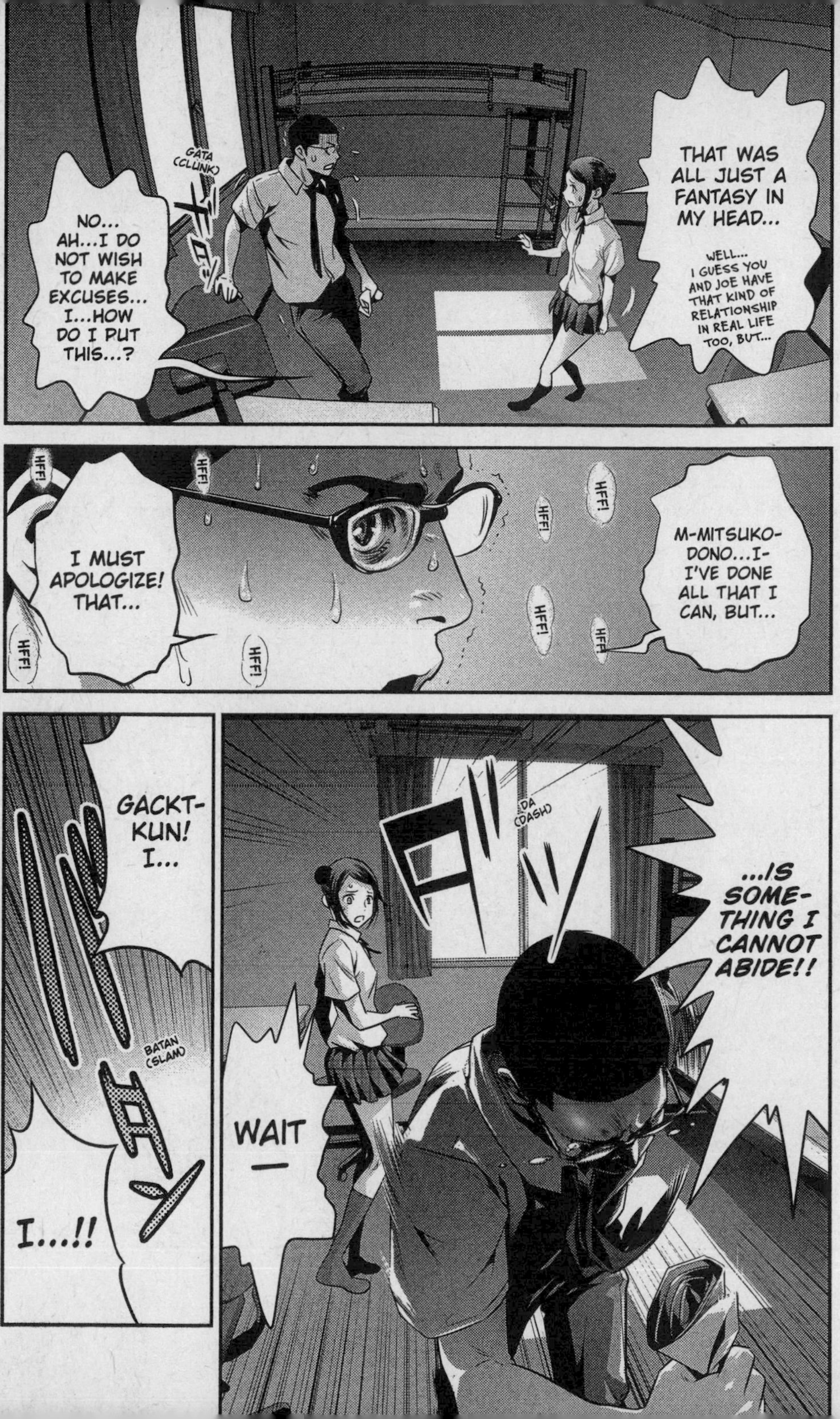
THAT WAS ALL JUST A FANTASY IN MY HEAD...
WELL... I GUESS YOU AND JOE HAVE THAT KIND OF RELATIONSHIP IN REAL LIFE TOO, BUT...
GATA (CLUNK)
NO... AH...I DO NOT WISH TO MAKE EXCUSES... I...HOW DO I PUT THIS...?
M-MITSUKO-DONO...I-I'VE DONE ALL THAT I CAN, BUT...
HFF!
HFF!
HFF!
HFF!
HFF!
HFF!
HFF!
HFF!
I MUST APOLOGIZE! THAT...
...IS SOMETHING I CANNOT ABIDE!!
DA (DASH)
WAIT—
GACKT-KUN! I...
BATAN (SLAM)
I...!!

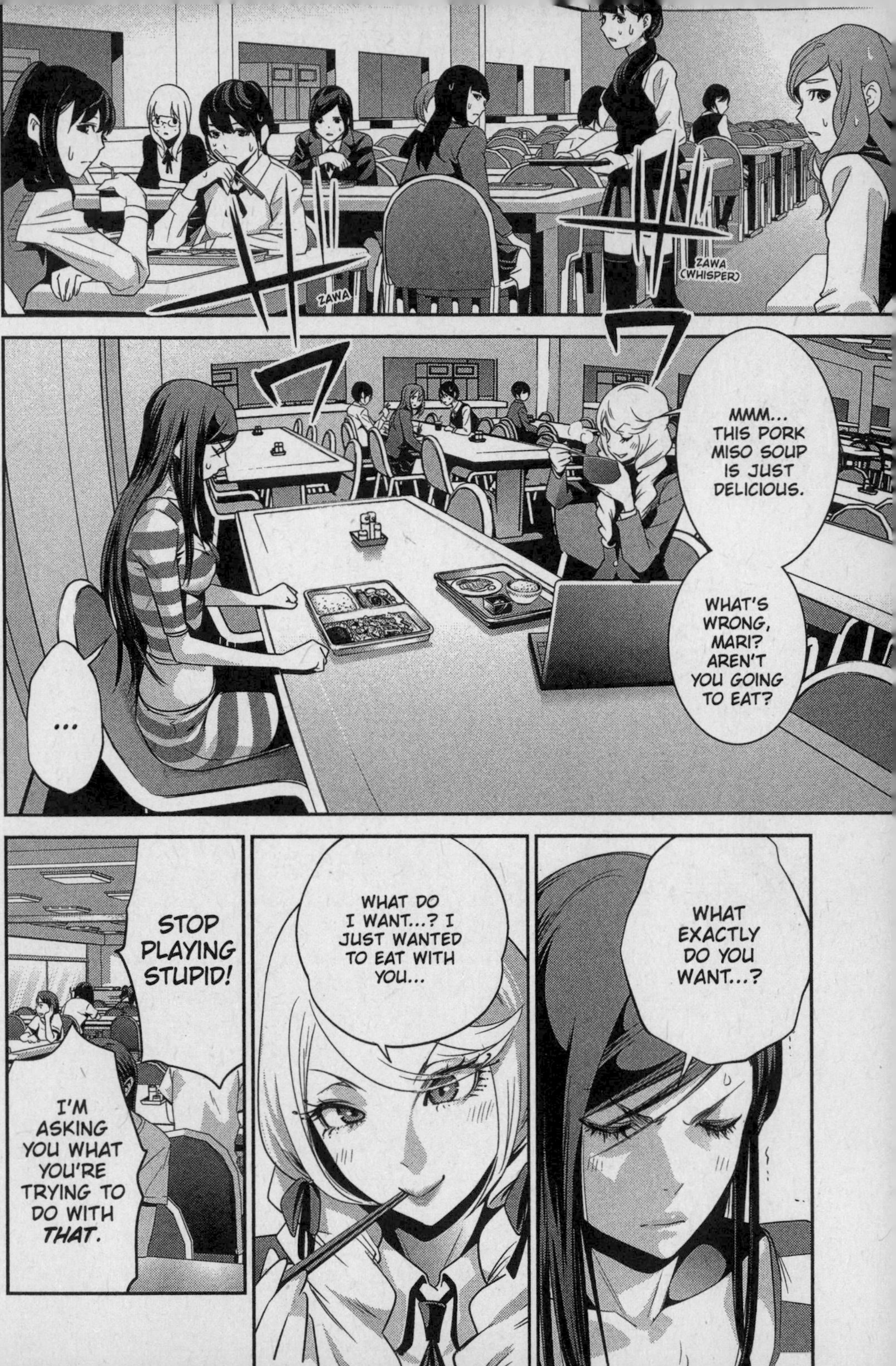
ZAWA (WHISPER)
ZAWA
MMM... THIS PORK MISO SOUP IS JUST DELICIOUS.
WHAT'S WRONG, MARI? AREN'T YOU GOING TO EAT?
...
WHAT EXACTLY DO YOU WANT...?
WHAT DO I WANT...? I JUST WANTED TO EAT WITH YOU...
STOP PLAYING STUPID!
I'M ASKING YOU WHAT YOU'RE TRYING TO DO WITH *THAT*.

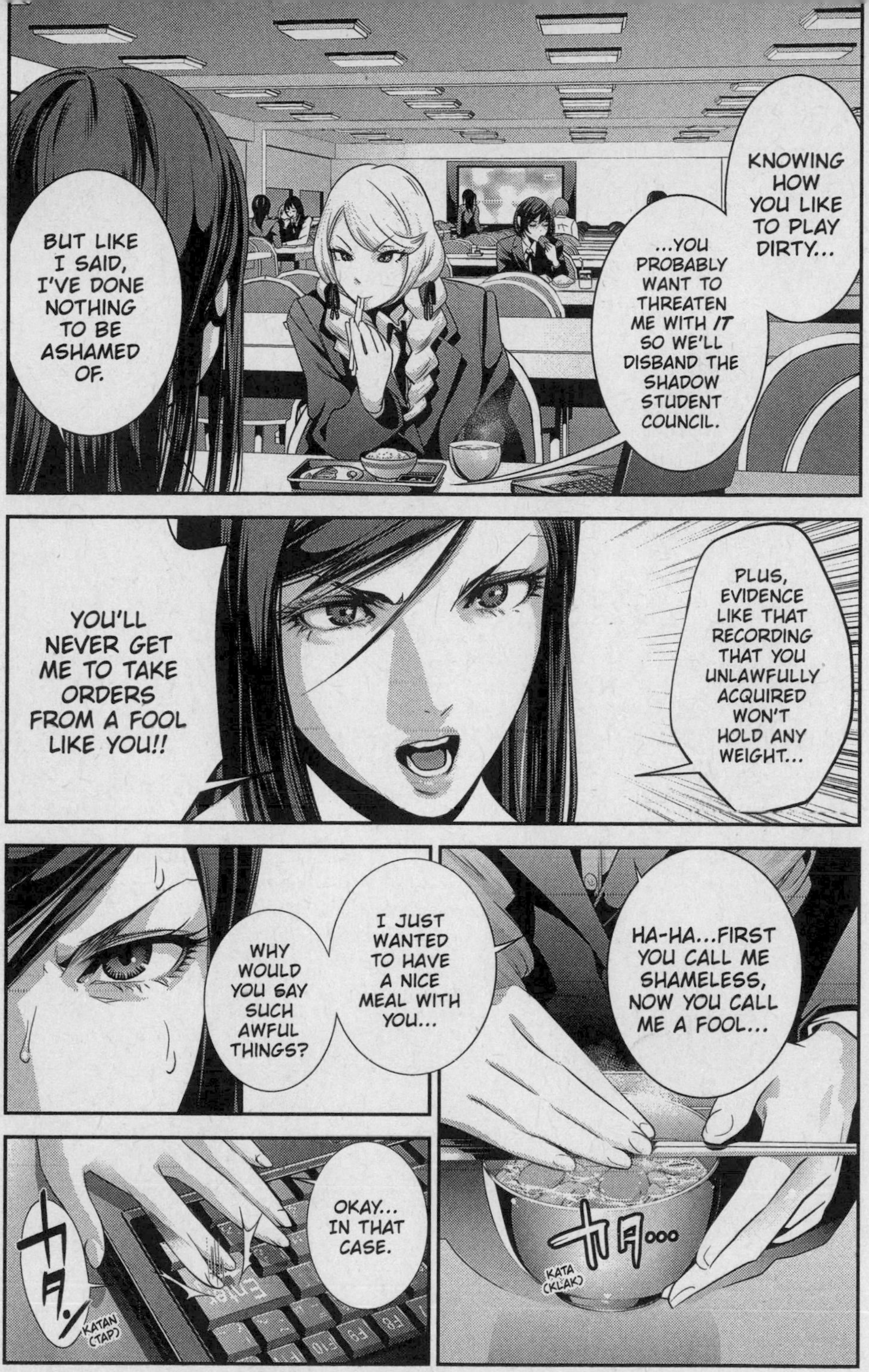
KNOWING HOW YOU LIKE TO PLAY DIRTY...
...YOU PROBABLY WANT TO THREATEN ME WITH *IT* SO WE'LL DISBAND THE SHADOW STUDENT COUNCIL.
BUT LIKE I SAID, I'VE DONE NOTHING TO BE ASHAMED OF.
PLUS, EVIDENCE LIKE THAT RECORDING THAT YOU UNLAWFULLY ACQUIRED WON'T HOLD ANY WEIGHT...
YOU'LL NEVER GET ME TO TAKE ORDERS FROM A FOOL LIKE YOU!!
HA-HA...FIRST YOU CALL ME SHAMELESS, NOW YOU CALL ME A FOOL...
I JUST WANTED TO HAVE A NICE MEAL WITH YOU...
WHY WOULD YOU SAY SUCH AWFUL THINGS?
カタ...
KATA (KLAK)
OKAY... IN THAT CASE.
カタン
KATAN (TAP)

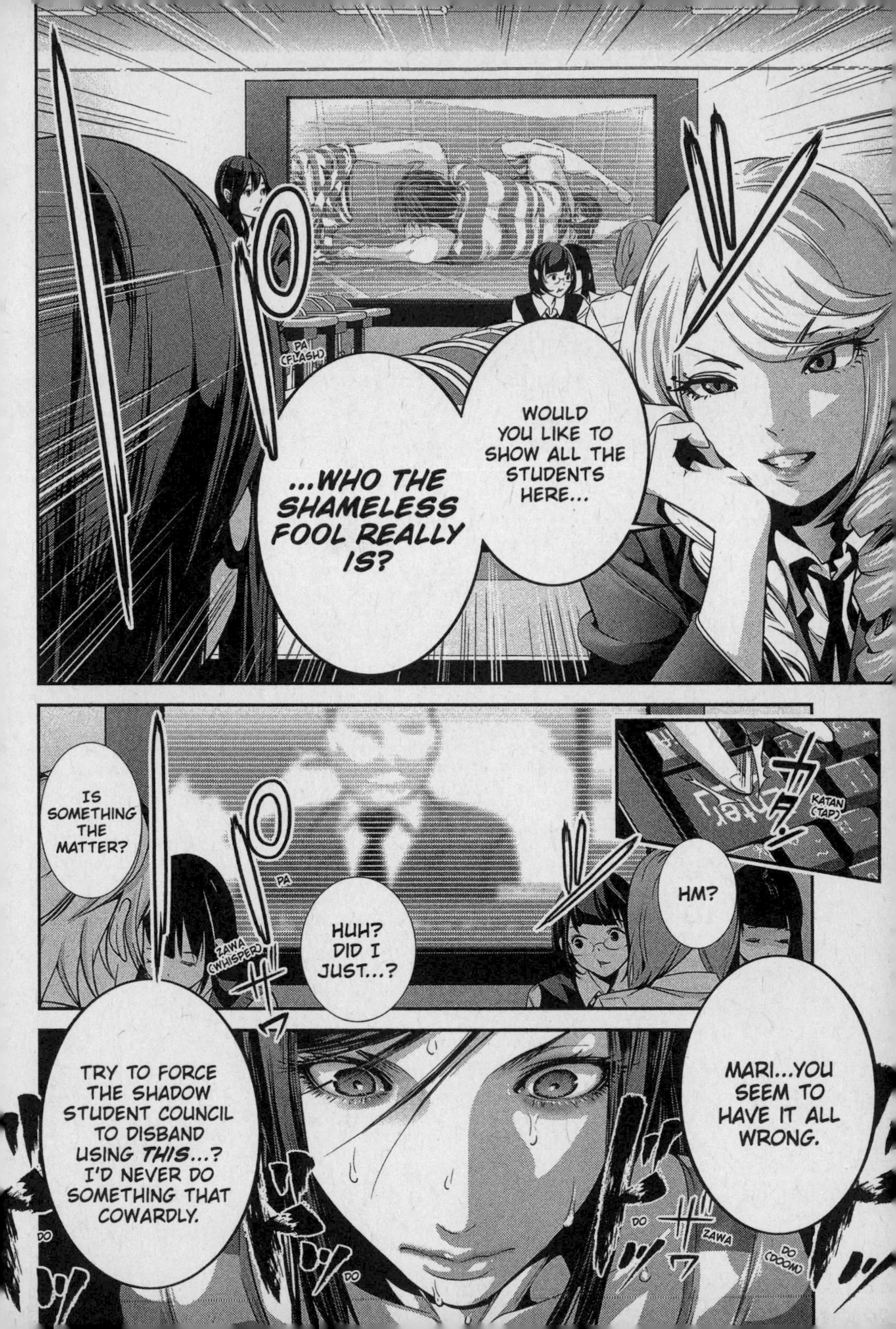
WOULD YOU LIKE TO SHOW ALL THE STUDENTS HERE...
...WHO THE SHAMELESS FOOL REALLY IS?
PA (FLASH)
KATAN (TAP)
HM?
HUH? DID I JUST...?
PA
IS SOMETHING THE MATTER?
ZAWA (WHISPER)
MARI...YOU SEEM TO HAVE IT ALL WRONG.
TRY TO FORCE THE SHADOW STUDENT COUNCIL TO DISBAND USING *THIS*...? I'D NEVER DO SOMETHING THAT COWARDLY.
DO (DOOM)
ZAWA
DO
DO
DO

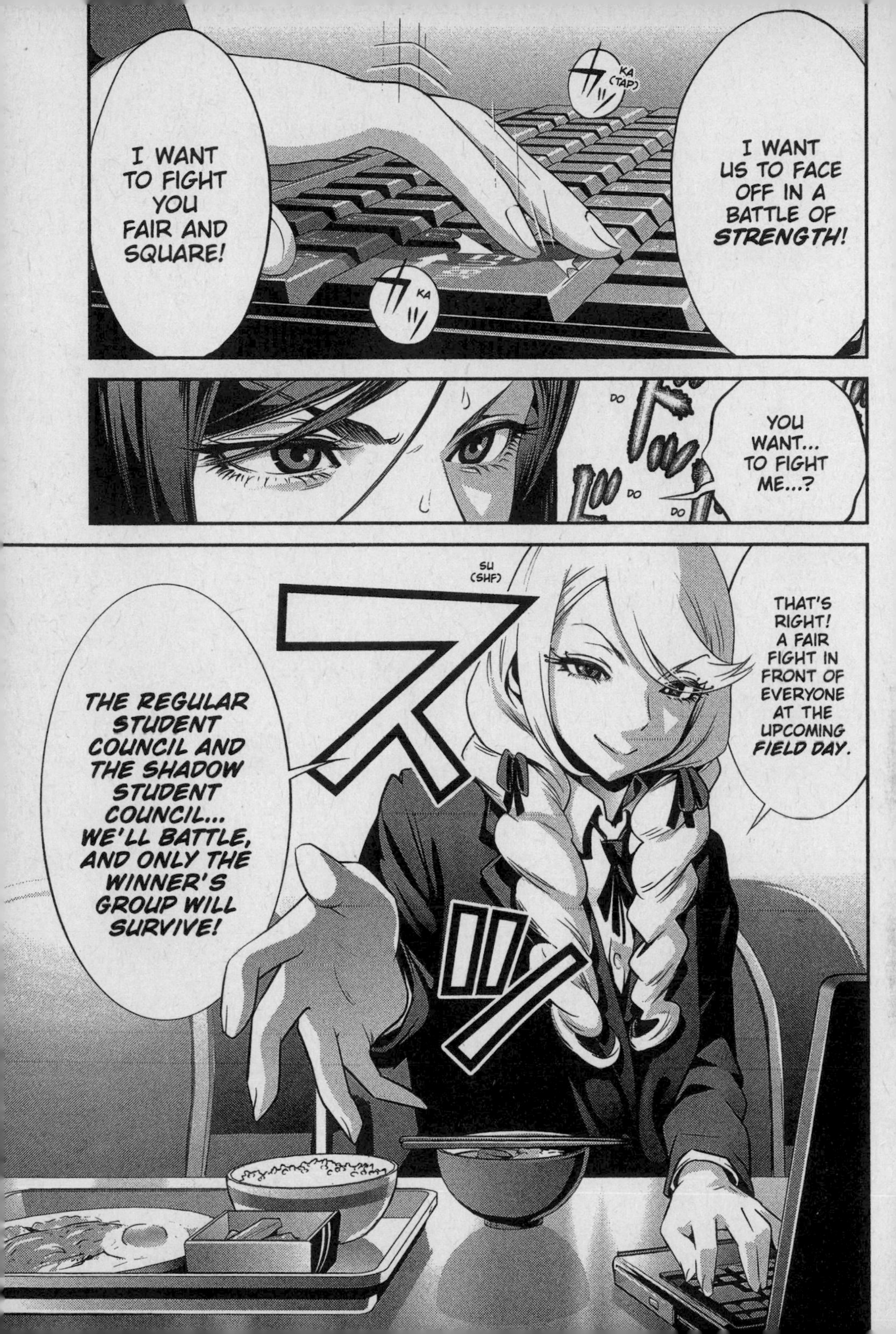

I WANT US TO FACE OFF IN A BATTLE OF STRENGTH!
KA (TAP)
KA
I WANT TO FIGHT YOU FAIR AND SQUARE!
DO
DO
DO
YOU WANT... TO FIGHT ME...?
SU (SHF)
THAT'S RIGHT! A FAIR FIGHT IN FRONT OF EVERYONE AT THE UPCOMING FIELD DAY.
THE REGULAR STUDENT COUNCIL AND THE SHADOW STUDENT COUNCIL... WE'LL BATTLE, AND ONLY THE WINNER'S GROUP WILL SURVIVE!

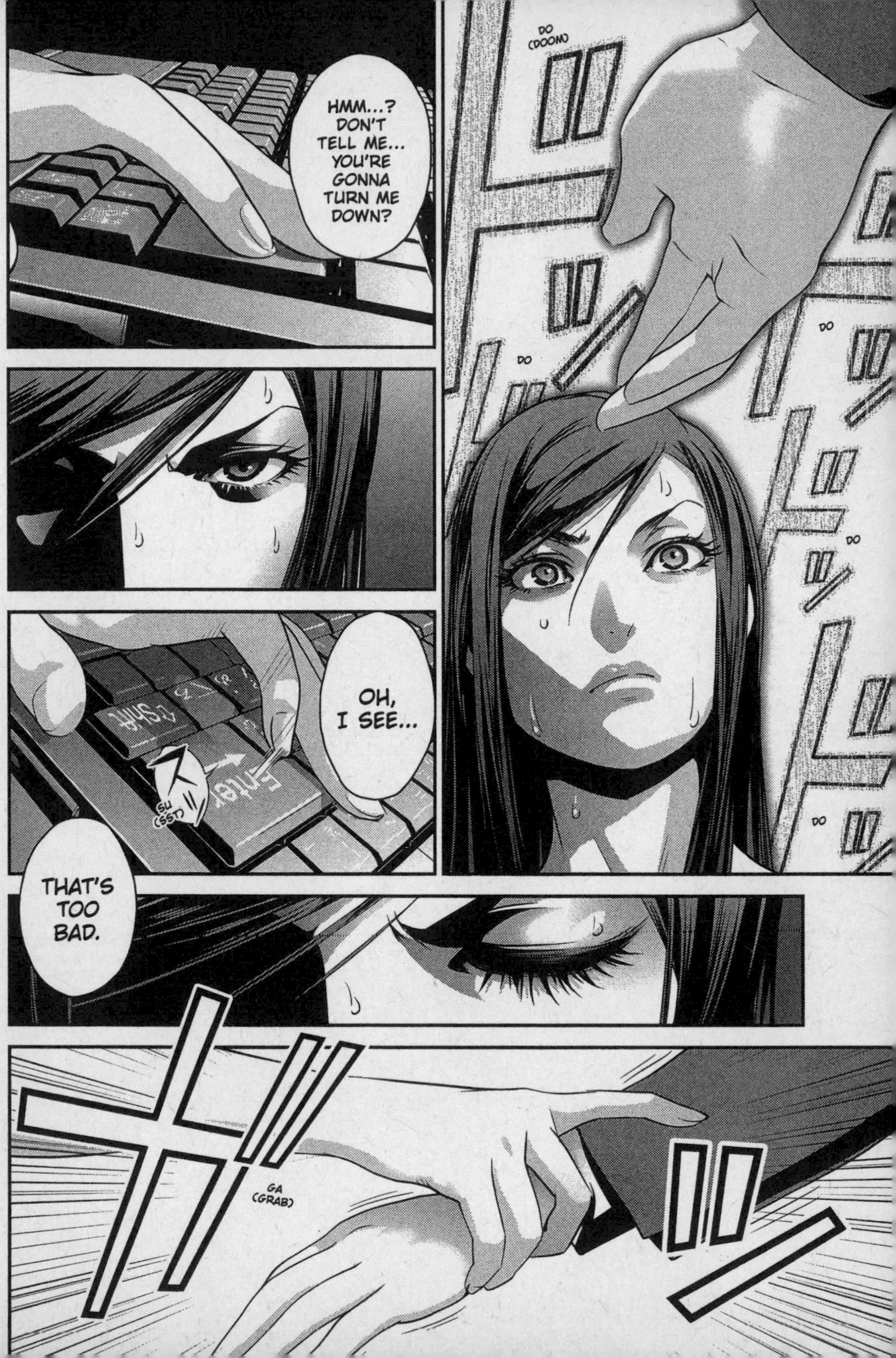
DO
(DOOM)
HMM...? DON'T TELL ME... YOU'RE GONNA TURN ME DOWN?
DO
DO
DO
DO
DO
OH, I SEE...
SU
(SST)
THAT'S TOO BAD.
GA
(GRAB)

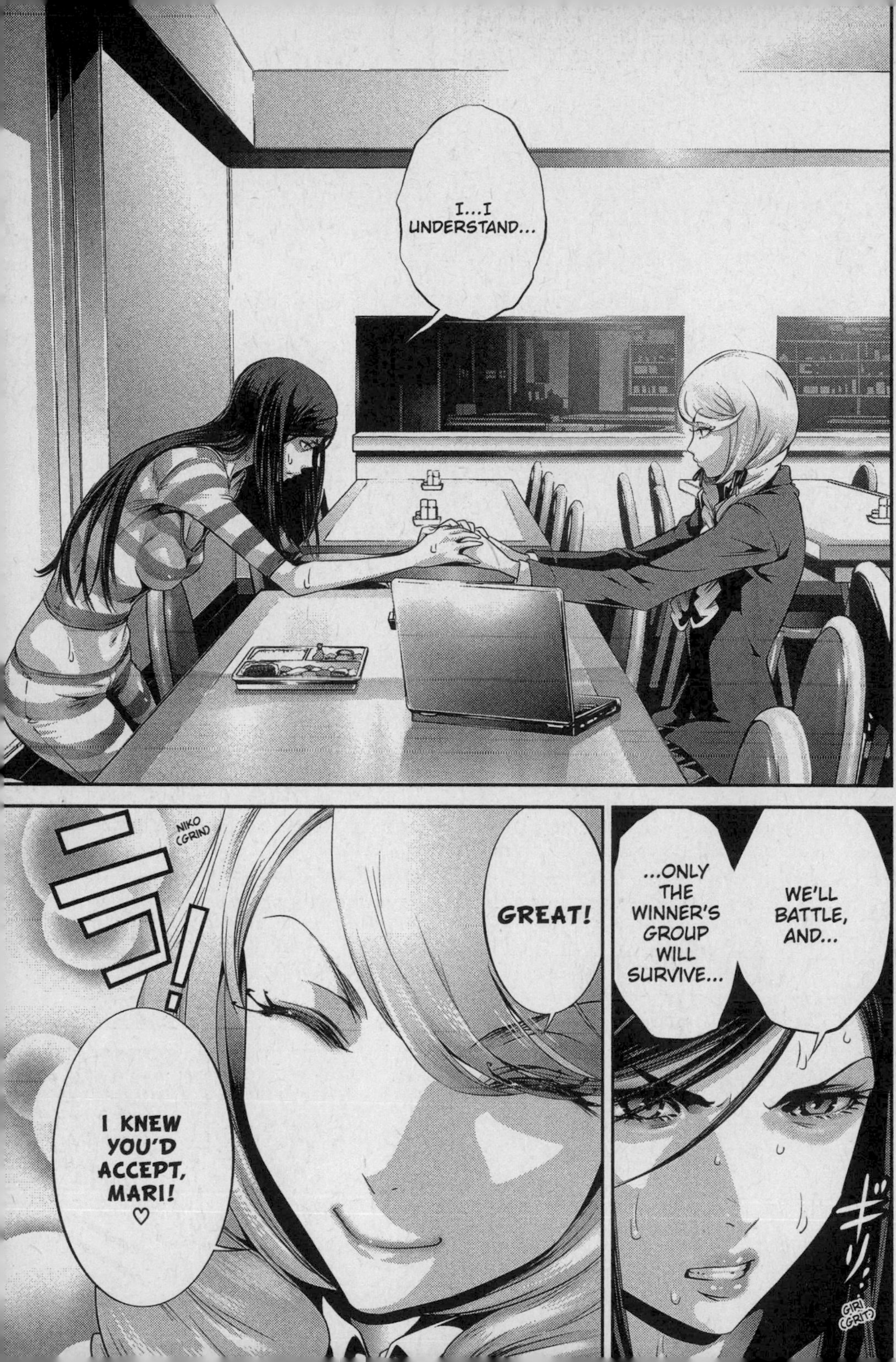
I...I UNDERSTAND...
WE'LL BATTLE, AND...
...ONLY THE WINNER'S GROUP WILL SURVIVE...
GIRI (GRIT)
GREAT!
NIKO (GRIN)
I KNEW YOU'D ACCEPT, MARI! ♡

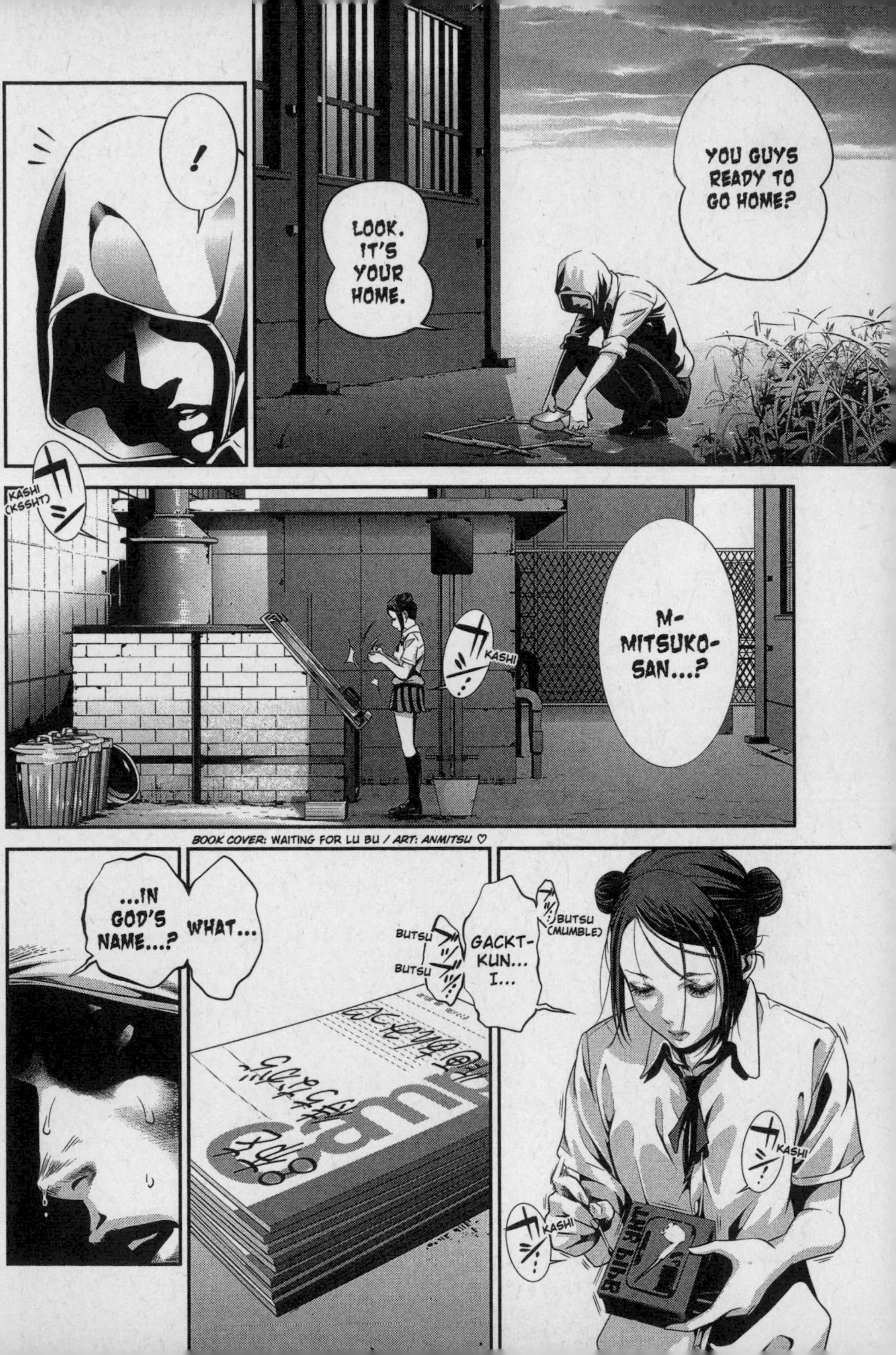
YOU GUYS READY TO GO HOME?
LOOK. IT'S YOUR HOME.
!
M-MITSUKO-SAN...?
KASHI
KASHI (KSSHT)
BOOK COVER: WAITING FOR LU BU / ART: ANMITSU ♡
BUTSU (MUMBLE)
GACKT-KUN... I...
BUTSU
BUTSU
KASHI
KASHI
WHAT...
...IN GOD'S NAME...?

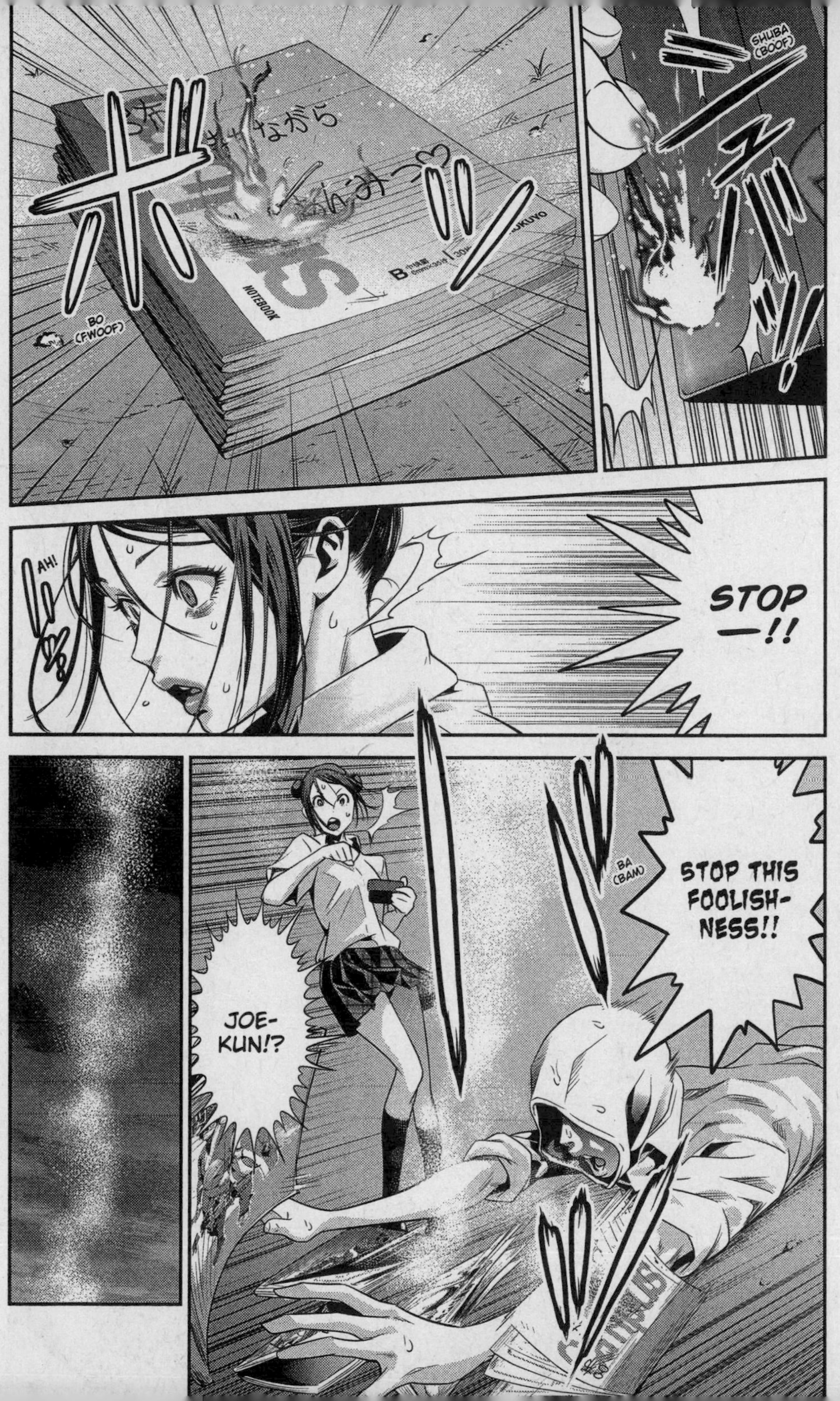
SHUBA (BOOF)
BO (F.WOOF)
NOTEBOOK
STOP—!!
AH!
BA (BAM)
STOP THIS FOOLISH-NESS!!
JOE-KUN!?

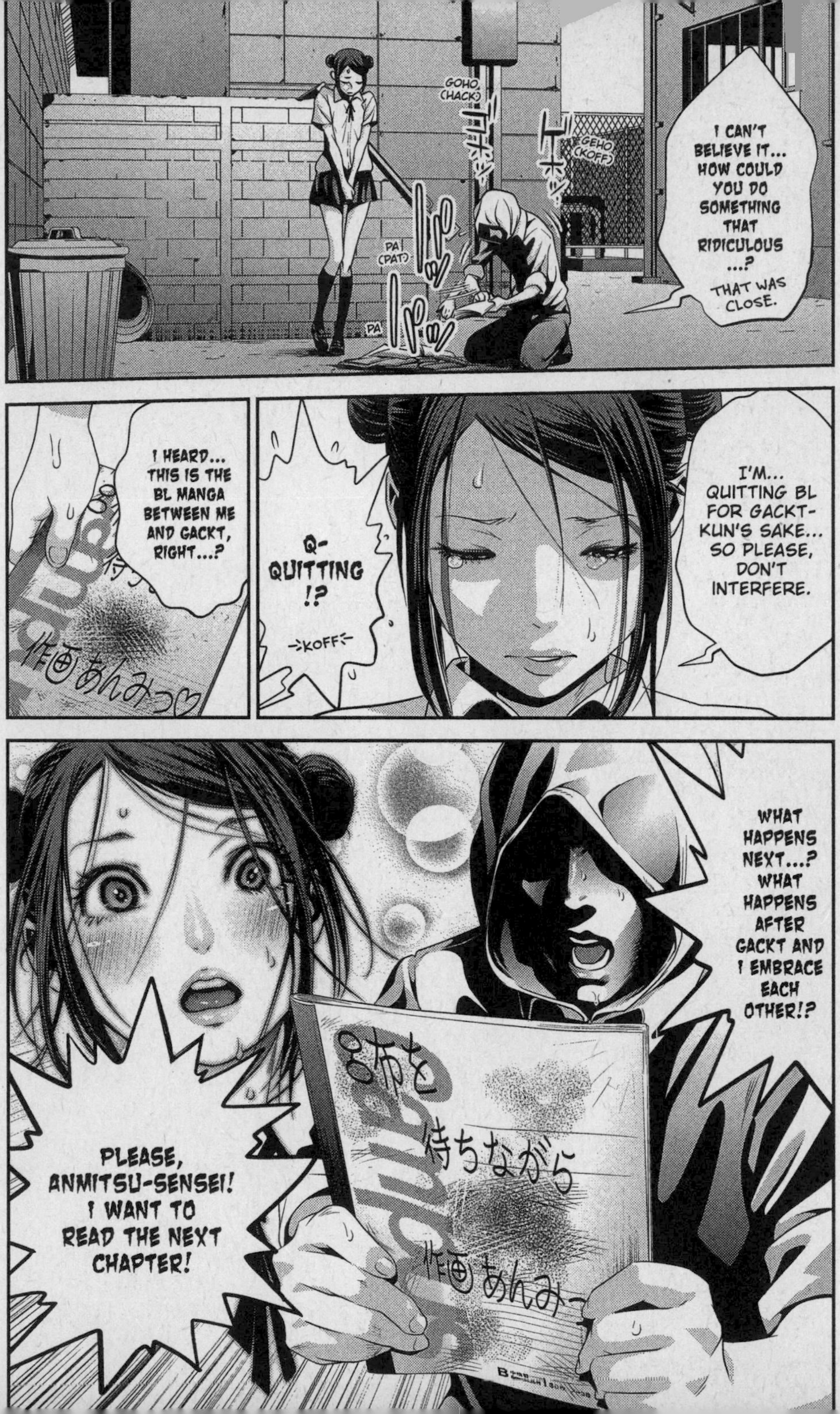
I CAN'T BELIEVE IT... HOW COULD YOU DO SOMETHING THAT RIDICULOUS ...?
THAT WAS CLOSE.
GEHO (KOFF)
GOHO (CHACK)
PA (PAT)
PA
I'M... QUITTING BL FOR GACKT-KUN'S SAKE... SO PLEASE, DON'T INTERFERE.
Q-QUITTING!?
KOFF
I HEARD... THIS IS THE BL MANGA BETWEEN ME AND GACKT, RIGHT...?
作画あんみつ♡
WHAT HAPPENS NEXT...? WHAT HAPPENS AFTER GACKT AND I EMBRACE EACH OTHER!?
PLEASE, ANMITSU-SENSEI! I WANT TO READ THE NEXT CHAPTER!
待ちながら
作画あんみつ

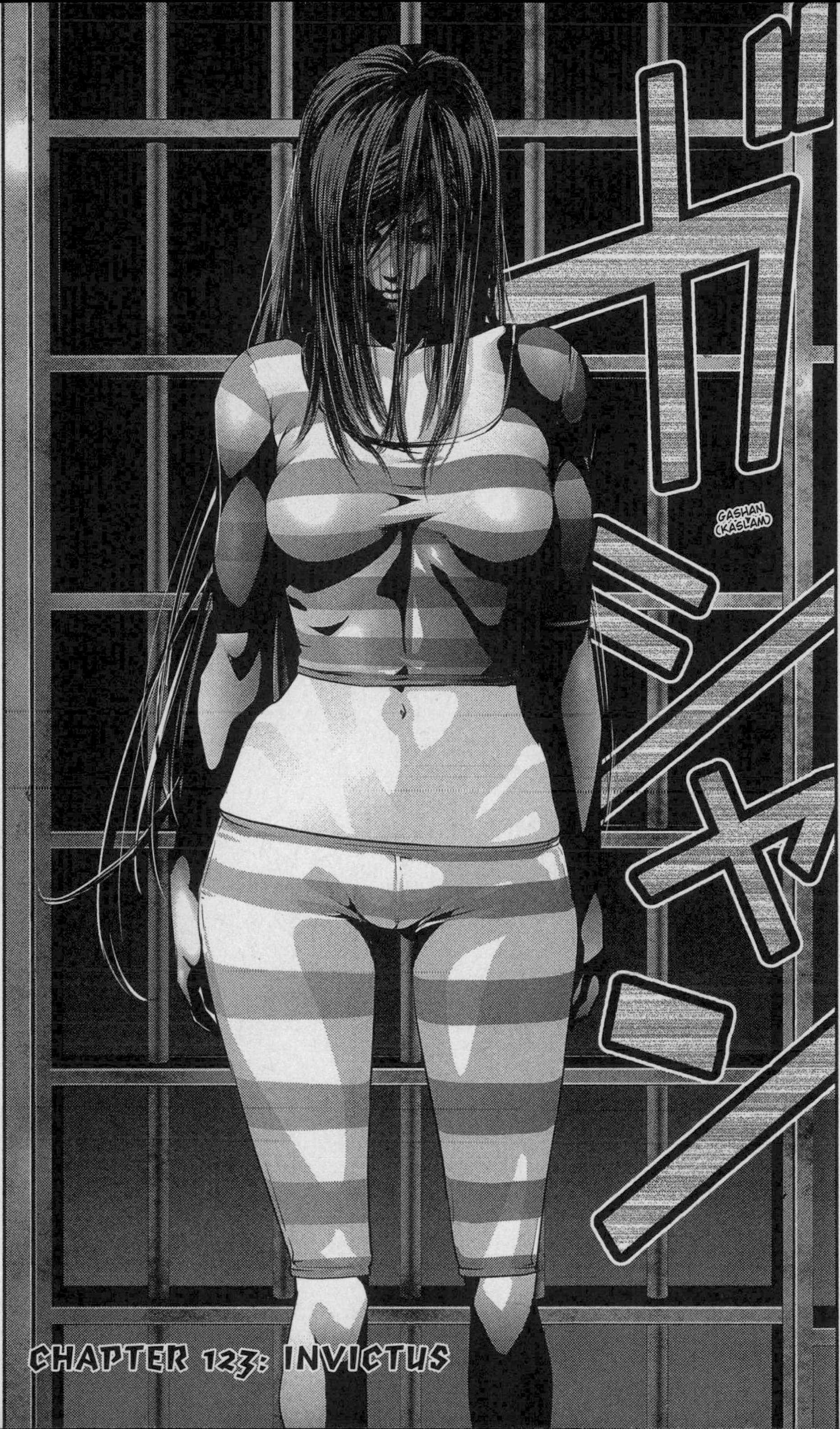
GASHAN (KASLAM)
CHAPTER 123: INVICTUS

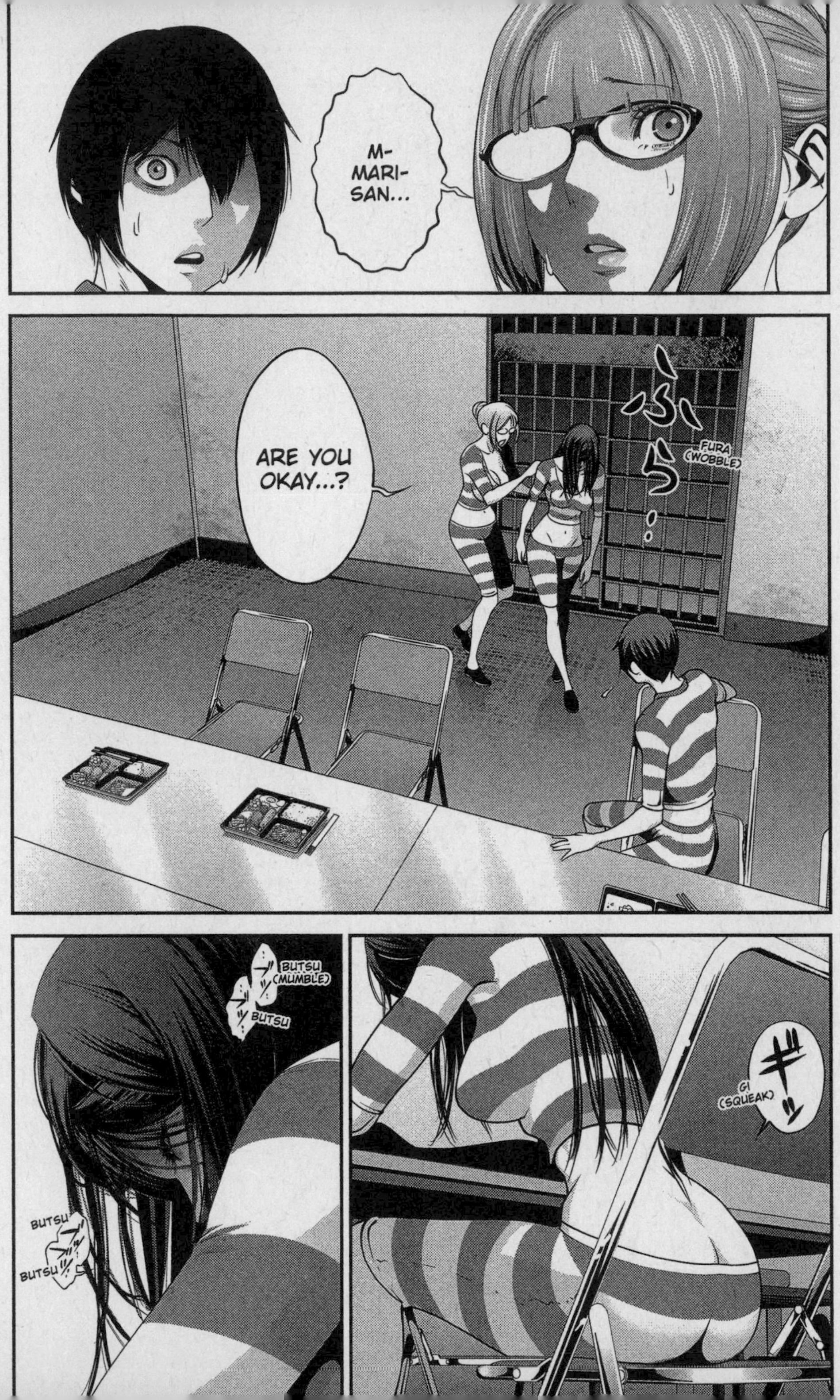
M-MARI-SAN...
ふら…
FURA (WOBBLE)
ARE YOU OKAY...?
ギッ
GI (SQUEAK)
BUTSU (MUMBLE)
BUTSU
BUTSU
BUTSU!!

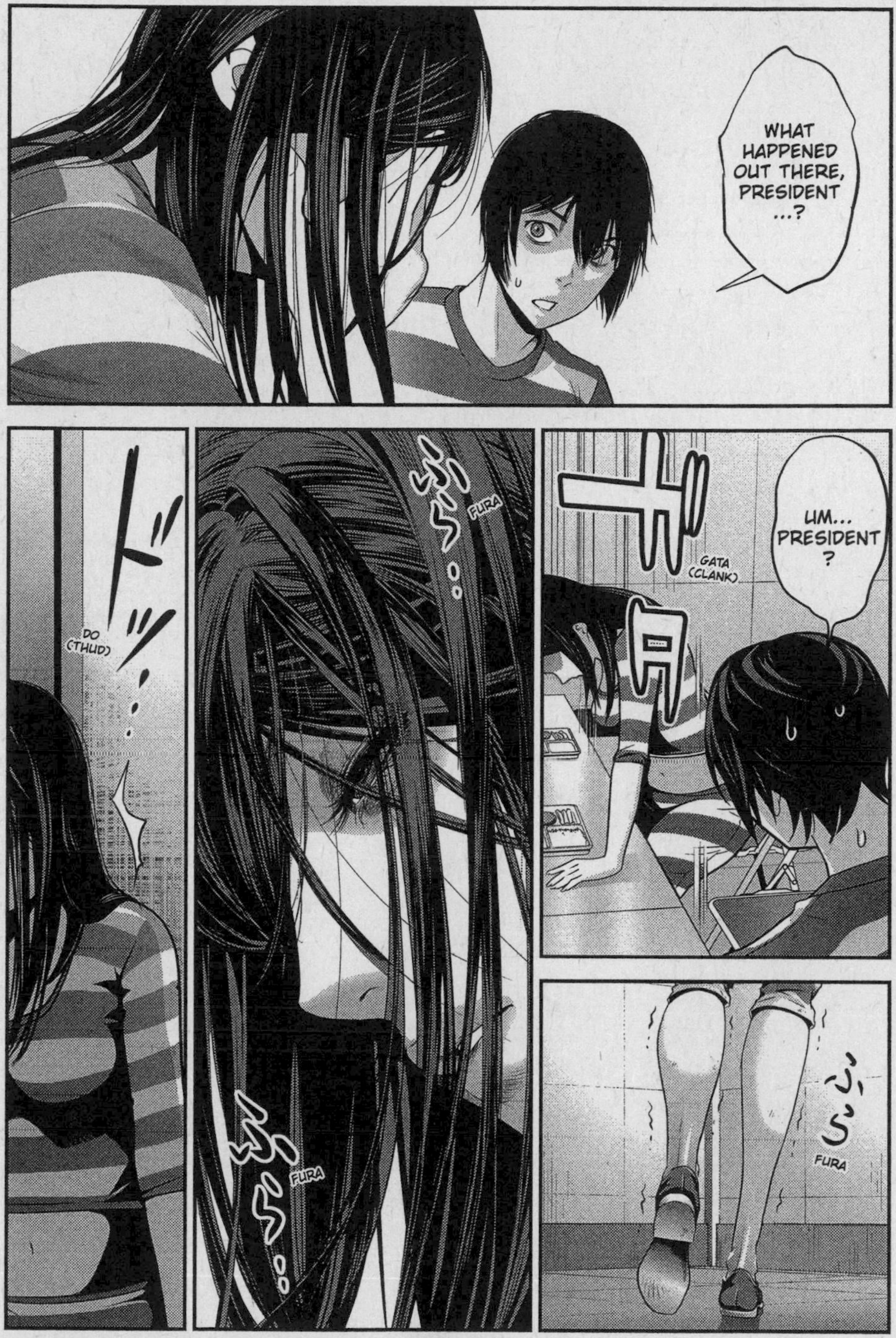
WHAT HAPPENED OUT THERE, PRESIDENT ...?
GATA (CLANK)
UM... PRESIDENT?
FURA
FURA
FURA
DO (THUD)

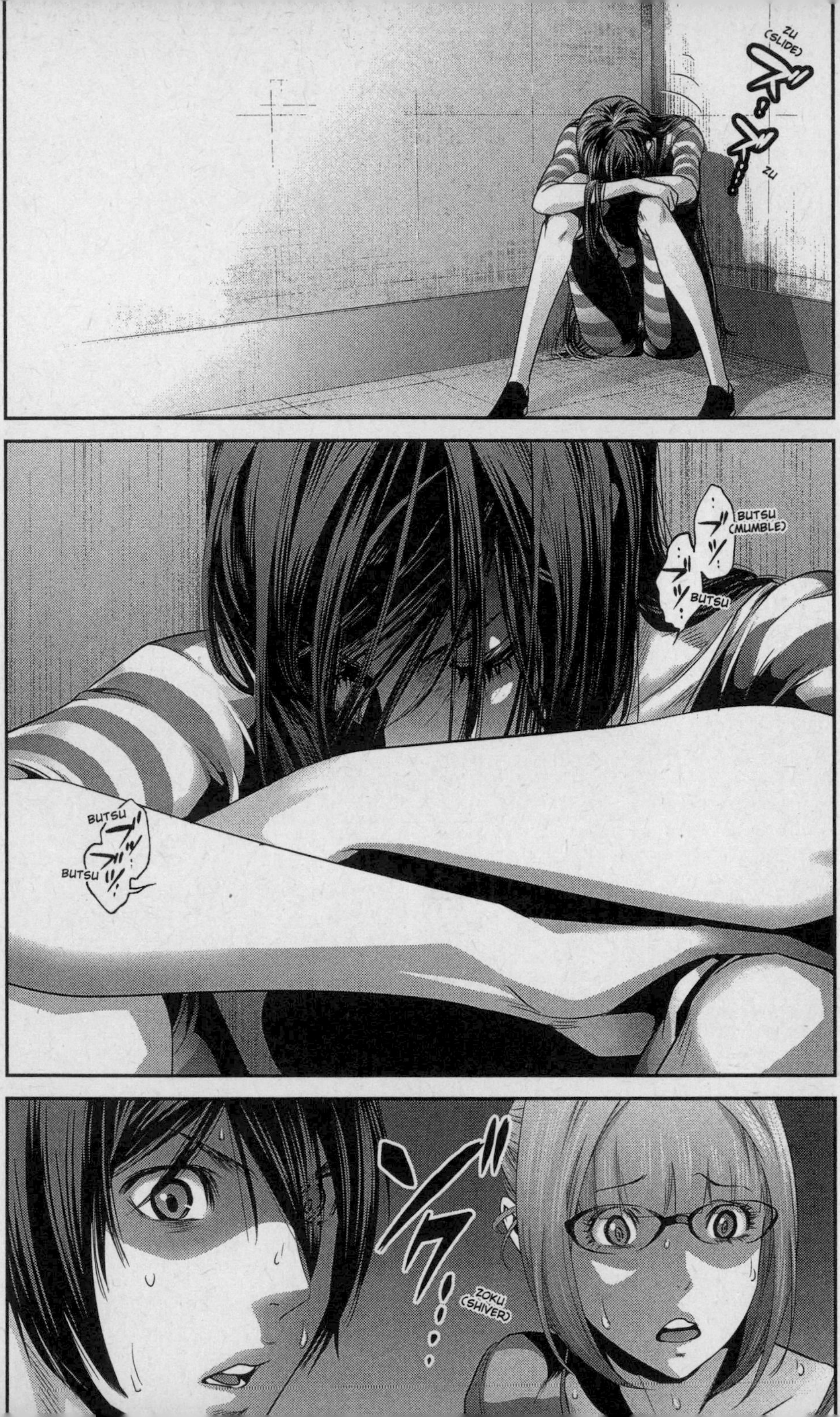
ZU (SLIDE)
ZU
BUTSU (MUMBLE)
BUTSU
BUTSU
BUTSU
ZOKU (SHIVER)

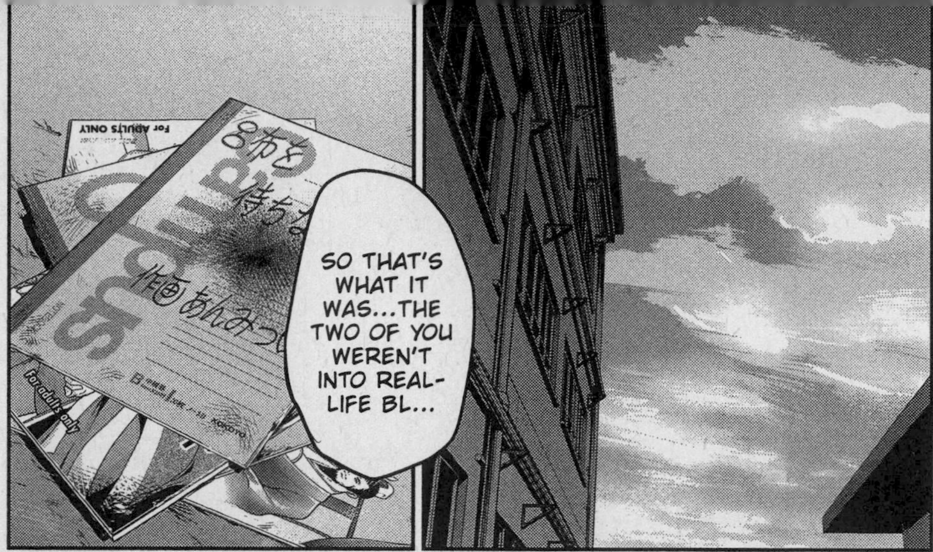
SO THAT'S WHAT IT WAS...THE TWO OF YOU WEREN'T INTO REAL-LIFE BL...

BOOK COVER: WAITING FOR LU BU / ART: ANMITSU ♡

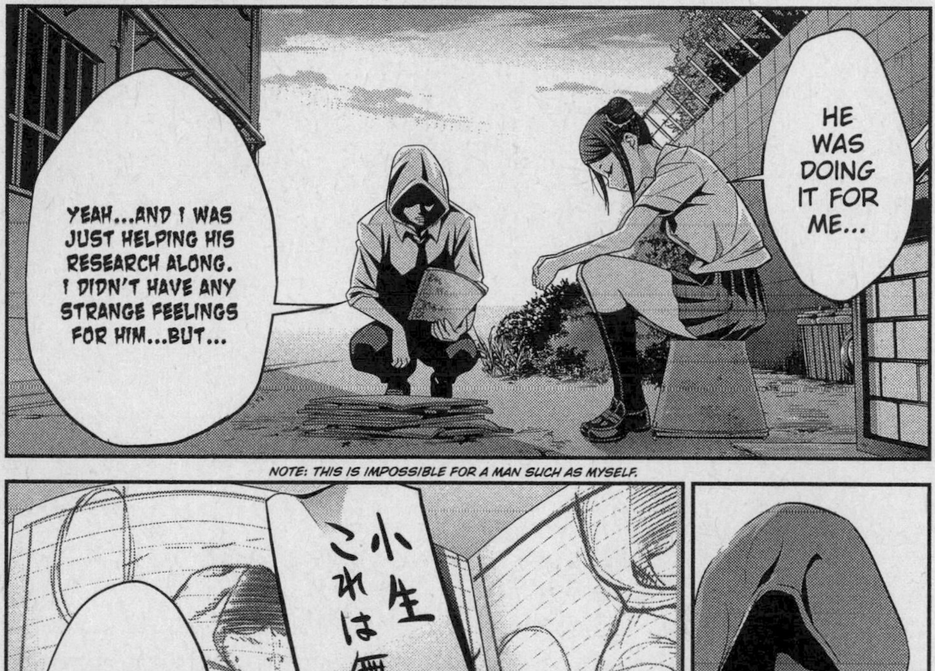
HE WAS DOING IT FOR ME...
YEAH...AND I WAS JUST HELPING HIS RESEARCH ALONG. I DIDN'T HAVE ANY STRANGE FEELINGS FOR HIM...BUT...

NOTE: THIS IS IMPOSSIBLE FOR A MAN SUCH AS MYSELF.

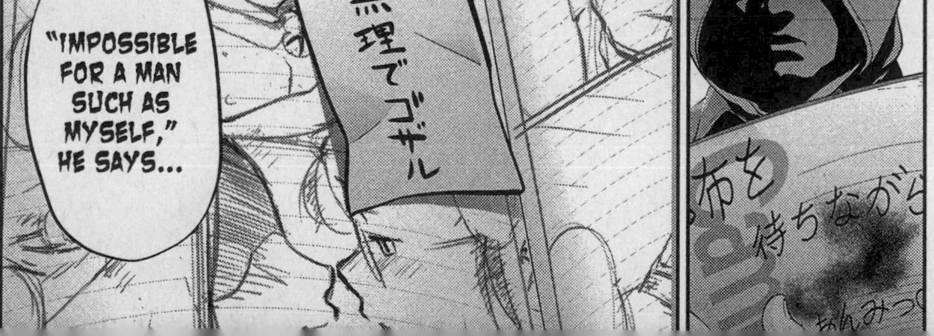
小生これは無理でゴザル
"IMPOSSIBLE FOR A MAN SUCH AS MYSELF," HE SAYS...

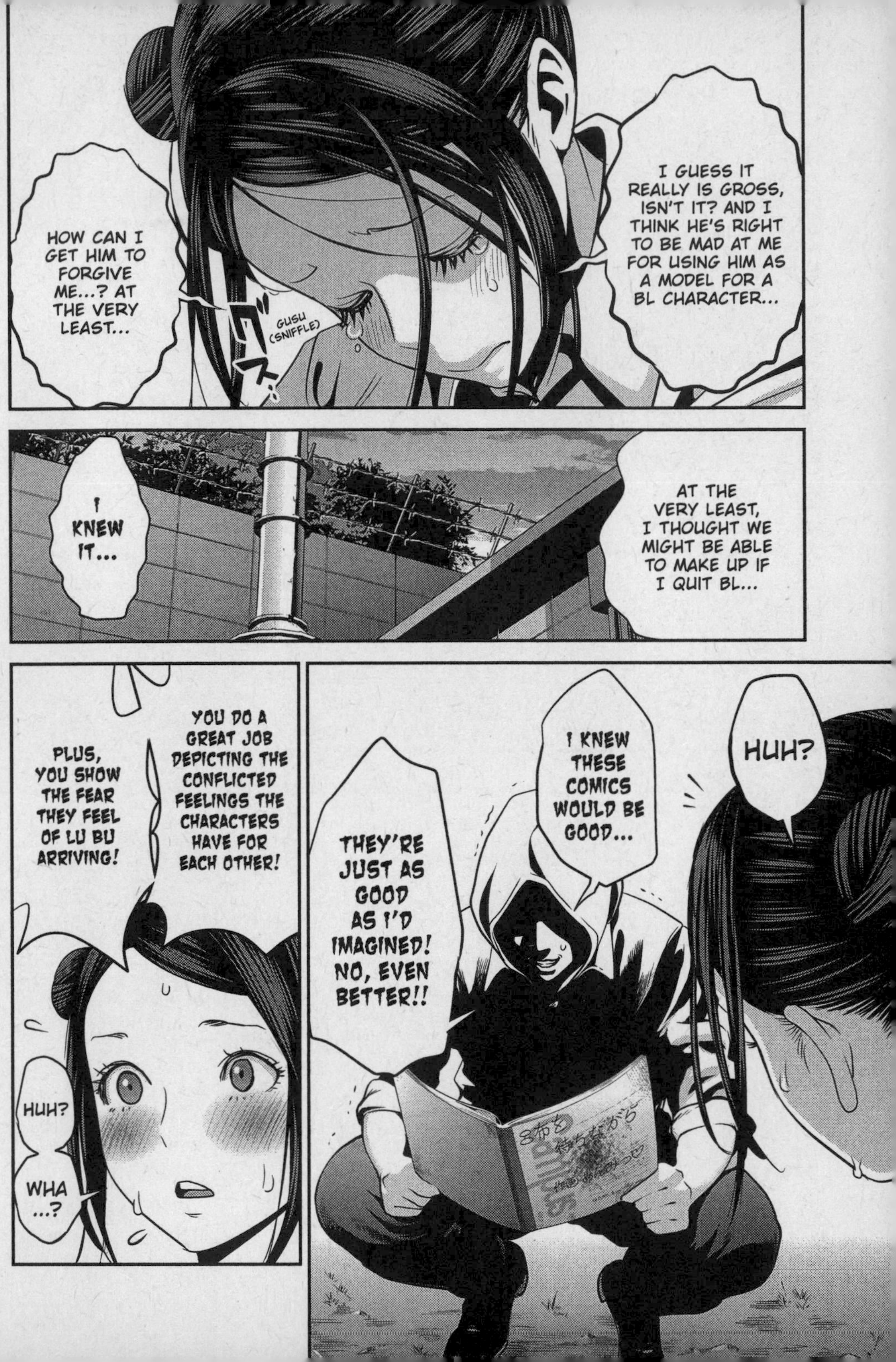
I GUESS IT REALLY IS GROSS, ISN'T IT? AND I THINK HE'S RIGHT TO BE MAD AT ME FOR USING HIM AS A MODEL FOR A BL CHARACTER...
GUSU (SNIFFLE)
HOW CAN I GET HIM TO FORGIVE ME...? AT THE VERY LEAST...
AT THE VERY LEAST, I THOUGHT WE MIGHT BE ABLE TO MAKE UP IF I QUIT BL...
I KNEW IT...
HUH?
I KNEW THESE COMICS WOULD BE GOOD...
THEY'RE JUST AS GOOD AS I'D IMAGINED! NO, EVEN BETTER!!
YOU DO A GREAT JOB DEPICTING THE CONFLICTED FEELINGS THE CHARACTERS HAVE FOR EACH OTHER!
PLUS, YOU SHOW THE FEAR THEY FEEL OF LU BU ARRIVING!
HUH?
WHA...?

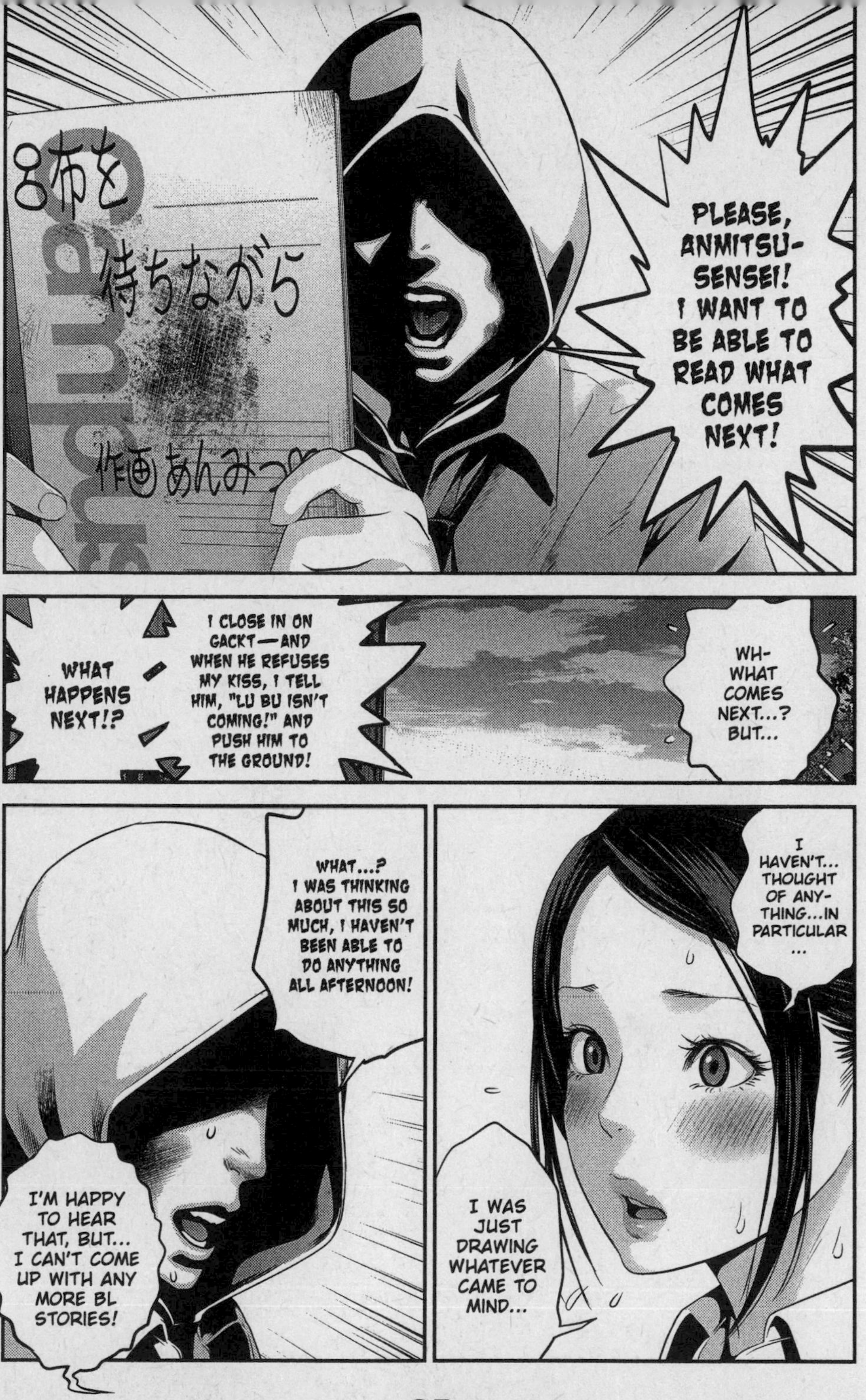

呂布を待ちながら
作画あんみつ
PLEASE, ANMITSU-SENSEI! I WANT TO BE ABLE TO READ WHAT COMES NEXT!
WH-WHAT COMES NEXT...? BUT...
I CLOSE IN ON GACKT—AND WHEN HE REFUSES MY KISS, I TELL HIM, "LU BU ISN'T COMING!" AND PUSH HIM TO THE GROUND!
WHAT HAPPENS NEXT!?
I HAVEN'T... THOUGHT OF ANY-THING...IN PARTICULAR...
I WAS JUST DRAWING WHATEVER CAME TO MIND...
WHAT...? I WAS THINKING ABOUT THIS SO MUCH, I HAVEN'T BEEN ABLE TO DO ANYTHING ALL AFTERNOON!
I'M HAPPY TO HEAR THAT, BUT... I CAN'T COME UP WITH ANY MORE BL STORIES!

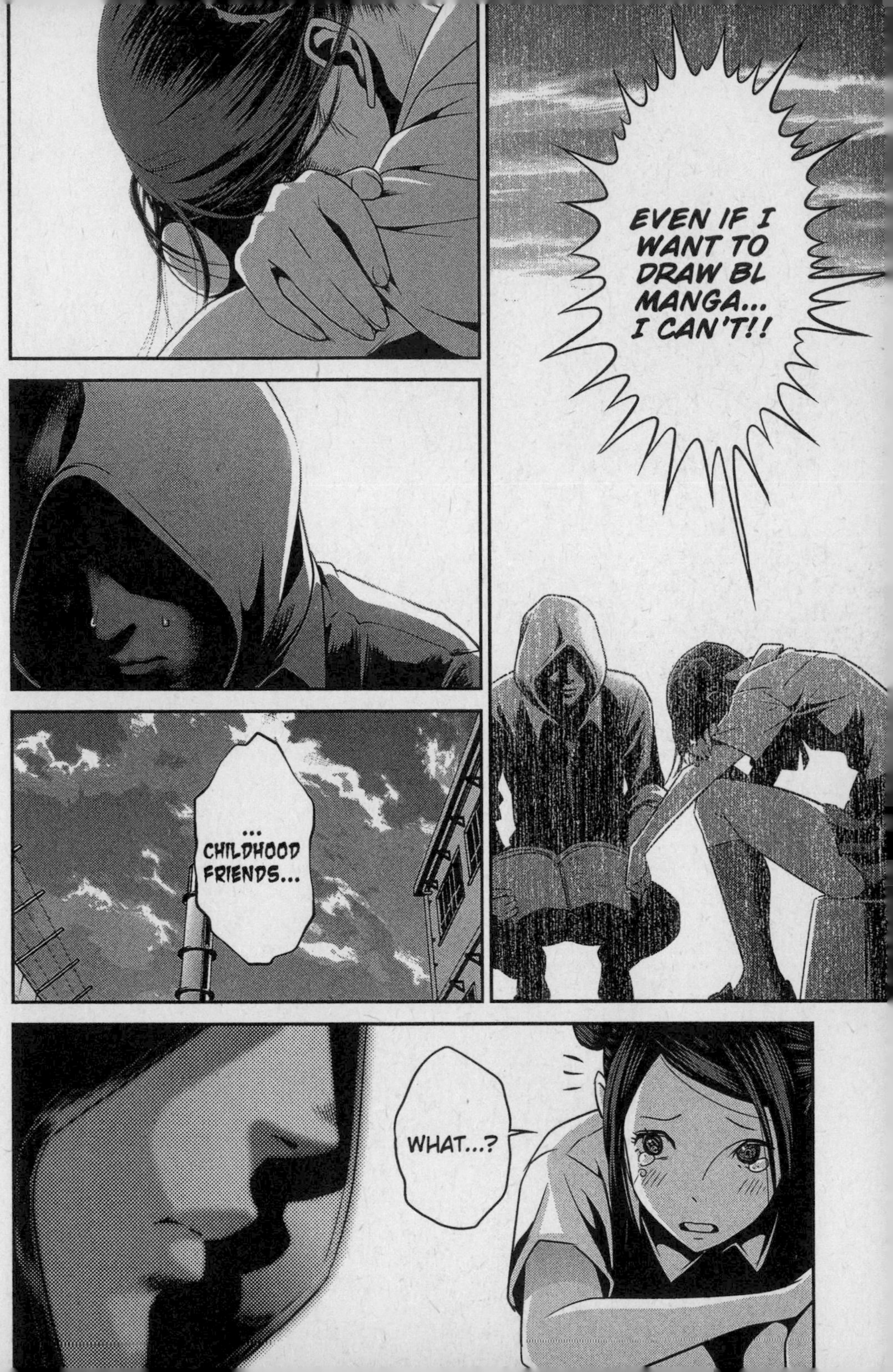
EVEN IF I WANT TO DRAW BL MANGA... I CAN'T!!
...CHILDHOOD FRIENDS...
WHAT...?

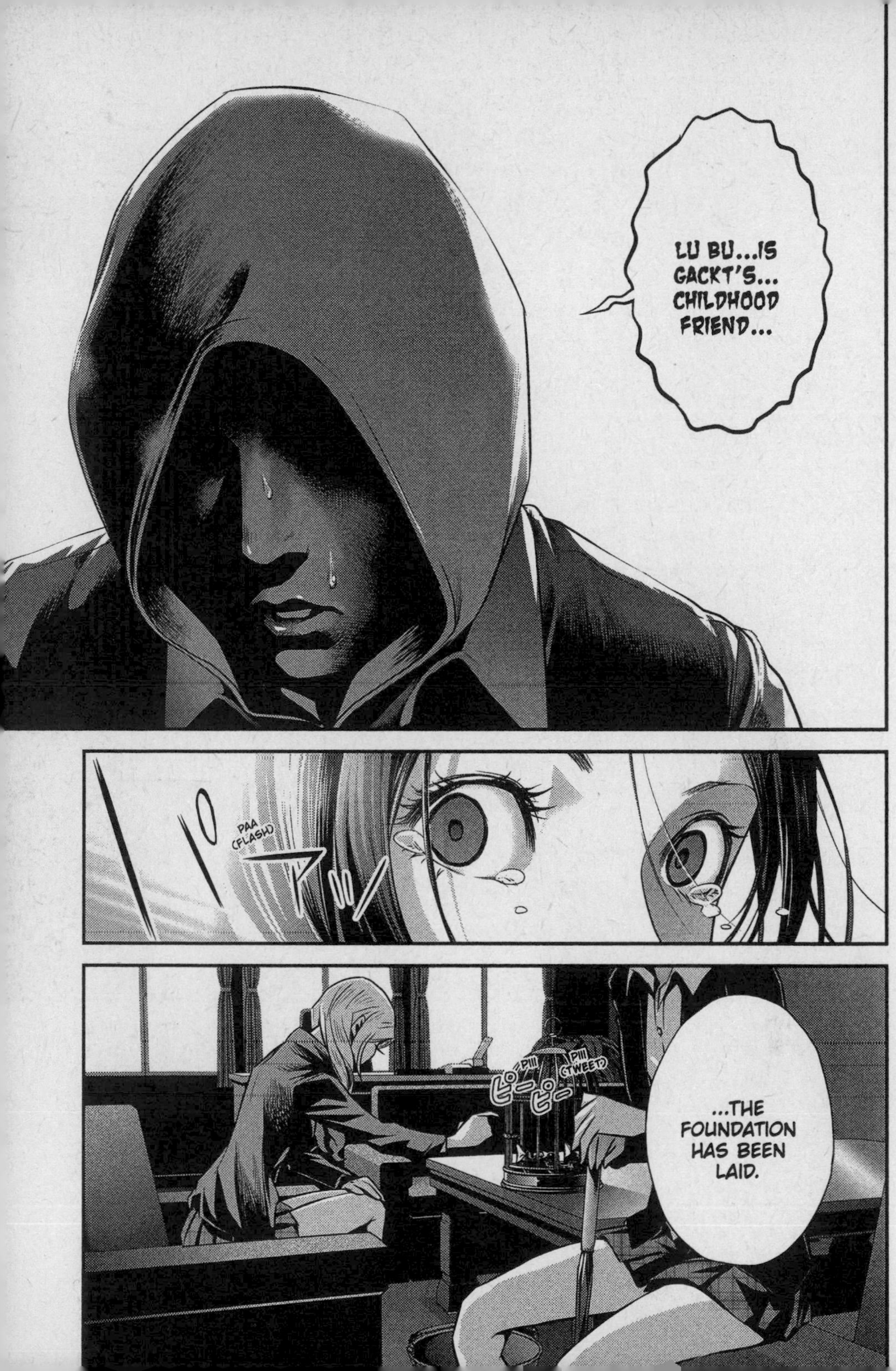
LU BU...IS GACKT'S... CHILDHOOD FRIEND...
PAA (FLASH)
PIII PIII (TWEET)
...THE FOUNDATION HAS BEEN LAID.

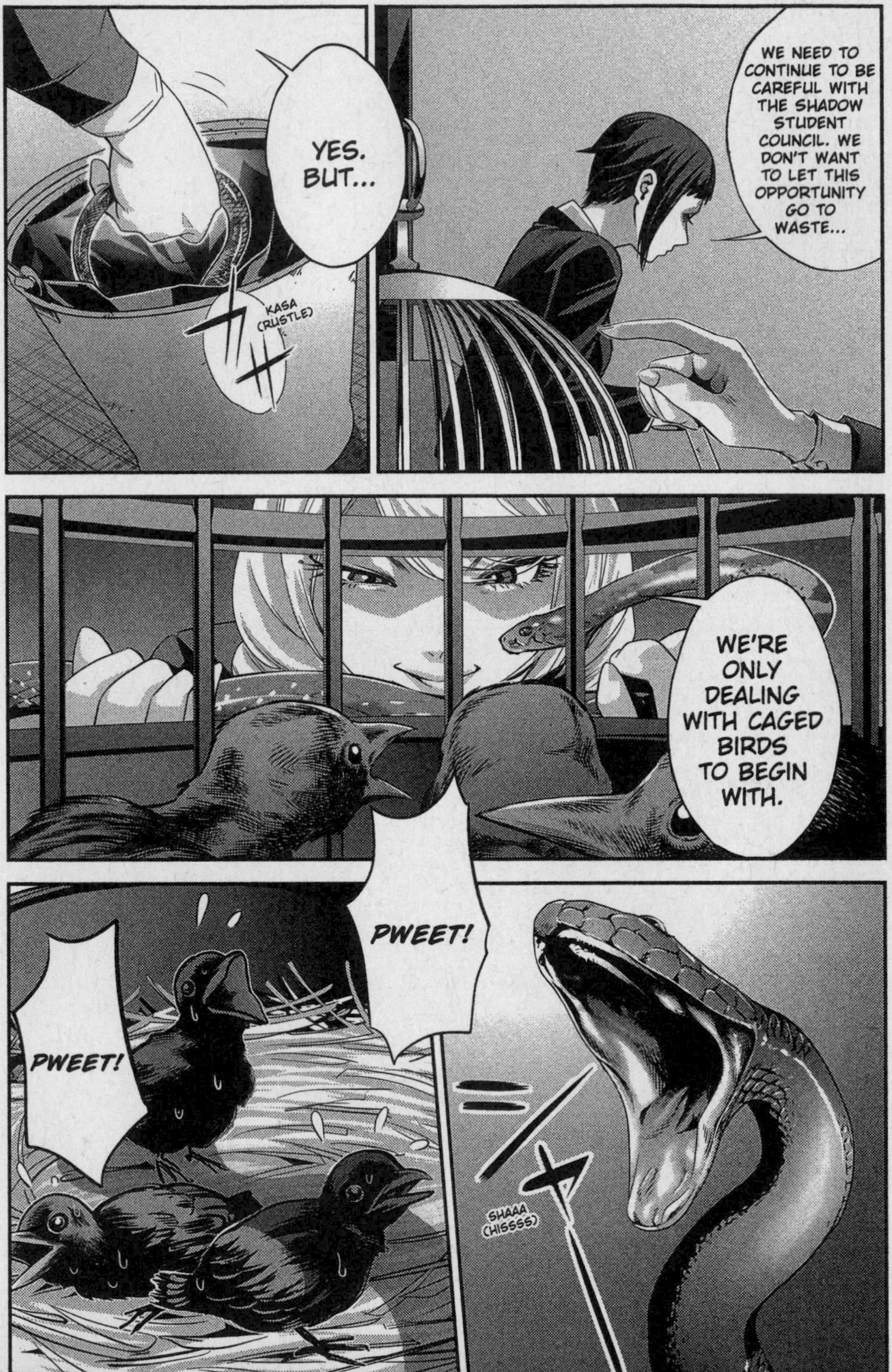
WE NEED TO CONTINUE TO BE CAREFUL WITH THE SHADOW STUDENT COUNCIL. WE DON'T WANT TO LET THIS OPPORTUNITY GO TO WASTE...
YES. BUT...
KASA (RUSTLE)
WE'RE ONLY DEALING WITH CAGED BIRDS TO BEGIN WITH.
SHAAA (HISSSS)
PWEET!
PWEET!

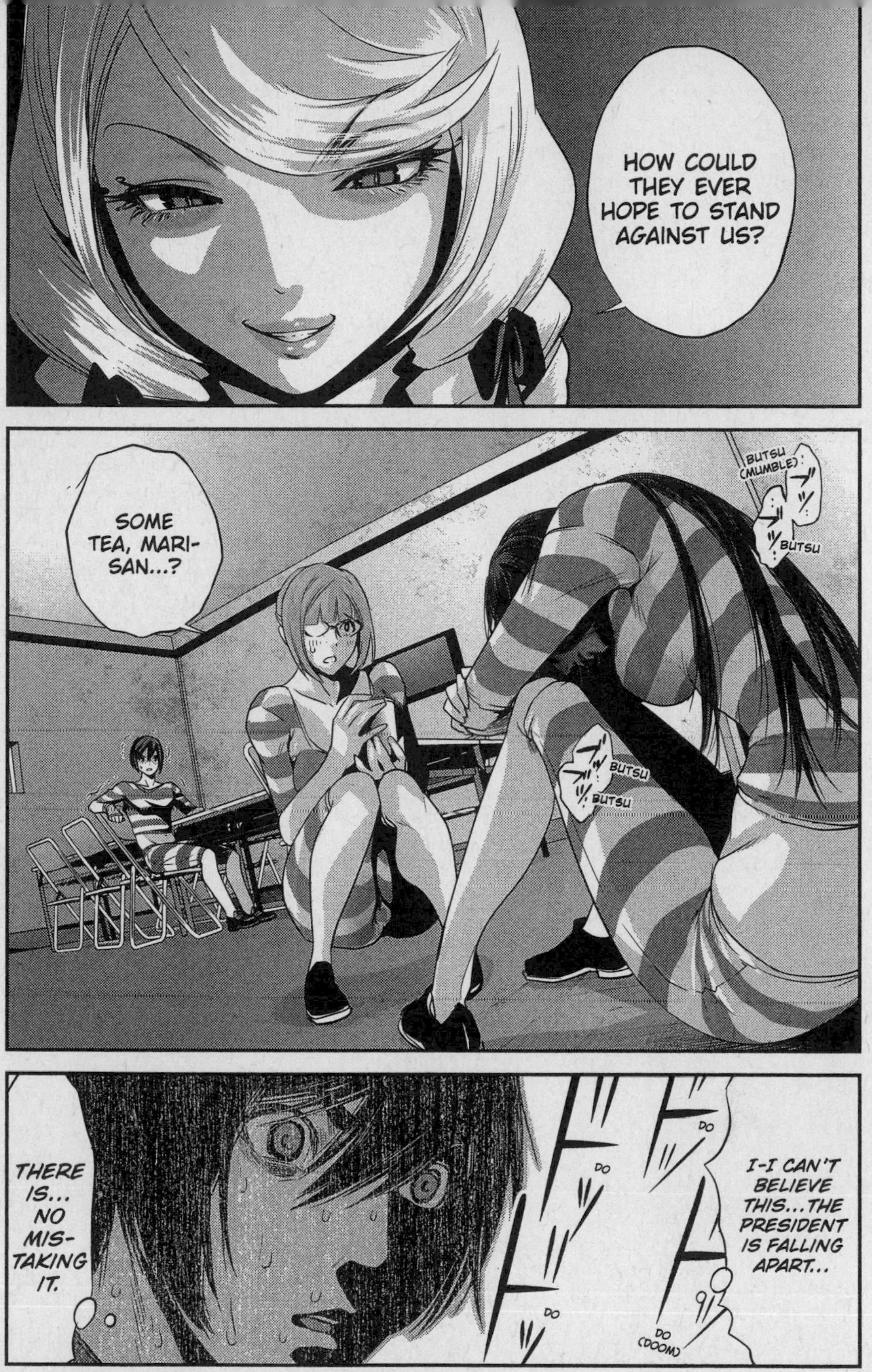
HOW COULD THEY EVER HOPE TO STAND AGAINST US?
BUTSU (MUMBLE) BUTSU
SOME TEA, MARI-SAN...?
BUTSU BUTSU
I-I CAN'T BELIEVE THIS...THE PRESIDENT IS FALLING APART...
DO DO DO DO (DOOM)
THERE IS... NO MIS-TAKING IT.

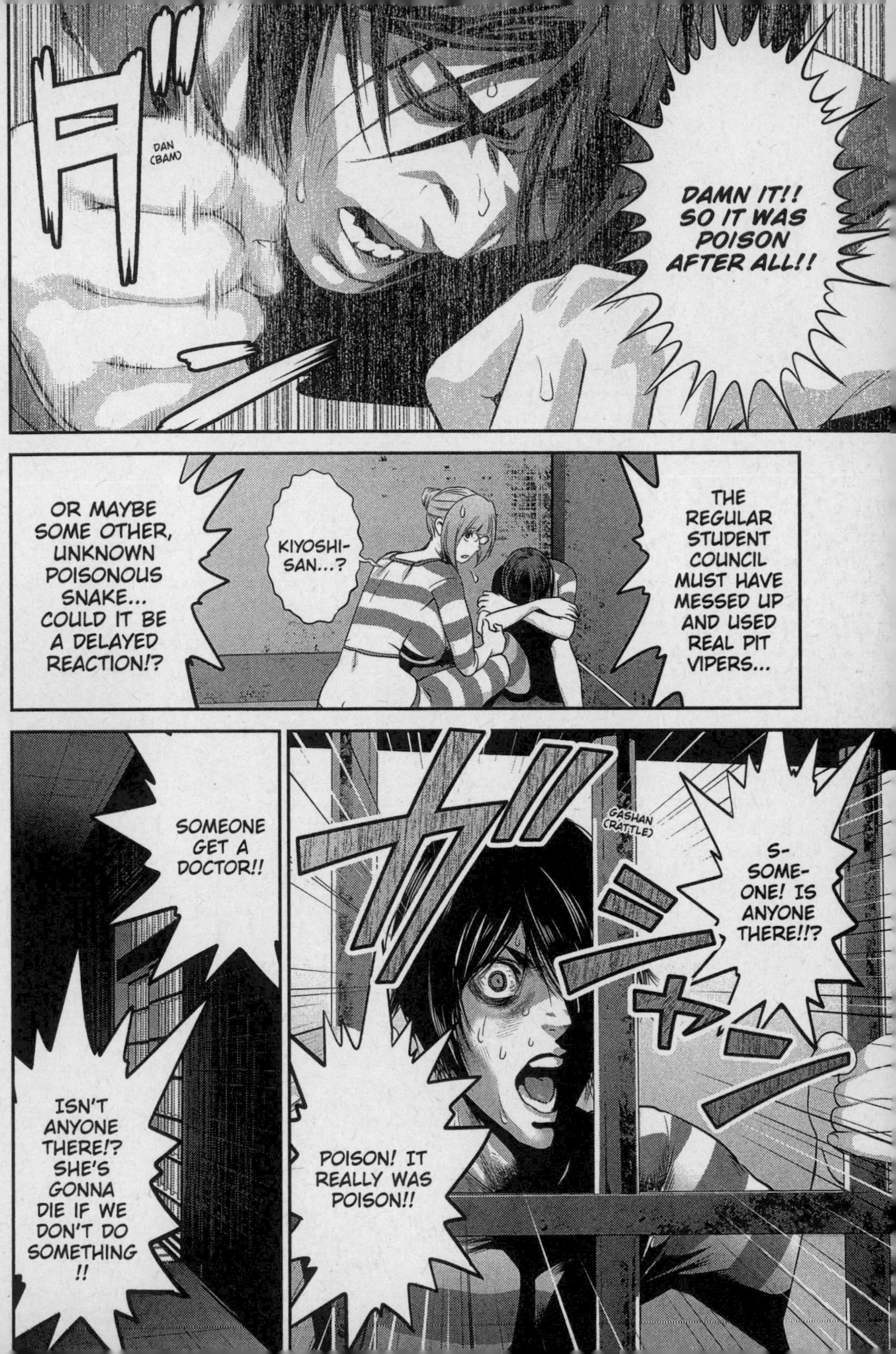
DAMN IT!! SO IT WAS POISON AFTER ALL!!
DAN (BAM)
THE REGULAR STUDENT COUNCIL MUST HAVE MESSED UP AND USED REAL PIT VIPERS...
KIYOSHI-SAN...?
OR MAYBE SOME OTHER, UNKNOWN POISONOUS SNAKE... COULD IT BE A DELAYED REACTION!?
GASHAN (RATTLE)
S-SOMEONE! IS ANYONE THERE!!?
POISON! IT REALLY WAS POISON!!
SOMEONE GET A DOCTOR!!
ISN'T ANYONE THERE!? SHE'S GONNA DIE IF WE DON'T DO SOMETHING!!

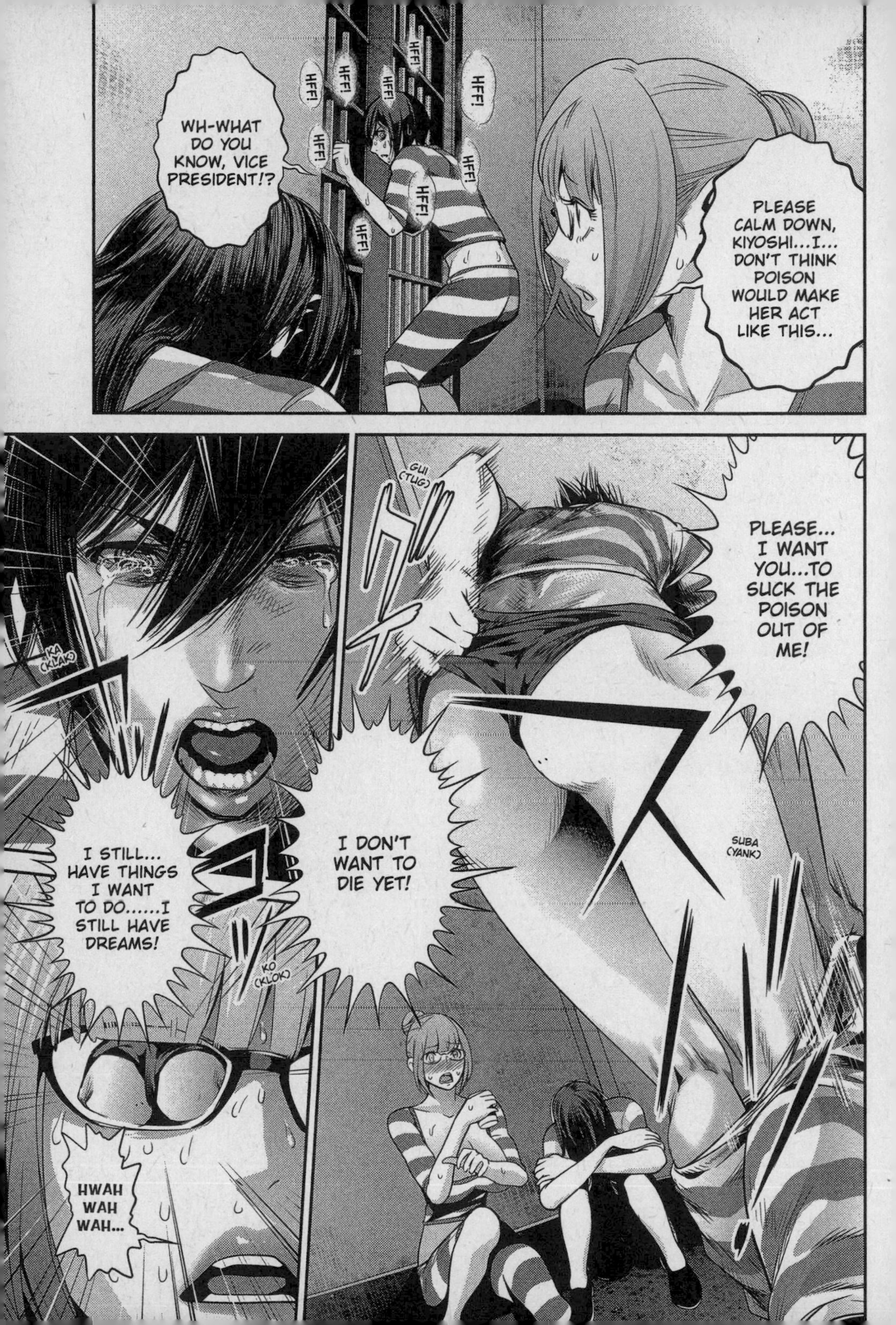
PLEASE CALM DOWN, KIYOSHI...I... DON'T THINK POISON WOULD MAKE HER ACT LIKE THIS...
HFF!
HFF!
HFF!
HFF!
HFF!
HFF!
HFF!
HFF!
WH-WHAT DO YOU KNOW, VICE PRESIDENT!?
GUI (TUG)
PLEASE... I WANT YOU...TO SUCK THE POISON OUT OF ME!
SUBA (YANK)
KA (KLAK)
I DON'T WANT TO DIE YET!
I STILL... HAVE THINGS I WANT TO DO......I STILL HAVE DREAMS!
KO (KLOK)
HWAH WAH WAH...

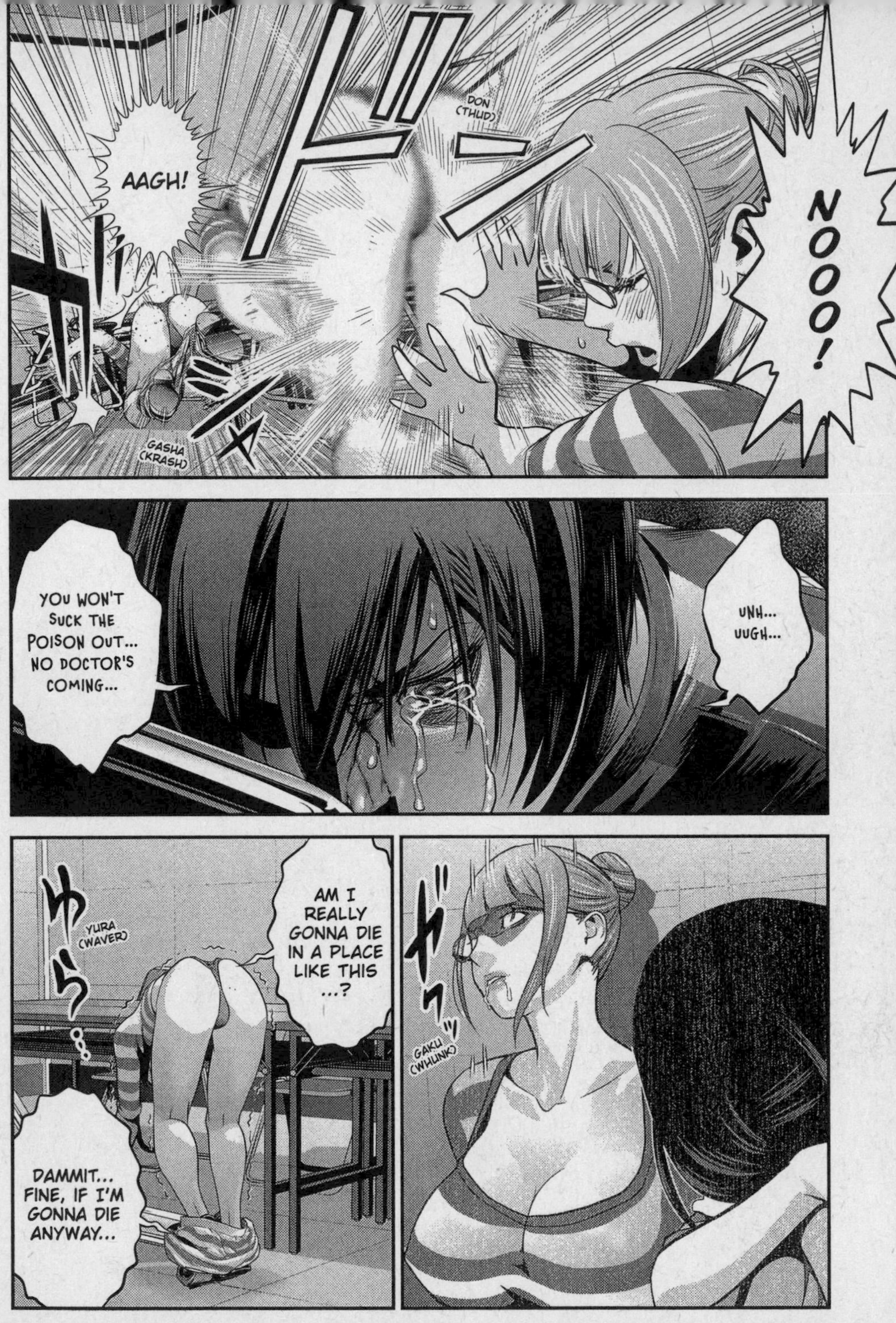
NOOOO!
DON (THUD)
AAGH!
GASHA (KRASH)
UNH... UUGH...
YOU WON'T SUCK THE POISON OUT... NO DOCTOR'S COMING...
GAKU (WHUNK)
AM I REALLY GONNA DIE IN A PLACE LIKE THIS ...?
YURA (WAVER)
DAMMIT... FINE, IF I'M GONNA DIE ANYWAY...

IF I'M GONNA DIE ANYWAY...

...I'LL BE GROPING SOME BOOBIES!!

DA

DA

DA
(DASH)

GA
(WHAP)

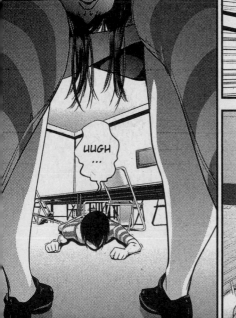

UUGH...

DOTA
(THUNK)

GON
(KLONG)

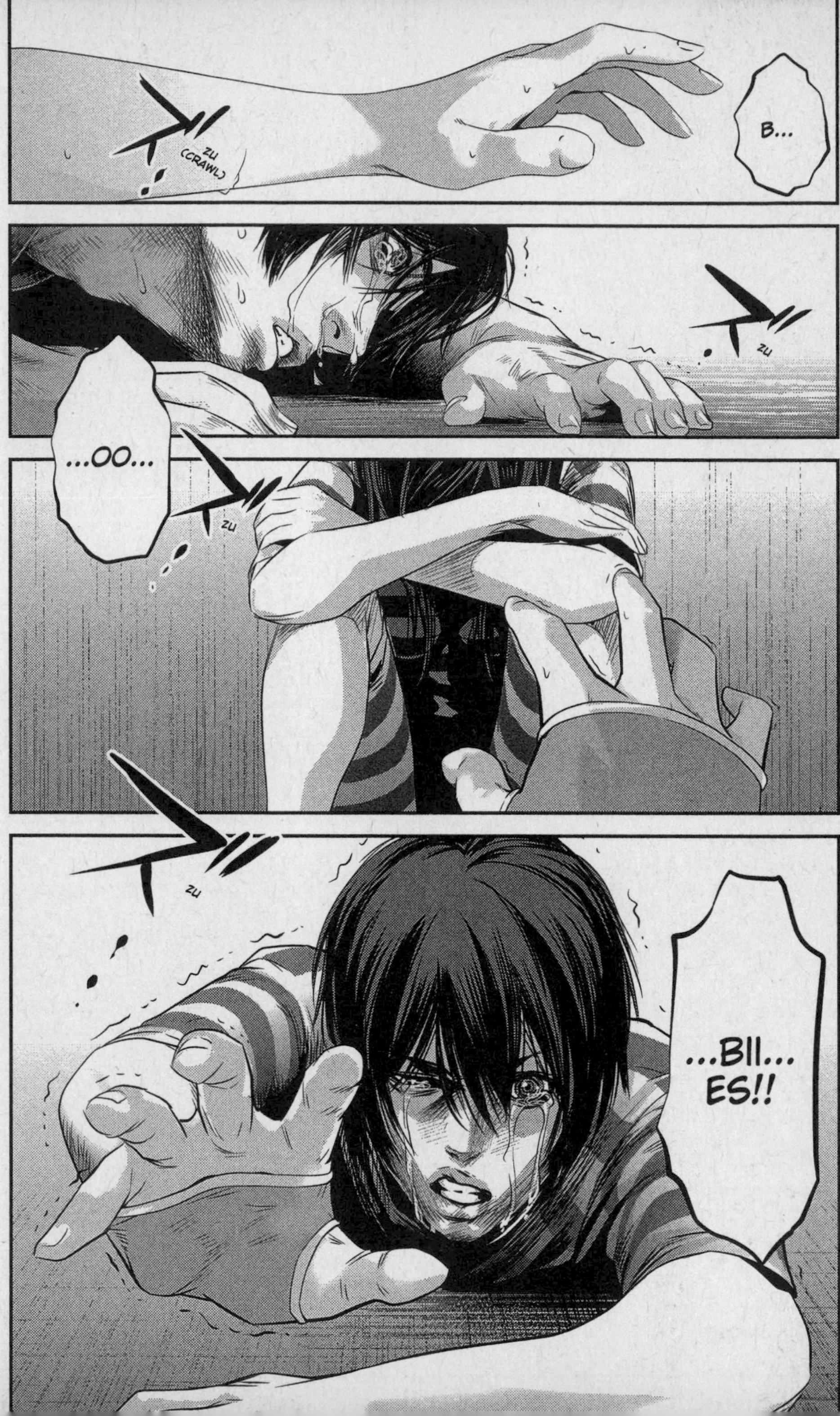
B...
ZU (CRAWL)
ZU
...OO...
ZU
...BII... ES!!
ZU

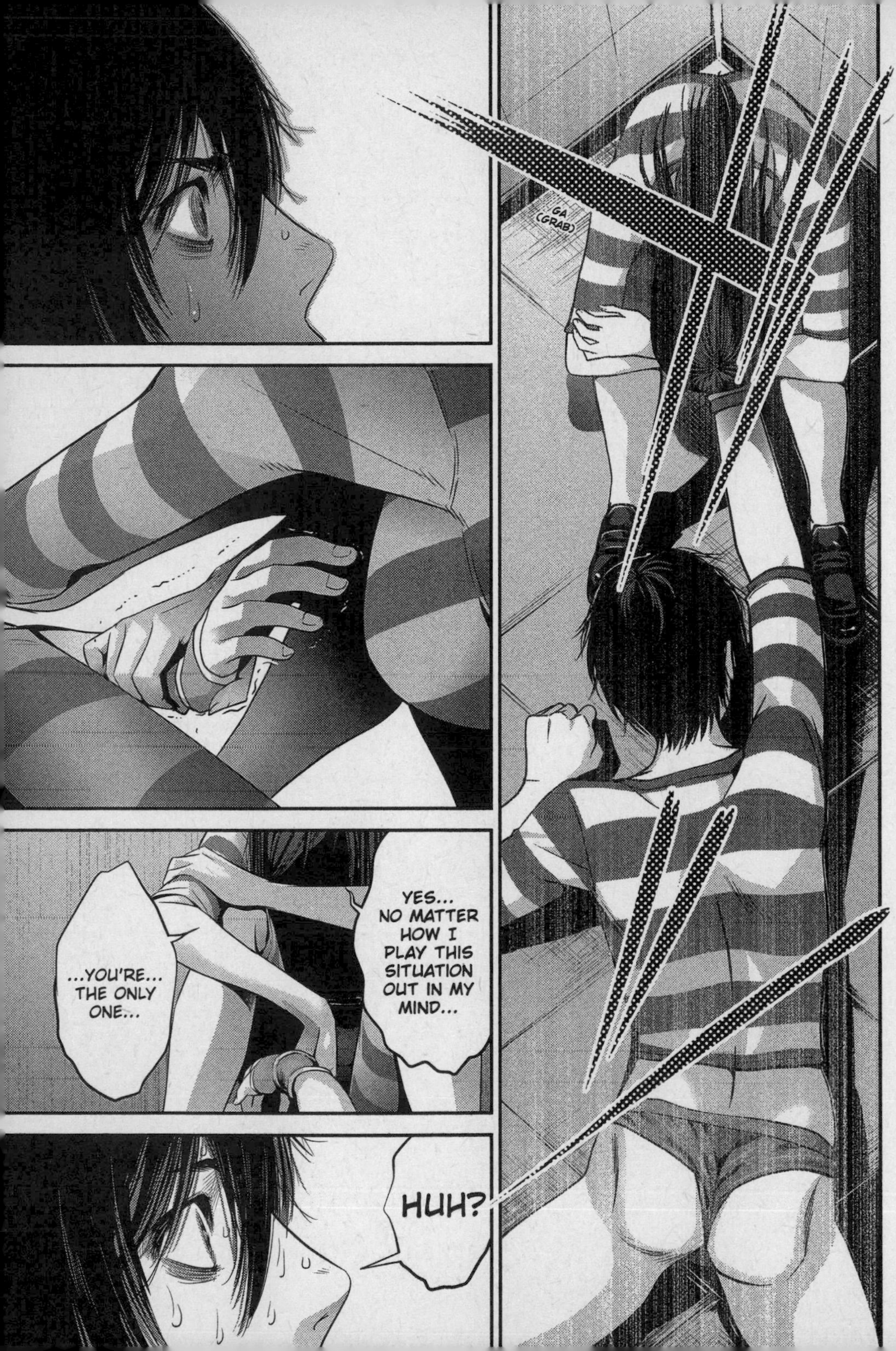
GA (GRAB)
YES... NO MATTER HOW I PLAY THIS SITUATION OUT IN MY MIND...
...YOU'RE... THE ONLY ONE...
HUH?

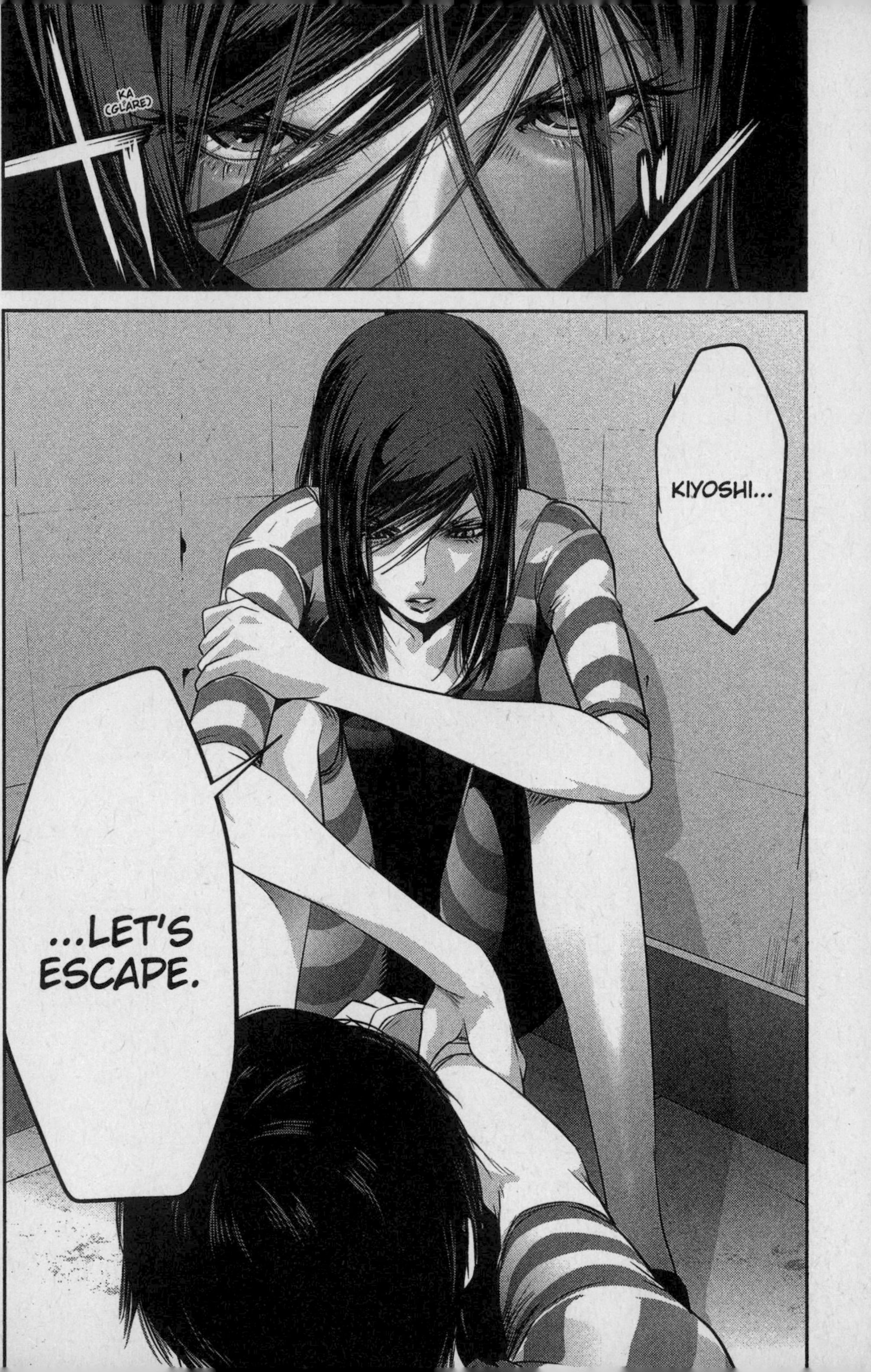
KA (GLARE)
KIYOSHI...
...LET'S ESCAPE.

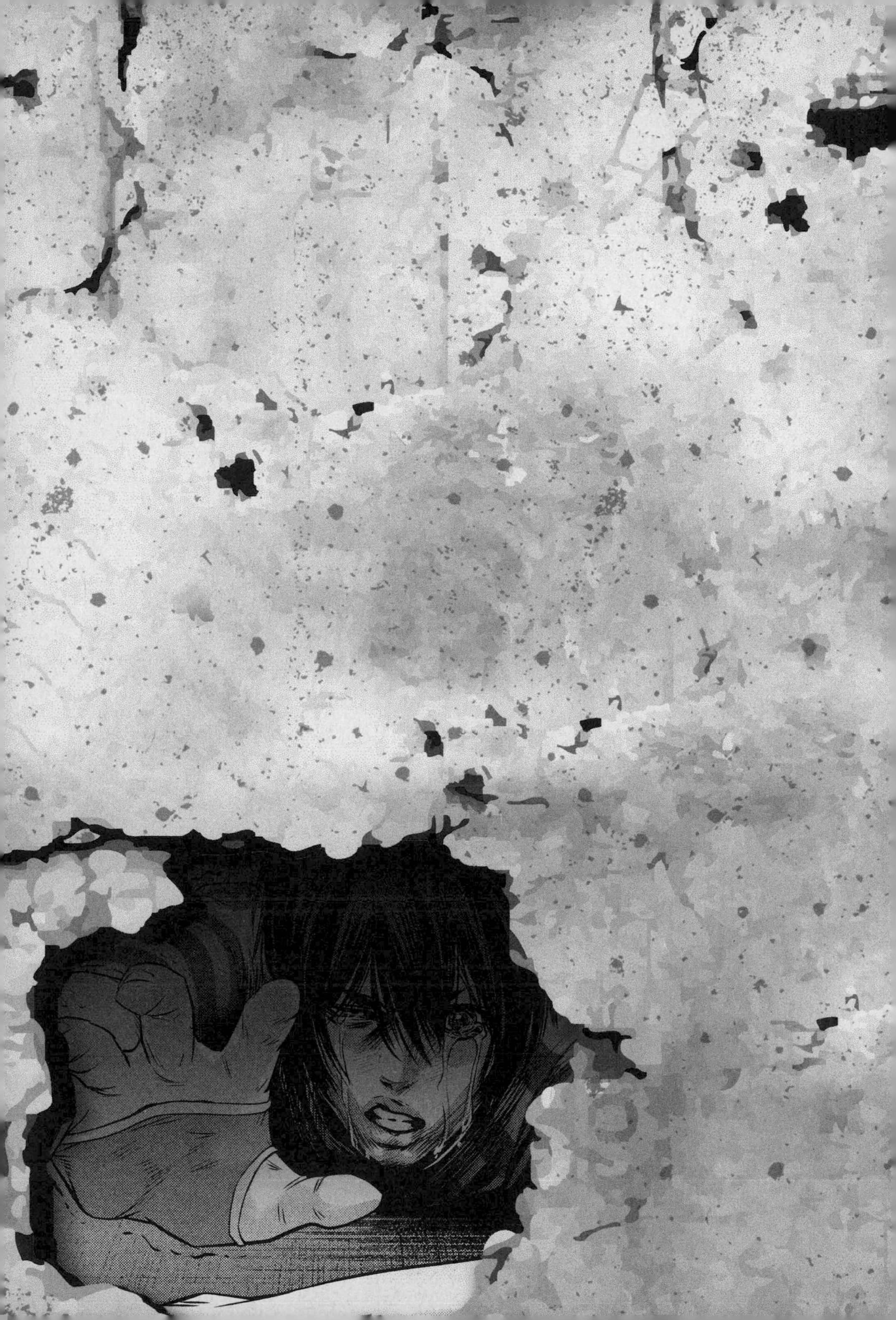

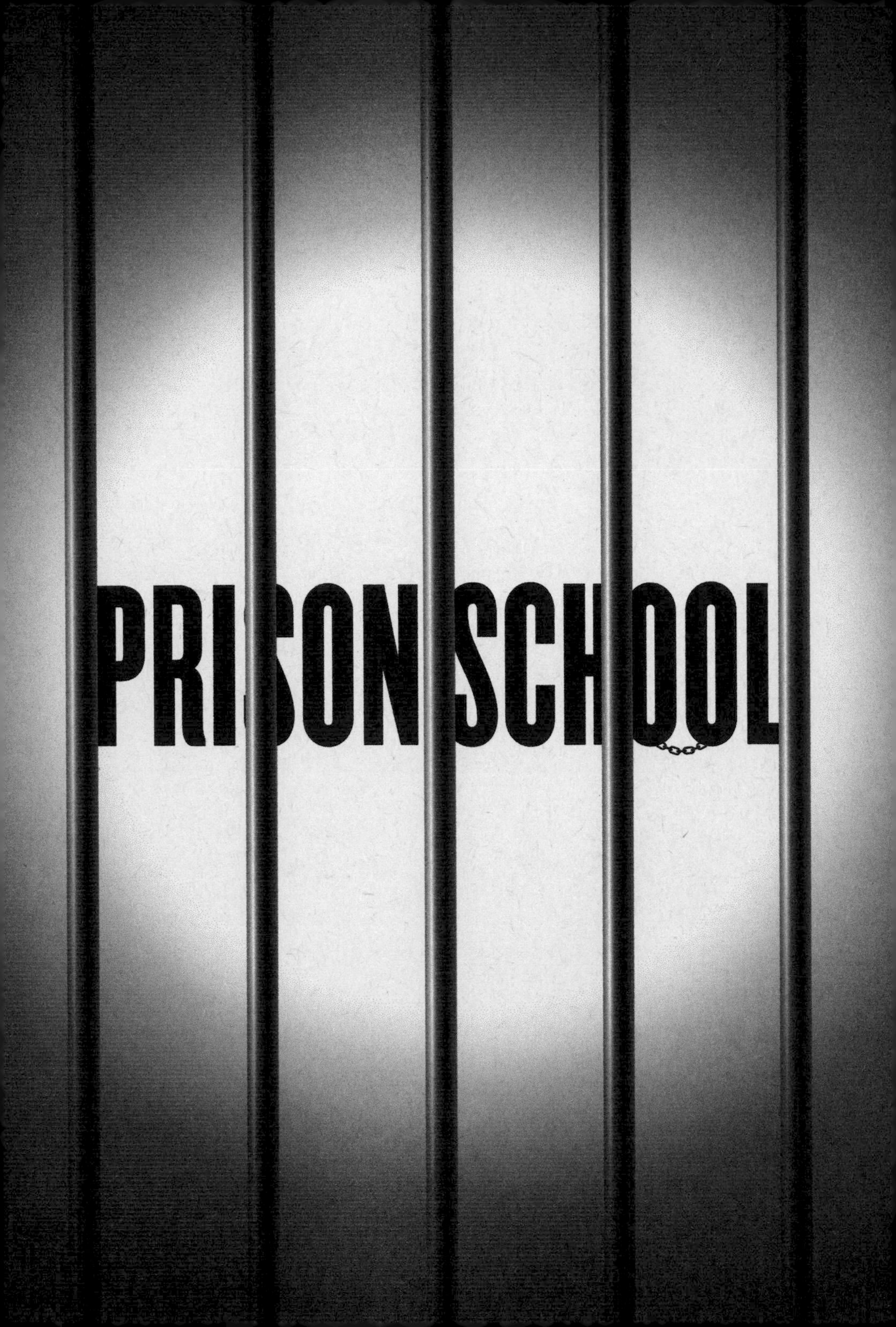
PRISON SCHOOL

CHAPTER 124: WASTED YOUTH

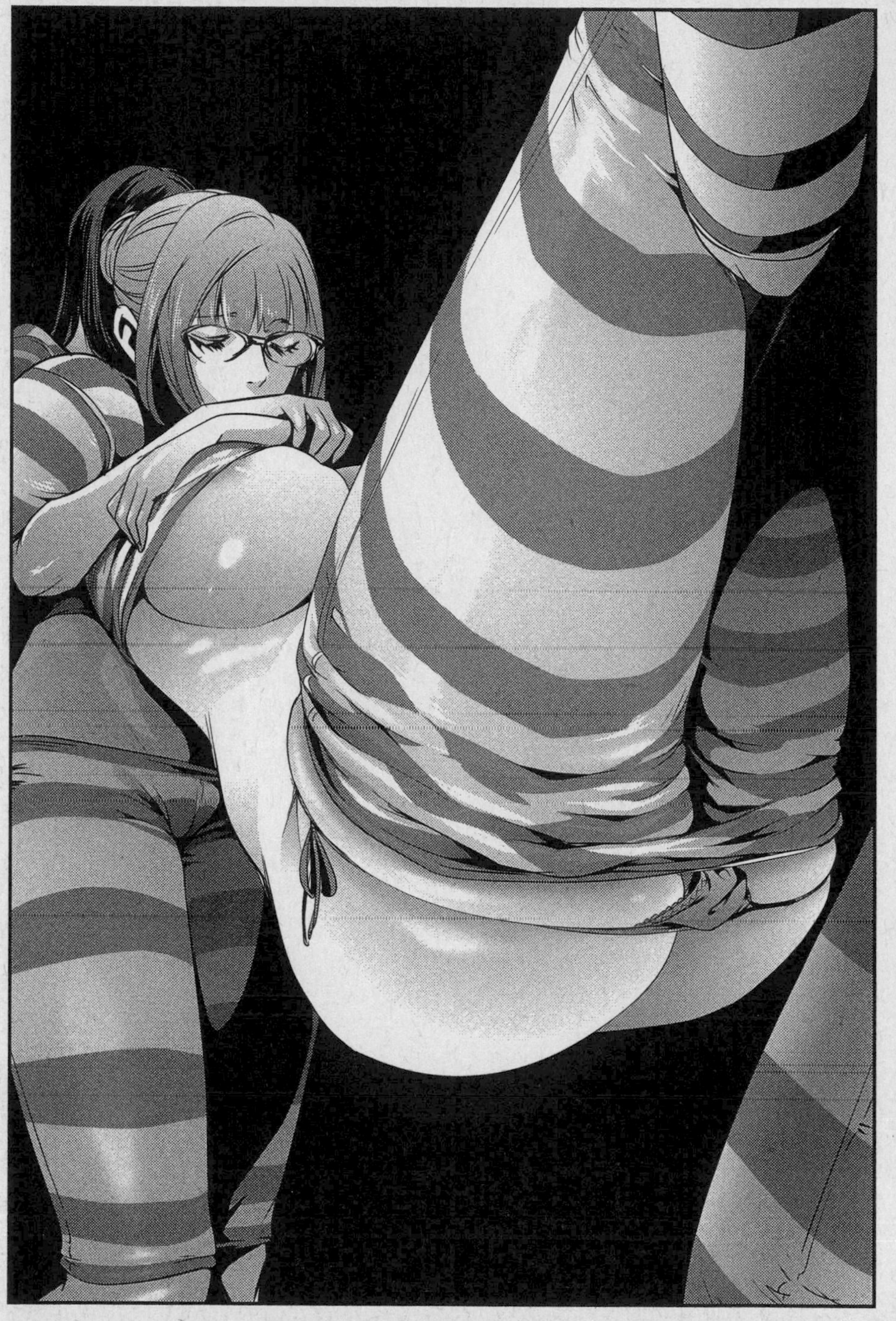

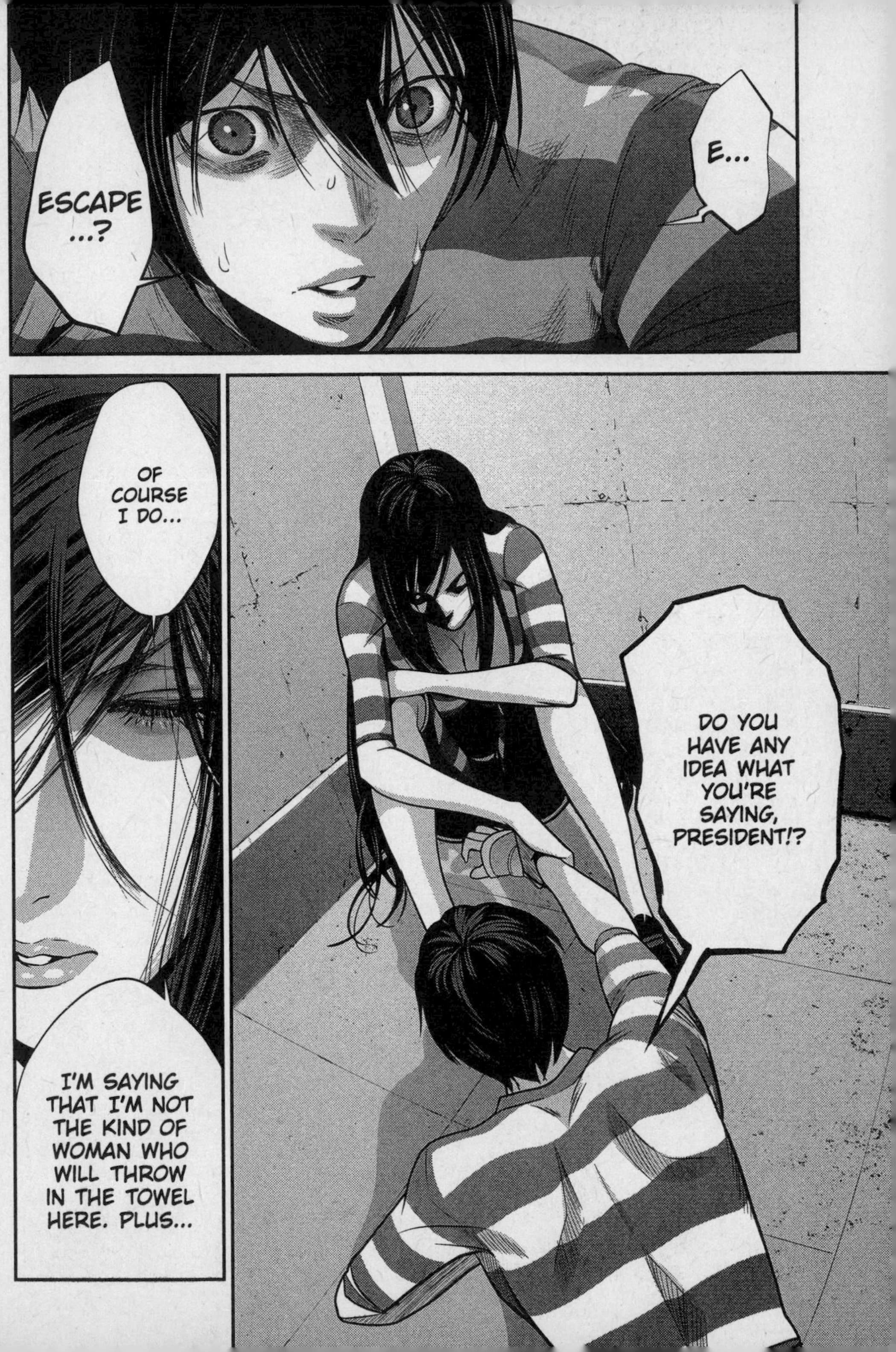
E...
ESCAPE ...?
DO YOU HAVE ANY IDEA WHAT YOU'RE SAYING, PRESIDENT!?
OF COURSE I DO...
I'M SAYING THAT I'M NOT THE KIND OF WOMAN WHO WILL THROW IN THE TOWEL HERE. PLUS...

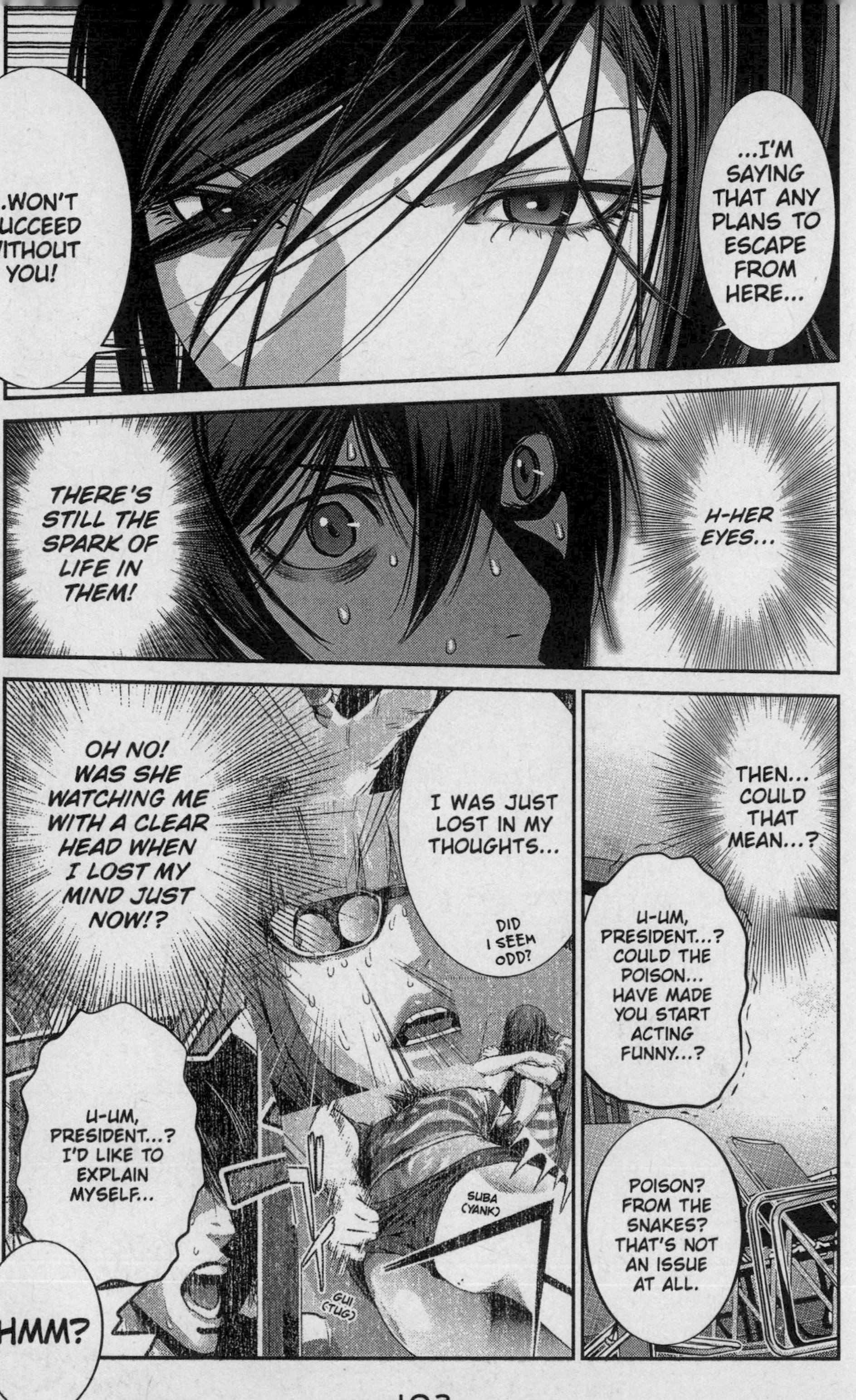
...I'M SAYING THAT ANY PLANS TO ESCAPE FROM HERE...
...WON'T SUCCEED WITHOUT YOU!
H-HER EYES...
THERE'S STILL THE SPARK OF LIFE IN THEM!
THEN... COULD THAT MEAN...?
U-UM, PRESIDENT...? COULD THE POISON... HAVE MADE YOU START ACTING FUNNY...?
POISON? FROM THE SNAKES? THAT'S NOT AN ISSUE AT ALL.
I WAS JUST LOST IN MY THOUGHTS...
DID I SEEM ODD?
OH NO! WAS SHE WATCHING ME WITH A CLEAR HEAD WHEN I LOST MY MIND JUST NOW!?
SUBA (YANK)
GUI (TUG)
U-UM, PRESIDENT...? I'D LIKE TO EXPLAIN MYSELF...
HMM?

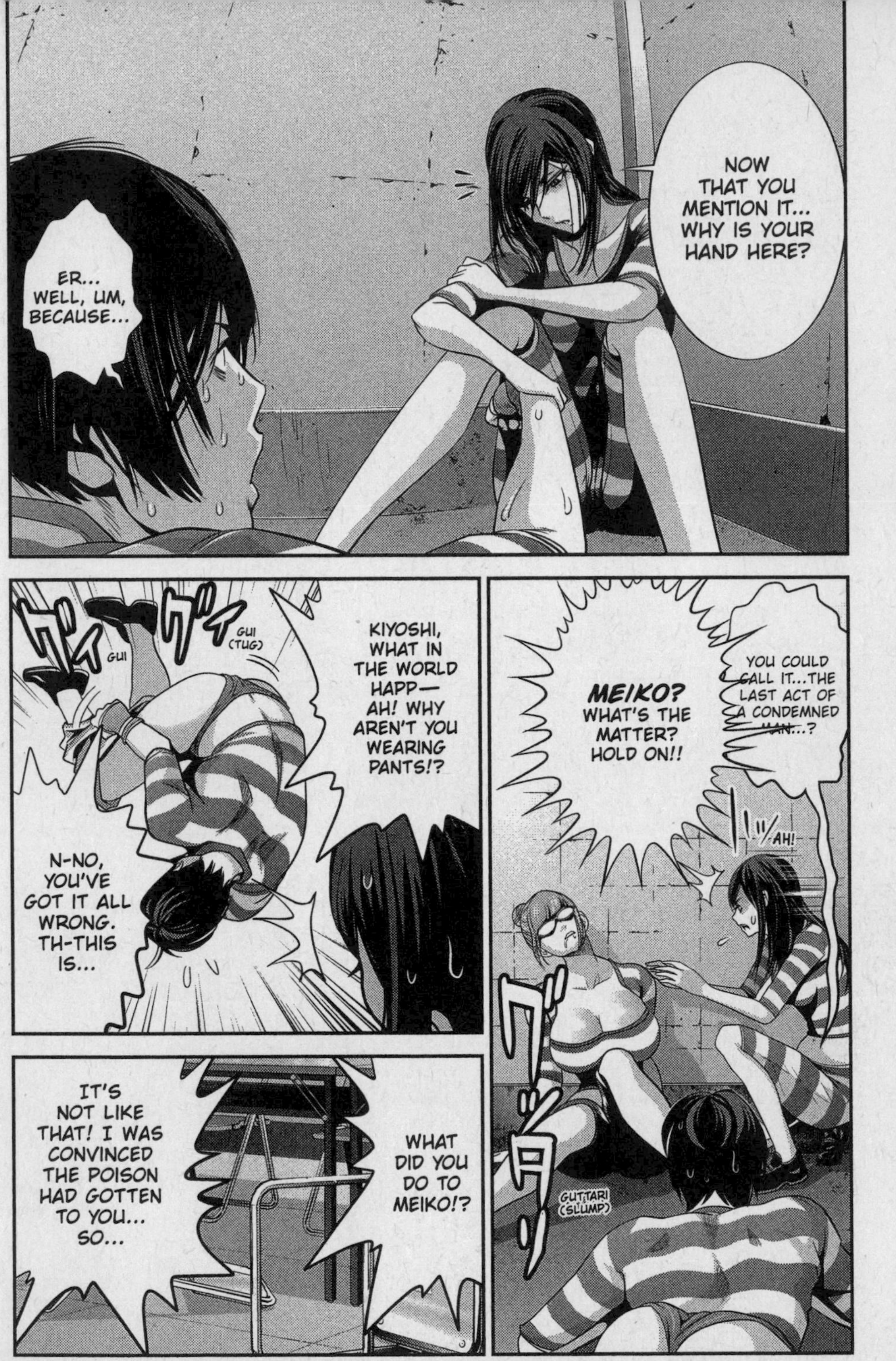
NOW THAT YOU MENTION IT... WHY IS YOUR HAND HERE?
ER... WELL, UM, BECAUSE...
YOU COULD CALL IT...THE LAST ACT OF A CONDEMNED MAN...?
MEIKO? WHAT'S THE MATTER? HOLD ON!!
AH!
GUTTARI (SLUMP)
GUI (TUG)
GUI
KIYOSHI, WHAT IN THE WORLD HAPP— AH! WHY AREN'T YOU WEARING PANTS!?
N-NO, YOU'VE GOT IT ALL WRONG. TH-THIS IS...
WHAT DID YOU DO TO MEIKO!?
IT'S NOT LIKE THAT! I WAS CONVINCED THE POISON HAD GOTTEN TO YOU... SO...

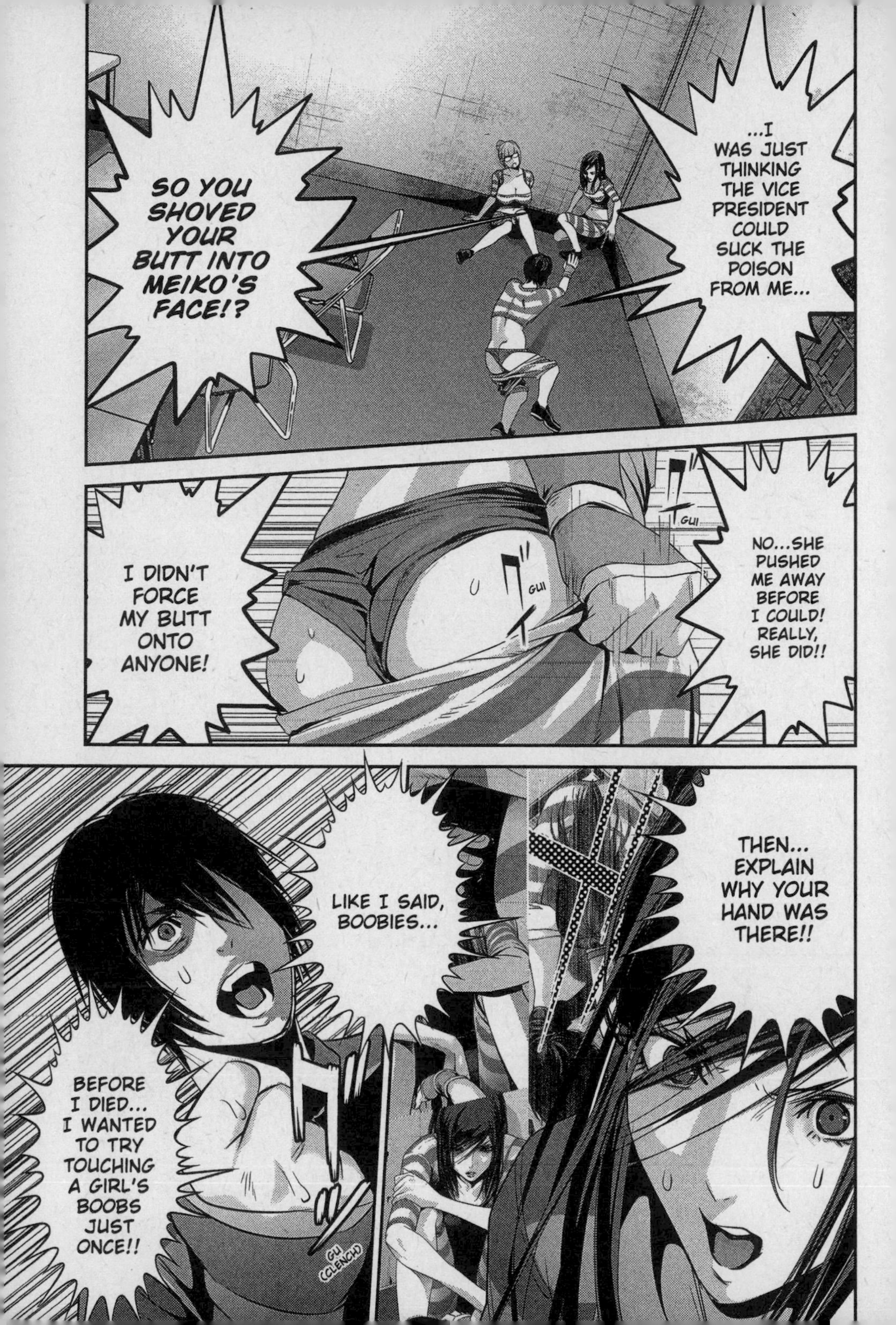

...I WAS JUST THINKING THE VICE PRESIDENT COULD SUCK THE POISON FROM ME...
SO YOU SHOVED YOUR BUTT INTO MEIKO'S FACE!?
GUI
GUI
NO...SHE PUSHED ME AWAY BEFORE I COULD! REALLY, SHE DID!!
I DIDN'T FORCE MY BUTT ONTO ANYONE!
THEN... EXPLAIN WHY YOUR HAND WAS THERE!!
LIKE I SAID, BOOBIES...
BEFORE I DIED... I WANTED TO TRY TOUCHING A GIRL'S BOOBS JUST ONCE!!
GU (CLENCH)

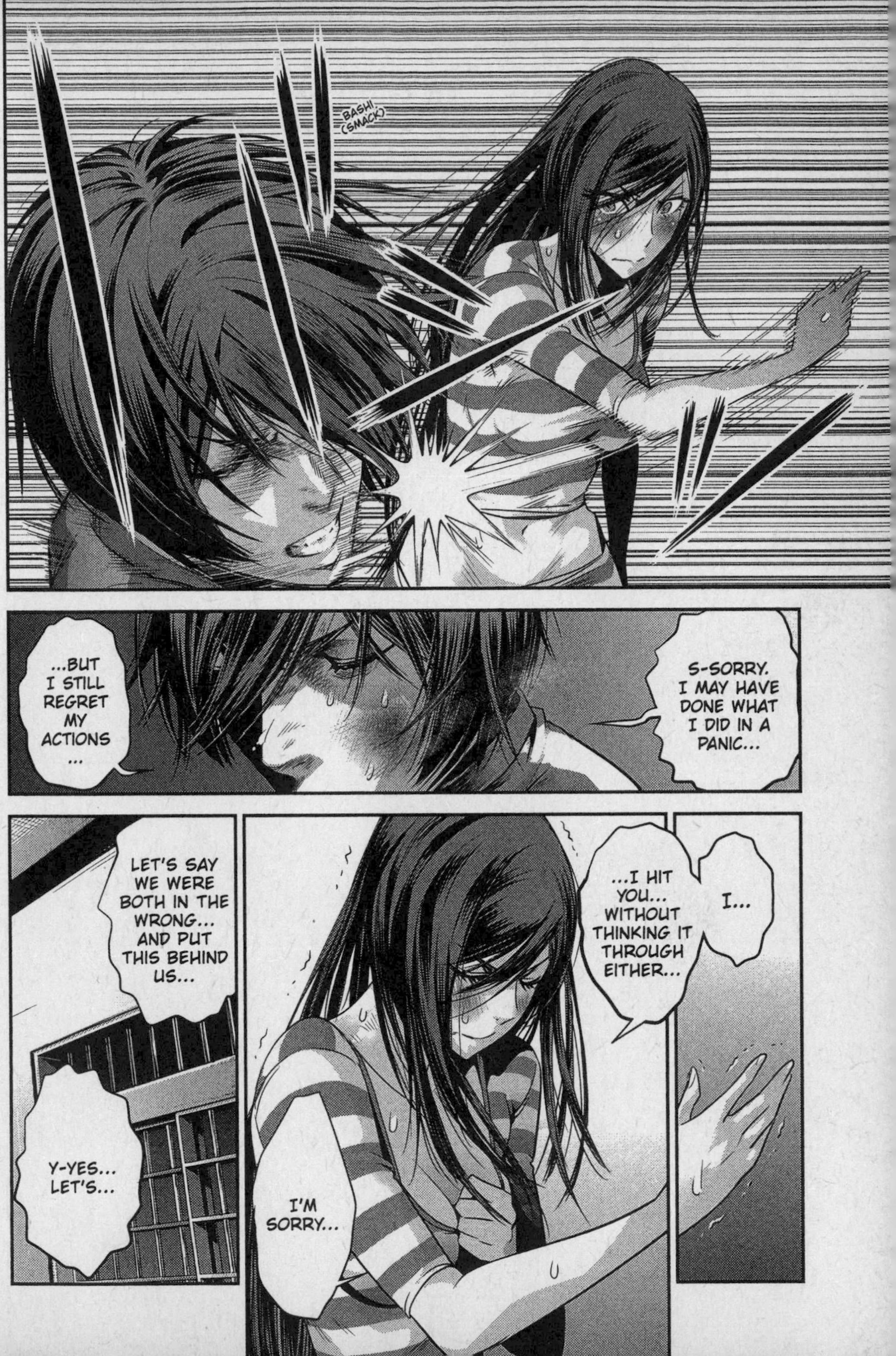
BASHI (SMACK)
S-SORRY. I MAY HAVE DONE WHAT I DID IN A PANIC...
...BUT I STILL REGRET MY ACTIONS ...
I...
...I HIT YOU... WITHOUT THINKING IT THROUGH EITHER...
I'M SORRY...
LET'S SAY WE WERE BOTH IN THE WRONG... AND PUT THIS BEHIND US...
Y-YES... LET'S...

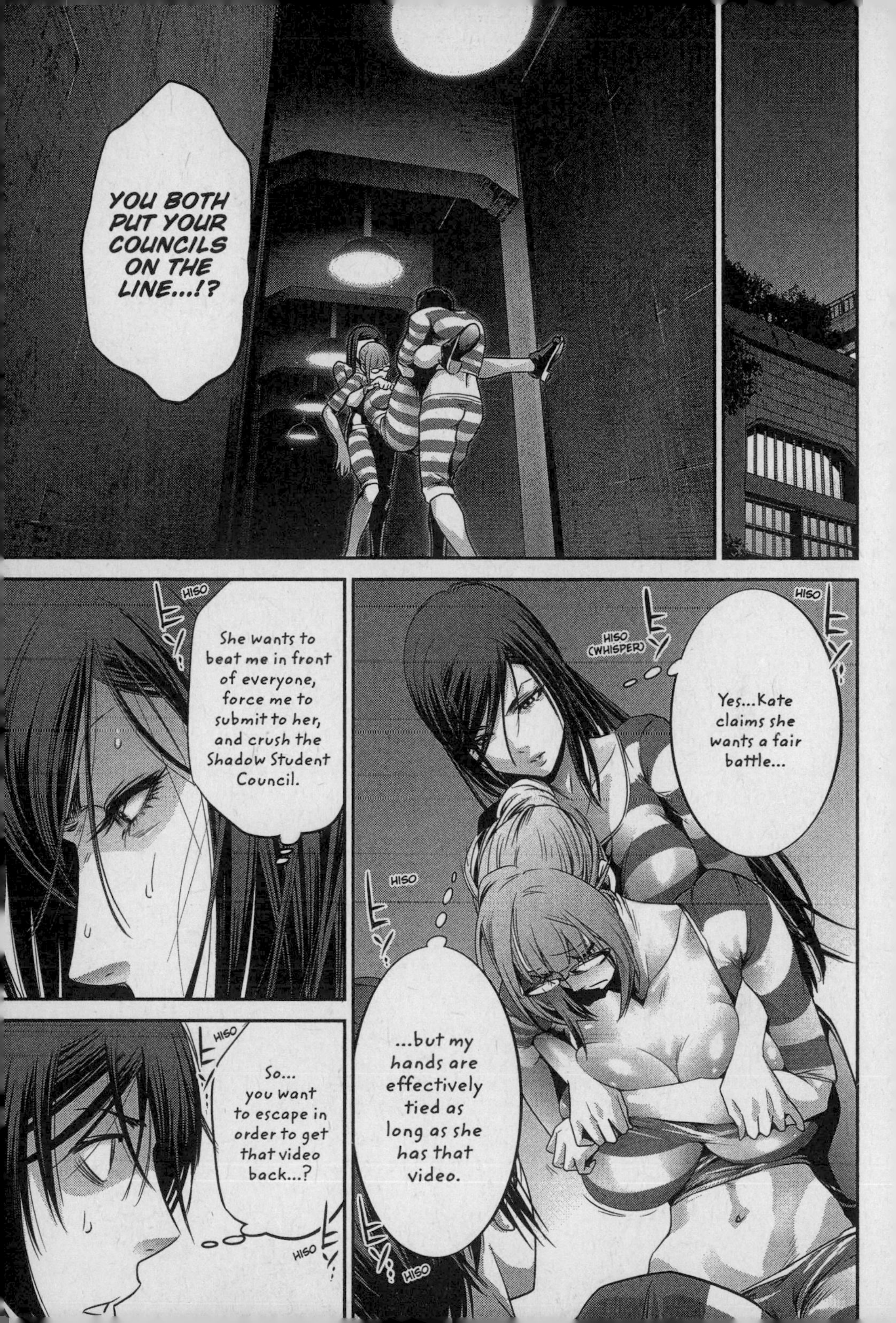
YOU BOTH PUT YOUR COUNCILS ON THE LINE...!?
HISO
HISO (WHISPER)
Yes...Kate claims she wants a fair battle...
HISO
...but my hands are effectively tied as long as she has that video.
HISO
HISO
She wants to beat me in front of everyone, force me to submit to her, and crush the Shadow Student Council.
HISO
So... you want to escape in order to get that video back...?
HISO

You realize it's a digital file, right? She can make as many copies as she wants.
ZURI (SLIP)
ZURI
ZURI
ZURI
Yeah...But then, why escape...?
ZURI
I have a plan.
ZURI
We just need to escape by field day...
ZURI
...and we need you to make that happen...
ZURI

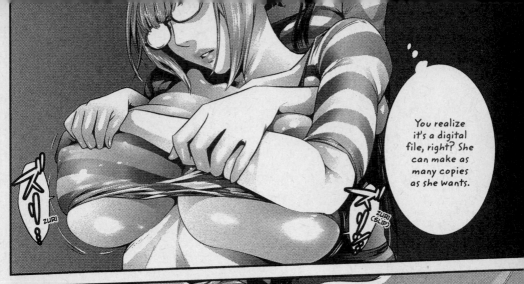

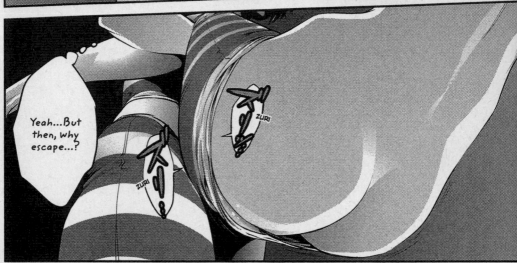

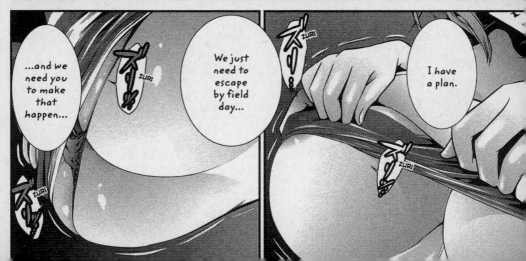

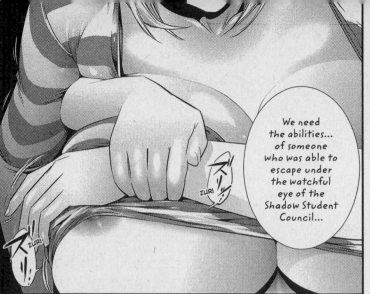

We need the abilities... of someone who was able to escape under the watchful eye of the Shadow Student Council...
ZURI
ZURI
But...
ZURI
ZURI
HEY, WHAT ARE YOU DOING? HURRY UP AND GET IN HERE.
HISO (WHISPER)
I'll tell you the details tomorrow.

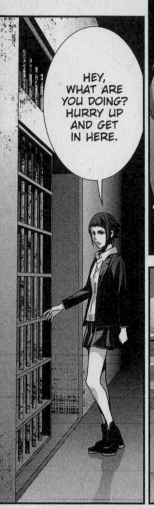

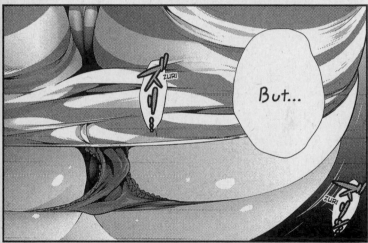

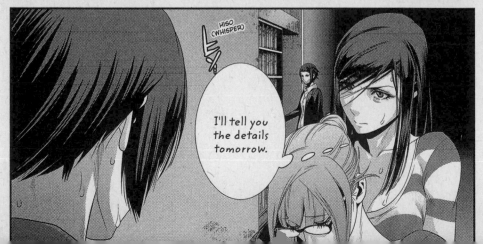

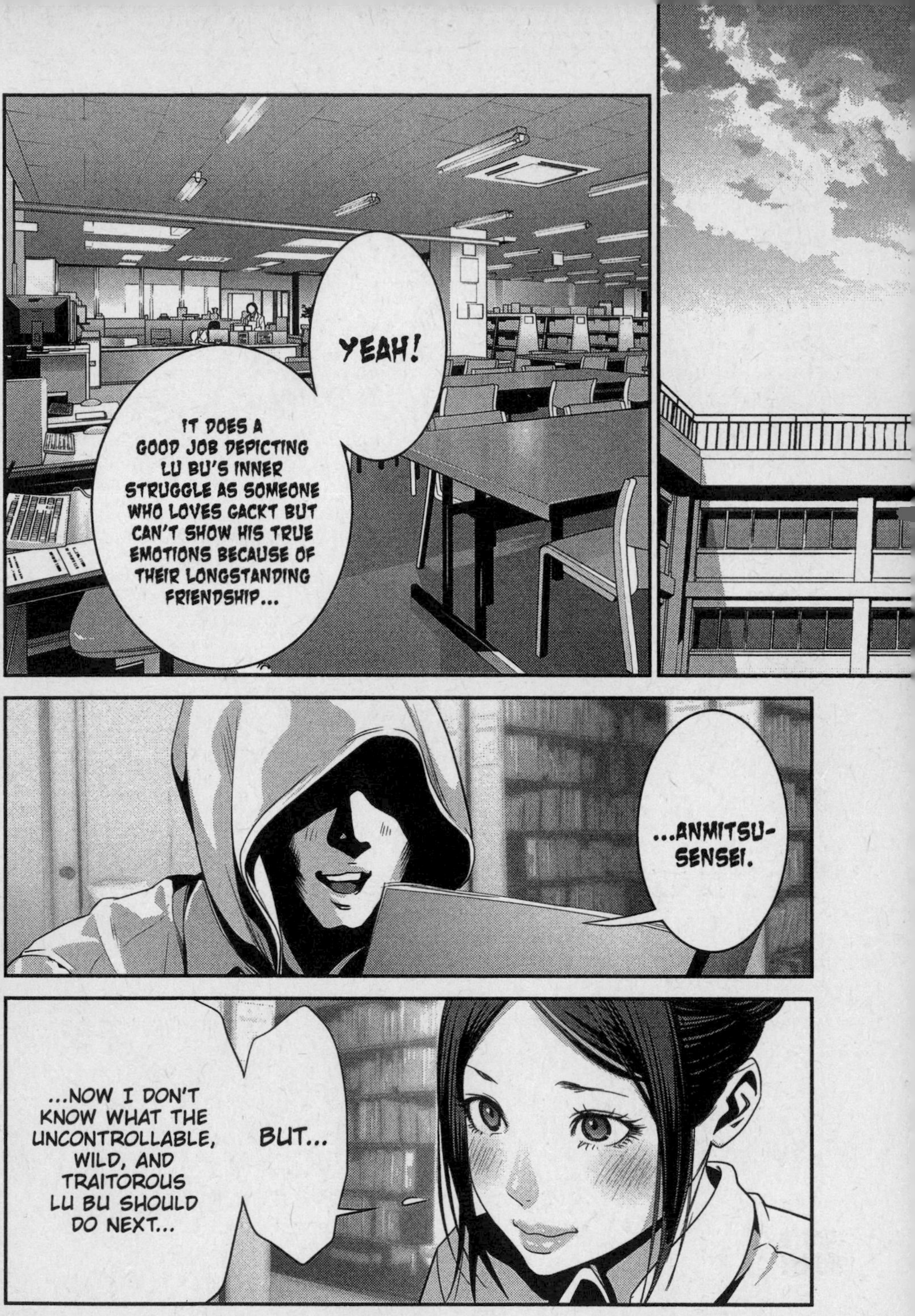
YEAH!
IT DOES A GOOD JOB DEPICTING LU BU'S INNER STRUGGLE AS SOMEONE WHO LOVES GACKT BUT CAN'T SHOW HIS TRUE EMOTIONS BECAUSE OF THEIR LONGSTANDING FRIENDSHIP...
...ANMITSU-SENSEI.
BUT...
...NOW I DON'T KNOW WHAT THE UNCONTROLLABLE, WILD, AND TRAITOROUS LU BU SHOULD DO NEXT...

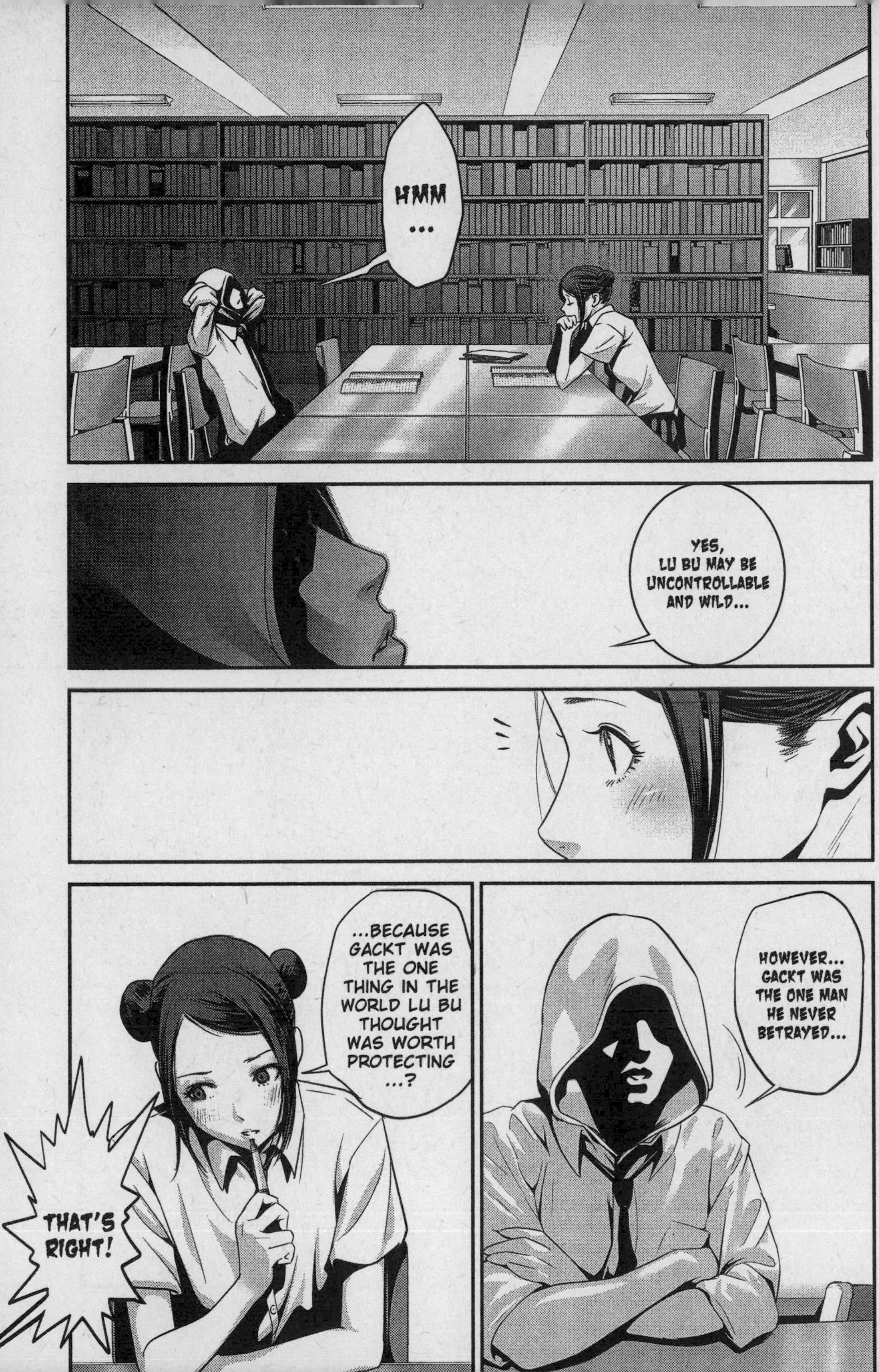
HMM...
YES, LU BU MAY BE UNCONTROLLABLE AND WILD...
HOWEVER... GACKT WAS THE ONE MAN HE NEVER BETRAYED...
...BECAUSE GACKT WAS THE ONE THING IN THE WORLD LU BU THOUGHT WAS WORTH PROTECTING...?
THAT'S RIGHT!

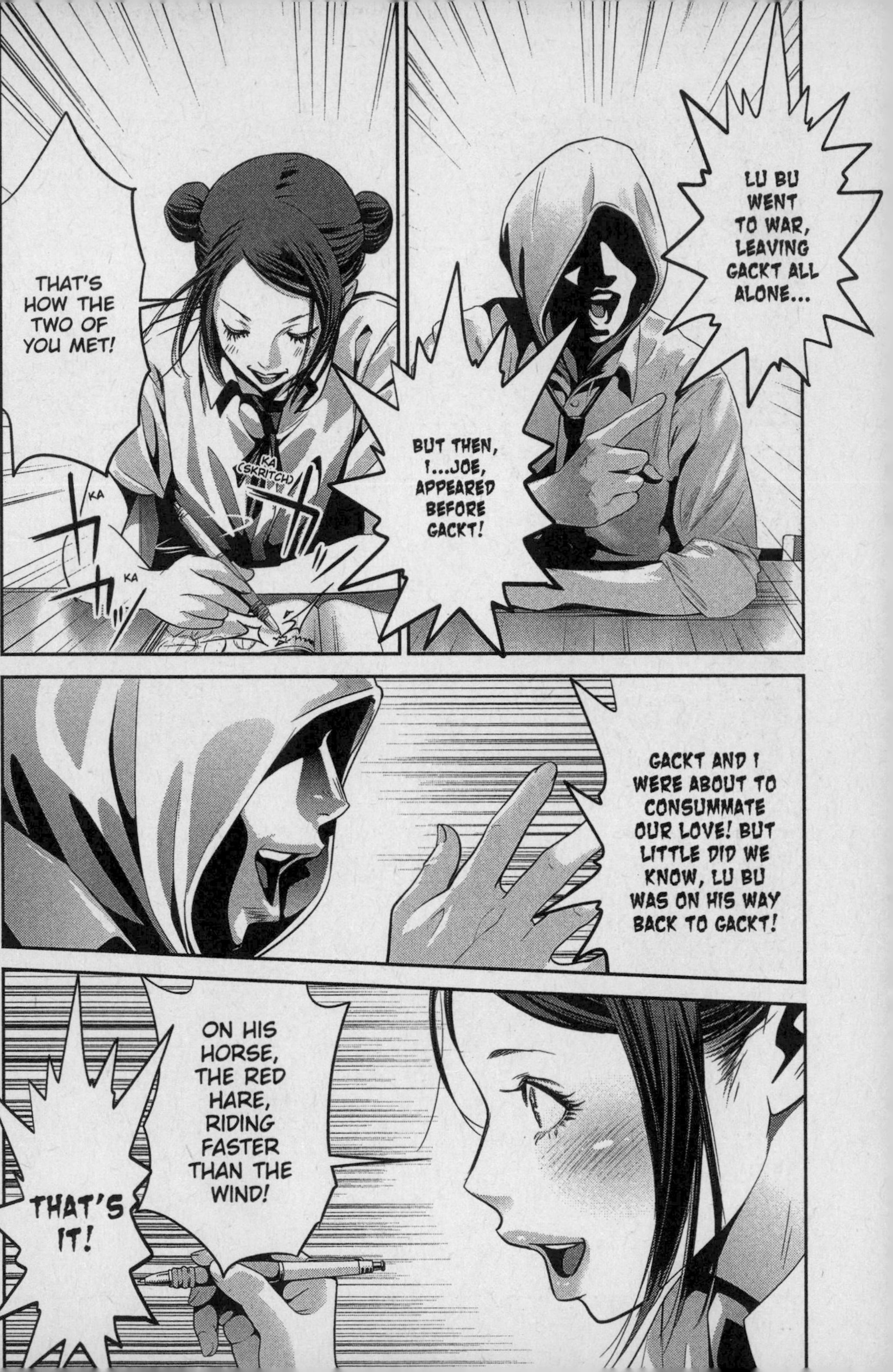
LU BU WENT TO WAR, LEAVING GACKT ALL ALONE...
BUT THEN, I...JOE, APPEARED BEFORE GACKT!
THAT'S HOW THE TWO OF YOU MET!
KA (SKRITCH)
KA
KA
GACKT AND I WERE ABOUT TO CONSUMMATE OUR LOVE! BUT LITTLE DID WE KNOW, LU BU WAS ON HIS WAY BACK TO GACKT!
ON HIS HORSE, THE RED HARE, RIDING FASTER THAN THE WIND!
THAT'S IT!

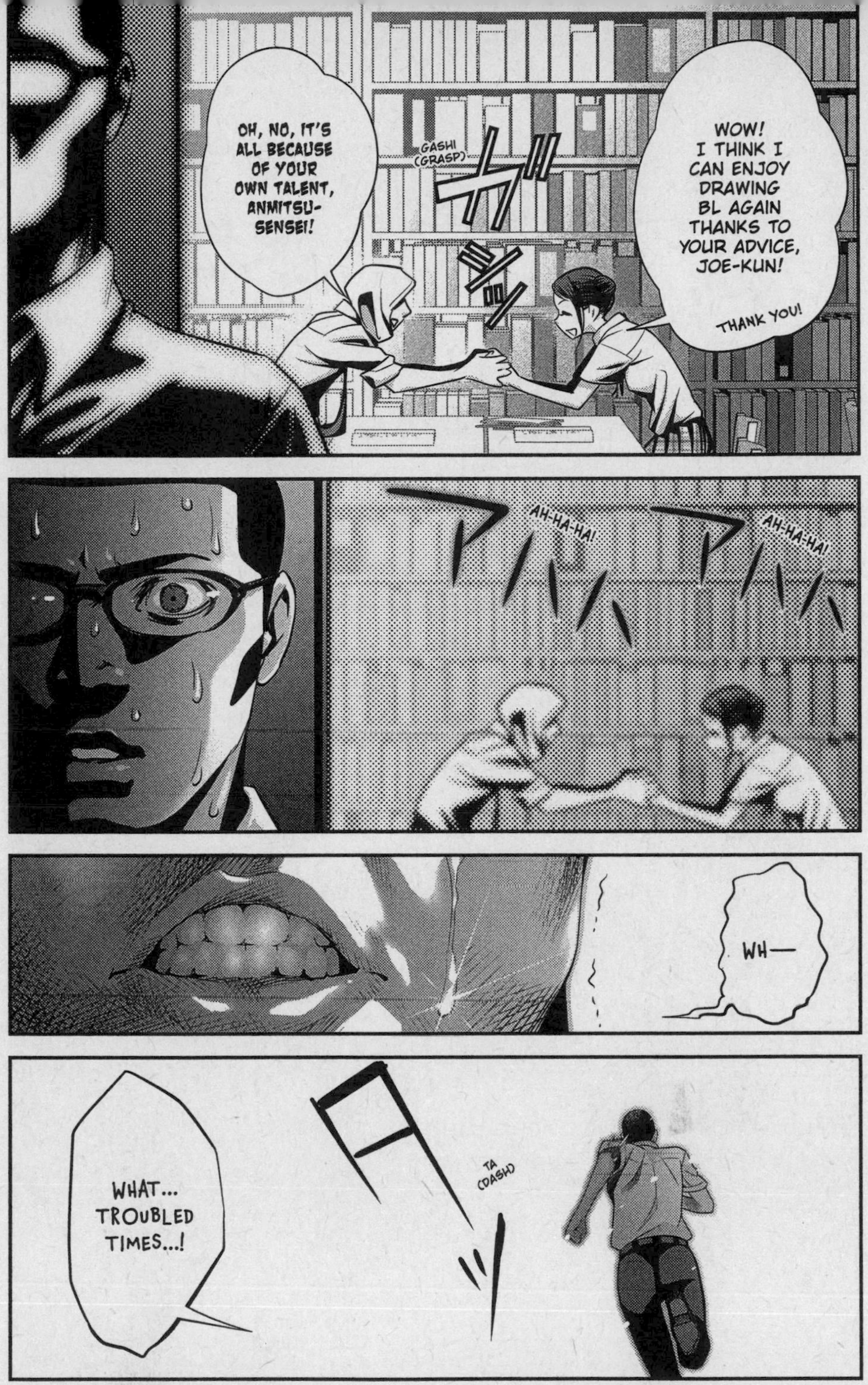
WOW! I THINK I CAN ENJOY DRAWING BL AGAIN THANKS TO YOUR ADVICE, JOE-KUN!
THANK YOU!
GASHI (GRASP)
OH, NO, IT'S ALL BECAUSE OF YOUR OWN TALENT, ANMITSU-SENSEI!
AH-HA-HA!
AH-HA-HA!
WH—
TA (DASH)
WHAT... TROUBLED TIMES...!

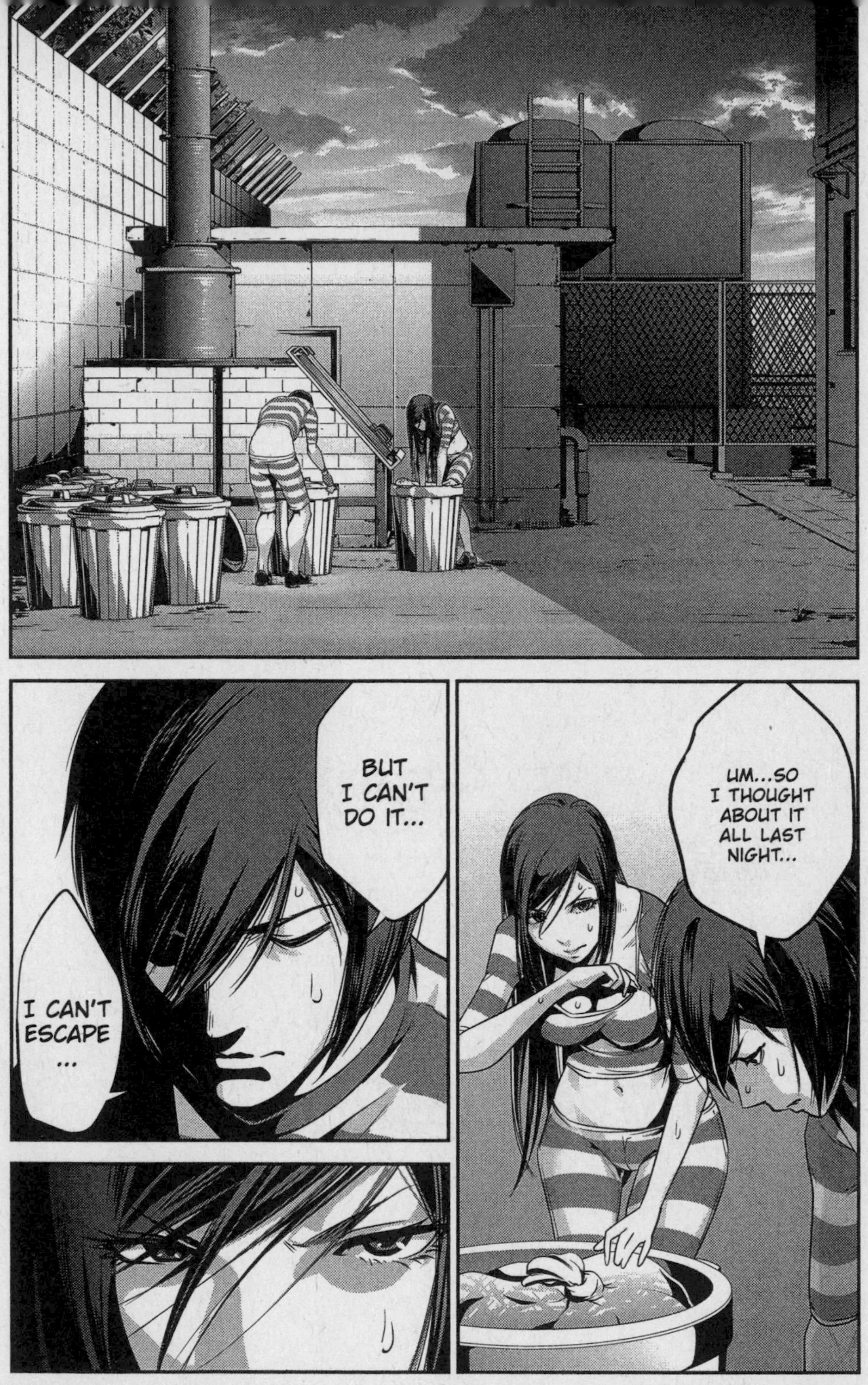
UM...SO I THOUGHT ABOUT IT ALL LAST NIGHT...
BUT I CAN'T DO IT...
I CAN'T ESCAPE ...

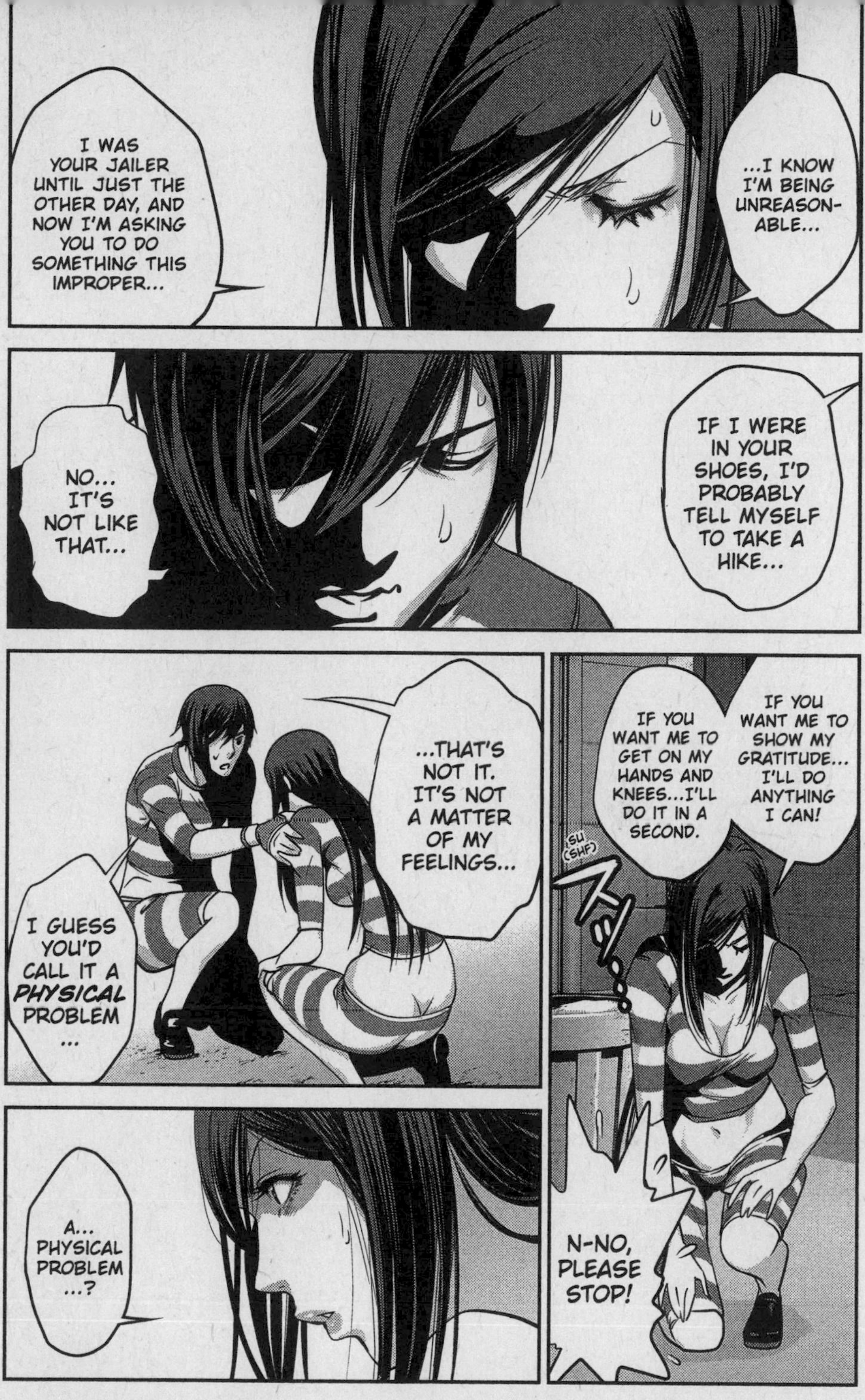
...I KNOW I'M BEING UNREASON-ABLE...
I WAS YOUR JAILER UNTIL JUST THE OTHER DAY, AND NOW I'M ASKING YOU TO DO SOMETHING THIS IMPROPER...
IF I WERE IN YOUR SHOES, I'D PROBABLY TELL MYSELF TO TAKE A HIKE...
NO... IT'S NOT LIKE THAT...
IF YOU WANT ME TO SHOW MY GRATITUDE... I'LL DO ANYTHING I CAN!
IF YOU WANT ME TO GET ON MY HANDS AND KNEES...I'LL DO IT IN A SECOND.
SU (SHF)
N-NO, PLEASE STOP!
...THAT'S NOT IT. IT'S NOT A MATTER OF MY FEELINGS...
I GUESS YOU'D CALL IT A ***PHYSICAL*** PROBLEM ...
A... PHYSICAL PROBLEM ...?

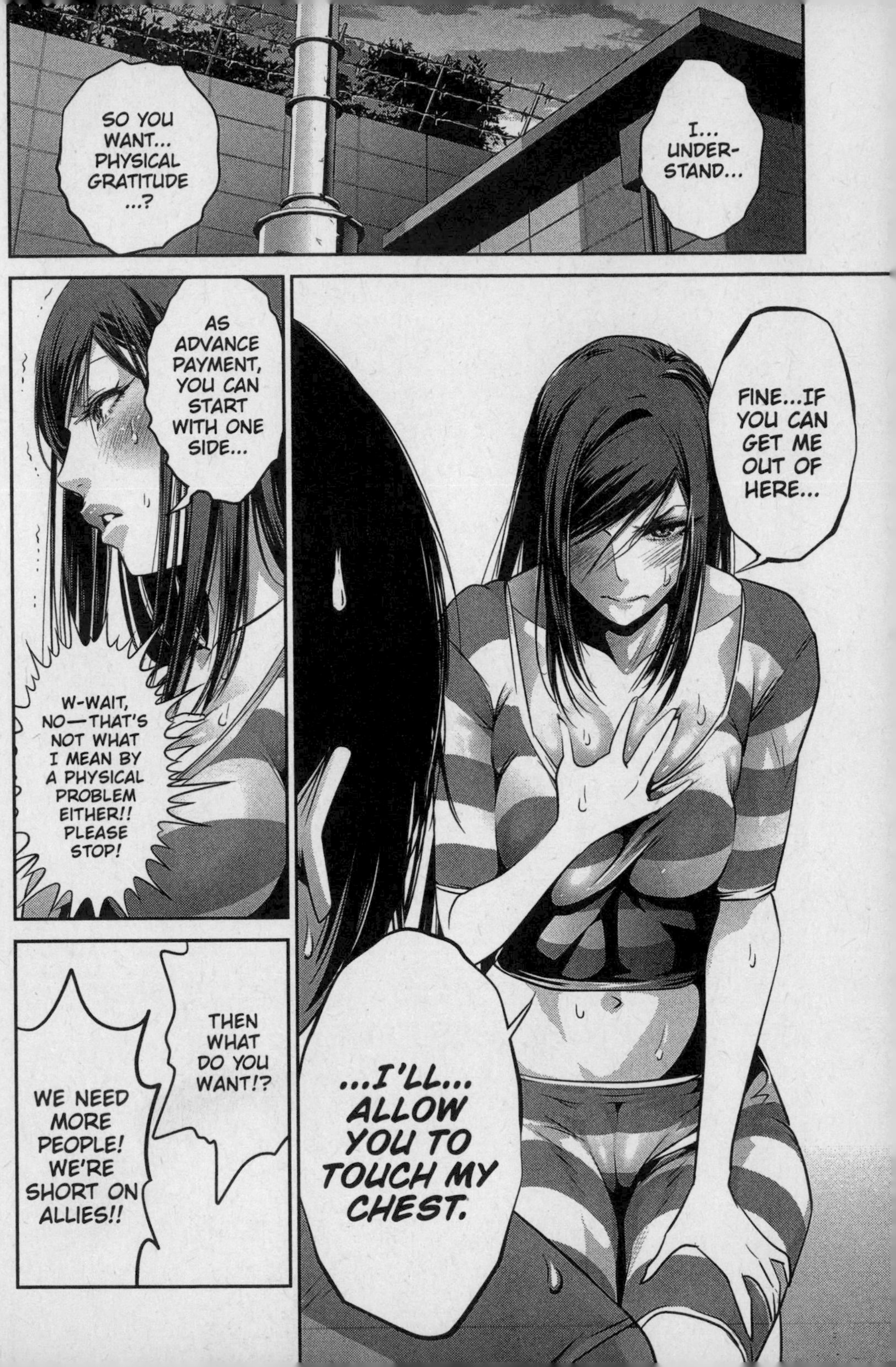
I... UNDER-STAND...
SO YOU WANT... PHYSICAL GRATITUDE ...?
FINE...IF YOU CAN GET ME OUT OF HERE...
...I'LL... ALLOW YOU TO TOUCH MY CHEST.
AS ADVANCE PAYMENT, YOU CAN START WITH ONE SIDE...
W-WAIT, NO—THAT'S NOT WHAT I MEAN BY A PHYSICAL PROBLEM EITHER!! PLEASE STOP!
THEN WHAT DO YOU WANT!?
WE NEED MORE PEOPLE! WE'RE SHORT ON ALLIES!!

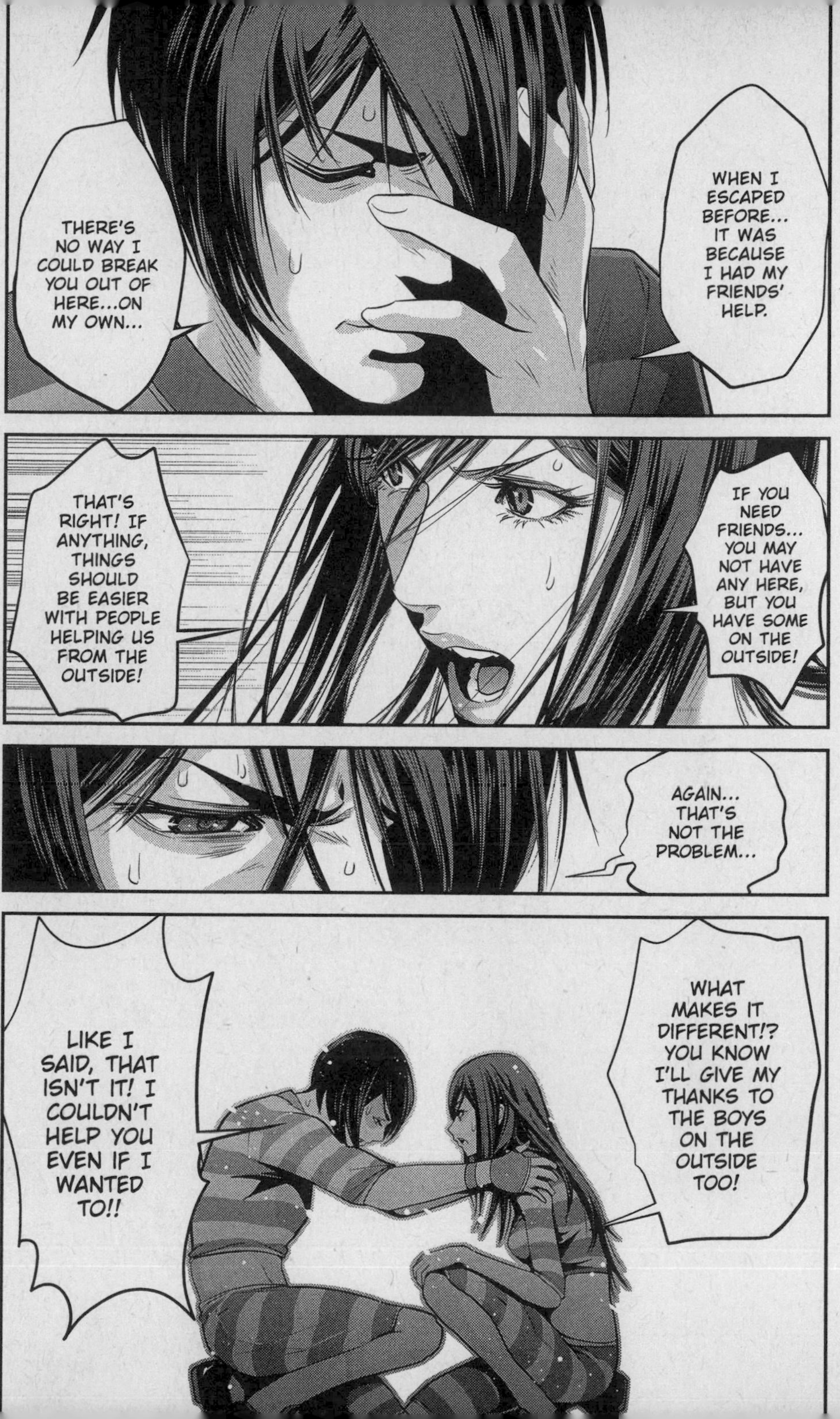
WHEN I ESCAPED BEFORE... IT WAS BECAUSE I HAD MY FRIENDS' HELP.
THERE'S NO WAY I COULD BREAK YOU OUT OF HERE...ON MY OWN...
IF YOU NEED FRIENDS... YOU MAY NOT HAVE ANY HERE, BUT YOU HAVE SOME ON THE OUTSIDE!
THAT'S RIGHT! IF ANYTHING, THINGS SHOULD BE EASIER WITH PEOPLE HELPING US FROM THE OUTSIDE!
AGAIN... THAT'S NOT THE PROBLEM...
WHAT MAKES IT DIFFERENT!? YOU KNOW I'LL GIVE MY THANKS TO THE BOYS ON THE OUTSIDE TOO!
LIKE I SAID, THAT ISN'T IT! I COULDN'T HELP YOU EVEN IF I WANTED TO!!

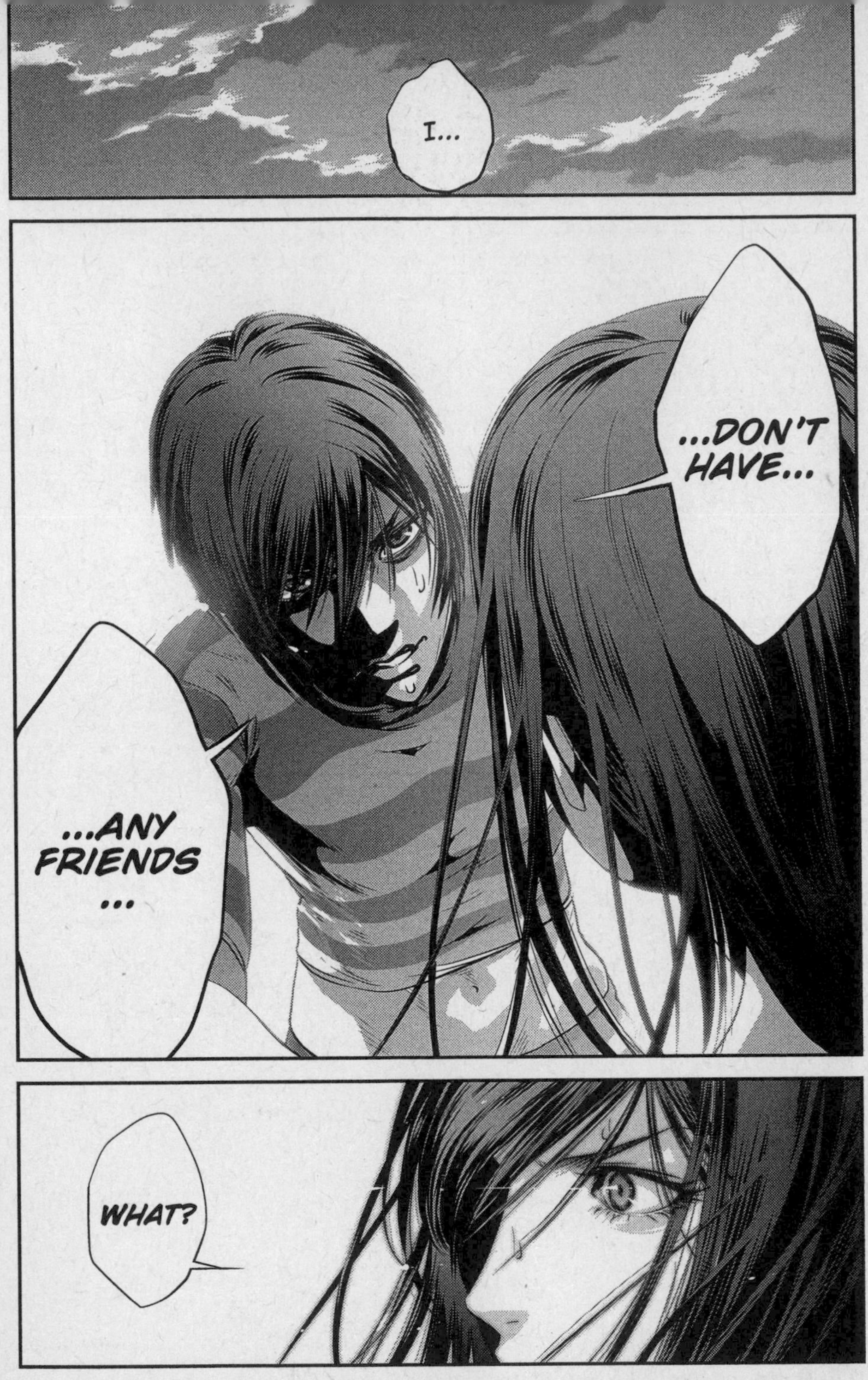
I...
...DON'T HAVE...
...ANY FRIENDS ...
WHAT?

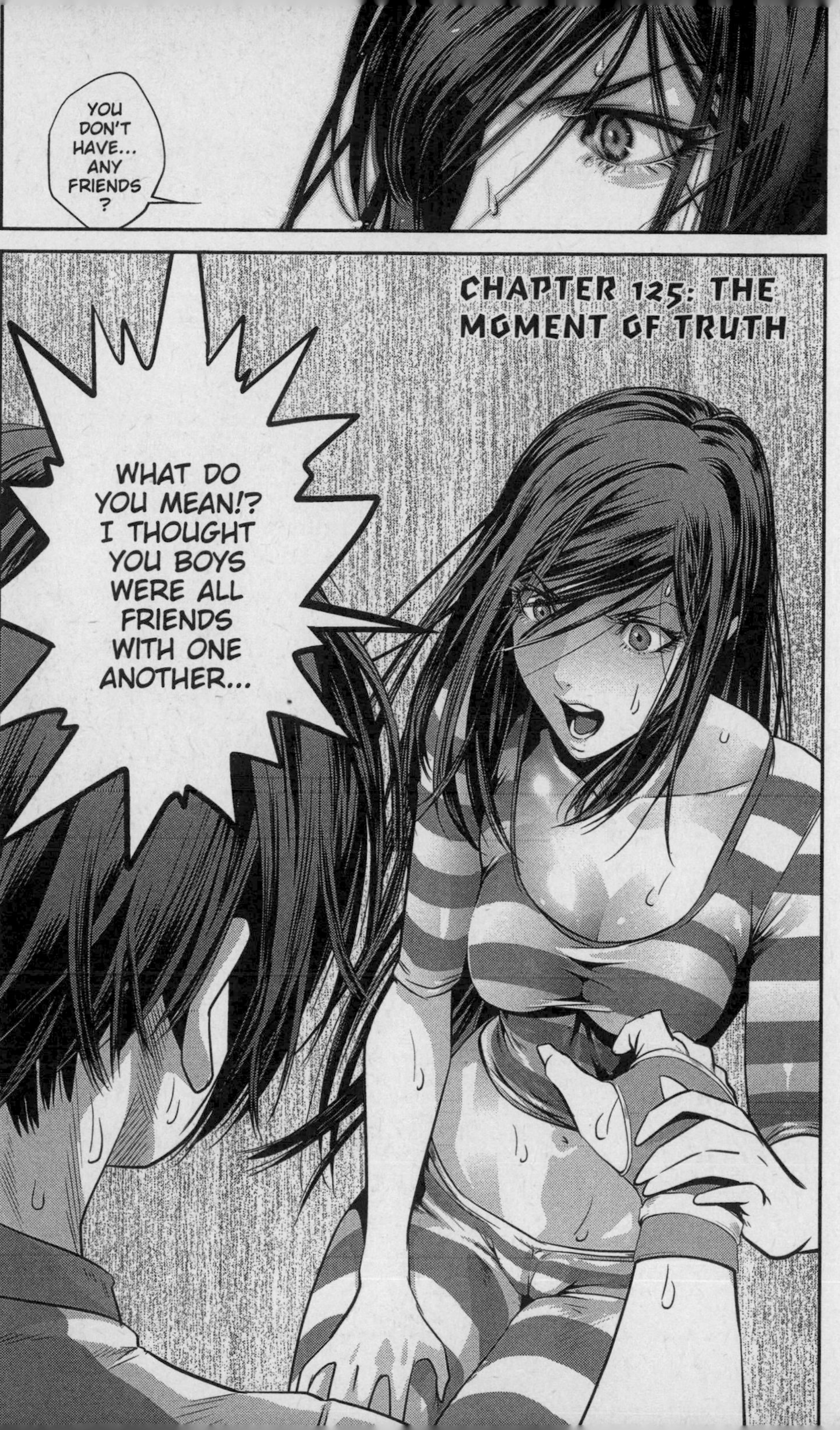
YOU DON'T HAVE... ANY FRIENDS?
CHAPTER 125: THE MOMENT OF TRUTH
WHAT DO YOU MEAN!? I THOUGHT YOU BOYS WERE ALL FRIENDS WITH ONE ANOTHER...

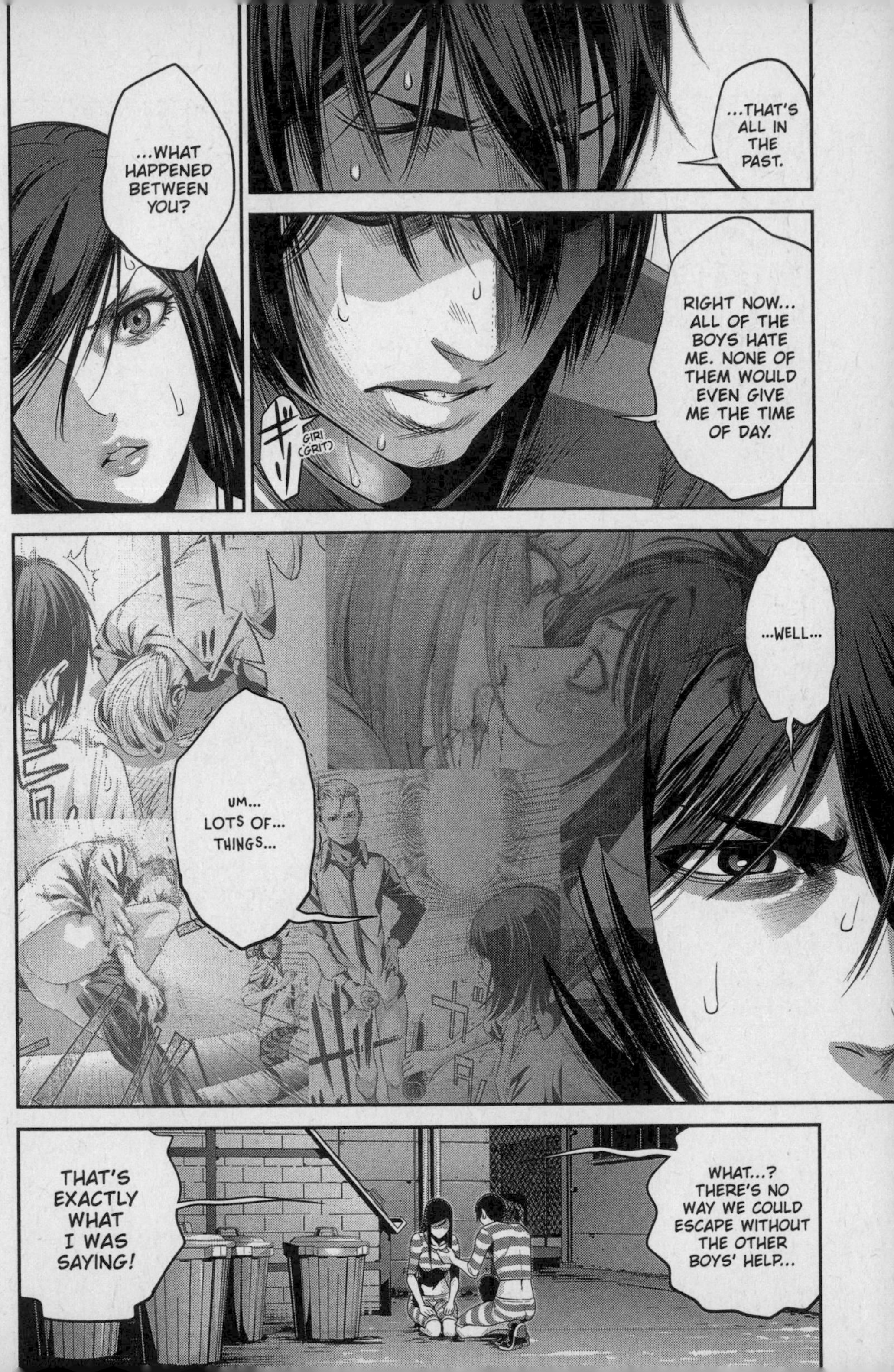
...WHAT HAPPENED BETWEEN YOU?
...THAT'S ALL IN THE PAST.
RIGHT NOW... ALL OF THE BOYS HATE ME. NONE OF THEM WOULD EVEN GIVE ME THE TIME OF DAY.
GIRI (GRIT)
...WELL...
UM... LOTS OF... THINGS...
WHAT...? THERE'S NO WAY WE COULD ESCAPE WITHOUT THE OTHER BOYS' HELP...
THAT'S EXACTLY WHAT I WAS SAYING!

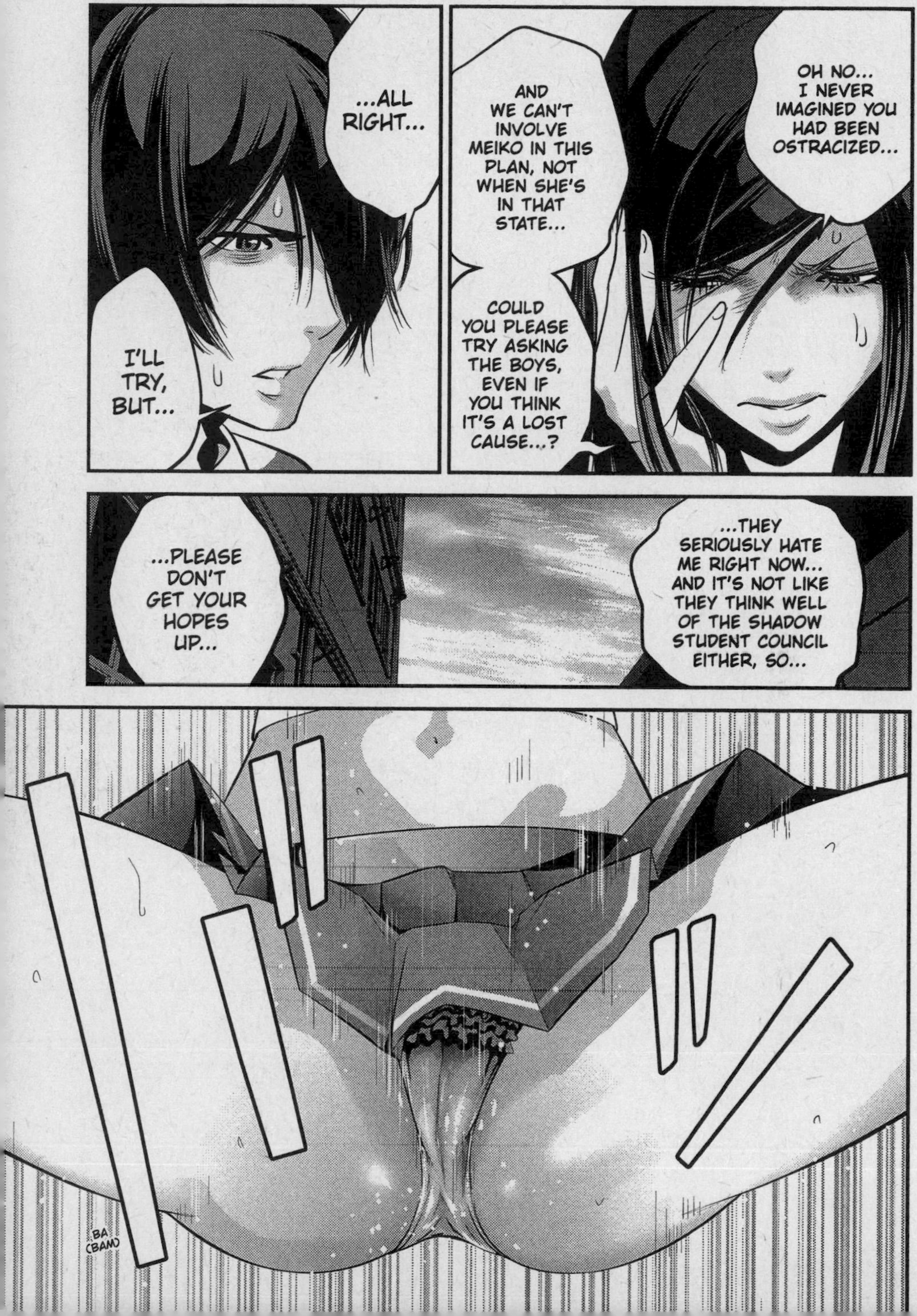
OH NO... I NEVER IMAGINED YOU HAD BEEN OSTRACIZED...
AND WE CAN'T INVOLVE MEIKO IN THIS PLAN, NOT WHEN SHE'S IN THAT STATE...
COULD YOU PLEASE TRY ASKING THE BOYS, EVEN IF YOU THINK IT'S A LOST CAUSE...?
...ALL RIGHT...
I'LL TRY, BUT...
...THEY SERIOUSLY HATE ME RIGHT NOW... AND IT'S NOT LIKE THEY THINK WELL OF THE SHADOW STUDENT COUNCIL EITHER, SO...
...PLEASE DON'T GET YOUR HOPES UP...
BA (BAM)

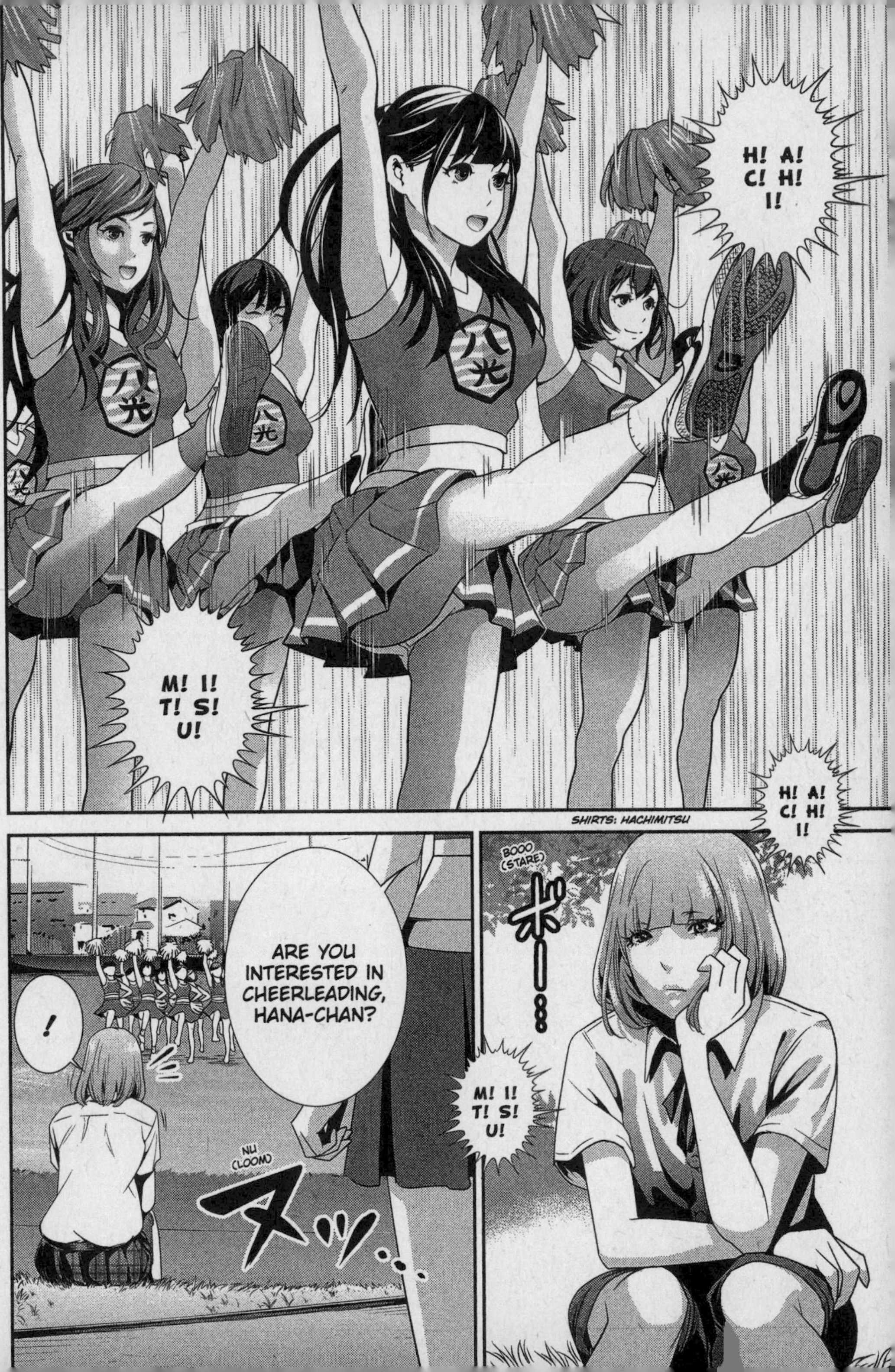
H! A! C! H! I!
M! I! T! S! U!
SHIRTS: HACHIMITSU
H! A! C! H! I!
BOOO (STARE)
M! I! T! S! U!
ARE YOU INTERESTED IN CHEERLEADING, HANA-CHAN?
NU (LOOM)
!

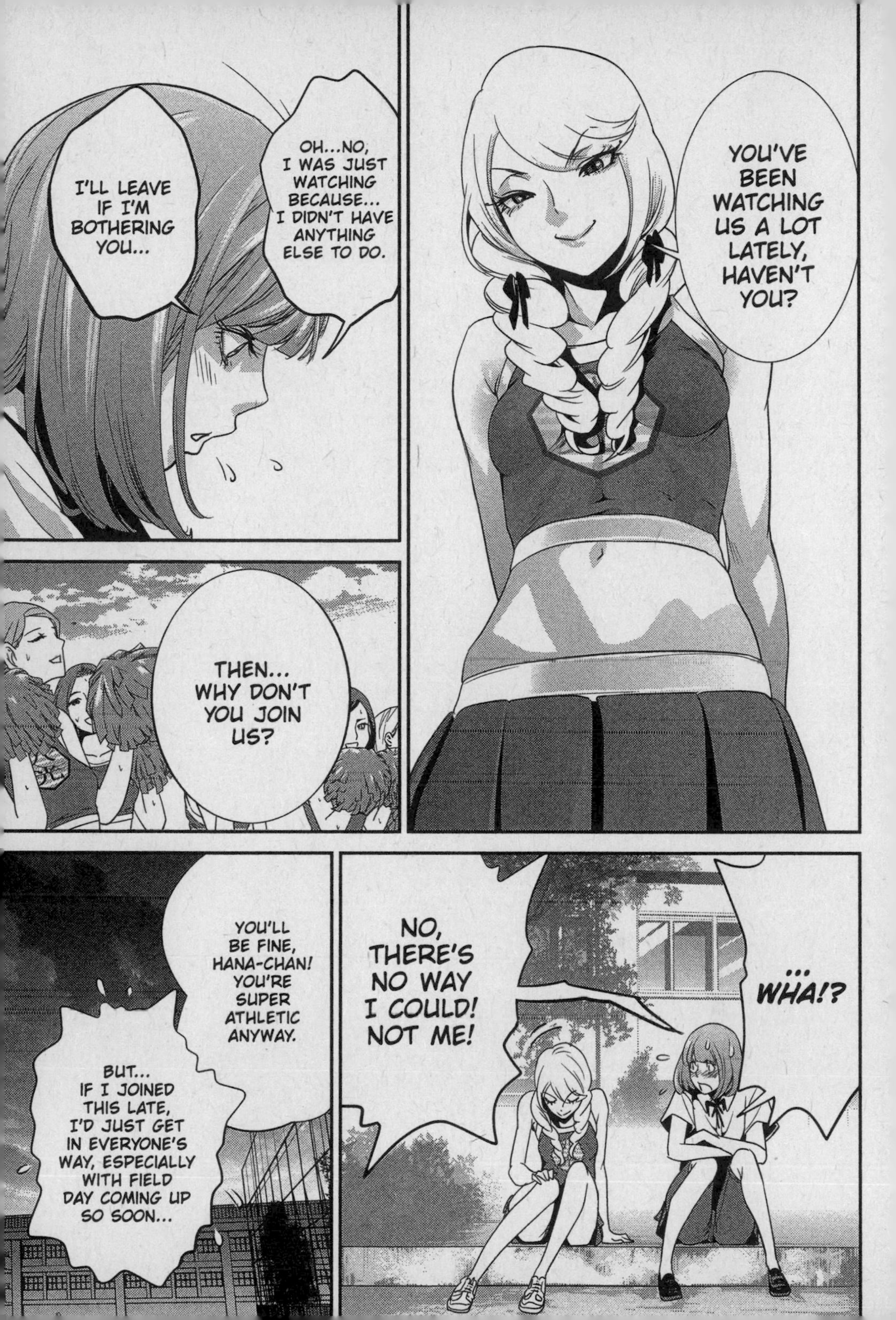
YOU'VE BEEN WATCHING US A LOT LATELY, HAVEN'T YOU?
OH...NO, I WAS JUST WATCHING BECAUSE... I DIDN'T HAVE ANYTHING ELSE TO DO.
I'LL LEAVE IF I'M BOTHERING YOU...
THEN... WHY DON'T YOU JOIN US?
...WHA!?
NO, THERE'S NO WAY I COULD! NOT ME!
YOU'LL BE FINE, HANA-CHAN! YOU'RE SUPER ATHLETIC ANYWAY.
BUT... IF I JOINED THIS LATE, I'D JUST GET IN EVERYONE'S WAY, ESPECIALLY WITH FIELD DAY COMING UP SO SOON...

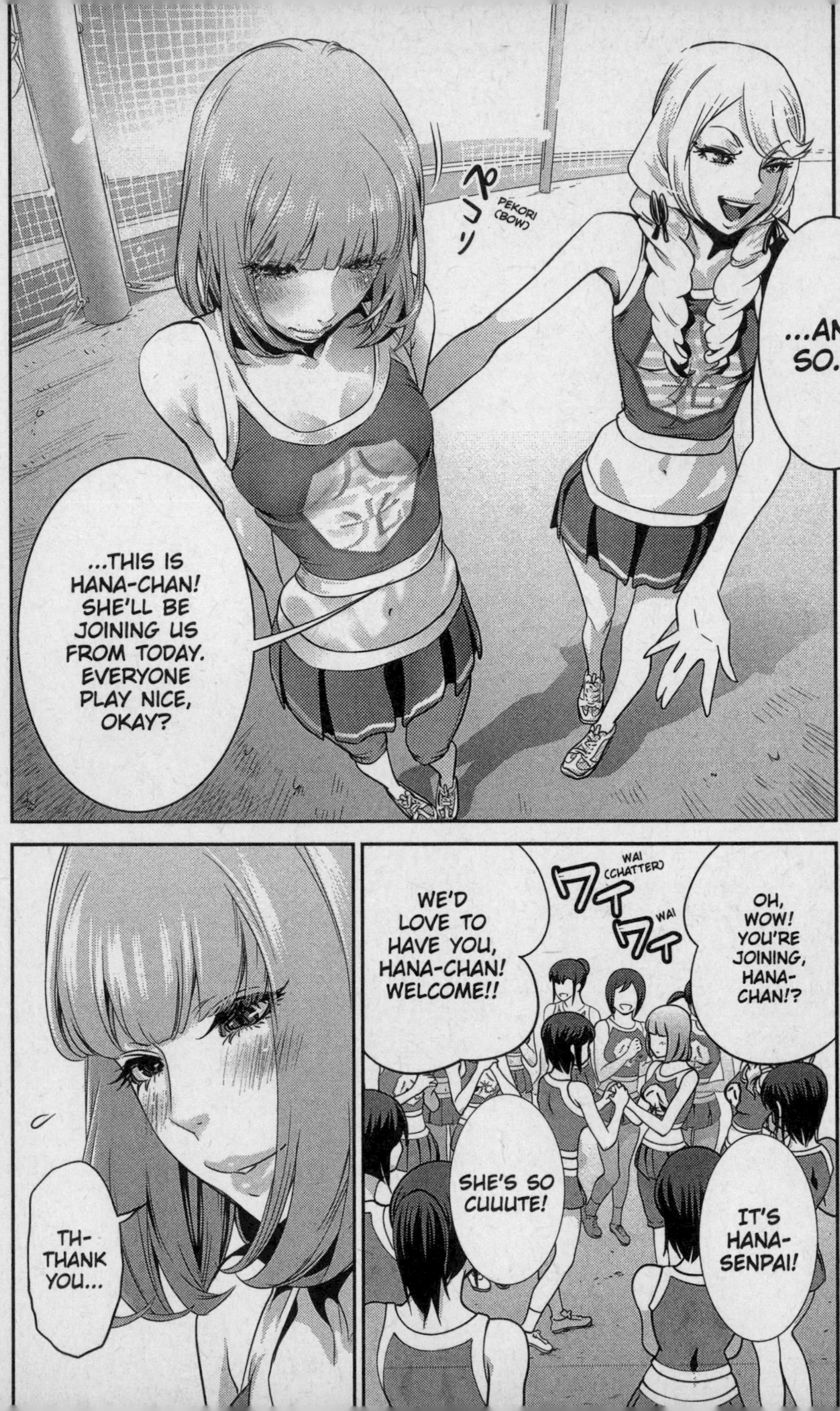
...AND SO...
ペコリ
PEKORI (BOW)
...THIS IS HANA-CHAN! SHE'LL BE JOINING US FROM TODAY. EVERYONE PLAY NICE, OKAY?
OH, WOW! YOU'RE JOINING, HANA-CHAN!?
ワイワイ
WAI (CHATTER) WAI
WE'D LOVE TO HAVE YOU, HANA-CHAN! WELCOME!!
IT'S HANA-SENPAI!
SHE'S SO CUUUTE!
TH-THANK YOU...

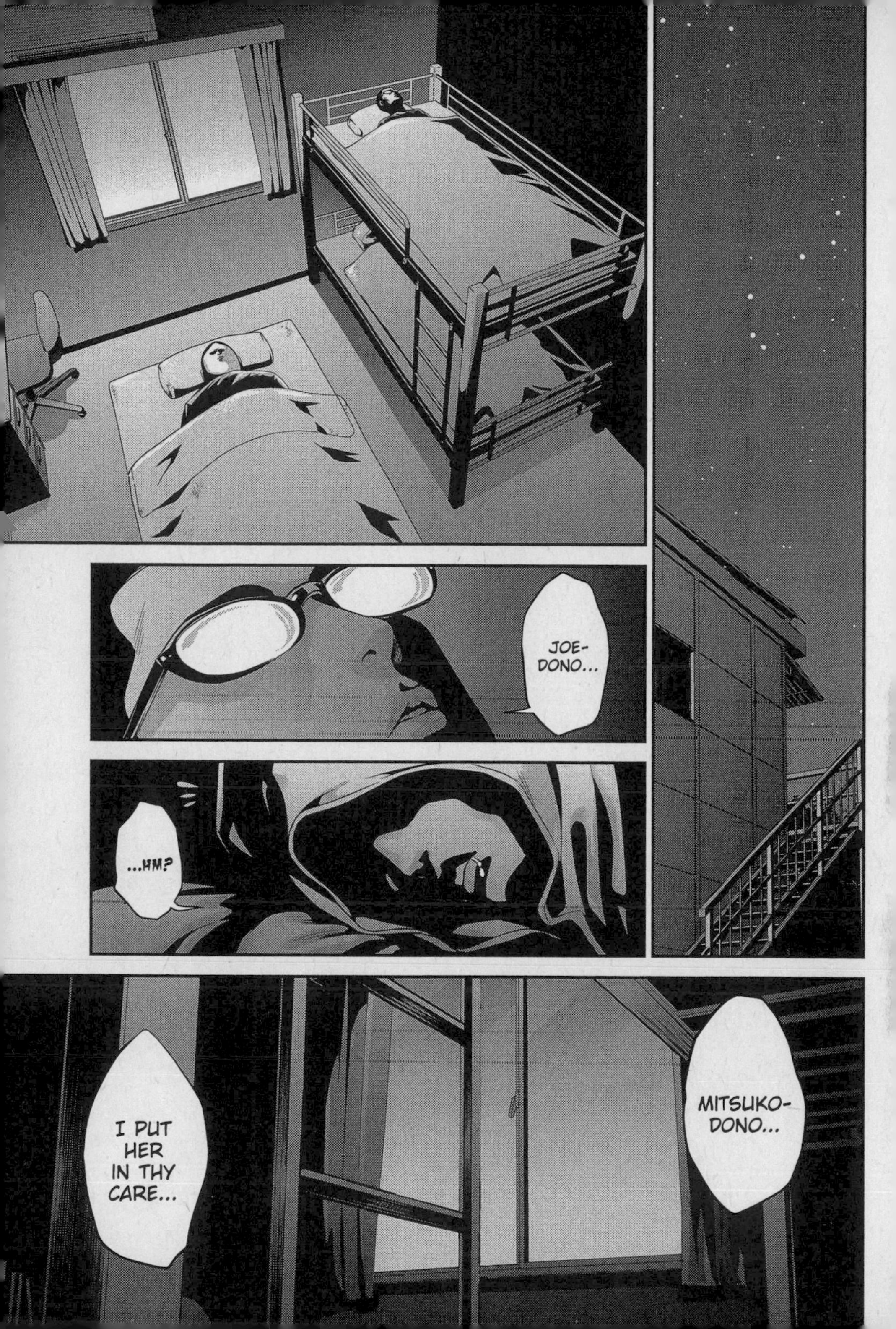
JOE-DONO...
...HM?
MITSUKO-DONO...
I PUT HER IN THY CARE...

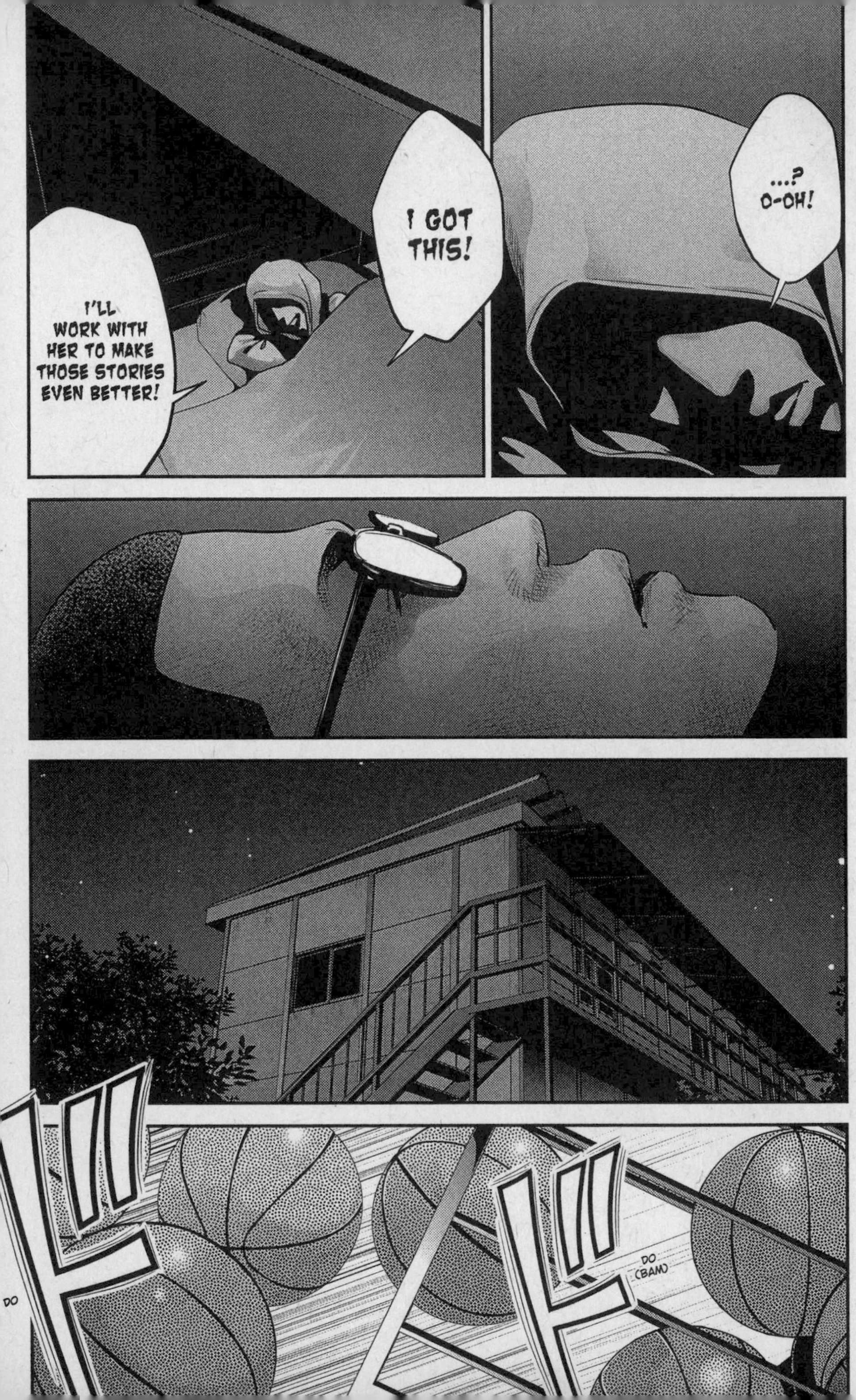
...?
O-OH!
I GOT THIS!
I'LL WORK WITH HER TO MAKE THOSE STORIES EVEN BETTER!
DO
DO (BAM)

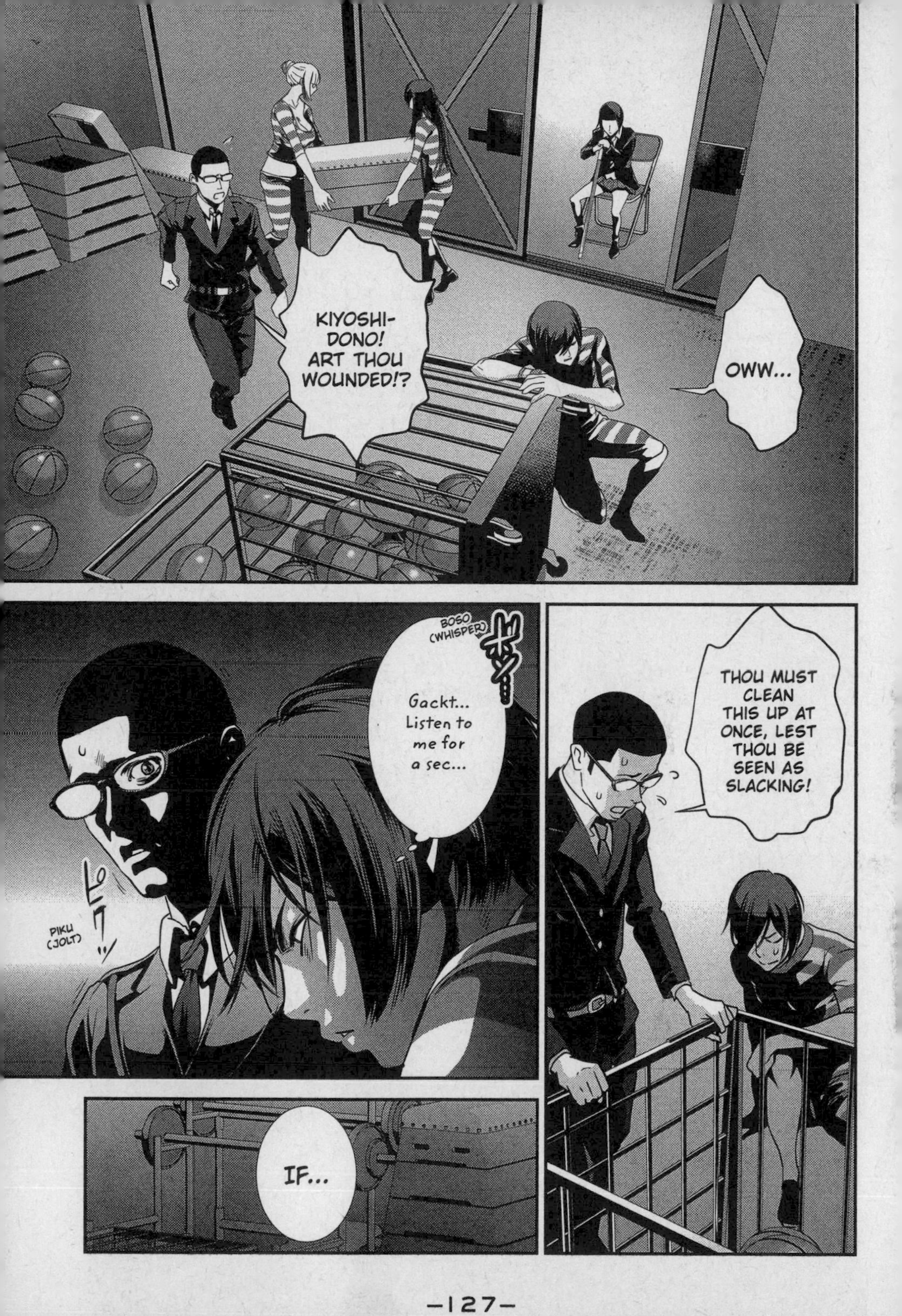
OWW...
KIYOSHI-DONO! ART THOU WOUNDED!?
THOU MUST CLEAN THIS UP AT ONCE, LEST THOU BE SEEN AS SLACKING!
BOSO (WHISPER)
Gackt... Listen to me for a sec...
PIKU (JOLT)
IF...

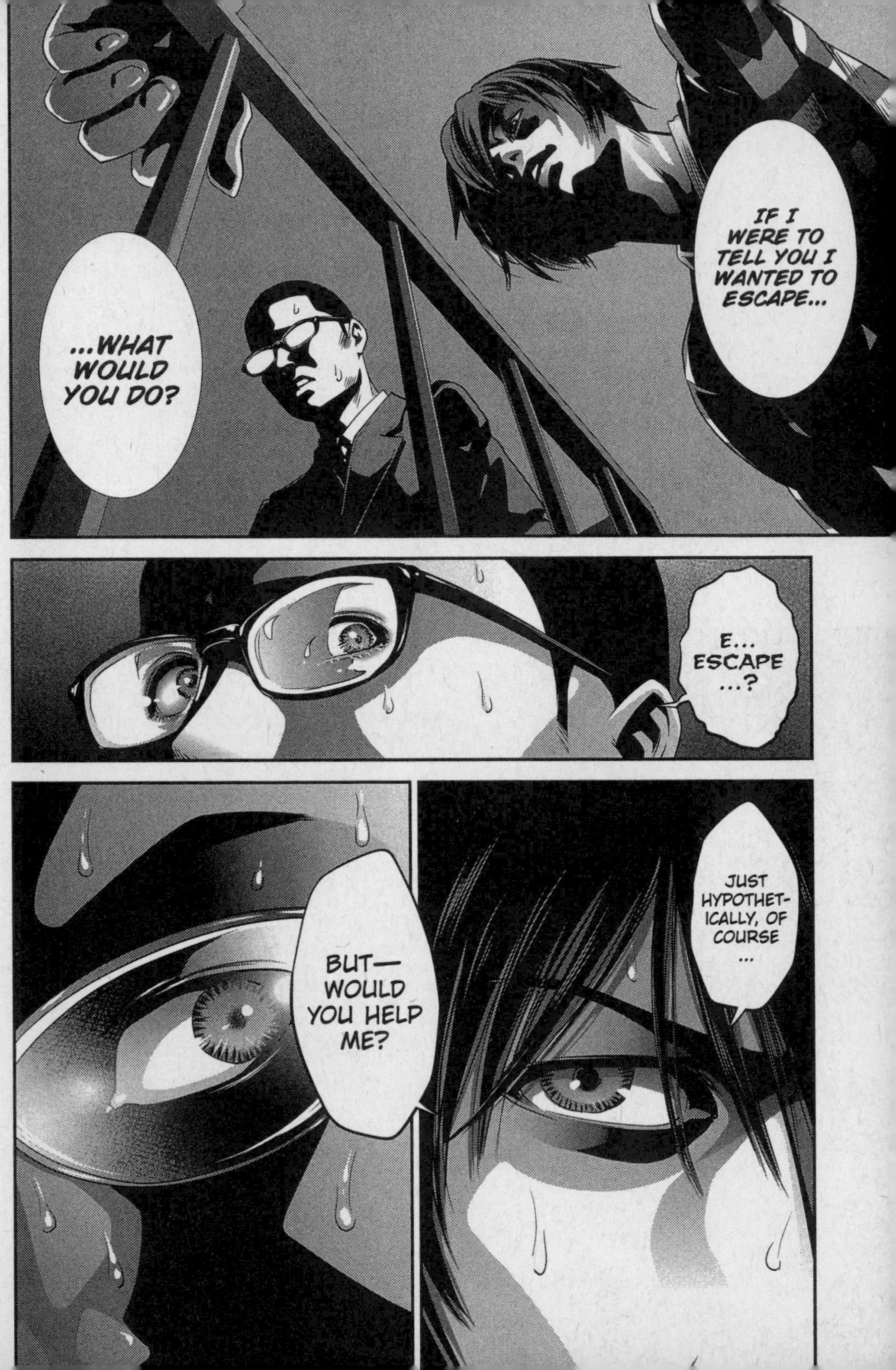
IF I WERE TO TELL YOU I WANTED TO ESCAPE...
...WHAT WOULD YOU DO?
E... ESCAPE ...?
JUST HYPOTHETICALLY, OF COURSE ...
BUT— WOULD YOU HELP ME?

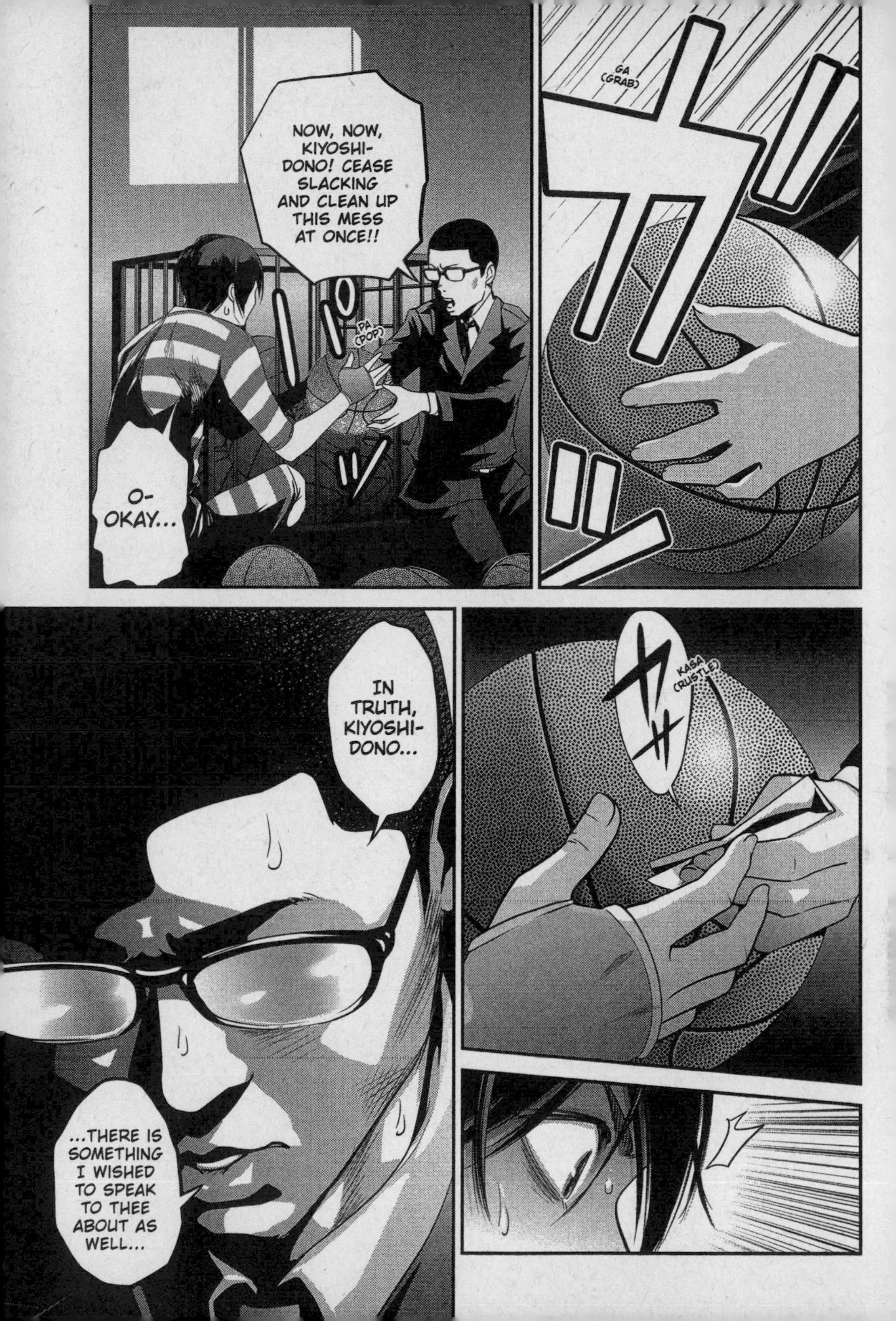
GA (GRAB)
NOW, NOW, KIYOSHI-DONO! CEASE SLACKING AND CLEAN UP THIS MESS AT ONCE!!
PA (POP)
O-OKAY...
KASA (RUSTLE)
IN TRUTH, KIYOSHI-DONO...
...THERE IS SOMETHING I WISHED TO SPEAK TO THEE ABOUT AS WELL...

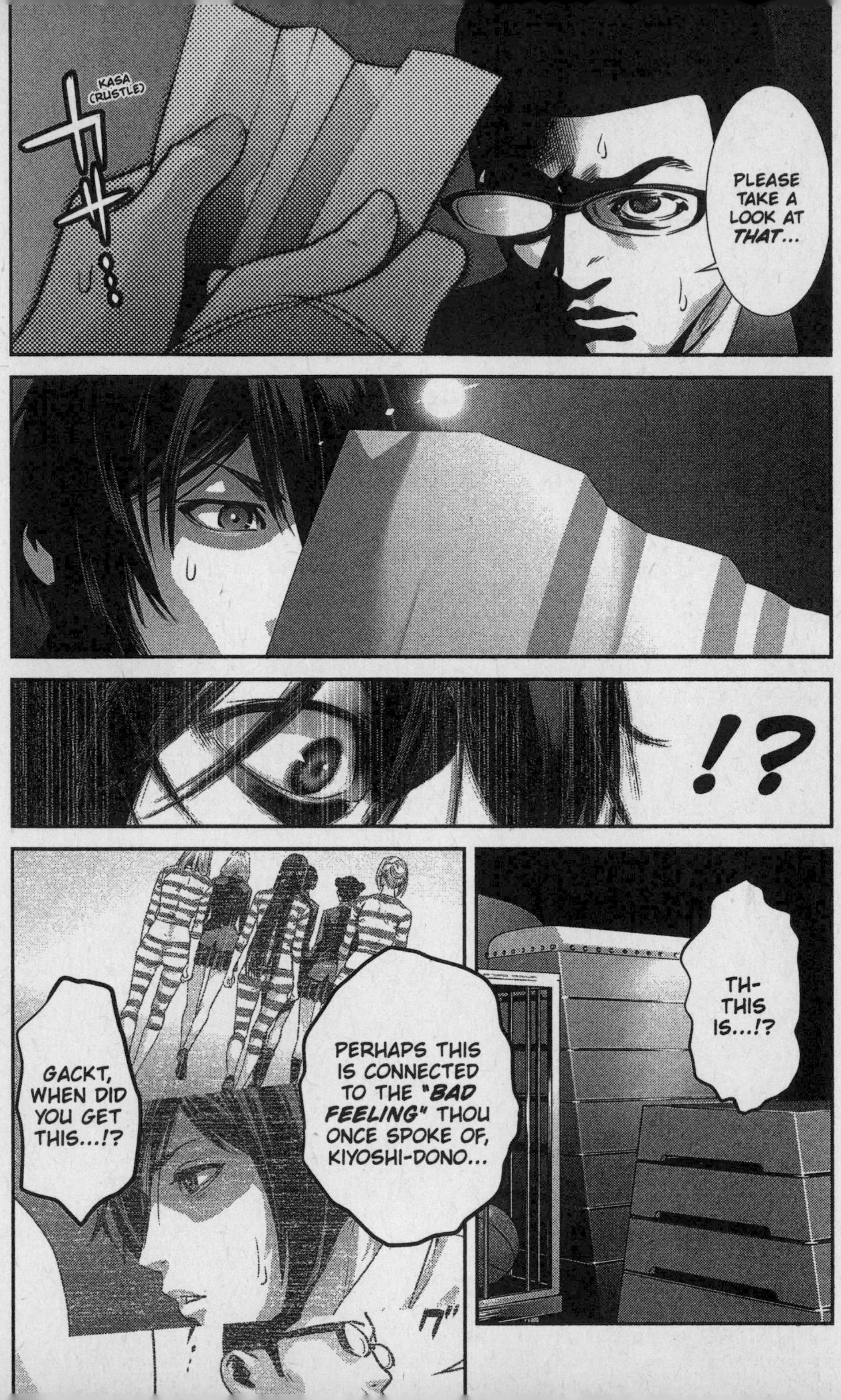
KASA (RUSTLE)
PLEASE TAKE A LOOK AT THAT...
!?
TH-THIS IS...!?
PERHAPS THIS IS CONNECTED TO THE "BAD FEELING" THOU ONCE SPOKE OF, KIYOSHI-DONO...
GACKT, WHEN DID YOU GET THIS...!?

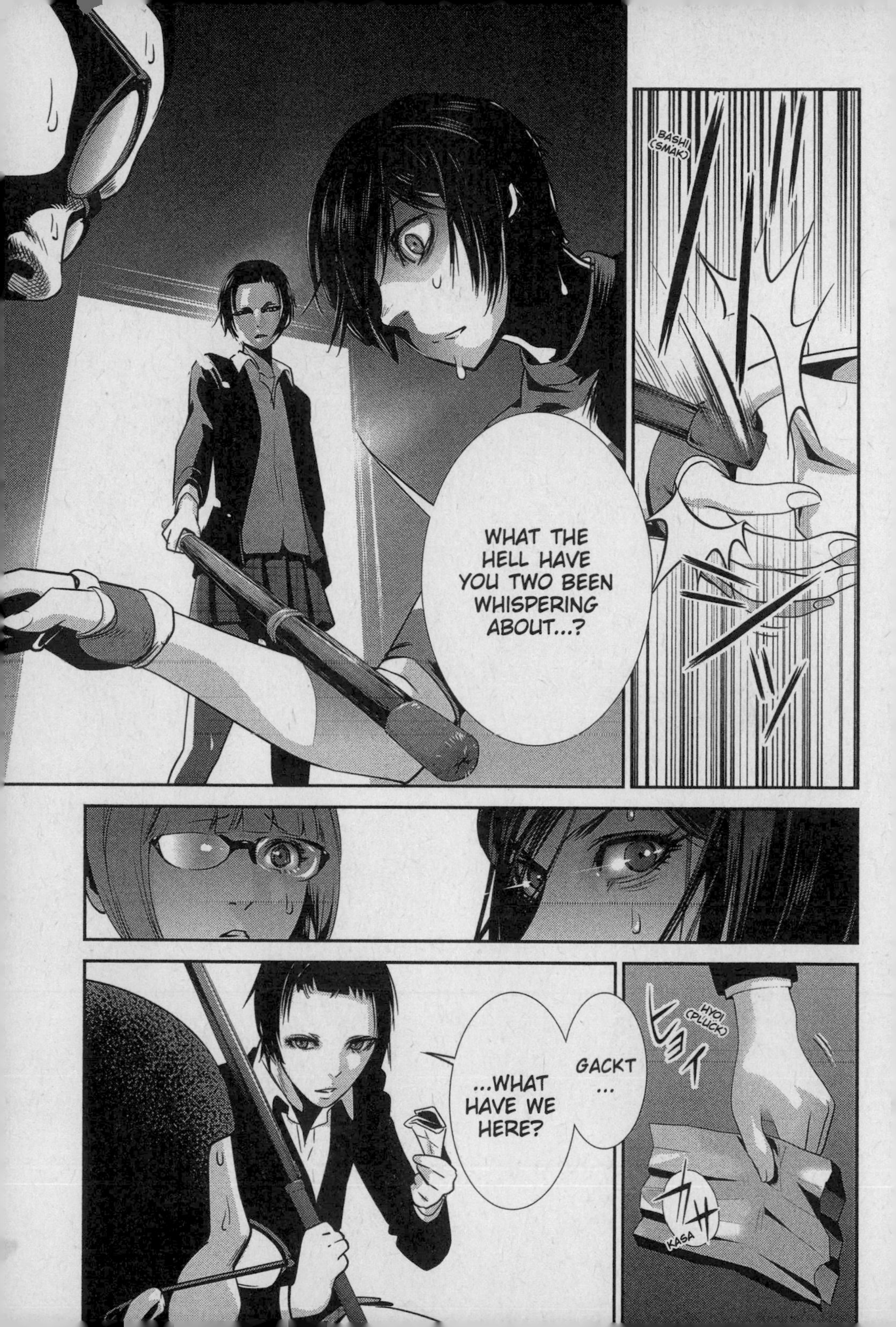
BASHI (SMAK)
WHAT THE HELL HAVE YOU TWO BEEN WHISPERING ABOUT...?
ヒョイ
HYOI (PLUCK)
カサ
KASA
GACKT ...
...WHAT HAVE WE HERE?

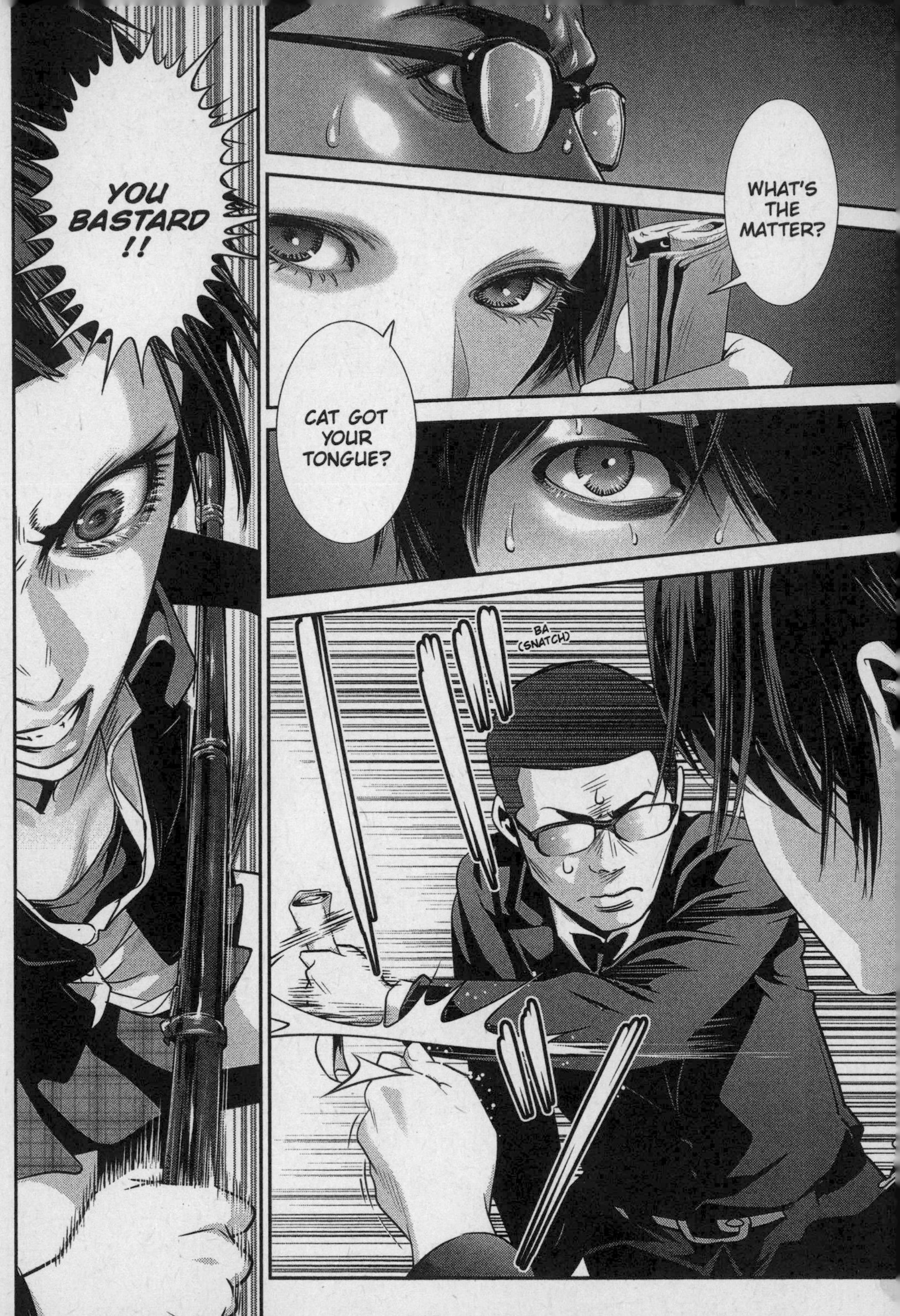
WHAT'S THE MATTER?
CAT GOT YOUR TONGUE?
BA (SNATCH)
YOU BASTARD !!

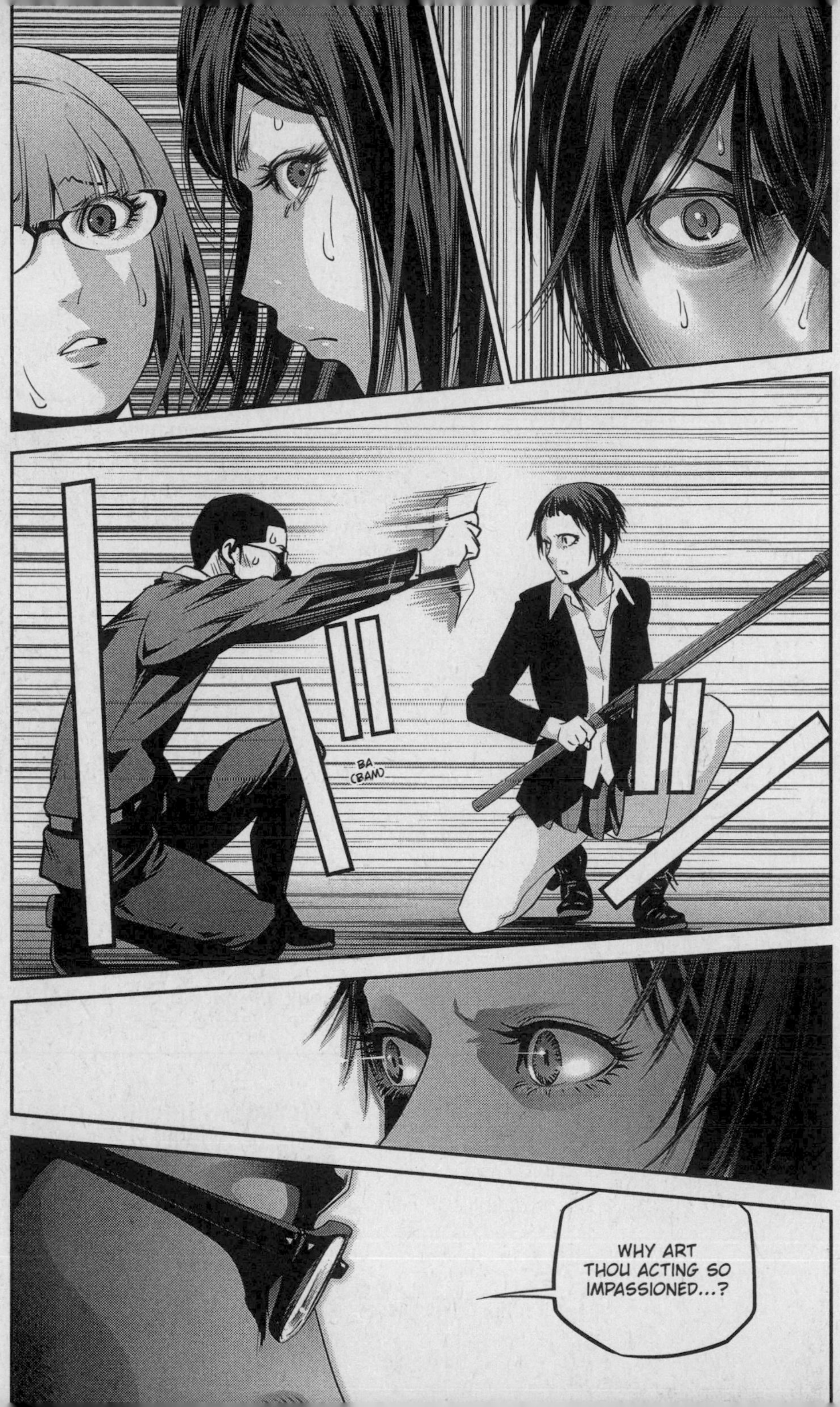
BA (BAM)
WHY ART THOU ACTING SO IMPASSIONED...?

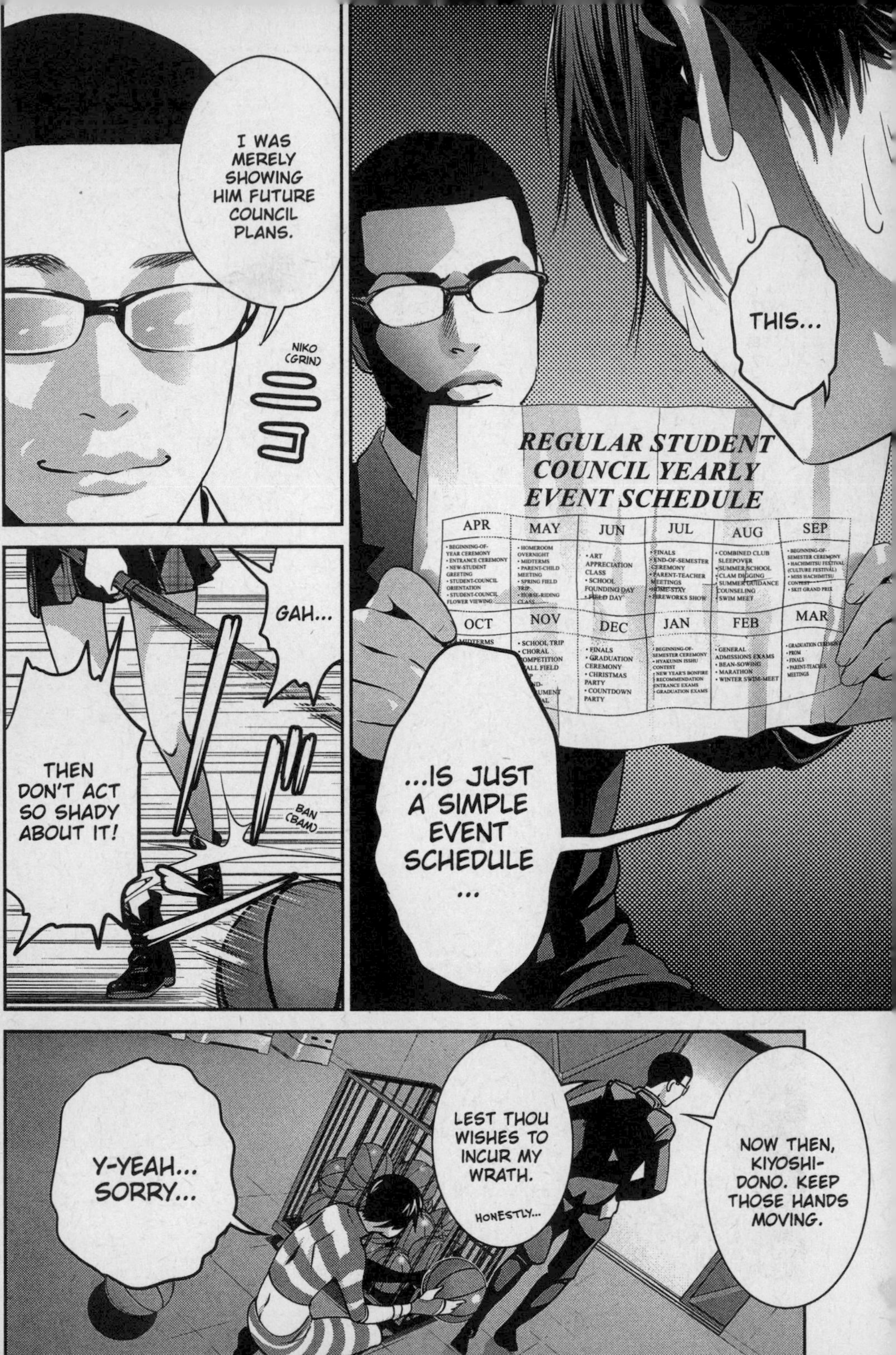
THIS...
REGULAR STUDENT COUNCIL YEARLY EVENT SCHEDULE
APR
• BEGINNING-OF-YEAR CEREMONY • ENTRANCE CEREMONY • NEW-STUDENT GREETING • STUDENT-COUNCIL ORIENTATION • STUDENT-COUNCIL FLOWER VIEWING
MAY
• HOMEROOM OVERNIGHT • MIDTERMS • PARENT-CHILD MEETING • SPRING FIELD TRIP • HORSE-RIDING CLASS
JUN
• ART APPRECIATION CLASS • SCHOOL FOUNDING DAY • FIELD DAY
JUL
• FINALS • END-OF-SEMESTER CEREMONY • PARENT-TEACHER MEETINGS • HOME-STAY • FIREWORKS SHOW
AUG
• COMBINED CLUB SLEEPOVER • SUMMER SCHOOL • CLAM DIGGING • SUMMER GUIDANCE COUNSELING • SWIM MEET
SEP
• BEGINNING-OF-SEMESTER CEREMONY • HACHIMITSU FESTIVAL (CULTURE FESTIVAL) • MISS HACHIMITSU CONTEST • SKIT GRAND PRIX
OCT
MIDTERMS
NOV
• SCHOOL TRIP • CHORAL
DEC
• FINALS • GRADUATION CEREMONY • CHRISTMAS PARTY • COUNTDOWN PARTY
JAN
• BEGINNING-OF-SEMESTER CEREMONY • HYAKUNIN ISSHU CONTEST • NEW YEAR'S BONFIRE • RECOMMENDATION ENTRANCE EXAMS • GRADUATION EXAMS
FEB
• GENERAL ADMISSIONS EXAMS • BEAN-SOWING • MARATHON • WINTER SWIM-MEET
MAR
• GRADUATION CEREMONY • PROM • FINALS • PARENT-TEACHER MEETINGS
...IS JUST A SIMPLE EVENT SCHEDULE ...
I WAS MERELY SHOWING HIM FUTURE COUNCIL PLANS.
NIKO (GRIN)
GAH...
THEN DON'T ACT SO SHADY ABOUT IT!
BAN (BAM)
NOW THEN, KIYOSHI-DONO. KEEP THOSE HANDS MOVING.
LEST THOU WISHES TO INCUR MY WRATH.
HONESTLY...
Y-YEAH... SORRY...

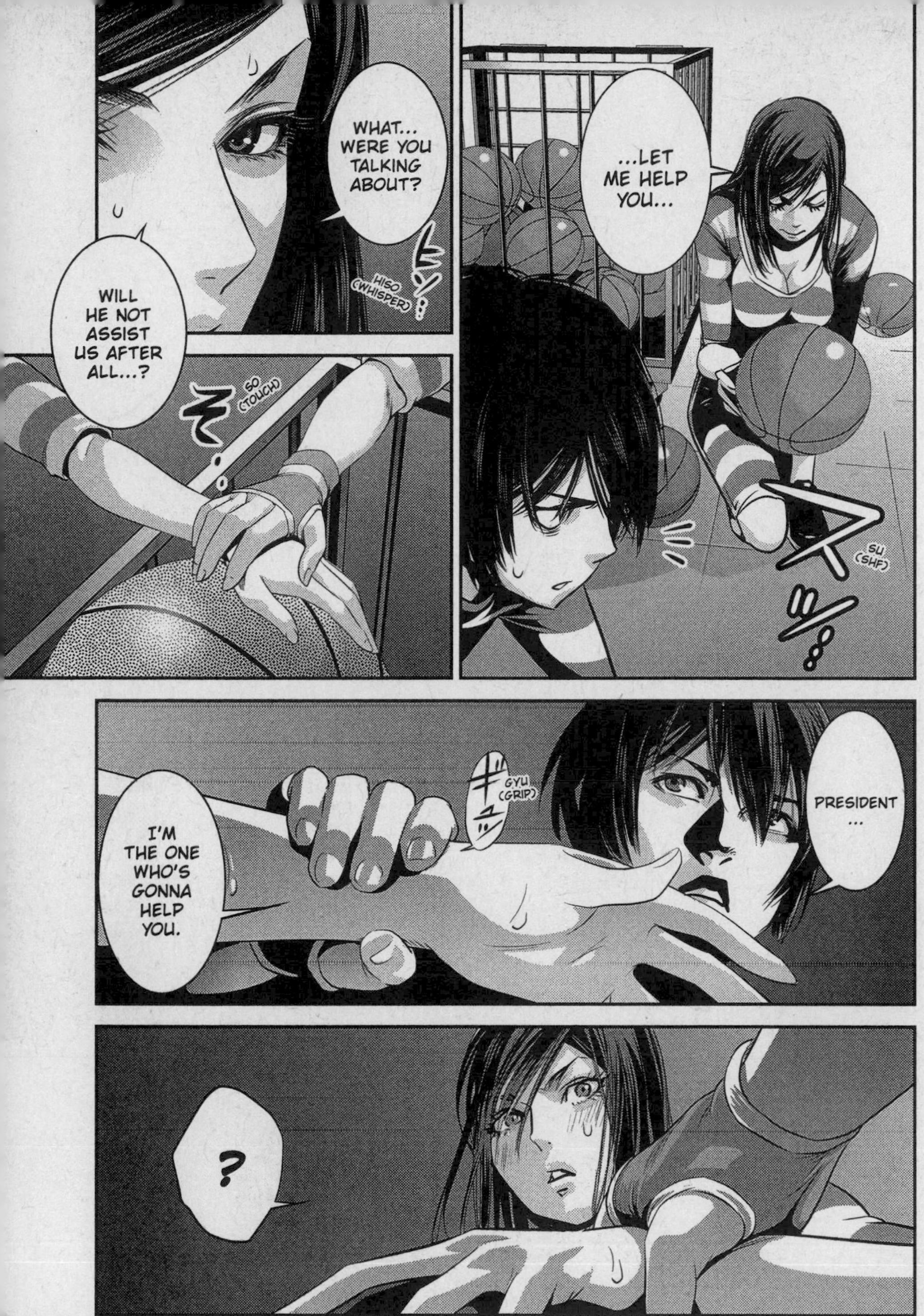
...LET ME HELP YOU...
SU (SHF)
WHAT... WERE YOU TALKING ABOUT?
HISO (WHISPER)
WILL HE NOT ASSIST US AFTER ALL...?
SO (TOUCH)
PRESIDENT ...
GYU (GRIP)
I'M THE ONE WHO'S GONNA HELP YOU.
?

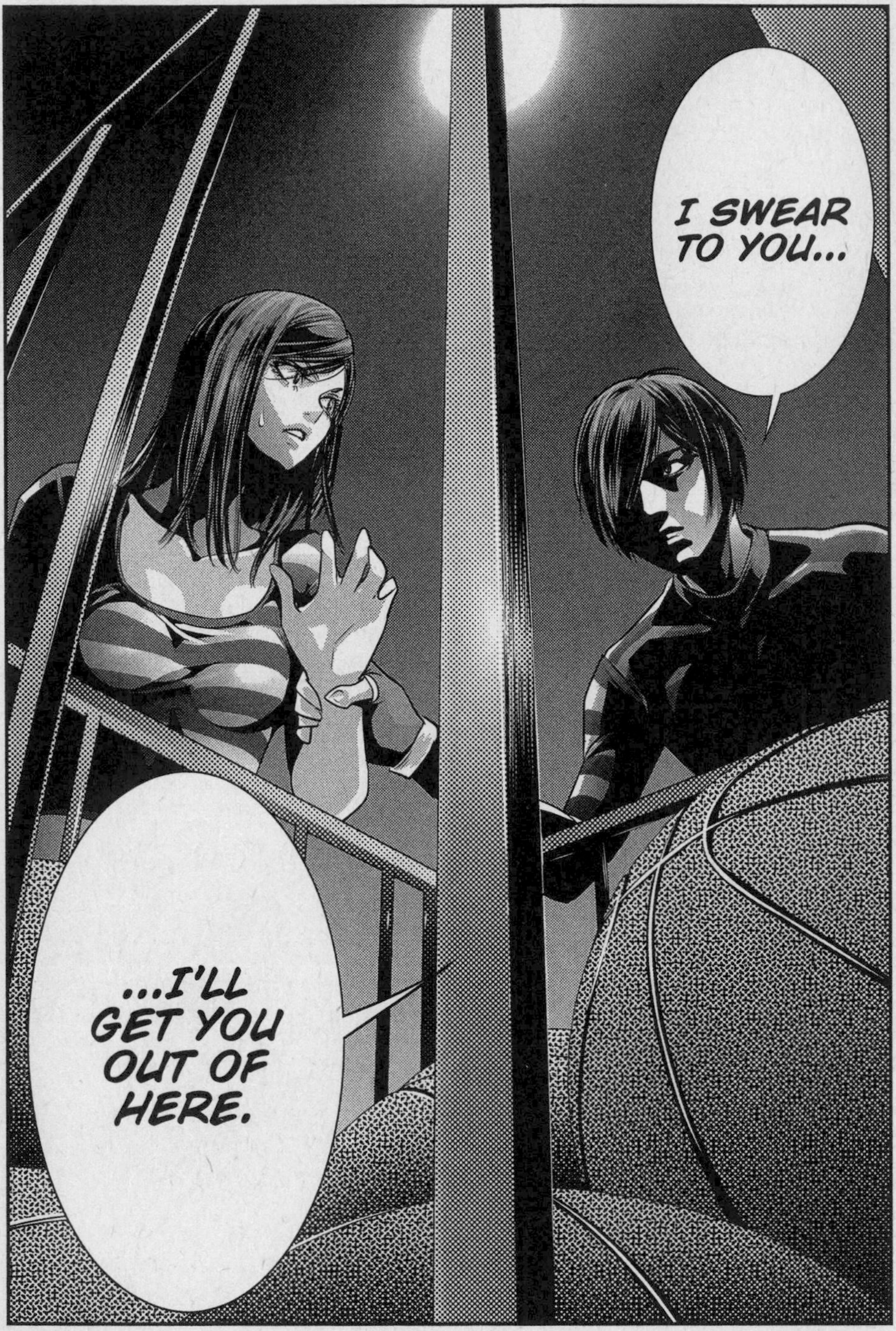
I SWEAR TO YOU...
...I'LL GET YOU OUT OF HERE.

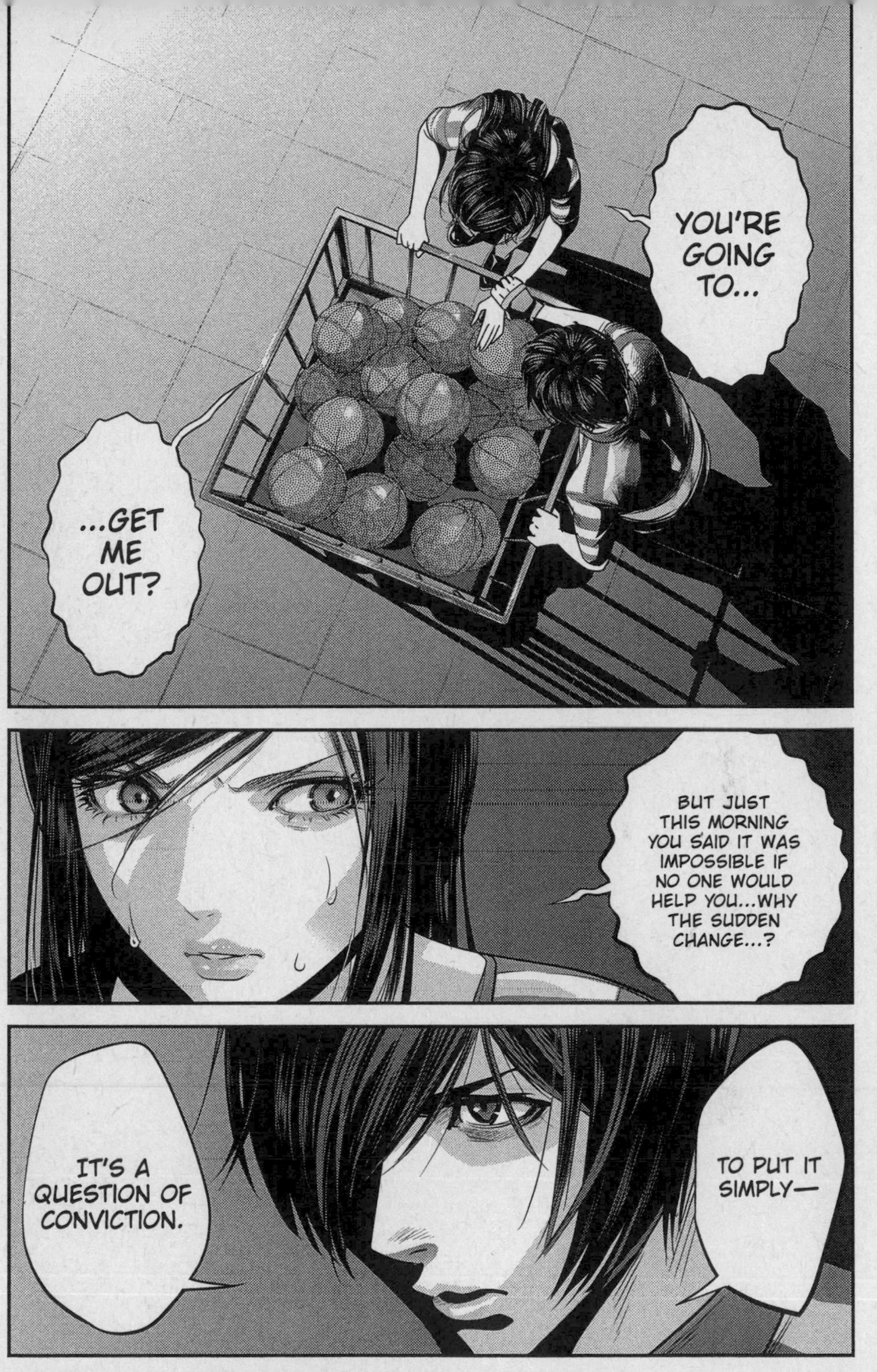
YOU'RE GOING TO...
...GET ME OUT?
BUT JUST THIS MORNING YOU SAID IT WAS IMPOSSIBLE IF NO ONE WOULD HELP YOU...WHY THE SUDDEN CHANGE...?
TO PUT IT SIMPLY—
IT'S A QUESTION OF CONVICTION.

CHAPTER 126: MEN ON A LEDGE

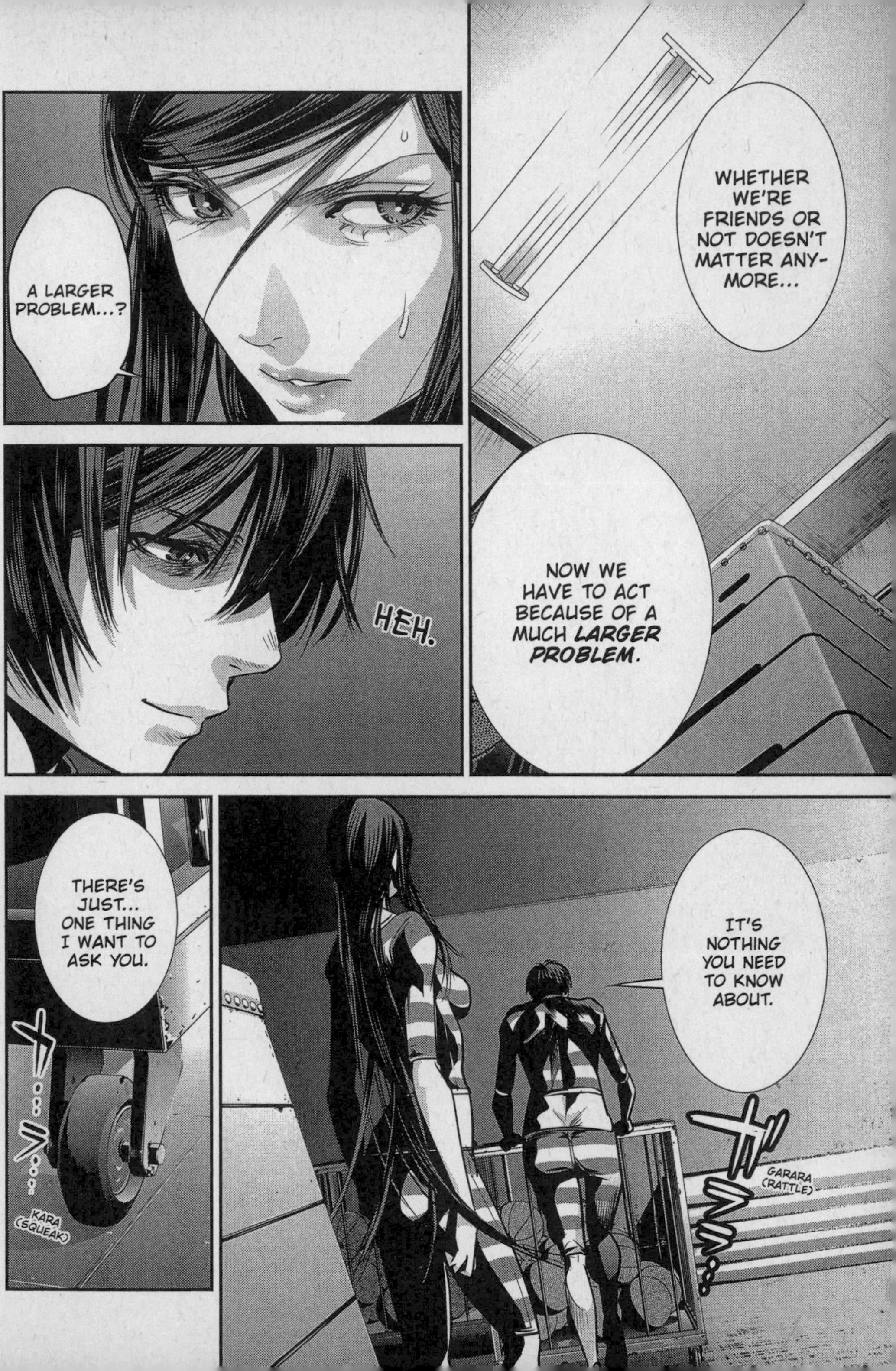

WHETHER WE'RE FRIENDS OR NOT DOESN'T MATTER ANY-MORE...
NOW WE HAVE TO ACT BECAUSE OF A MUCH *LARGER PROBLEM*.
A LARGER PROBLEM...?
HEH.
IT'S NOTHING YOU NEED TO KNOW ABOUT.
GARARA (RATTLE)
THERE'S JUST... ONE THING I WANT TO ASK YOU.
KARA (SQUEAK)

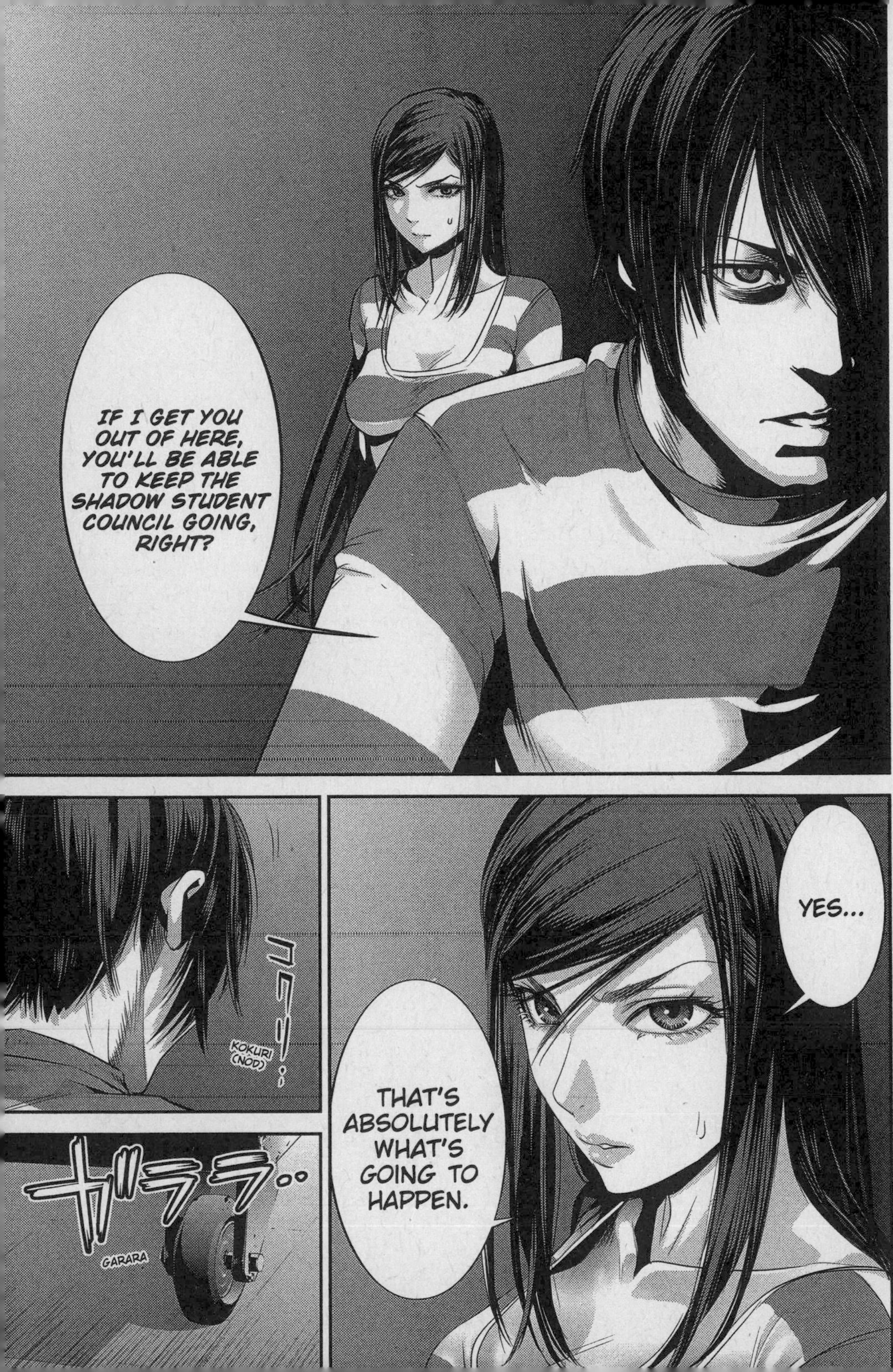
IF I GET YOU OUT OF HERE, YOU'LL BE ABLE TO KEEP THE SHADOW STUDENT COUNCIL GOING, RIGHT?
YES...
THAT'S ABSOLUTELY WHAT'S GOING TO HAPPEN.
KOKURI (NOD)
GARARA

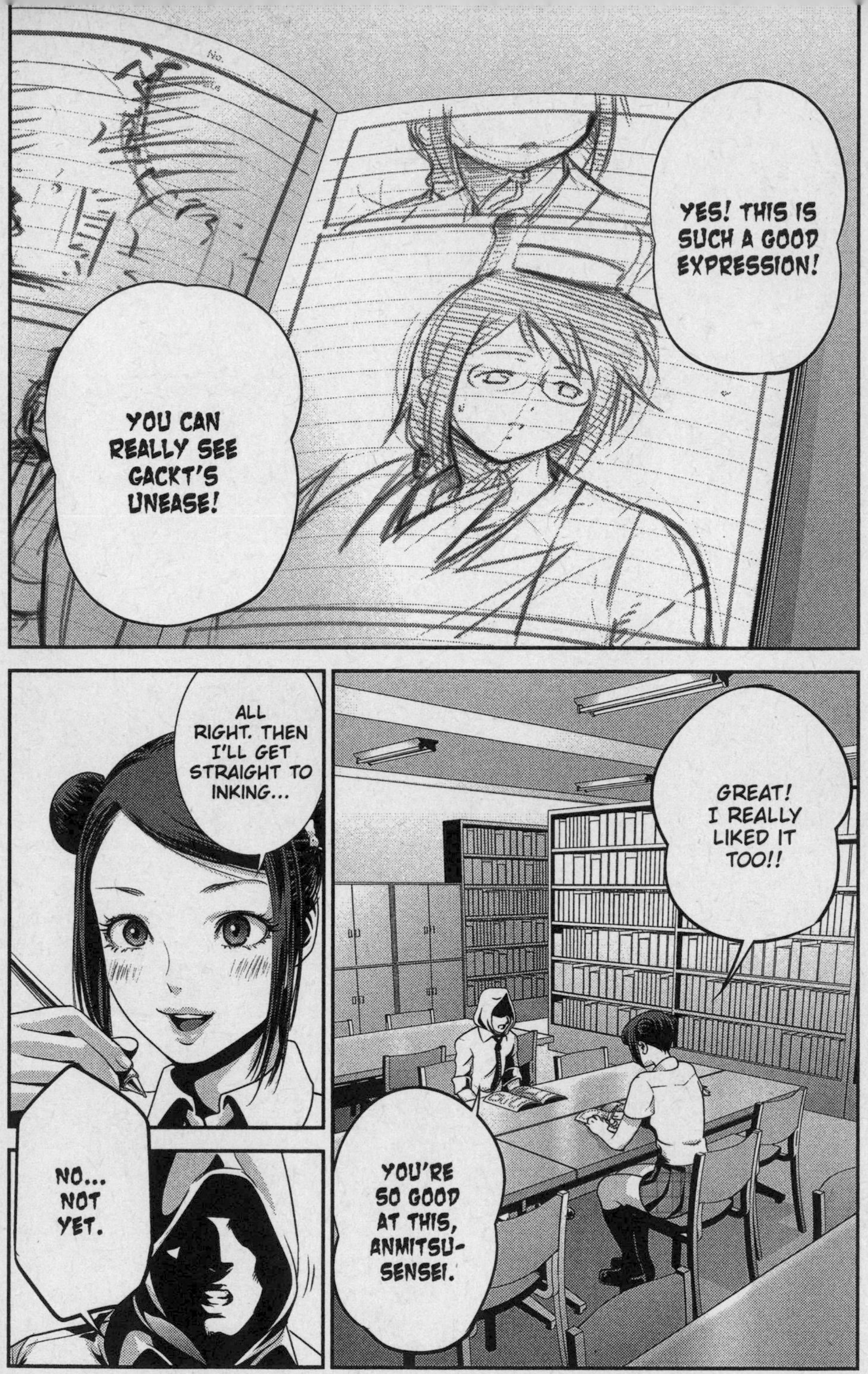
YES! THIS IS SUCH A GOOD EXPRESSION!
YOU CAN REALLY SEE GACKT'S UNEASE!
GREAT! I REALLY LIKED IT TOO!!
YOU'RE SO GOOD AT THIS, ANMITSU-SENSEI.
ALL RIGHT. THEN I'LL GET STRAIGHT TO INKING...
NO... NOT YET.

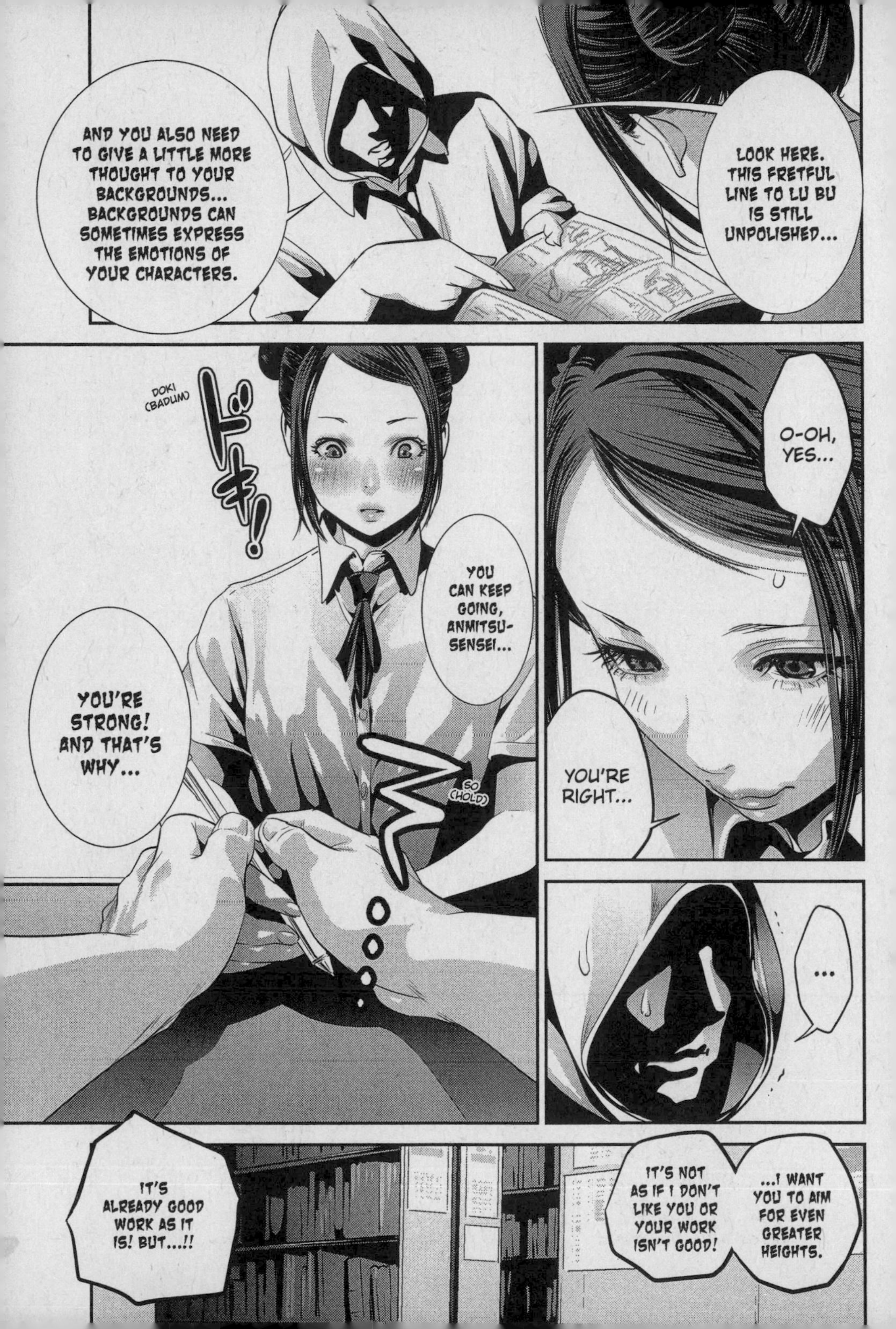
LOOK HERE. THIS FRETFUL LINE TO LU BU IS STILL UNPOLISHED...
AND YOU ALSO NEED TO GIVE A LITTLE MORE THOUGHT TO YOUR BACKGROUNDS... BACKGROUNDS CAN SOMETIMES EXPRESS THE EMOTIONS OF YOUR CHARACTERS.
O-OH, YES...
YOU'RE RIGHT...
DOKI (BADUM)
YOU CAN KEEP GOING, ANMITSU-SENSEI...
YOU'RE STRONG! AND THAT'S WHY...
SO (HOLD)
...
...I WANT YOU TO AIM FOR EVEN GREATER HEIGHTS.
IT'S NOT AS IF I DON'T LIKE YOU OR YOUR WORK ISN'T GOOD!
IT'S ALREADY GOOD WORK AS IT IS! BUT...!!

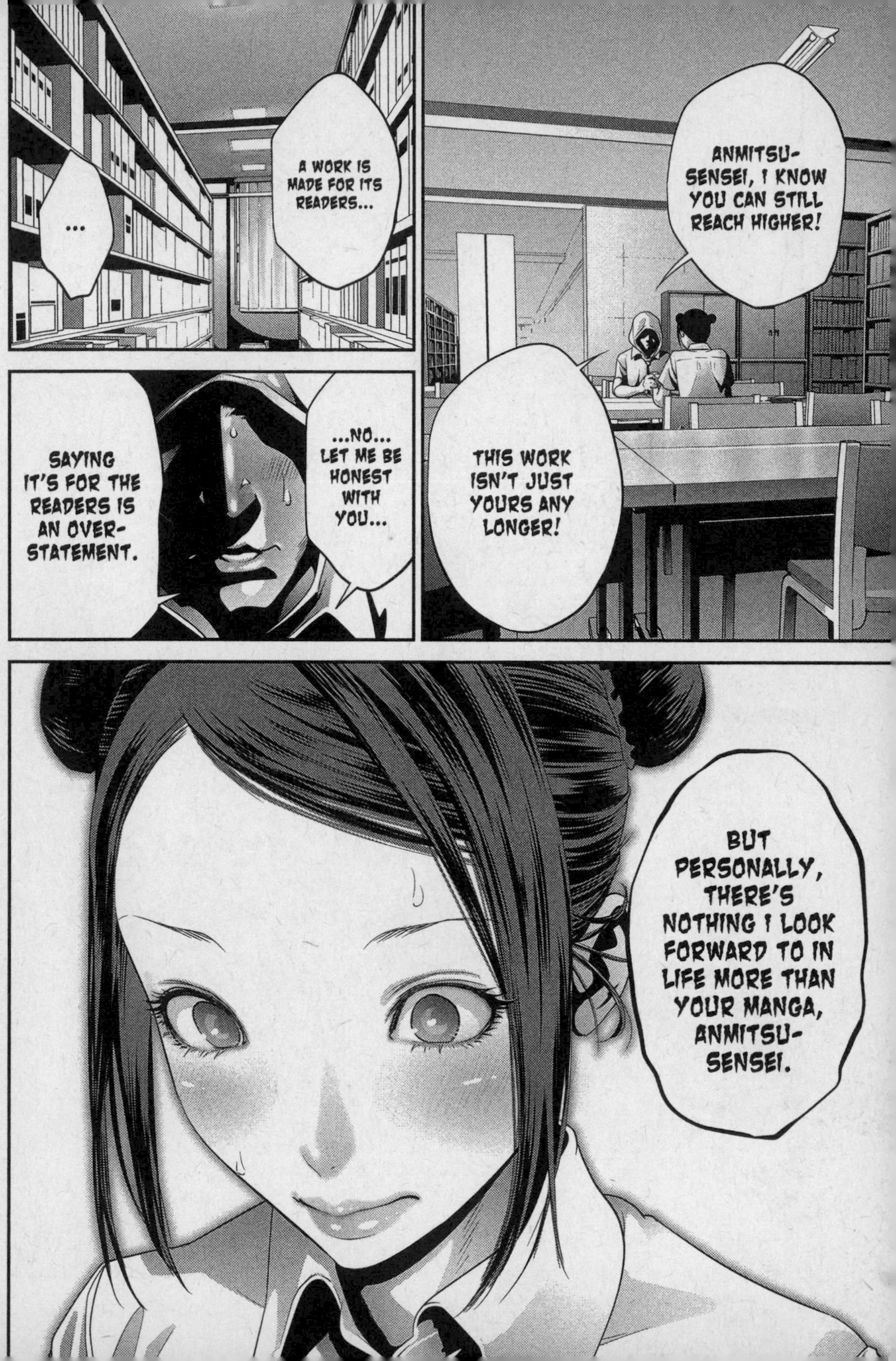
ANMITSU-SENSEI, I KNOW YOU CAN STILL REACH HIGHER!
THIS WORK ISN'T JUST YOURS ANY LONGER!
A WORK IS MADE FOR ITS READERS...
...
...NO... LET ME BE HONEST WITH YOU...
SAYING IT'S FOR THE READERS IS AN OVER-STATEMENT.
BUT PERSONALLY, THERE'S NOTHING I LOOK FORWARD TO IN LIFE MORE THAN YOUR MANGA, ANMITSU-SENSEI.

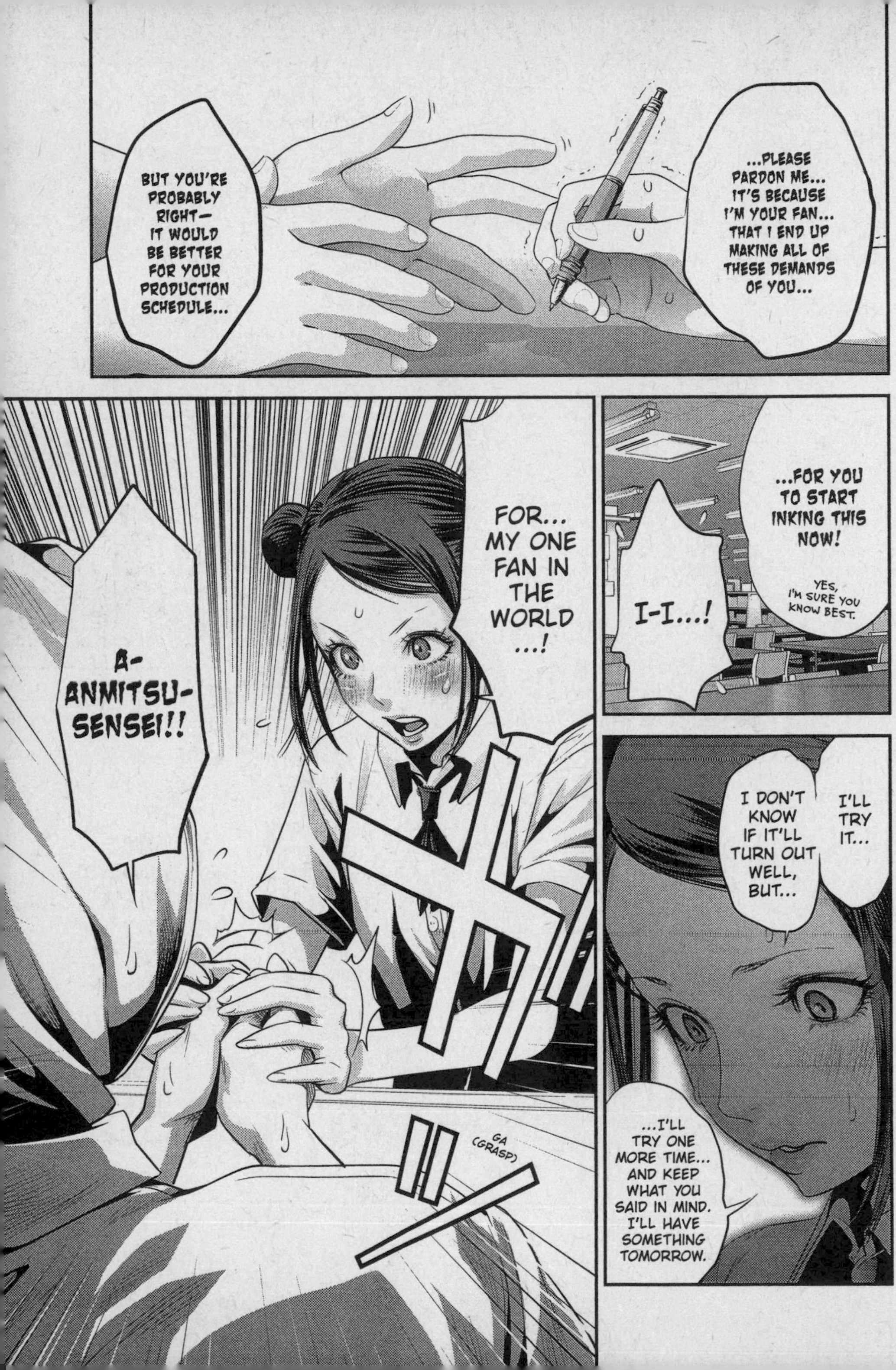
...PLEASE PARDON ME... IT'S BECAUSE I'M YOUR FAN... THAT I END UP MAKING ALL OF THESE DEMANDS OF YOU...
BUT YOU'RE PROBABLY RIGHT— IT WOULD BE BETTER FOR YOUR PRODUCTION SCHEDULE...
...FOR YOU TO START INKING THIS NOW!
YES, I'M SURE YOU KNOW BEST.
I-I...!
I'LL TRY IT...
I DON'T KNOW IF IT'LL TURN OUT WELL, BUT...
...I'LL TRY ONE MORE TIME... AND KEEP WHAT YOU SAID IN MIND. I'LL HAVE SOMETHING TOMORROW.
FOR... MY ONE FAN IN THE WORLD ...!
A-ANMITSU-SENSEI!!
GA (GRASP)

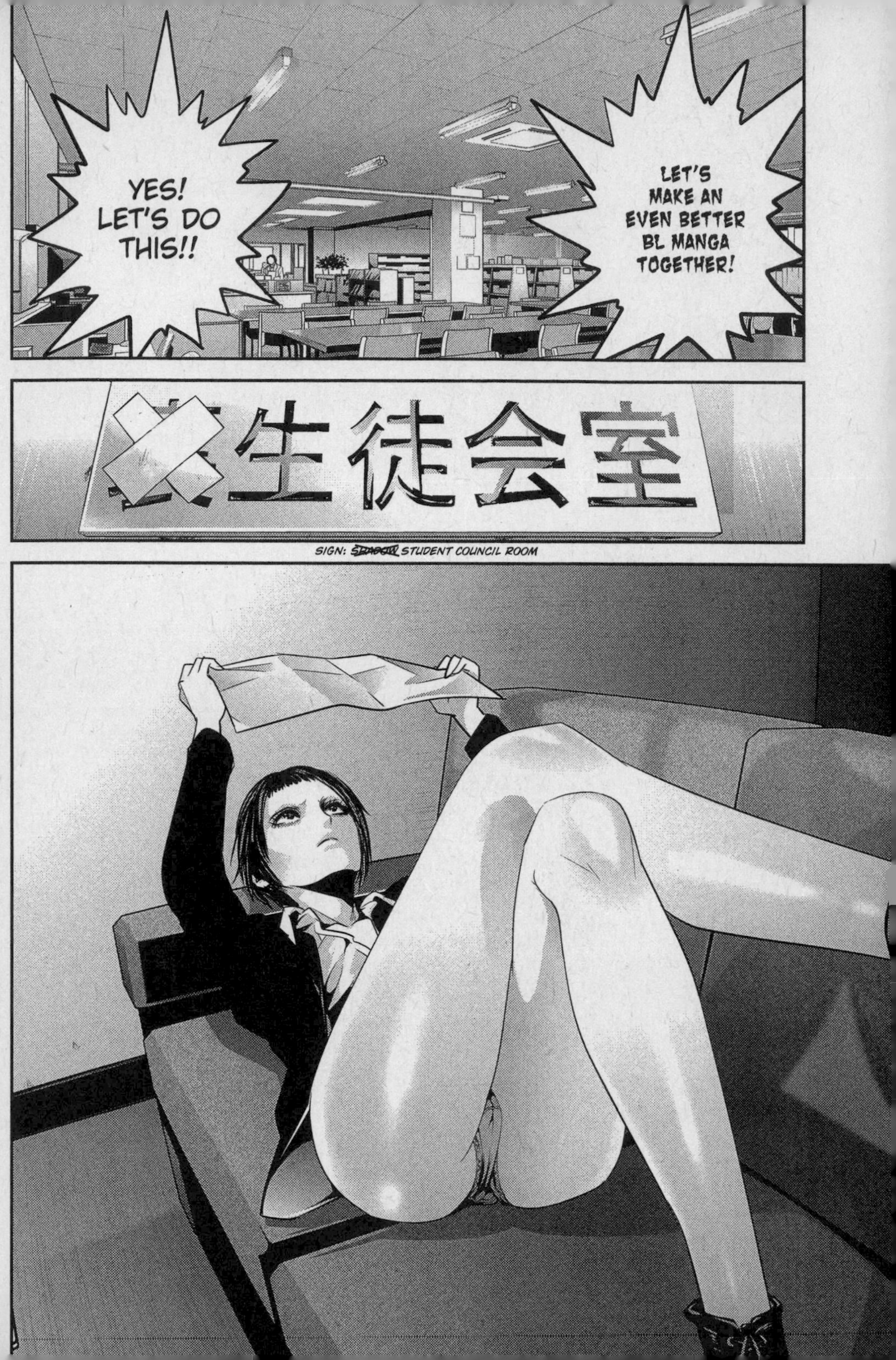
LET'S MAKE AN EVEN BETTER BL MANGA TOGETHER!
YES! LET'S DO THIS!!
生徒会室
SIGN: ~~SHADOW~~ STUDENT COUNCIL ROOM

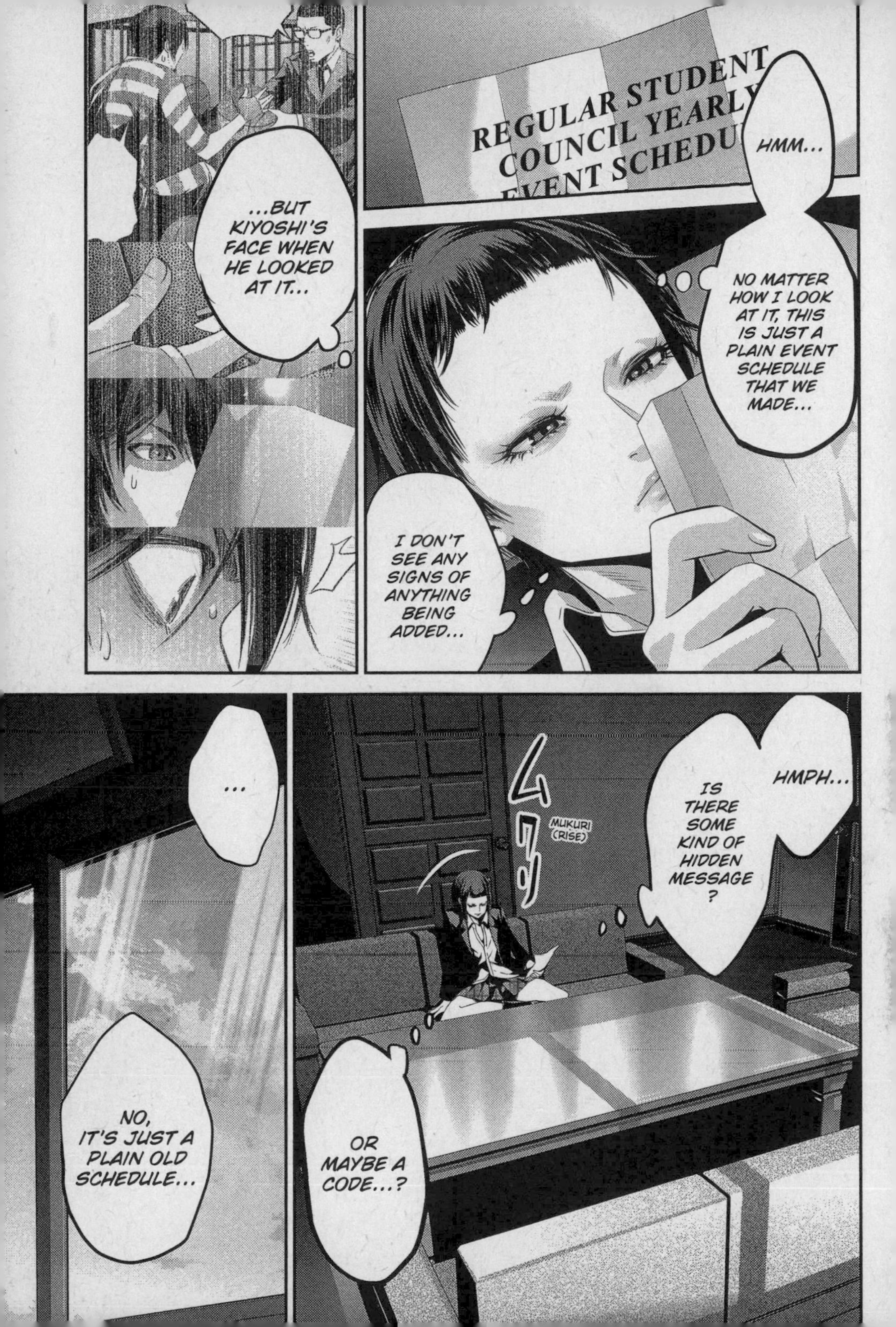
REGULAR STUDENT COUNCIL YEARLY EVENT SCHEDU
HMM...
NO MATTER HOW I LOOK AT IT, THIS IS JUST A PLAIN EVENT SCHEDULE THAT WE MADE...
I DON'T SEE ANY SIGNS OF ANYTHING BEING ADDED...
...BUT KIYOSHI'S FACE WHEN HE LOOKED AT IT...
HMPH...
IS THERE SOME KIND OF HIDDEN MESSAGE ?
MUKURI (RISE)
OR MAYBE A CODE...?
...
NO, IT'S JUST A PLAIN OLD SCHEDULE...

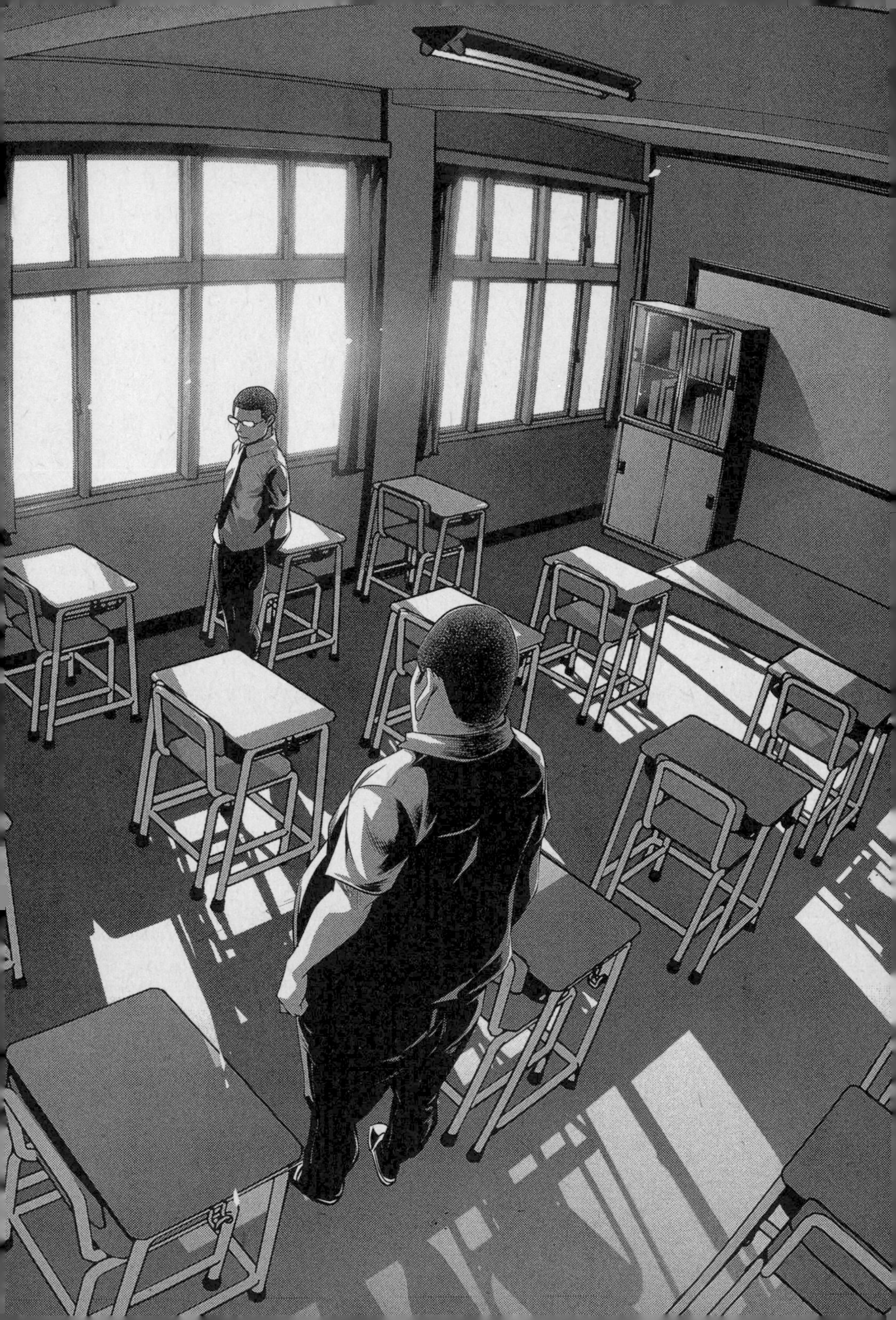

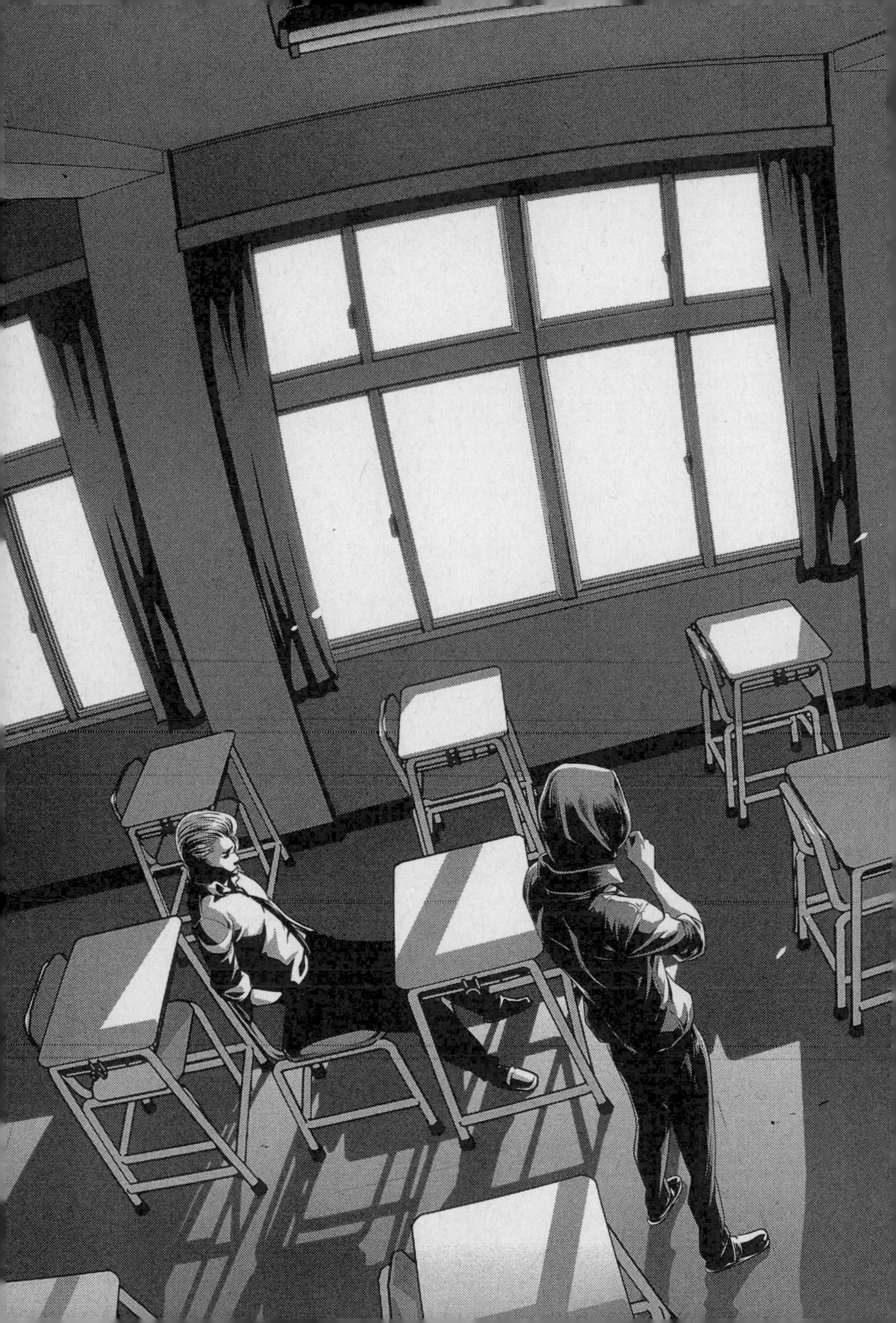

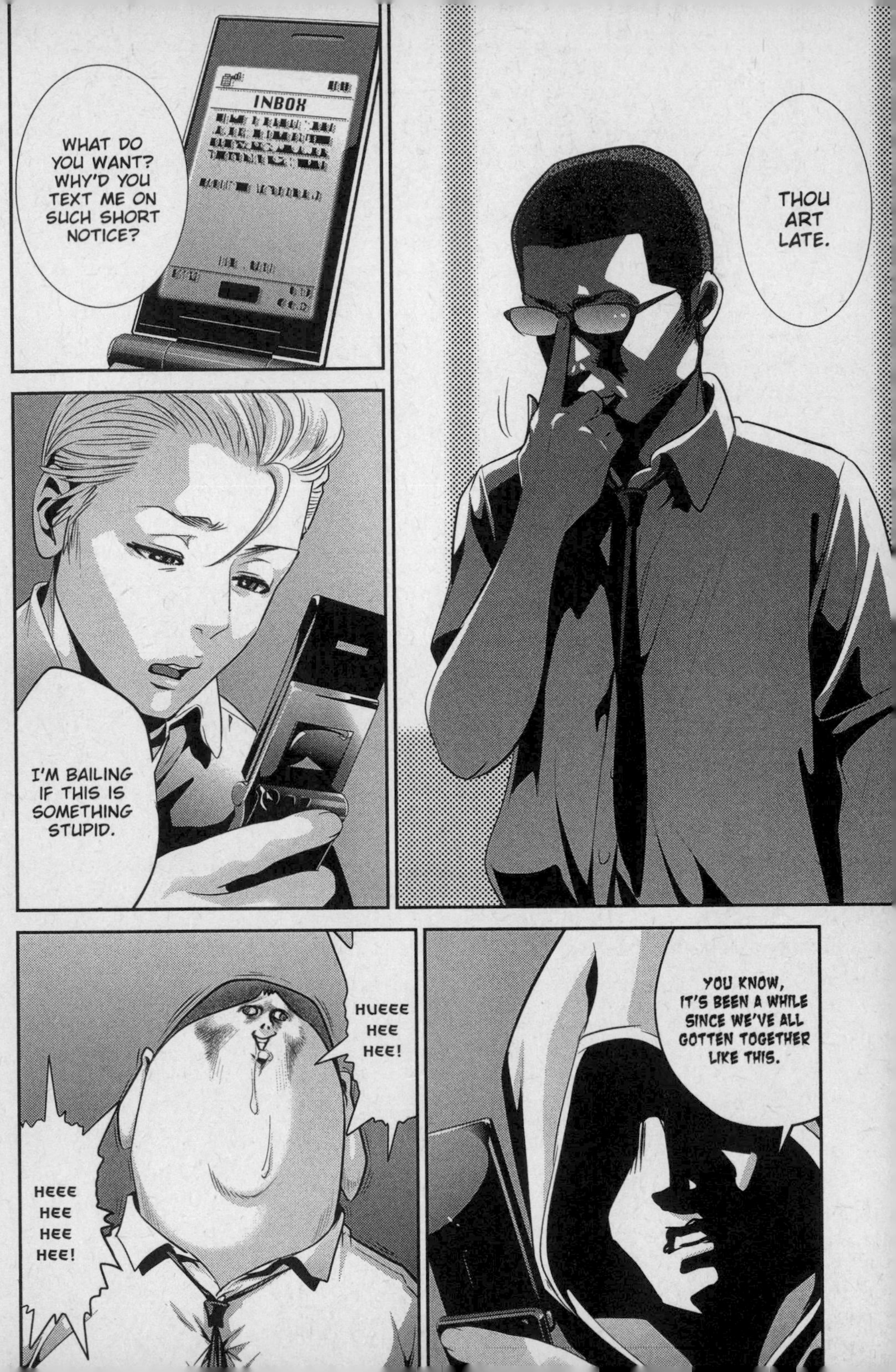
THOU ART LATE.
INBOX
WHAT DO YOU WANT? WHY'D YOU TEXT ME ON SUCH SHORT NOTICE?
I'M BAILING IF THIS IS SOMETHING STUPID.
YOU KNOW, IT'S BEEN A WHILE SINCE WE'VE ALL GOTTEN TOGETHER LIKE THIS.
HUEEE HEE HEE!
HEEE HEE HEE HEE!

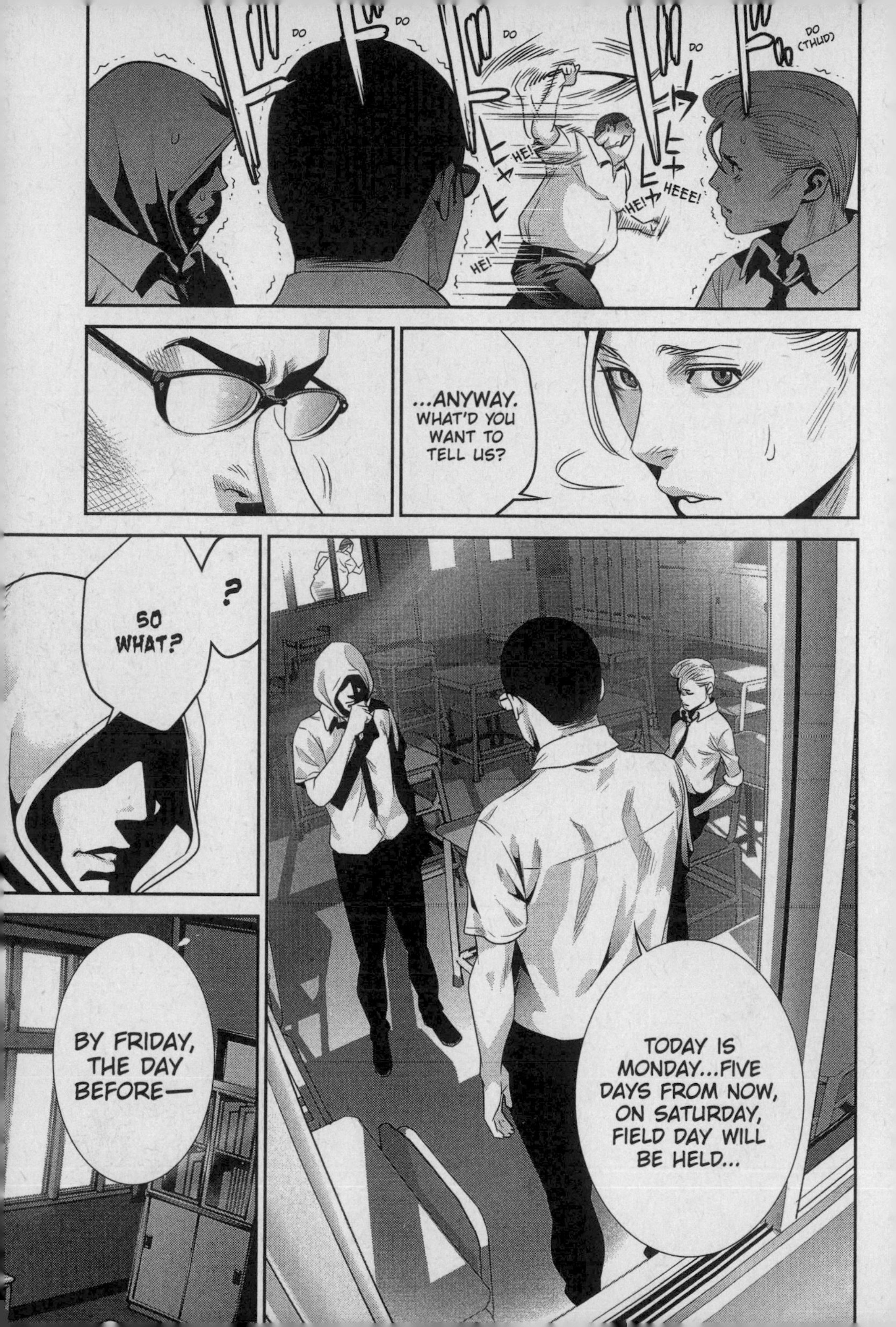
DO
DO
DO
DO
DO (THUD)
HE!
HEEEE!
HE!
HE!
...ANYWAY. WHAT'D YOU WANT TO TELL US?
?
SO WHAT?
TODAY IS MONDAY...FIVE DAYS FROM NOW, ON SATURDAY, FIELD DAY WILL BE HELD...
BY FRIDAY, THE DAY BEFORE—

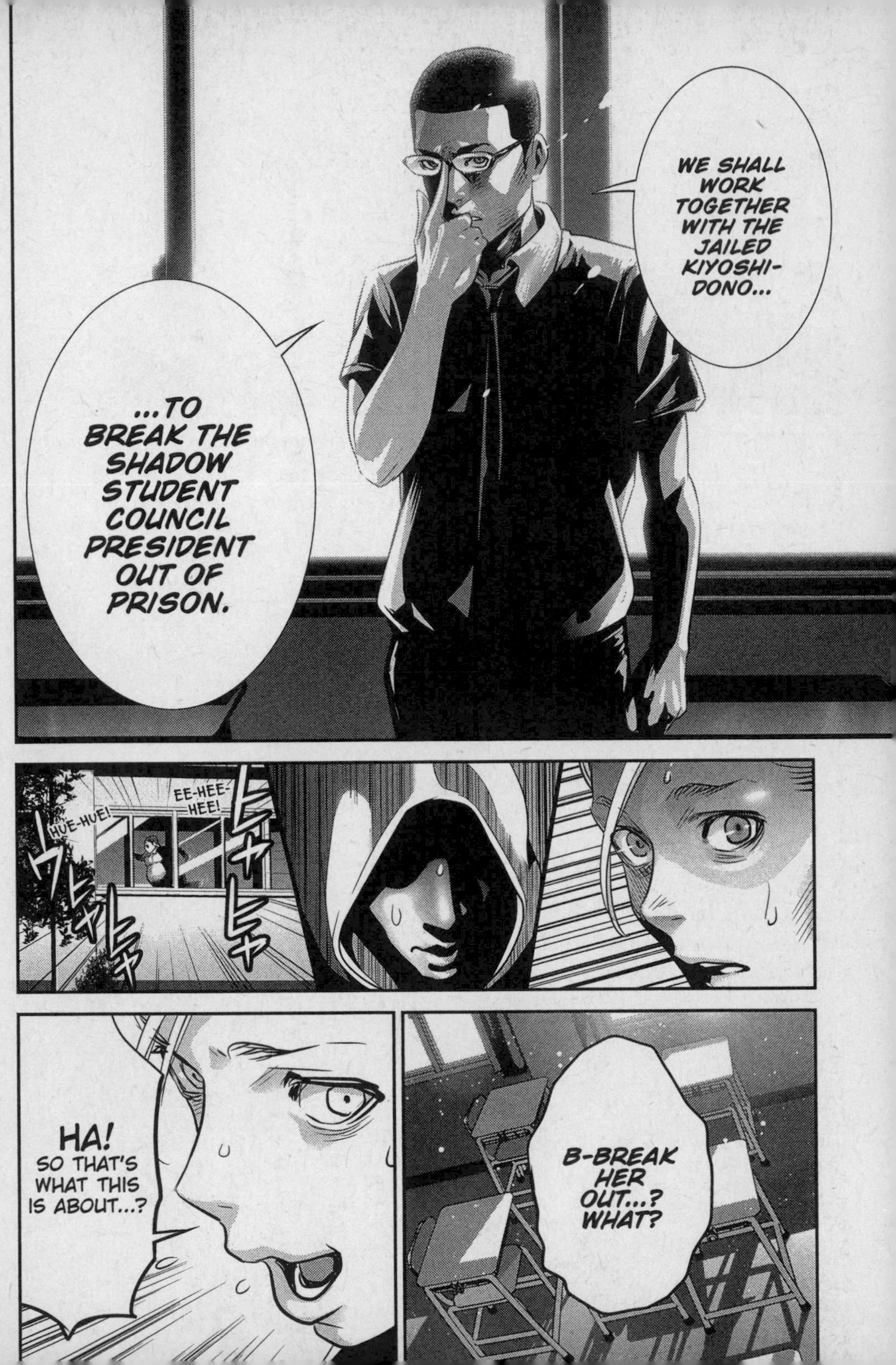
WE SHALL WORK TOGETHER WITH THE JAILED KIYOSHI-DONO...
...TO BREAK THE SHADOW STUDENT COUNCIL PRESIDENT OUT OF PRISON.
EE-HEE-HEE!
HUE-HUE!
B-BREAK HER OUT...? WHAT?
HA! SO THAT'S WHAT THIS IS ABOUT...?

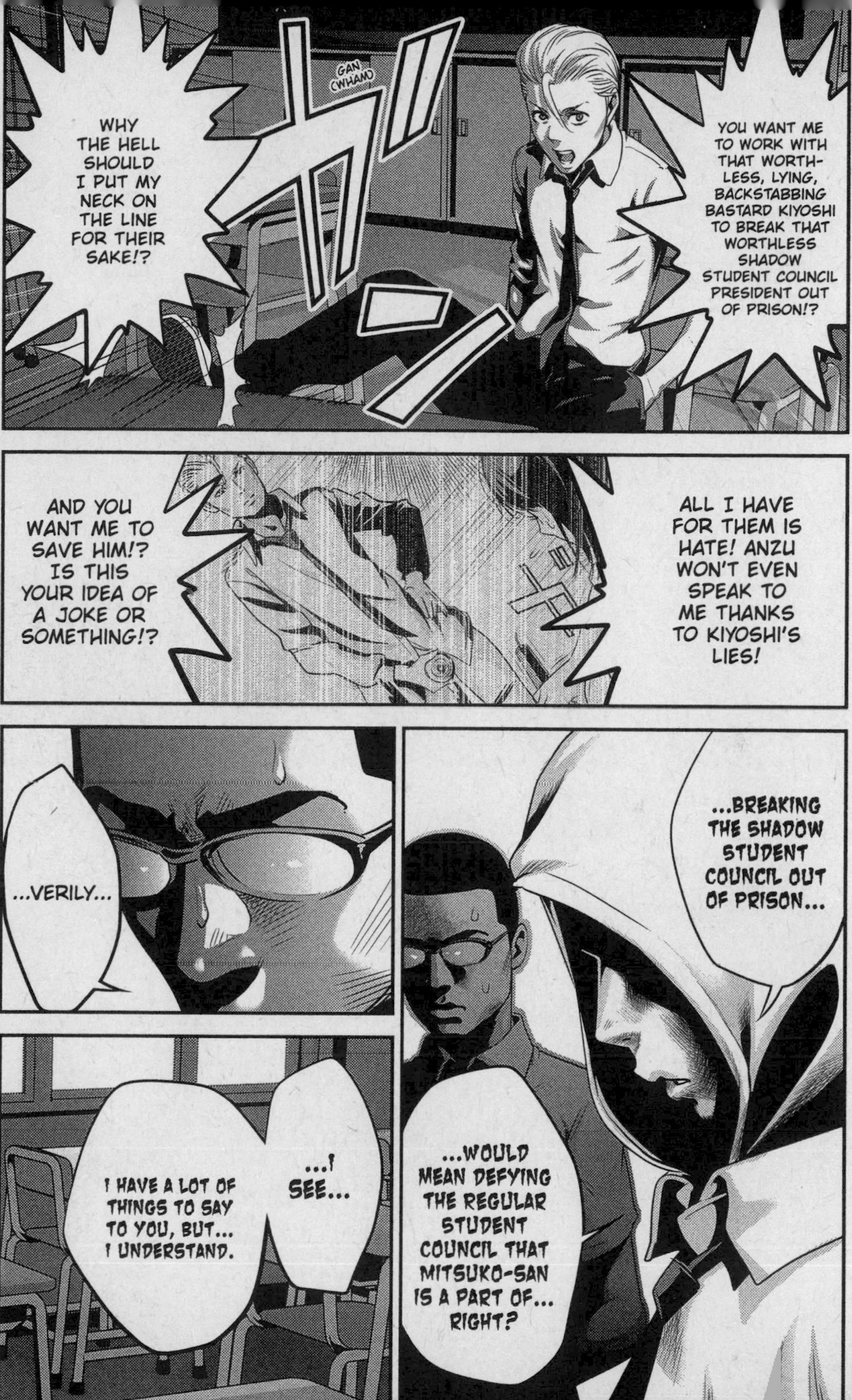
YOU WANT ME TO WORK WITH THAT WORTHLESS, LYING, BACKSTABBING BASTARD KIYOSHI TO BREAK THAT WORTHLESS SHADOW STUDENT COUNCIL PRESIDENT OUT OF PRISON!?
GAN (WHAM)
WHY THE HELL SHOULD I PUT MY NECK ON THE LINE FOR THEIR SAKE!?
ALL I HAVE FOR THEM IS HATE! ANZU WON'T EVEN SPEAK TO ME THANKS TO KIYOSHI'S LIES!
AND YOU WANT ME TO SAVE HIM!? IS THIS YOUR IDEA OF A JOKE OR SOMETHING!?
...BREAKING THE SHADOW STUDENT COUNCIL OUT OF PRISON...
...VERILY...
...WOULD MEAN DEFYING THE REGULAR STUDENT COUNCIL THAT MITSUKO-SAN IS A PART OF... RIGHT?
...I SEE...
I HAVE A LOT OF THINGS TO SAY TO YOU, BUT... I UNDERSTAND.

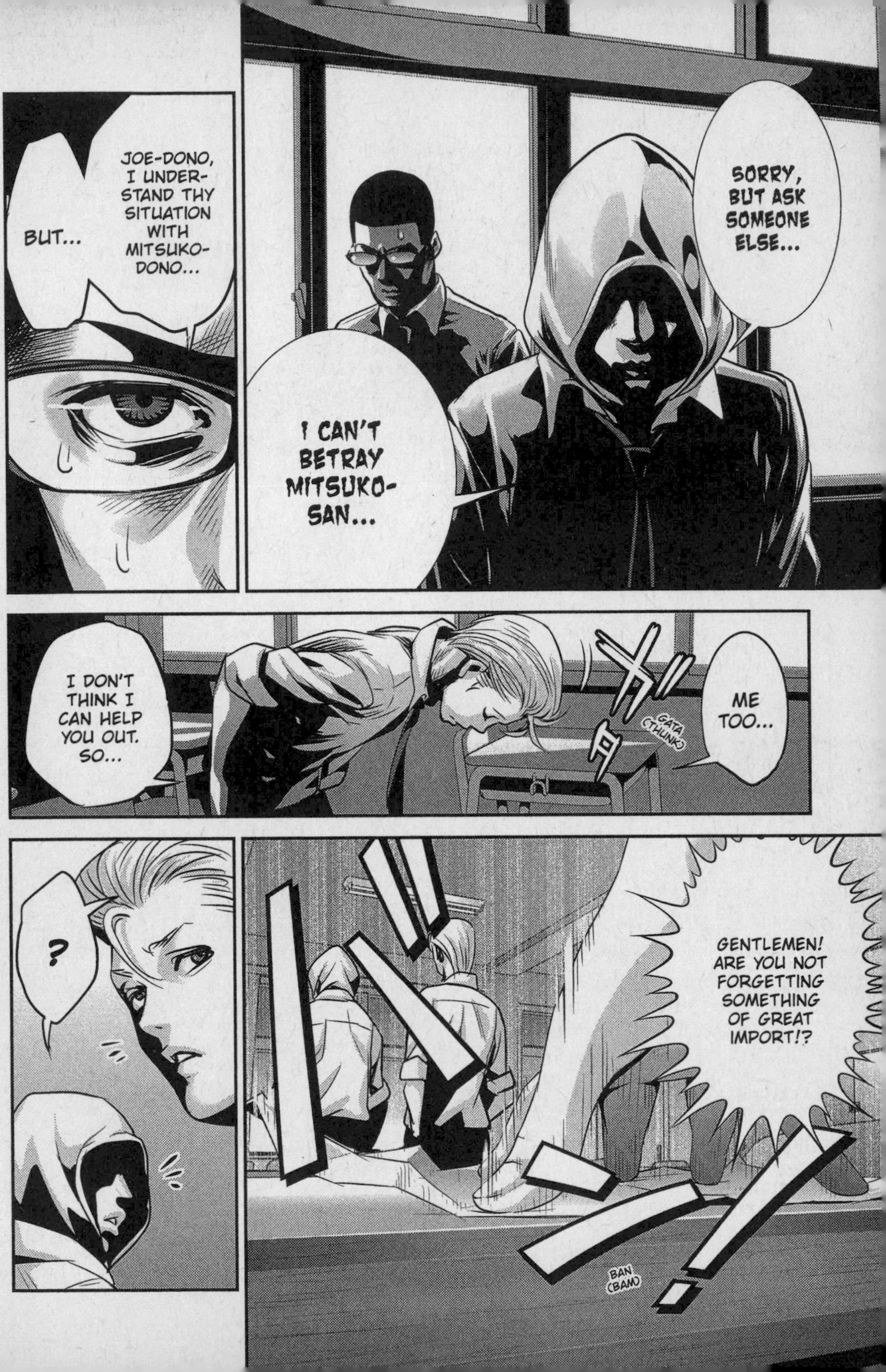
SORRY, BUT ASK SOMEONE ELSE...
I CAN'T BETRAY MITSUKO-SAN...
JOE-DONO, I UNDERSTAND THY SITUATION WITH MITSUKO-DONO...
BUT...
ME TOO...
GATA (THUNK)
I DON'T THINK I CAN HELP YOU OUT. SO...
GENTLEMEN! ARE YOU NOT FORGETTING SOMETHING OF GREAT IMPORT!?
BAN (BAM)
?

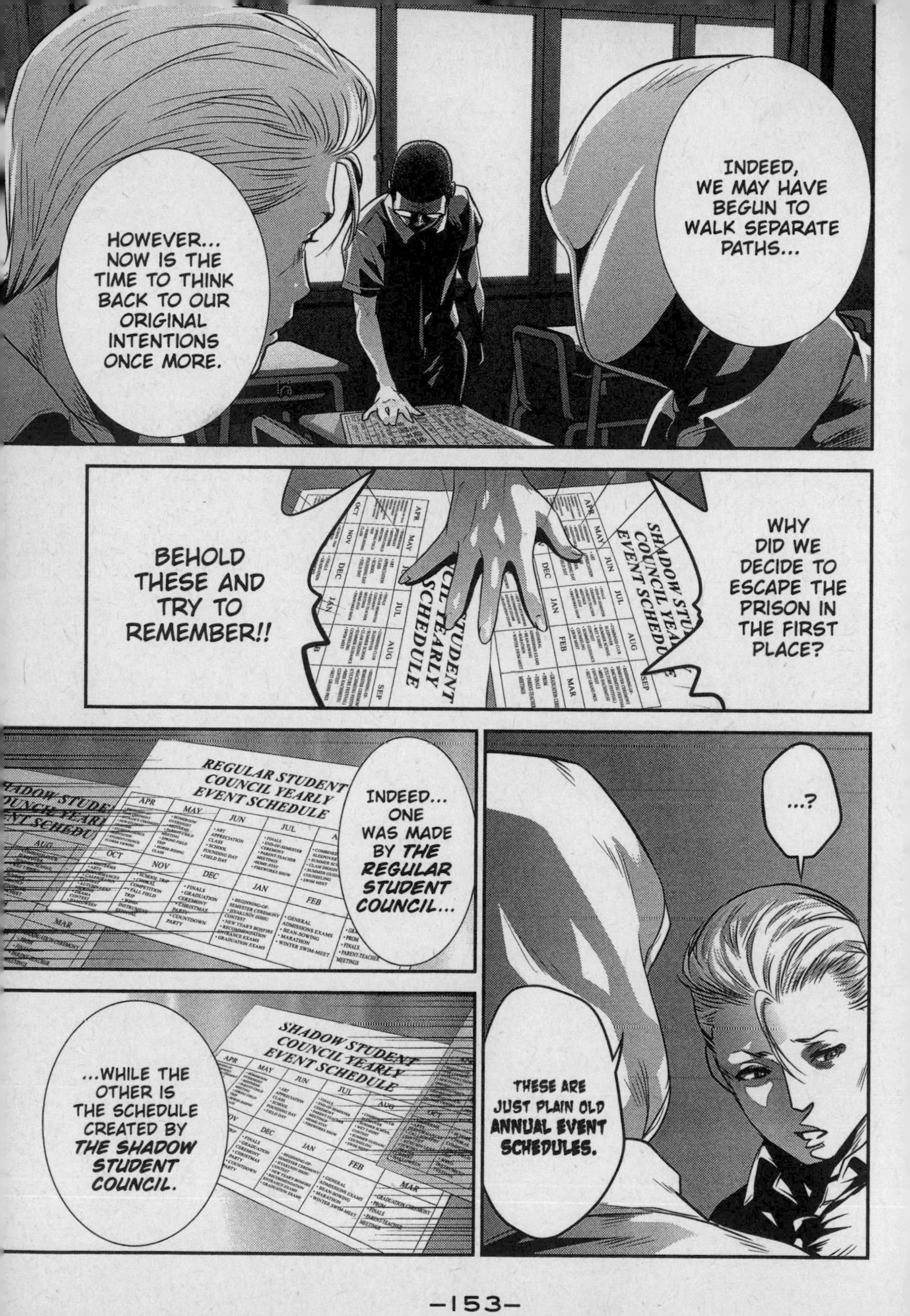
INDEED, WE MAY HAVE BEGUN TO WALK SEPARATE PATHS...
HOWEVER... NOW IS THE TIME TO THINK BACK TO OUR ORIGINAL INTENTIONS ONCE MORE.
WHY DID WE DECIDE TO ESCAPE THE PRISON IN THE FIRST PLACE?
BEHOLD THESE AND TRY TO REMEMBER!!
...?
REGULAR STUDENT COUNCIL YEARLY EVENT SCHEDULE
INDEED... ONE WAS MADE BY ***THE REGULAR STUDENT COUNCIL***...
SHADOW STUDENT COUNCIL YEARLY EVENT SCHEDULE
...WHILE THE OTHER IS THE SCHEDULE CREATED BY ***THE SHADOW STUDENT COUNCIL***.
THESE ARE JUST PLAIN OLD **ANNUAL EVENT SCHEDULES.**

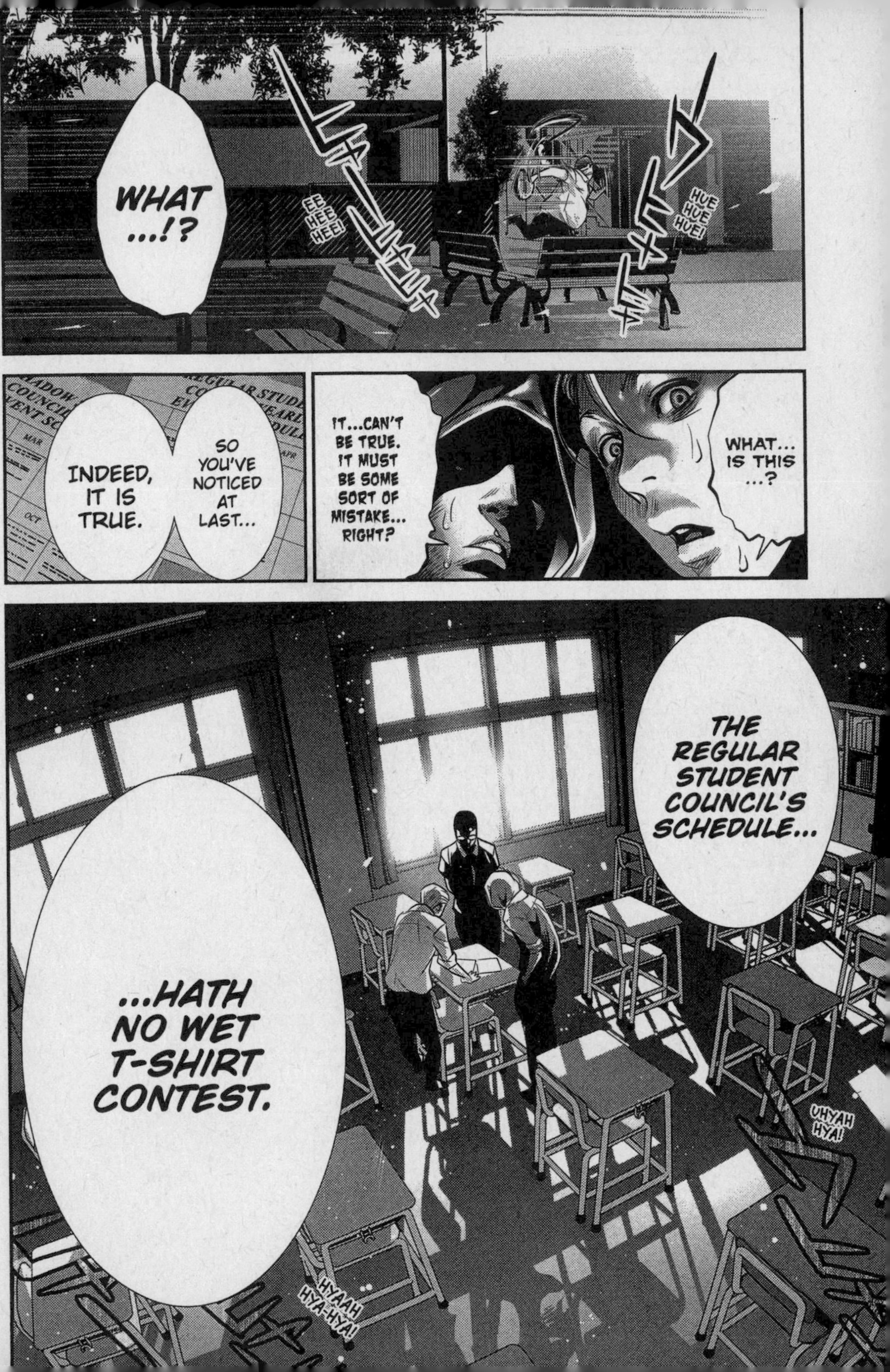
WHAT ...!?
HUE HUE HUE!
EE HEE HEE!
WHAT... IS THIS ...?
IT...CAN'T BE TRUE. IT MUST BE SOME SORT OF MISTAKE... RIGHT?
SO YOU'VE NOTICED AT LAST...
INDEED, IT IS TRUE.
THE REGULAR STUDENT COUNCIL'S SCHEDULE...
...HATH NO WET T-SHIRT CONTEST.
UHYAH HYA!
HYAAH HYA-HYA!

CHAPTER 127: INNOCENT VOICES

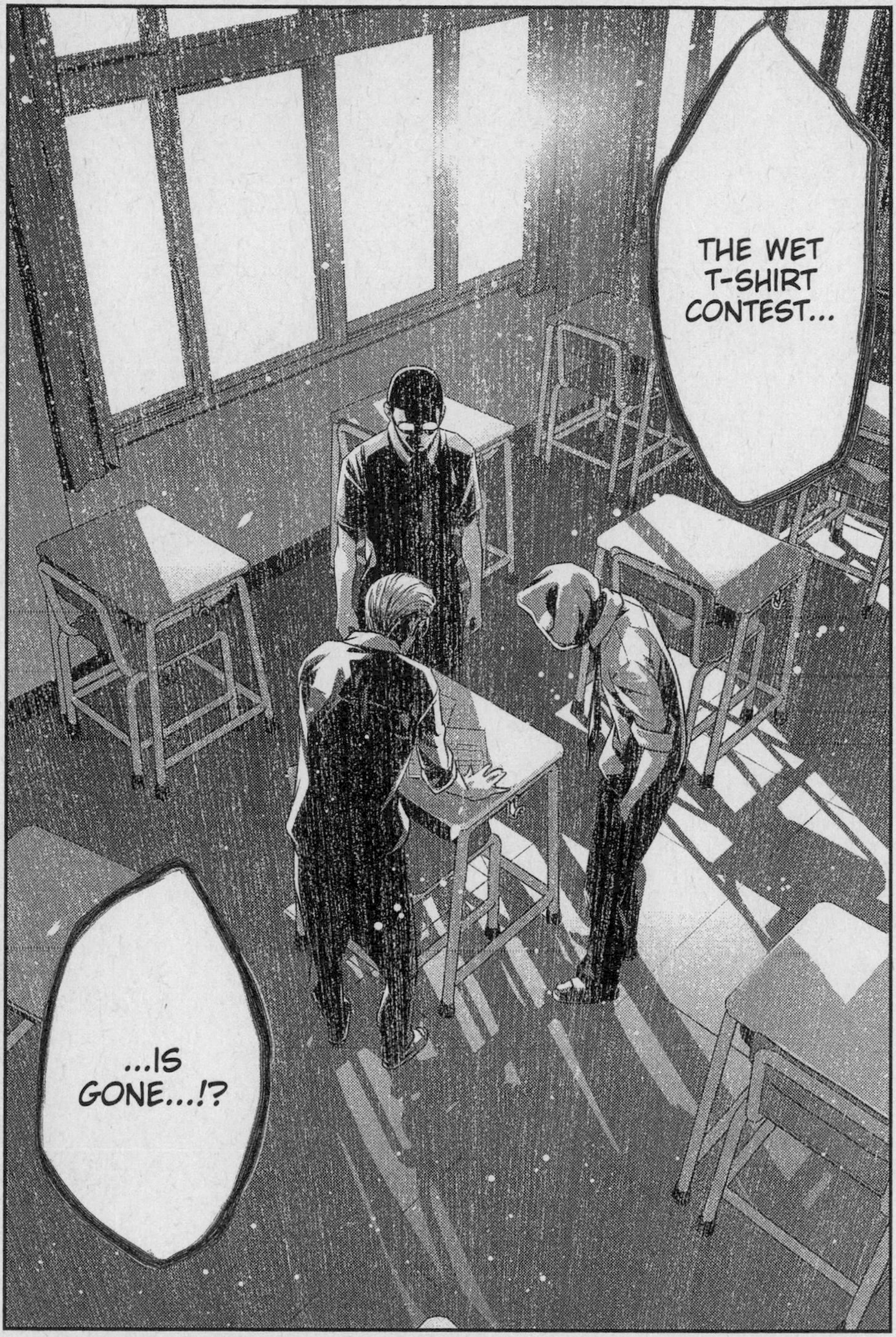
THE WET T-SHIRT CONTEST...
...IS GONE...!?

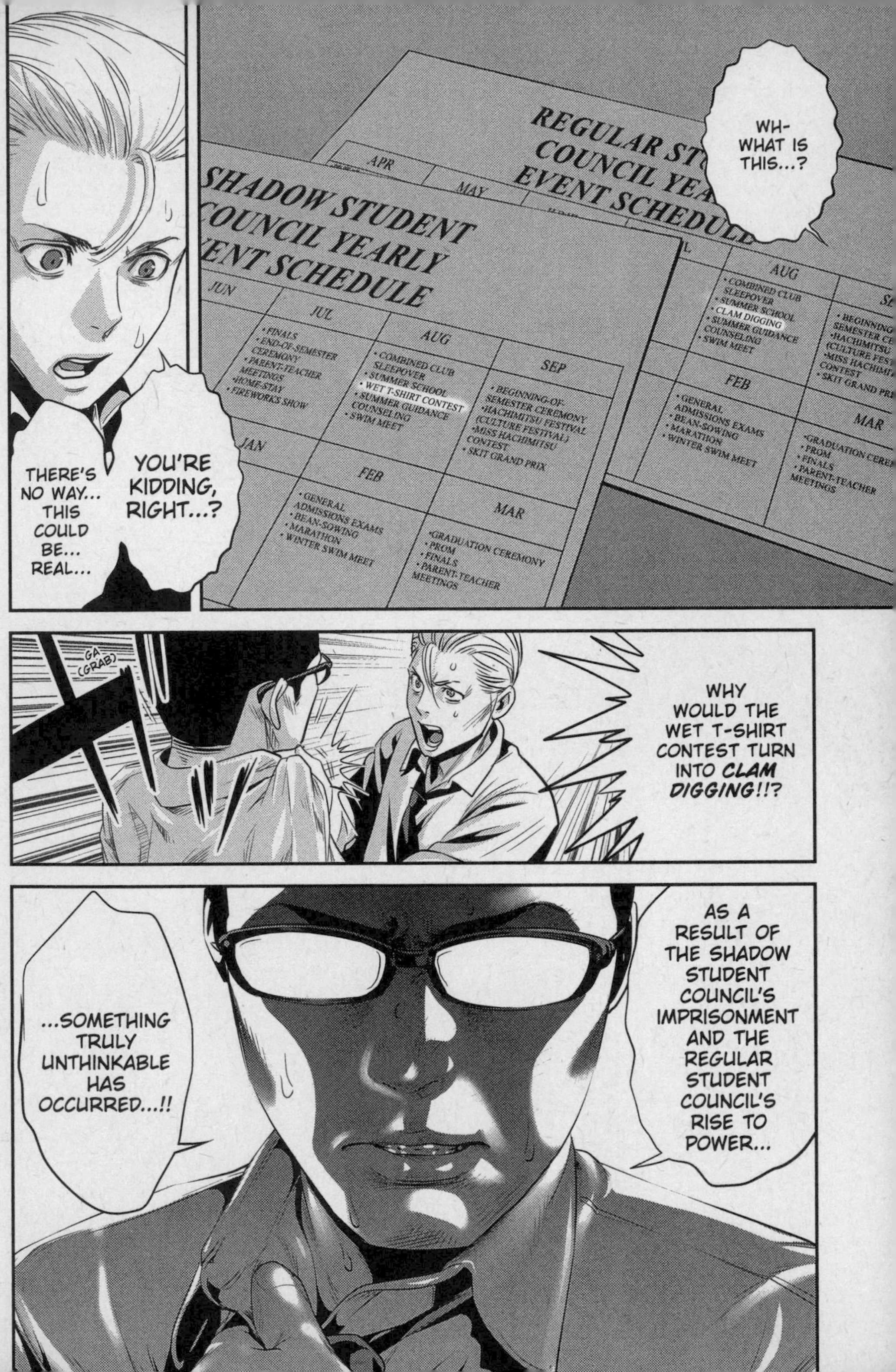
WH- WHAT IS THIS...?
REGULAR STUDENT COUNCIL YEARLY EVENT SCHEDULE
SHADOW STUDENT COUNCIL YEARLY EVENT SCHEDULE
JUN
JUL
• FINALS • END-OF-SEMESTER CEREMONY • PARENT-TEACHER MEETINGS •HOME-STAY • FIREWORKS SHOW
AUG
• COMBINED CLUB SLEEPOVER • SUMMER SCHOOL • WET T-SHIRT CONTEST • SUMMER GUIDANCE COUNSELING • SWIM MEET
SEP
• BEGINNING-OF-SEMESTER CEREMONY •HACHIMITSU FESTIVAL (CULTURE FESTIVAL) •MISS HACHIMITSU CONTEST • SKIT GRAND PRIX
JAN
FEB
• GENERAL ADMISSIONS EXAMS • BEAN-SOWING • MARATHON • WINTER SWIM MEET
MAR
•GRADUATION CEREMONY • PROM • FINALS • PARENT-TEACHER MEETINGS
AUG
• COMBINED CLUB SLEEPOVER • SUMMER SCHOOL • CLAM DIGGING • SUMMER GUIDANCE COUNSELING • SWIM MEET
FEB
• GENERAL ADMISSIONS EXAMS • BEAN-SOWING • MARATHON • WINTER SWIM MEET
MAR
YOU'RE KIDDING, RIGHT...?
THERE'S NO WAY... THIS COULD BE... REAL...
WHY WOULD THE WET T-SHIRT CONTEST TURN INTO CLAM DIGGING!!?
GA (GRAB)
AS A RESULT OF THE SHADOW STUDENT COUNCIL'S IMPRISONMENT AND THE REGULAR STUDENT COUNCIL'S RISE TO POWER...
...SOMETHING TRULY UNTHINKABLE HAS OCCURRED...!!

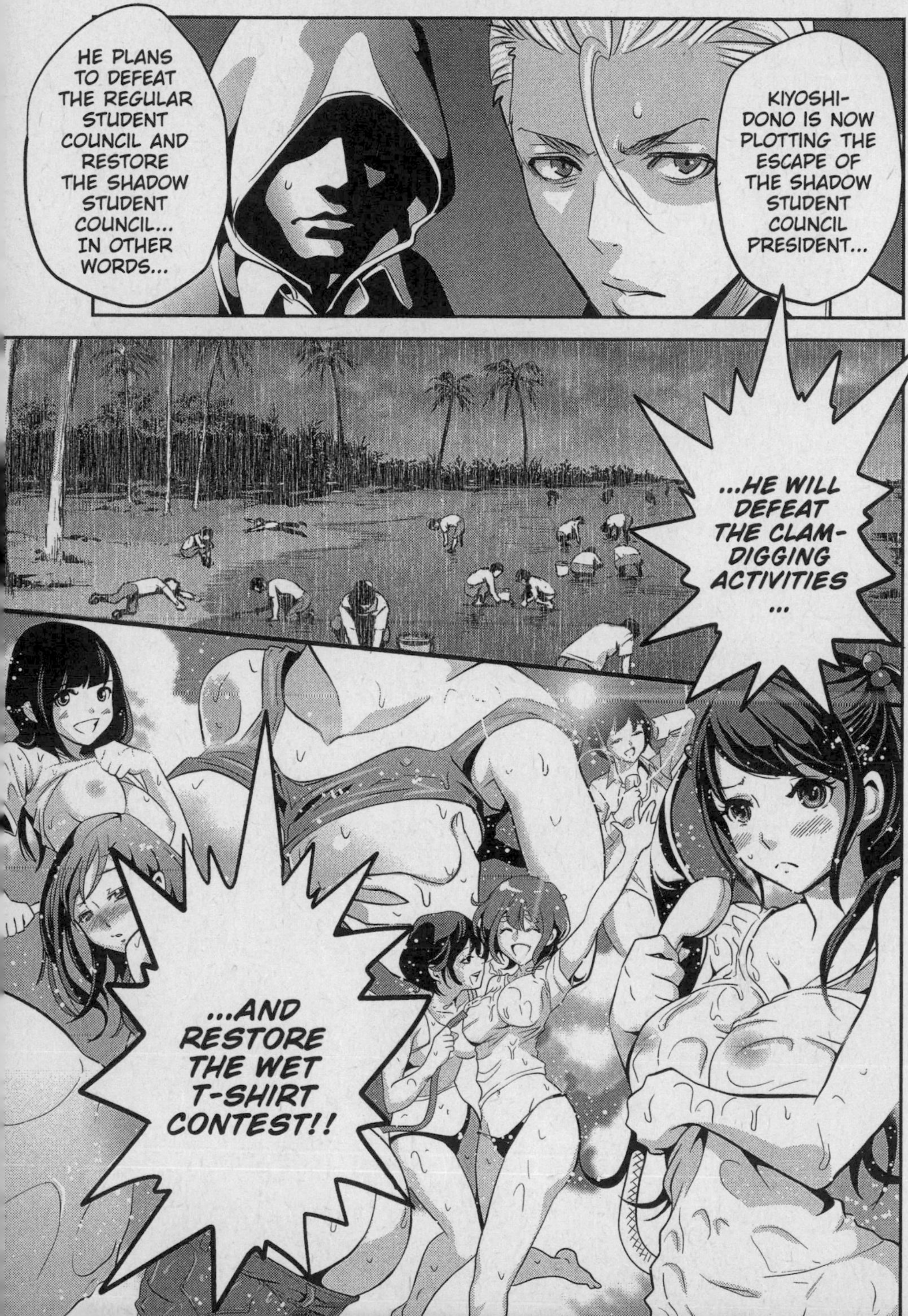
KIYOSHI-DONO IS NOW PLOTTING THE ESCAPE OF THE SHADOW STUDENT COUNCIL PRESIDENT...
HE PLANS TO DEFEAT THE REGULAR STUDENT COUNCIL AND RESTORE THE SHADOW STUDENT COUNCIL... IN OTHER WORDS...
...HE WILL DEFEAT THE CLAM-DIGGING ACTIVITIES ...
...AND RESTORE THE WET T-SHIRT CONTEST!!

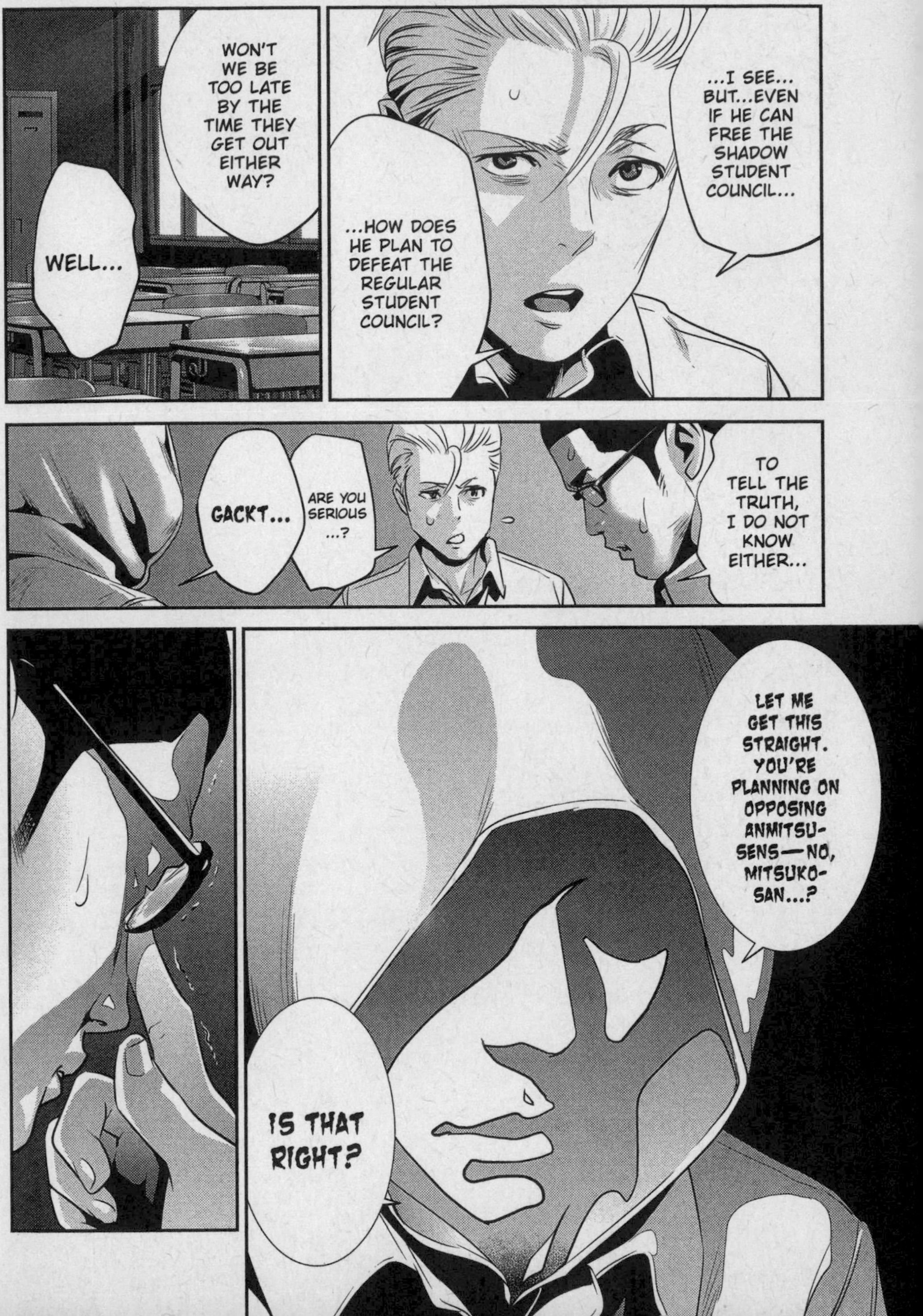

...I SEE... BUT...EVEN IF HE CAN FREE THE SHADOW STUDENT COUNCIL...
...HOW DOES HE PLAN TO DEFEAT THE REGULAR STUDENT COUNCIL?
WON'T WE BE TOO LATE BY THE TIME THEY GET OUT EITHER WAY?
WELL...
TO TELL THE TRUTH, I DO NOT KNOW EITHER...
ARE YOU SERIOUS ...?
GACKT...
LET ME GET THIS STRAIGHT. YOU'RE PLANNING ON OPPOSING ANMITSU-SENS—NO, MITSUKO-SAN...?
IS THAT RIGHT?

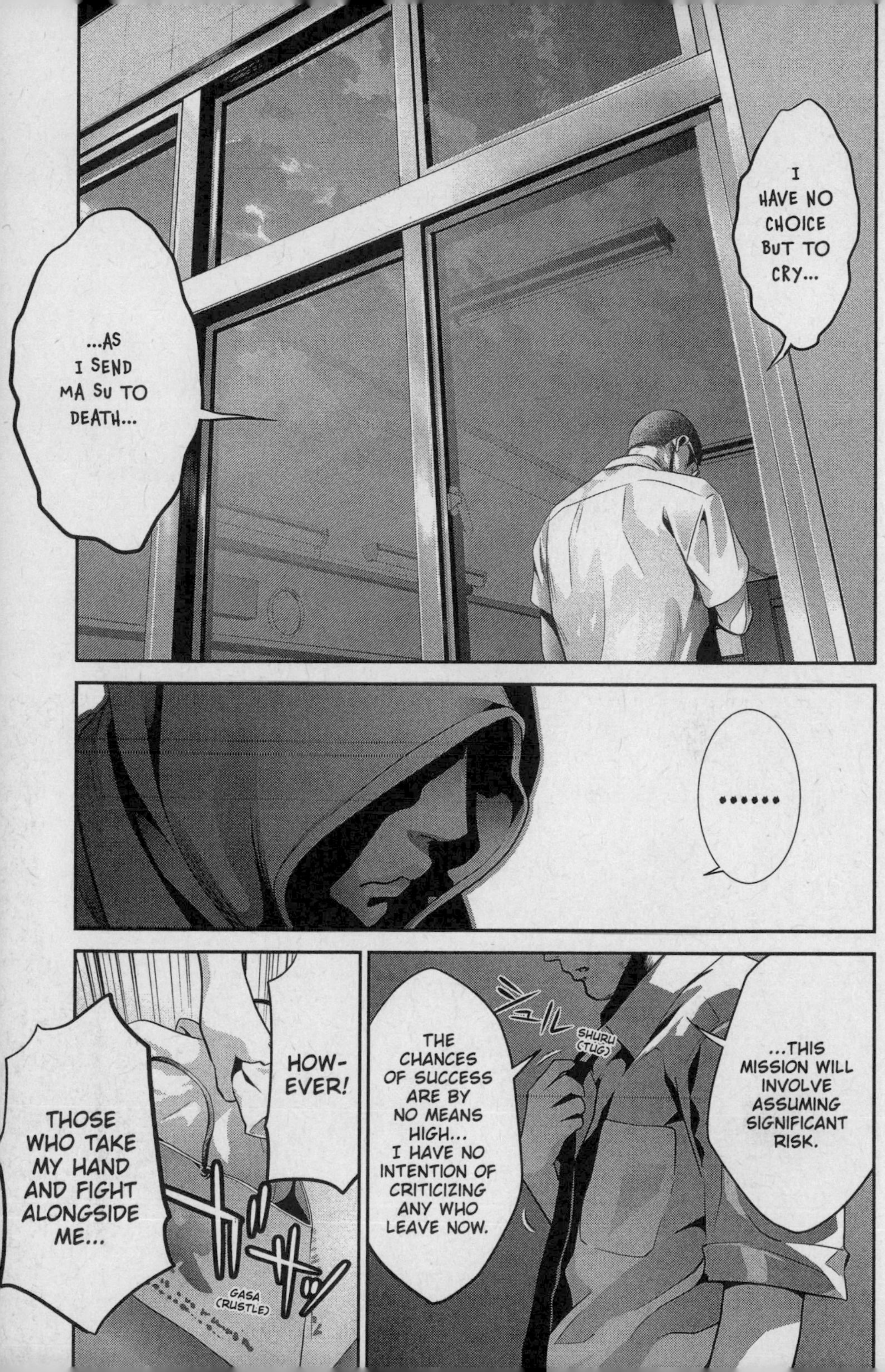
I HAVE NO CHOICE BUT TO CRY...
...AS I SEND MA SU TO DEATH...
......
...THIS MISSION WILL INVOLVE ASSUMING SIGNIFICANT RISK.
SHURU (TUG)
THE CHANCES OF SUCCESS ARE BY NO MEANS HIGH... I HAVE NO INTENTION OF CRITICIZING ANY WHO LEAVE NOW.
HOW-EVER!
THOSE WHO TAKE MY HAND AND FIGHT ALONGSIDE ME...
GASA (RUSTLE)

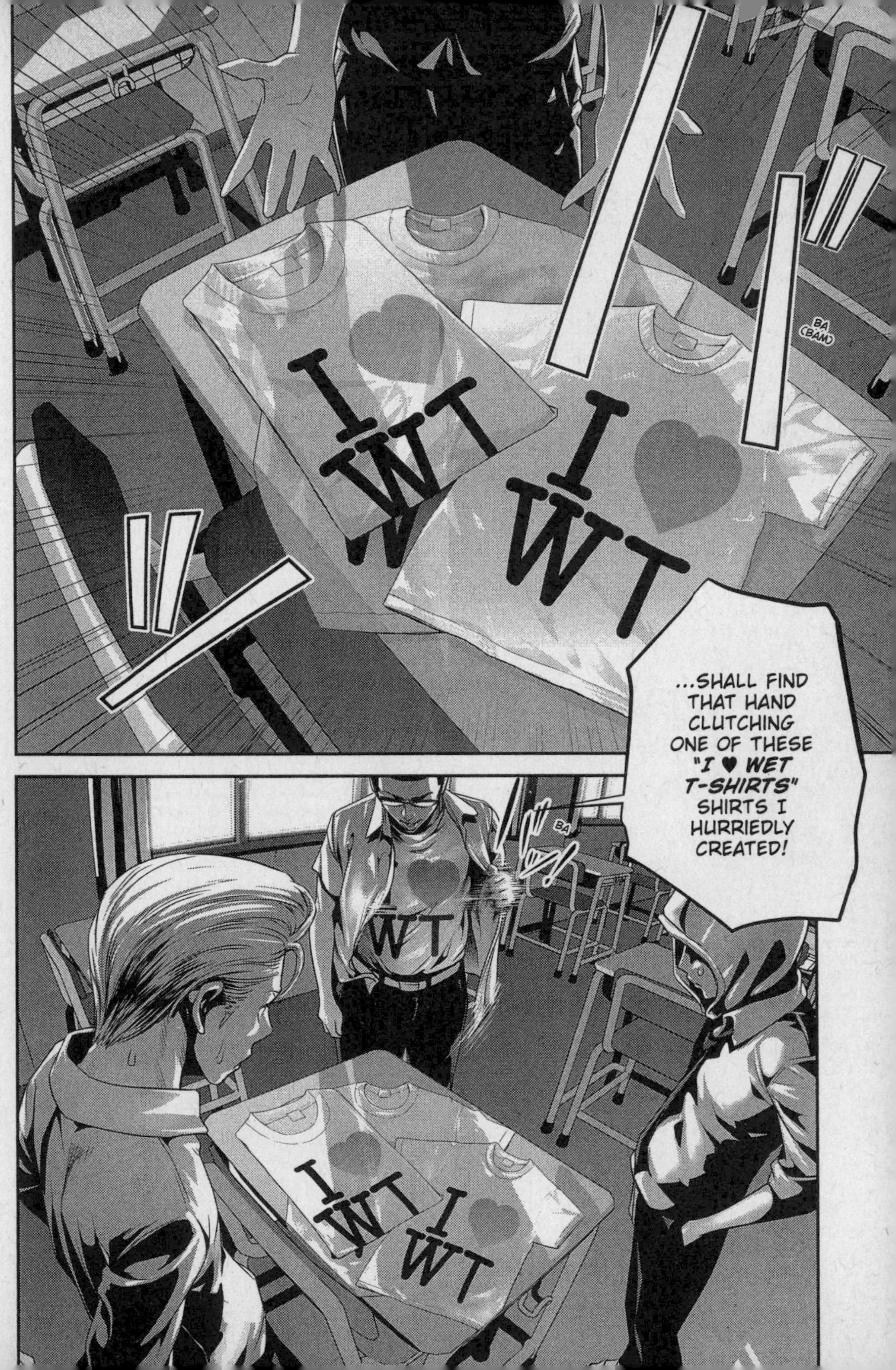
BA (BAM)
...SHALL FIND THAT HAND CLUTCHING ONE OF THESE "I ♥ WET T-SHIRTS" SHIRTS I HURRIEDLY CREATED!
BA

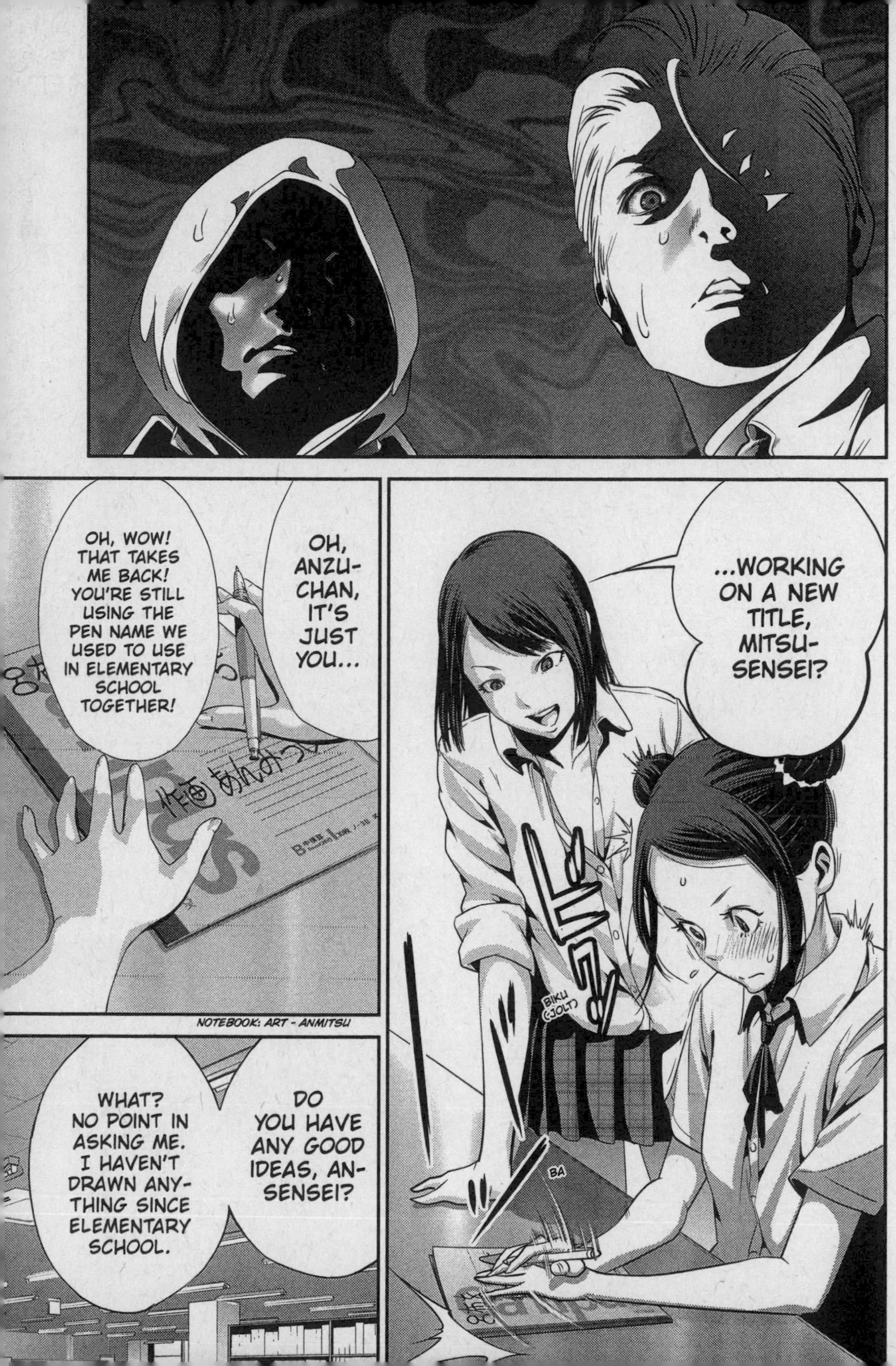
...WORKING ON A NEW TITLE, MITSU-SENSEI?
BIKU (JOLT)
BA
OH, ANZU-CHAN, IT'S JUST YOU...
OH, WOW! THAT TAKES ME BACK! YOU'RE STILL USING THE PEN NAME WE USED TO USE IN ELEMENTARY SCHOOL TOGETHER!
NOTEBOOK: ART - ANMITSU
DO YOU HAVE ANY GOOD IDEAS, AN-SENSEI?
WHAT? NO POINT IN ASKING ME. I HAVEN'T DRAWN ANYTHING SINCE ELEMENTARY SCHOOL.

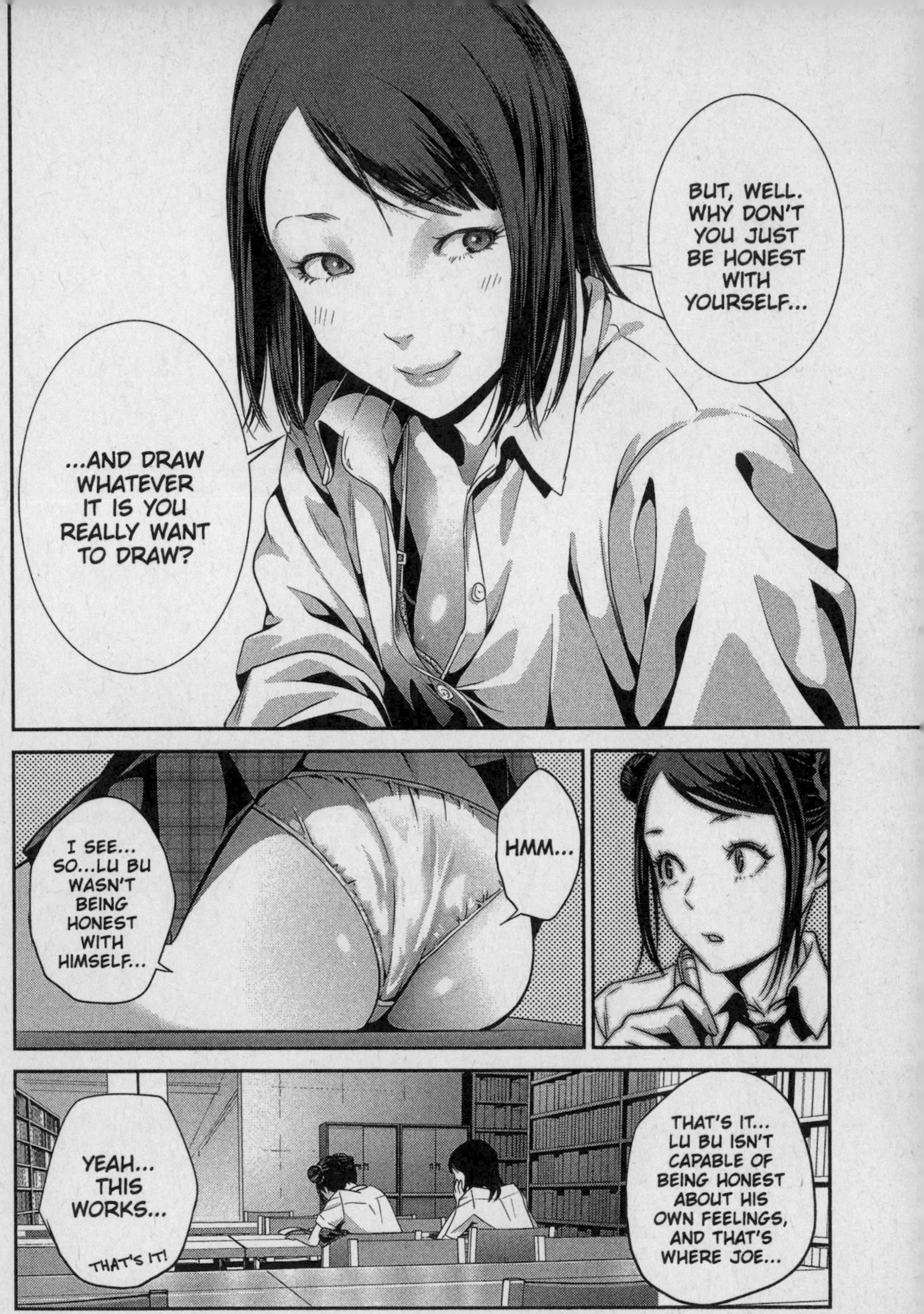
BUT, WELL. WHY DON'T YOU JUST BE HONEST WITH YOURSELF...
...AND DRAW WHATEVER IT IS YOU REALLY WANT TO DRAW?
HMM...
I SEE... SO...LU BU WASN'T BEING HONEST WITH HIMSELF...
THAT'S IT... LU BU ISN'T CAPABLE OF BEING HONEST ABOUT HIS OWN FEELINGS, AND THAT'S WHERE JOE...
YEAH... THIS WORKS...
THAT'S IT!

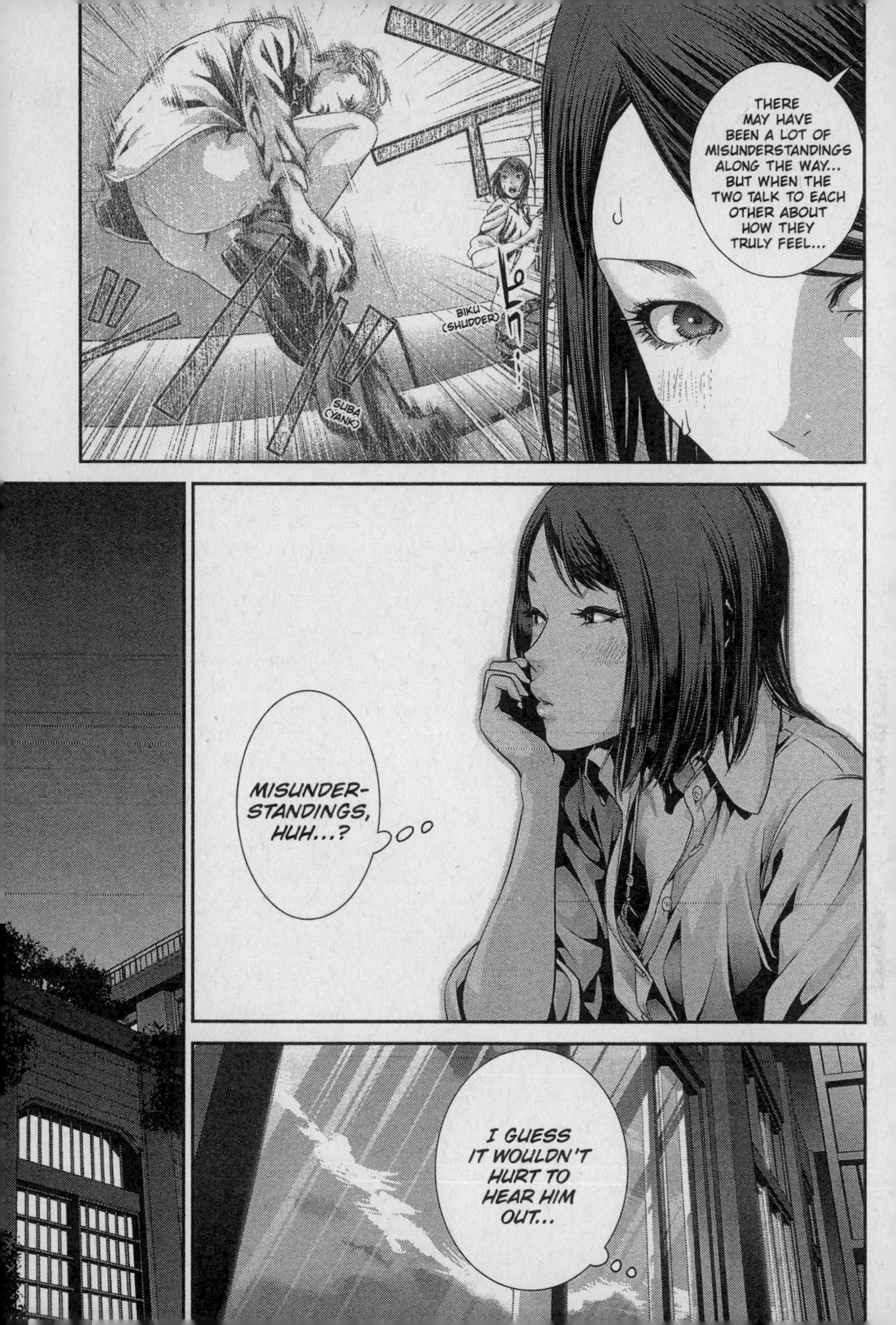

THERE MAY HAVE BEEN A LOT OF MISUNDERSTANDINGS ALONG THE WAY... BUT WHEN THE TWO TALK TO EACH OTHER ABOUT HOW THEY TRULY FEEL...
BIKU (SHUDDER)
SUBA (YANK)
MISUNDER-STANDINGS, HUH...?
I GUESS IT WOULDN'T HURT TO HEAR HIM OUT...

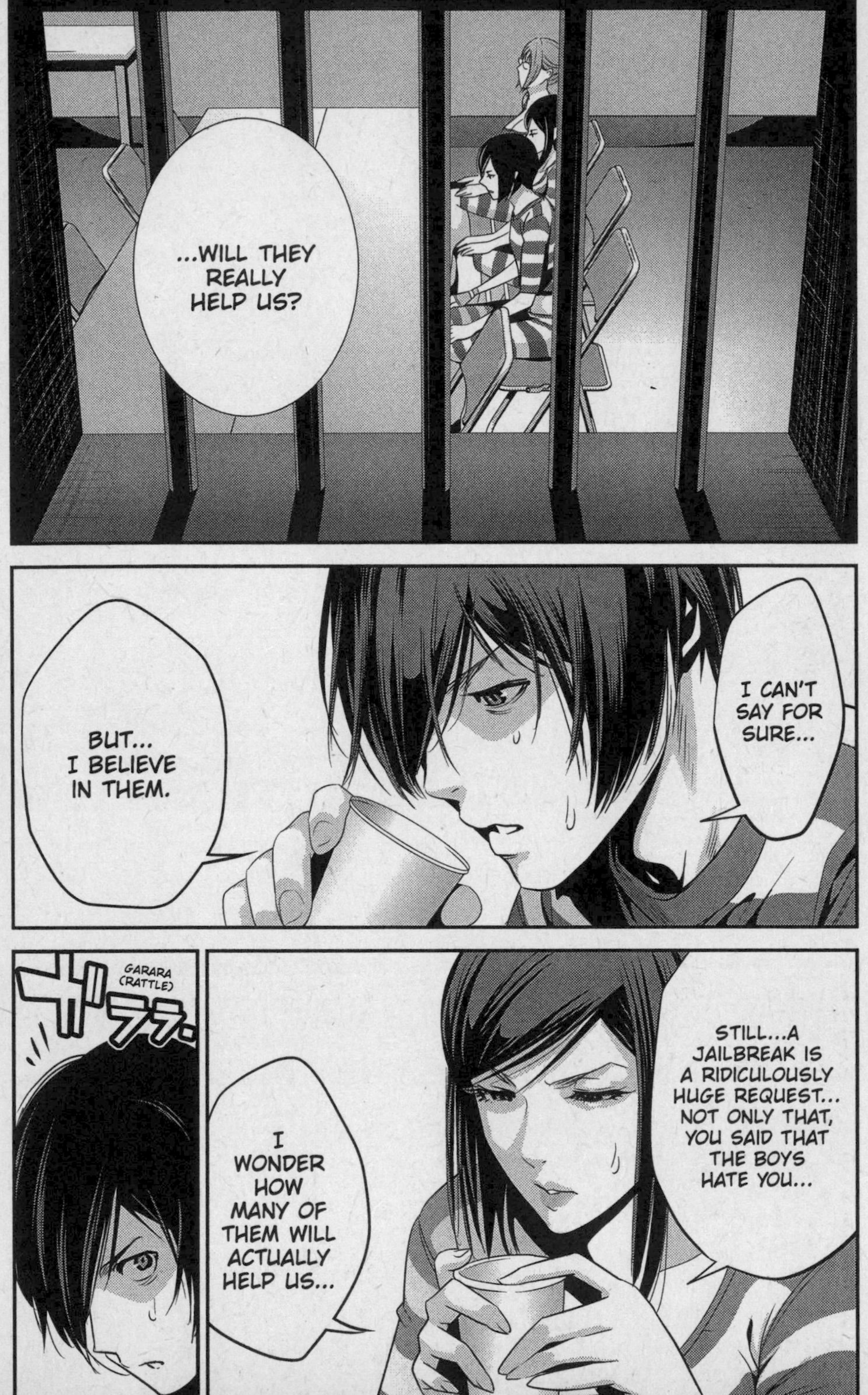
...WILL THEY REALLY HELP US?
I CAN'T SAY FOR SURE...
BUT... I BELIEVE IN THEM.
STILL...A JAILBREAK IS A RIDICULOUSLY HUGE REQUEST... NOT ONLY THAT, YOU SAID THAT THE BOYS HATE YOU...
I WONDER HOW MANY OF THEM WILL ACTUALLY HELP US...
GARARA (RATTLE)

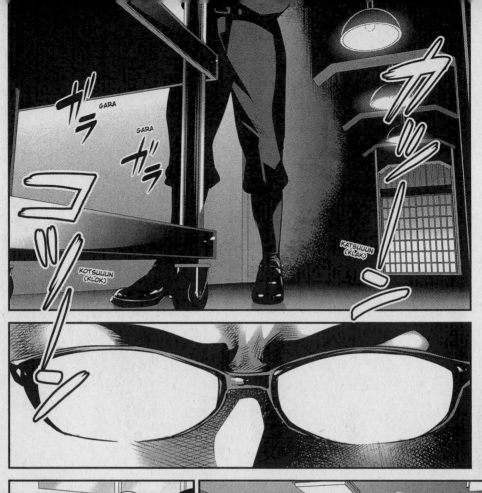

GARA

GARA

KATSUUUN
(KL'AK)

KOTSUUUN
(KL'OK)

MIND
IF I SIT
HERE?

KACHA
CKACHIKO

ZAWA
CCHATTE

ZAWA

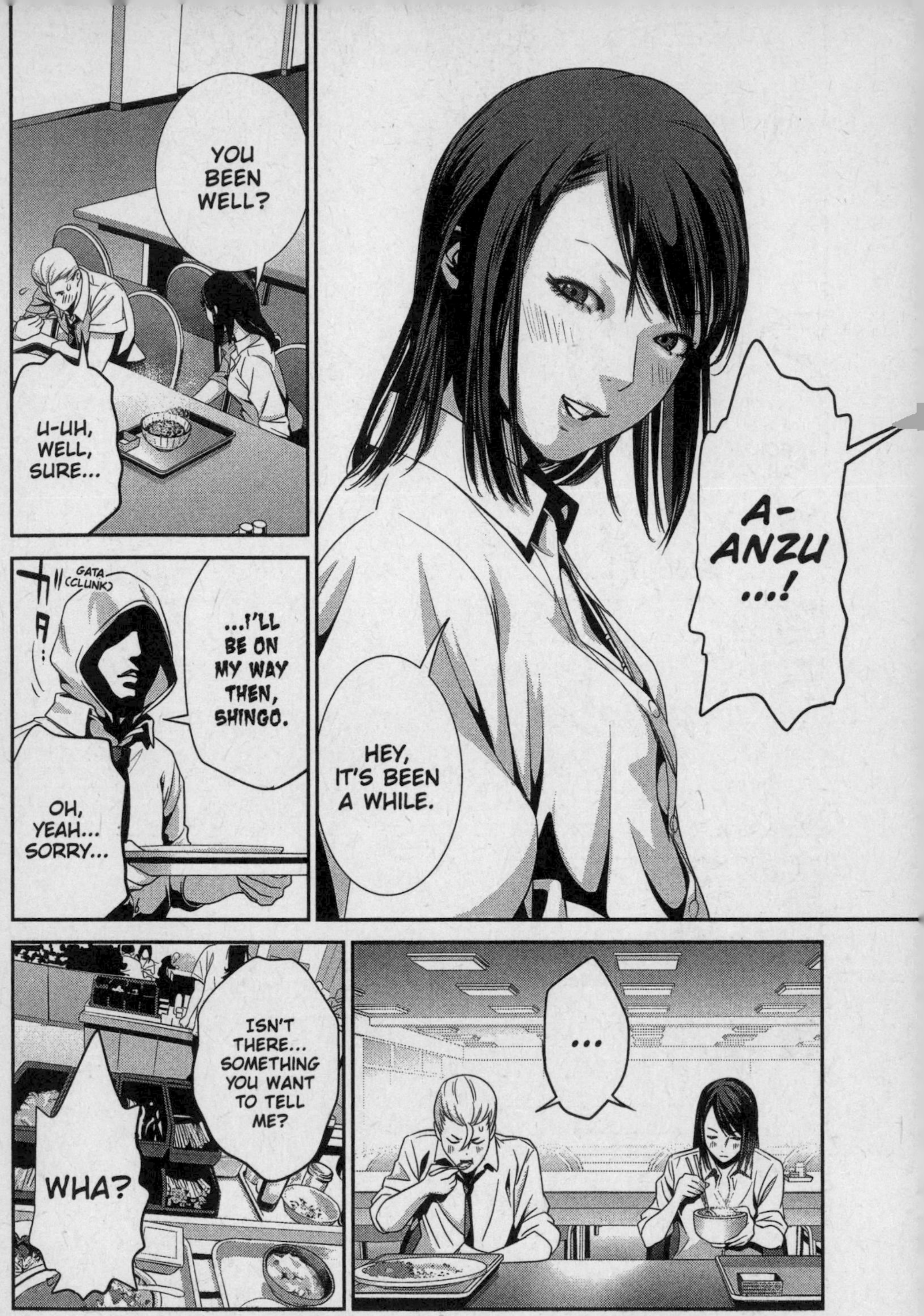
A-ANZU...!
HEY, IT'S BEEN A WHILE.
YOU BEEN WELL?
U-UH, WELL, SURE...
GATA (CLUNK)
...I'LL BE ON MY WAY THEN, SHINGO.
OH, YEAH... SORRY...
...
ISN'T THERE... SOMETHING YOU WANT TO TELL ME?
WHA?

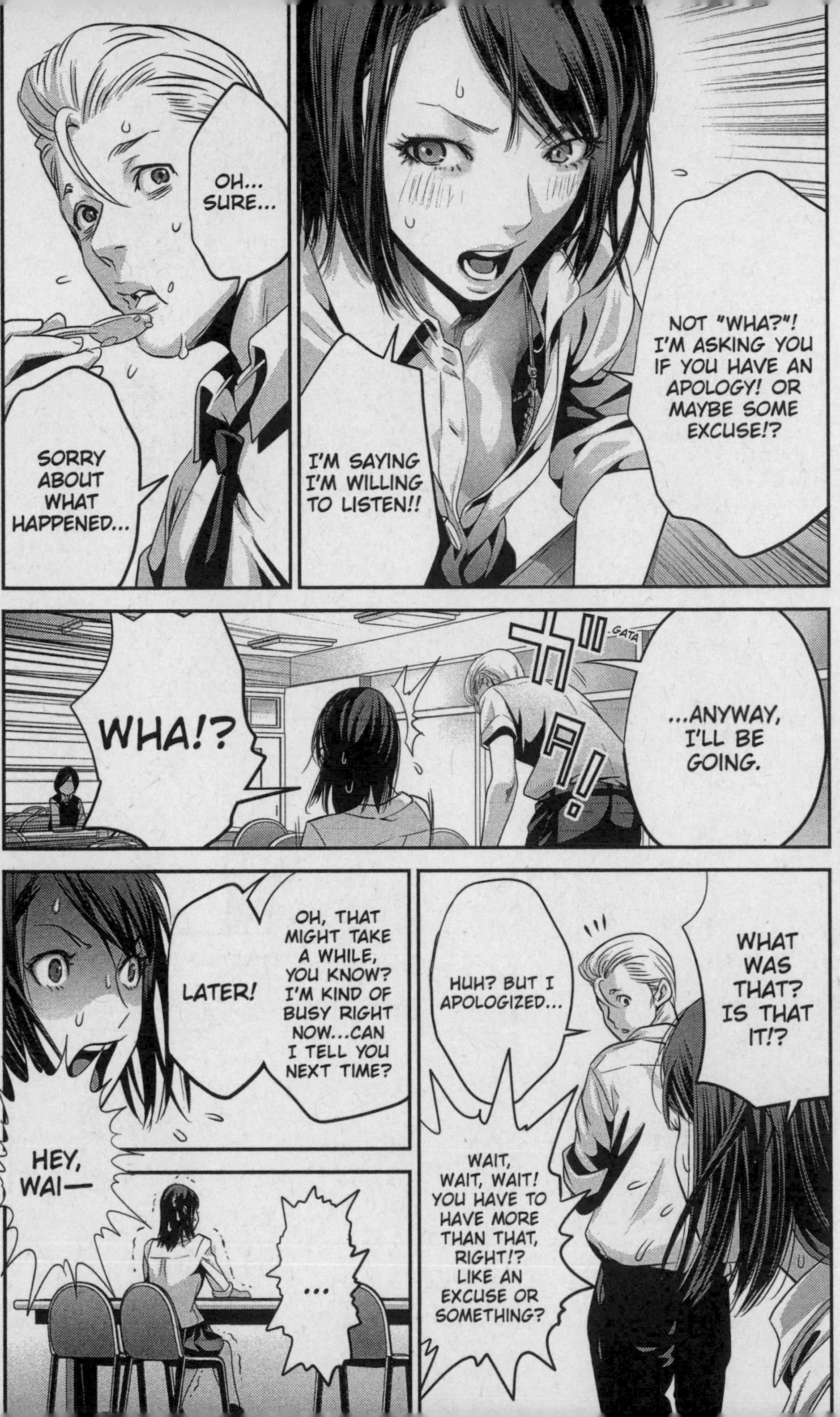
NOT "WHA?"! I'M ASKING YOU IF YOU HAVE AN APOLOGY! OR MAYBE SOME EXCUSE!?
I'M SAYING I'M WILLING TO LISTEN!!
OH... SURE...
SORRY ABOUT WHAT HAPPENED...
...ANYWAY, I'LL BE GOING.
GATA
WHA!?
WHAT WAS THAT? IS THAT IT!?
HUH? BUT I APOLOGIZED...
WAIT, WAIT, WAIT! YOU HAVE TO HAVE MORE THAN THAT, RIGHT!? LIKE AN EXCUSE OR SOMETHING?
OH, THAT MIGHT TAKE A WHILE, YOU KNOW? I'M KIND OF BUSY RIGHT NOW...CAN I TELL YOU NEXT TIME?
LATER!
HEY, WAI—
...

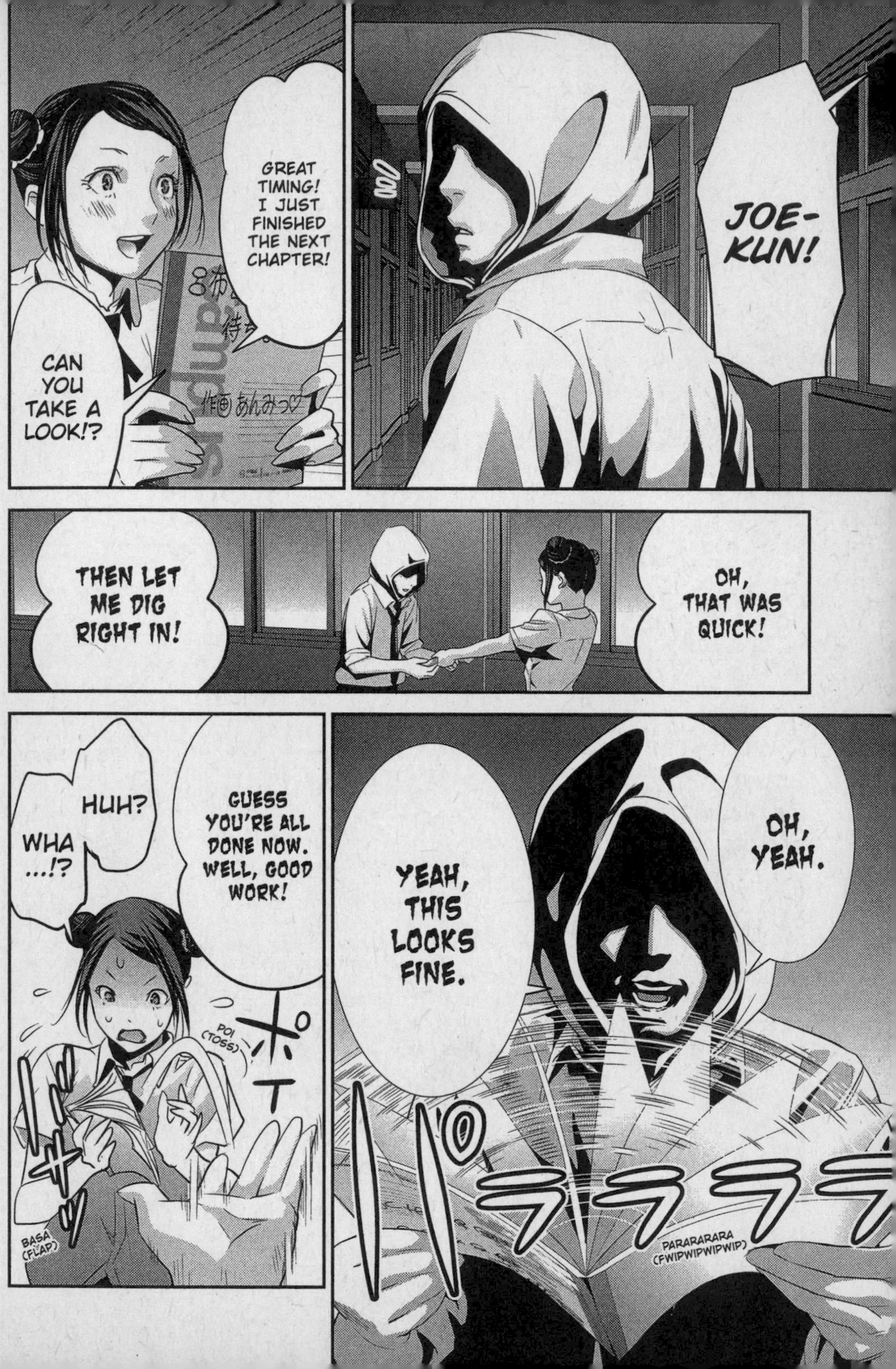

JOE-KUN!
GREAT TIMING! I JUST FINISHED THE NEXT CHAPTER!
作画 あんみつ♡
CAN YOU TAKE A LOOK!?
OH, THAT WAS QUICK!
THEN LET ME DIG RIGHT IN!
OH, YEAH.
YEAH, THIS LOOKS FINE.
PARARARARA (FWIPWIPWIPWIP)
GUESS YOU'RE ALL DONE NOW. WELL, GOOD WORK!
POI (TOSS)
HUH?
WHA ...!?
BASA (FLAP)

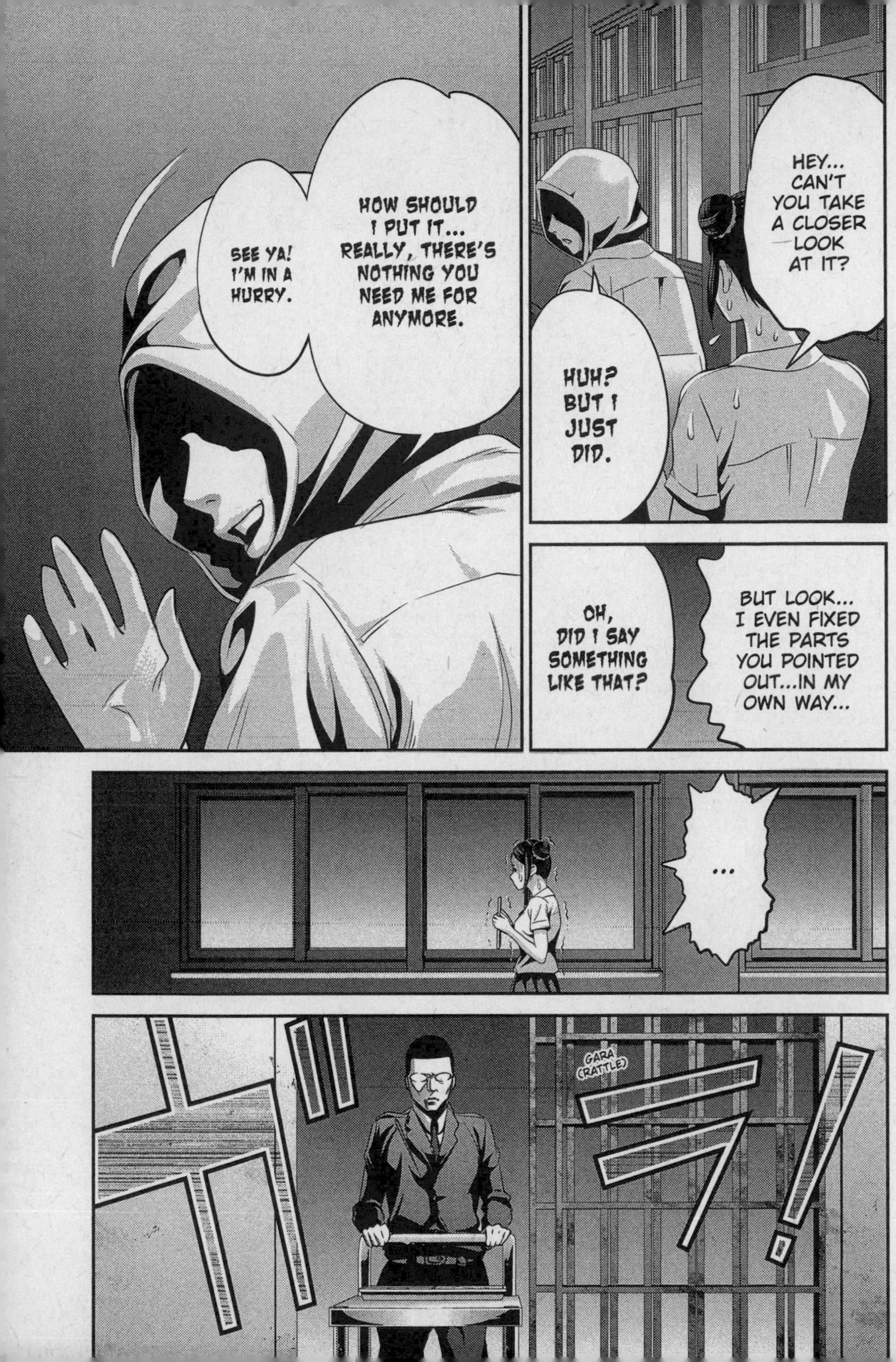
HEY... CAN'T YOU TAKE A CLOSER LOOK AT IT?
HUH? BUT I JUST DID.
BUT LOOK... I EVEN FIXED THE PARTS YOU POINTED OUT...IN MY OWN WAY...
OH, DID I SAY SOMETHING LIKE THAT?
HOW SHOULD I PUT IT... REALLY, THERE'S NOTHING YOU NEED ME FOR ANYMORE.
SEE YA! I'M IN A HURRY.
...
GARA (RATTLE)

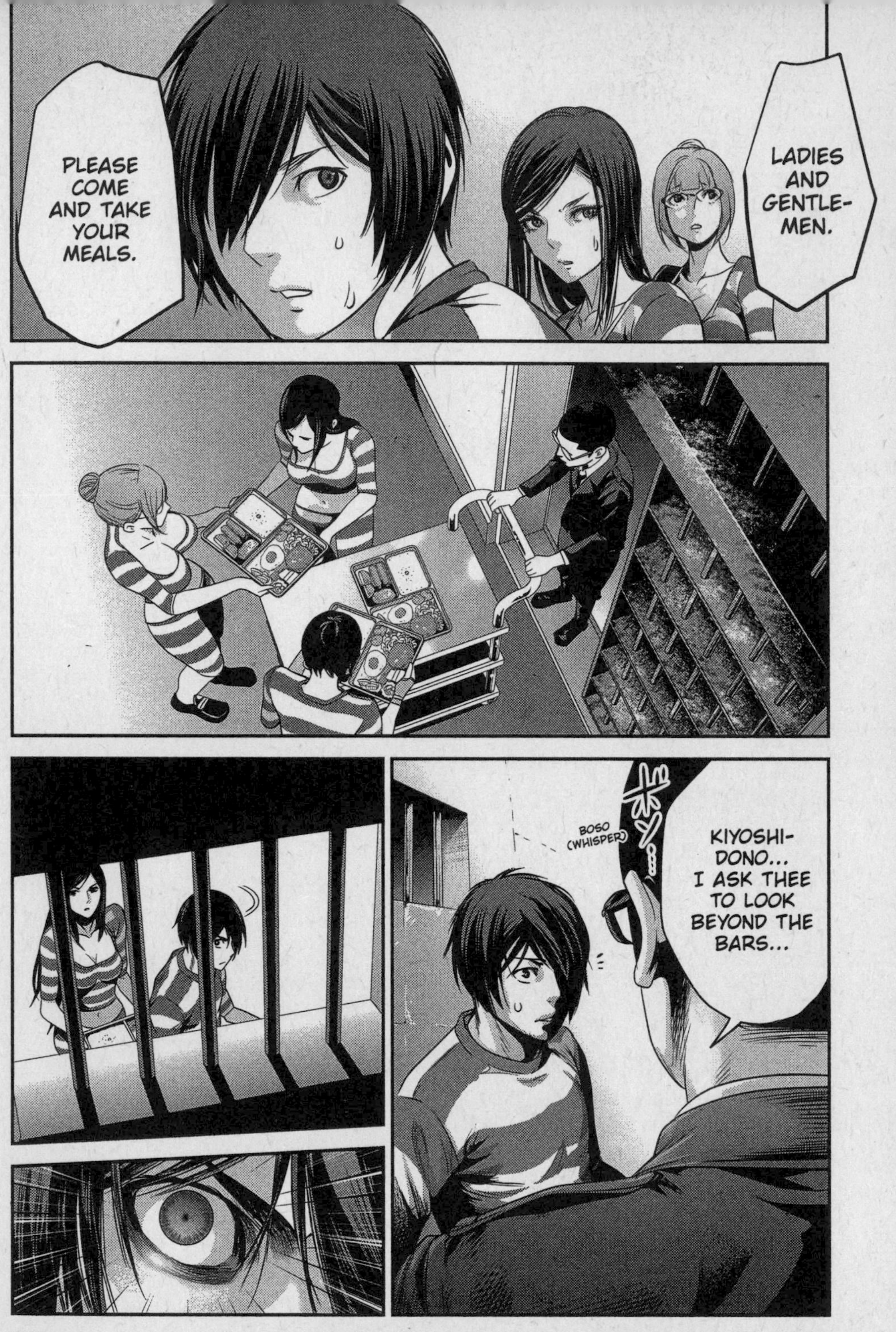
LADIES AND GENTLE-MEN.
PLEASE COME AND TAKE YOUR MEALS.
BOSO (WHISPER)
KIYOSHI-DONO... I ASK THEE TO LOOK BEYOND THE BARS...

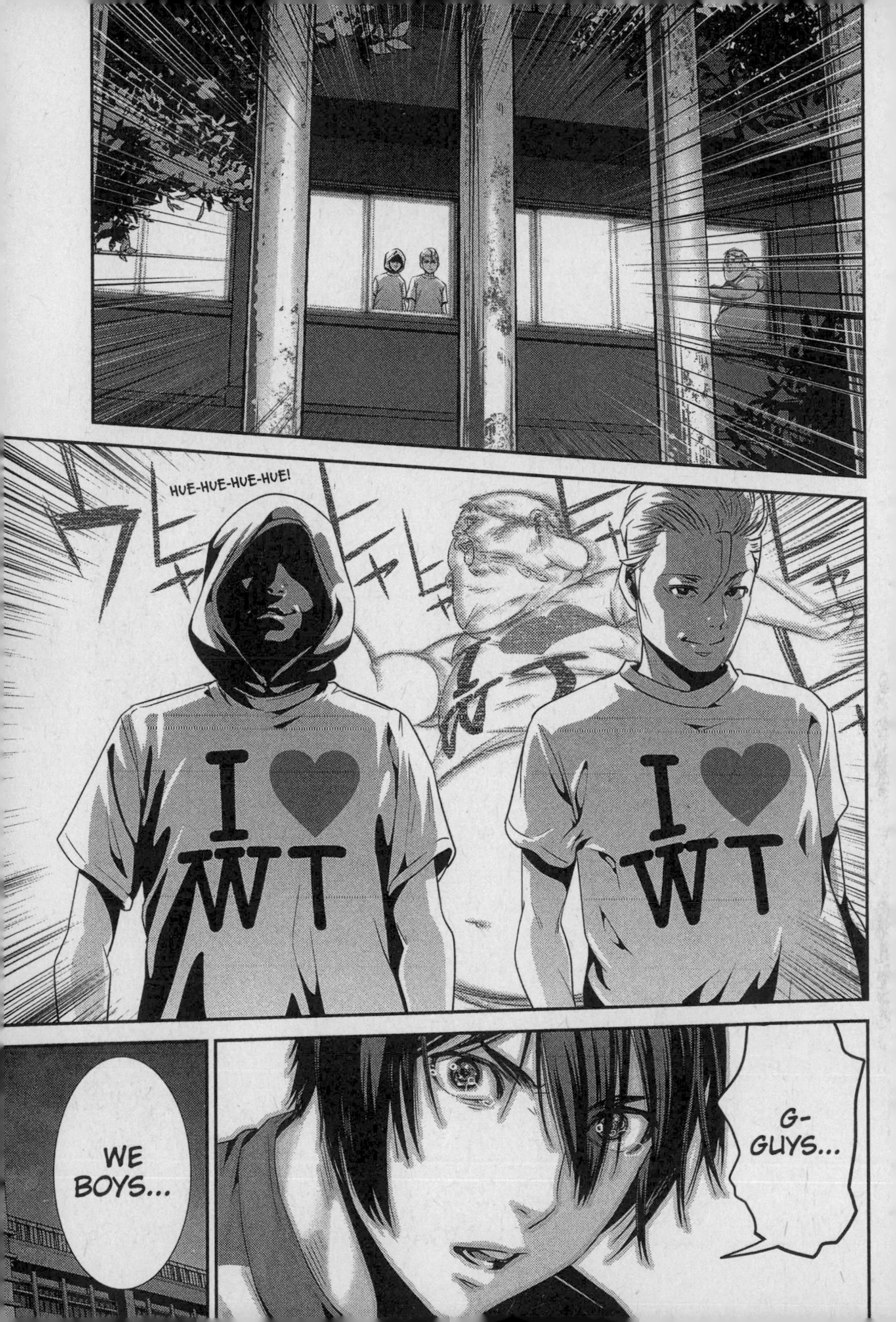
HUE-HUE-HUE-HUE!
I ♥ WT
I ♥ WT
G-GUYS...
WE BOYS...

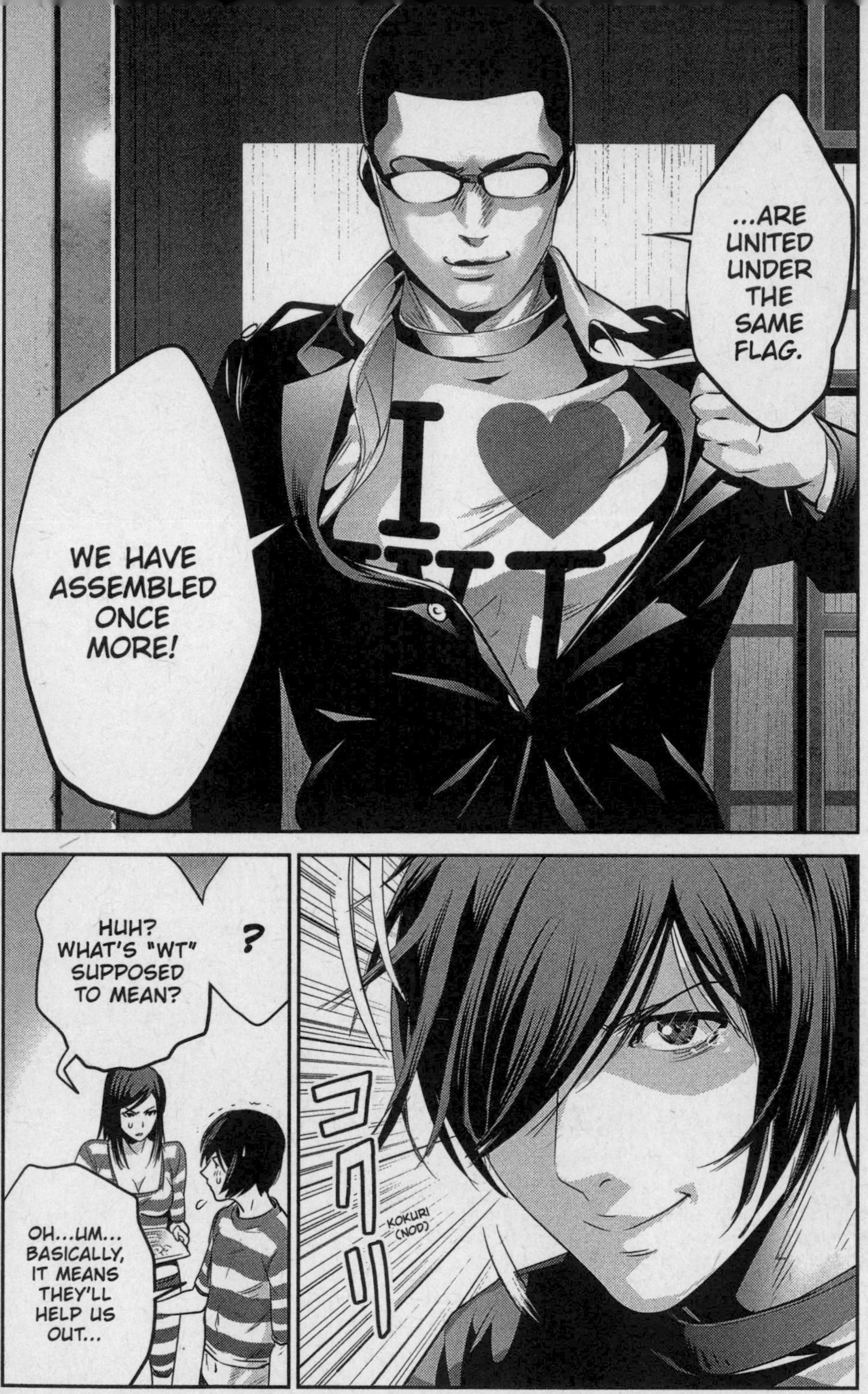
...ARE UNITED UNDER THE SAME FLAG.
WE HAVE ASSEMBLED ONCE MORE!
KOKURI (NOD)
HUH? WHAT'S "WT" SUPPOSED TO MEAN?
?
OH...UM... BASICALLY, IT MEANS THEY'LL HELP US OUT...

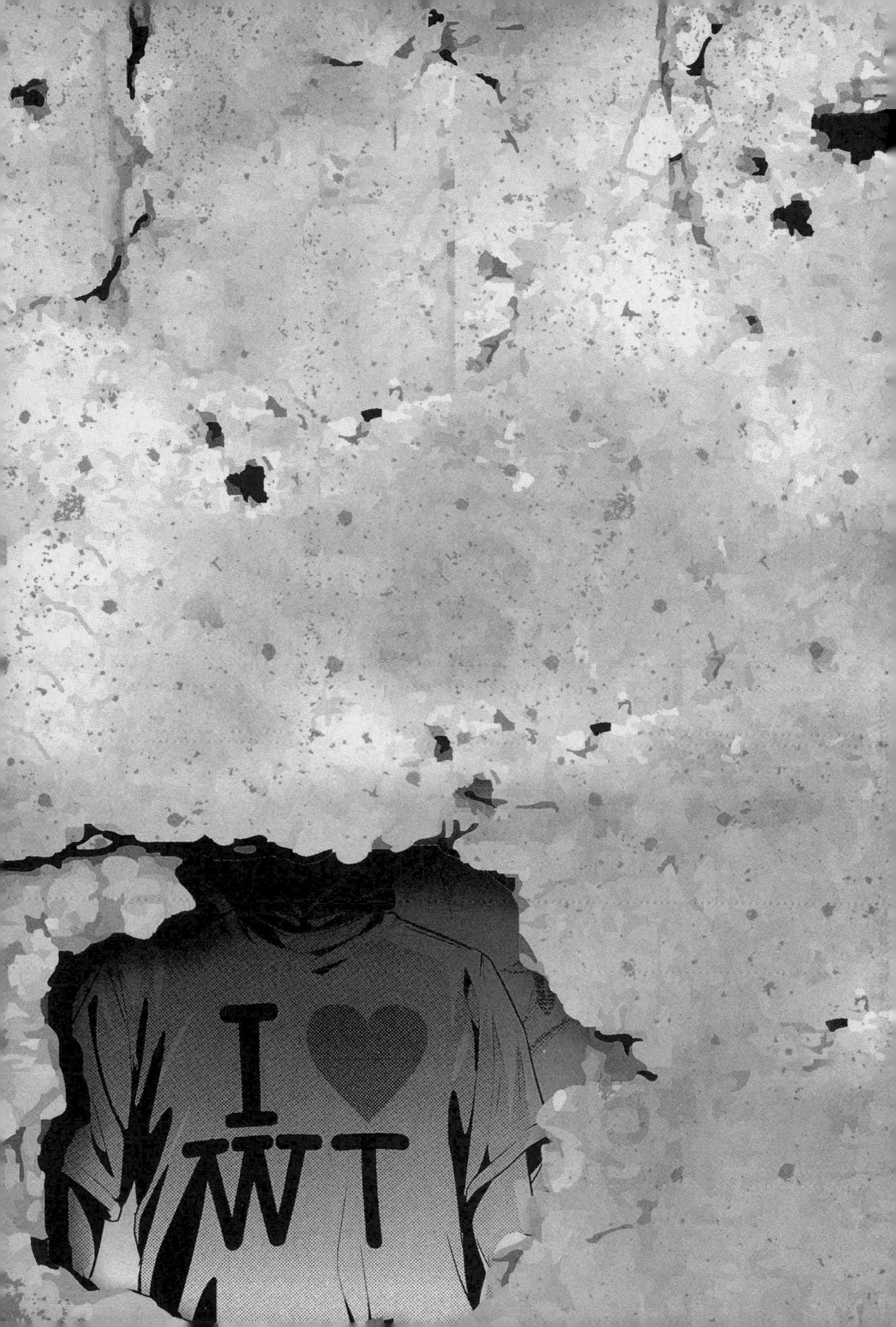
I ♥ WT

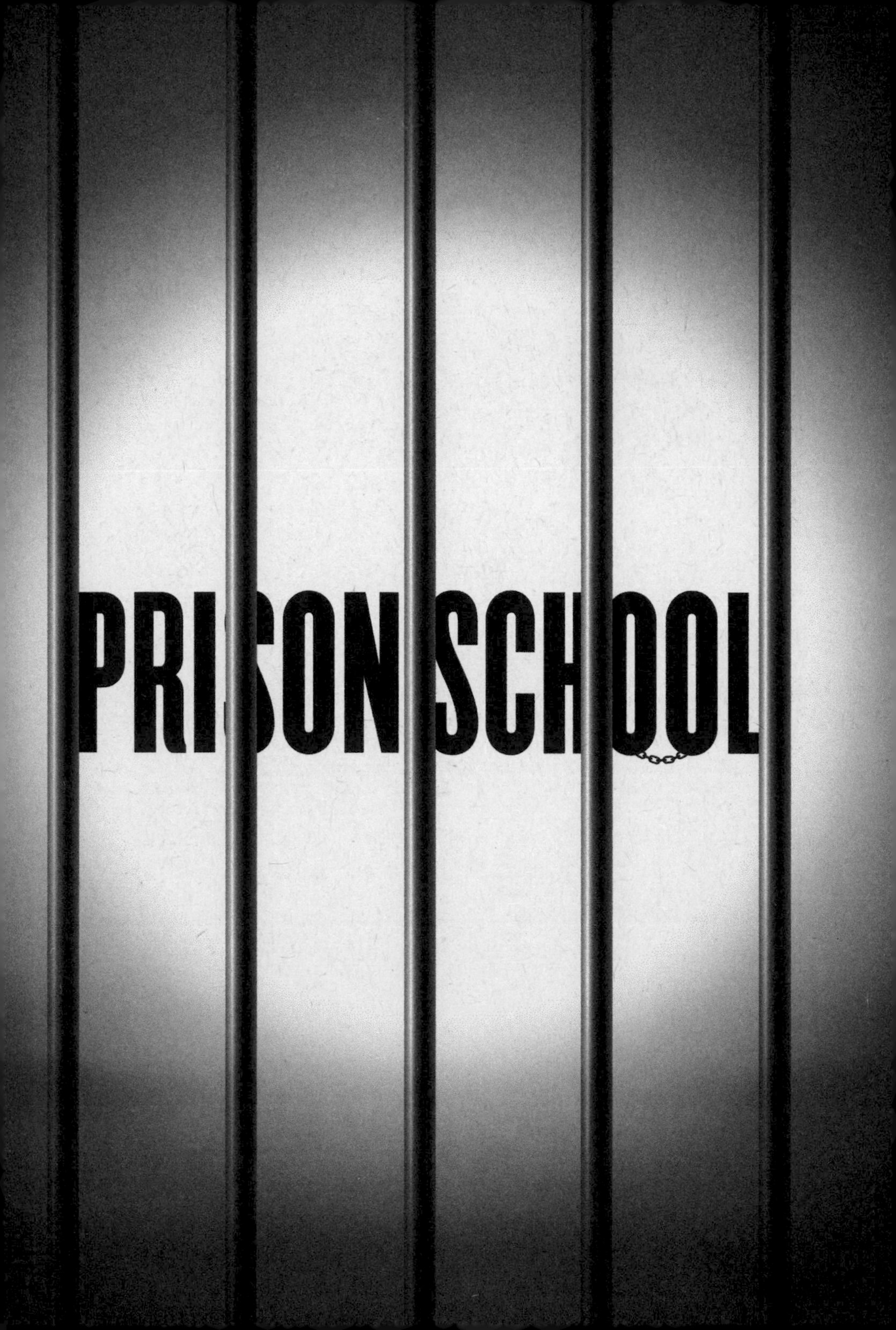
PRISON SCHOOL

CHAPTER 128: CATCH ME IF YOU CAN

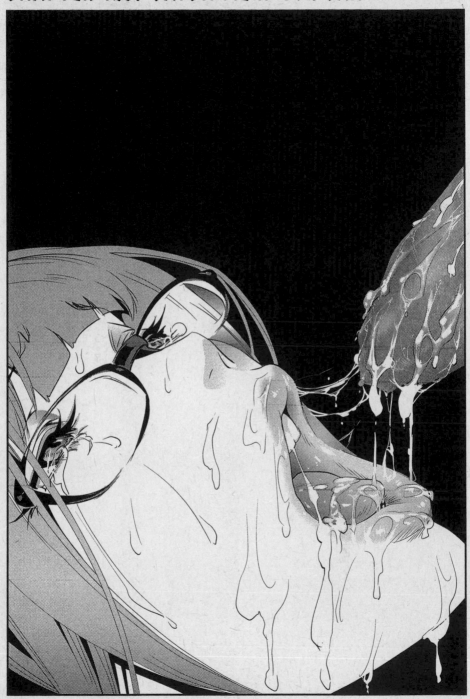

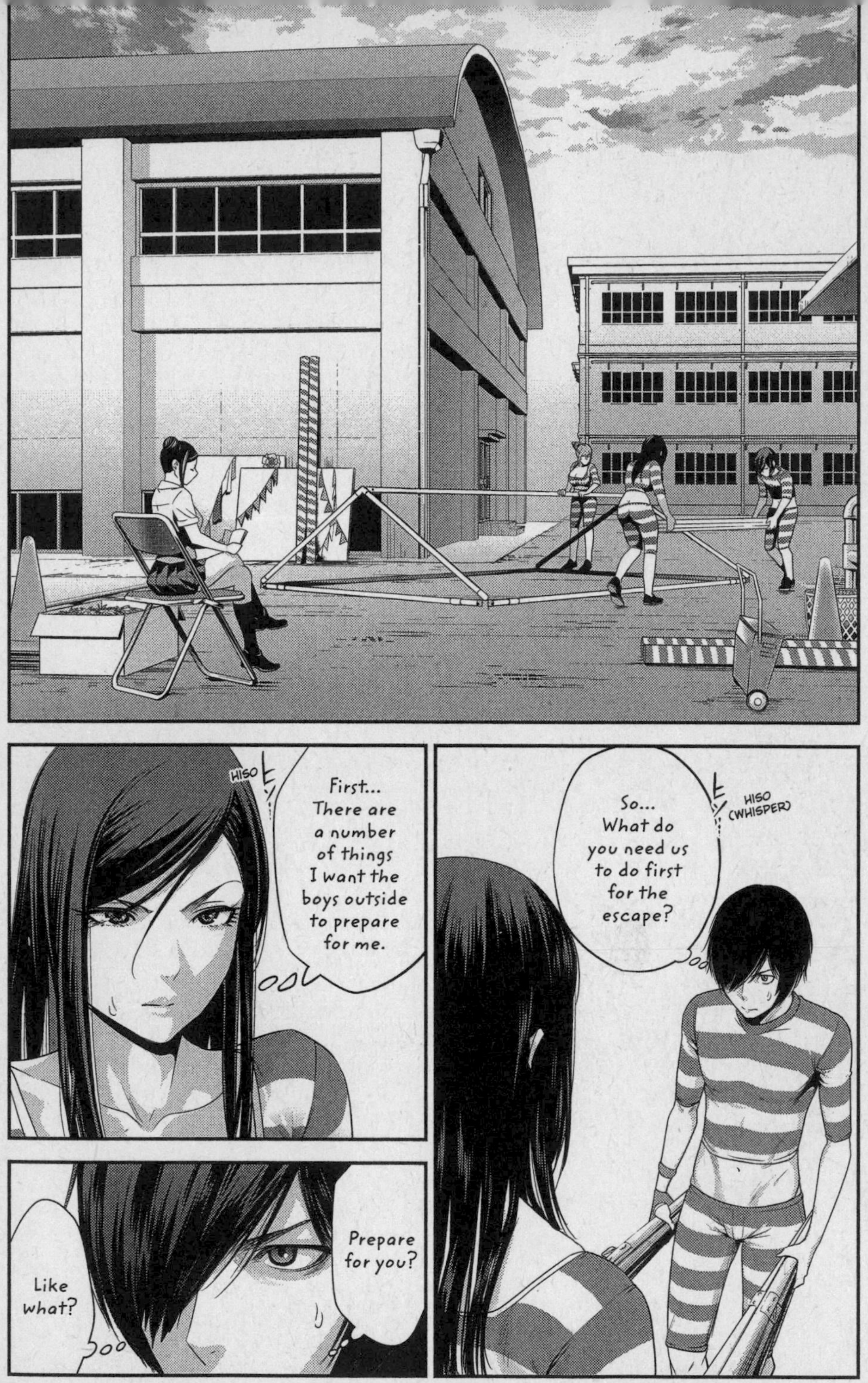
HISO (WHISPER)
So... What do you need us to do first for the escape?
HISO
First... There are a number of things I want the boys outside to prepare for me.
Prepare for you?
Like what?

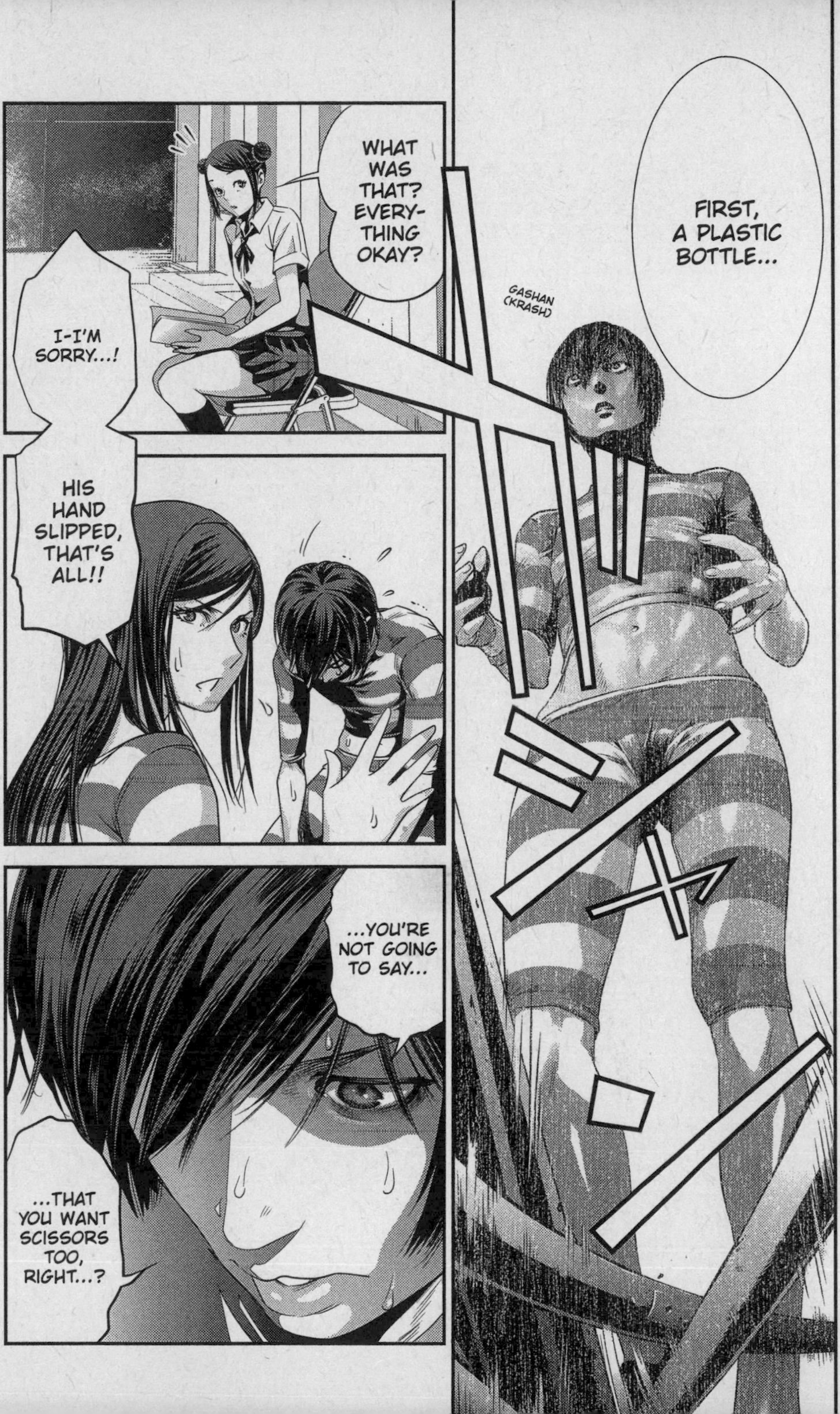
FIRST, A PLASTIC BOTTLE...
GASHAN (KRASH)
WHAT WAS THAT? EVERY-THING OKAY?
I-I'M SORRY...!
HIS HAND SLIPPED, THAT'S ALL!!
...YOU'RE NOT GOING TO SAY...
...THAT YOU WANT SCISSORS TOO, RIGHT...?

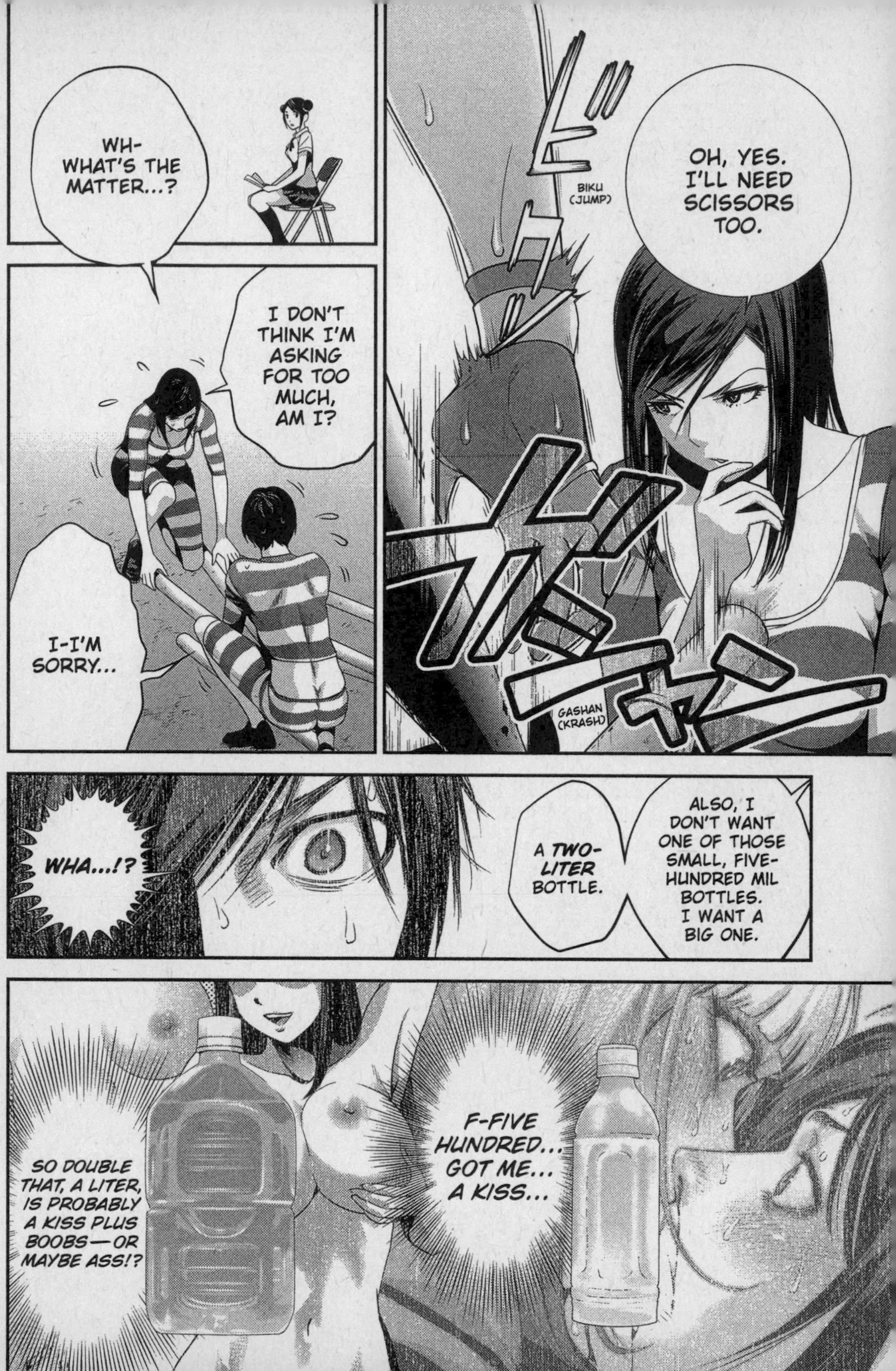
OH, YES. I'LL NEED SCISSORS TOO.
BIKU (JUMP)
GASHAN (KRASH)
WH- WHAT'S THE MATTER...?
I DON'T THINK I'M ASKING FOR TOO MUCH, AM I?
I-I'M SORRY...
ALSO, I DON'T WANT ONE OF THOSE SMALL, FIVE-HUNDRED MIL BOTTLES. I WANT A BIG ONE.
A TWO-LITER BOTTLE.
WHA...!?
F-FIVE HUNDRED... GOT ME... A KISS...
SO DOUBLE THAT, A LITER, IS PROBABLY A KISS PLUS BOOBS—OR MAYBE ASS!?

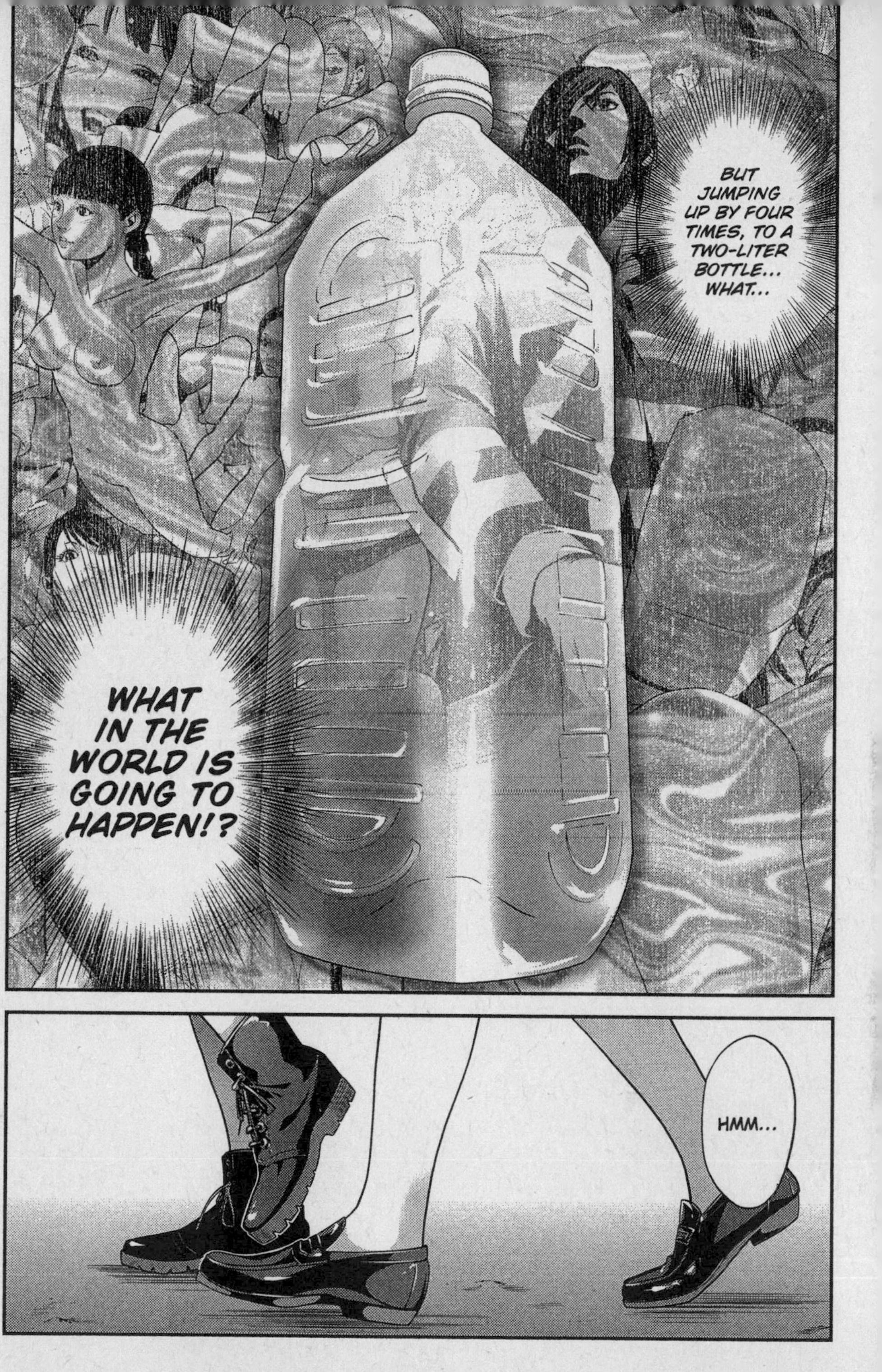
BUT JUMPING UP BY FOUR TIMES, TO A TWO-LITER BOTTLE... WHAT...
WHAT IN THE WORLD IS GOING TO HAPPEN!?
HMM...

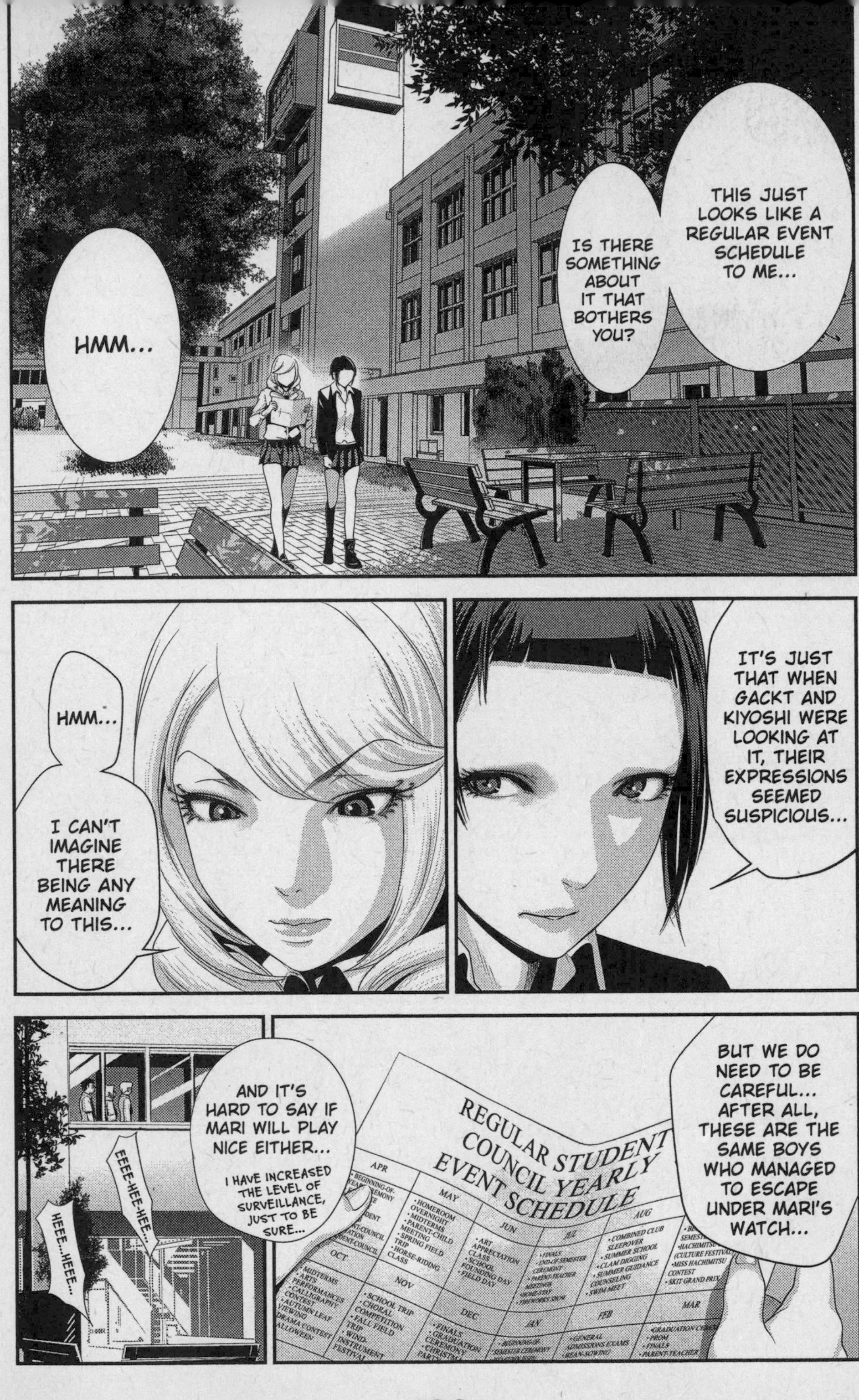
THIS JUST LOOKS LIKE A REGULAR EVENT SCHEDULE TO ME...
IS THERE SOMETHING ABOUT IT THAT BOTHERS YOU?
HMM...
IT'S JUST THAT WHEN GACKT AND KIYOSHI WERE LOOKING AT IT, THEIR EXPRESSIONS SEEMED SUSPICIOUS...
HMM...
I CAN'T IMAGINE THERE BEING ANY MEANING TO THIS...
BUT WE DO NEED TO BE CAREFUL... AFTER ALL, THESE ARE THE SAME BOYS WHO MANAGED TO ESCAPE UNDER MARI'S WATCH...
REGULAR STUDENT COUNCIL YEARLY EVENT SCHEDULE
AND IT'S HARD TO SAY IF MARI WILL PLAY NICE EITHER...
I HAVE INCREASED THE LEVEL OF SURVEILLANCE, JUST TO BE SURE...
EEEE-HEE-HEE...
HEEE...HEEE...

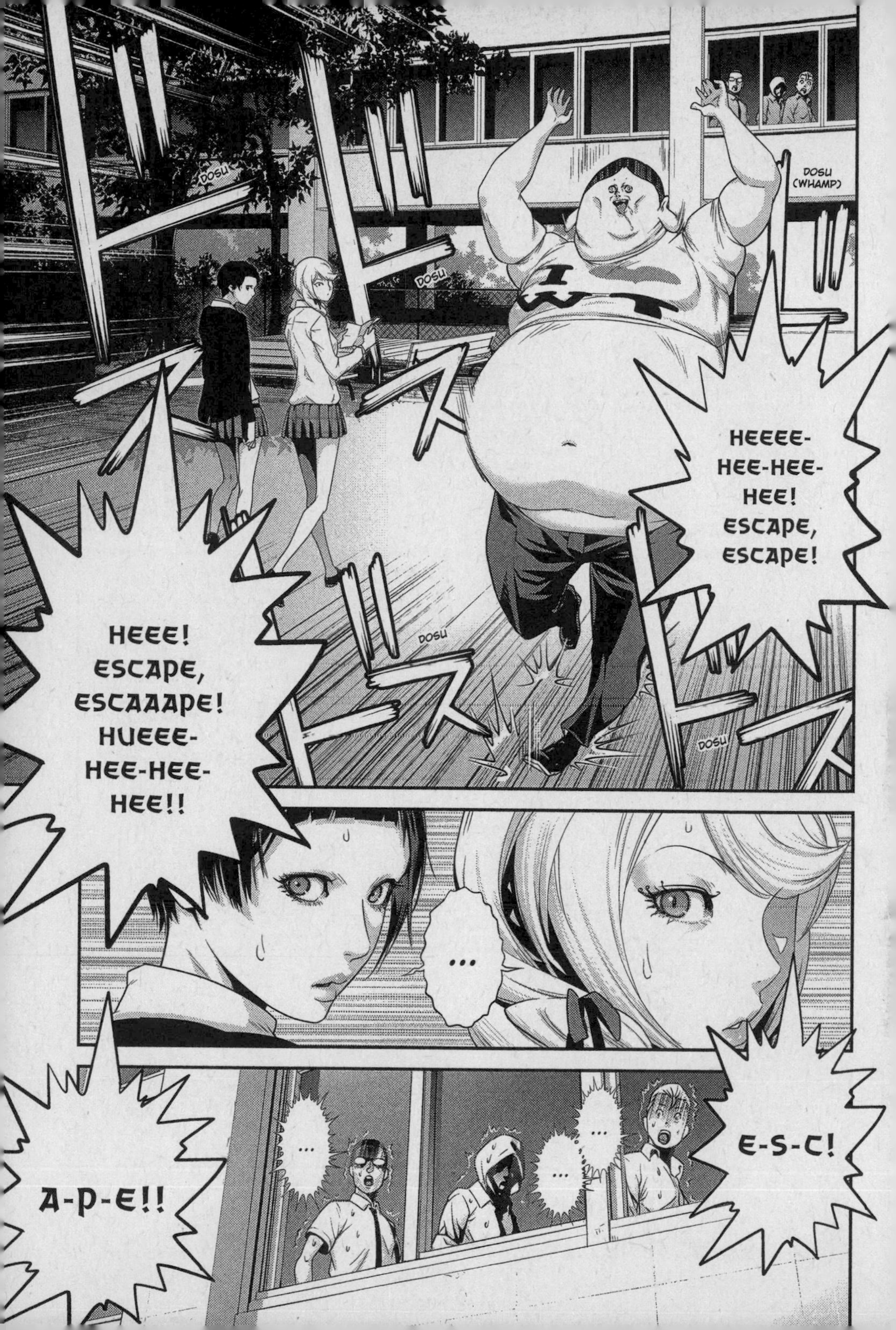

DOSU (WHAMP)
DOSU
DOSU
HEEEE-HEE-HEE-HEE! ESCAPE, ESCAPE!
HEEE! ESCAPE, ESCAAAPE! HUEEE-HEE-HEE-HEE!!
DOSU
DOSU
...
E-S-C!
...
...
...
A-P-E!!

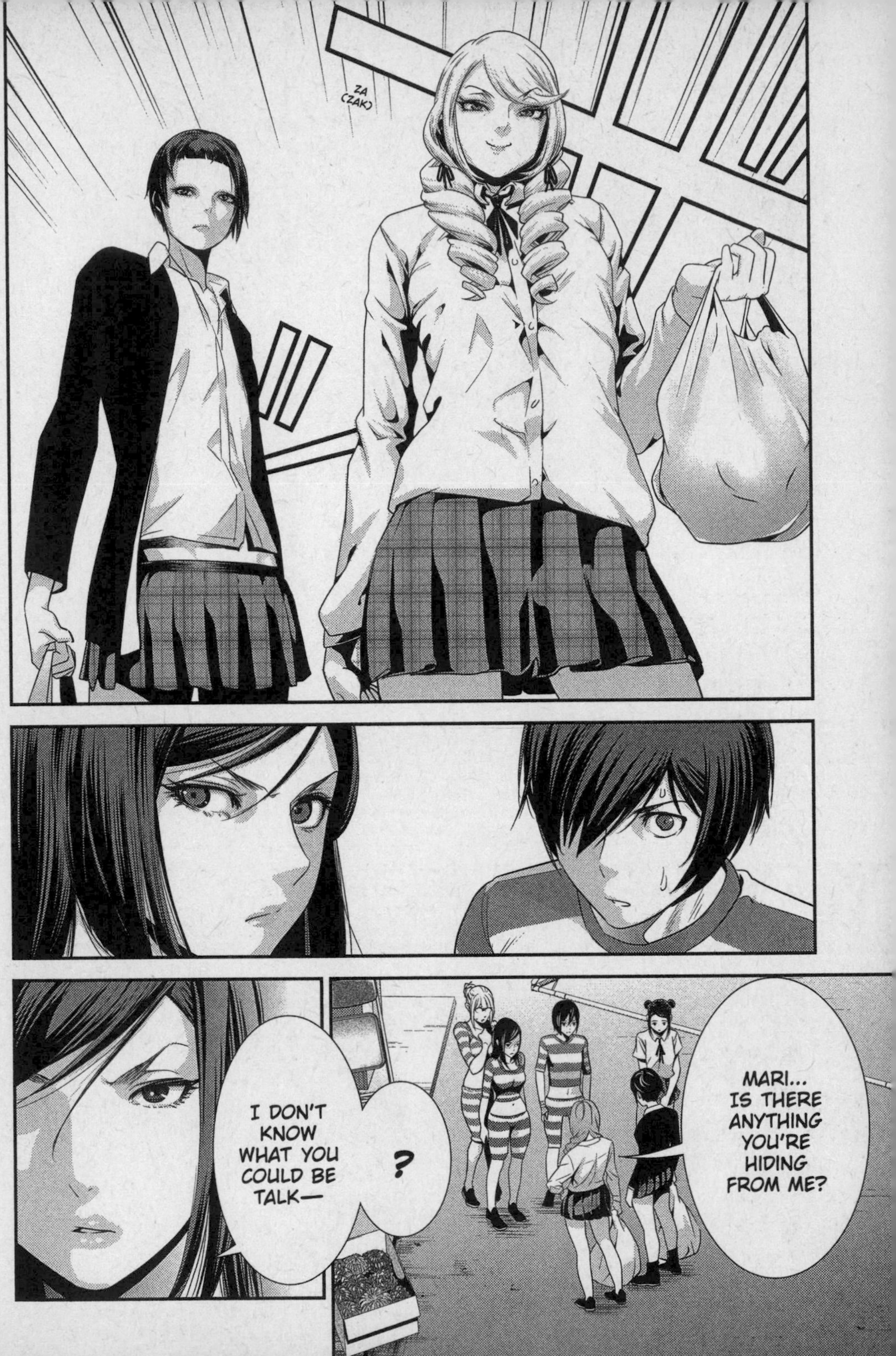
ZA (ZAK)
MARI... IS THERE ANYTHING YOU'RE HIDING FROM ME?
?
I DON'T KNOW WHAT YOU COULD BE TALK—

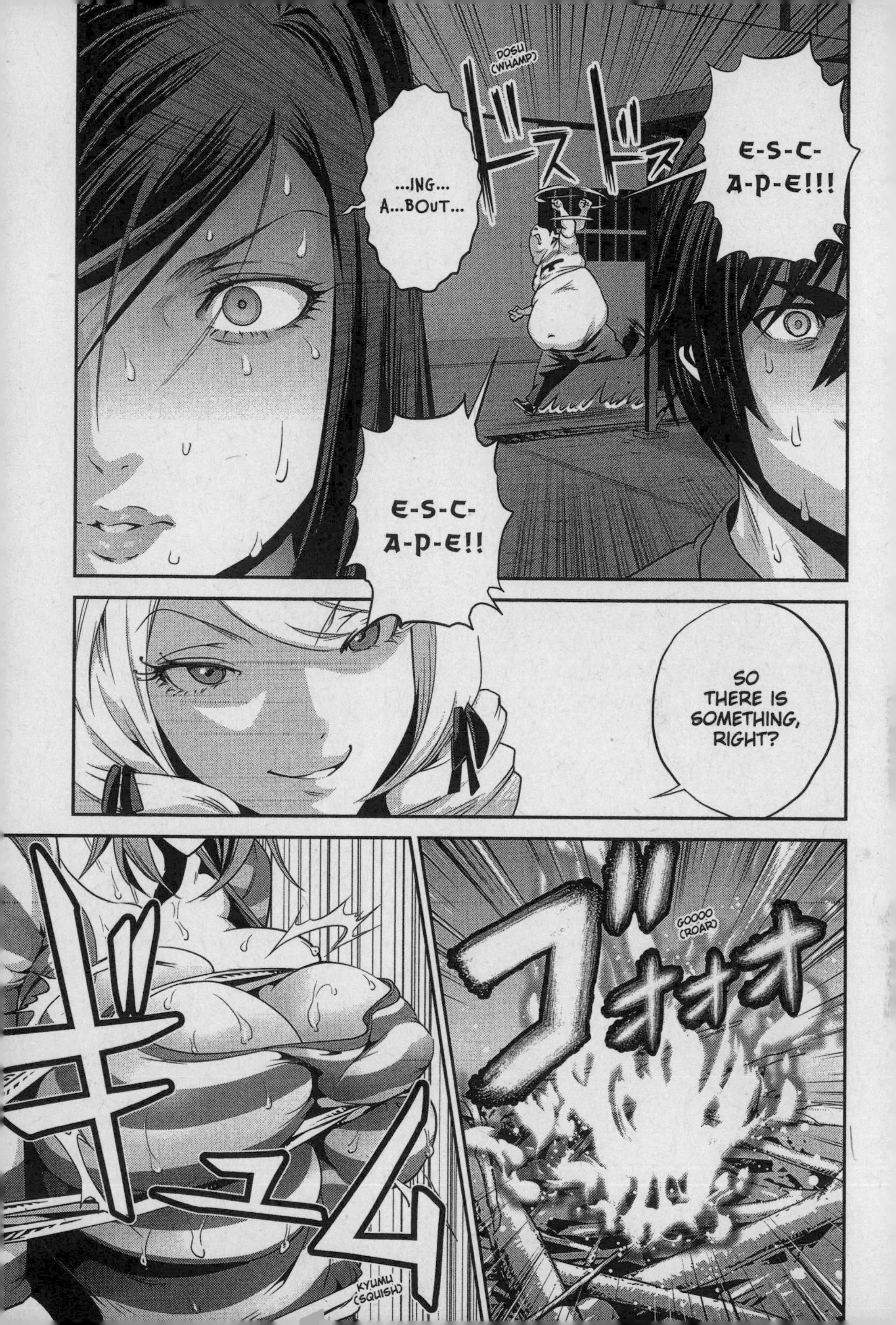
E-S-C-A-P-E!!!
ドスドス
DOSU (WHAMP)
...ING... A...BOUT...
E-S-C-A-P-E!!
SO THERE IS SOMETHING, RIGHT?
ゴオオオ
GOOOO (ROAR)
ギュム
KYUMU (SQUISH)

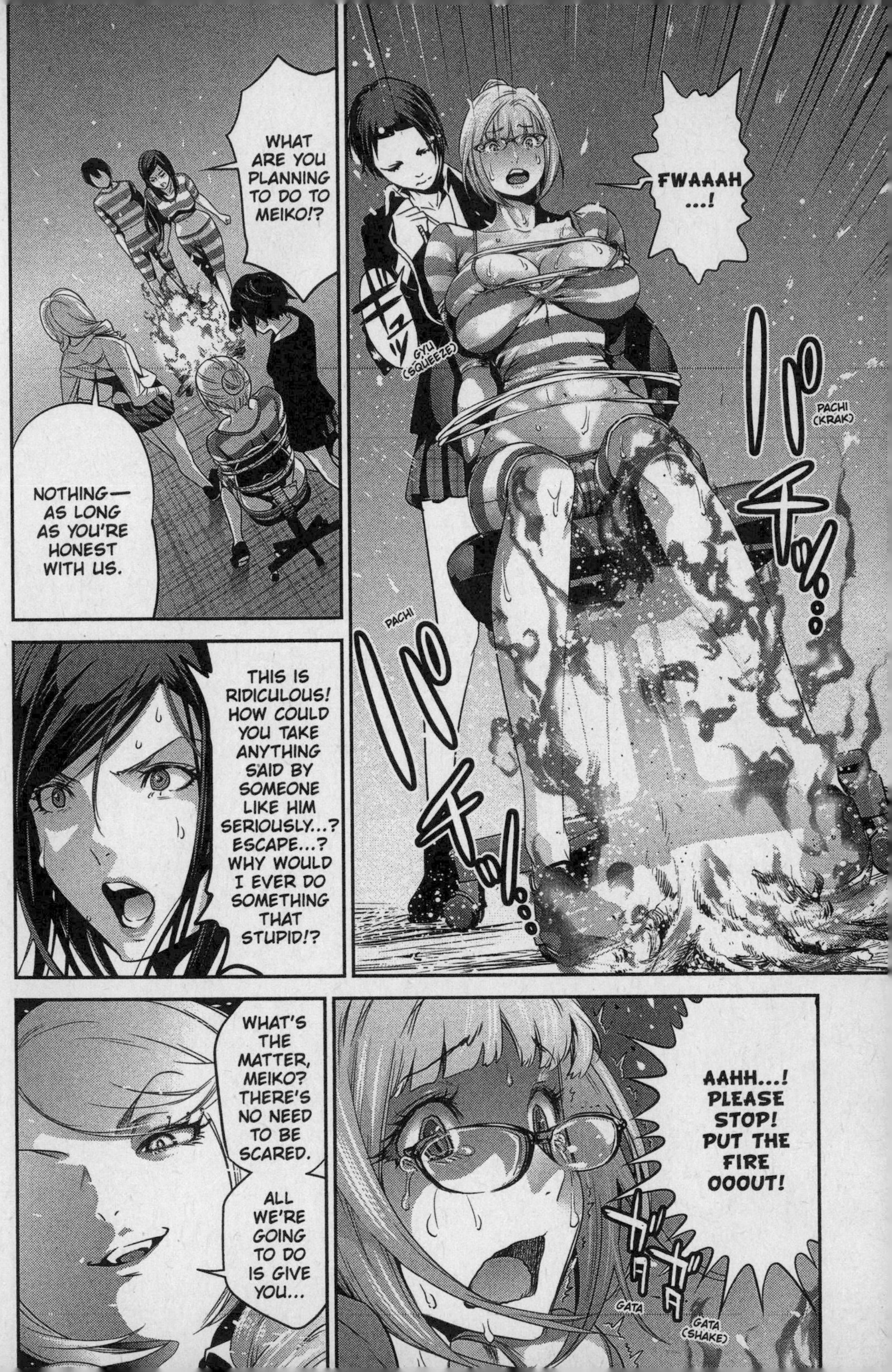

FWAAAH ...!
GYU (SQUEEZE)
PACHI (KRAK)
PACHI
WHAT ARE YOU PLANNING TO DO TO MEIKO!?
NOTHING— AS LONG AS YOU'RE HONEST WITH US.
THIS IS RIDICULOUS! HOW COULD YOU TAKE ANYTHING SAID BY SOMEONE LIKE HIM SERIOUSLY...? ESCAPE...? WHY WOULD I EVER DO SOMETHING THAT STUPID!?
AAHH...! PLEASE STOP! PUT THE FIRE OOOUT!
GATA
GATA (SHAKE)
WHAT'S THE MATTER, MEIKO? THERE'S NO NEED TO BE SCARED.
ALL WE'RE GOING TO DO IS GIVE YOU...

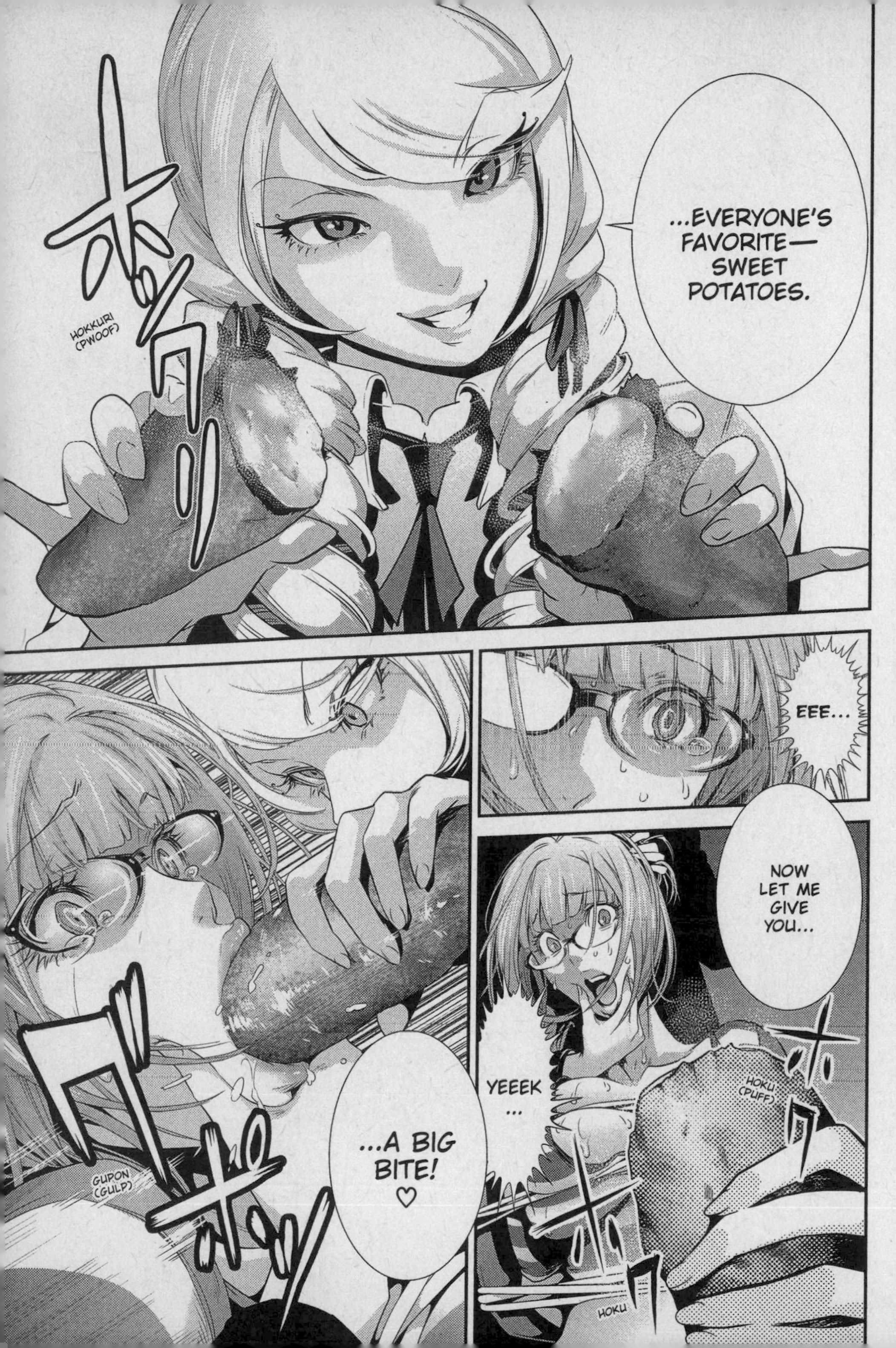

...EVERYONE'S FAVORITE—SWEET POTATOES.
HOKKURI (PWOOF)
EEE...
NOW LET ME GIVE YOU...
YEEEK ...
HOKU (PUFF)
HOKU
...A BIG BITE! ♡
GUPON (GULP)

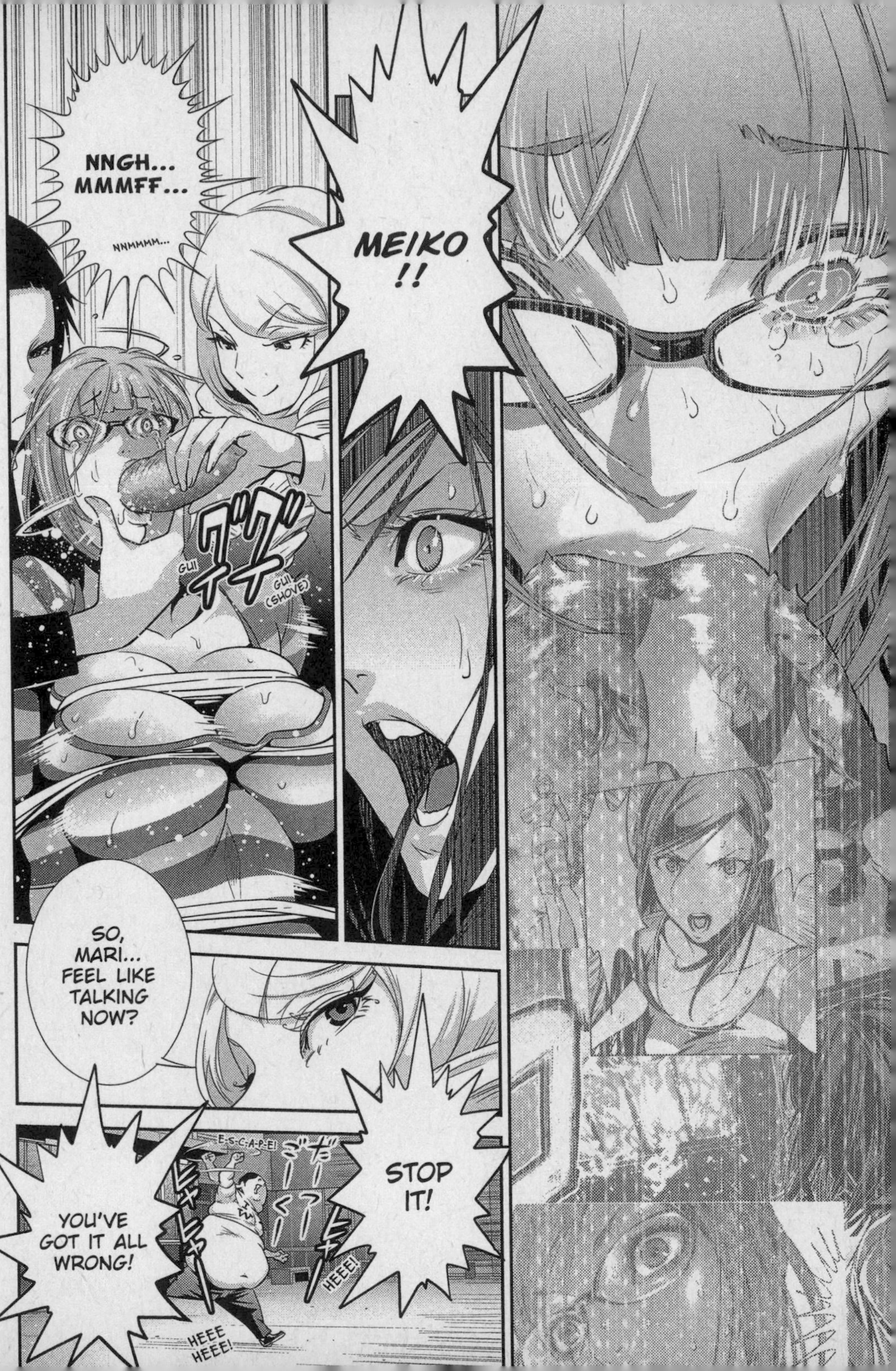

MEIKO !!
NNGH... MMMFF...
NNMMMM...
GUI
GUI (SHOVE)
SO, MARI... FEEL LIKE TALKING NOW?
STOP IT!
E-S-C-A-P-E!
YOU'VE GOT IT ALL WRONG!
HEEE!
HEEE HEEE!

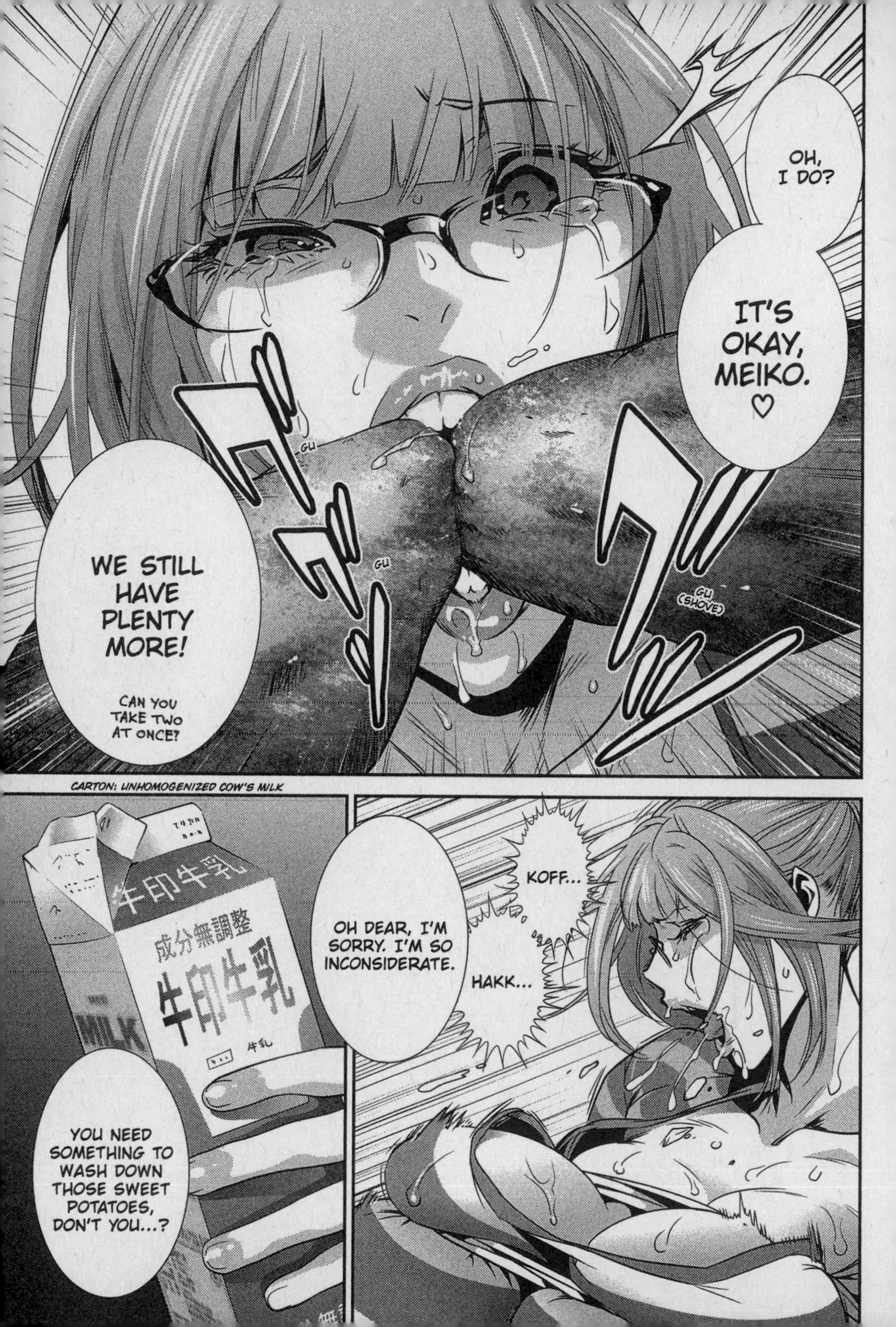
OH, I DO?
IT'S OKAY, MEIKO. ♡
GU
GU
GU (SHOVE)
WE STILL HAVE PLENTY MORE!
CAN YOU TAKE TWO AT ONCE?
CARTON: UNHOMOGENIZED COW'S MILK
KOFF...
HAKK...
OH DEAR, I'M SORRY. I'M SO INCONSIDERATE.
牛印牛乳
成分無調整
牛印牛乳
MILK
牛乳
YOU NEED SOMETHING TO WASH DOWN THOSE SWEET POTATOES, DON'T YOU...?

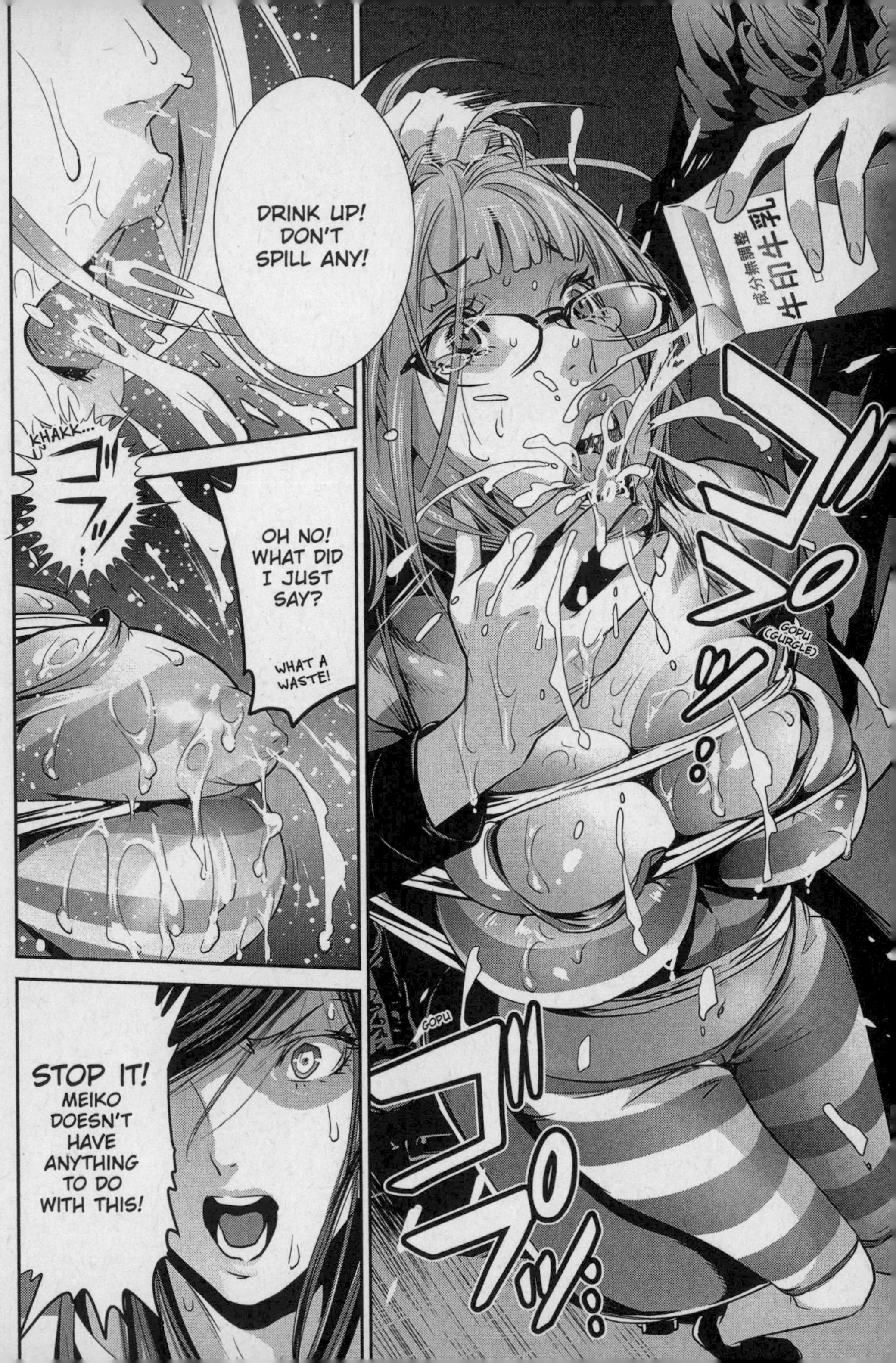

DRINK UP! DON'T SPILL ANY!
牛印牛乳
成分無調整
GOPU (GURGLE)
GOPU
KHAKK...
OH NO! WHAT DID I JUST SAY?
WHAT A WASTE!
STOP IT! MEIKO DOESN'T HAVE ANYTHING TO DO WITH THIS!

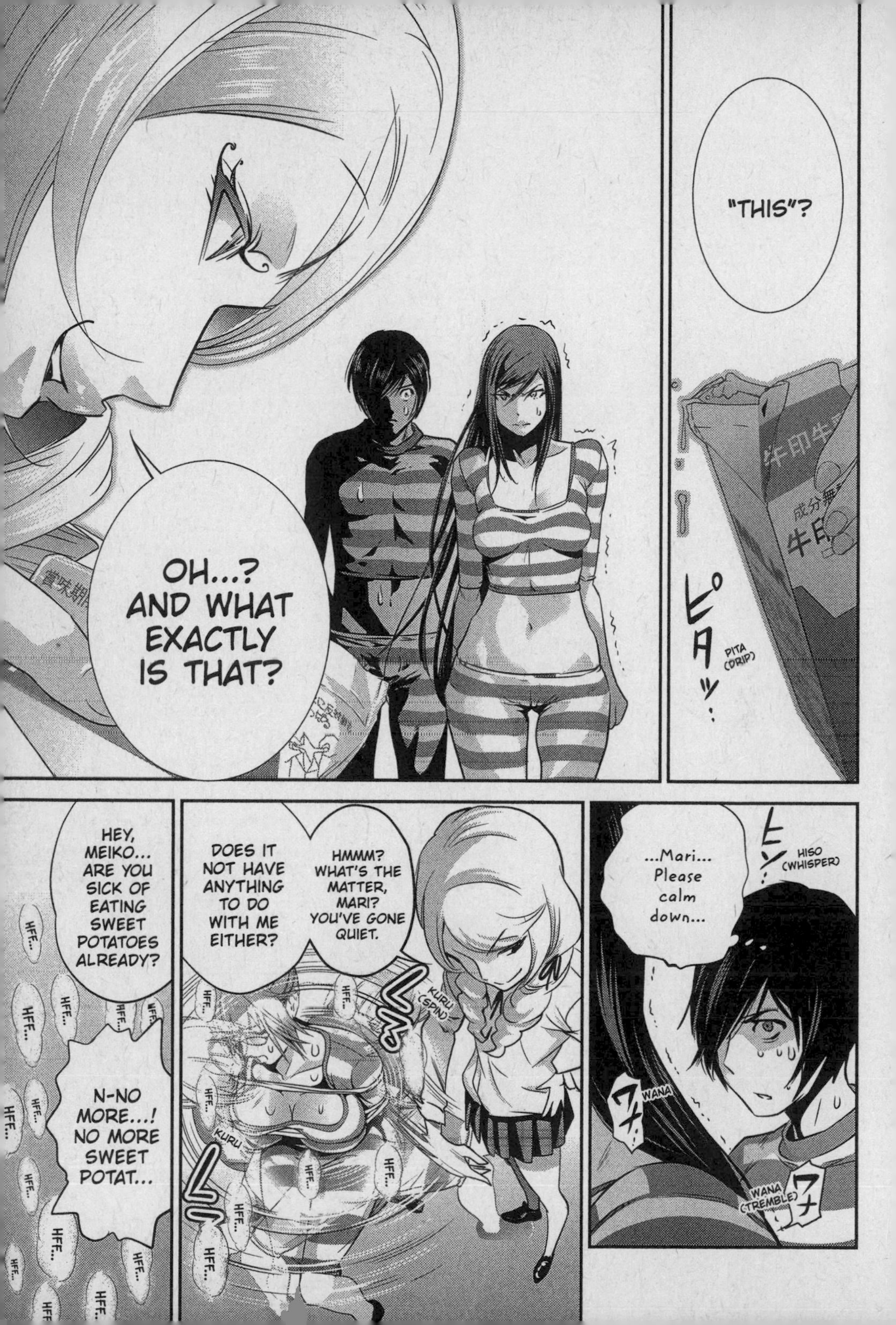
"THIS"?
ピタッ
PITA (DRIP)
OH...? AND WHAT EXACTLY IS THAT?
...Mari... Please calm down...
ヒソ
HISO (WHISPER)
ワナ
WANA
ワナ
WANA (TREMBLE)
HMMM? WHAT'S THE MATTER, MARI? YOU'VE GONE QUIET.
DOES IT NOT HAVE ANYTHING TO DO WITH ME EITHER?
KURU (SPIN)
KURU
HEY, MEIKO... ARE YOU SICK OF EATING SWEET POTATOES ALREADY?
N-NO MORE...! NO MORE SWEET POTAT...
HFF...

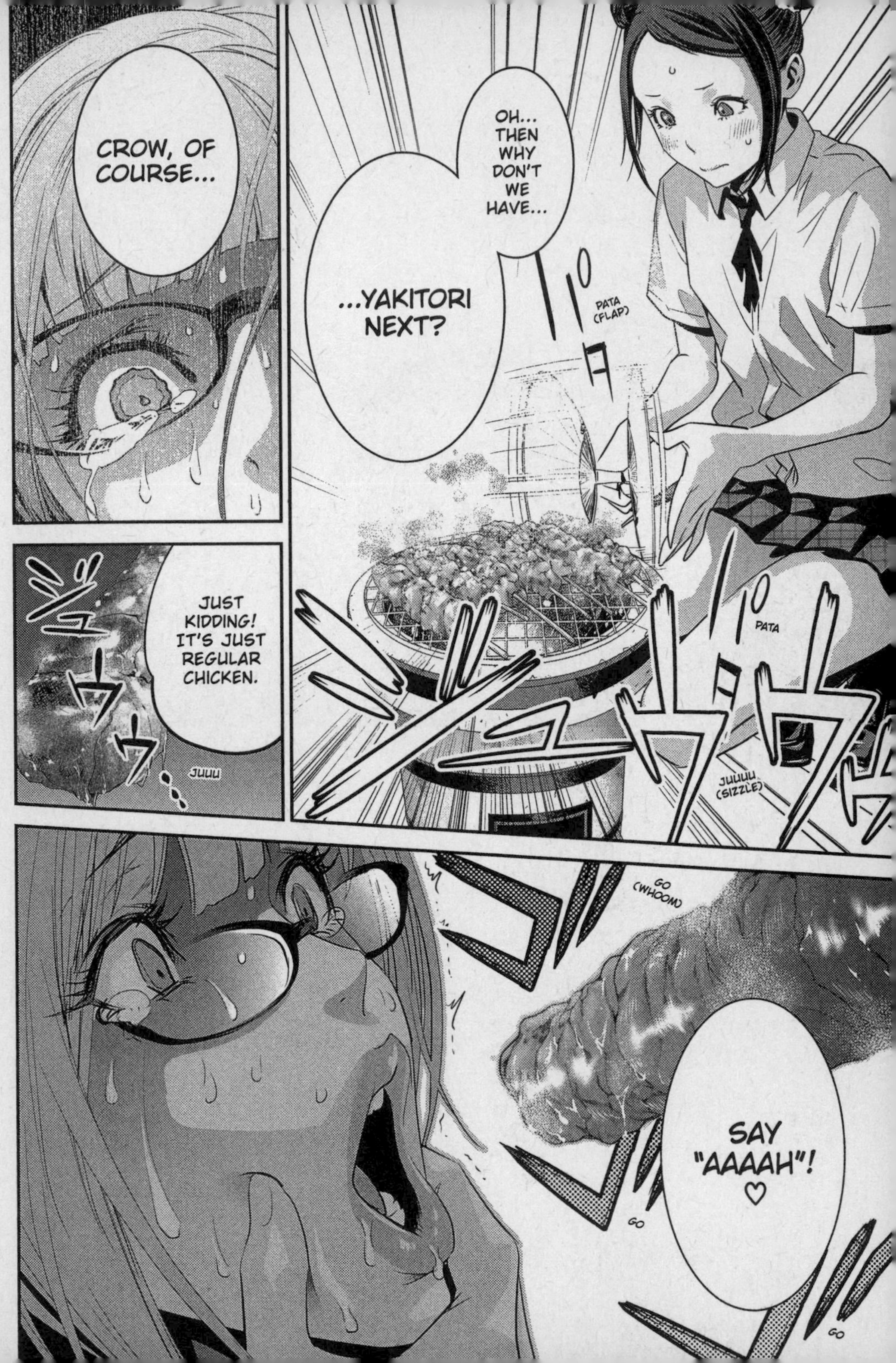

OH... THEN WHY DON'T WE HAVE...
PATA (FLAP)
...YAKITORI NEXT?
CROW, OF COURSE...
PATA
JUUUU (SIZZLE)
JUST KIDDING! IT'S JUST REGULAR CHICKEN.
JUUU
GO (WHOOM)
SAY "AAAAH"! ♡
GO
GO

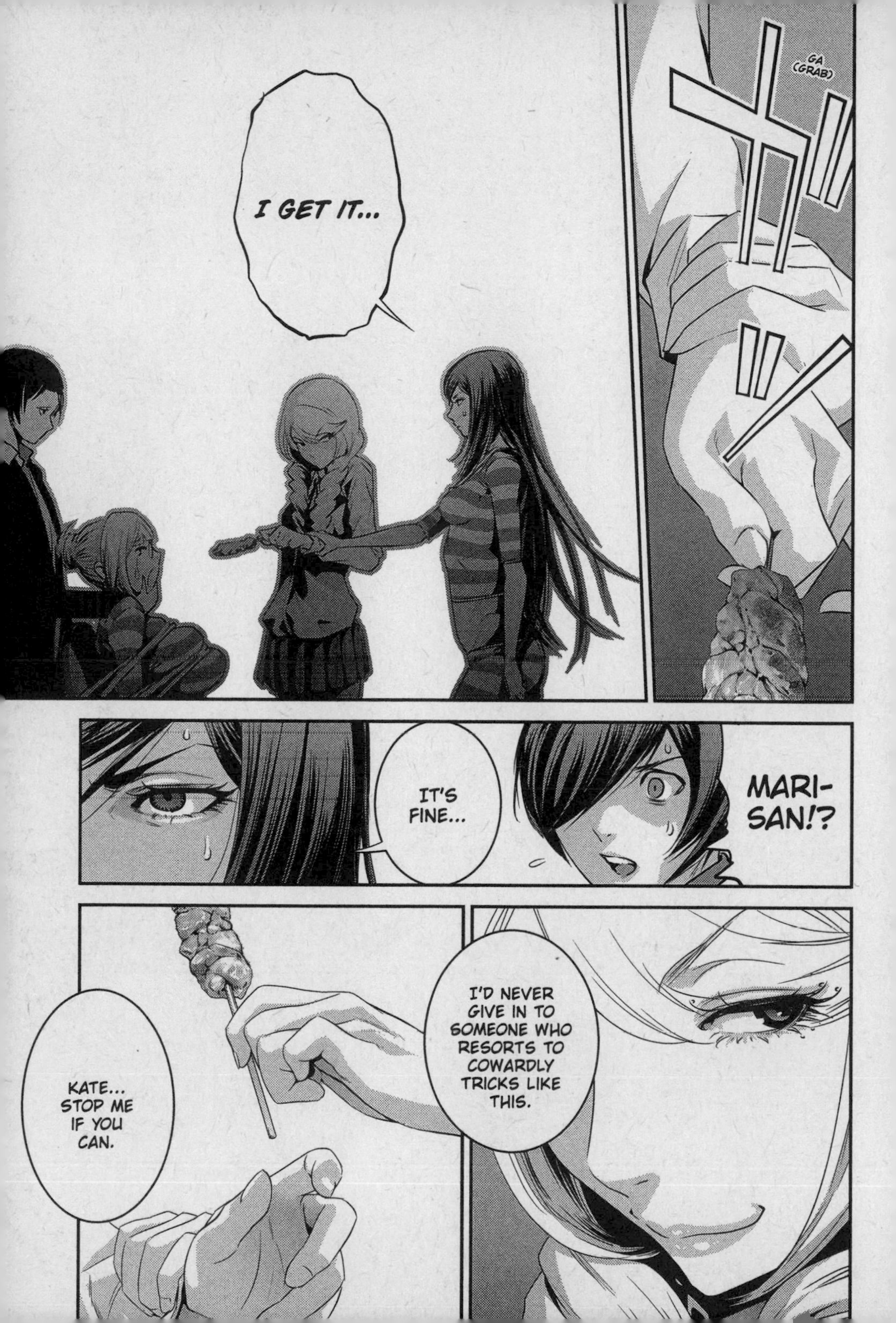
GA (GRAB)
I GET IT...
MARI-SAN!?
IT'S FINE...
I'D NEVER GIVE IN TO SOMEONE WHO RESORTS TO COWARDLY TRICKS LIKE THIS.
KATE... STOP ME IF YOU CAN.

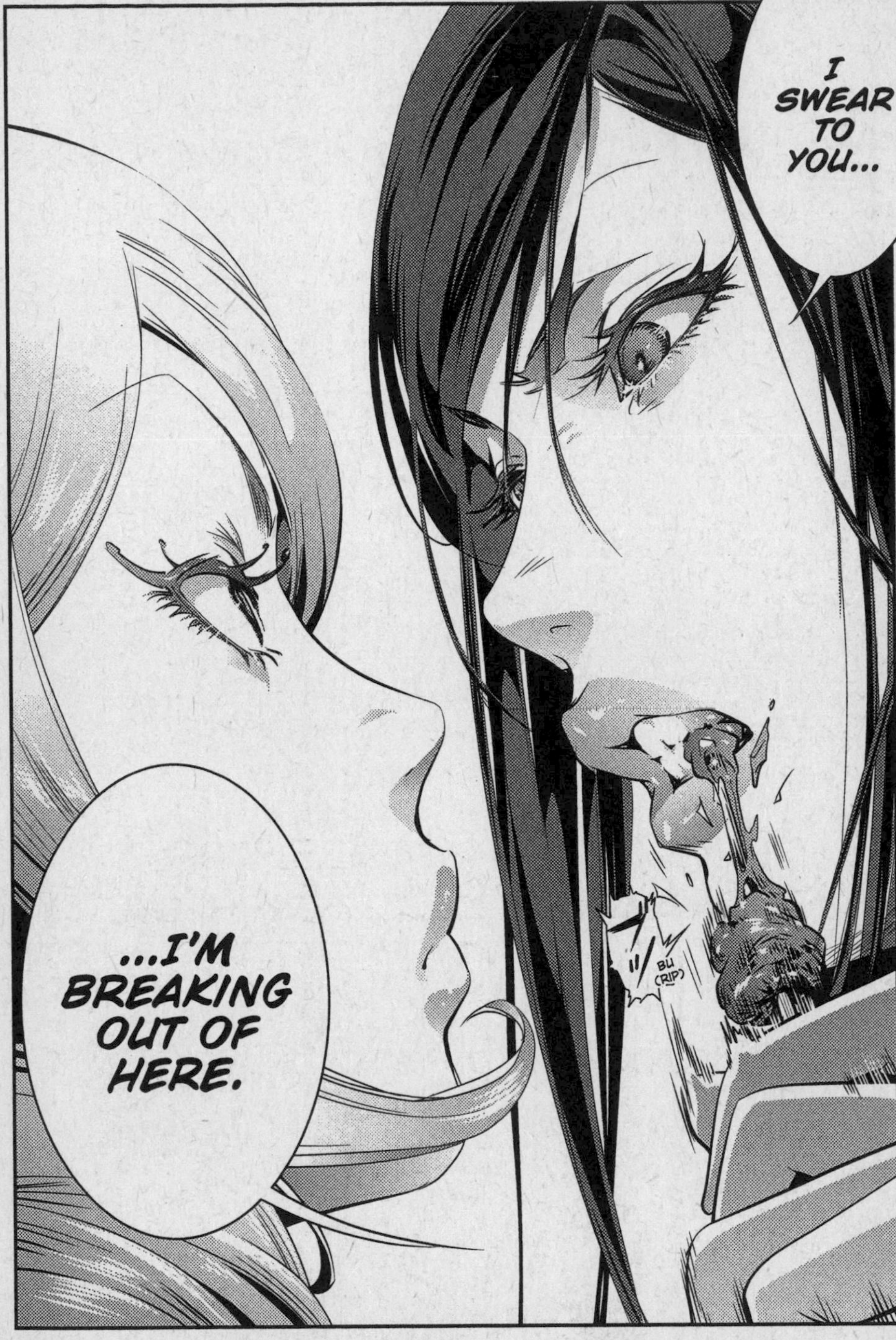
I SWEAR TO YOU...
BU (RIP)
...I'M BREAKING OUT OF HERE.

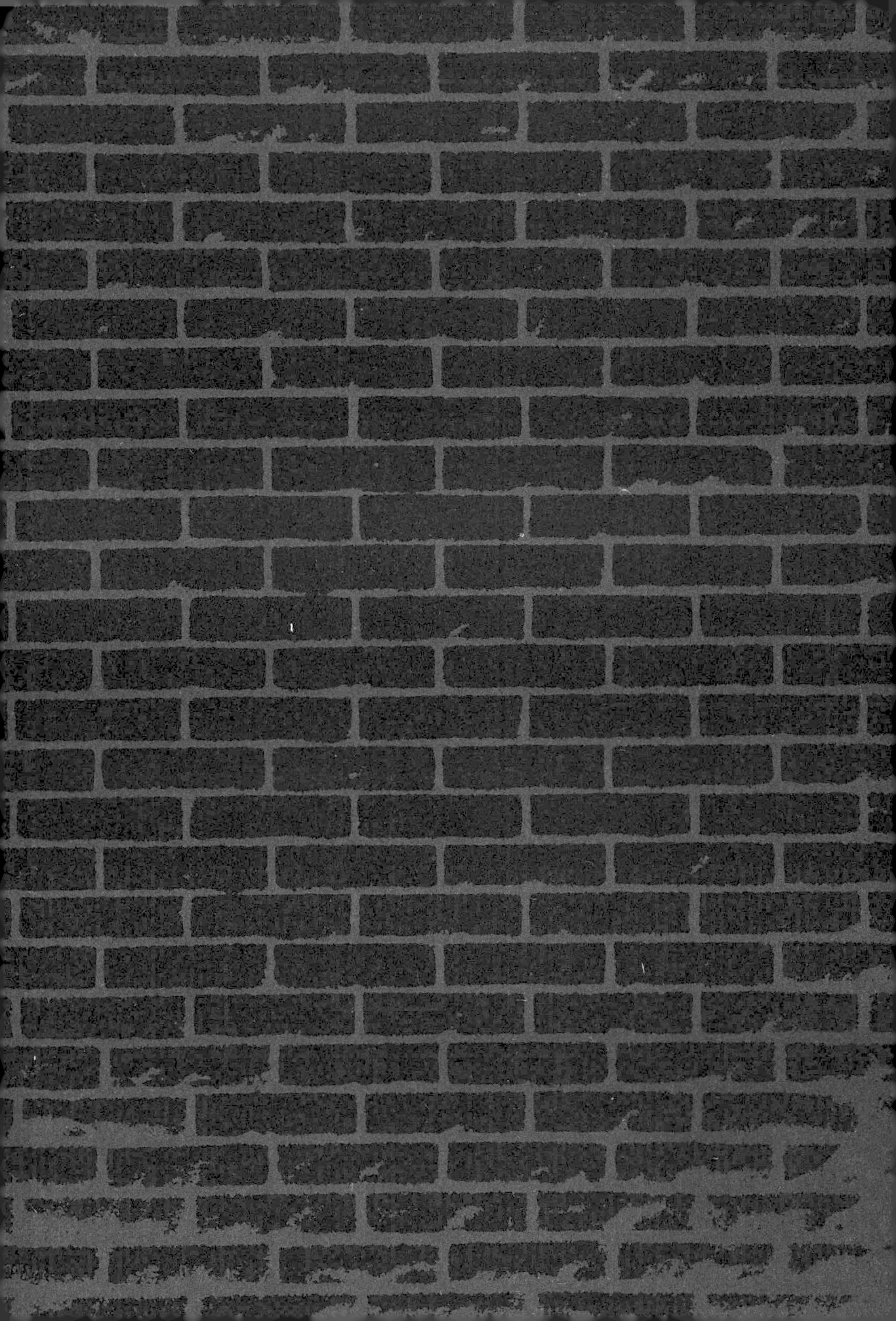

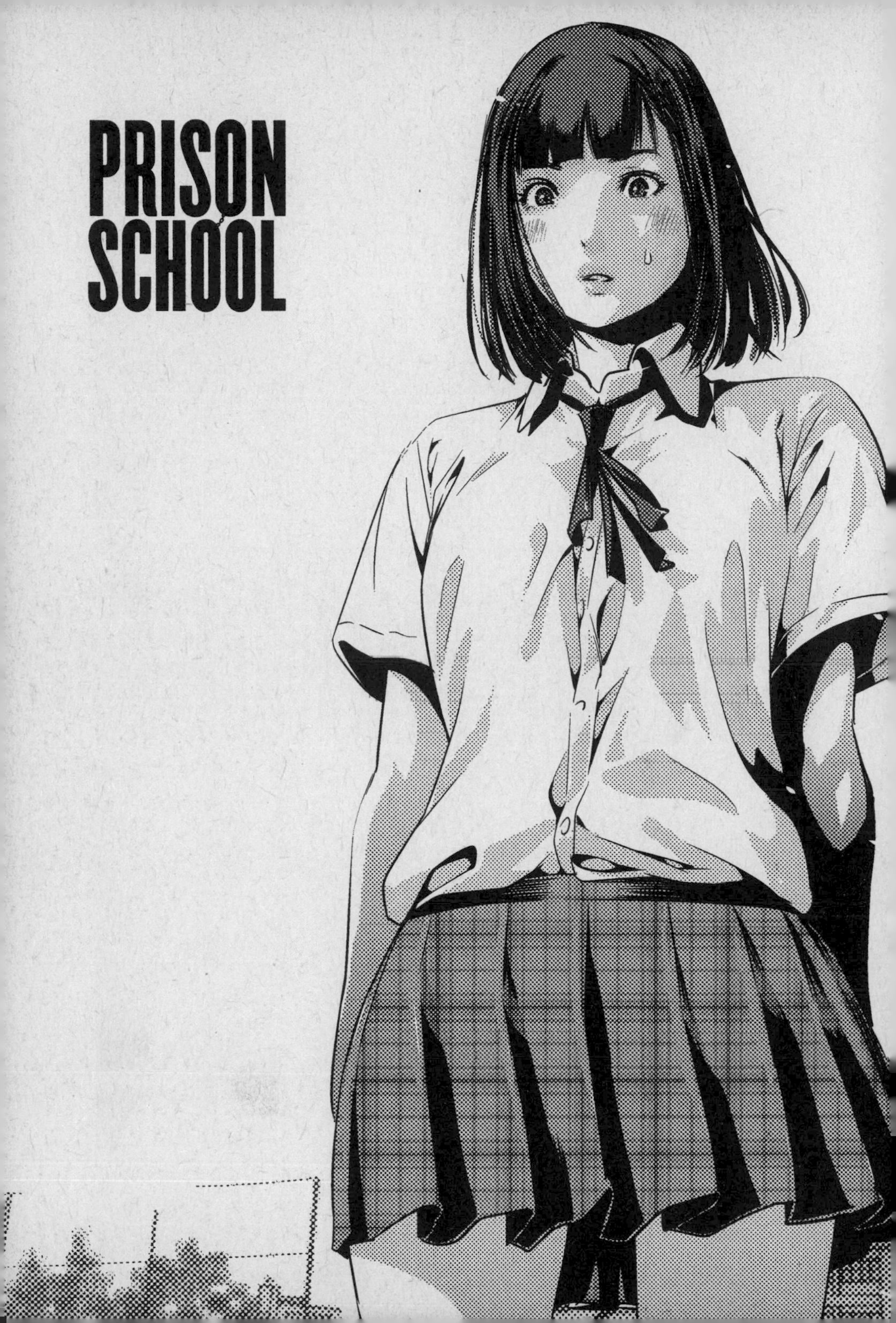
PRISON
SCHOOL

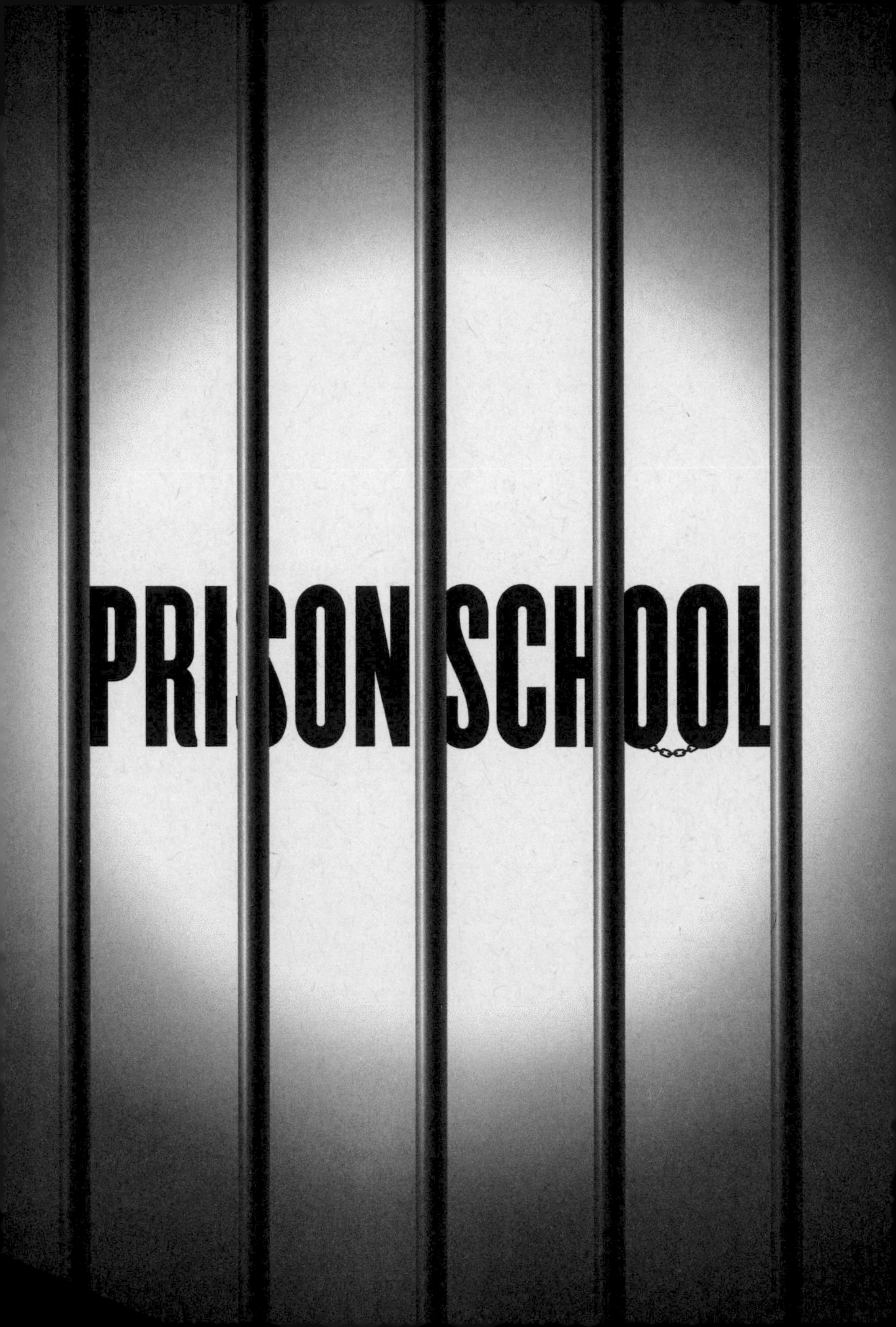
PRISON SCHOOL

CHAPTER 129: WITNESS

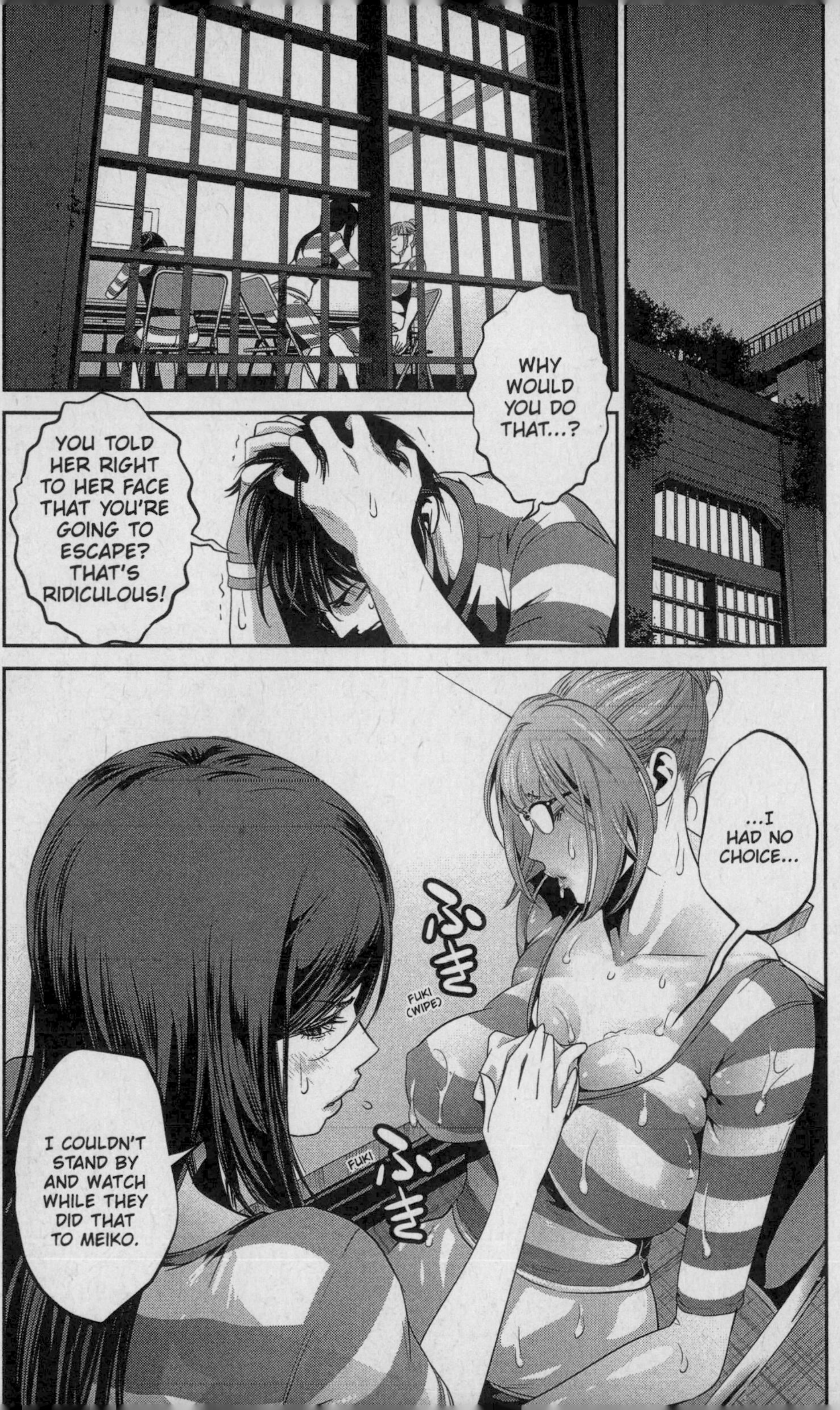

WHY WOULD YOU DO THAT...?
YOU TOLD HER RIGHT TO HER FACE THAT YOU'RE GOING TO ESCAPE? THAT'S RIDICULOUS!
...I HAD NO CHOICE...
ふき
FUKI (WIPE)
ふき
FUKI
I COULDN'T STAND BY AND WATCH WHILE THEY DID THAT TO MEIKO.

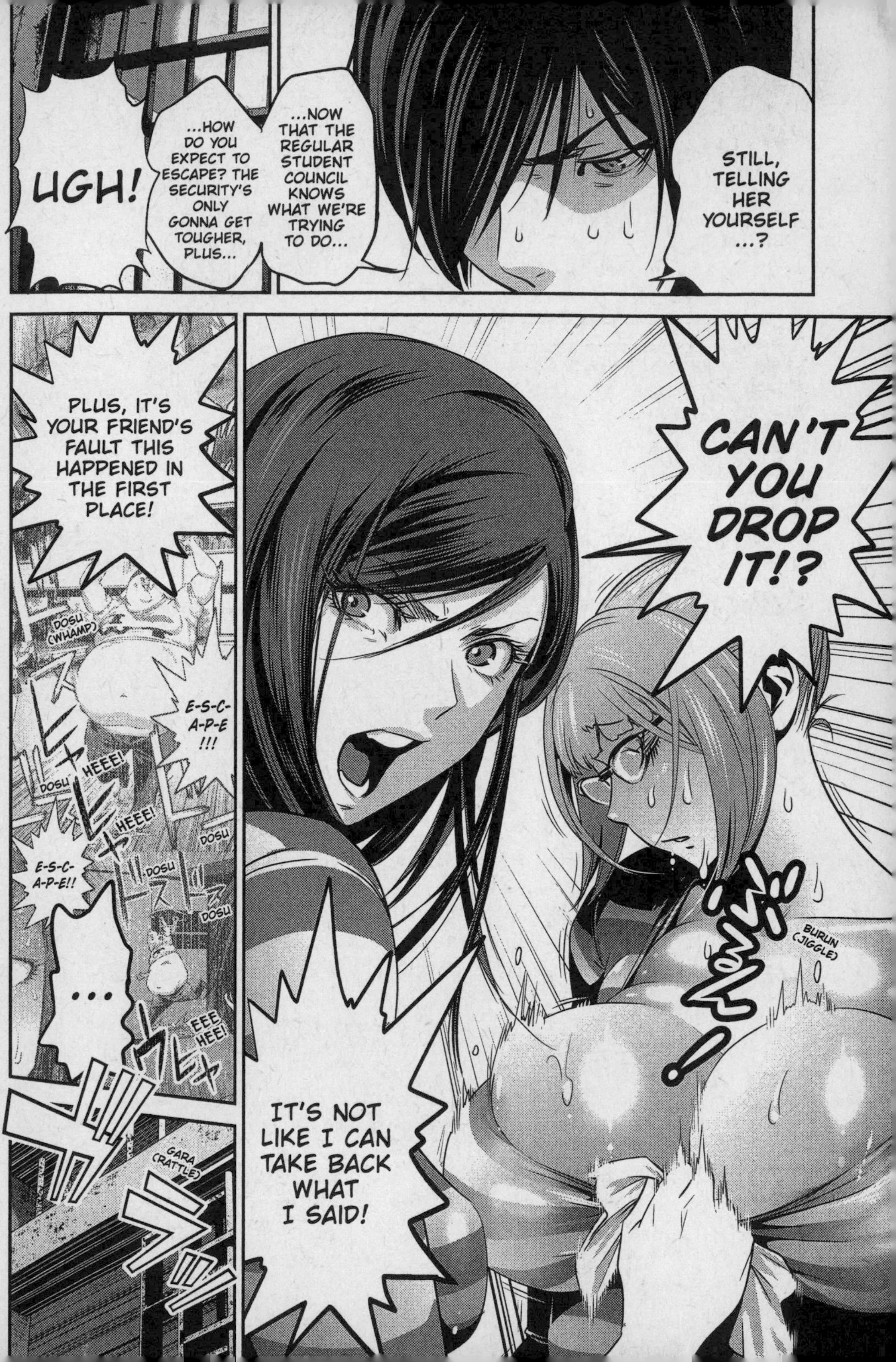
STILL, TELLING HER YOURSELF ...?
...NOW THAT THE REGULAR STUDENT COUNCIL KNOWS WHAT WE'RE TRYING TO DO...
...HOW DO YOU EXPECT TO ESCAPE? THE SECURITY'S ONLY GONNA GET TOUGHER, PLUS...
UGH!
CAN'T YOU DROP IT!?
BURUN (JIGGLE)
IT'S NOT LIKE I CAN TAKE BACK WHAT I SAID!
PLUS, IT'S YOUR FRIEND'S FAULT THIS HAPPENED IN THE FIRST PLACE!
DOSU (WHAMP)
E-S-C-A-P-E !!!
HEEE!
DOSU
HEEE!
DOSU
E-S-C-A-P-E!!
DOSU
DOSU
...
EEE HEE!
GARA (RATTLE)

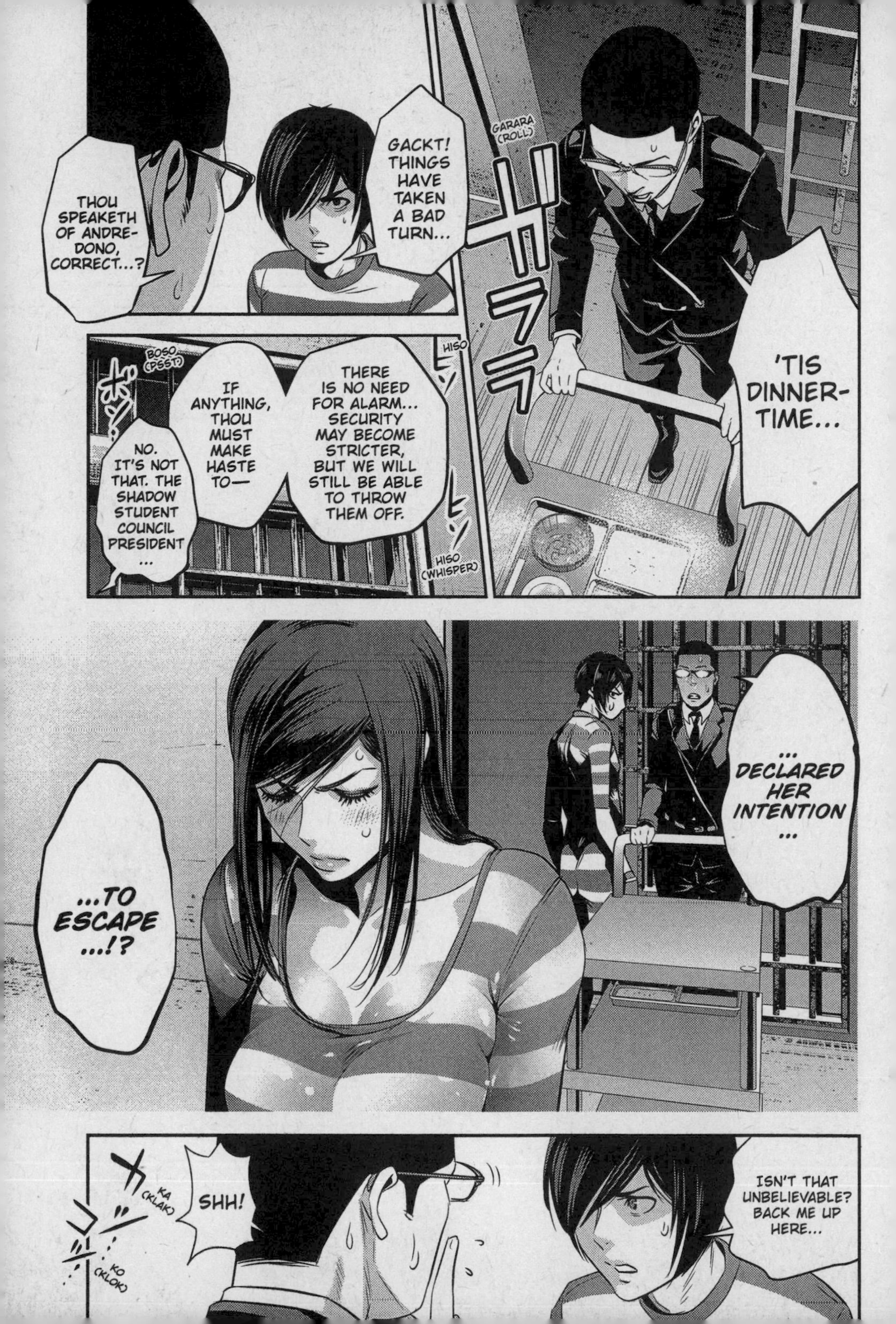
GARARA (ROLL)
'TIS DINNER-TIME...
GACKT! THINGS HAVE TAKEN A BAD TURN...
THOU SPEAKETH OF ANDRE-DONO, CORRECT...?
HISO
HISO (WHISPER)
THERE IS NO NEED FOR ALARM... SECURITY MAY BECOME STRICTER, BUT WE WILL STILL BE ABLE TO THROW THEM OFF.
IF ANYTHING, THOU MUST MAKE HASTE TO—
BOSO (PSST)
NO. IT'S NOT THAT. THE SHADOW STUDENT COUNCIL PRESIDENT ...
... DECLARED HER INTENTION ...
...TO ESCAPE ...!?
ISN'T THAT UNBELIEVABLE? BACK ME UP HERE...
SHH!
KA (KLAK)
KO (KLOK)

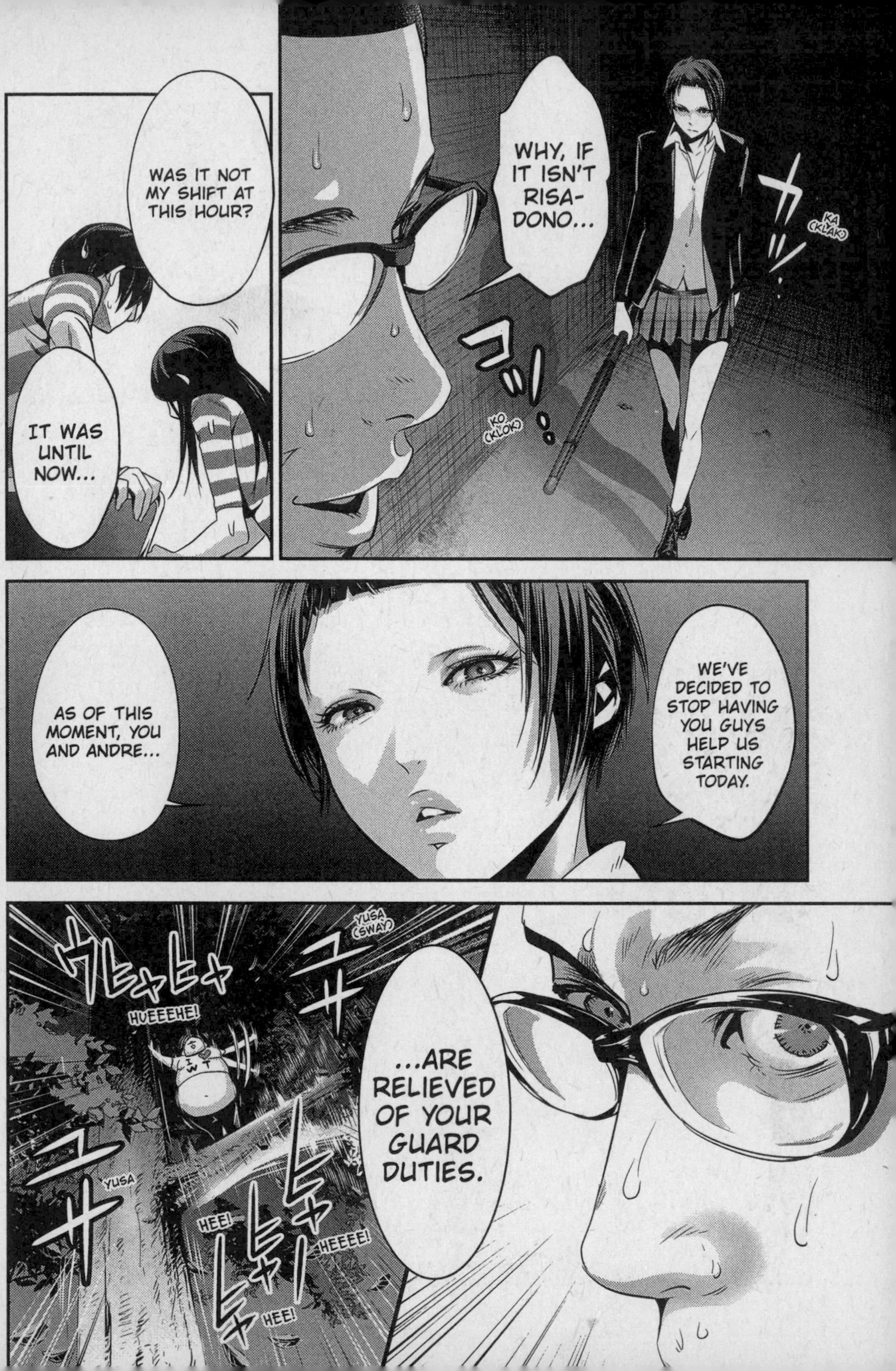
KA (KLAK)
WHY, IF IT ISN'T RISA-DONO...
KO (KLOK)
WAS IT NOT MY SHIFT AT THIS HOUR?
IT WAS UNTIL NOW...
WE'VE DECIDED TO STOP HAVING YOU GUYS HELP US STARTING TODAY.
AS OF THIS MOMENT, YOU AND ANDRE...
...ARE RELIEVED OF YOUR GUARD DUTIES.
YUSA (SWAY)
HUEEEHE!
YUSA
HEE!
HEEEE!
HEE!

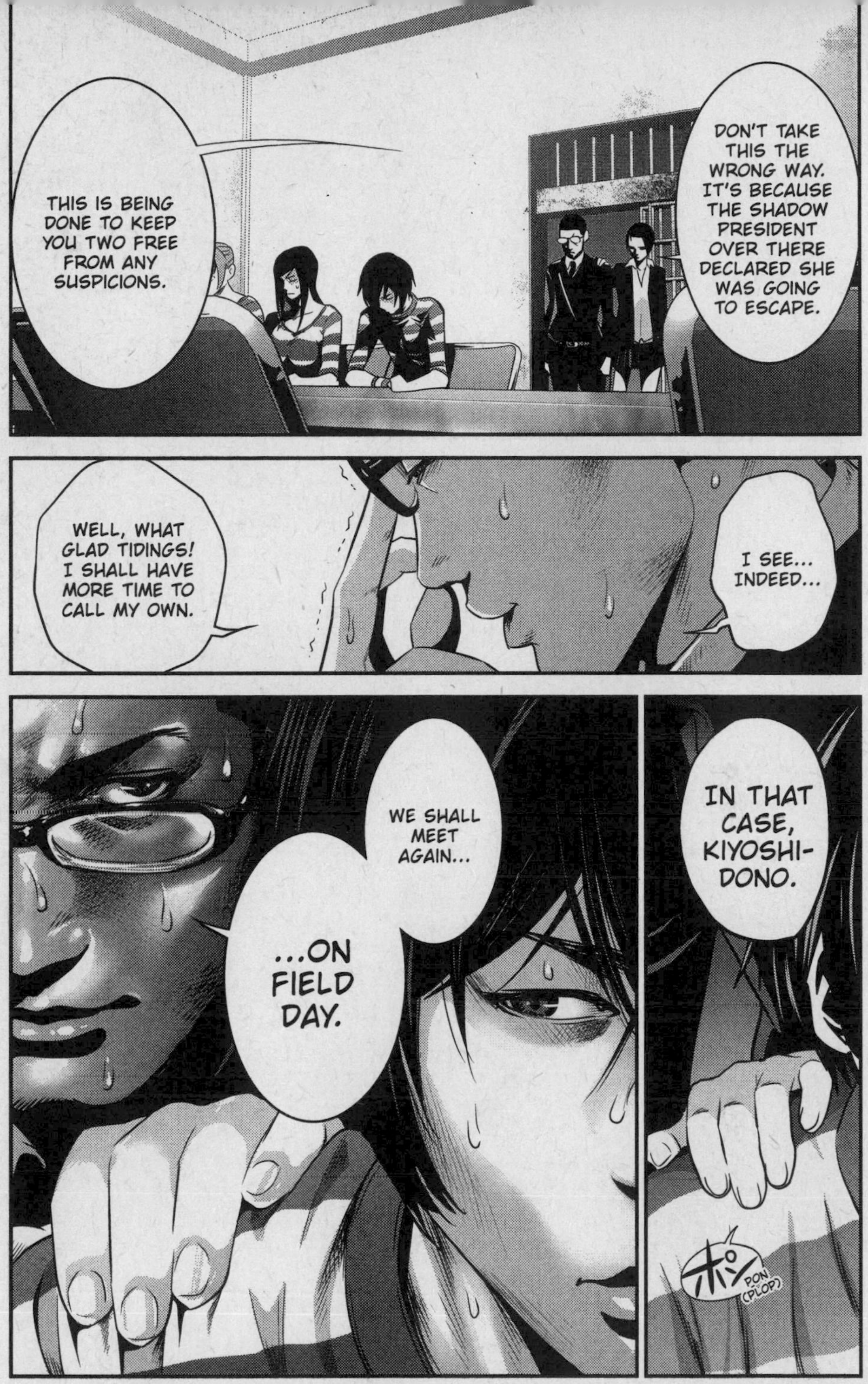

DON'T TAKE THIS THE WRONG WAY. IT'S BECAUSE THE SHADOW PRESIDENT OVER THERE DECLARED SHE WAS GOING TO ESCAPE.
THIS IS BEING DONE TO KEEP YOU TWO FREE FROM ANY SUSPICIONS.
I SEE... INDEED...
WELL, WHAT GLAD TIDINGS! I SHALL HAVE MORE TIME TO CALL MY OWN.
IN THAT CASE, KIYOSHI-DONO.
ポン
PON (PLOP)
WE SHALL MEET AGAIN...
...ON FIELD DAY.

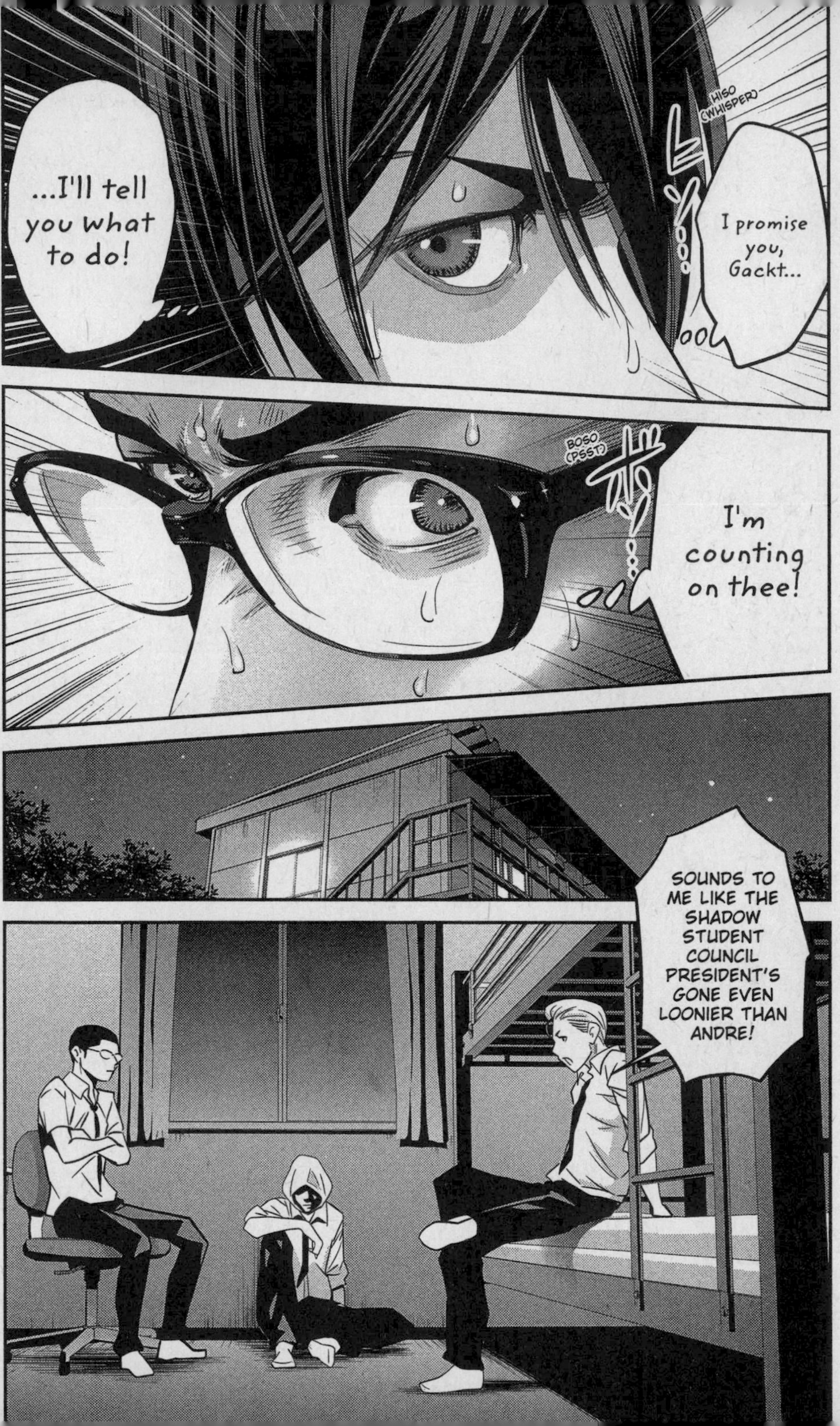
HISO (WHISPER)
I promise you, Gackt...
...I'll tell you what to do!
BOSO (PSST)
I'm counting on thee!
SOUNDS TO ME LIKE THE SHADOW STUDENT COUNCIL PRESIDENT'S GONE EVEN LOONIER THAN ANDRE!

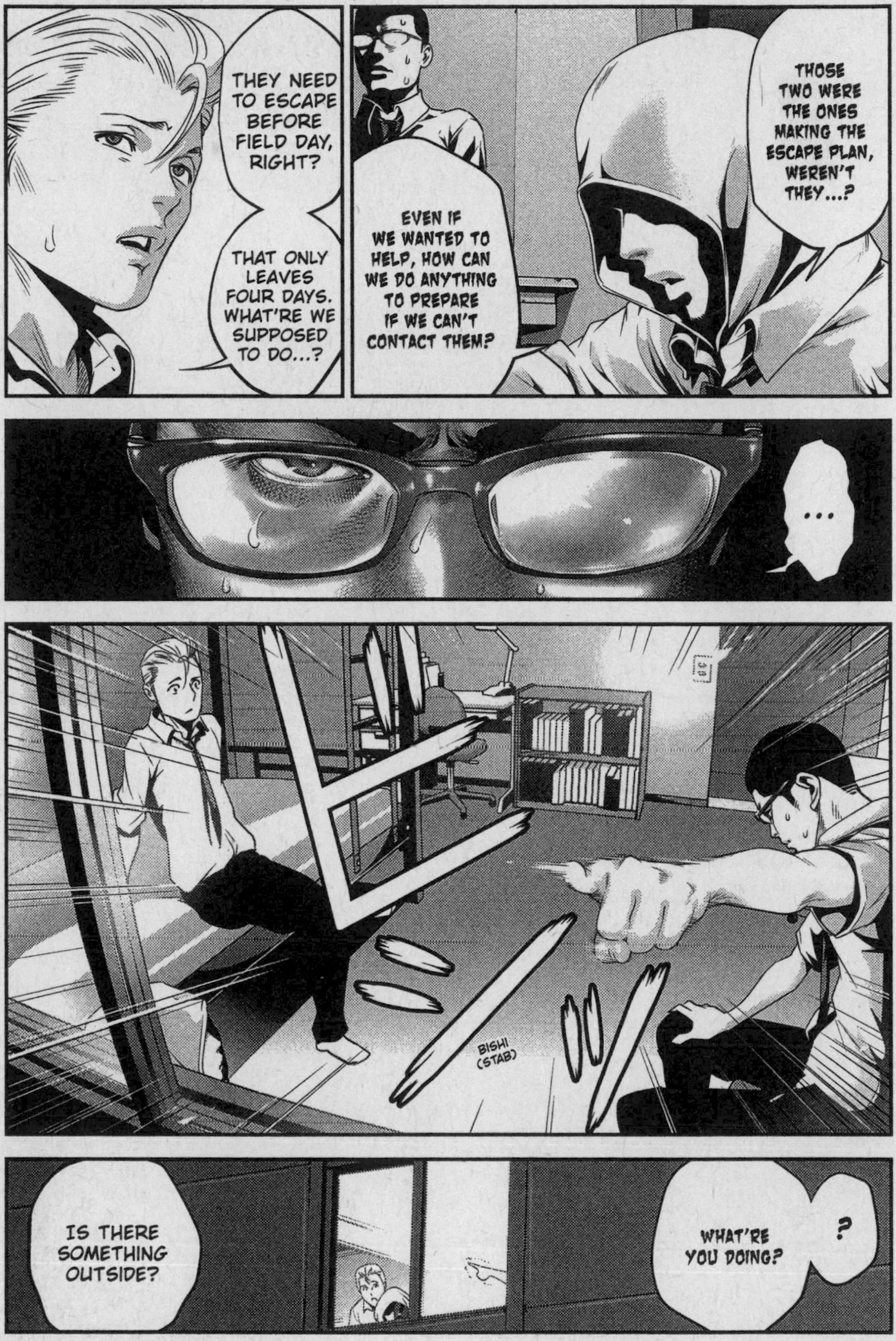
THOSE TWO WERE THE ONES MAKING THE ESCAPE PLAN, WEREN'T THEY...?
EVEN IF WE WANTED TO HELP, HOW CAN WE DO ANYTHING TO PREPARE IF WE CAN'T CONTACT THEM?
THEY NEED TO ESCAPE BEFORE FIELD DAY, RIGHT?
THAT ONLY LEAVES FOUR DAYS. WHAT'RE WE SUPPOSED TO DO...?
...
BISHI (STAB)
?
WHAT'RE YOU DOING?
IS THERE SOMETHING OUTSIDE?

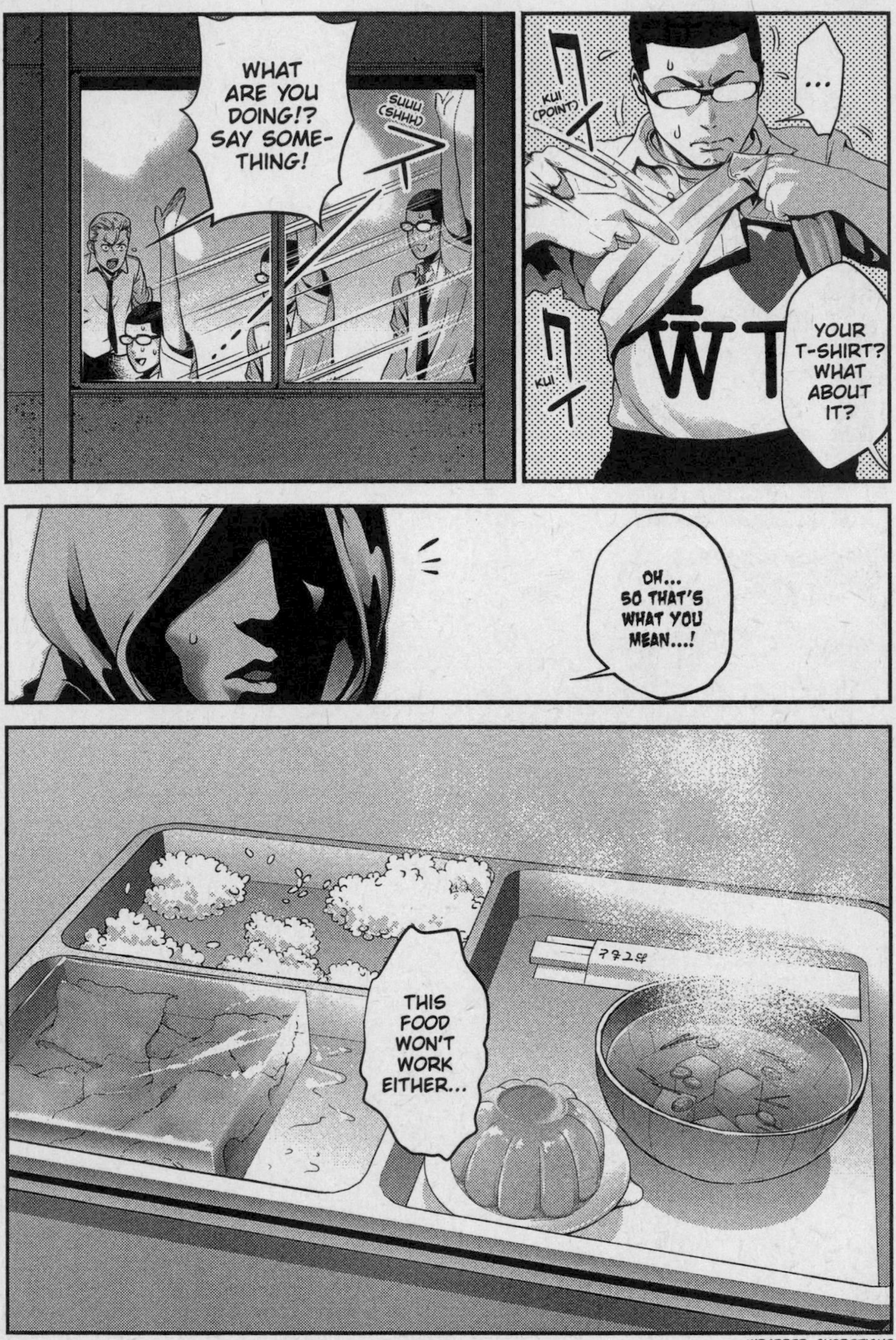

KUI (POINT)
...
KUI
YOUR T-SHIRT? WHAT ABOUT IT?
WHAT ARE YOU DOING!? SAY SOME-THING!
SUUU (SHHH)
WT
OH... SO THAT'S WHAT YOU MEAN...!
THIS FOOD WON'T WORK EITHER...

WRAPPER: CHOPSTICKS

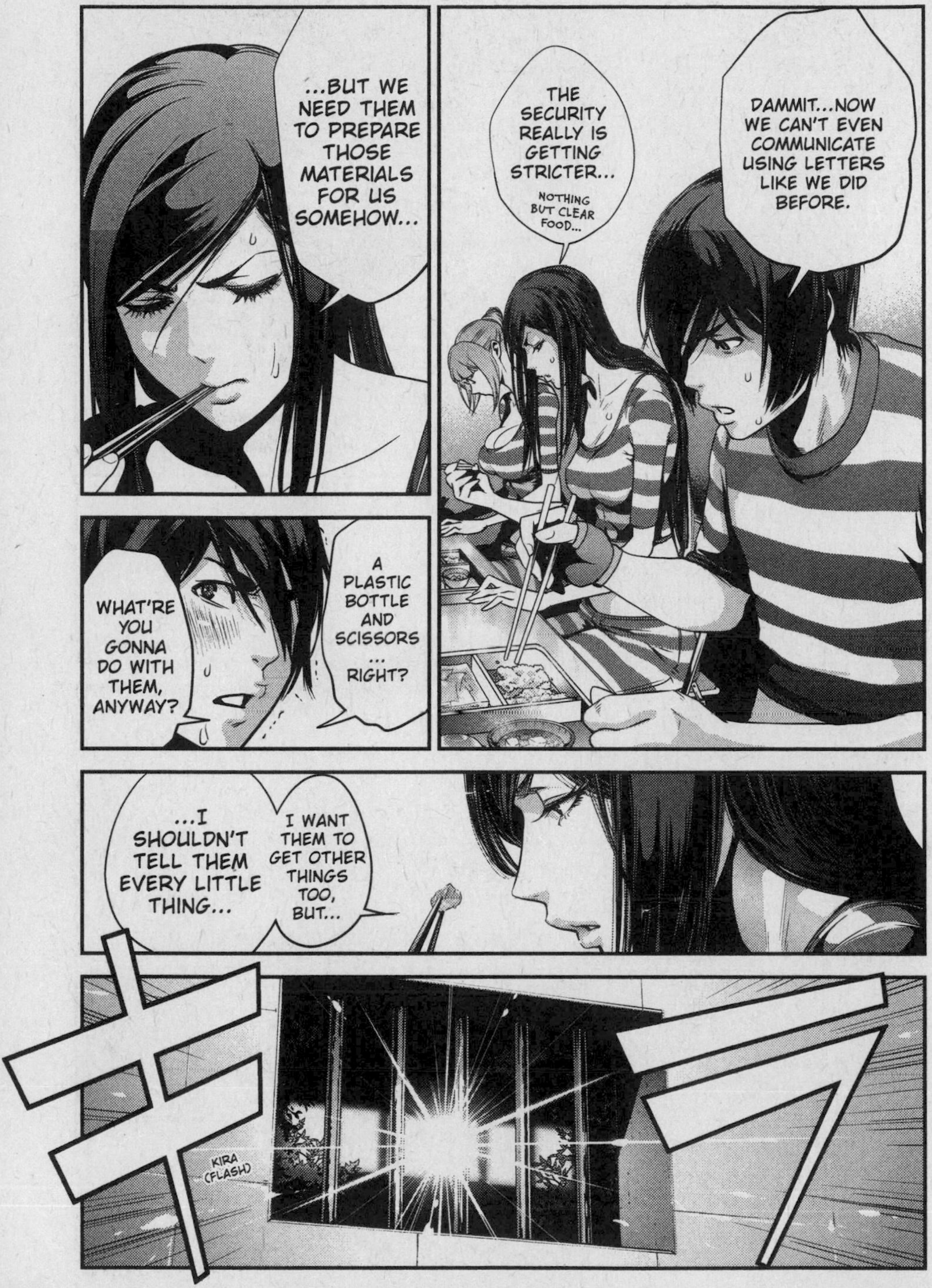
DAMMIT...NOW WE CAN'T EVEN COMMUNICATE USING LETTERS LIKE WE DID BEFORE.
THE SECURITY REALLY IS GETTING STRICTER...
NOTHING BUT CLEAR FOOD...
...BUT WE NEED THEM TO PREPARE THOSE MATERIALS FOR US SOMEHOW...
A PLASTIC BOTTLE AND SCISSORS ... RIGHT?
WHAT'RE YOU GONNA DO WITH THEM, ANYWAY?
I WANT THEM TO GET OTHER THINGS TOO, BUT...
...I SHOULDN'T TELL THEM EVERY LITTLE THING...
KIRA (FLASH)

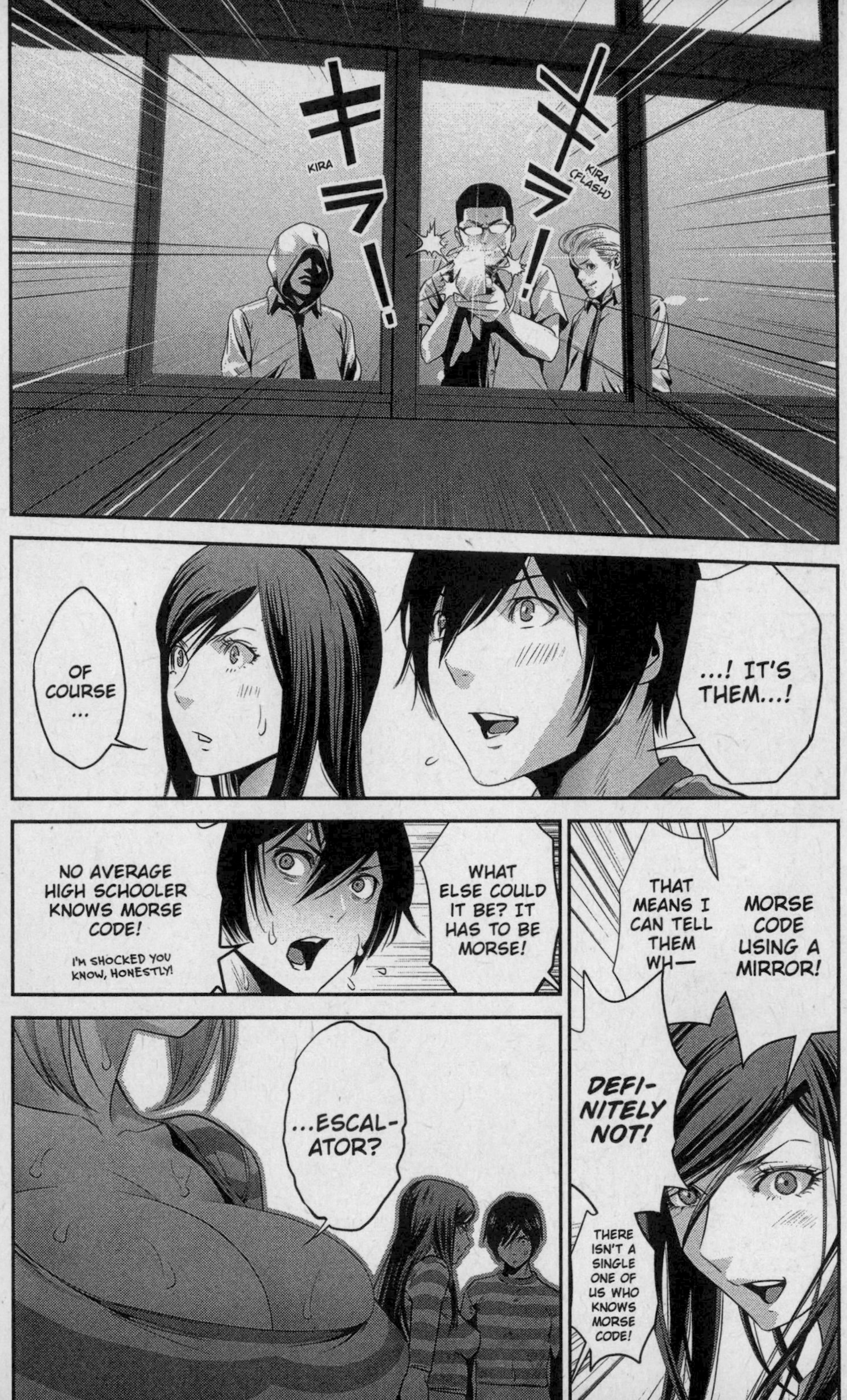
キラ!
KIRA (FLASH)
キラ!
KIRA
...! IT'S THEM...!
OF COURSE ...
MORSE CODE USING A MIRROR!
THAT MEANS I CAN TELL THEM WH—
WHAT ELSE COULD IT BE? IT HAS TO BE MORSE!
NO AVERAGE HIGH SCHOOLER KNOWS MORSE CODE!
I'M SHOCKED YOU KNOW, HONESTLY!
DEFI-NITELY NOT!
THERE ISN'T A SINGLE ONE OF US WHO KNOWS MORSE CODE!
...ESCAL-ATOR?

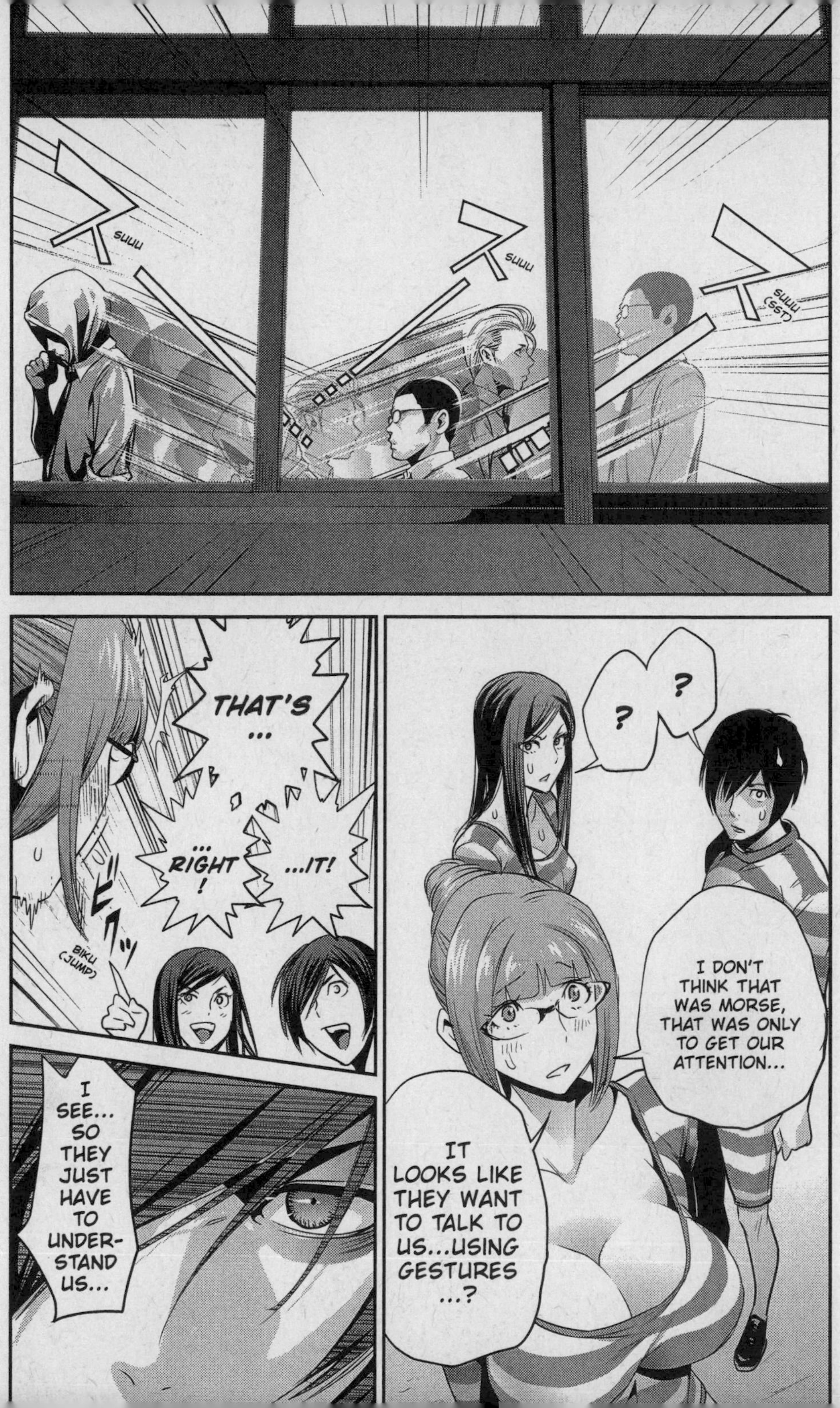

SUUU (SST)
SUUU
SUUU
?
?
I DON'T THINK THAT WAS MORSE, THAT WAS ONLY TO GET OUR ATTENTION...
THAT'S ...
...IT!
... RIGHT !
BIKU (JUMP)
IT LOOKS LIKE THEY WANT TO TALK TO US...USING GESTURES ...?
I SEE... SO THEY JUST HAVE TO UNDER-STAND US...

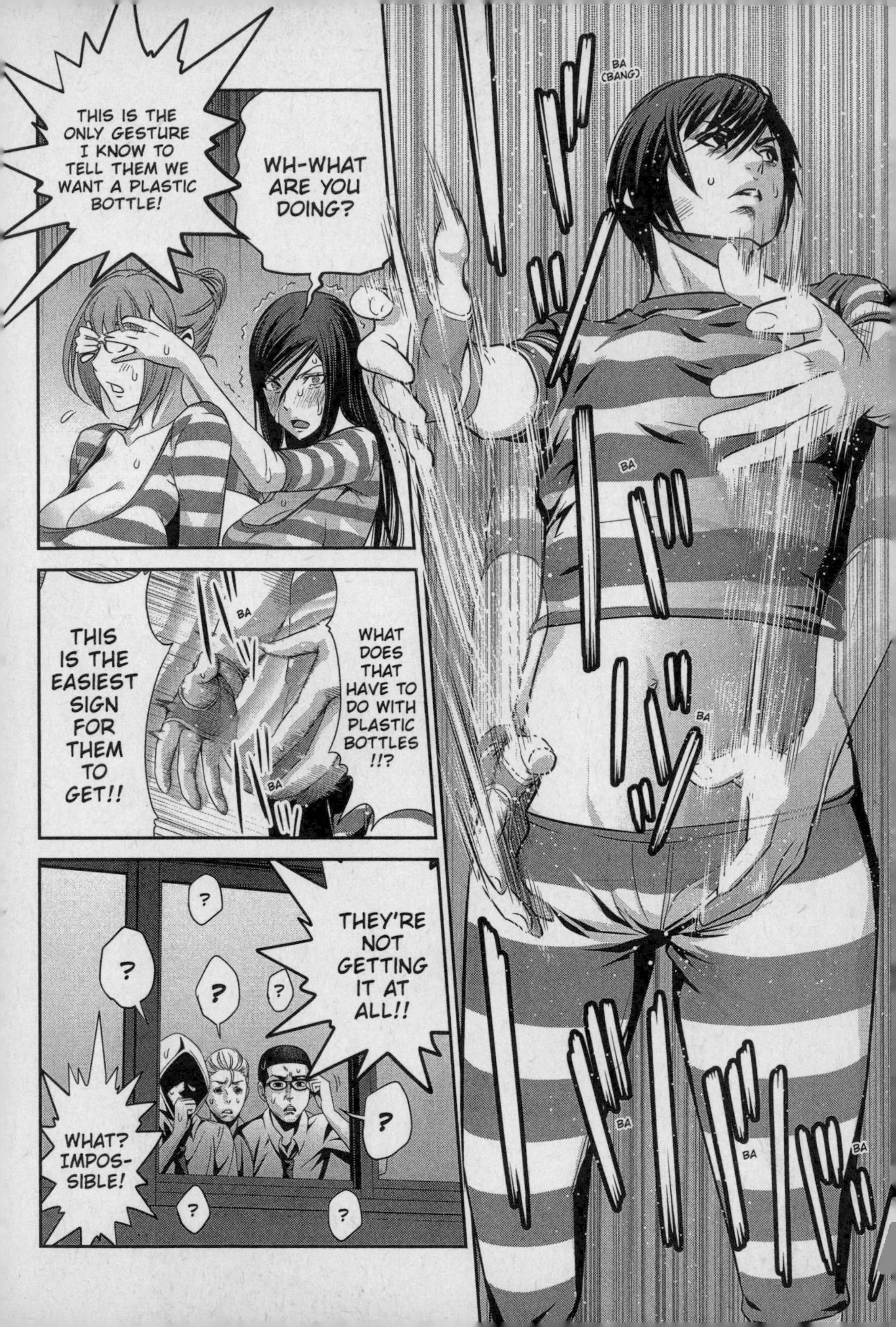
BA
(BANG)
BA
BA
BA
BA
BA
WH-WHAT ARE YOU DOING?
THIS IS THE ONLY GESTURE I KNOW TO TELL THEM WE WANT A PLASTIC BOTTLE!
BA
BA
WHAT DOES THAT HAVE TO DO WITH PLASTIC BOTTLES!!?
THIS IS THE EASIEST SIGN FOR THEM TO GET!!
THEY'RE NOT GETTING IT AT ALL!!
?
?
?
?
?
?
?
WHAT? IMPOSSIBLE!

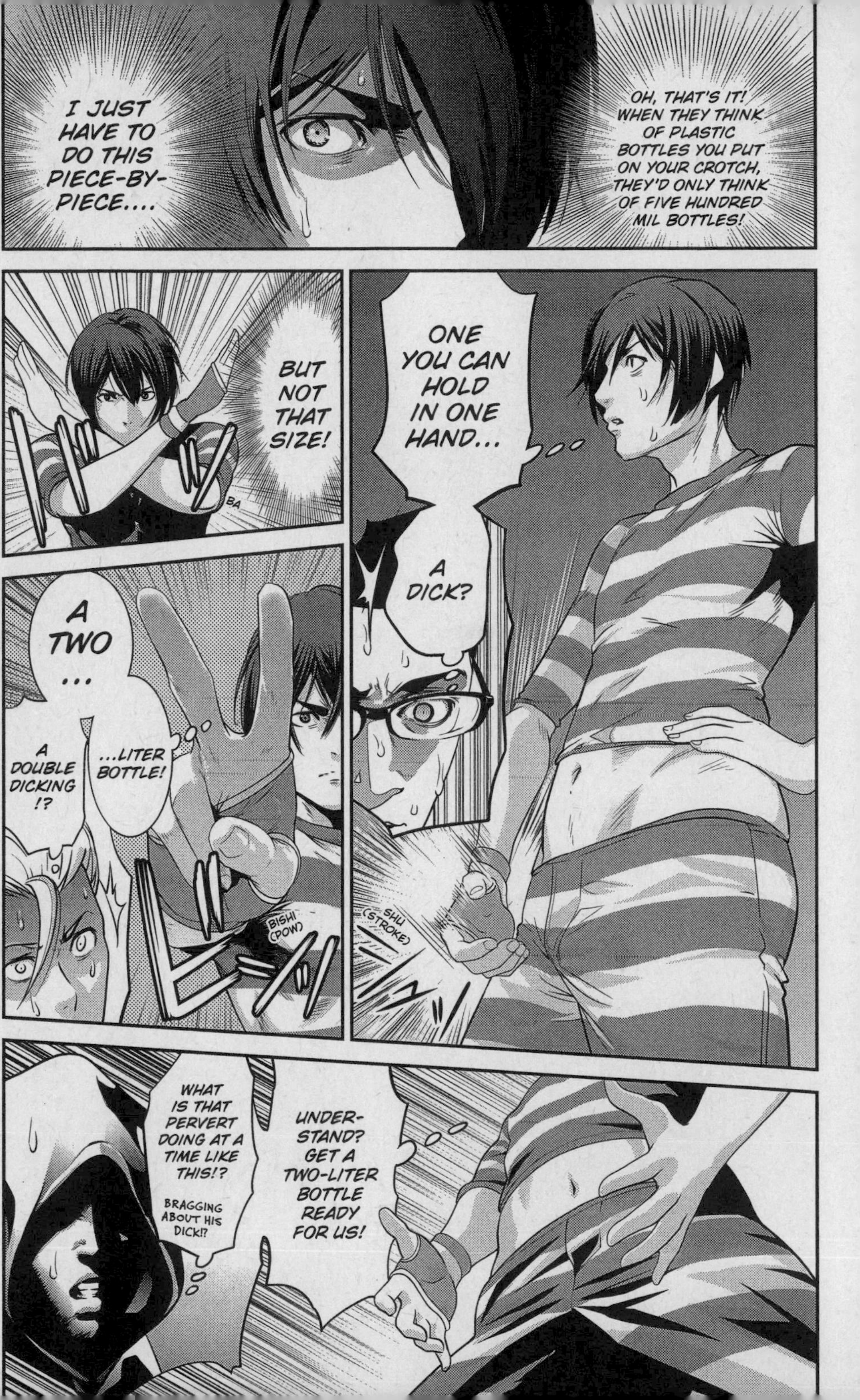
OH, THAT'S IT! WHEN THEY THINK OF PLASTIC BOTTLES YOU PUT ON YOUR CROTCH, THEY'D ONLY THINK OF FIVE HUNDRED MIL BOTTLES!
I JUST HAVE TO DO THIS PIECE-BY-PIECE....
ONE YOU CAN HOLD IN ONE HAND...
BUT NOT THAT SIZE!
BA
A DICK?
A TWO...
...LITER BOTTLE!
A DOUBLE DICKING!?
SHU (STROKE)
BISHI (POW)
UNDER-STAND? GET A TWO-LITER BOTTLE READY FOR US!
WHAT IS THAT PERVERT DOING AT A TIME LIKE THIS!?
BRAGGING ABOUT HIS DICK!?

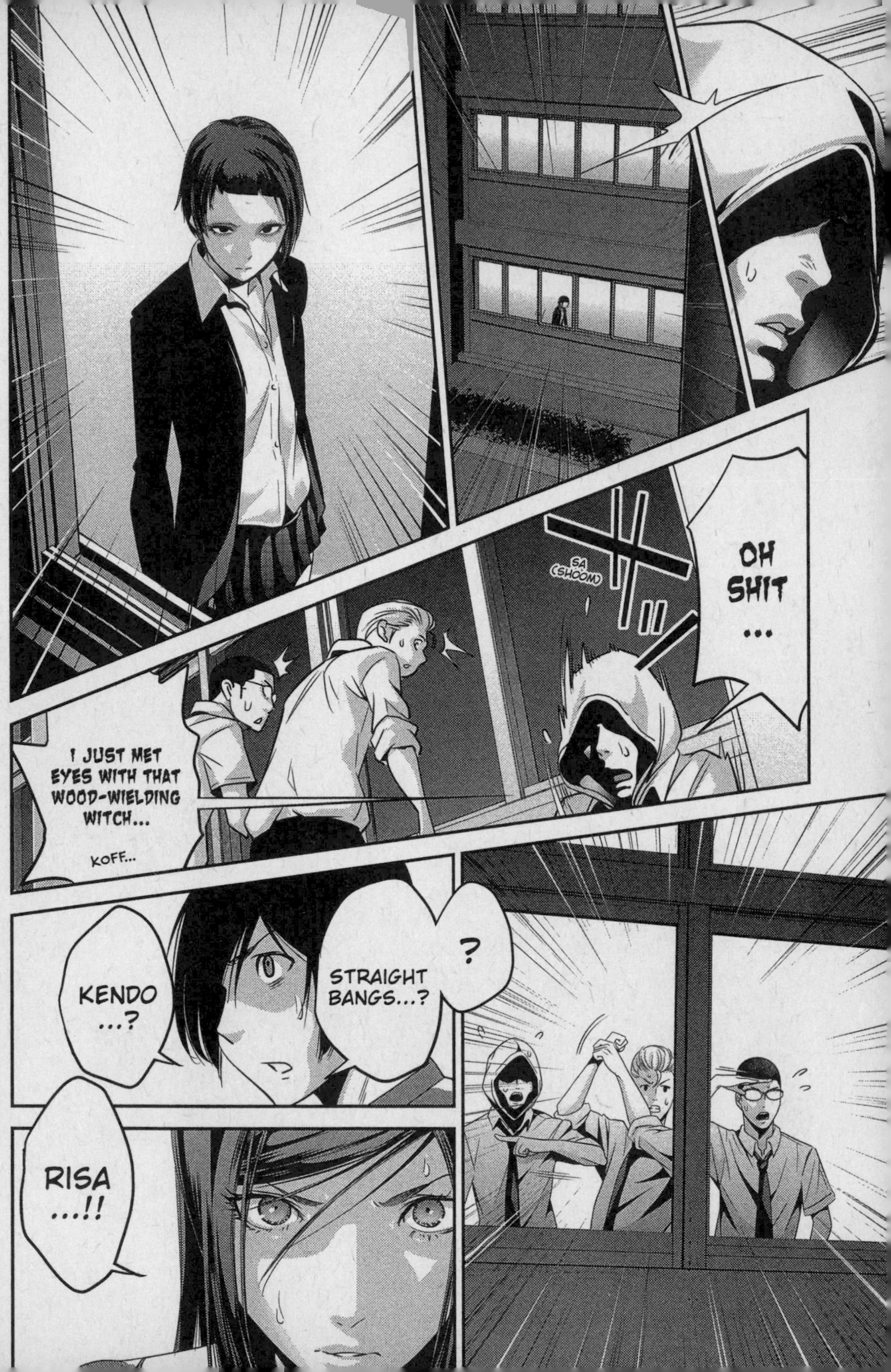

OH SHIT ...
SA (SHOOM)
I JUST MET EYES WITH THAT WOOD-WIELDING WITCH...
KOFF...
?
STRAIGHT BANGS...?
KENDO ...?
RISA ...!!

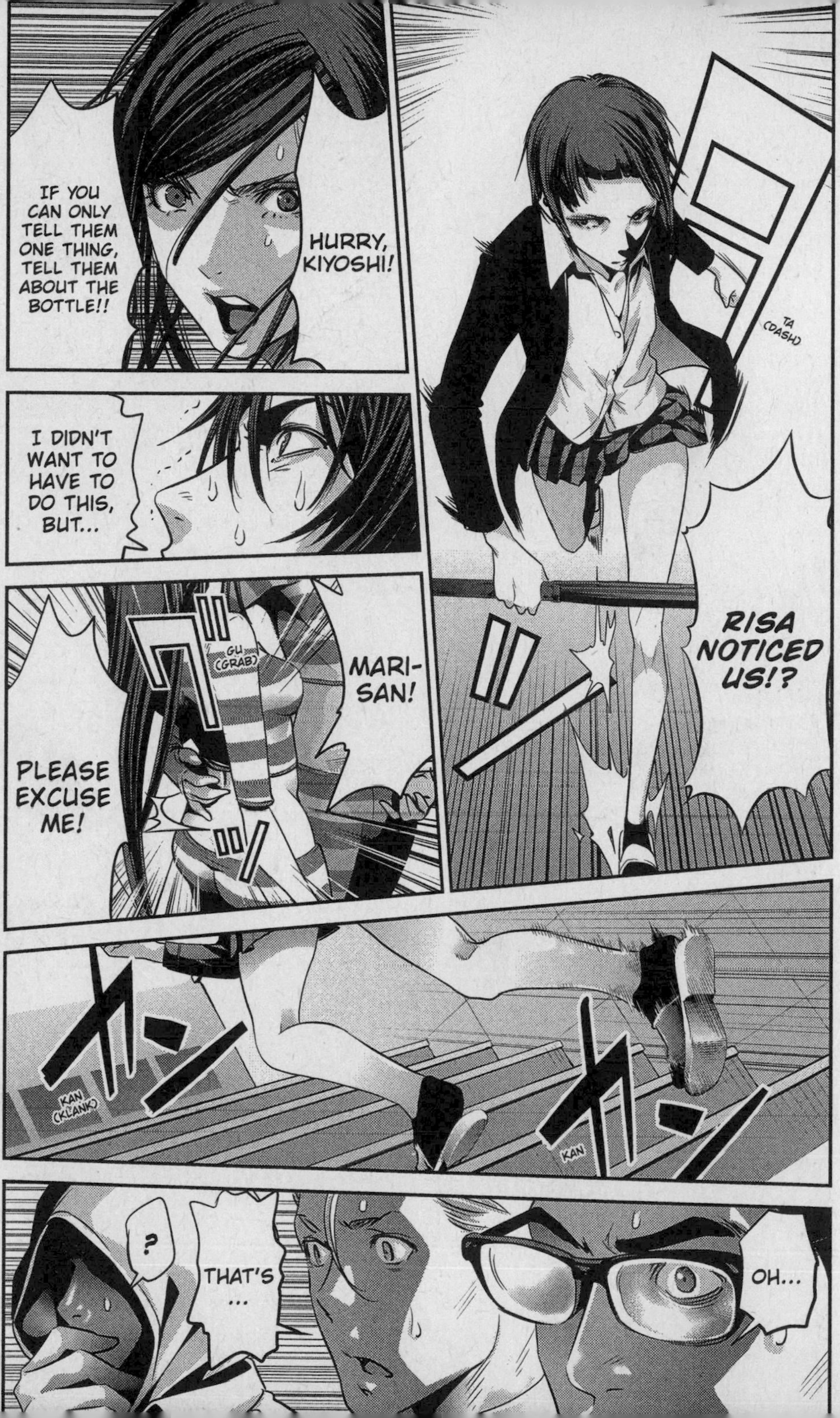
TA (DASH)
RISA NOTICED US!?
HURRY, KIYOSHI!
IF YOU CAN ONLY TELL THEM ONE THING, TELL THEM ABOUT THE BOTTLE!!
I DIDN'T WANT TO HAVE TO DO THIS, BUT...
MARI-SAN!
GU (GRAB)
PLEASE EXCUSE ME!
KAN
KAN (KLANK)
OH...
THAT'S...
?

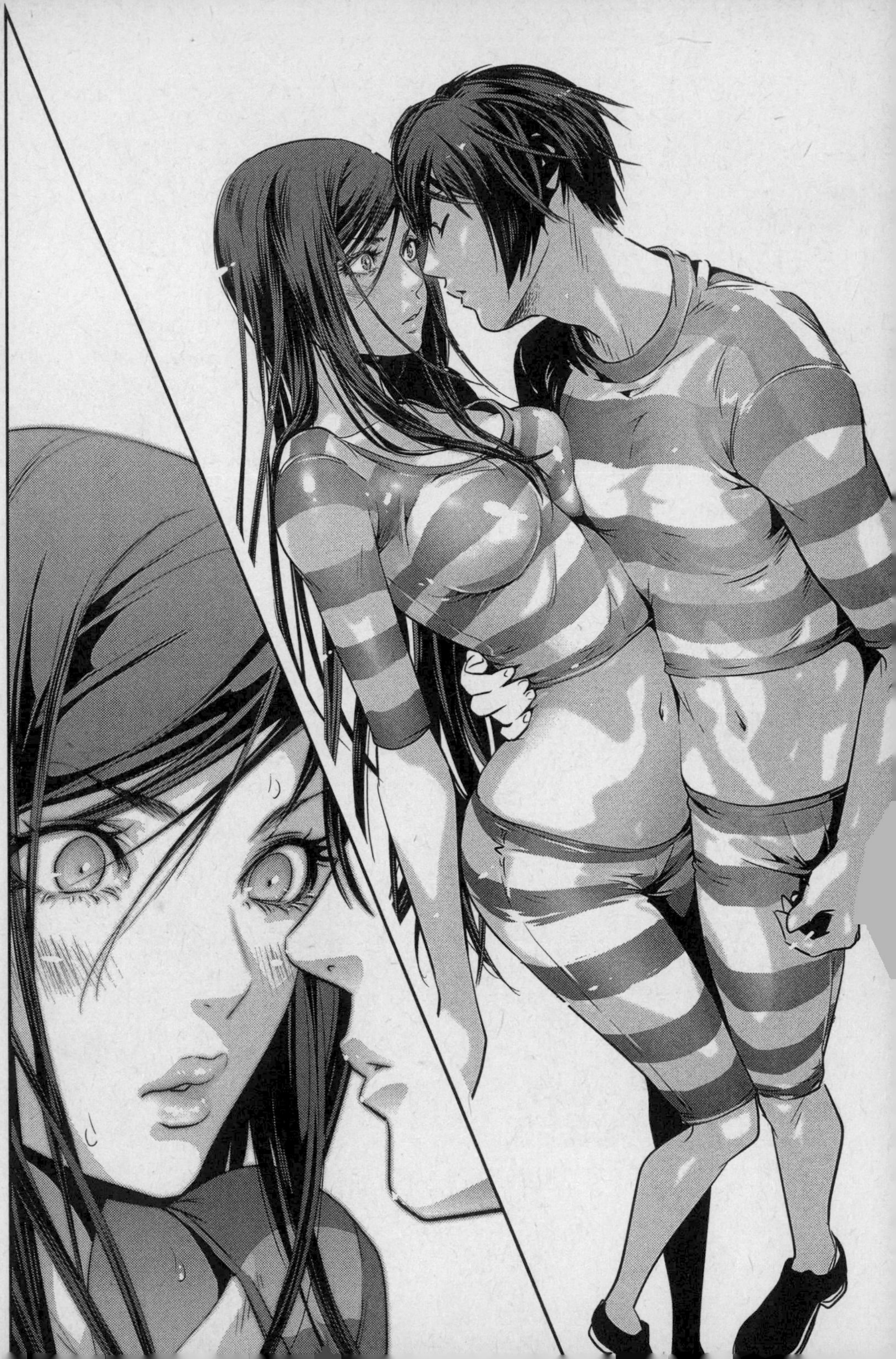

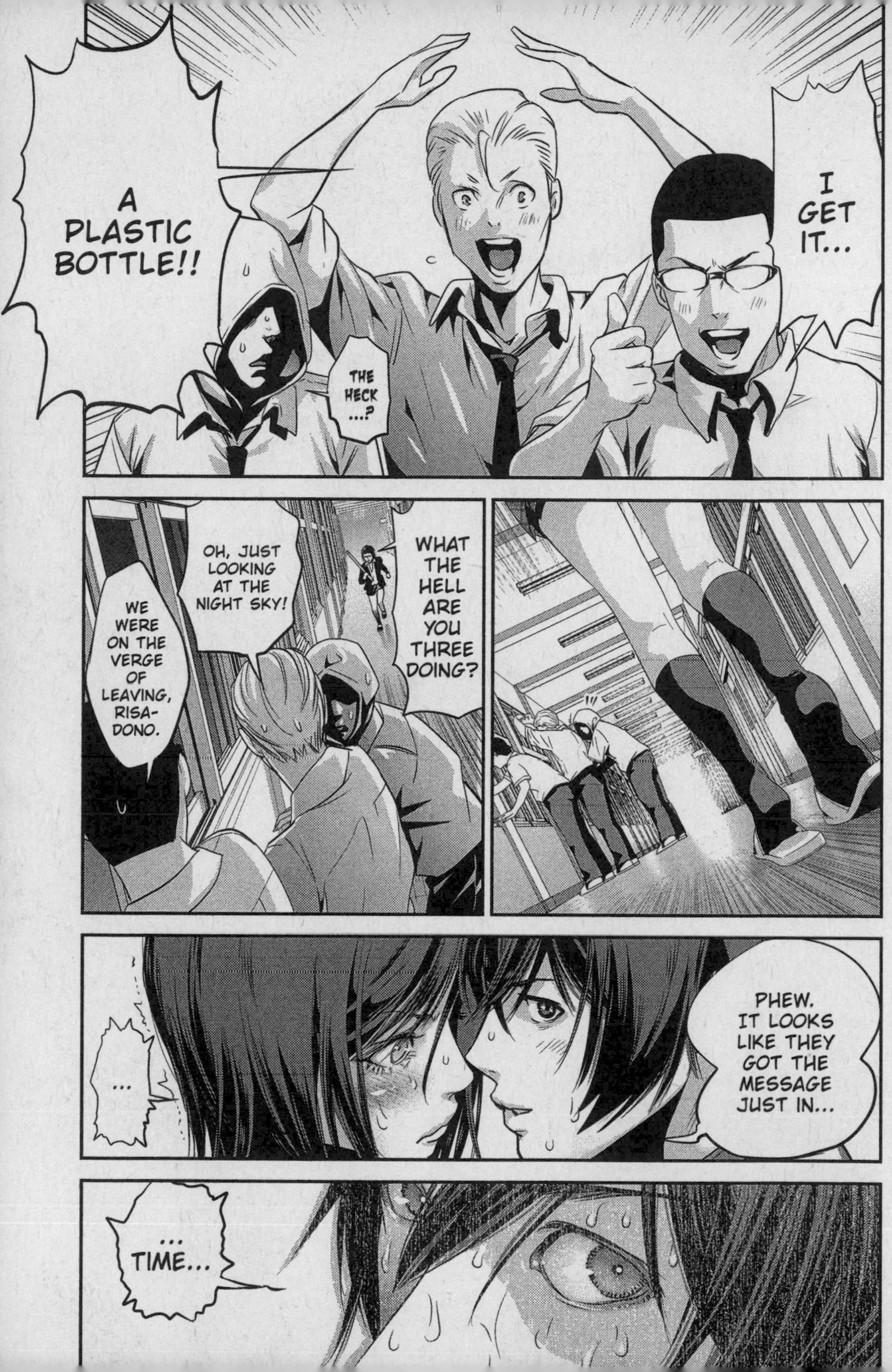

I GET IT...
A PLASTIC BOTTLE!!
THE HECK ...?
WHAT THE HELL ARE YOU THREE DOING?
OH, JUST LOOKING AT THE NIGHT SKY!
WE WERE ON THE VERGE OF LEAVING, RISA-DONO.
PHEW. IT LOOKS LIKE THEY GOT THE MESSAGE JUST IN...
...
... TIME...

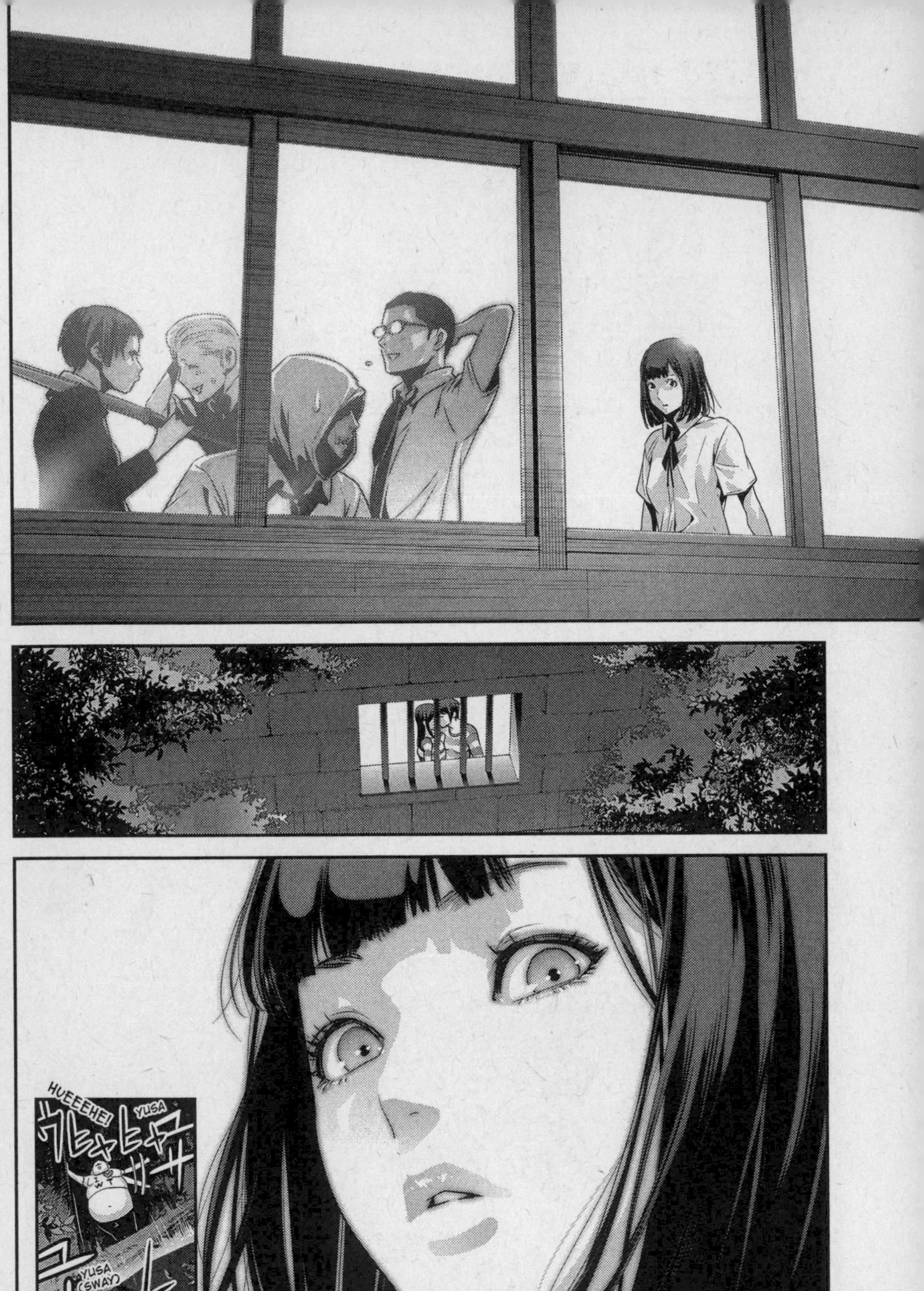
HUEEEHE!
YUSA
YUSA (SWAY)
HEE!
HEE!

CHAPTER 130: VANTAGE POINT

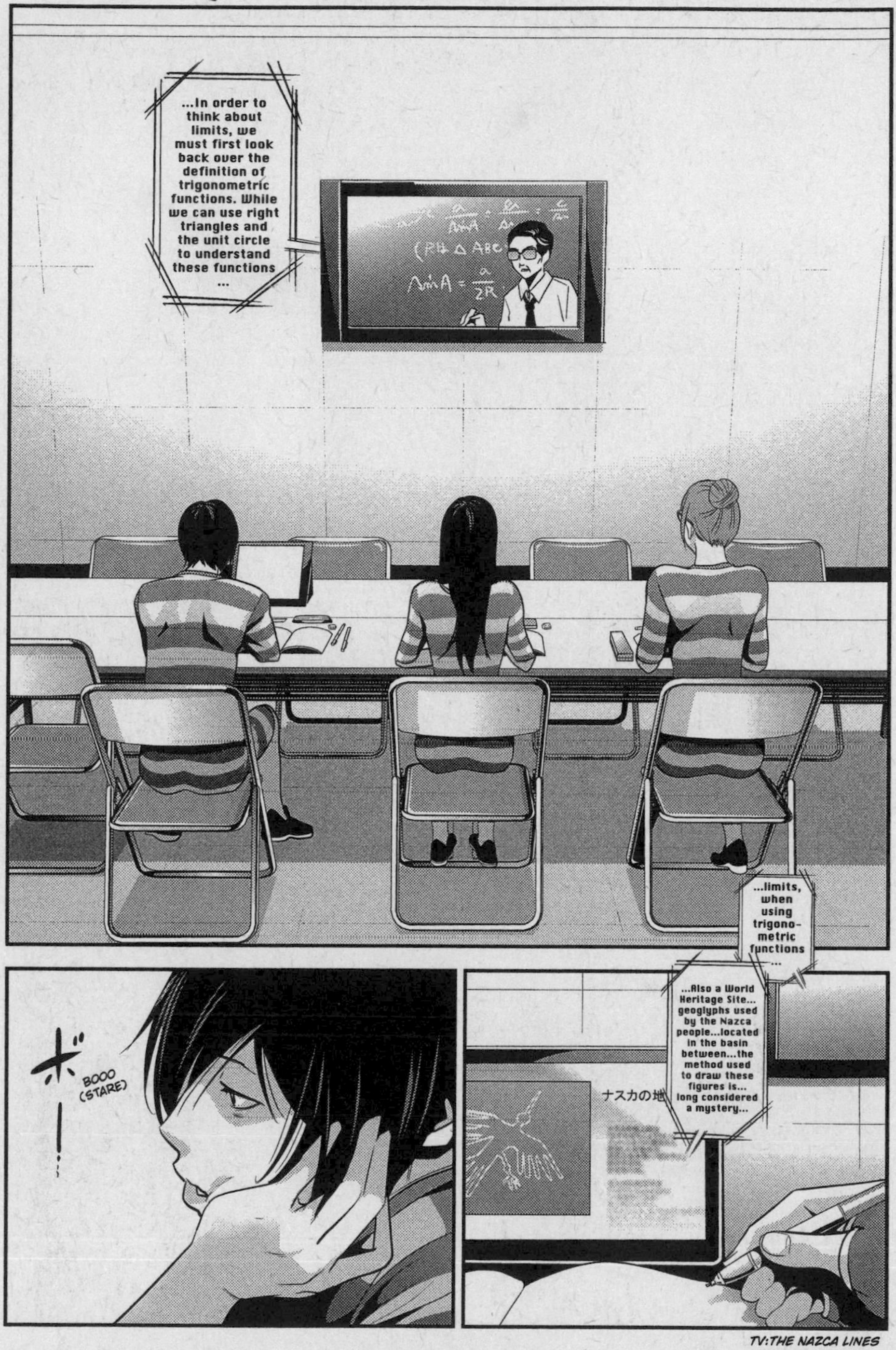
...In order to think about limits, we must first look back over the definition of trigonometric functions. While we can use right triangles and the unit circle to understand these functions ...
...limits, when using trigonometric functions ...
...Also a World Heritage Site... geoglyphs used by the Nazca people...located in the basin between...the method used to draw these figures is... long considered a mystery...
ナスカの地
BOOO (STARE)

TV: THE NAZCA LINES

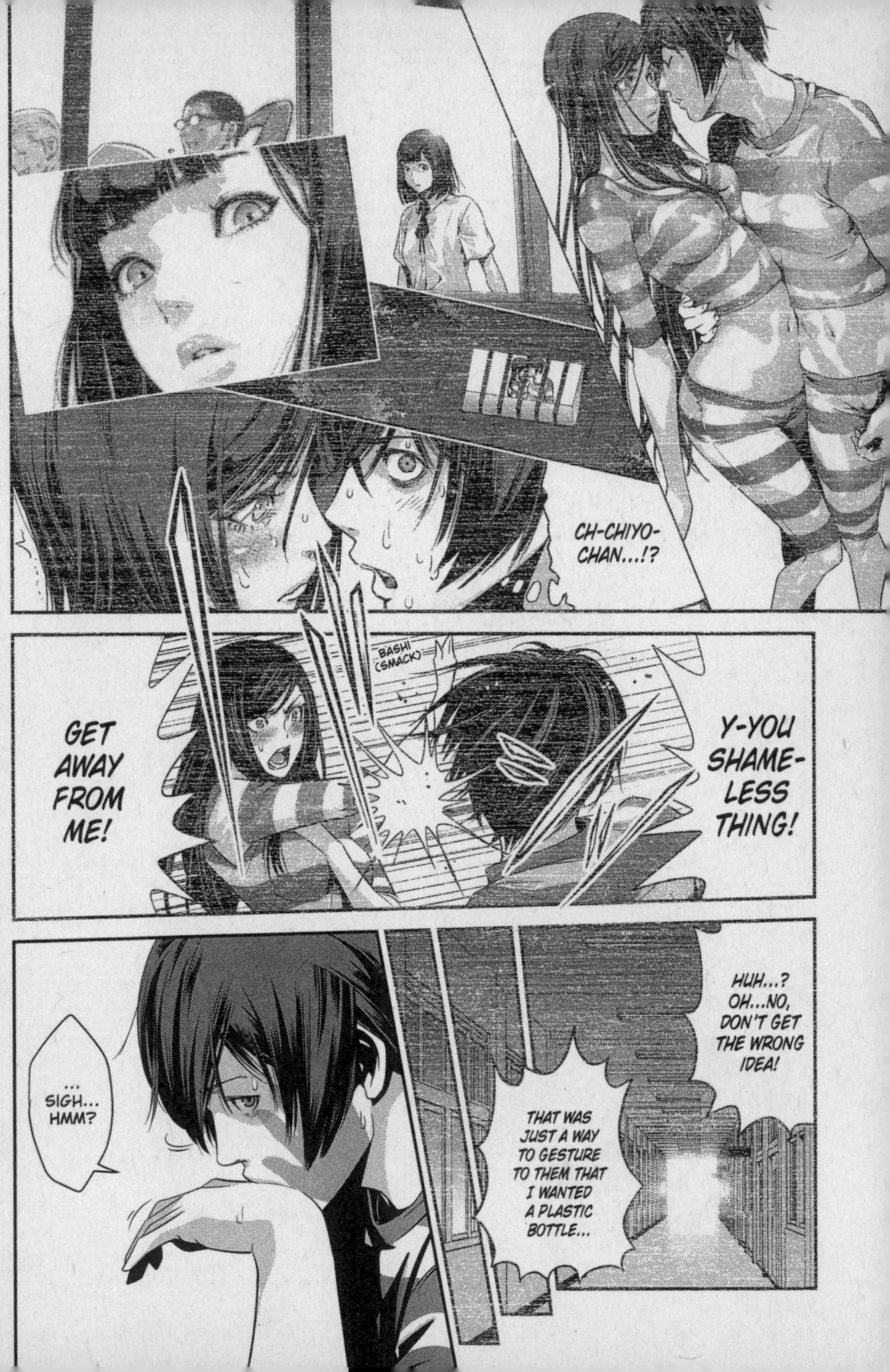
CH-CHIYO-CHAN...!?
BASHI (SMACK)
Y-YOU SHAME-LESS THING!
GET AWAY FROM ME!
HUH...? OH...NO, DON'T GET THE WRONG IDEA!
THAT WAS JUST A WAY TO GESTURE TO THEM THAT I WANTED A PLASTIC BOTTLE...
... SIGH... HMM?

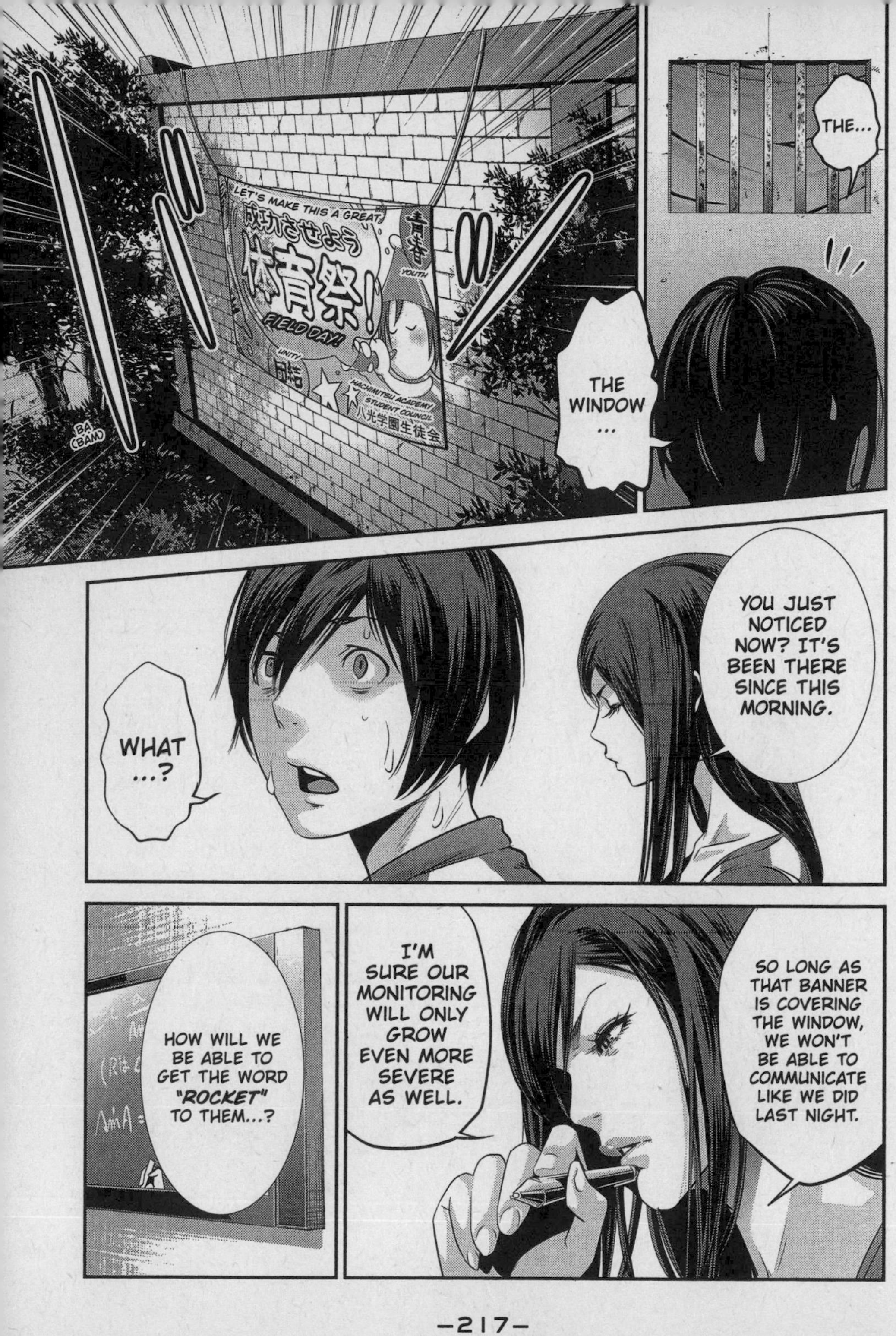
THE...
THE WINDOW...
LET'S MAKE THIS A GREAT
成功させよう
体育祭!
FIELD DAY!
青春
YOUTH
UNITY
団結
HACHIMITSU ACADEMY STUDENT COUNCIL
八光学園生徒会
BA (BAM)
YOU JUST NOTICED NOW? IT'S BEEN THERE SINCE THIS MORNING.
WHAT...?
SO LONG AS THAT BANNER IS COVERING THE WINDOW, WE WON'T BE ABLE TO COMMUNICATE LIKE WE DID LAST NIGHT.
I'M SURE OUR MONITORING WILL ONLY GROW EVEN MORE SEVERE AS WELL.
HOW WILL WE BE ABLE TO GET THE WORD "ROCKET" TO THEM...?

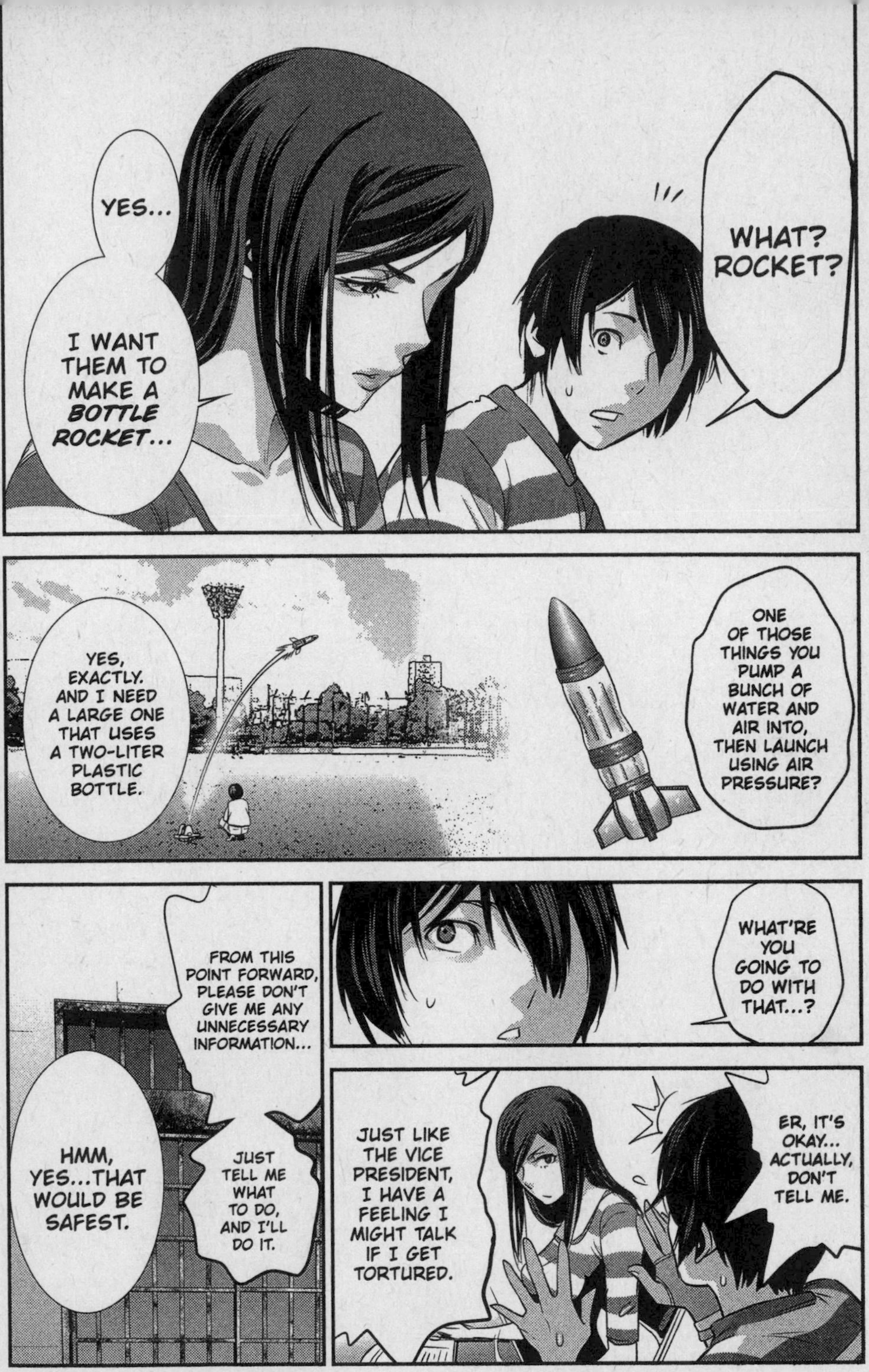
WHAT? ROCKET?
YES...
I WANT THEM TO MAKE A *BOTTLE ROCKET*...
ONE OF THOSE THINGS YOU PUMP A BUNCH OF WATER AND AIR INTO, THEN LAUNCH USING AIR PRESSURE?
YES, EXACTLY. AND I NEED A LARGE ONE THAT USES A TWO-LITER PLASTIC BOTTLE.
WHAT'RE YOU GOING TO DO WITH THAT...?
FROM THIS POINT FORWARD, PLEASE DON'T GIVE ME ANY UNNECESSARY INFORMATION...
ER, IT'S OKAY... ACTUALLY, DON'T TELL ME.
JUST LIKE THE VICE PRESIDENT, I HAVE A FEELING I MIGHT TALK IF I GET TORTURED.
JUST TELL ME WHAT TO DO, AND I'LL DO IT.
HMM, YES...THAT WOULD BE SAFEST.

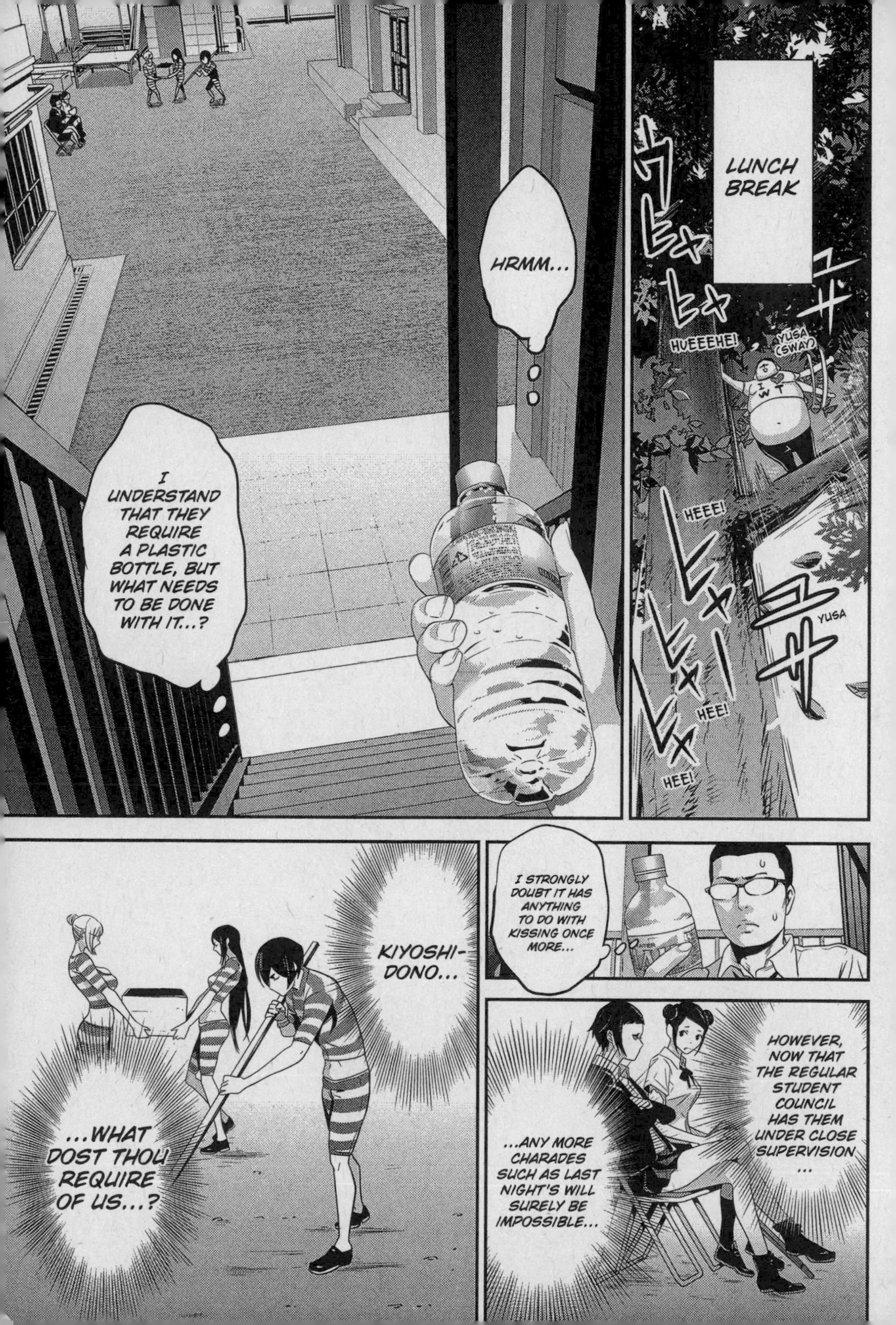

LUNCH BREAK
HUEEEHE!
YUSA (SWAY)
HEEE!
HEE!
HEE!
YUSA
HRMM...
I UNDERSTAND THAT THEY REQUIRE A PLASTIC BOTTLE, BUT WHAT NEEDS TO BE DONE WITH IT...?
I STRONGLY DOUBT IT HAS ANYTHING TO DO WITH KISSING ONCE MORE...
KIYOSHI-DONO...
...WHAT DOST THOU REQUIRE OF US...?
HOWEVER, NOW THAT THE REGULAR STUDENT COUNCIL HAS THEM UNDER CLOSE SUPERVISION...
...ANY MORE CHARADES SUCH AS LAST NIGHT'S WILL SURELY BE IMPOSSIBLE...

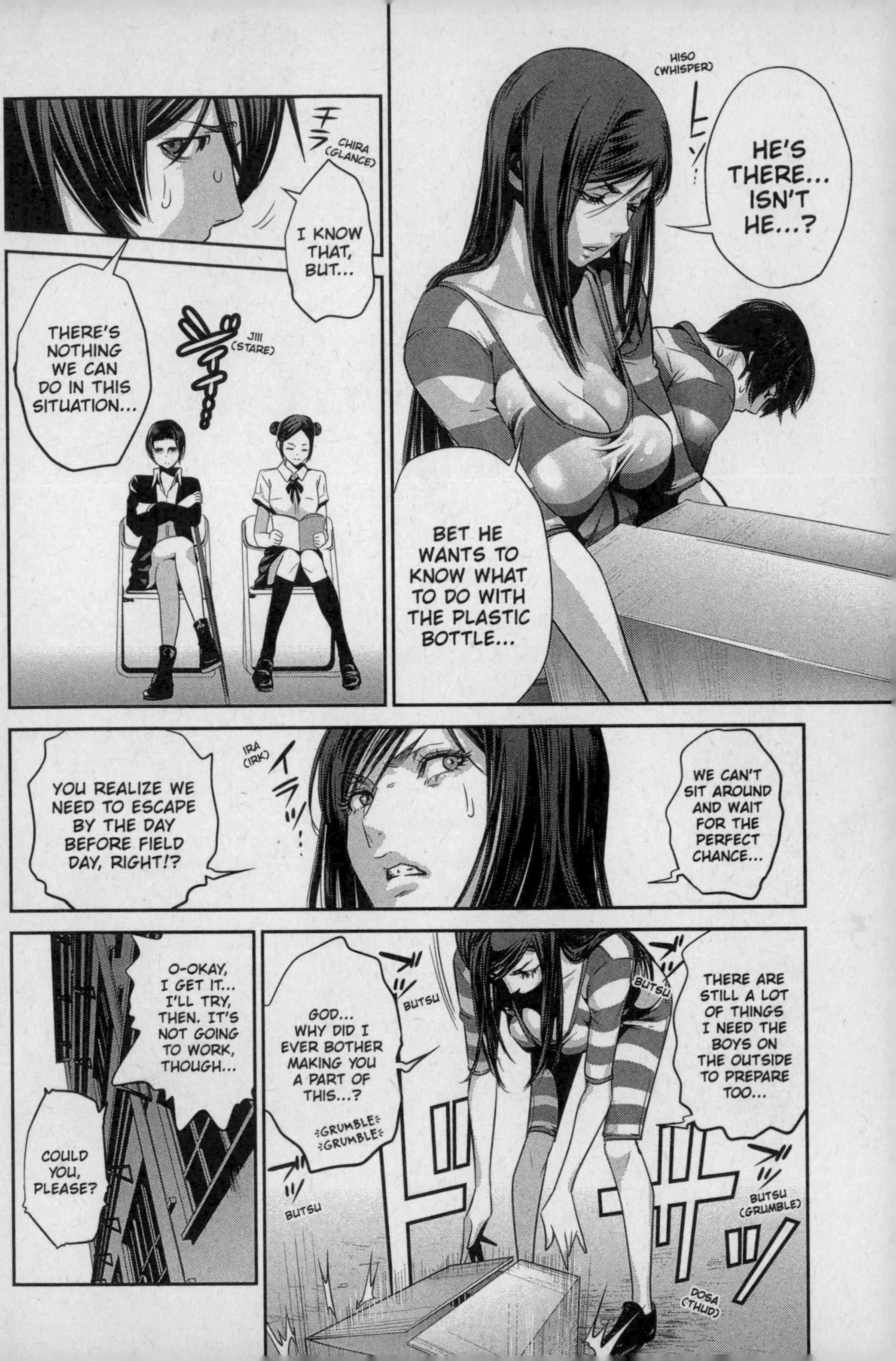
HISO (WHISPER)
HE'S THERE... ISN'T HE...?
BET HE WANTS TO KNOW WHAT TO DO WITH THE PLASTIC BOTTLE...
CHIRA (GLANCE)
I KNOW THAT, BUT...
THERE'S NOTHING WE CAN DO IN THIS SITUATION...
JIII (STARE)
WE CAN'T SIT AROUND AND WAIT FOR THE PERFECT CHANCE...
IRA (IRK)
YOU REALIZE WE NEED TO ESCAPE BY THE DAY BEFORE FIELD DAY, RIGHT!?
BUTSU
THERE ARE STILL A LOT OF THINGS I NEED THE BOYS ON THE OUTSIDE TO PREPARE TOO...
BUTSU
GOD... WHY DID I EVER BOTHER MAKING YOU A PART OF THIS...?
GRUMBLE GRUMBLE
BUTSU
BUTSU (GRUMBLE)
DOSA (THUD)
O-OKAY, I GET IT... I'LL TRY, THEN. IT'S NOT GOING TO WORK, THOUGH...
COULD YOU, PLEASE?

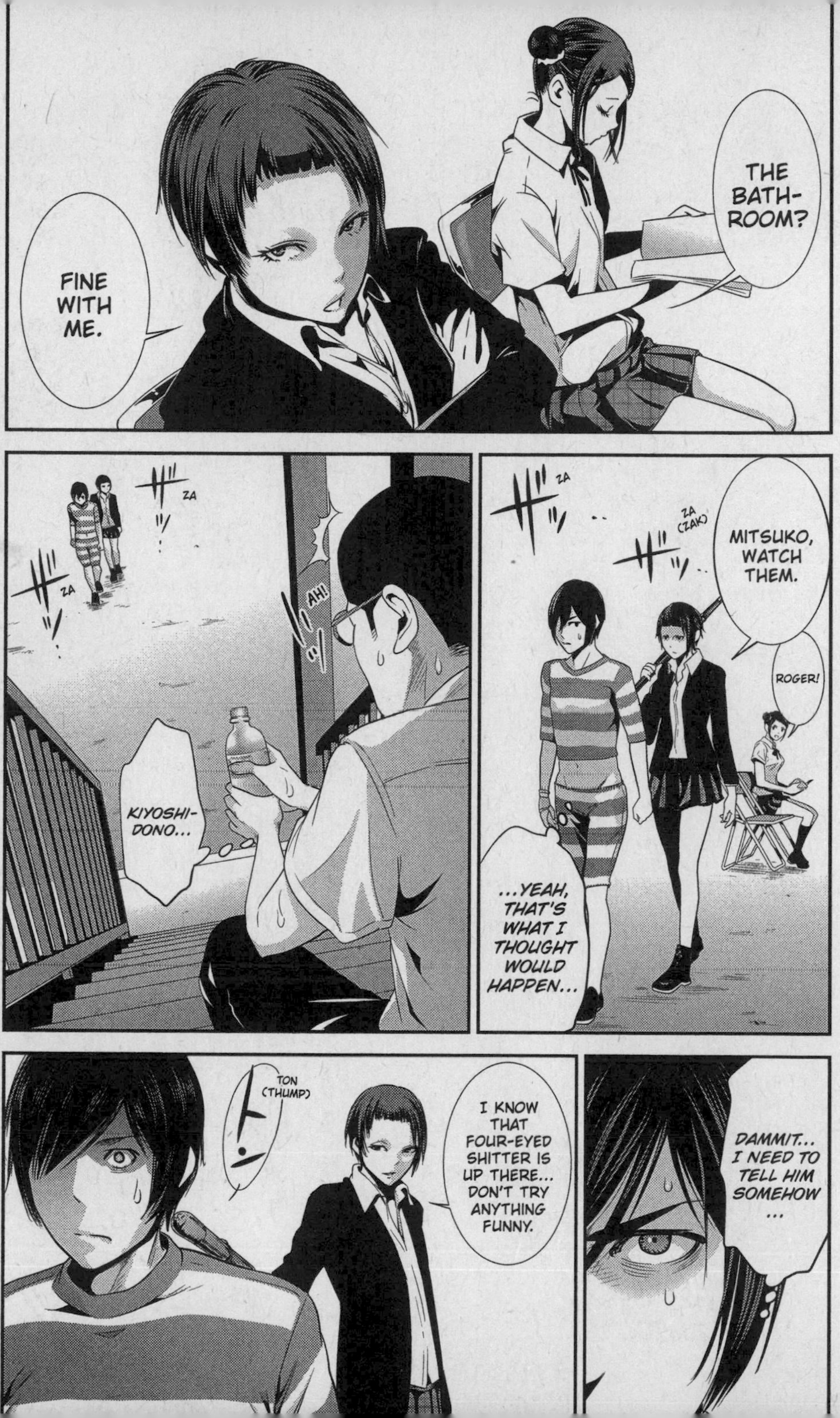
THE BATH-ROOM?
FINE WITH ME.
ZA
ZA (ZAK)
MITSUKO, WATCH THEM.
ROGER!
...YEAH, THAT'S WHAT I THOUGHT WOULD HAPPEN...
ZA
ZA
AH!
KIYOSHI-DONO...
DAMMIT... I NEED TO TELL HIM SOMEHOW...
I KNOW THAT FOUR-EYED SHITTER IS UP THERE... DON'T TRY ANYTHING FUNNY.
TON (THUMP)

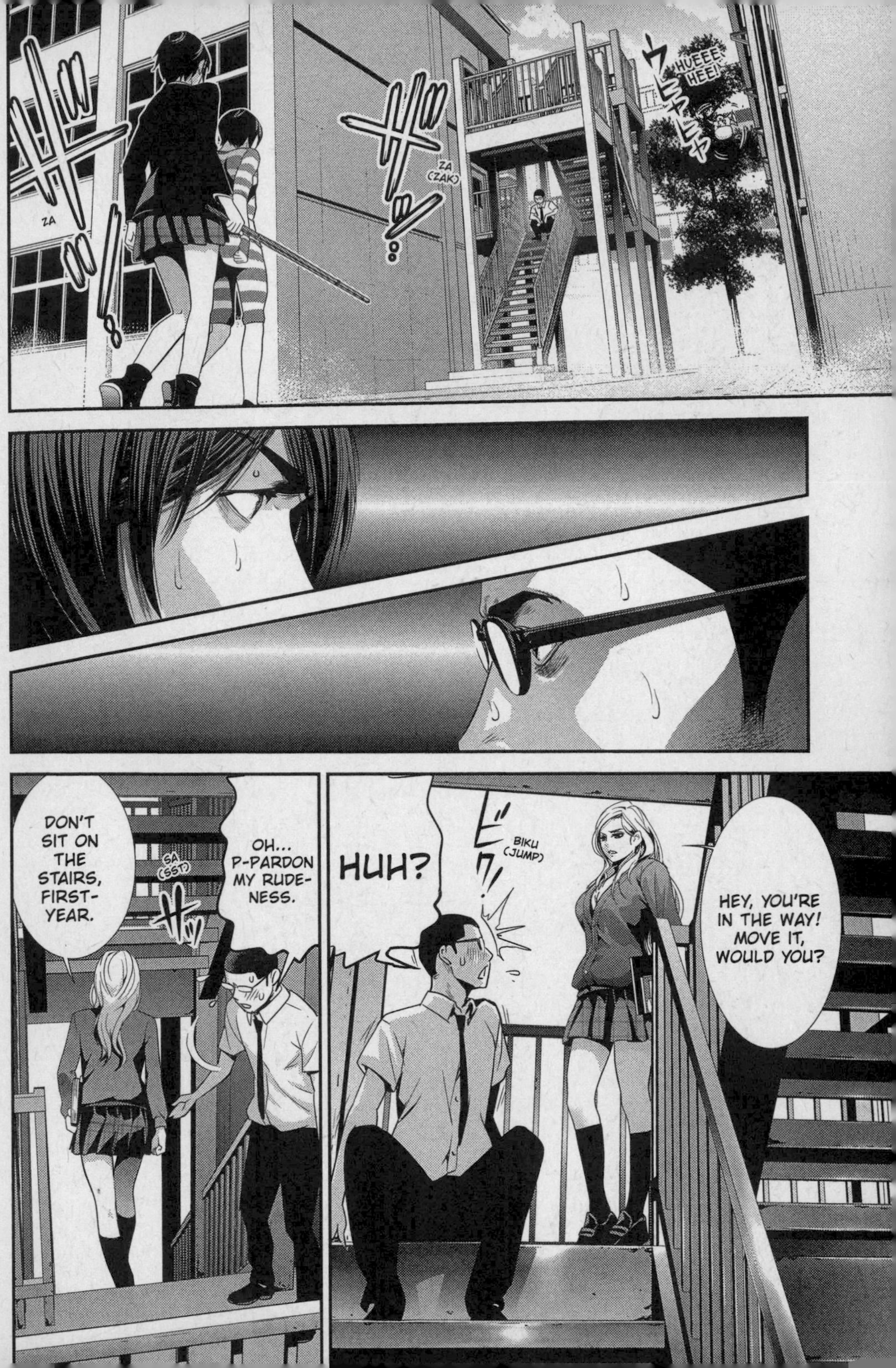
HUEEE HEE!
ZA (ZAK)
ZA
HEY, YOU'RE IN THE WAY! MOVE IT, WOULD YOU?
BIKU (JUMP)
HUH?
OH... P-PARDON MY RUDENESS.
SA (SST)
DON'T SIT ON THE STAIRS, FIRST-YEAR.

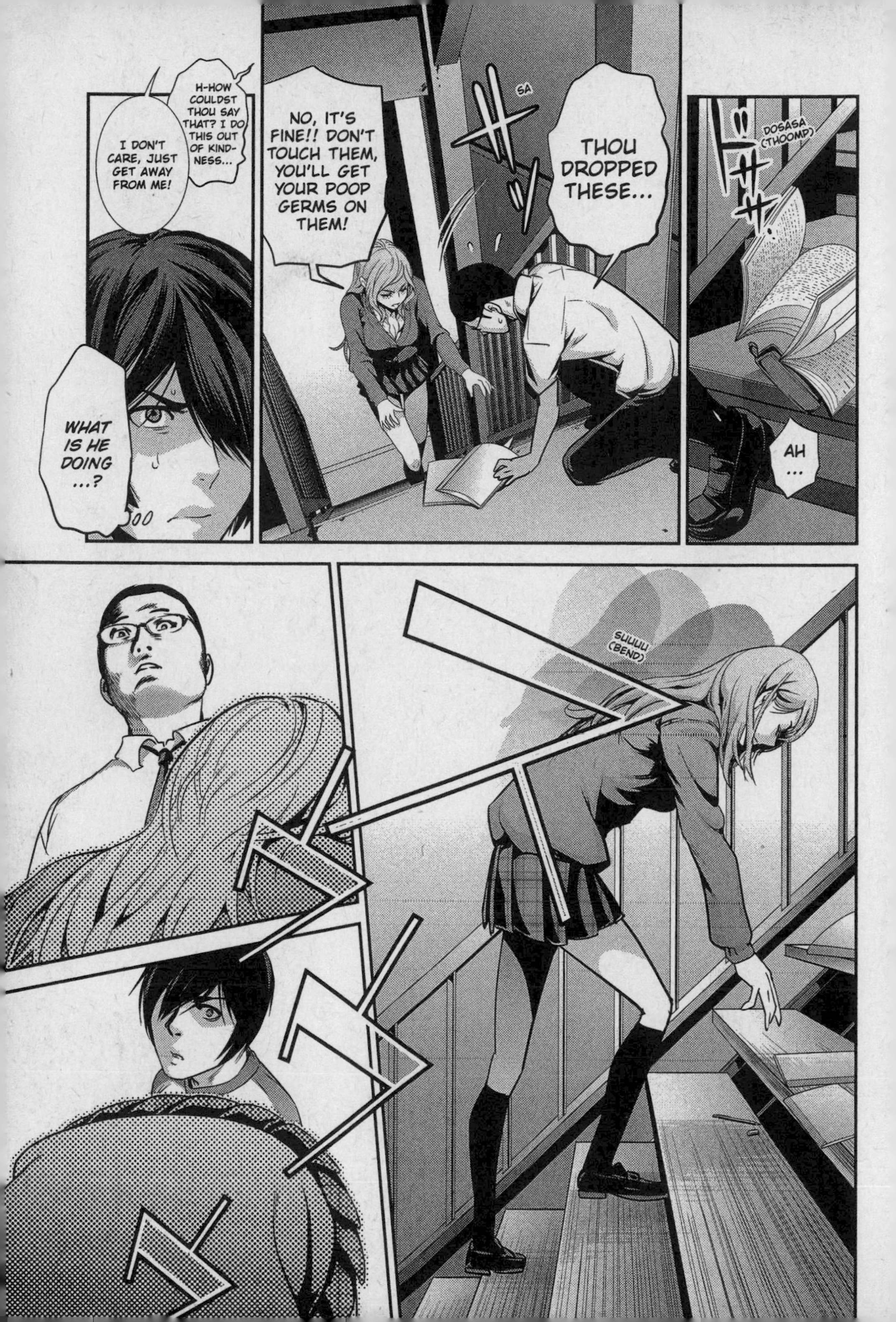
DOSASA (THOOMP)
AH ...
SA
THOU DROPPED THESE...
NO, IT'S FINE!! DON'T TOUCH THEM, YOU'LL GET YOUR POOP GERMS ON THEM!
H-HOW COULDST THOU SAY THAT? I DO THIS OUT OF KINDNESS...
I DON'T CARE, JUST GET AWAY FROM ME!
WHAT IS HE DOING ...?
SUUUU (BEND)

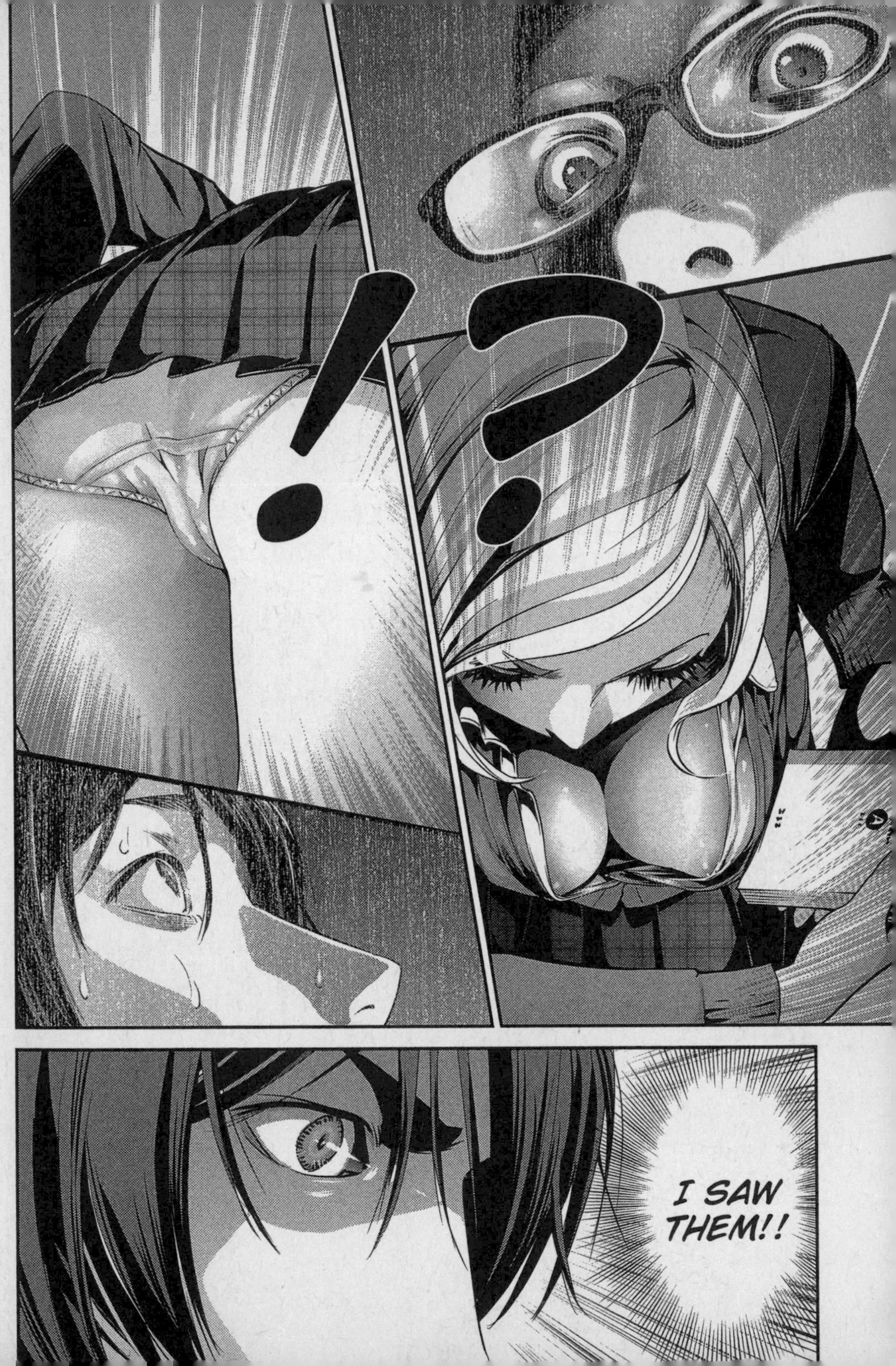
!?
I SAW THEM!!

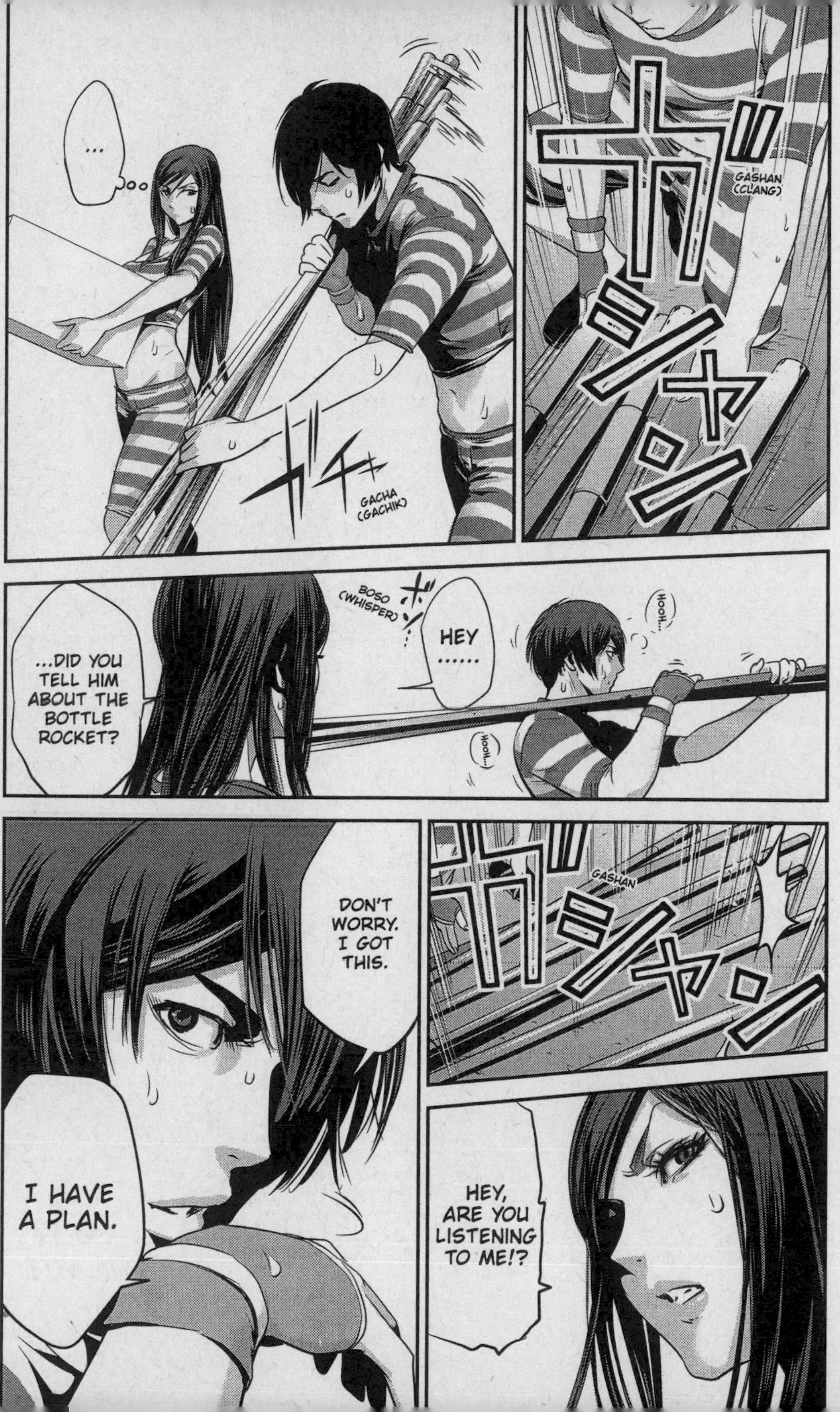
GASHAN (CLANG)
...
GACHA (GACHIK)
Hooh...
Hooh...
BOSO (WHISPER)
HEY ......
...DID YOU TELL HIM ABOUT THE BOTTLE ROCKET?
GASHAN
HEY, ARE YOU LISTENING TO ME!?
DON'T WORRY. I GOT THIS.
I HAVE A PLAN.

KIYOSHI-DONO SEEMS TO BE WORKING UNUSUALLY HARD AFTER RETURNING TO HIS LABOR...

BUT RATHER THAN CONCENTRATING ON THY WORK, KIYOSHI, THOU MUST TELL ME WHAT TO DO WITH THIS PLASTIC BOTTLE...!

ZUZU
(DRAG)

KATA
(KLUNK)

CHIRA
(GLANCE)

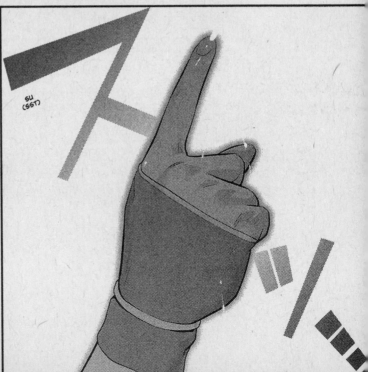

SU
(SST)

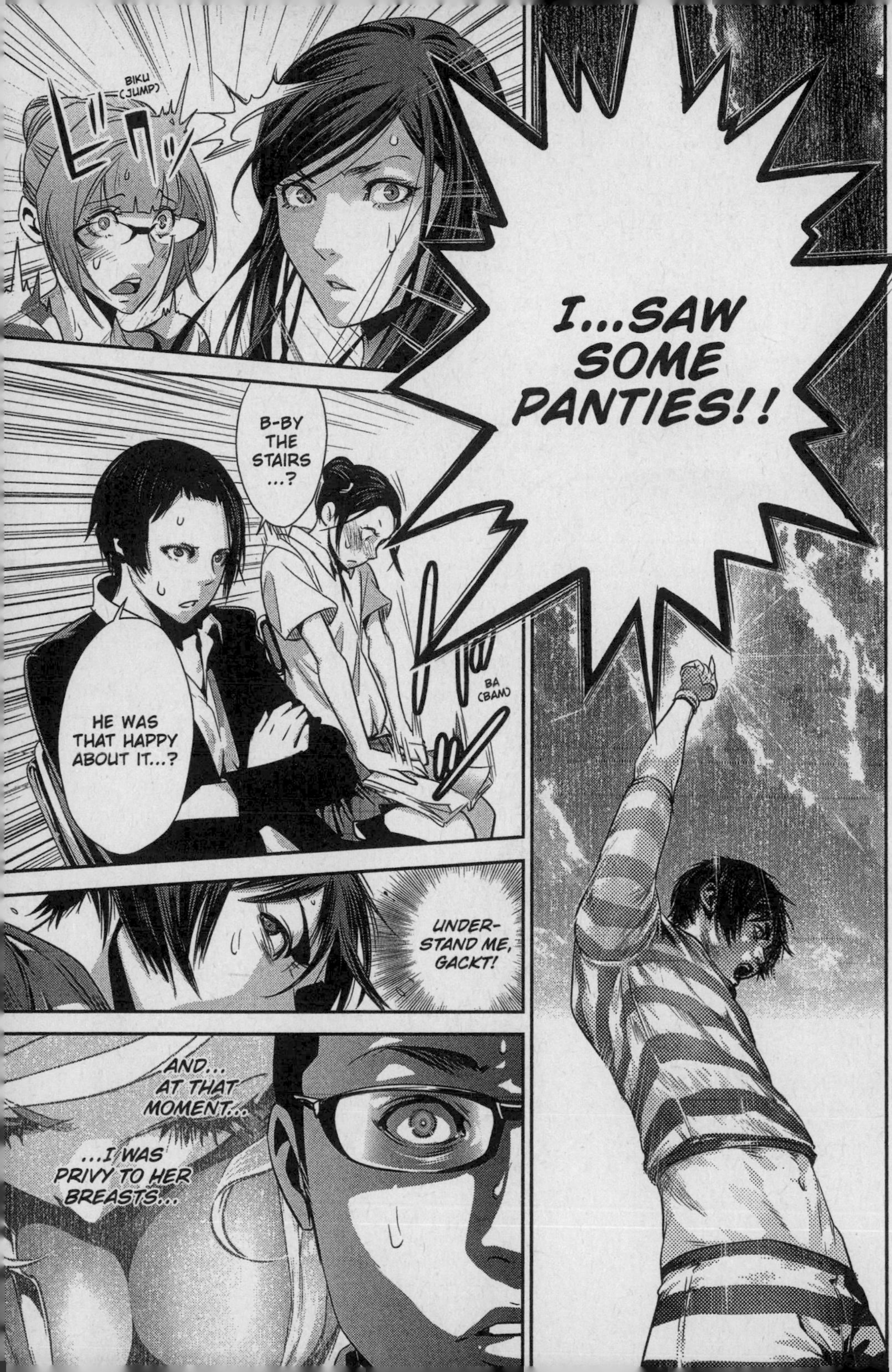
I...SAW SOME PANTIES!!
BIKU (JUMP)
B-BY THE STAIRS ...?
HE WAS THAT HAPPY ABOUT IT...?
BA (BAM)
UNDER-STAND ME, GACKT!
AND... AT THAT MOMENT...
...I WAS PRIVY TO HER BREASTS...

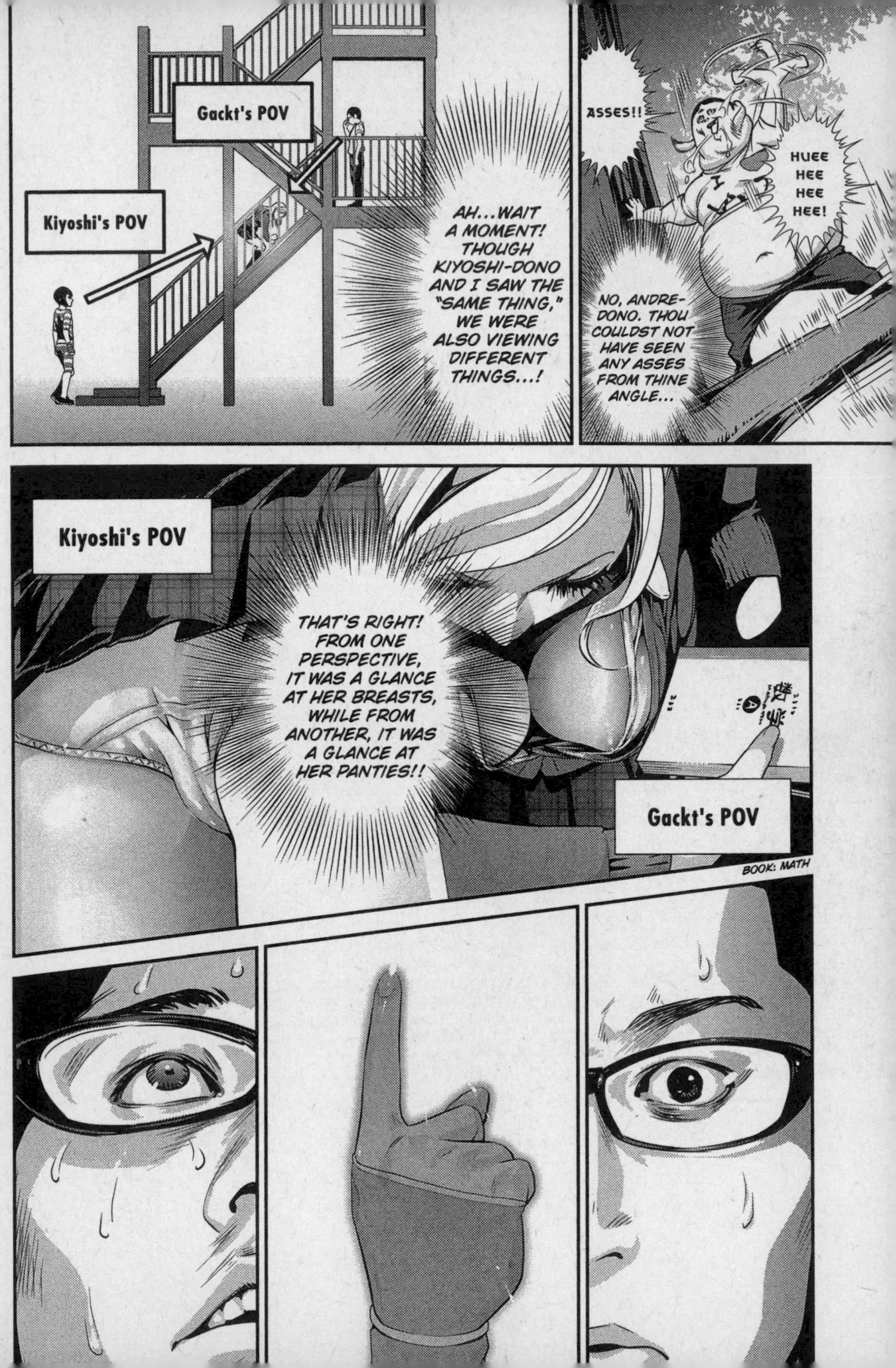
ASSES!!
HUEE HEE HEE HEE!
NO, ANDRE-DONO. THOU COULDST NOT HAVE SEEN ANY ASSES FROM THINE ANGLE...
Gackt's POV
Kiyoshi's POV
AH...WAIT A MOMENT! THOUGH KIYOSHI-DONO AND I SAW THE "SAME THING," WE WERE ALSO VIEWING DIFFERENT THINGS...!
Kiyoshi's POV
THAT'S RIGHT! FROM ONE PERSPECTIVE, IT WAS A GLANCE AT HER BREASTS, WHILE FROM ANOTHER, IT WAS A GLANCE AT HER PANTIES!!
Gackt's POV
BOOK: MATH

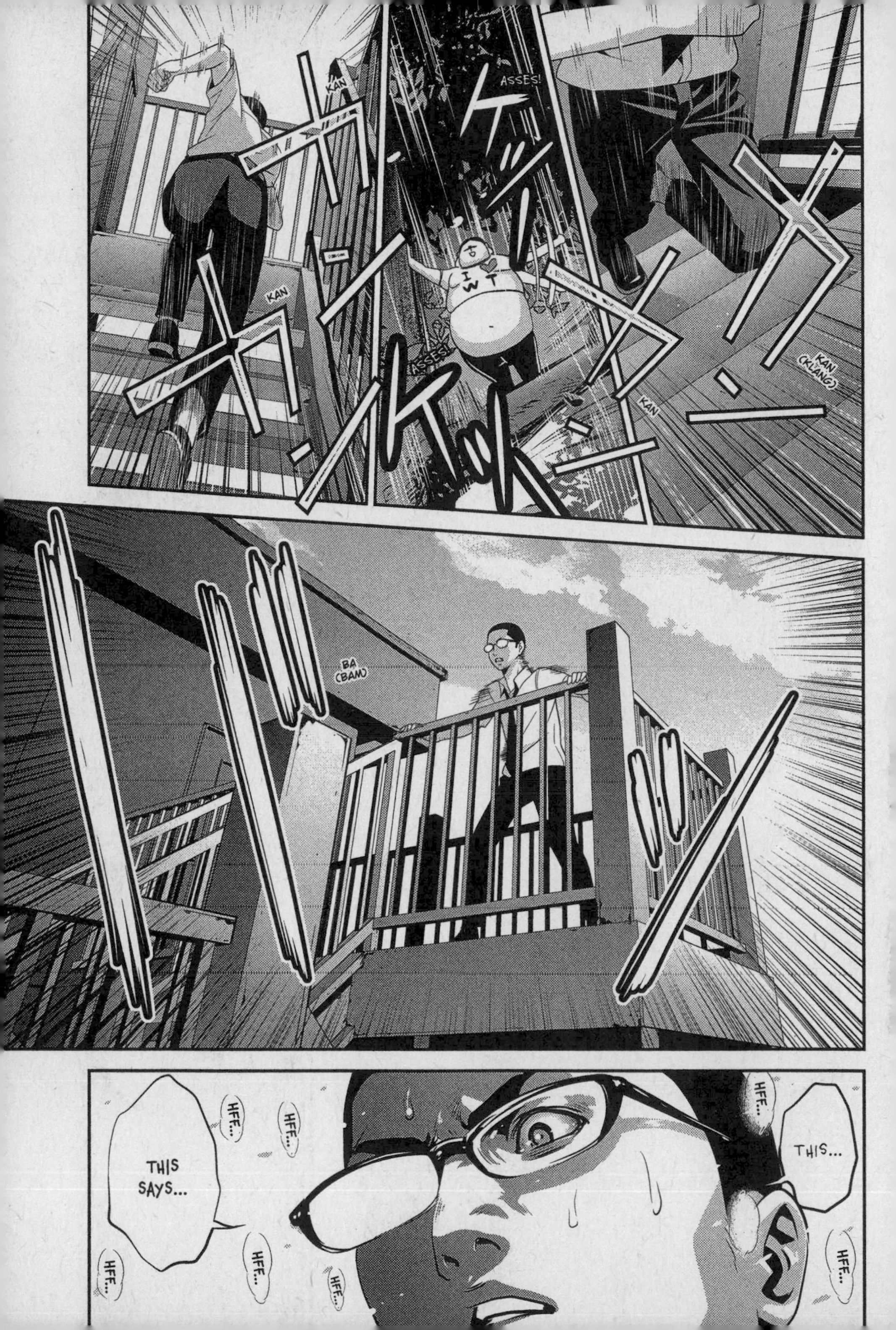
ASSES!
KAN
KAN (KLANG)
KAN
KAN
ASSES!
I W T
BA (BAM)
HFF...
THIS...
HFF...
HFF...
HFF...
THIS SAYS...
HFF...
HFF...
HFF...

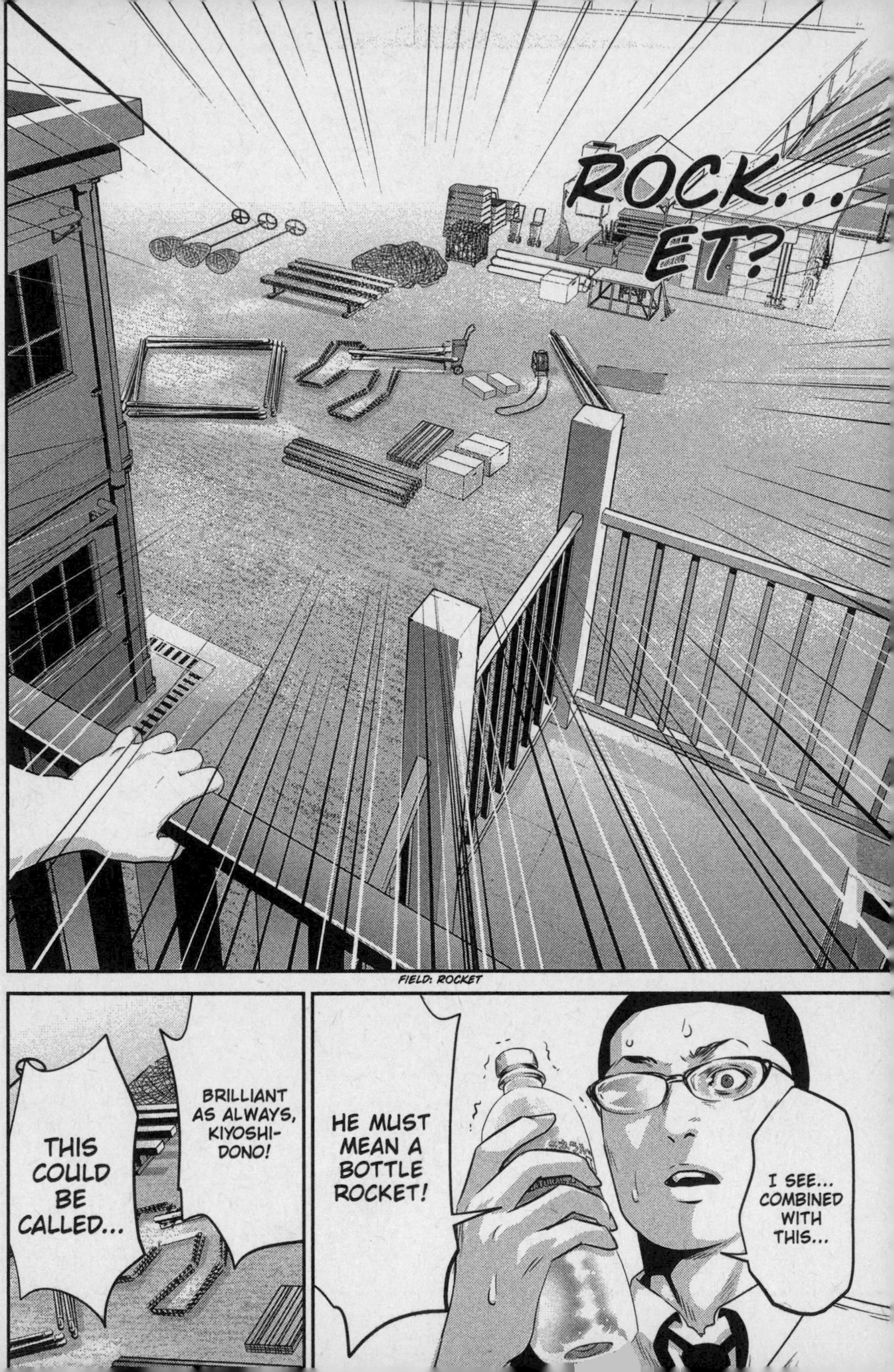
ROCK... ET?
FIELD: ROCKET
I SEE... COMBINED WITH THIS...
HE MUST MEAN A BOTTLE ROCKET!
BRILLIANT AS ALWAYS, KIYOSHI-DONO!
THIS COULD BE CALLED...

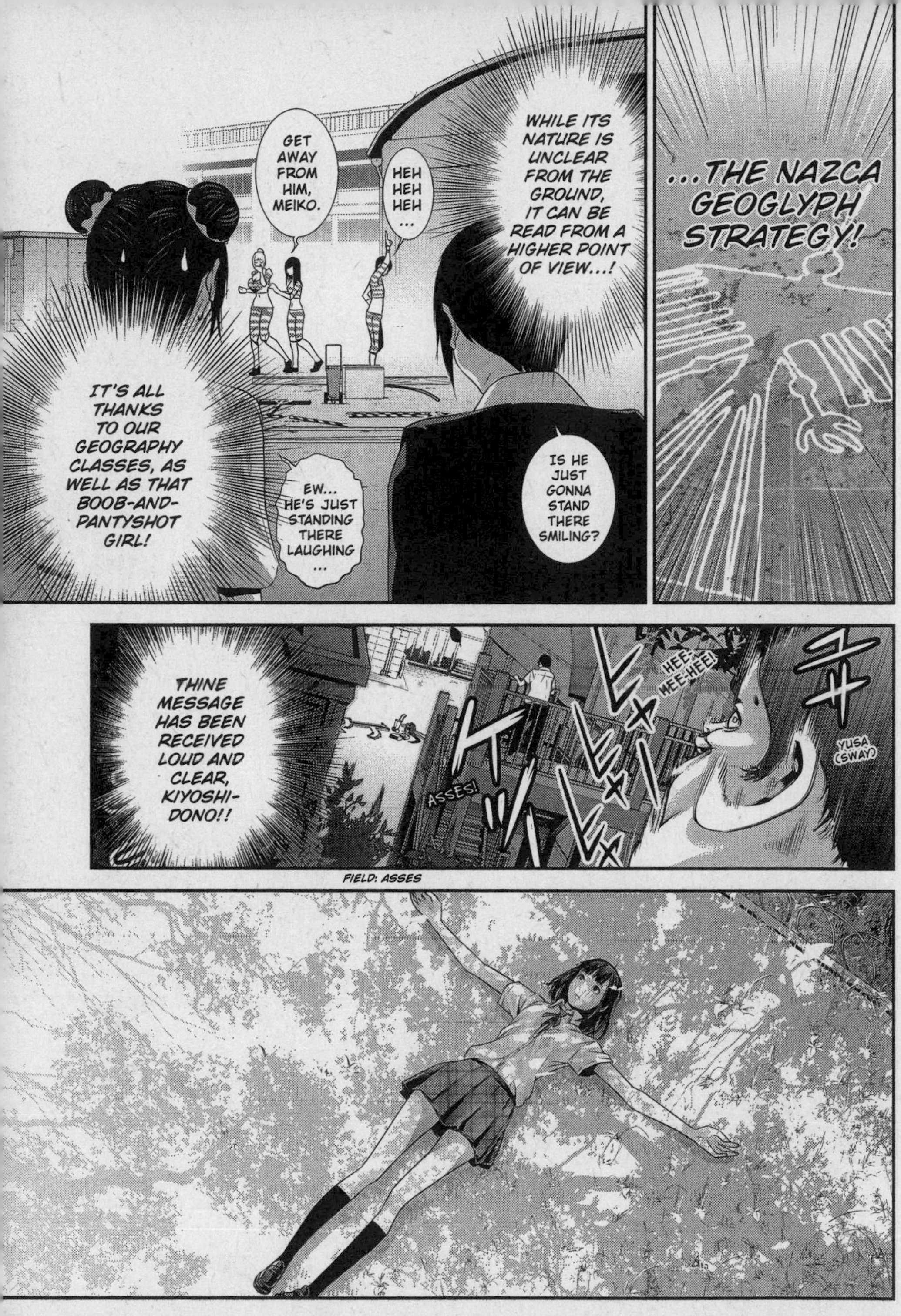
...THE NAZCA GEOGLYPH STRATEGY!
WHILE ITS NATURE IS UNCLEAR FROM THE GROUND, IT CAN BE READ FROM A HIGHER POINT OF VIEW...!
HEH HEH HEH ...
GET AWAY FROM HIM, MEIKO.
IS HE JUST GONNA STAND THERE SMILING?
EW... HE'S JUST STANDING THERE LAUGHING ...
IT'S ALL THANKS TO OUR GEOGRAPHY CLASSES, AS WELL AS THAT BOOB-AND-PANTYSHOT GIRL!
HEE-HEE-HEE!
YUSA (SWAY)
ASSES!
THINE MESSAGE HAS BEEN RECEIVED LOUD AND CLEAR, KIYOSHI-DONO!!
FIELD: ASSES

I DON'T UNDER-STAND...

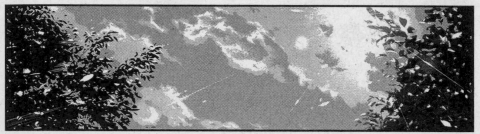

WHAT ARE...

...THESE FEELINGS...?

CHAPTER 131: THE RIGHT STUFF

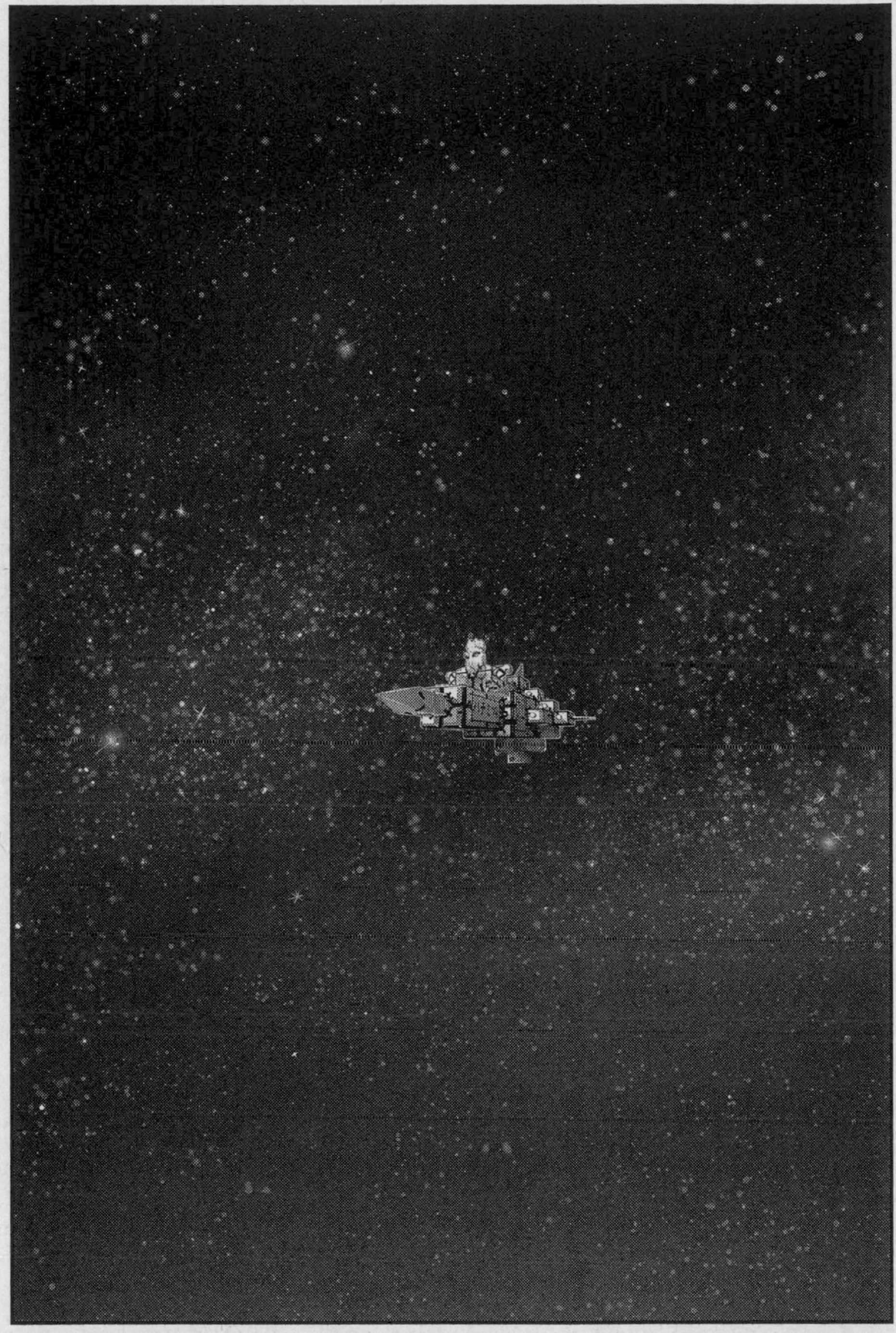

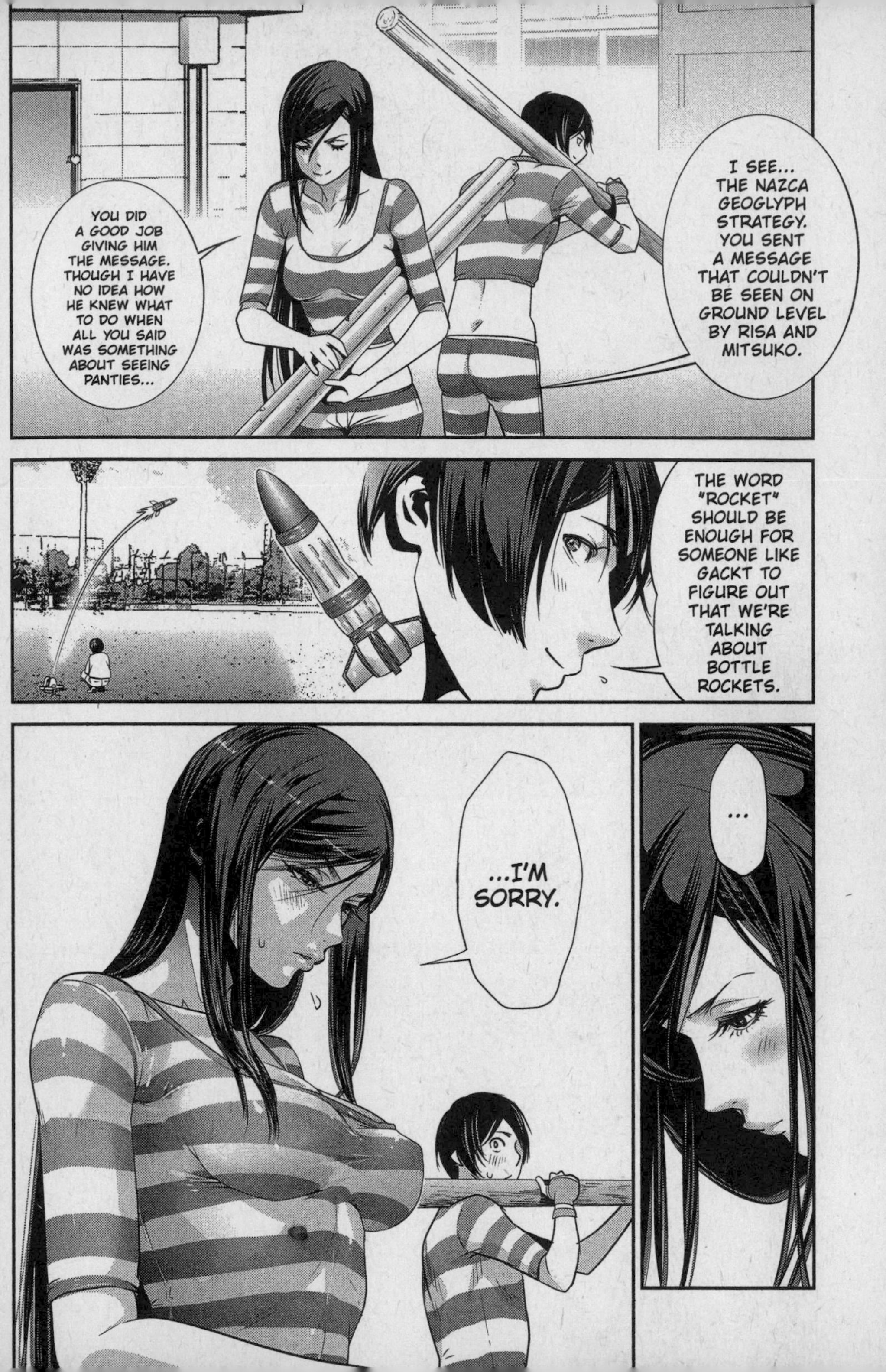
I SEE... THE NAZCA GEOGLYPH STRATEGY. YOU SENT A MESSAGE THAT COULDN'T BE SEEN ON GROUND LEVEL BY RISA AND MITSUKO.
YOU DID A GOOD JOB GIVING HIM THE MESSAGE. THOUGH I HAVE NO IDEA HOW HE KNEW WHAT TO DO WHEN ALL YOU SAID WAS SOMETHING ABOUT SEEING PANTIES...
THE WORD "ROCKET" SHOULD BE ENOUGH FOR SOMEONE LIKE GACKT TO FIGURE OUT THAT WE'RE TALKING ABOUT BOTTLE ROCKETS.
...
...I'M SORRY.

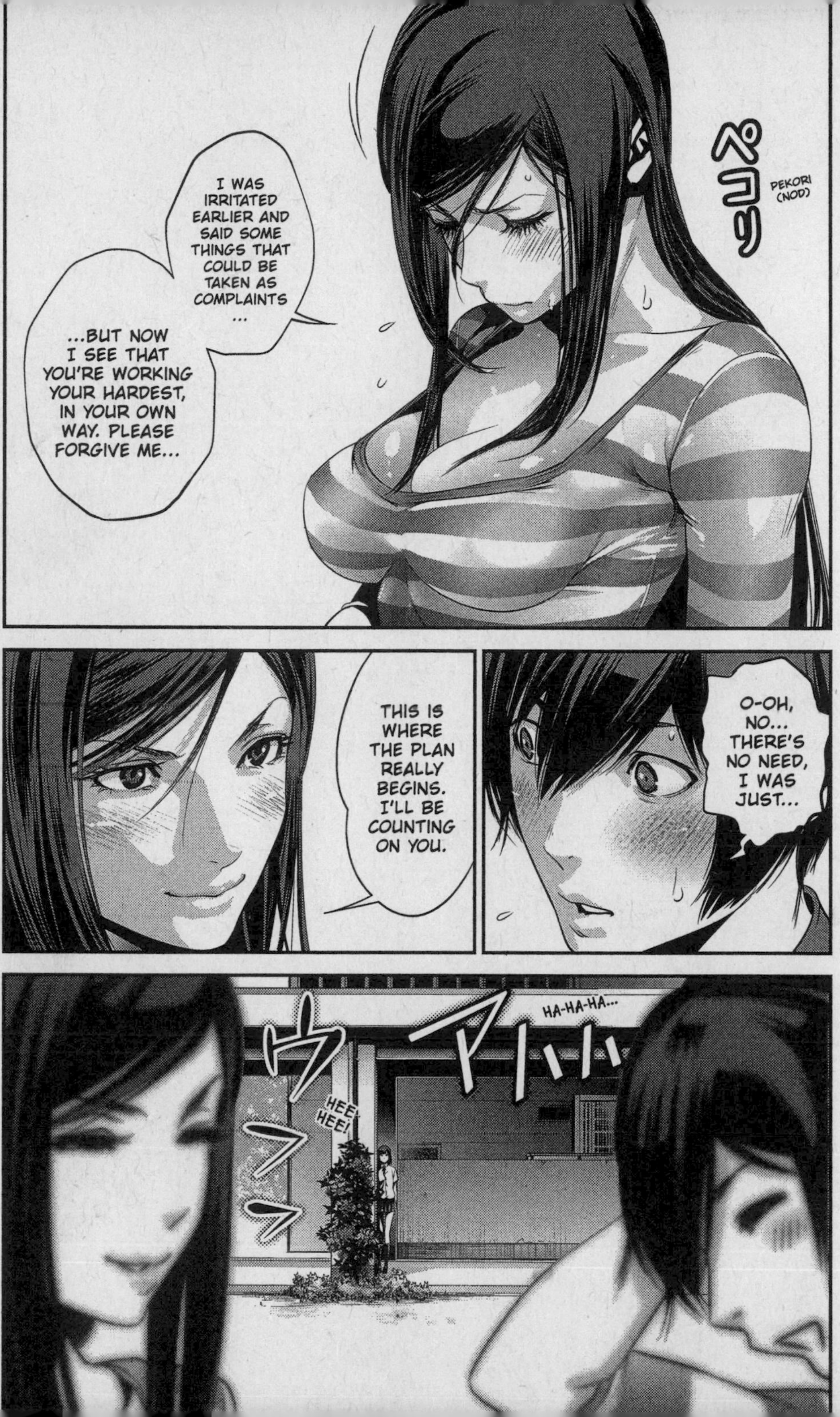
ペコッ
PEKORI (NOD)
I WAS IRRITATED EARLIER AND SAID SOME THINGS THAT COULD BE TAKEN AS COMPLAINTS ...
...BUT NOW I SEE THAT YOU'RE WORKING YOUR HARDEST, IN YOUR OWN WAY. PLEASE FORGIVE ME...
O-OH, NO... THERE'S NO NEED, I WAS JUST...
THIS IS WHERE THE PLAN REALLY BEGINS. I'LL BE COUNTING ON YOU.
アハハ
HA-HA-HA...
ウフフフ
HEE! HEE!

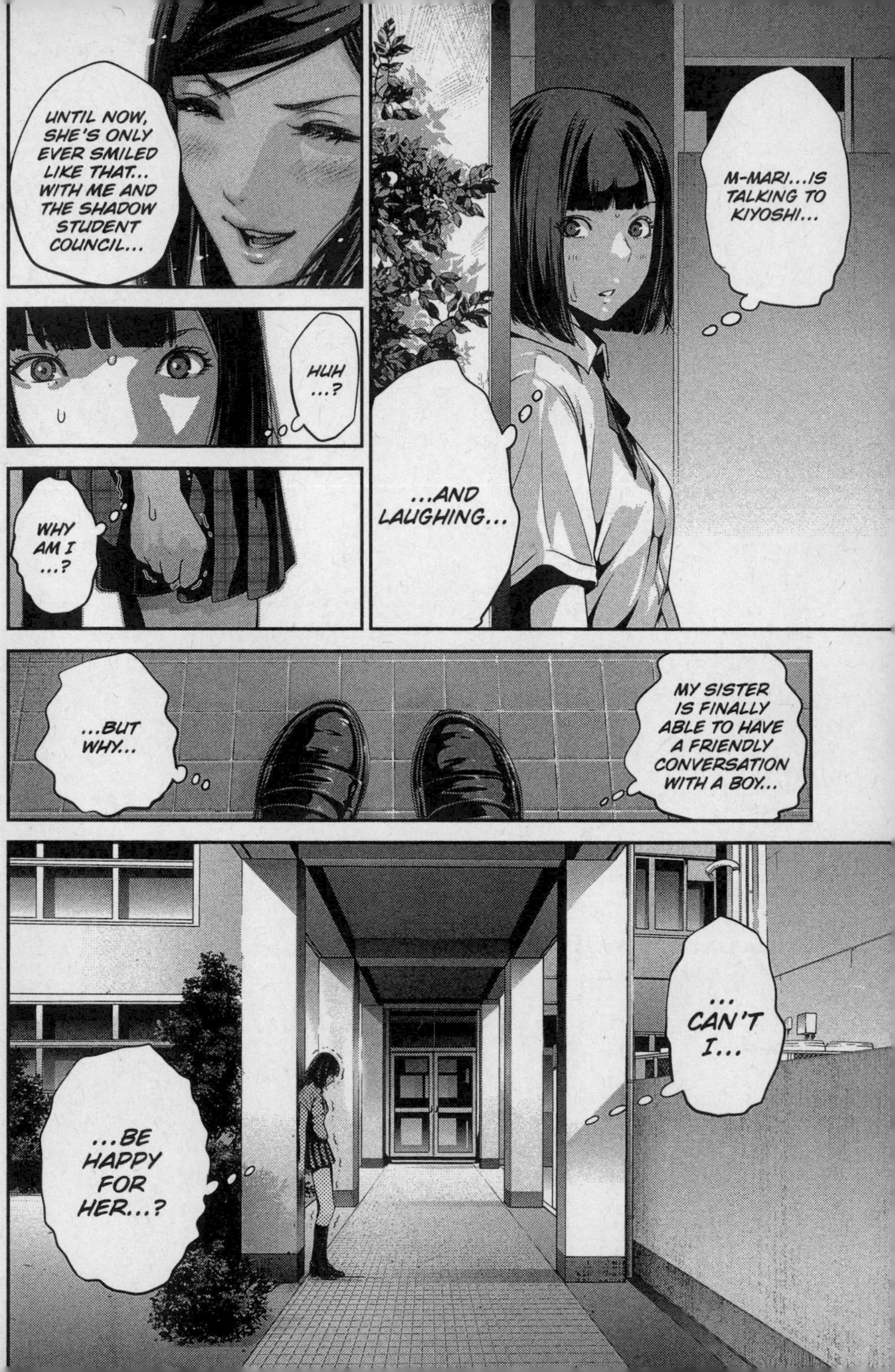
M-MARI...IS TALKING TO KIYOSHI...
...AND LAUGHING...
UNTIL NOW, SHE'S ONLY EVER SMILED LIKE THAT... WITH ME AND THE SHADOW STUDENT COUNCIL...
HUH ...?
WHY AM I ...?
MY SISTER IS FINALLY ABLE TO HAVE A FRIENDLY CONVERSATION WITH A BOY...
...BUT WHY...
... CAN'T I...
...BE HAPPY FOR HER...?

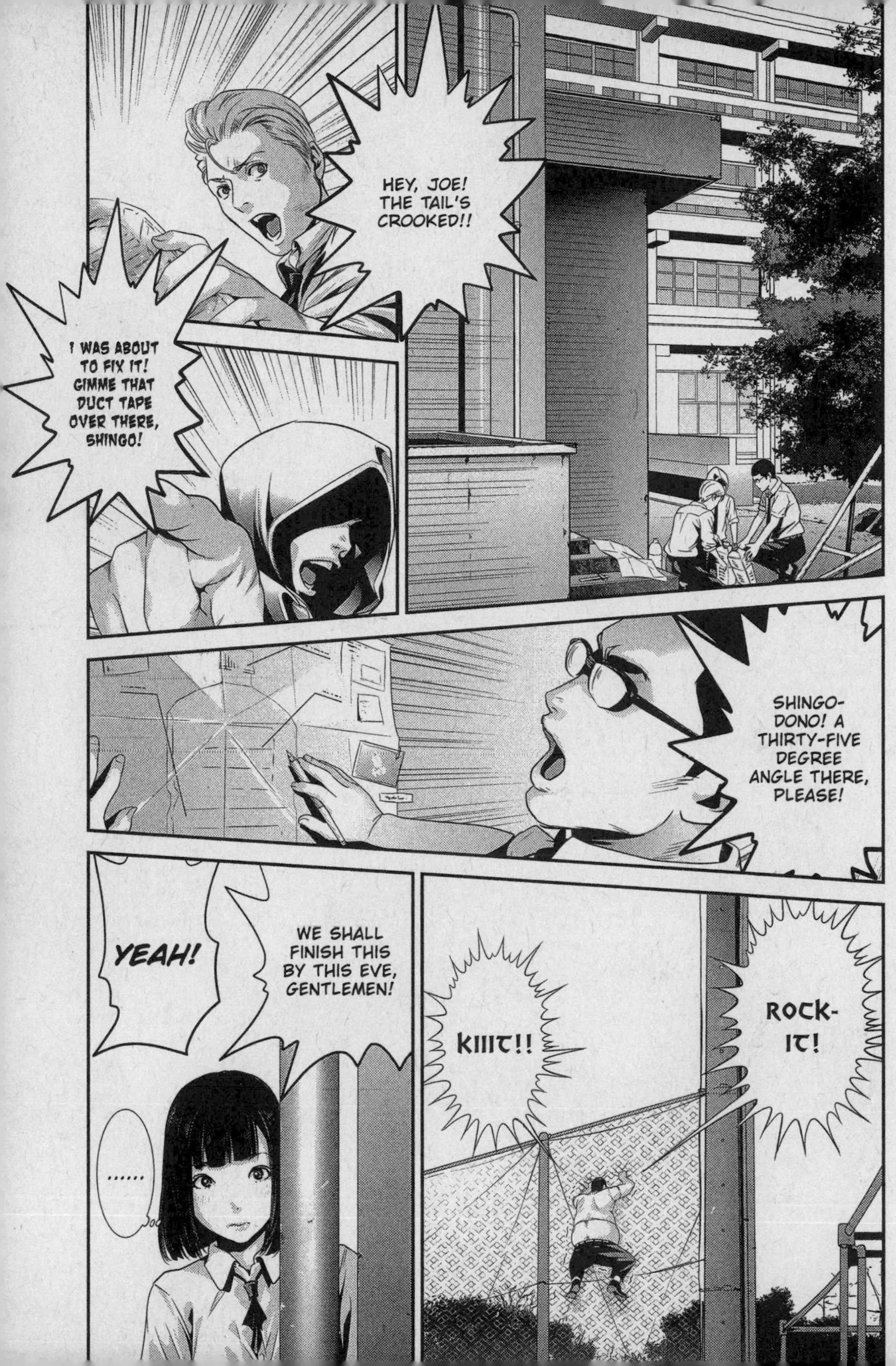
HEY, JOE! THE TAIL'S CROOKED!!
I WAS ABOUT TO FIX IT! GIMME THAT DUCT TAPE OVER THERE, SHINGO!
SHINGO-DONO! A THIRTY-FIVE DEGREE ANGLE THERE, PLEASE!
WE SHALL FINISH THIS BY THIS EVE, GENTLEMEN!
YEAH!
......
ROCK-IT!
KIIIT!!

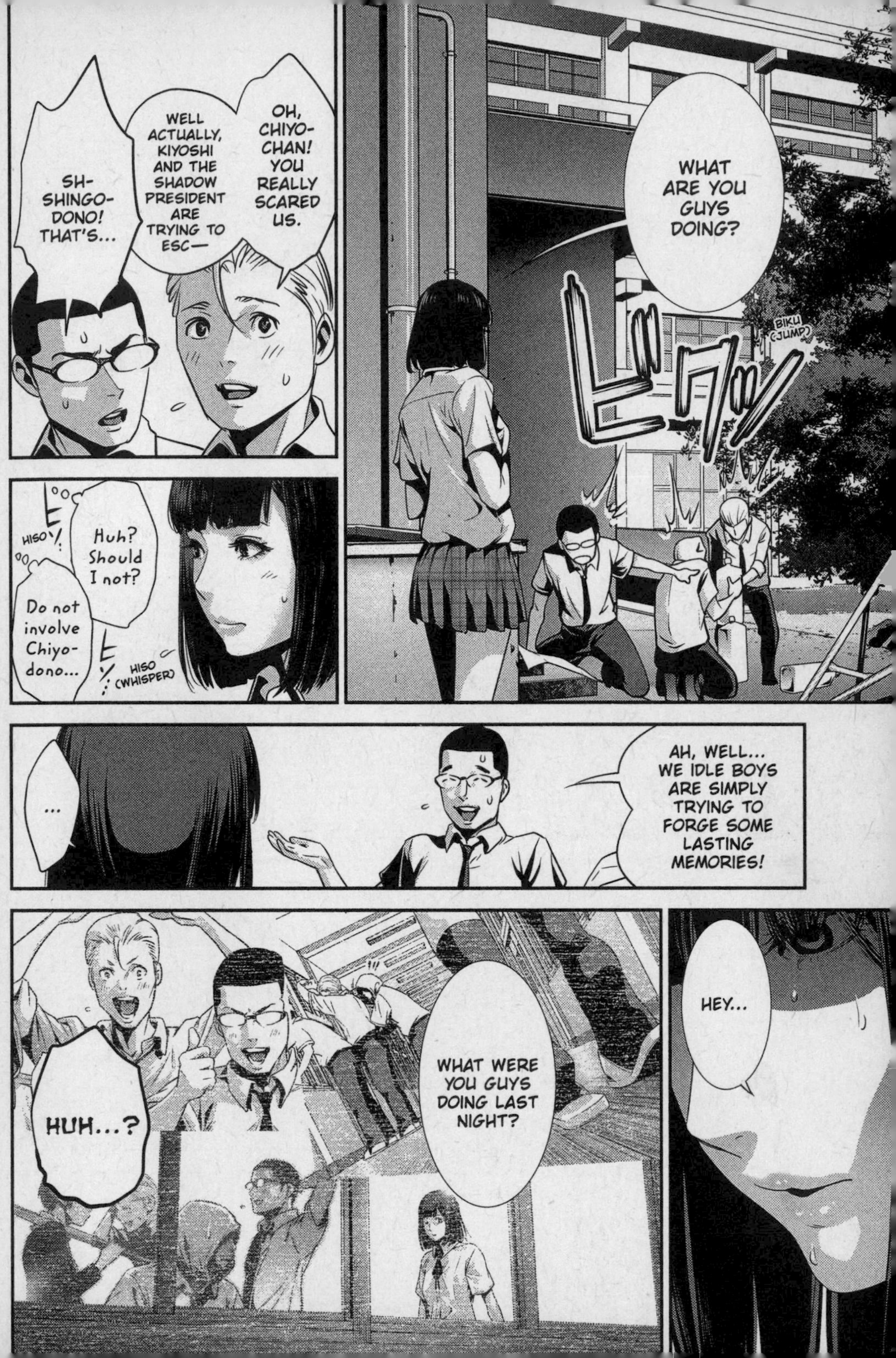
WHAT ARE YOU GUYS DOING?
BIKU (JUMP)
OH, CHIYO-CHAN! YOU REALLY SCARED US.
WELL ACTUALLY, KIYOSHI AND THE SHADOW PRESIDENT ARE TRYING TO ESC—
SH-SHINGO-DONO! THAT'S...
HISO
Huh? Should I not?
Do not involve Chiyo-dono...
HISO (WHISPER)
AH, WELL... WE IDLE BOYS ARE SIMPLY TRYING TO FORGE SOME LASTING MEMORIES!
...
HEY...
WHAT WERE YOU GUYS DOING LAST NIGHT?
HUH...?

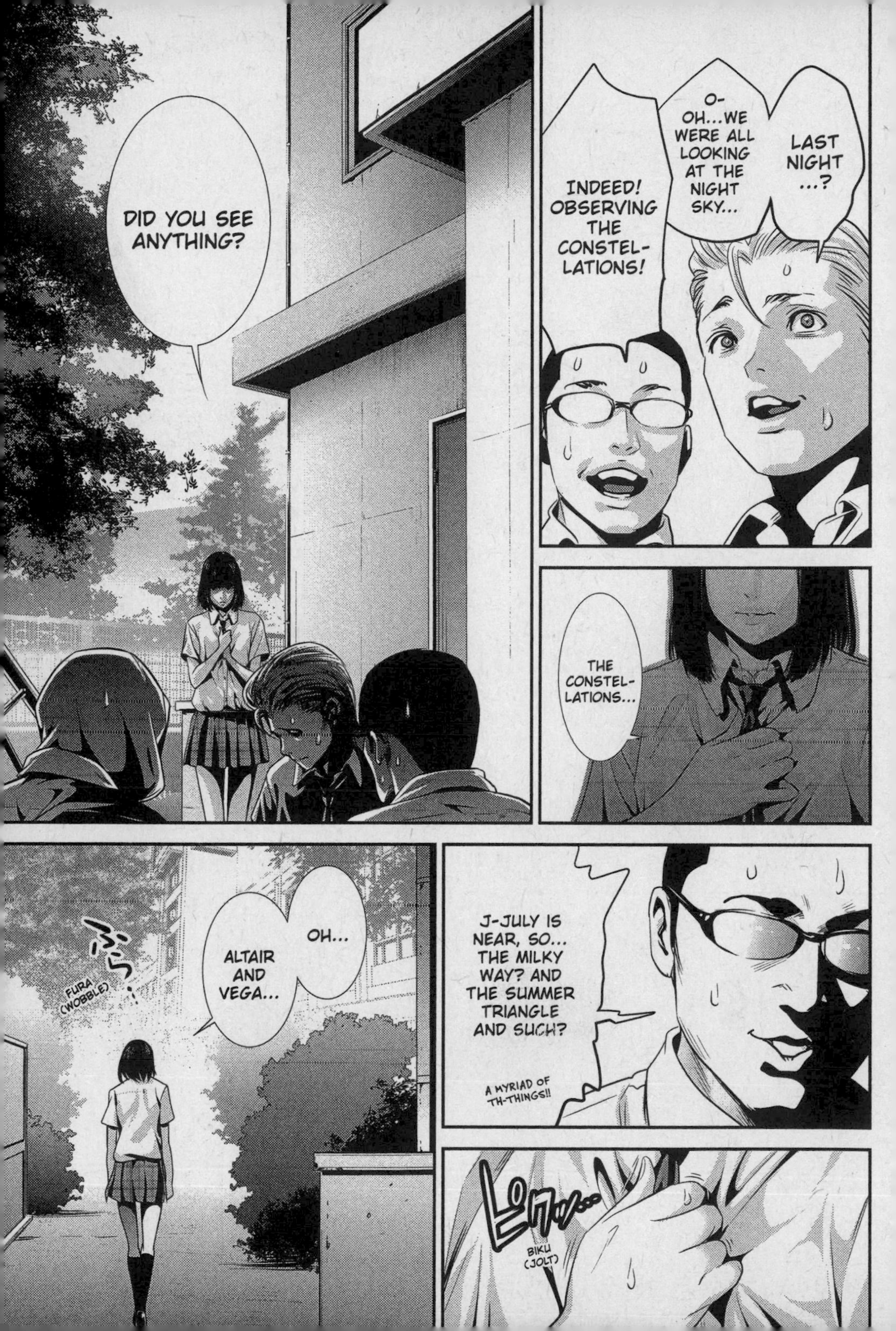
LAST NIGHT ...?
O-OH...WE WERE ALL LOOKING AT THE NIGHT SKY...
INDEED! OBSERVING THE CONSTEL-LATIONS!
DID YOU SEE ANYTHING?
THE CONSTEL-LATIONS...
J-JULY IS NEAR, SO... THE MILKY WAY? AND THE SUMMER TRIANGLE AND SUCH?
A MYRIAD OF TH-THINGS!!
OH...
ALTAIR AND VEGA...
FURA (WOBBLE)
BIKU (JOLT)

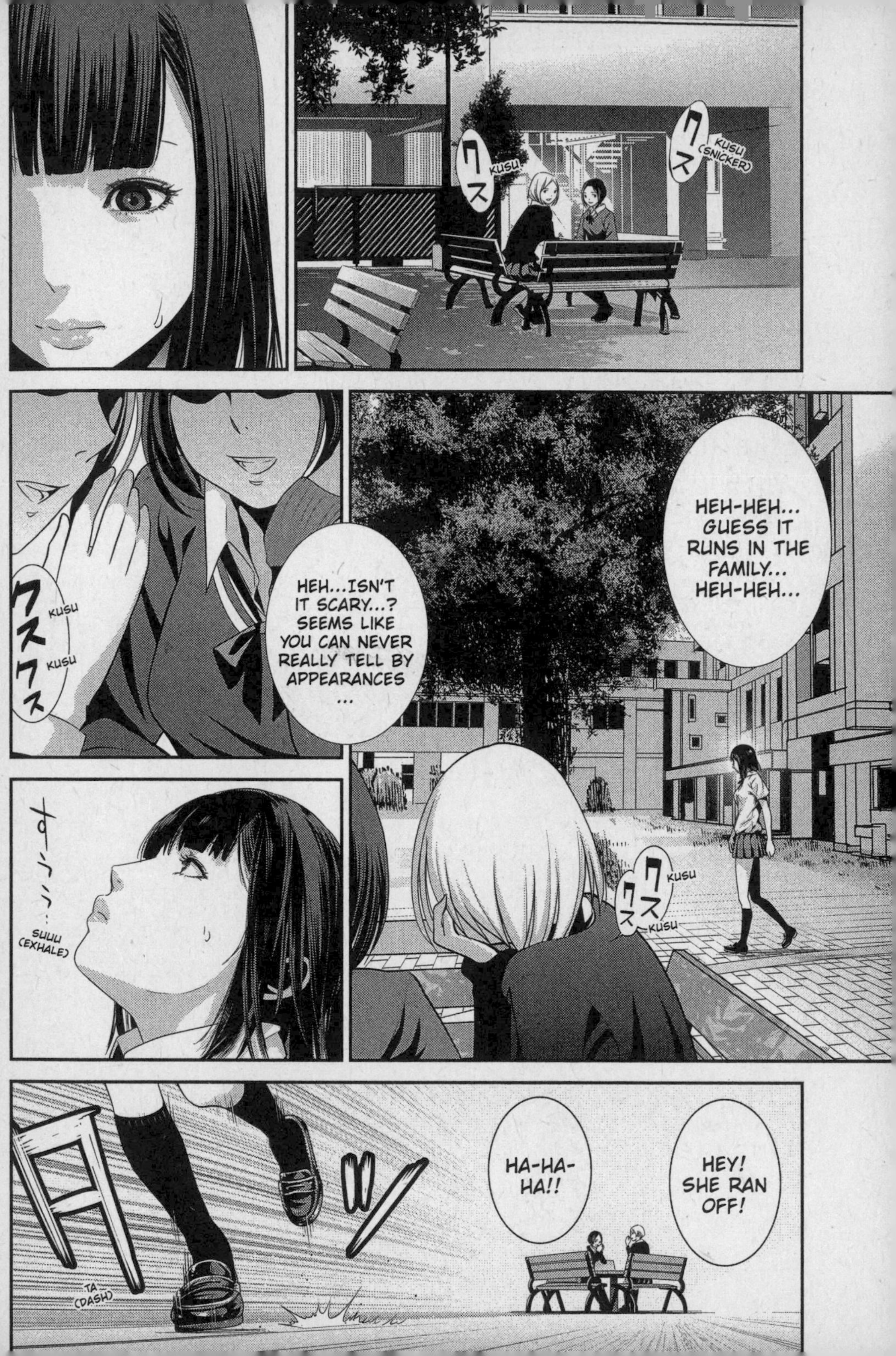
クス KUSU (SNICKER)
クス KUSU
HEH-HEH... GUESS IT RUNS IN THE FAMILY... HEH-HEH...
HEH...ISN'T IT SCARY...? SEEMS LIKE YOU CAN NEVER REALLY TELL BY APPEARANCES ...
クスクス KUSU KUSU
クスクス KUSU KUSU
すぅぅ… SUUU (EXHALE)
HEY! SHE RAN OFF!
HA-HA-HA!!
TA (DASH)

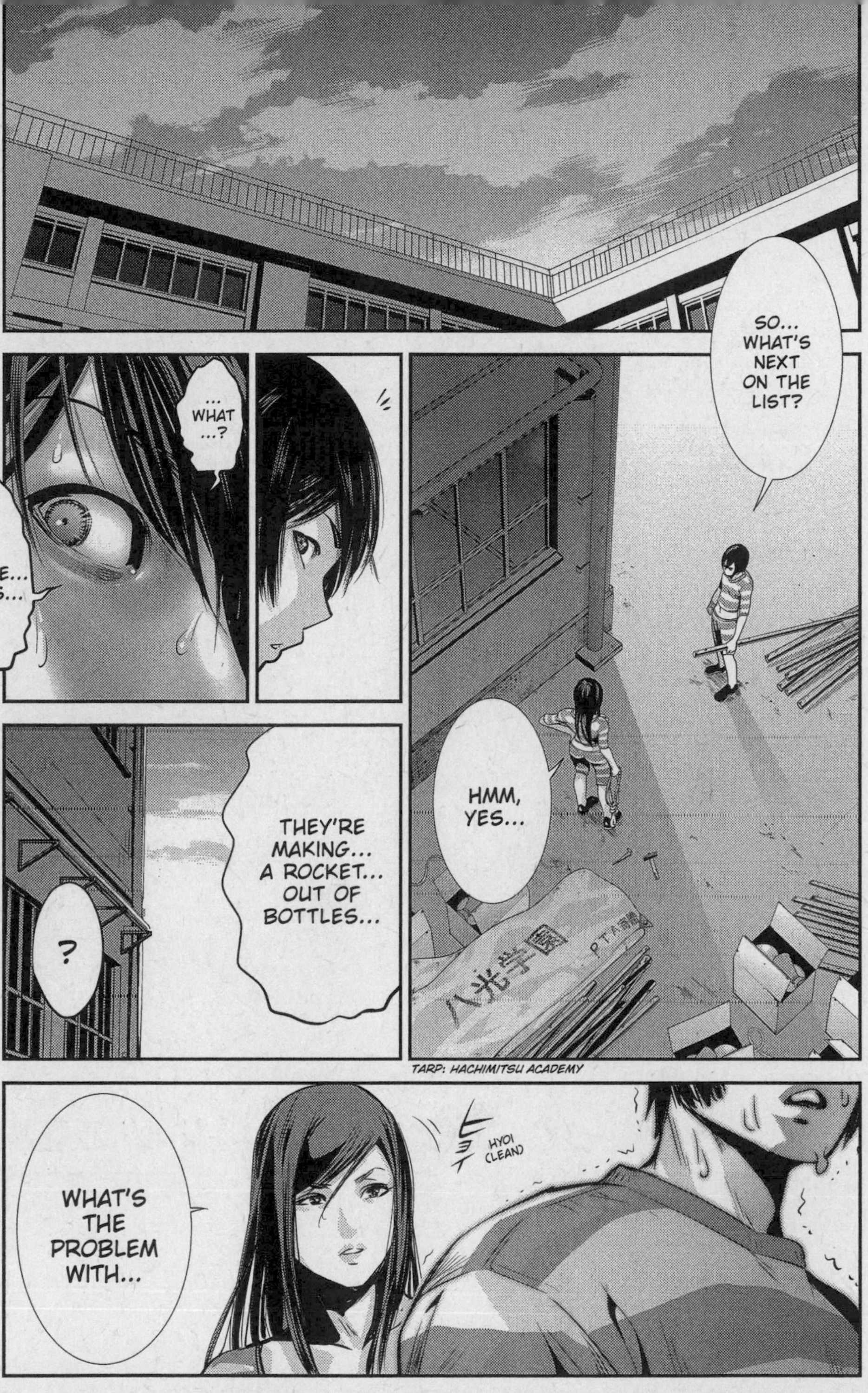
SO... WHAT'S NEXT ON THE LIST?
HMM, YES...
...WHAT...?
THOSE... GUYS...
THEY'RE MAKING... A ROCKET... OUT OF BOTTLES...
?
HYOI (LEAN)
WHAT'S THE PROBLEM WITH...

TARP: HACHIMITSU ACADEMY

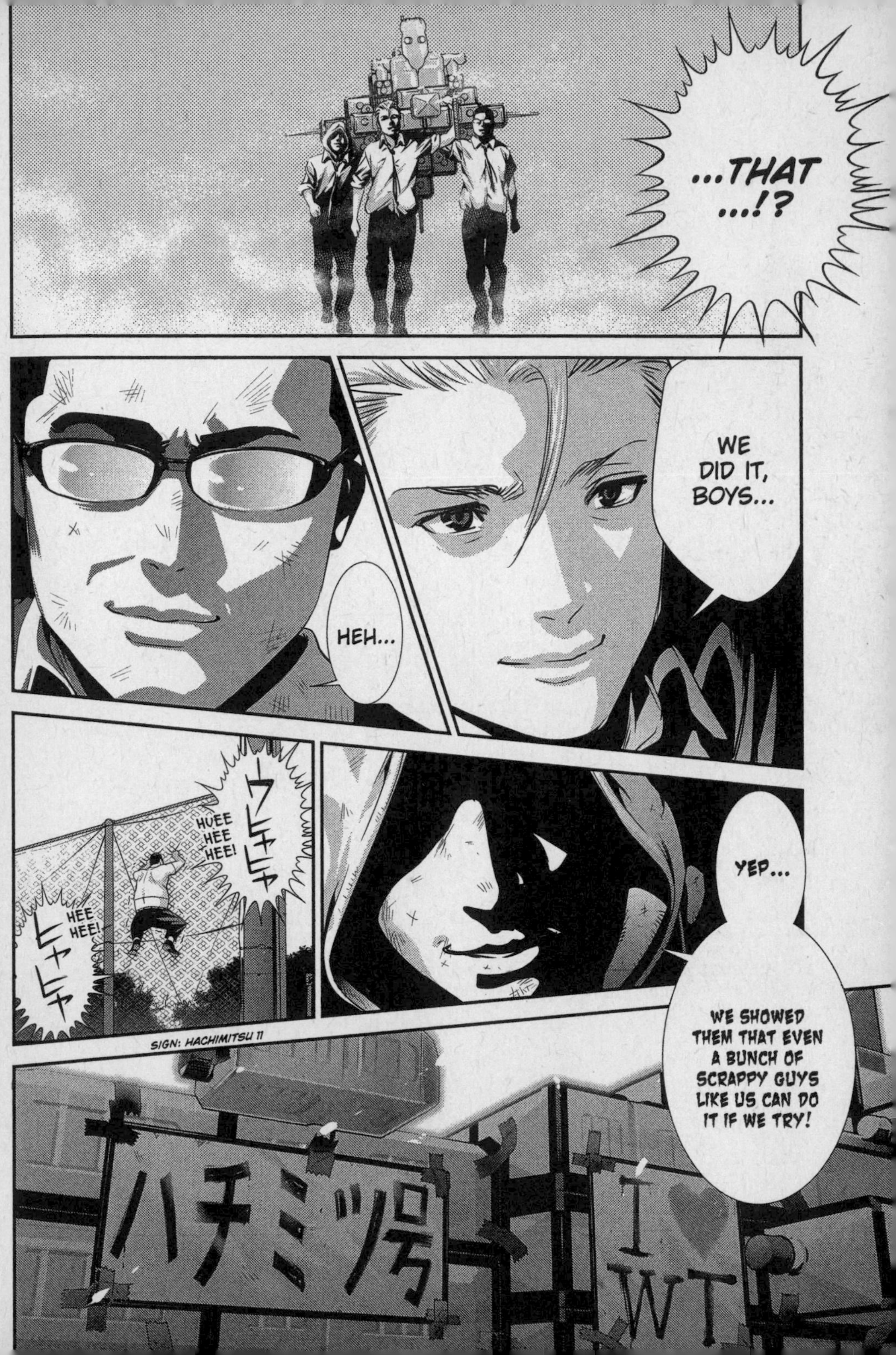
...THAT ...!?
WE DID IT, BOYS...
HEH...
YEP...
WE SHOWED THEM THAT EVEN A BUNCH OF SCRAPPY GUYS LIKE US CAN DO IT IF WE TRY!
HUEE HEE HEE!
HEE HEE!
SIGN: HACHIMITSU 11
I ♥ WT

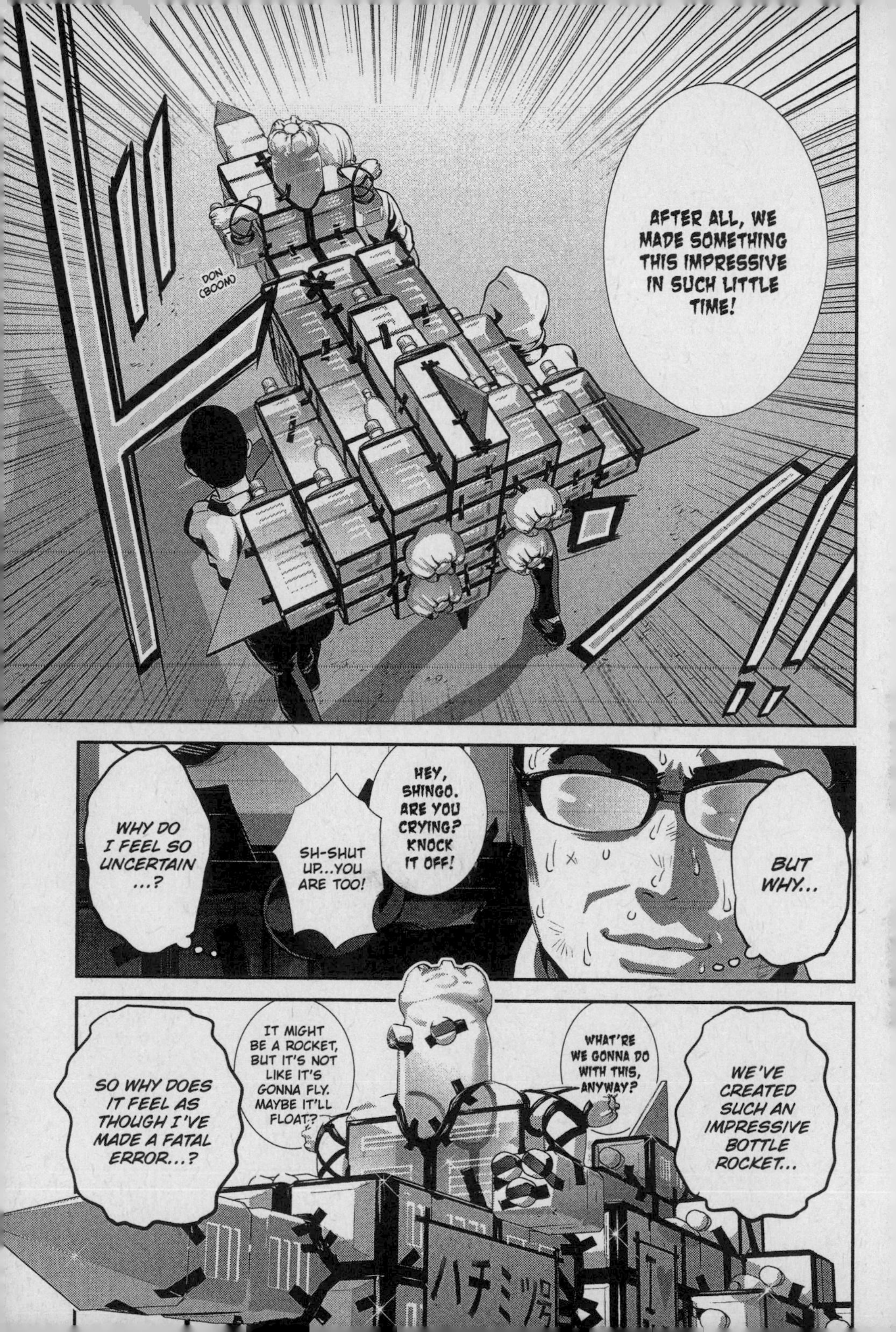
AFTER ALL, WE MADE SOMETHING THIS IMPRESSIVE IN SUCH LITTLE TIME!
DON (BOOM)
BUT WHY...
HEY, SHINGO. ARE YOU CRYING? KNOCK IT OFF!
SH-SHUT UP...YOU ARE TOO!
WHY DO I FEEL SO UNCERTAIN ...?
WE'VE CREATED SUCH AN IMPRESSIVE BOTTLE ROCKET...
WHAT'RE WE GONNA DO WITH THIS, ANYWAY?
IT MIGHT BE A ROCKET, BUT IT'S NOT LIKE IT'S GONNA FLY. MAYBE IT'LL FLOAT?
SO WHY DOES IT FEEL AS THOUGH I'VE MADE A FATAL ERROR...?
ハチミツ号

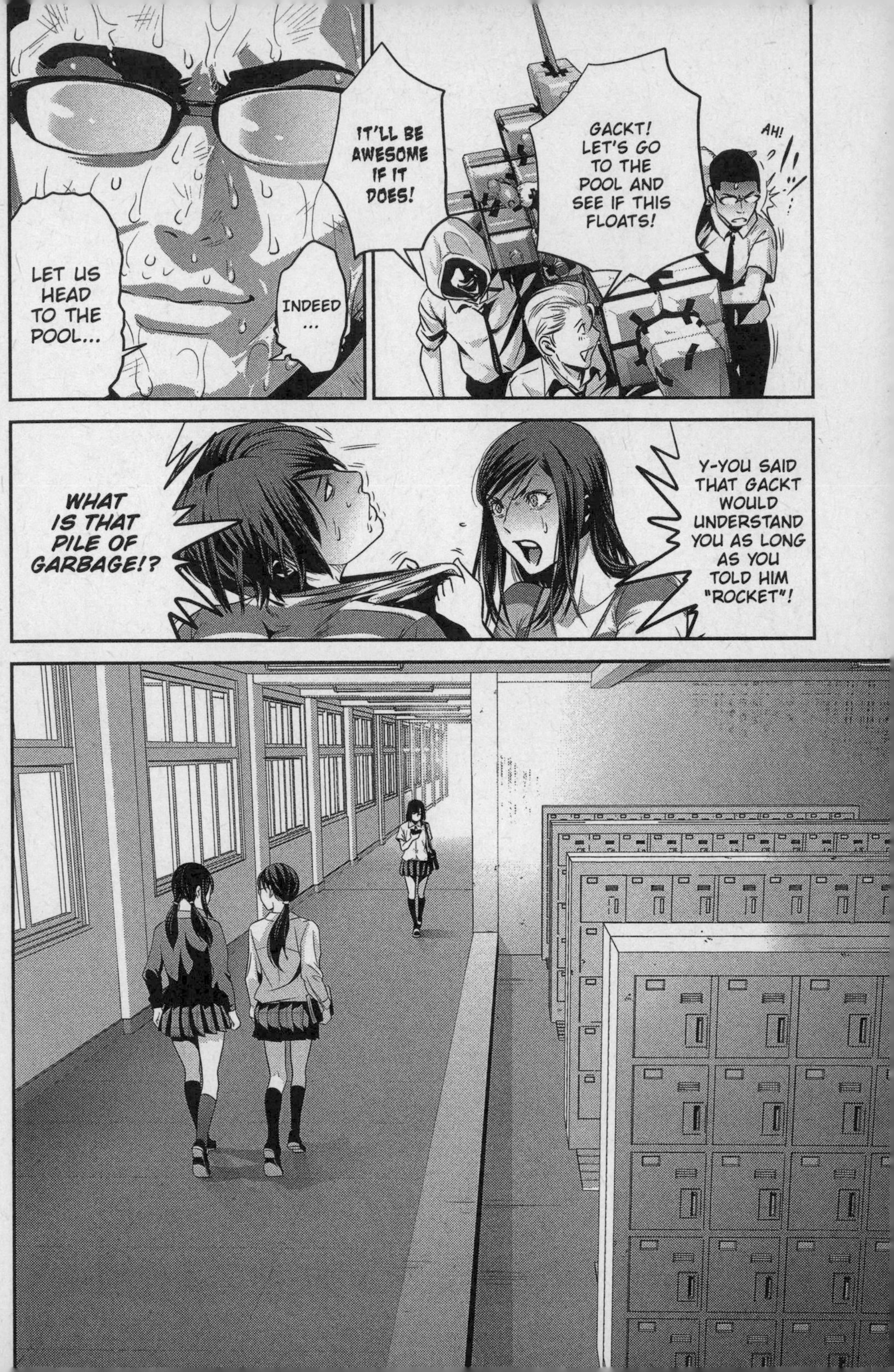
AH!
GACKT! LET'S GO TO THE POOL AND SEE IF THIS FLOATS!
IT'LL BE AWESOME IF IT DOES!
INDEED...
LET US HEAD TO THE POOL...
Y-YOU SAID THAT GACKT WOULD UNDERSTAND YOU AS LONG AS YOU TOLD HIM "ROCKET"!
WHAT IS THAT PILE OF GARBAGE!?

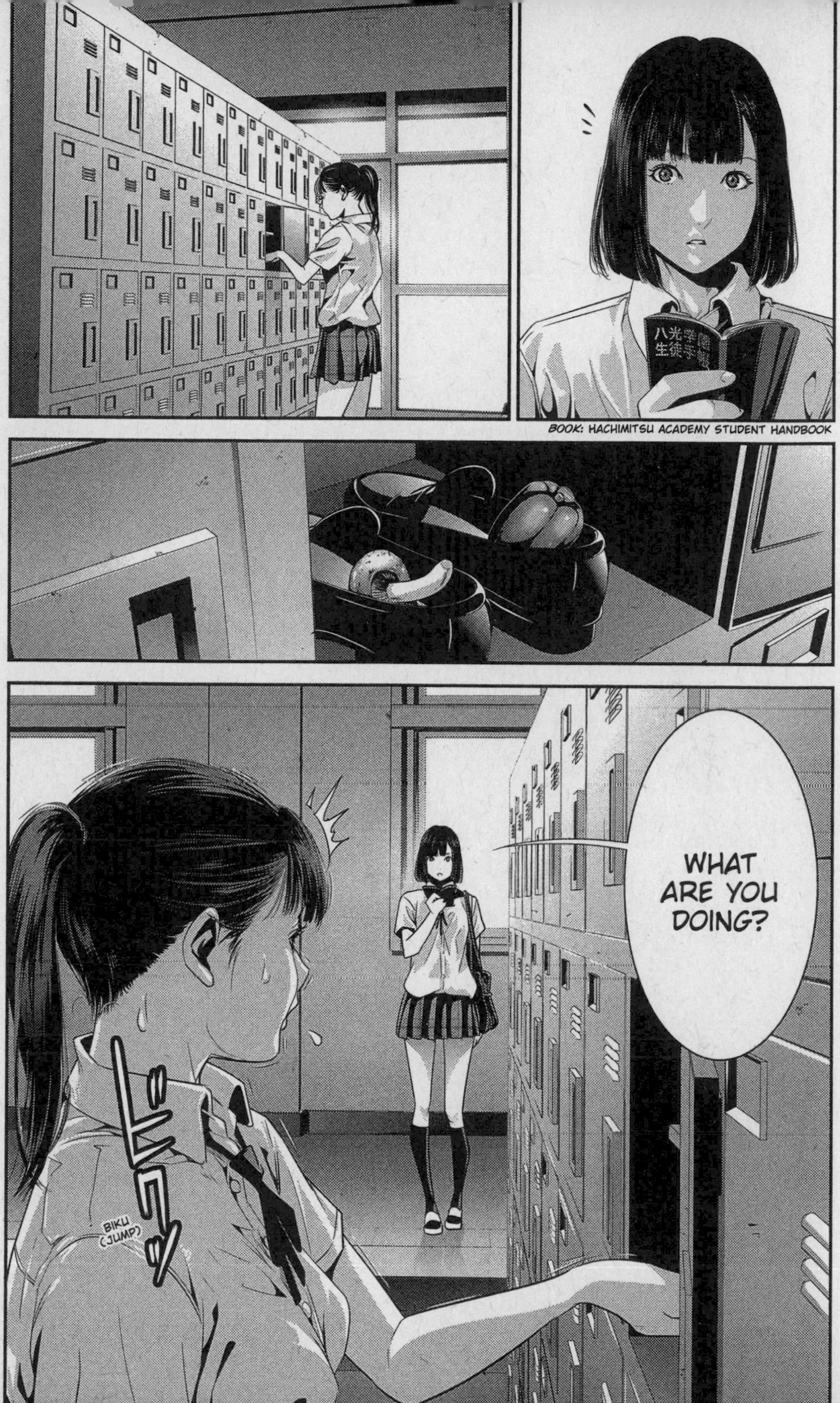
BOOK: HACHIMITSU ACADEMY STUDENT HANDBOOK
WHAT ARE YOU DOING?
BIKU (JUMP)

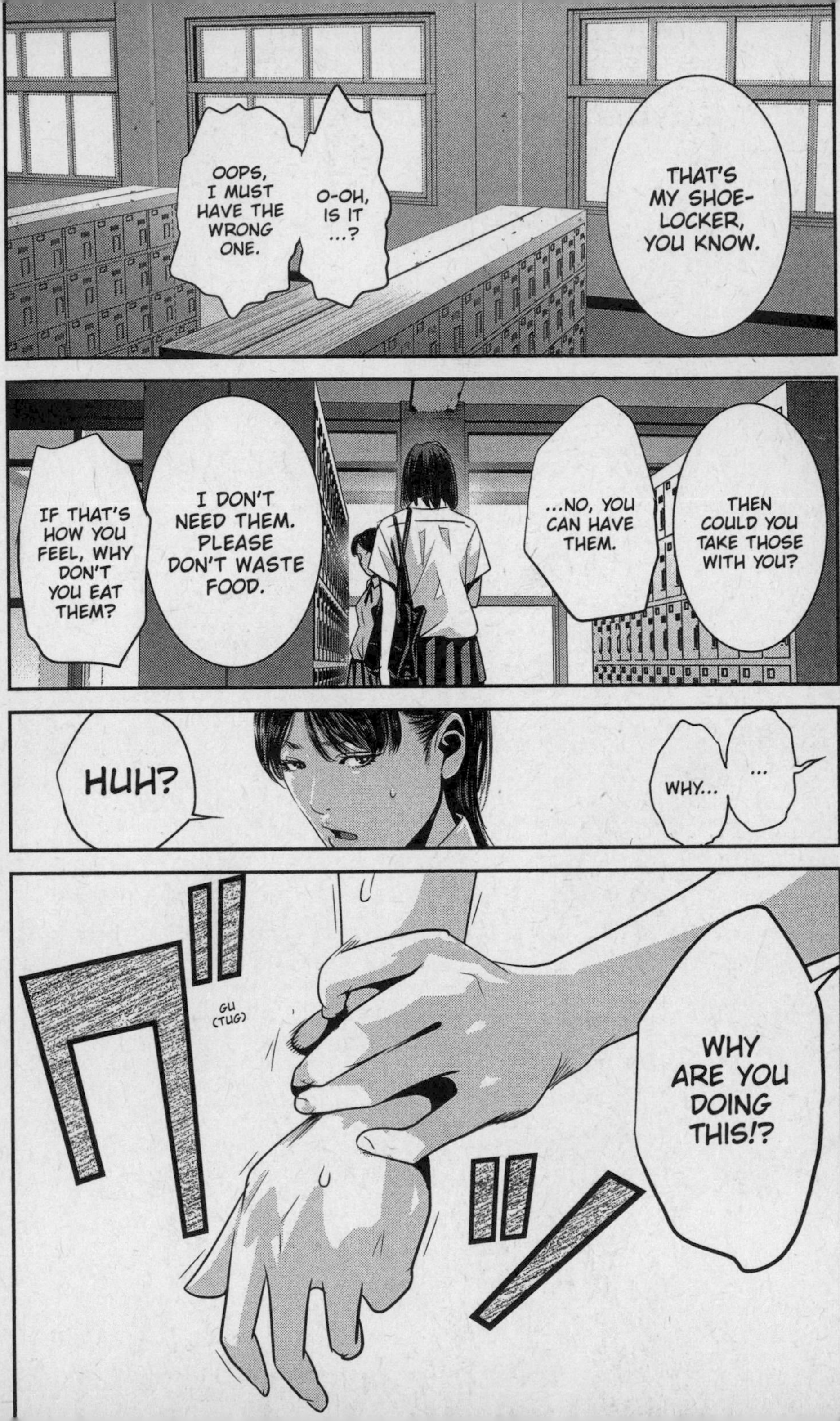
THAT'S MY SHOE-LOCKER, YOU KNOW.
O-OH, IS IT ...?
OOPS, I MUST HAVE THE WRONG ONE.
THEN COULD YOU TAKE THOSE WITH YOU?
...NO, YOU CAN HAVE THEM.
I DON'T NEED THEM. PLEASE DON'T WASTE FOOD.
IF THAT'S HOW YOU FEEL, WHY DON'T YOU EAT THEM?
WHY... ...
HUH?
WHY ARE YOU DOING THIS!?
GU (TUG)

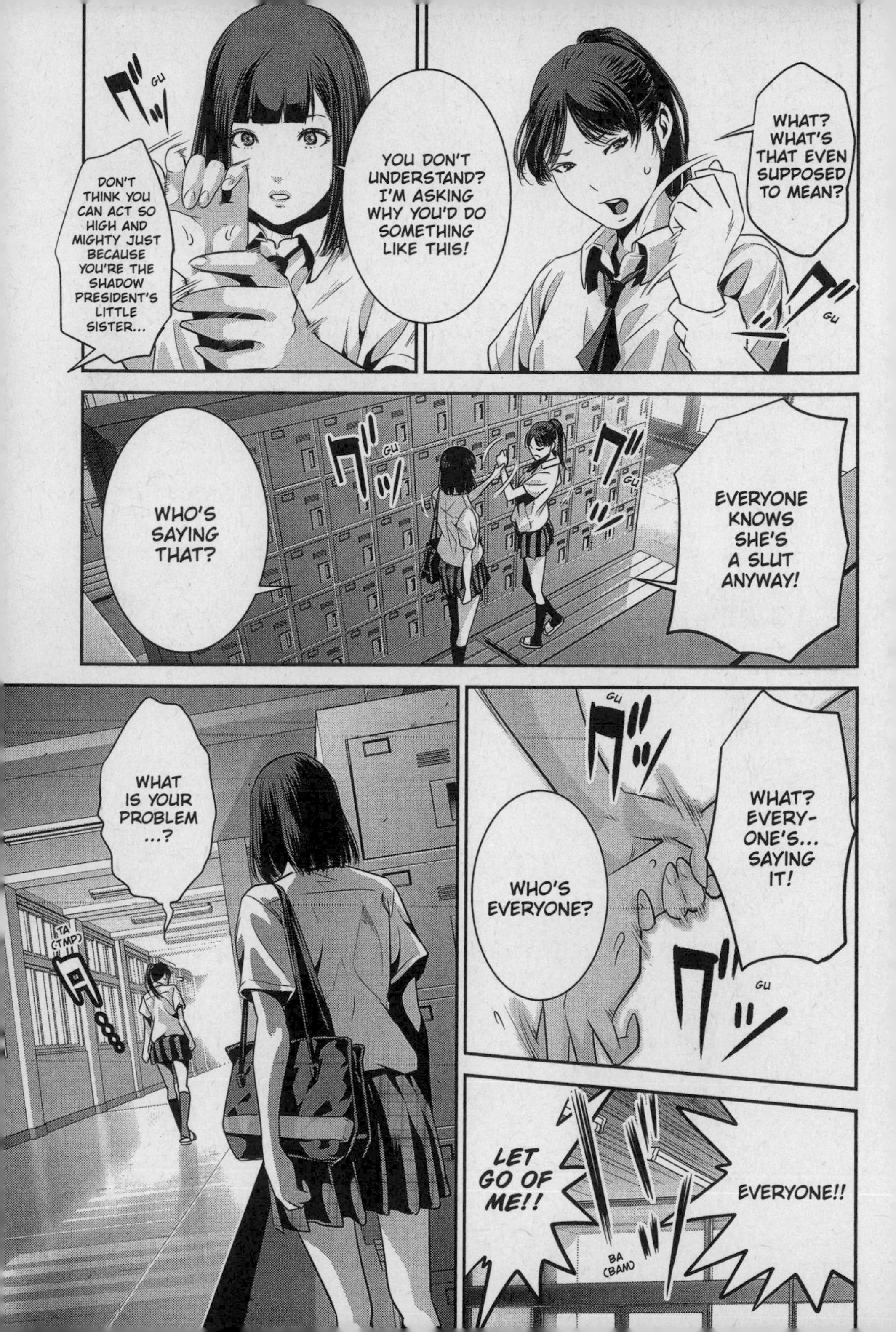

WHAT? WHAT'S THAT EVEN SUPPOSED TO MEAN?
GU
YOU DON'T UNDERSTAND? I'M ASKING WHY YOU'D DO SOMETHING LIKE THIS!
GU
DON'T THINK YOU CAN ACT SO HIGH AND MIGHTY JUST BECAUSE YOU'RE THE SHADOW PRESIDENT'S LITTLE SISTER...
EVERYONE KNOWS SHE'S A SLUT ANYWAY!
GU
GU
WHO'S SAYING THAT?
WHAT? EVERY-ONE'S... SAYING IT!
GU
GU
WHO'S EVERYONE?
EVERYONE!!
LET GO OF ME!!
BA (BAM)
WHAT IS YOUR PROBLEM ...?
TA (TMP)

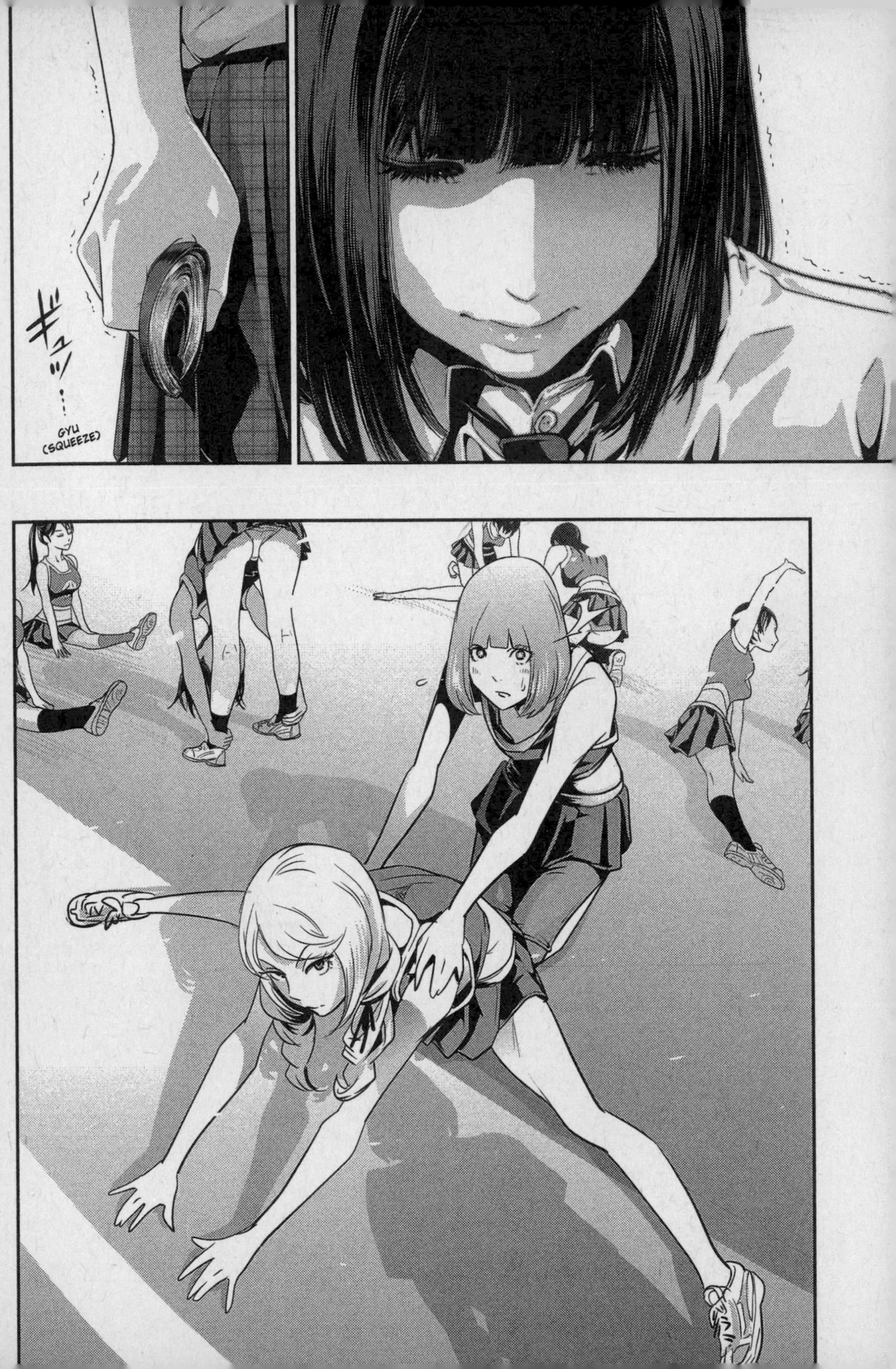
ギュッ…
GYU (SQUEEZE)

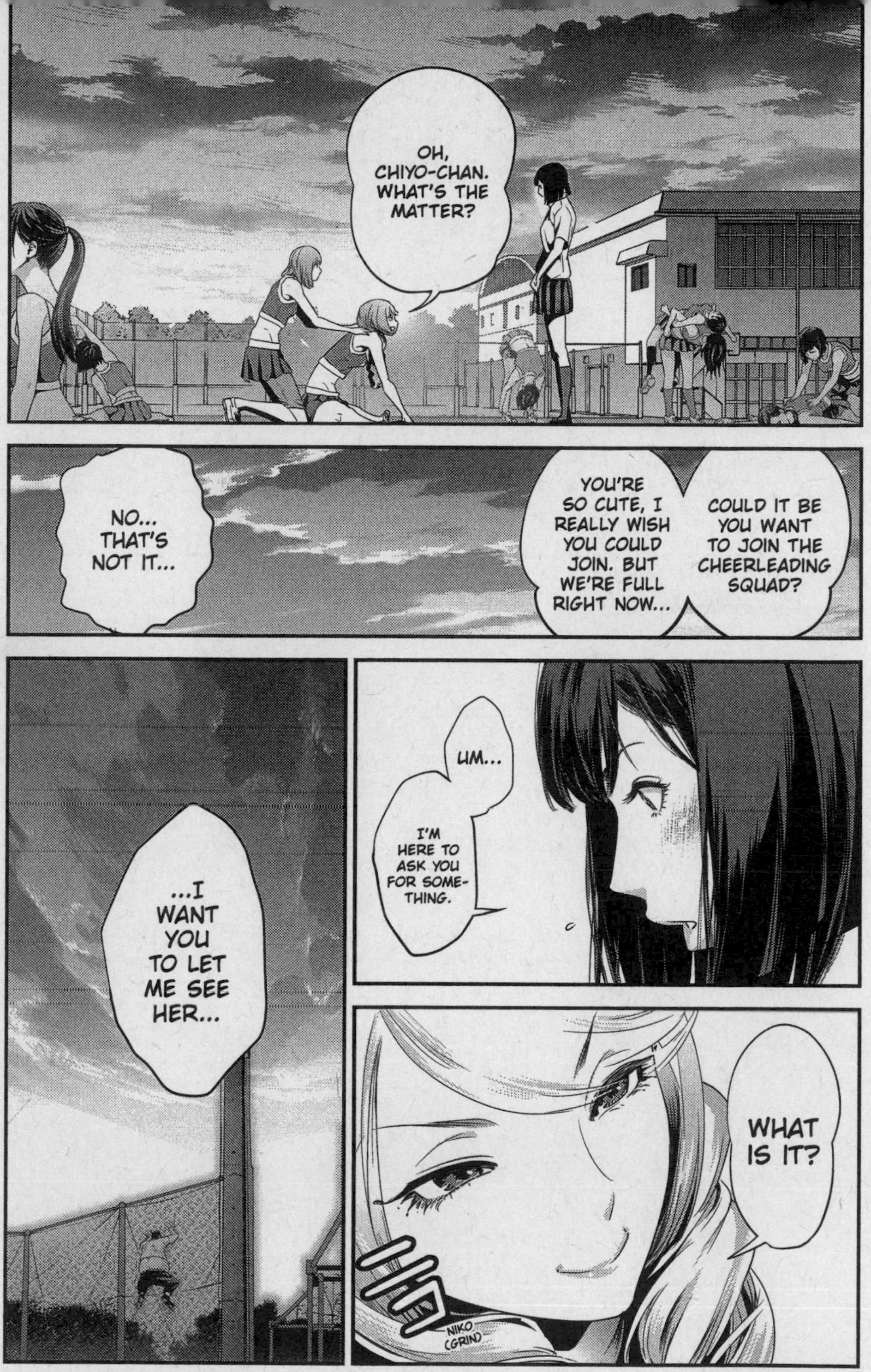
OH, CHIYO-CHAN. WHAT'S THE MATTER?
COULD IT BE YOU WANT TO JOIN THE CHEERLEADING SQUAD?
YOU'RE SO CUTE, I REALLY WISH YOU COULD JOIN. BUT WE'RE FULL RIGHT NOW...
NO... THAT'S NOT IT...
UM...
I'M HERE TO ASK YOU FOR SOME-THING.
WHAT IS IT?
NIKO (GRIN)
...I WANT YOU TO LET ME SEE HER...

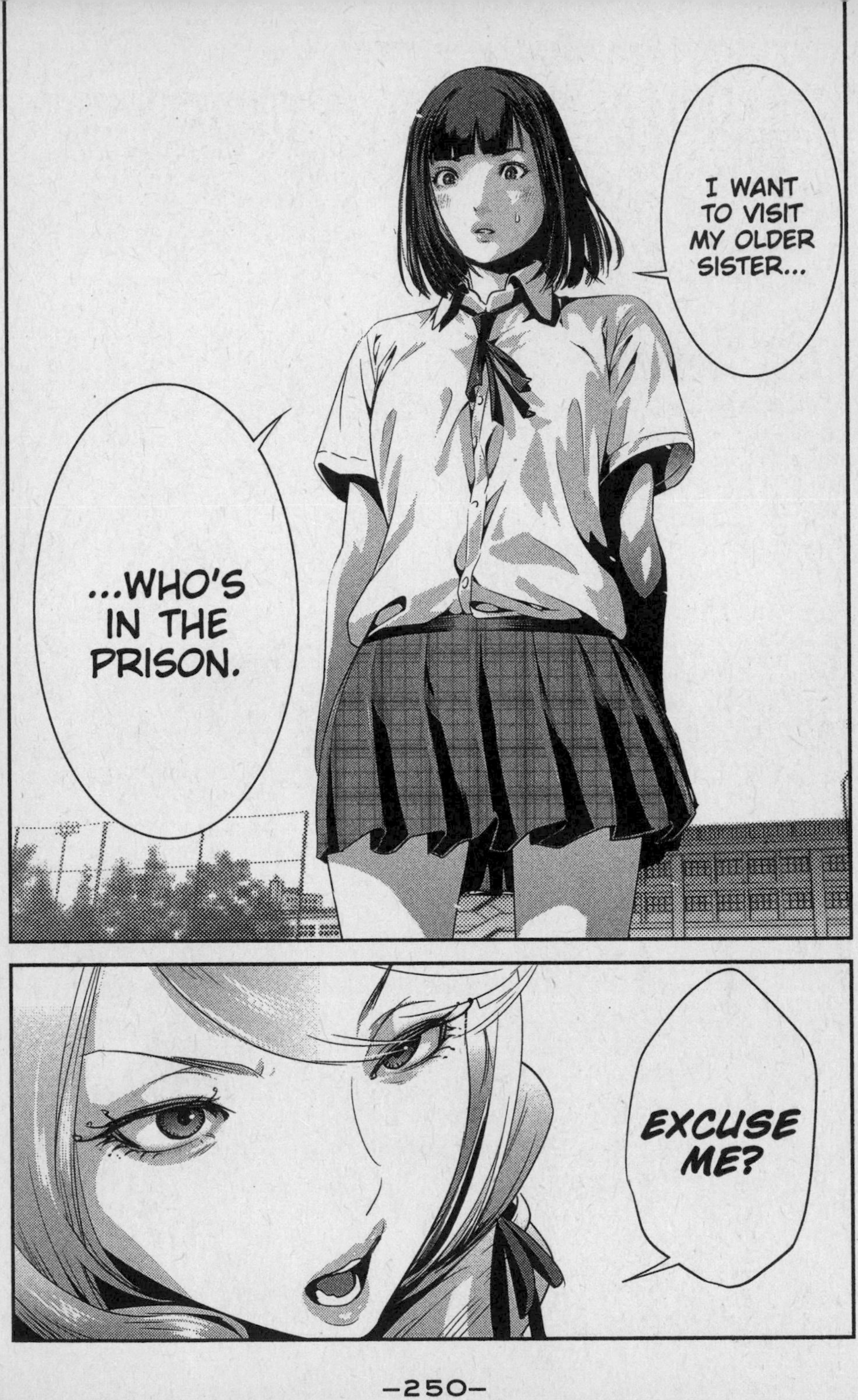
I WANT TO VISIT MY OLDER SISTER...
...WHO'S IN THE PRISON.
EXCUSE ME?

CHAPTER 132: SNOW WHITE

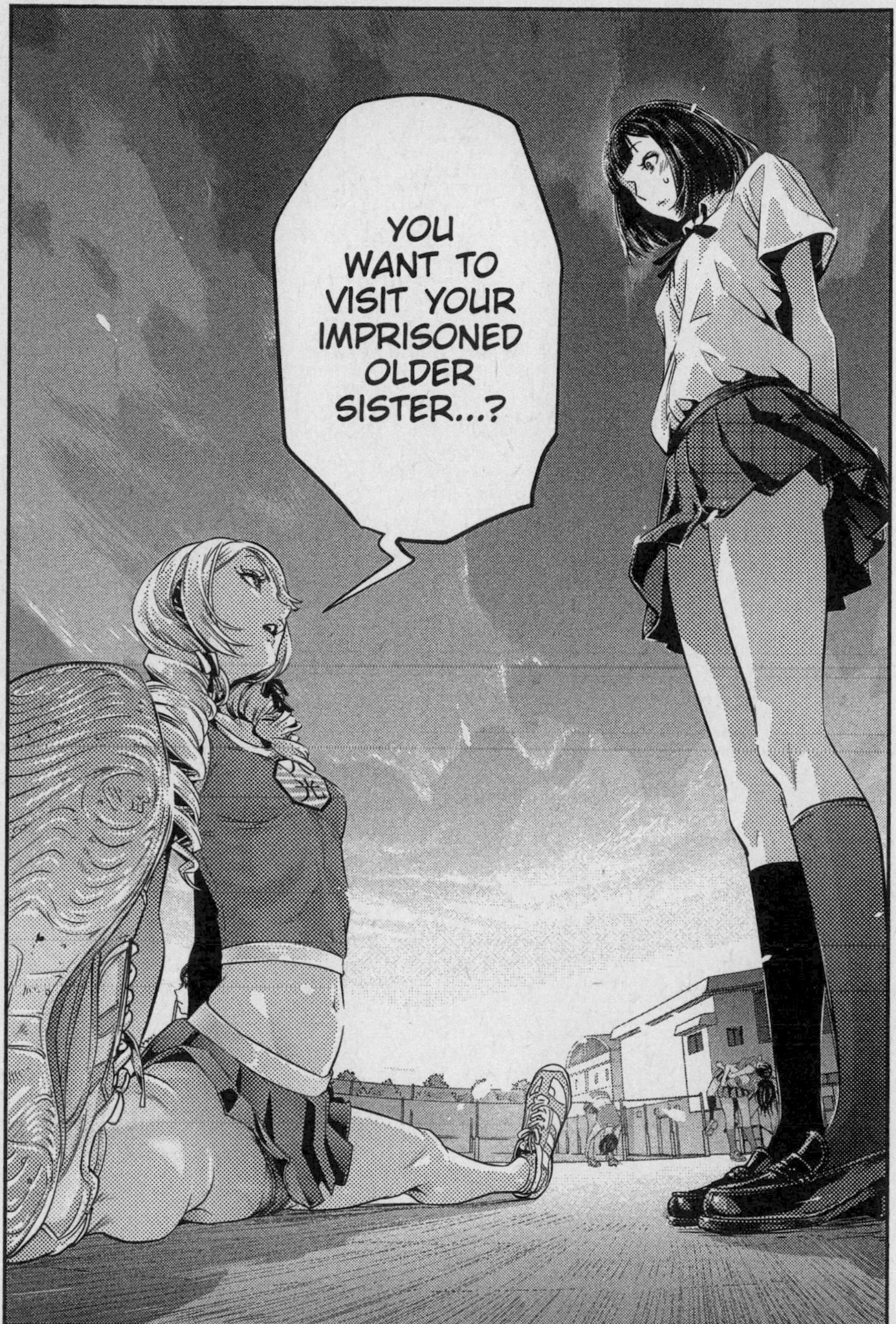
YOU WANT TO VISIT YOUR IMPRISONED OLDER SISTER...?

SHIRT: HACHIMITSU

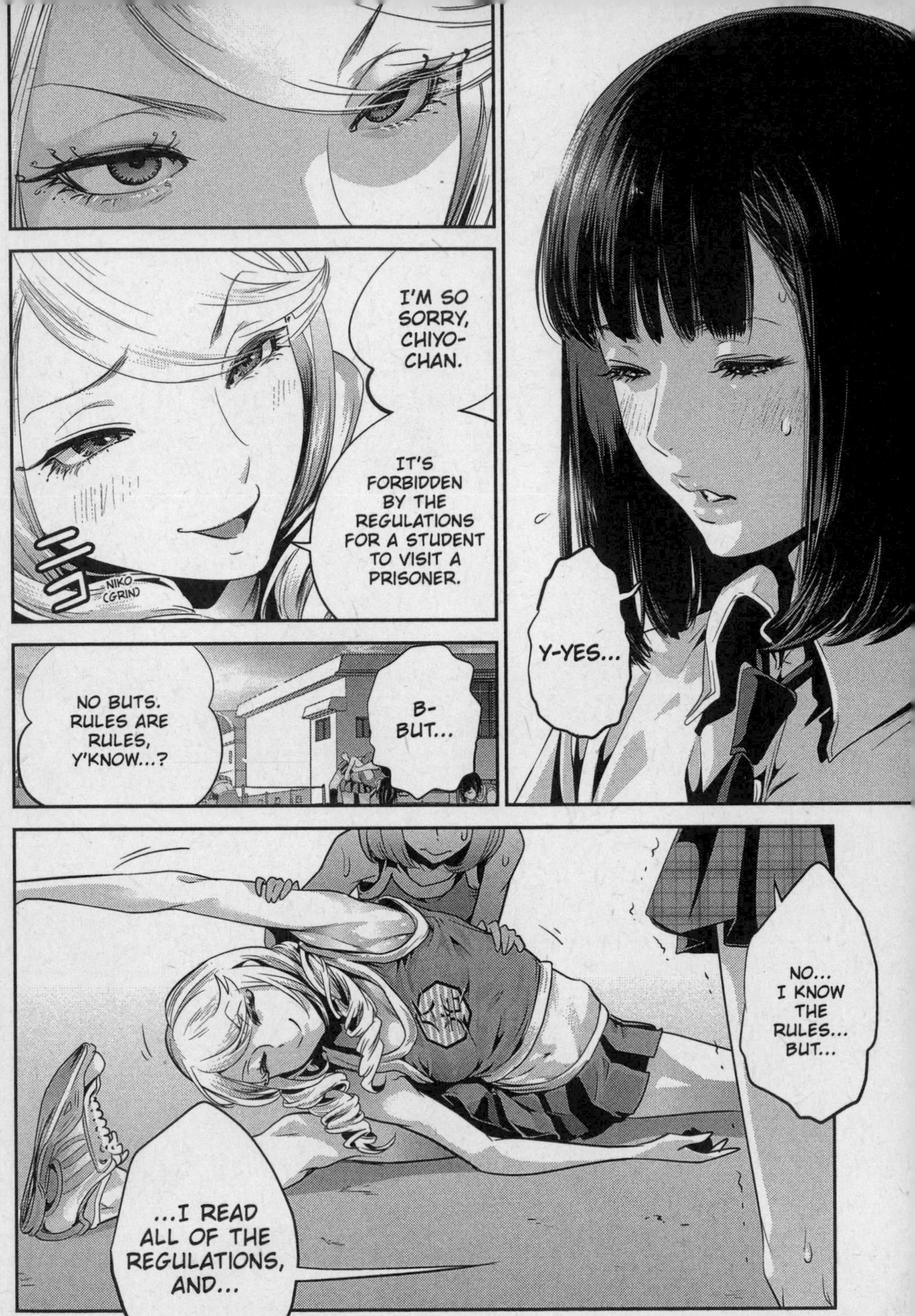
I'M SO SORRY, CHIYO-CHAN.
IT'S FORBIDDEN BY THE REGULATIONS FOR A STUDENT TO VISIT A PRISONER.
NIKO (GRIN)
B-BUT...
NO BUTS. RULES ARE RULES, Y'KNOW...?
Y-YES...
NO... I KNOW THE RULES... BUT...
...I READ ALL OF THE REGULATIONS, AND...

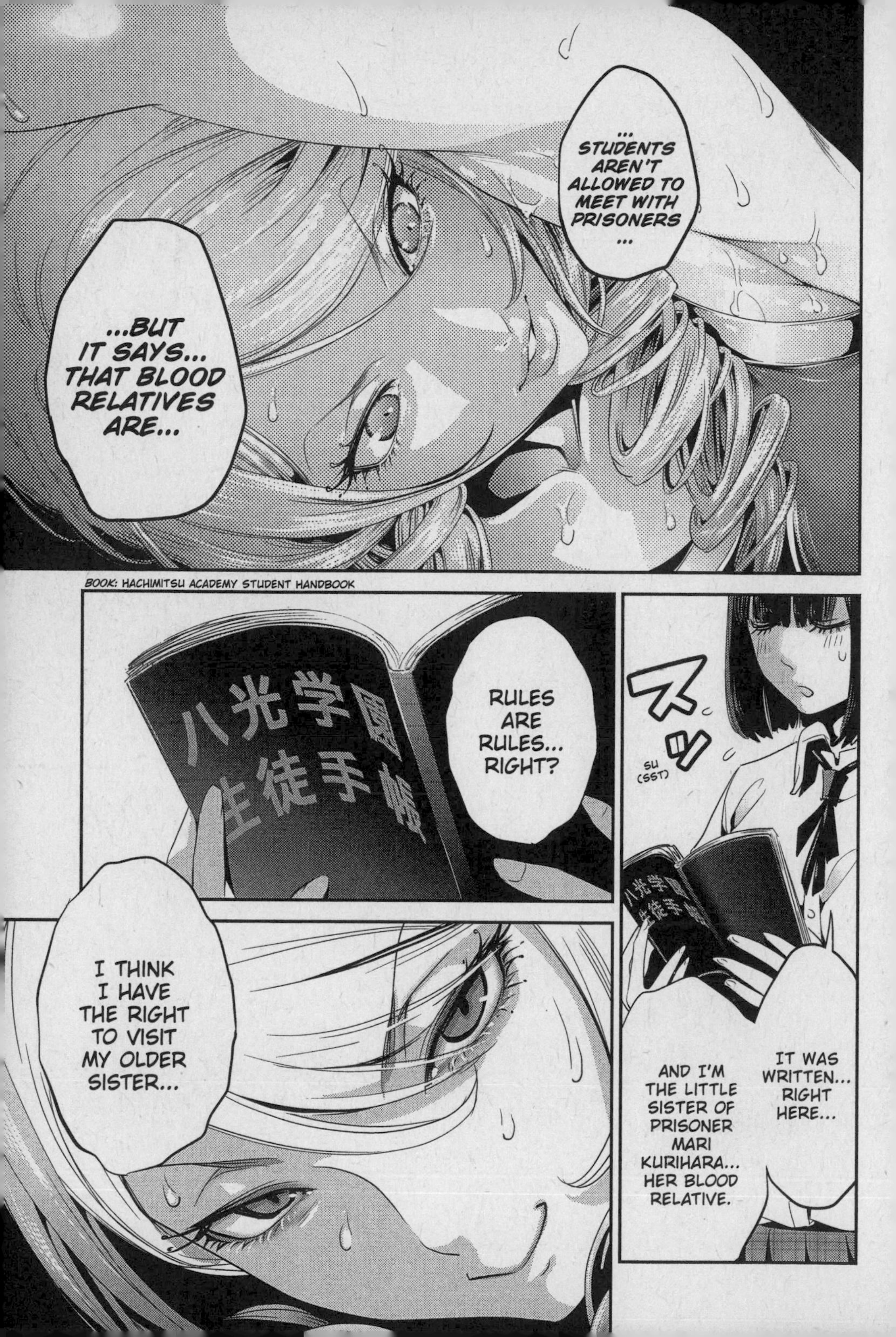
...
STUDENTS AREN'T ALLOWED TO MEET WITH PRISONERS
...
...BUT IT SAYS... THAT BLOOD RELATIVES ARE...
BOOK: HACHIMITSU ACADEMY STUDENT HANDBOOK
RULES ARE RULES... RIGHT?
八光学園 生徒手帳
SU (SST)
I THINK I HAVE THE RIGHT TO VISIT MY OLDER SISTER...
IT WAS WRITTEN... RIGHT HERE...
AND I'M THE LITTLE SISTER OF PRISONER MARI KURIHARA... HER BLOOD RELATIVE.

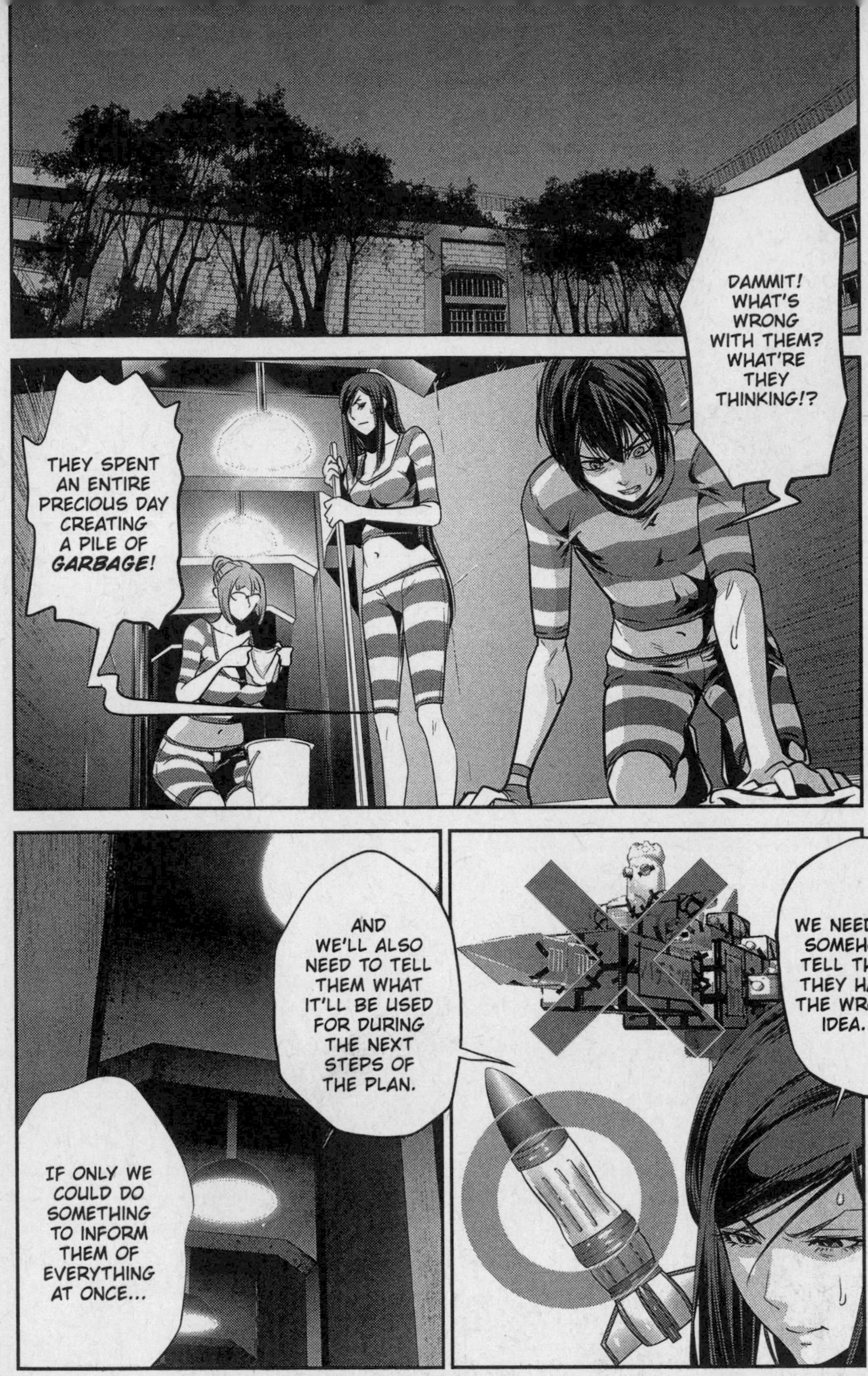
DAMMIT! WHAT'S WRONG WITH THEM? WHAT'RE THEY THINKING!?
THEY SPENT AN ENTIRE PRECIOUS DAY CREATING A PILE OF GARBAGE!
WE NEED TO SOMEHOW TELL THEM THEY HAVE THE WRONG IDEA...
AND WE'LL ALSO NEED TO TELL THEM WHAT IT'LL BE USED FOR DURING THE NEXT STEPS OF THE PLAN.
IF ONLY WE COULD DO SOMETHING TO INFORM THEM OF EVERYTHING AT ONCE...

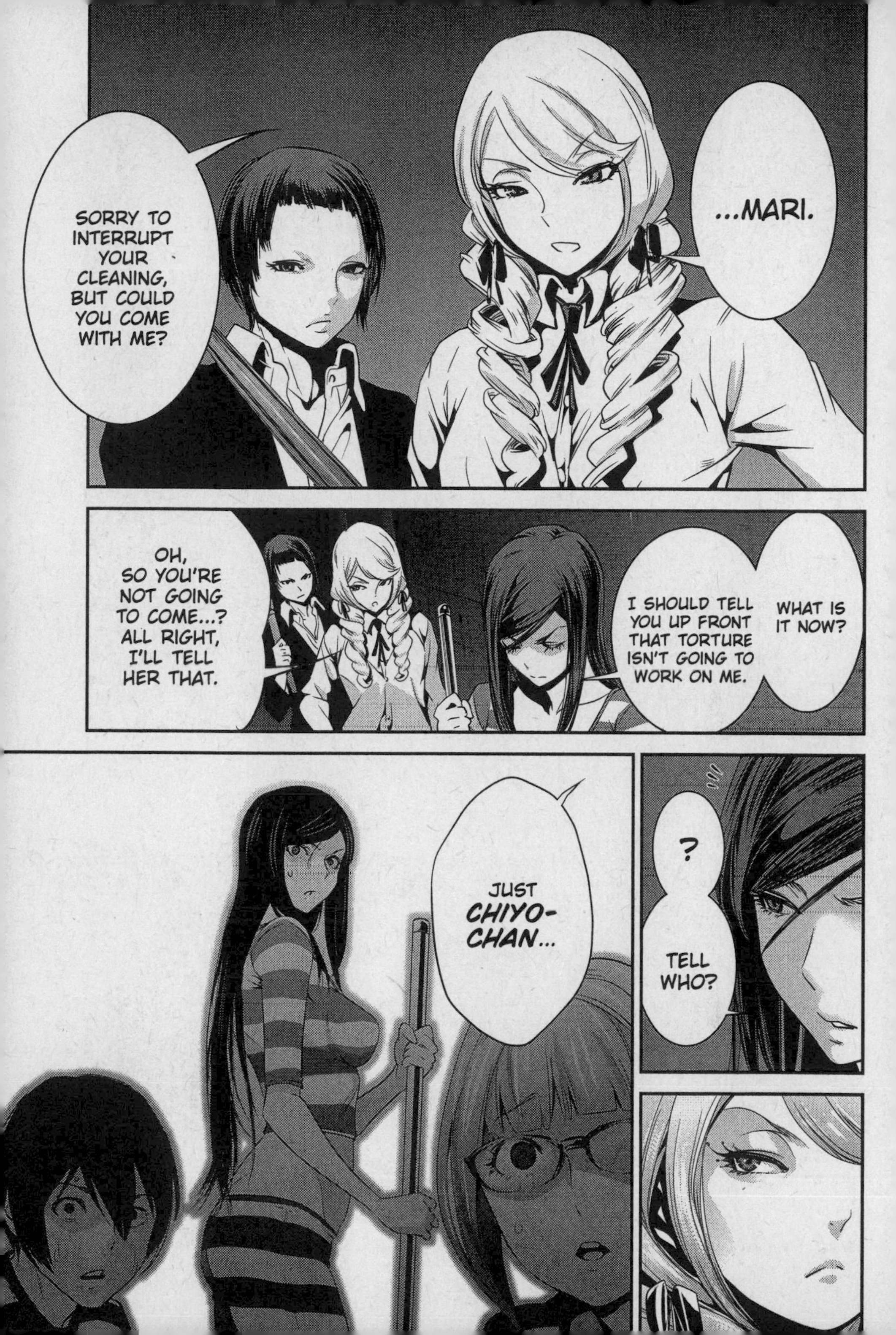
...MARI.
SORRY TO INTERRUPT YOUR CLEANING, BUT COULD YOU COME WITH ME?
WHAT IS IT NOW?
I SHOULD TELL YOU UP FRONT THAT TORTURE ISN'T GOING TO WORK ON ME.
OH, SO YOU'RE NOT GOING TO COME...? ALL RIGHT, I'LL TELL HER THAT.
?
TELL WHO?
JUST CHIYO-CHAN...

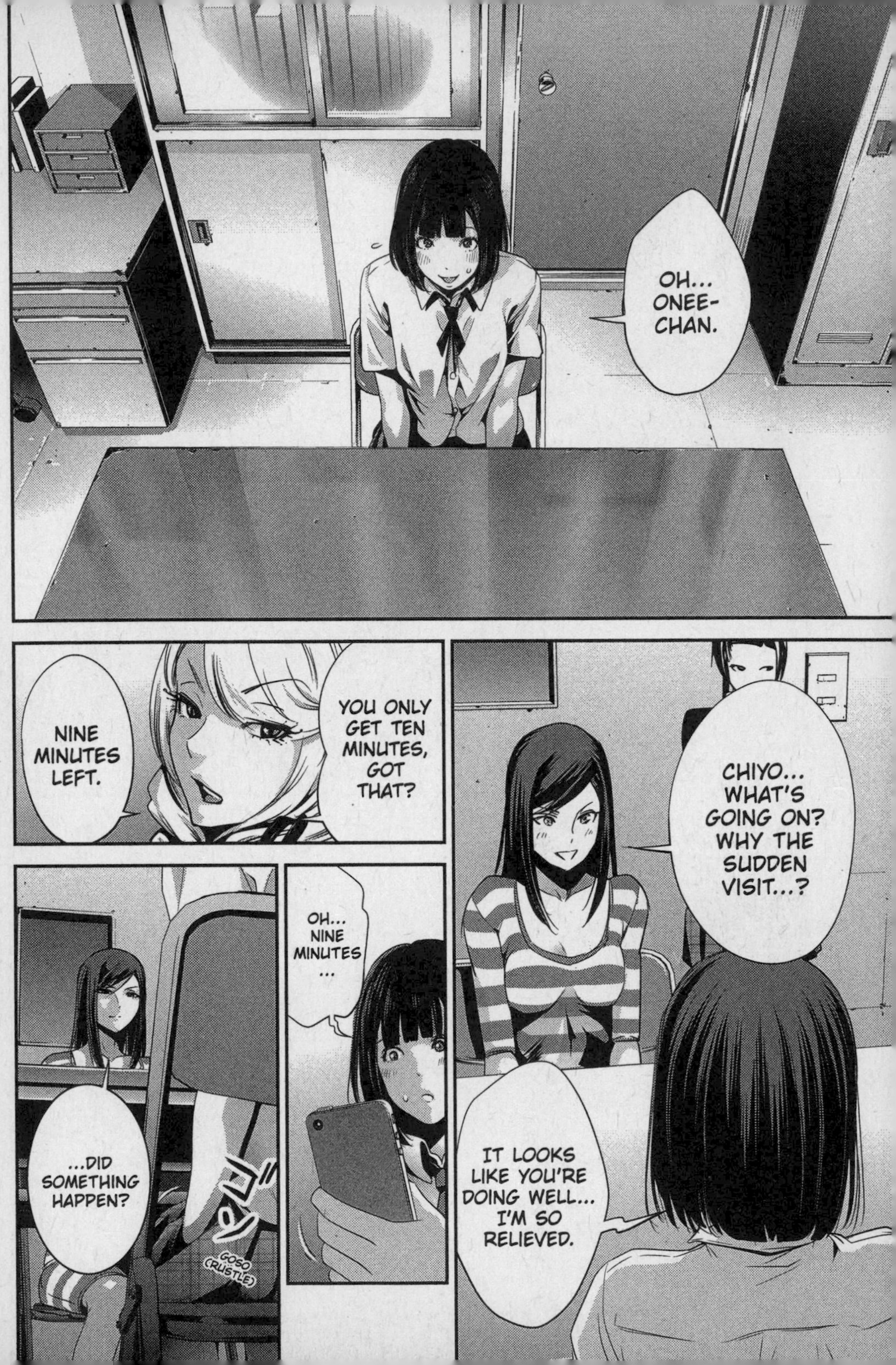
OH... ONEE-CHAN.
CHIYO... WHAT'S GOING ON? WHY THE SUDDEN VISIT...?
YOU ONLY GET TEN MINUTES, GOT THAT?
NINE MINUTES LEFT.
IT LOOKS LIKE YOU'RE DOING WELL... I'M SO RELIEVED.
OH... NINE MINUTES ...
...DID SOMETHING HAPPEN?
GOSO (RUSTLE)

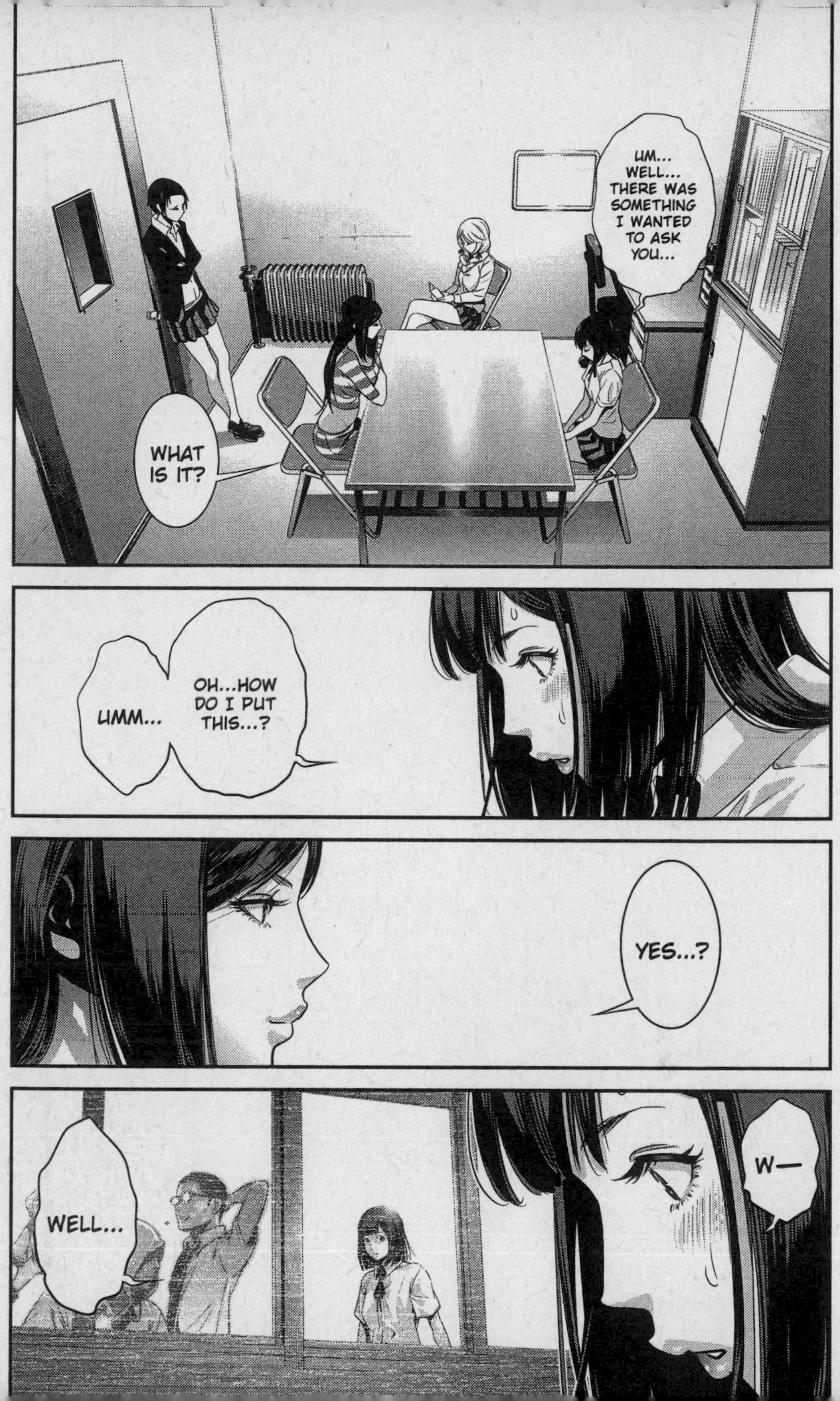
UM... WELL... THERE WAS SOMETHING I WANTED TO ASK YOU...
WHAT IS IT?
OH...HOW DO I PUT THIS...?
UMM...
YES...?
W—
WELL...

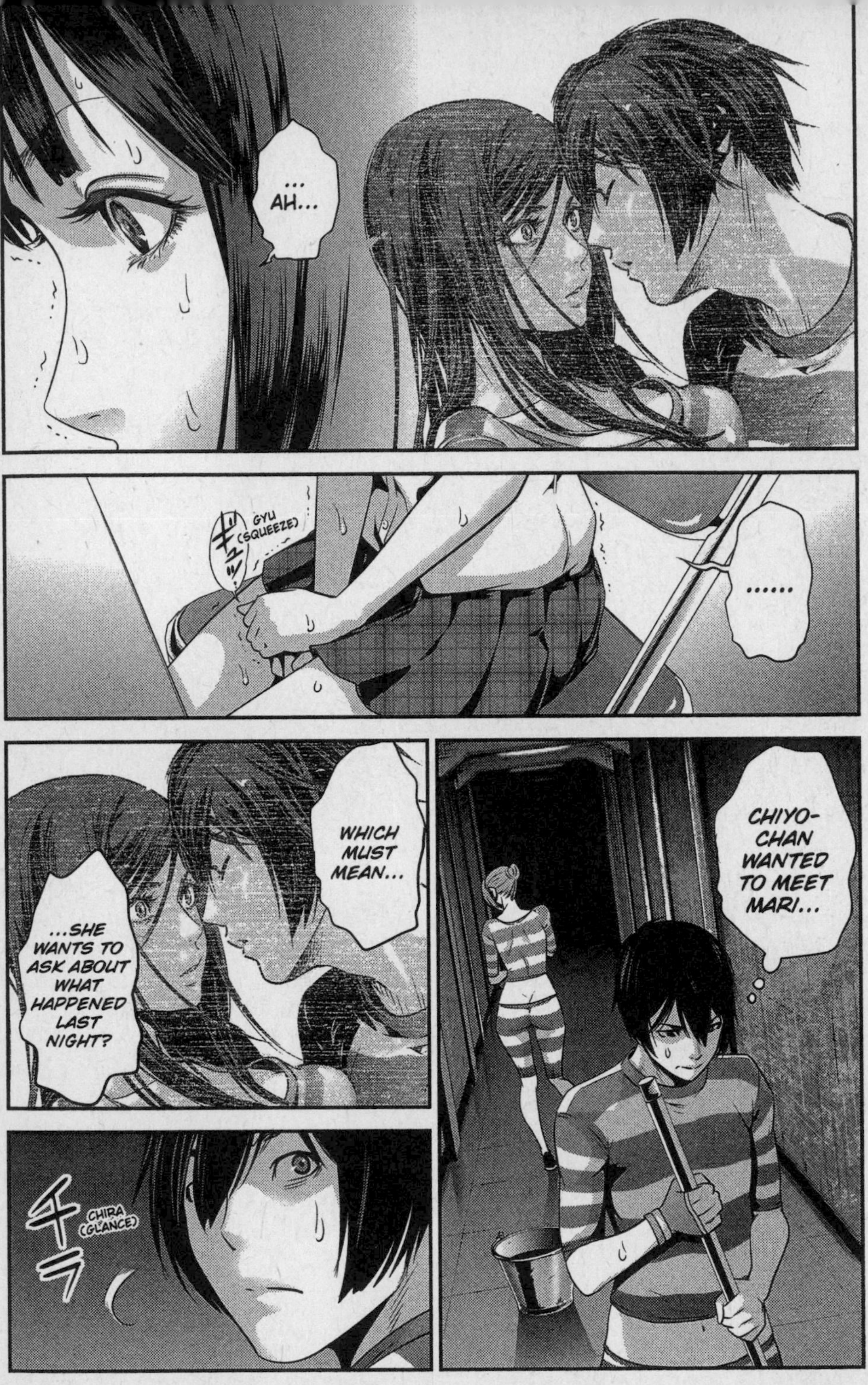
... AH...
......
ギュッ
GYU (SQUEEZE)
CHIYO-CHAN WANTED TO MEET MARI...
WHICH MUST MEAN...
...SHE WANTS TO ASK ABOUT WHAT HAPPENED LAST NIGHT?
チラ
CHIRA (GLANCE)

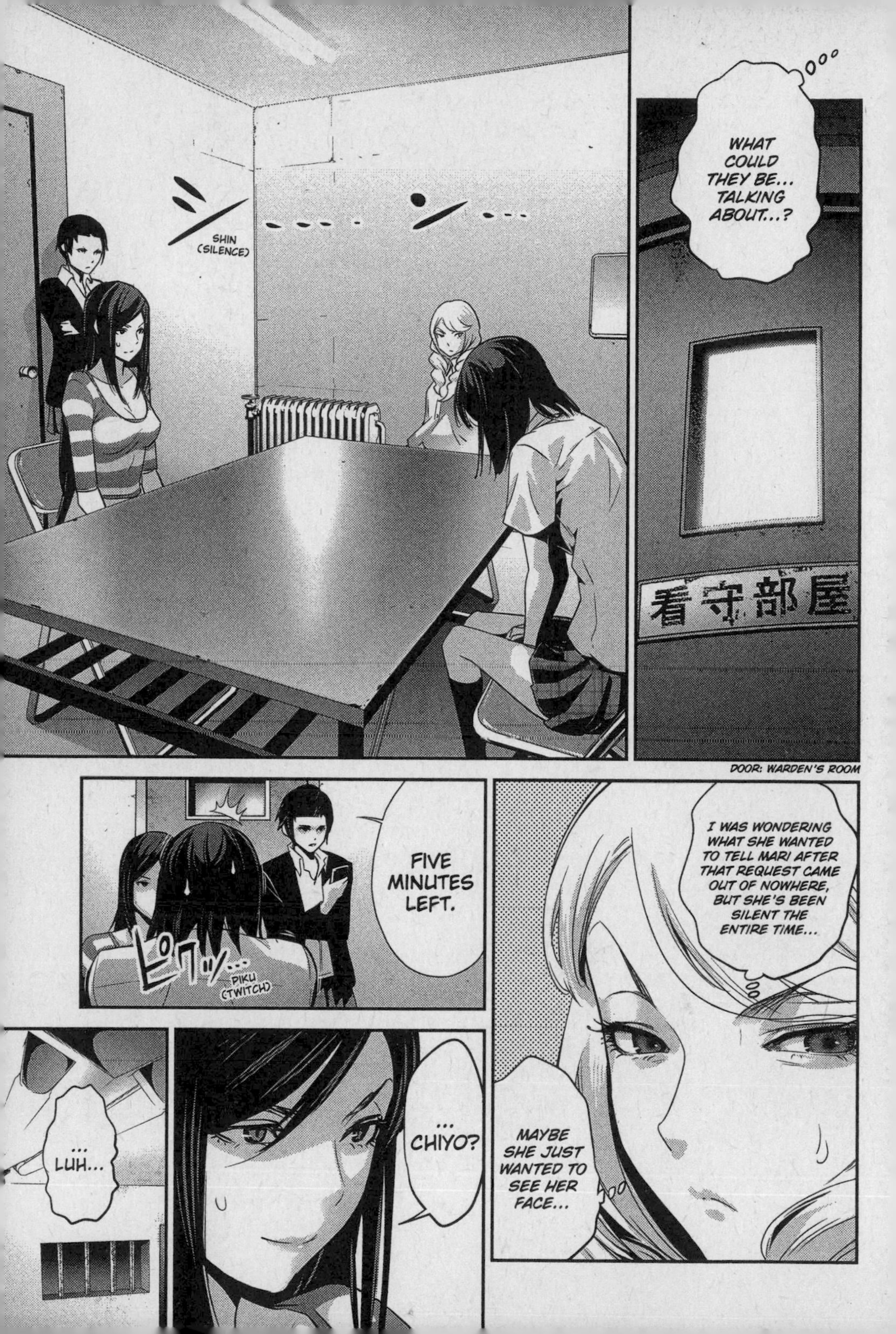
WHAT COULD THEY BE... TALKING ABOUT...?
看守部屋
DOOR: WARDEN'S ROOM
シーン・・・・・・
SHIN (SILENCE)
I WAS WONDERING WHAT SHE WANTED TO TELL MARI AFTER THAT REQUEST CAME OUT OF NOWHERE, BUT SHE'S BEEN SILENT THE ENTIRE TIME...
FIVE MINUTES LEFT.
ピクッ...
PIKU (TWITCH)
MAYBE SHE JUST WANTED TO SEE HER FACE...
...CHIYO?
...LUH...

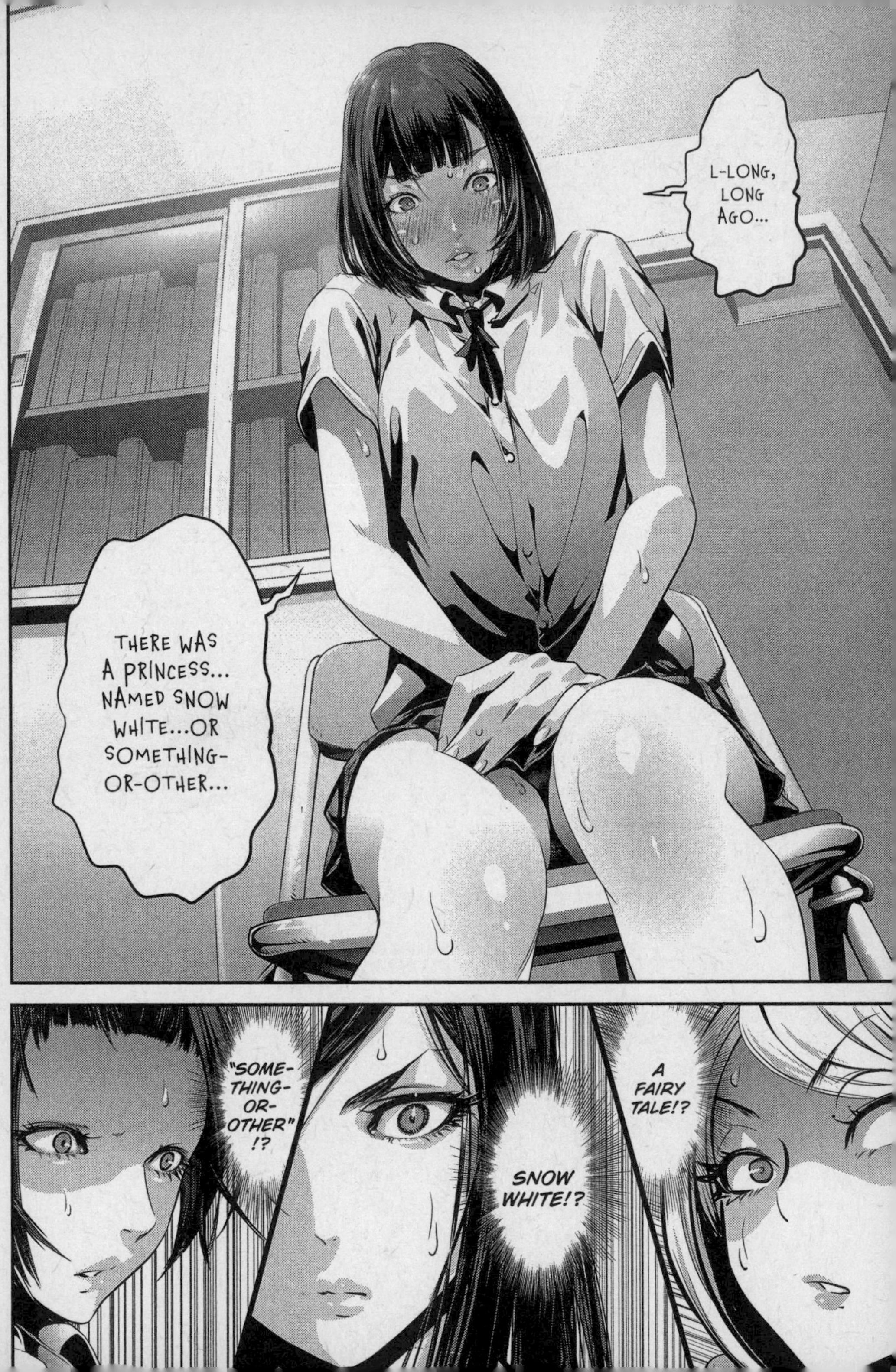
L-LONG, LONG AGO...
THERE WAS A PRINCESS... NAMED SNOW WHITE...OR SOMETHING-OR-OTHER...
A FAIRY TALE!?
SNOW WHITE!?
"SOME-THING-OR-OTHER" !?

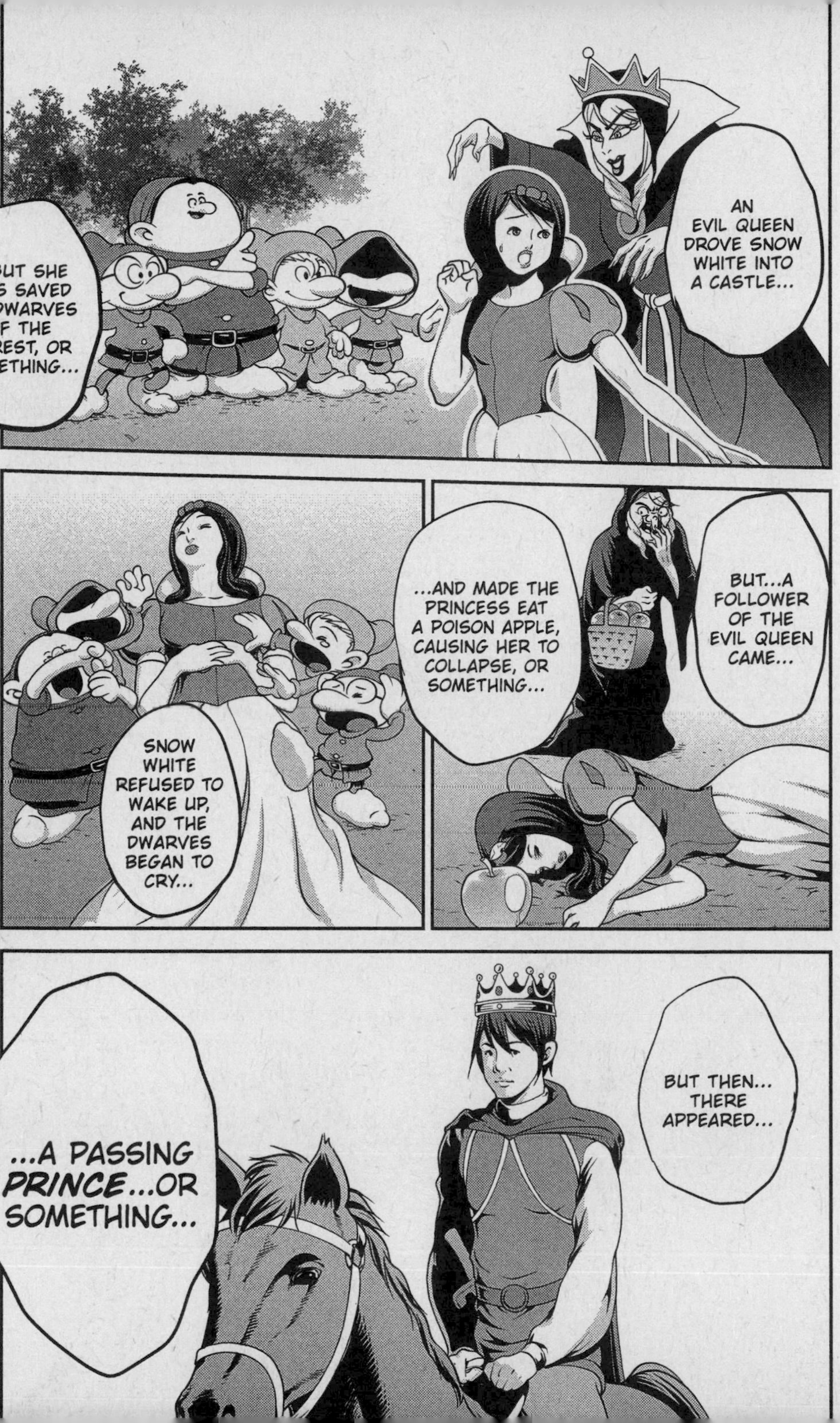

AN EVIL QUEEN DROVE SNOW WHITE INTO A CASTLE...
...BUT SHE WAS SAVED BY DWARVES OF THE FOREST, OR SOMETHING...
BUT...A FOLLOWER OF THE EVIL QUEEN CAME...
...AND MADE THE PRINCESS EAT A POISON APPLE, CAUSING HER TO COLLAPSE, OR SOMETHING...
SNOW WHITE REFUSED TO WAKE UP, AND THE DWARVES BEGAN TO CRY...
BUT THEN... THERE APPEARED...
...A PASSING PRINCE...OR SOMETHING...

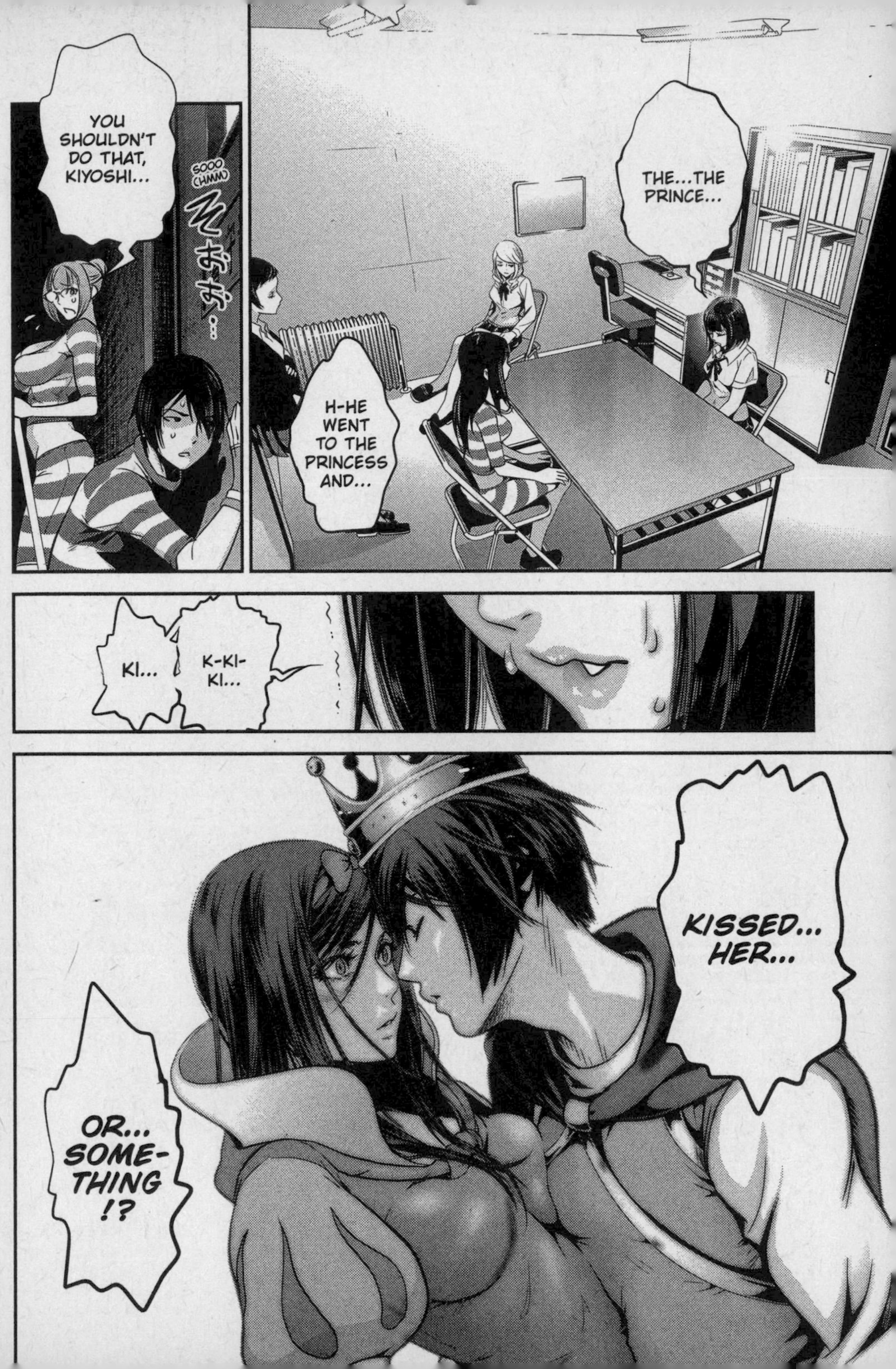
THE...THE PRINCE...
H-HE WENT TO THE PRINCESS AND...
SOOO (HMM)
そおぉ…
YOU SHOULDN'T DO THAT, KIYOSHI...
K-KI-KI...
KI...
KISSED... HER...
OR... SOMETHING!?

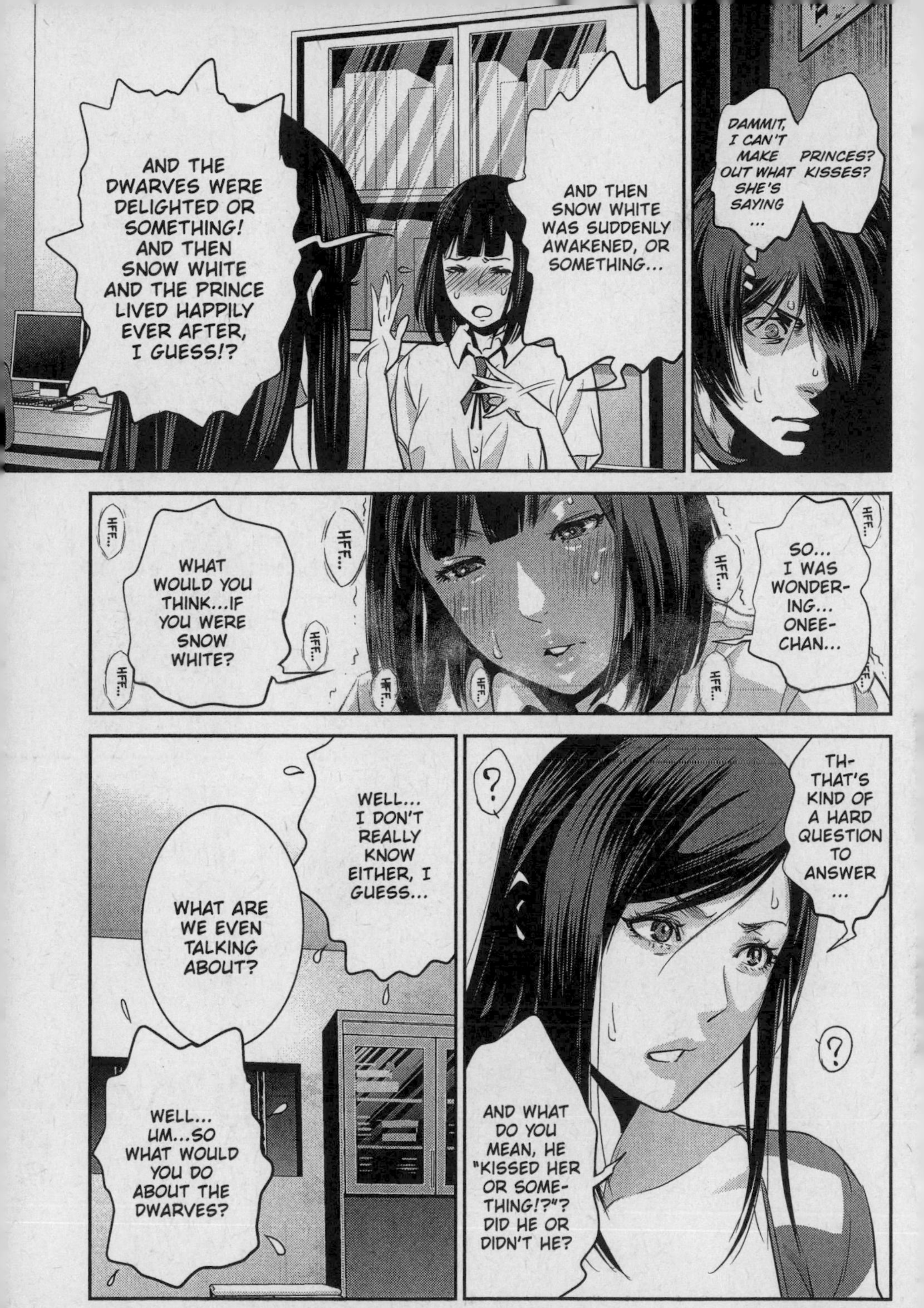
PRINCES? KISSES?
DAMMIT, I CAN'T MAKE OUT WHAT SHE'S SAYING...
AND THEN SNOW WHITE WAS SUDDENLY AWAKENED, OR SOMETHING...
AND THE DWARVES WERE DELIGHTED OR SOMETHING! AND THEN SNOW WHITE AND THE PRINCE LIVED HAPPILY EVER AFTER, I GUESS!?
HFF...
SO... I WAS WONDERING... ONEE-CHAN...
HFF...
HFF...
WHAT WOULD YOU THINK...IF YOU WERE SNOW WHITE?
HFF...
TH-THAT'S KIND OF A HARD QUESTION TO ANSWER...
?
?
AND WHAT DO YOU MEAN, HE "KISSED HER OR SOME-THING!?"? DID HE OR DIDN'T HE?
WELL... I DON'T REALLY KNOW EITHER, I GUESS...
WHAT ARE WE EVEN TALKING ABOUT?
WELL... UM...SO WHAT WOULD YOU DO ABOUT THE DWARVES?

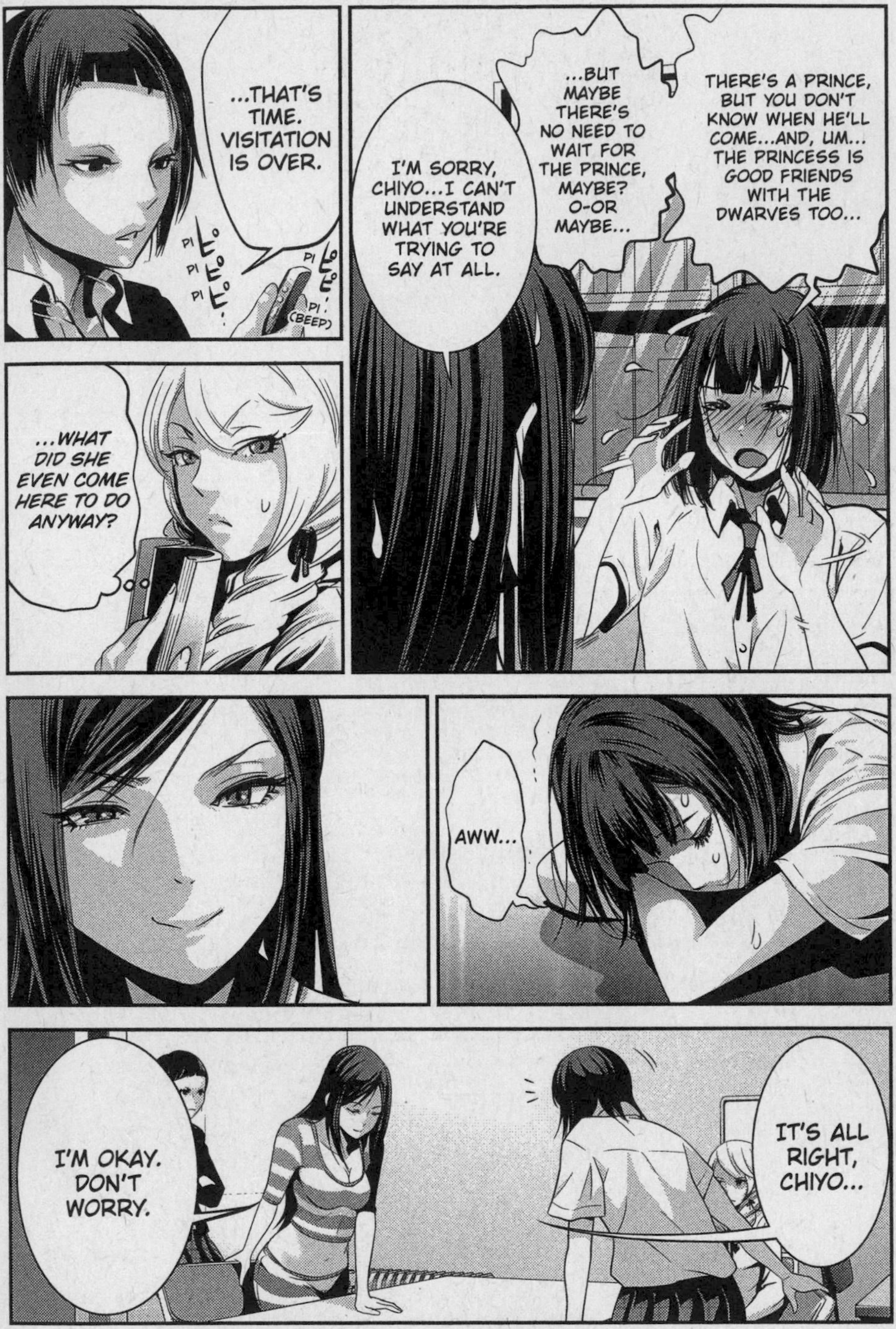
THERE'S A PRINCE, BUT YOU DON'T KNOW WHEN HE'LL COME...AND, UM... THE PRINCESS IS GOOD FRIENDS WITH THE DWARVES TOO...
...BUT MAYBE THERE'S NO NEED TO WAIT FOR THE PRINCE, MAYBE? O-OR MAYBE...
I'M SORRY, CHIYO...I CAN'T UNDERSTAND WHAT YOU'RE TRYING TO SAY AT ALL.
...THAT'S TIME. VISITATION IS OVER.
PI PI PI PI PI (BEEP)
...WHAT DID SHE EVEN COME HERE TO DO ANYWAY?
AWW...
IT'S ALL RIGHT, CHIYO...
I'M OKAY. DON'T WORRY.

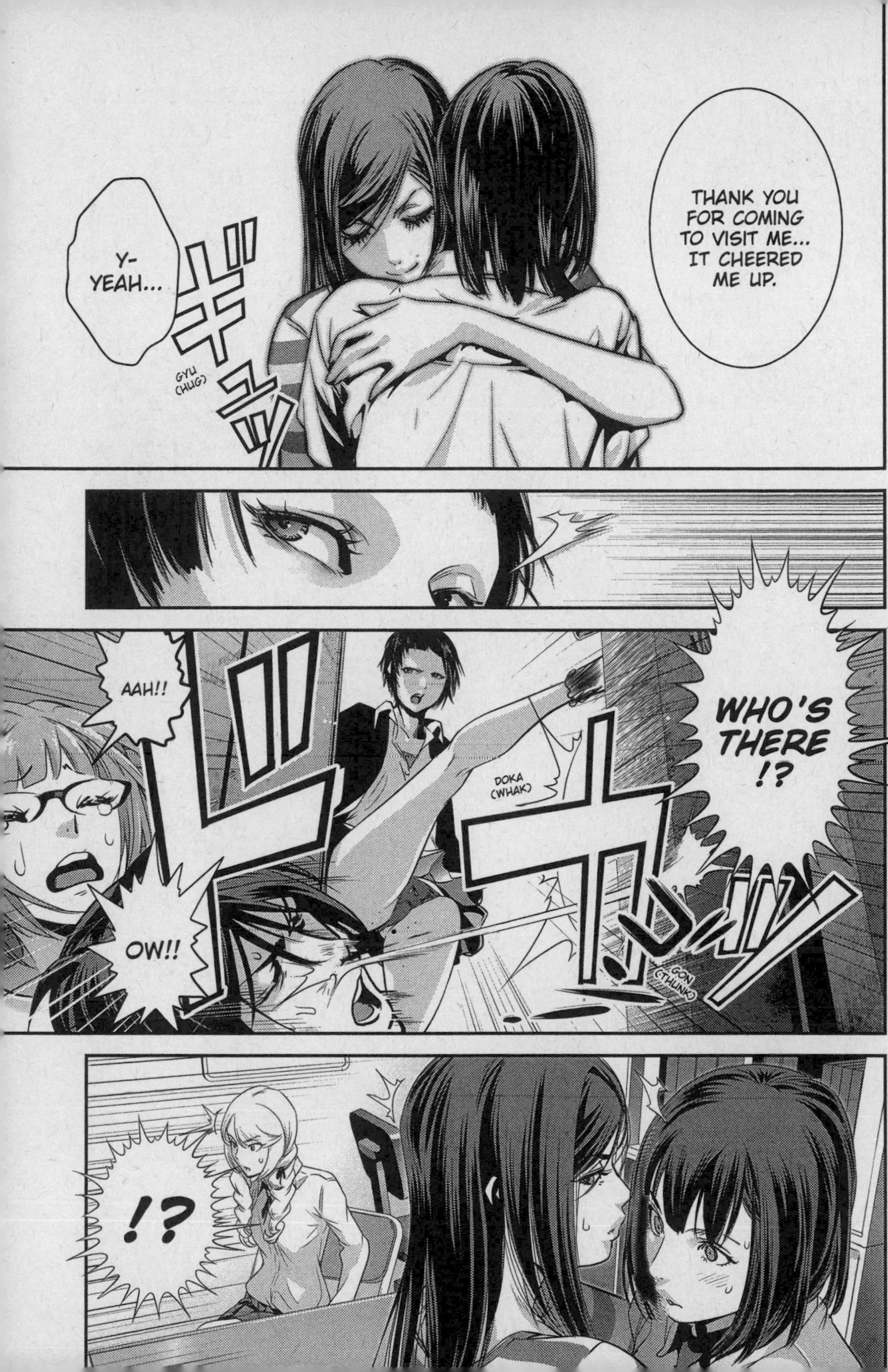

THANK YOU FOR COMING TO VISIT ME... IT CHEERED ME UP.
Y-YEAH...
GYU (HUG)
WHO'S THERE !?
AAH!!
DOKA (WHAK)
OW!!
GON (THUNK)
!?

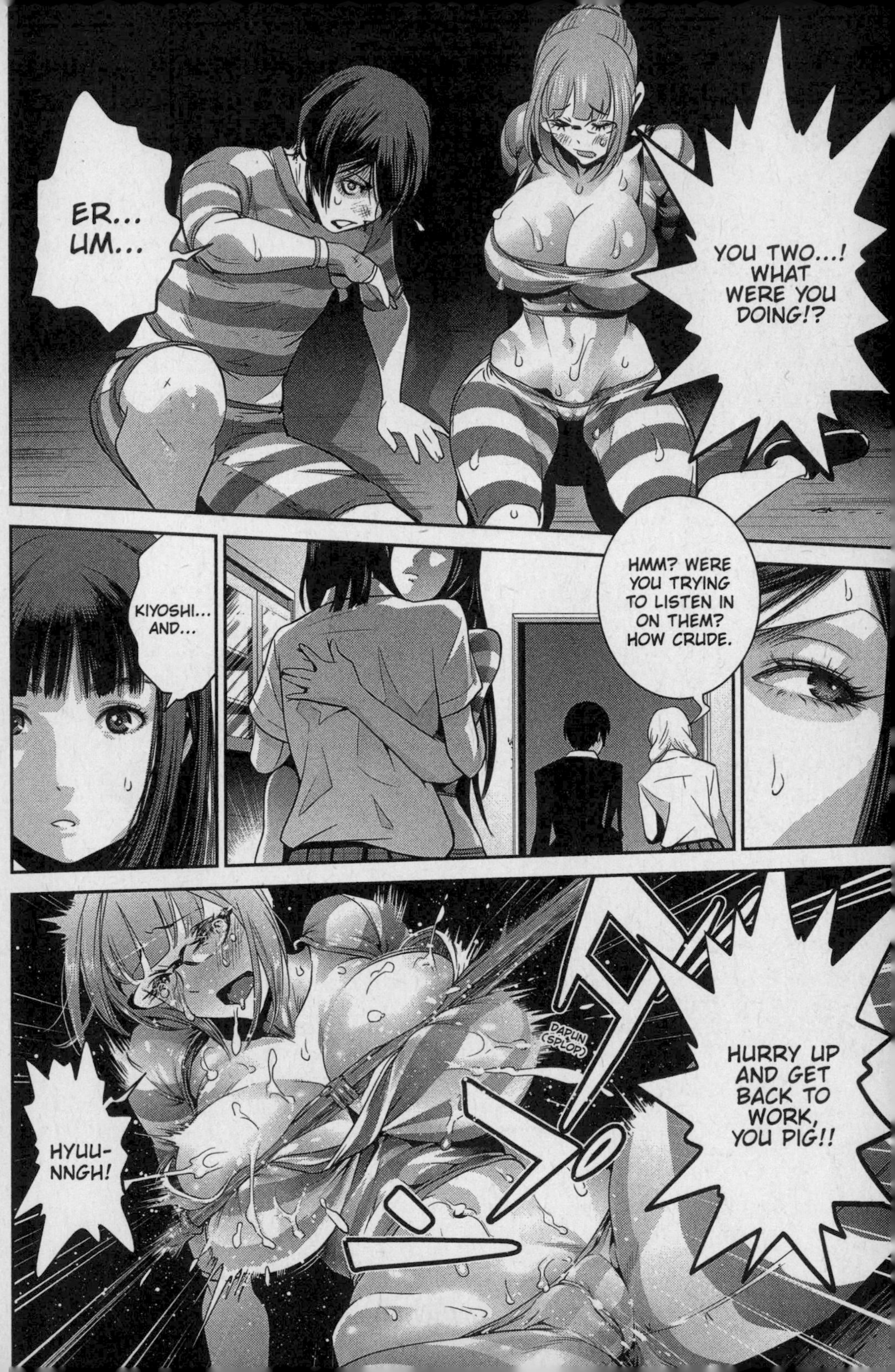
YOU TWO...! WHAT WERE YOU DOING!?
ER... UM...
HMM? WERE YOU TRYING TO LISTEN IN ON THEM? HOW CRUDE.
KIYOSHI... AND...
HURRY UP AND GET BACK TO WORK, YOU PIG!!
DAPUN (SPLOP)
HYUU-NNGH!

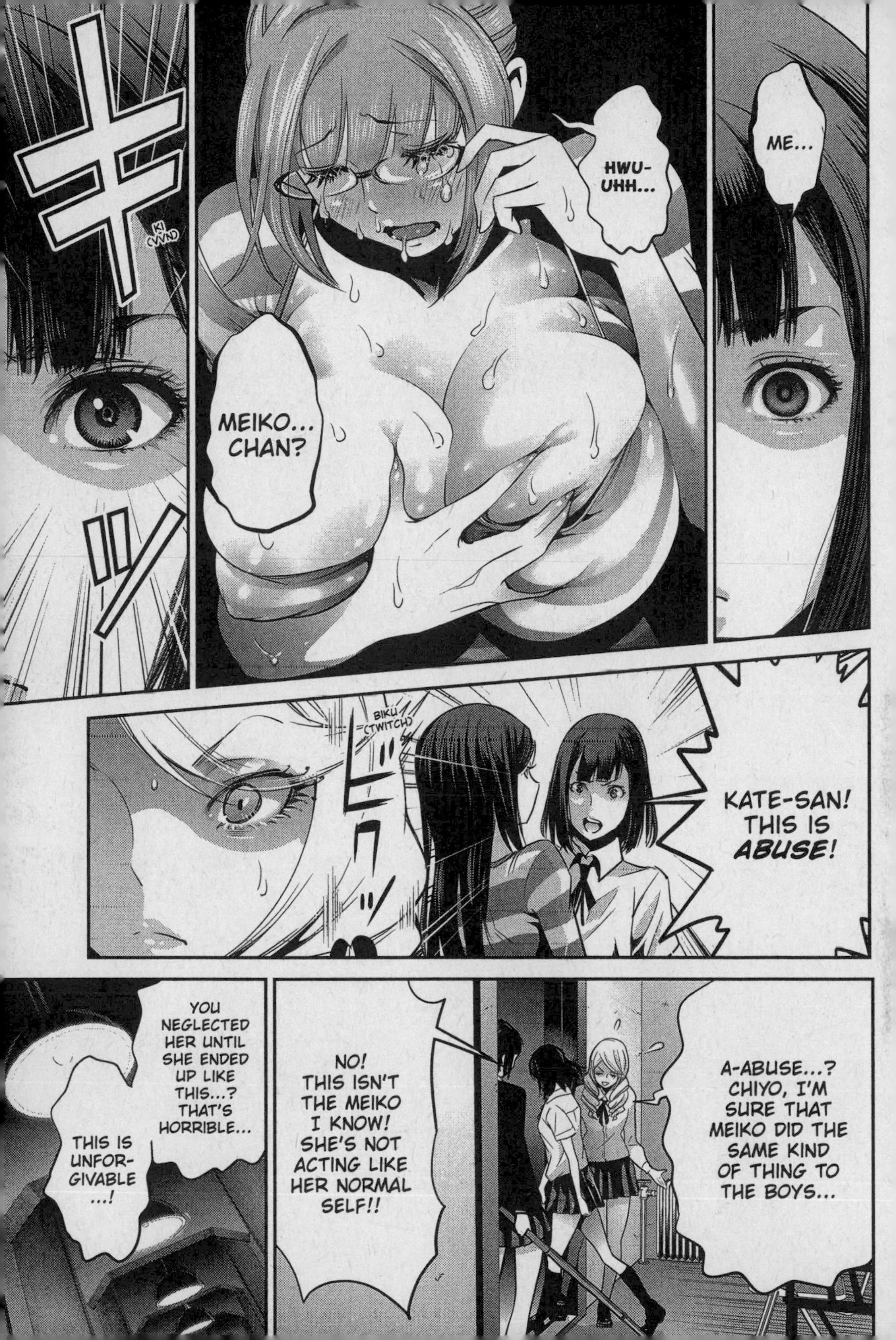
ME...
HWU-UHH...
MEIKO... CHAN?
KATE-SAN! THIS IS ABUSE!
BIKU (TWITCH)
A-ABUSE...? CHIYO, I'M SURE THAT MEIKO DID THE SAME KIND OF THING TO THE BOYS...
NO! THIS ISN'T THE MEIKO I KNOW! SHE'S NOT ACTING LIKE HER NORMAL SELF!!
YOU NEGLECTED HER UNTIL SHE ENDED UP LIKE THIS...? THAT'S HORRIBLE...
THIS IS UNFORGIVABLE...!

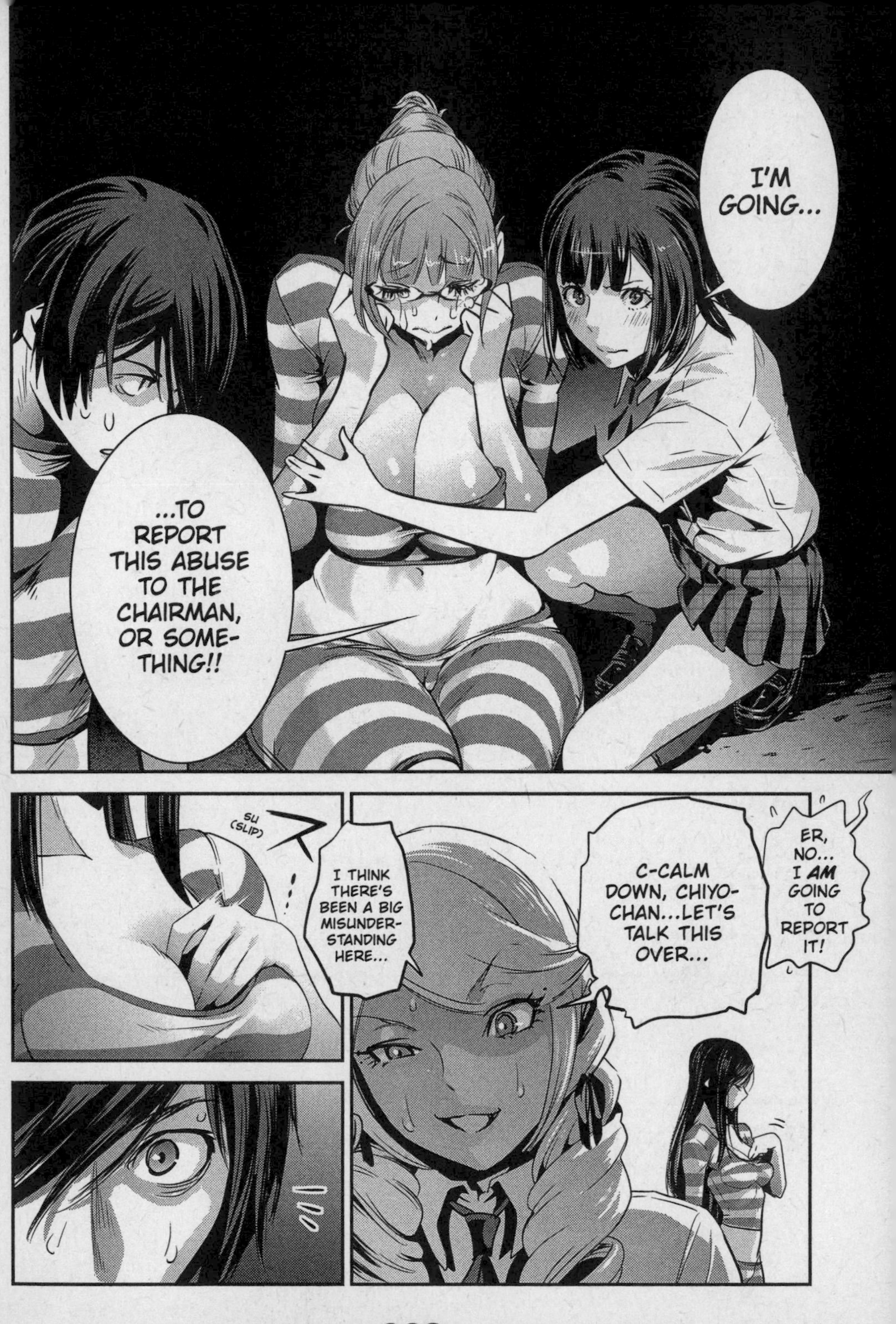
I'M GOING...
...TO REPORT THIS ABUSE TO THE CHAIRMAN, OR SOME-THING!!
ER, NO... I *AM* GOING TO REPORT IT!
C-CALM DOWN, CHIYO-CHAN...LET'S TALK THIS OVER...
I THINK THERE'S BEEN A BIG MISUNDER-STANDING HERE...
SU (SLIP)

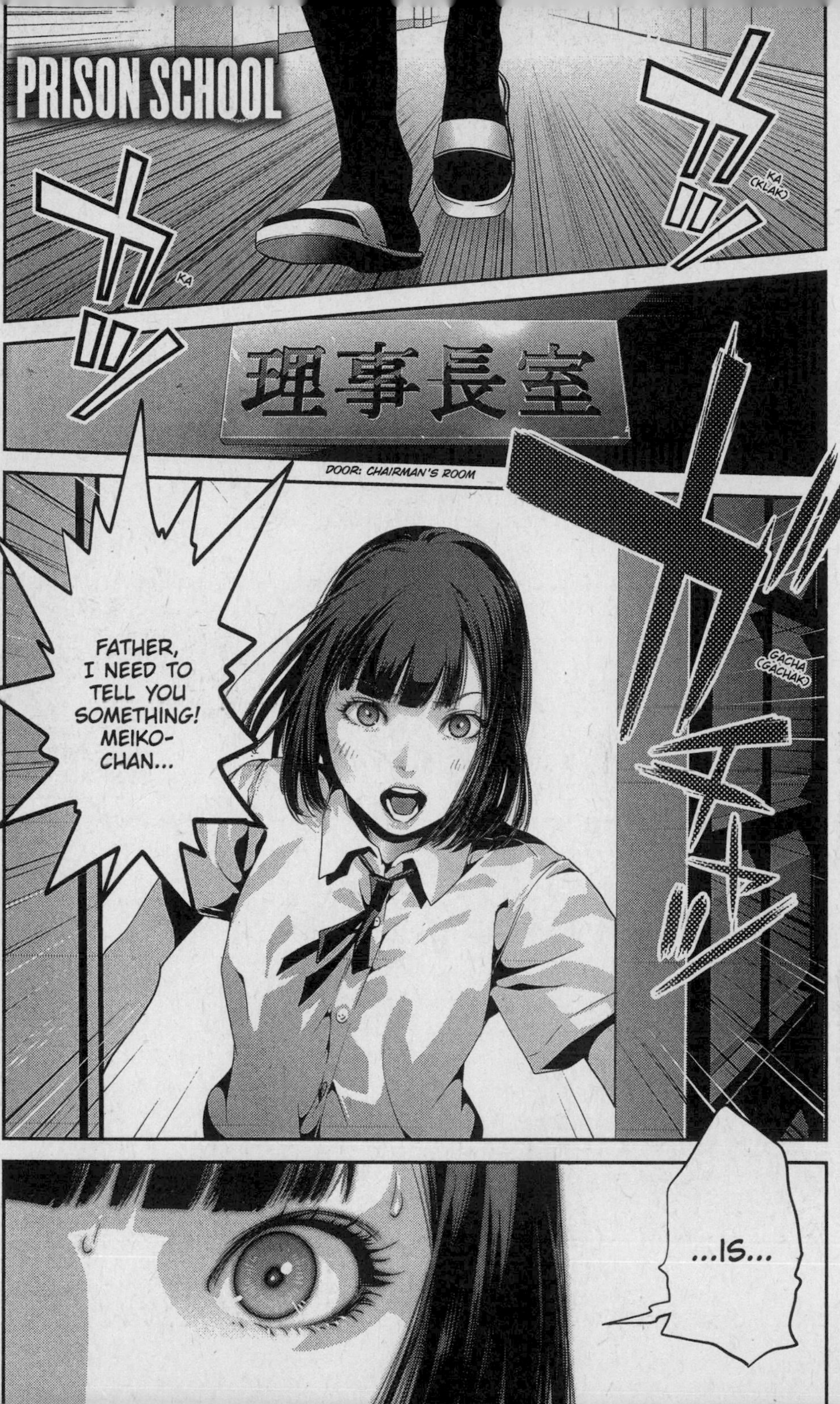
PRISON SCHOOL
KA (KLAK)
KA
理事長室
DOOR: CHAIRMAN'S ROOM
GACHA (GACHAK)
FATHER, I NEED TO TELL YOU SOMETHING! MEIKO-CHAN...
...IS...

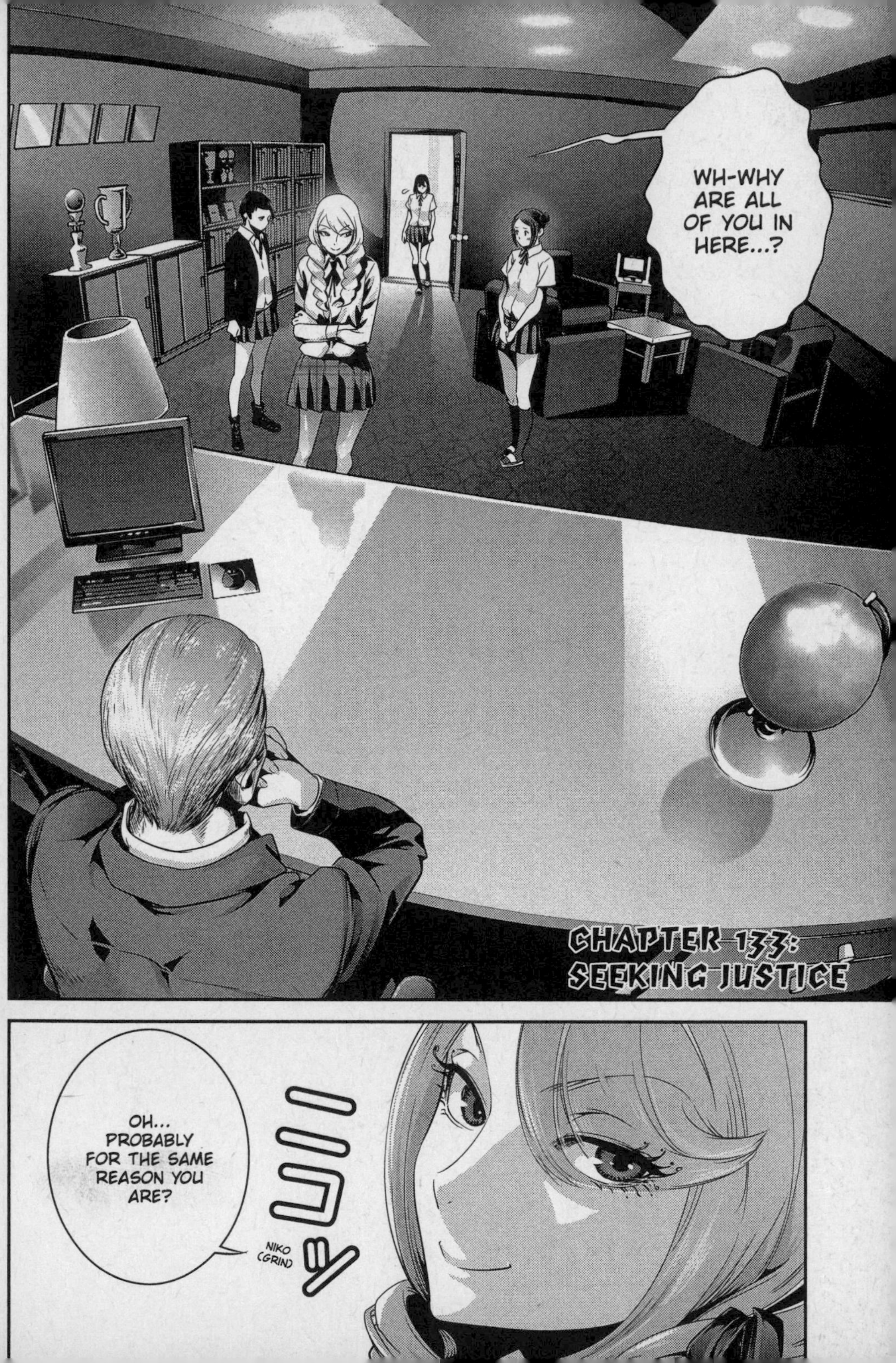
WH-WHY ARE ALL OF YOU IN HERE...?
CHAPTER 133: SEEKING JUSTICE
OH... PROBABLY FOR THE SAME REASON YOU ARE?
NIKO (GRIN)

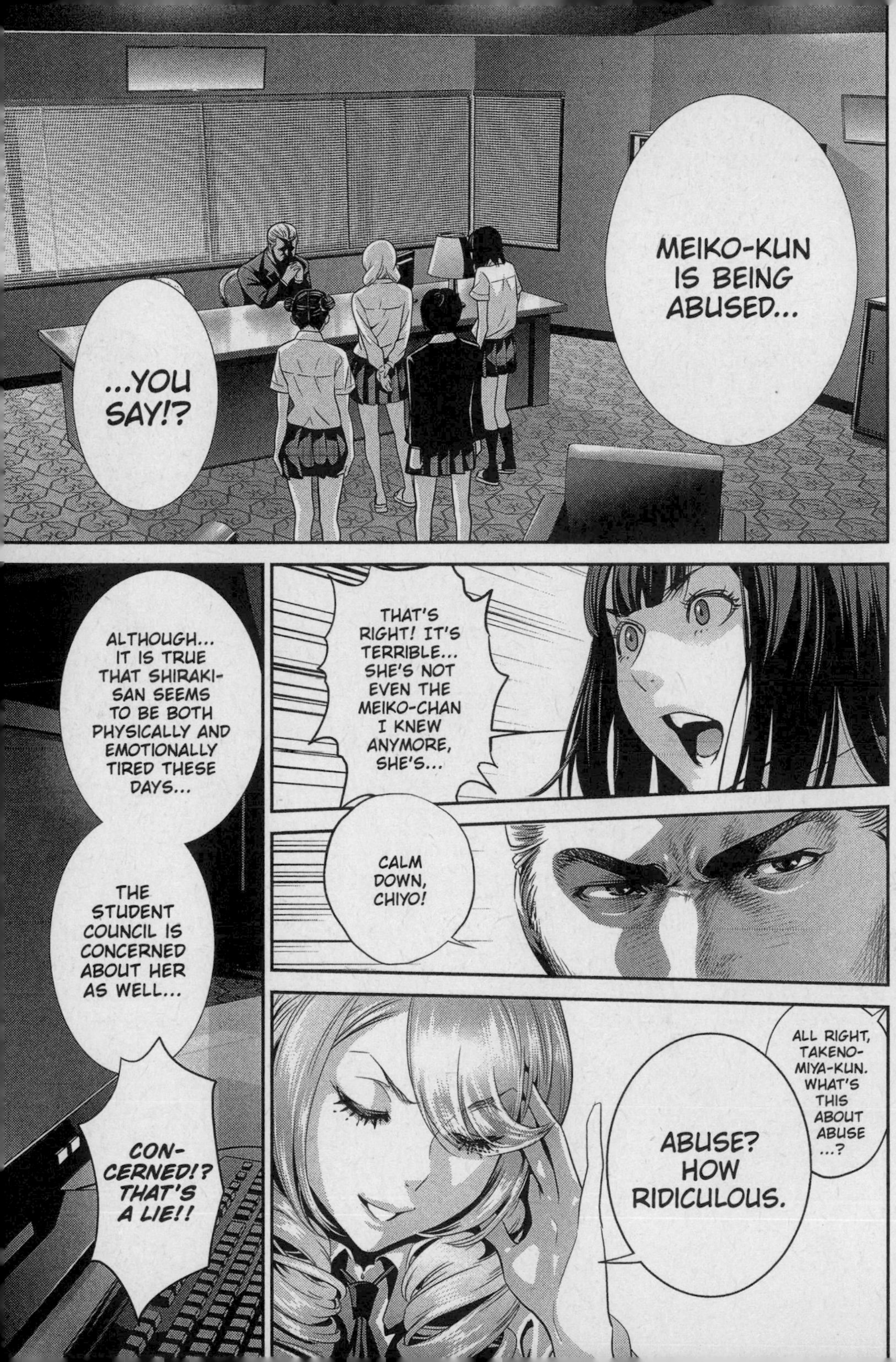
MEIKO-KUN IS BEING ABUSED...
...YOU SAY!?
ALTHOUGH... IT IS TRUE THAT SHIRAKI-SAN SEEMS TO BE BOTH PHYSICALLY AND EMOTIONALLY TIRED THESE DAYS...
THE STUDENT COUNCIL IS CONCERNED ABOUT HER AS WELL...
CON-CERNED!? THAT'S A LIE!!
THAT'S RIGHT! IT'S TERRIBLE... SHE'S NOT EVEN THE MEIKO-CHAN I KNEW ANYMORE, SHE'S...
CALM DOWN, CHIYO!
ALL RIGHT, TAKENO-MIYA-KUN. WHAT'S THIS ABOUT ABUSE ...?
ABUSE? HOW RIDICULOUS.

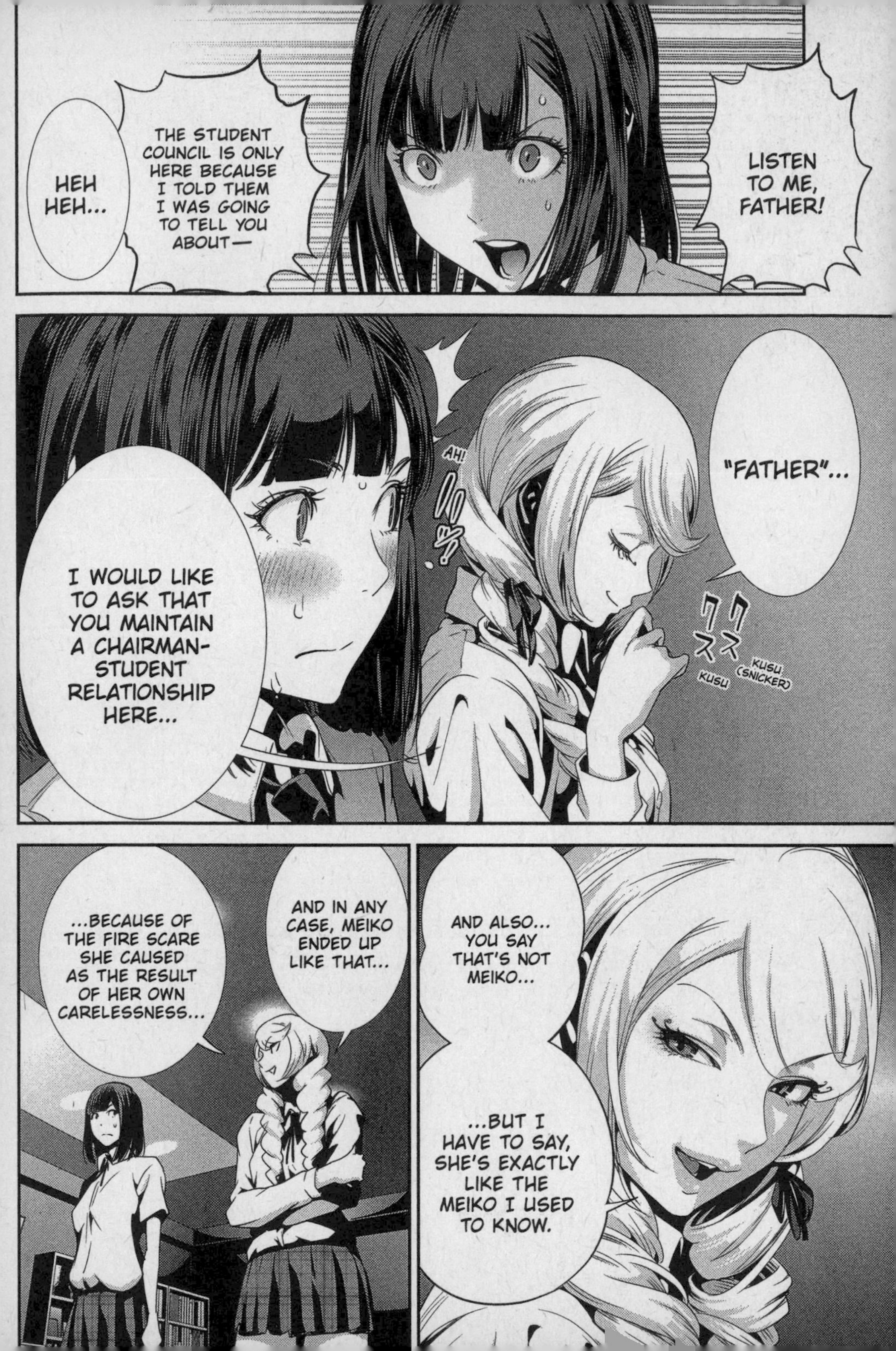
LISTEN TO ME, FATHER!
THE STUDENT COUNCIL IS ONLY HERE BECAUSE I TOLD THEM I WAS GOING TO TELL YOU ABOUT—
HEH HEH...
"FATHER"...
AH!
クス クス
KUSU KUSU (SNICKER)
I WOULD LIKE TO ASK THAT YOU MAINTAIN A CHAIRMAN-STUDENT RELATIONSHIP HERE...
AND ALSO... YOU SAY THAT'S NOT MEIKO...
...BUT I HAVE TO SAY, SHE'S EXACTLY LIKE THE MEIKO I USED TO KNOW.
AND IN ANY CASE, MEIKO ENDED UP LIKE THAT...
...BECAUSE OF THE FIRE SCARE SHE CAUSED AS THE RESULT OF HER OWN CARELESSNESS...

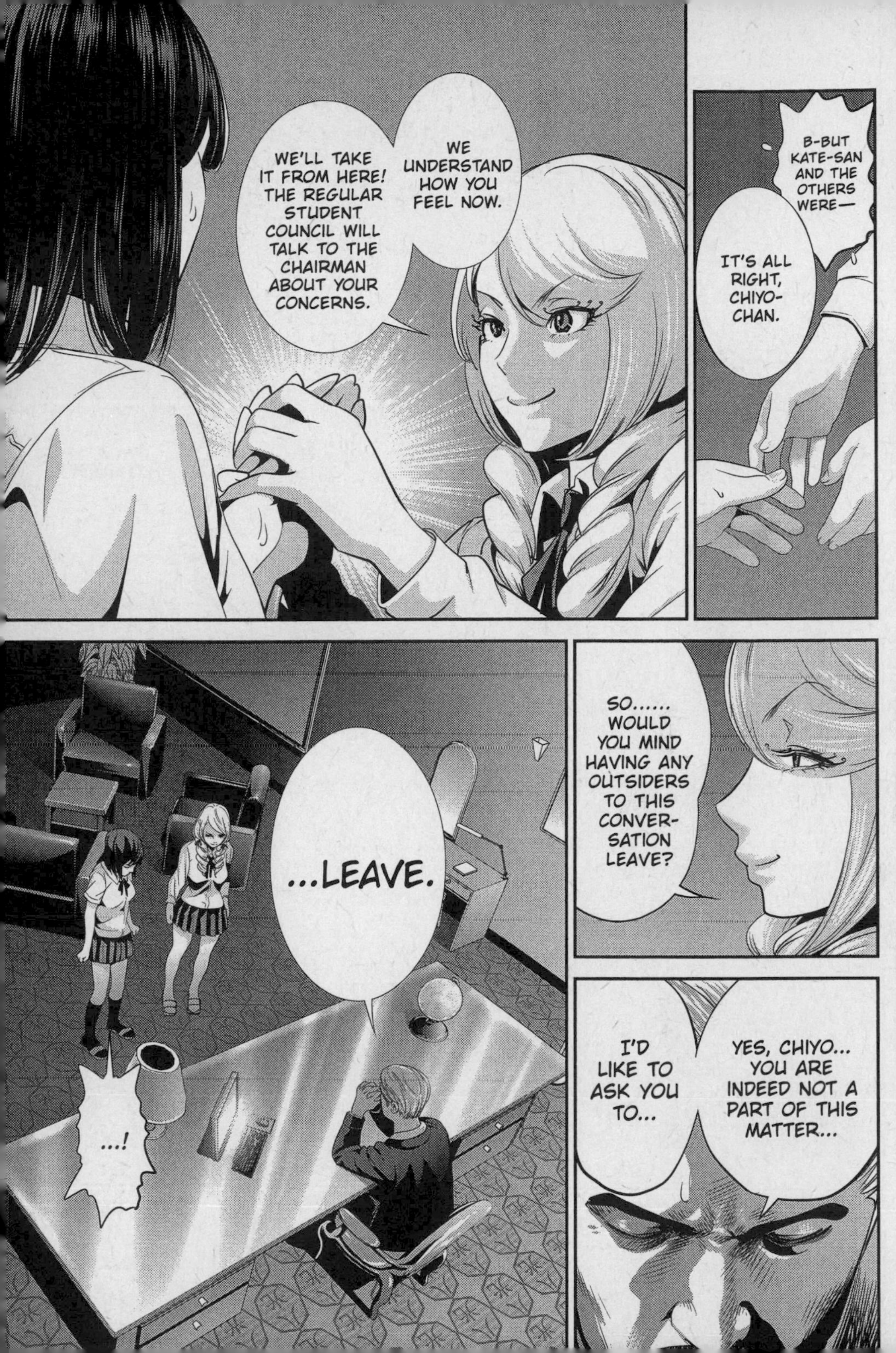
B-BUT KATE-SAN AND THE OTHERS WERE—
IT'S ALL RIGHT, CHIYO-CHAN.
WE UNDERSTAND HOW YOU FEEL NOW.
WE'LL TAKE IT FROM HERE! THE REGULAR STUDENT COUNCIL WILL TALK TO THE CHAIRMAN ABOUT YOUR CONCERNS.
SO...... WOULD YOU MIND HAVING ANY OUTSIDERS TO THIS CONVER-SATION LEAVE?
YES, CHIYO... YOU ARE INDEED NOT A PART OF THIS MATTER...
I'D LIKE TO ASK YOU TO...
...LEAVE.
...!

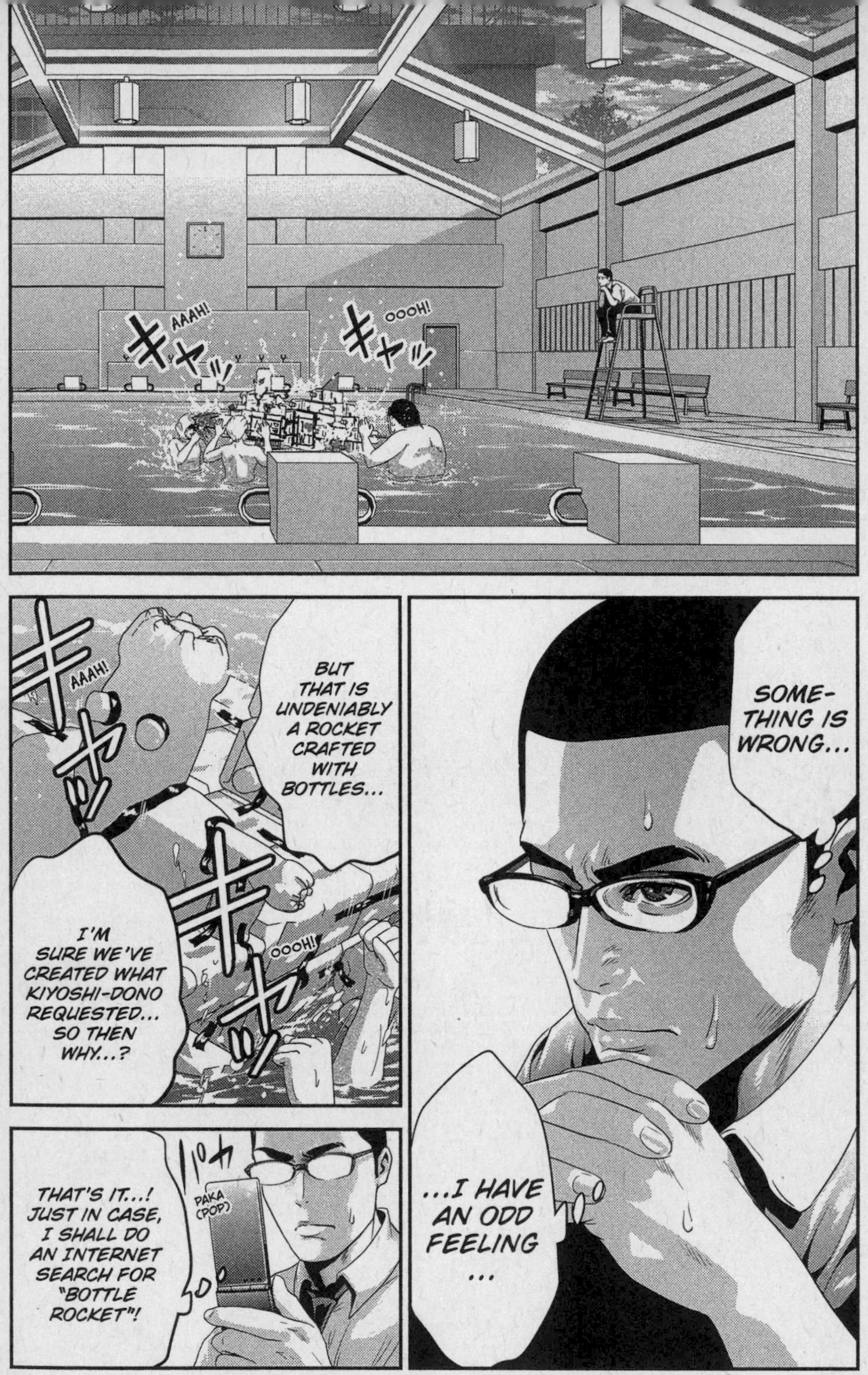
OOOH!
AAAH!
SOME-THING IS WRONG...
...I HAVE AN ODD FEELING ...
BUT THAT IS UNDENIABLY A ROCKET CRAFTED WITH BOTTLES...
AAAH!
OOOH!
I'M SURE WE'VE CREATED WHAT KIYOSHI-DONO REQUESTED... SO THEN WHY...?
PAKA (POP)
THAT'S IT...! JUST IN CASE, I SHALL DO AN INTERNET SEARCH FOR "BOTTLE ROCKET"!

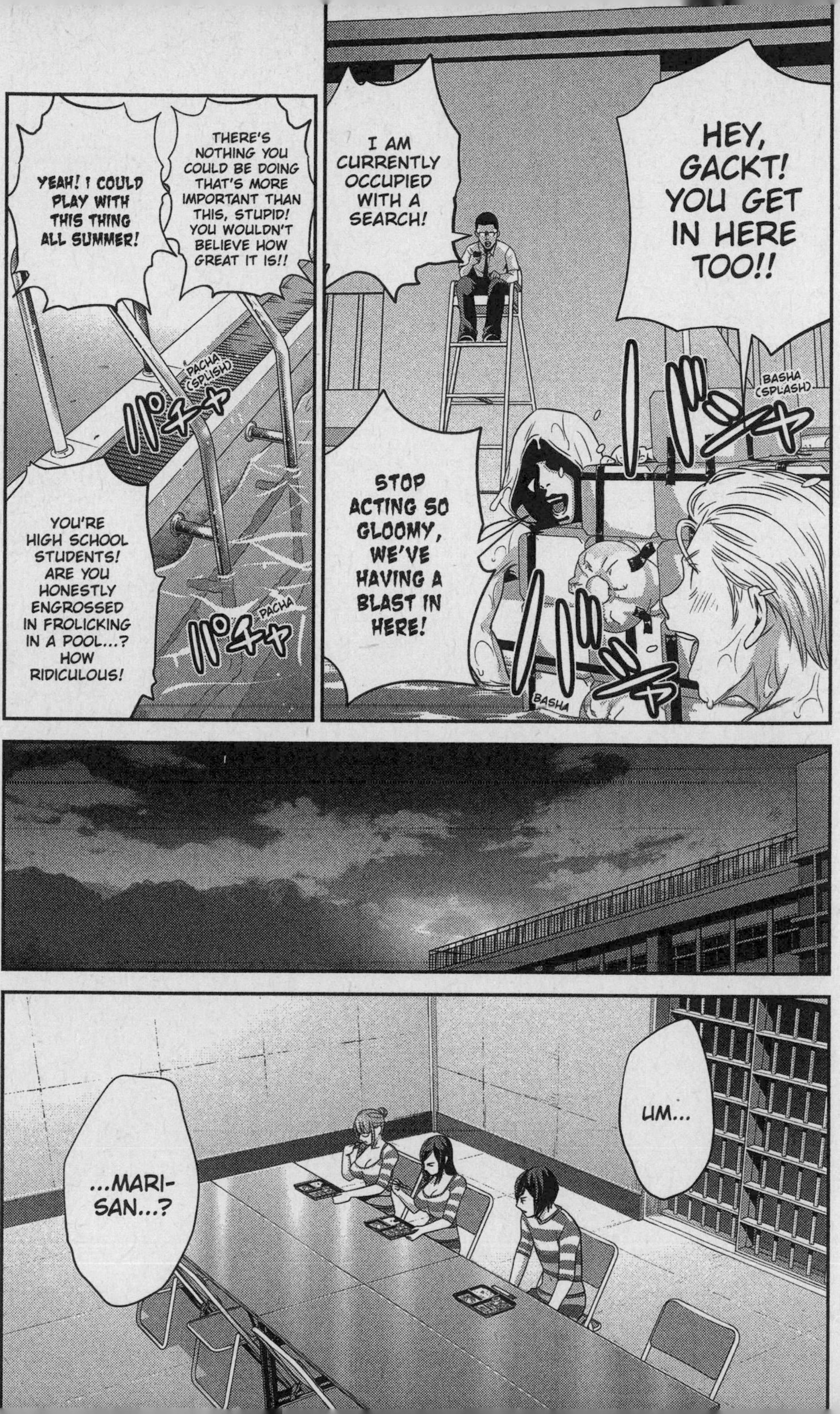
HEY, GACKT! YOU GET IN HERE TOO!!
I AM CURRENTLY OCCUPIED WITH A SEARCH!
BASHA (SPLASH)
STOP ACTING SO GLOOMY, WE'VE HAVING A BLAST IN HERE!
BASHA
THERE'S NOTHING YOU COULD BE DOING THAT'S MORE IMPORTANT THAN THIS, STUPID! YOU WOULDN'T BELIEVE HOW GREAT IT IS!!
YEAH! I COULD PLAY WITH THIS THING ALL SUMMER!
PACHA (SPLISH)
YOU'RE HIGH SCHOOL STUDENTS! ARE YOU HONESTLY ENGROSSED IN FROLICKING IN A POOL...? HOW RIDICULOUS!
PACHA
UM...
...MARI-SAN...?

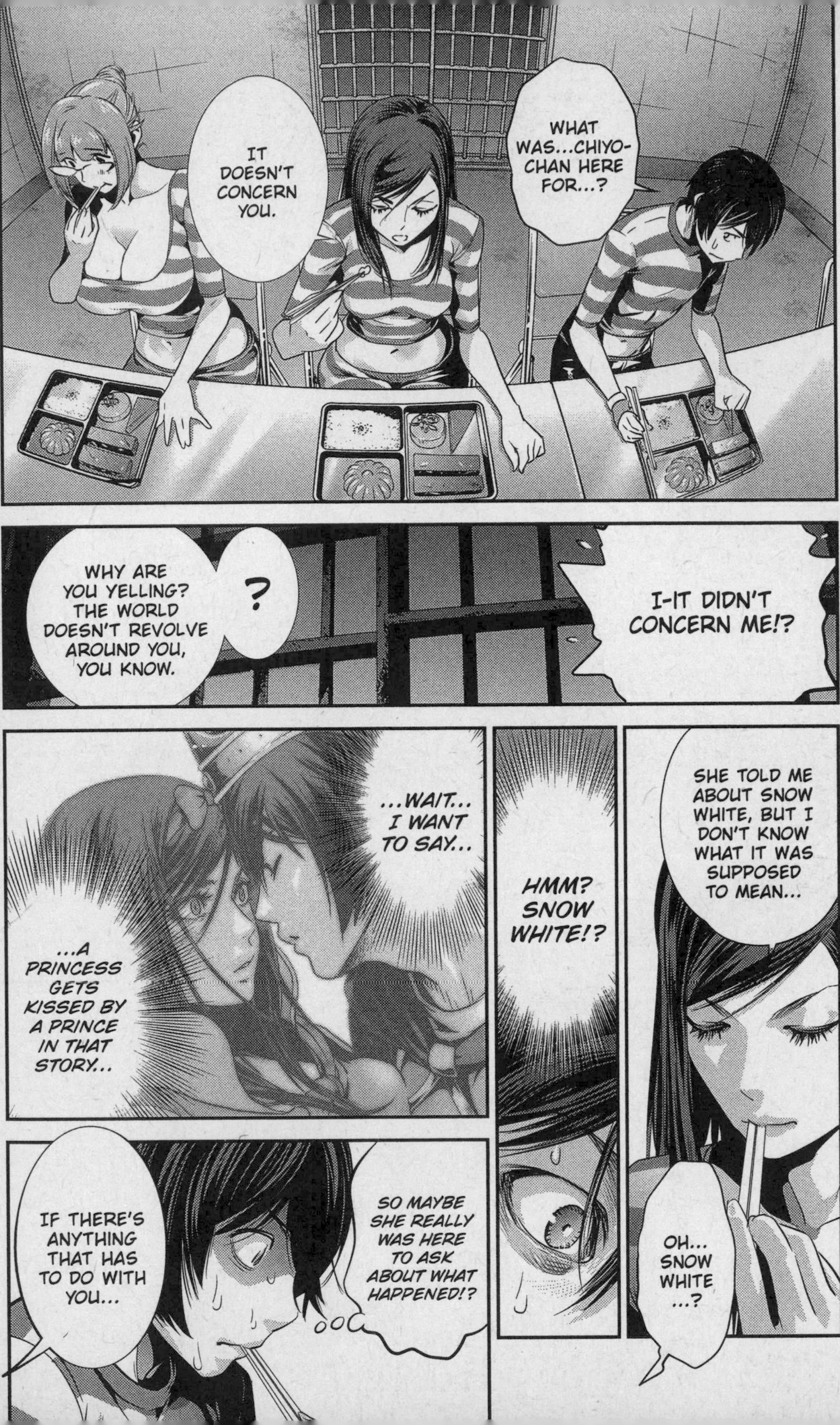

WHAT WAS...CHIYO-CHAN HERE FOR...?
IT DOESN'T CONCERN YOU.
I-IT DIDN'T CONCERN ME!?
?
WHY ARE YOU YELLING? THE WORLD DOESN'T REVOLVE AROUND YOU, YOU KNOW.
SHE TOLD ME ABOUT SNOW WHITE, BUT I DON'T KNOW WHAT IT WAS SUPPOSED TO MEAN...
OH... SNOW WHITE ...?
HMM? SNOW WHITE!?
...WAIT... I WANT TO SAY...
...A PRINCESS GETS KISSED BY A PRINCE IN THAT STORY...
SO MAYBE SHE REALLY WAS HERE TO ASK ABOUT WHAT HAPPENED!?
IF THERE'S ANYTHING THAT HAS TO DO WITH YOU...

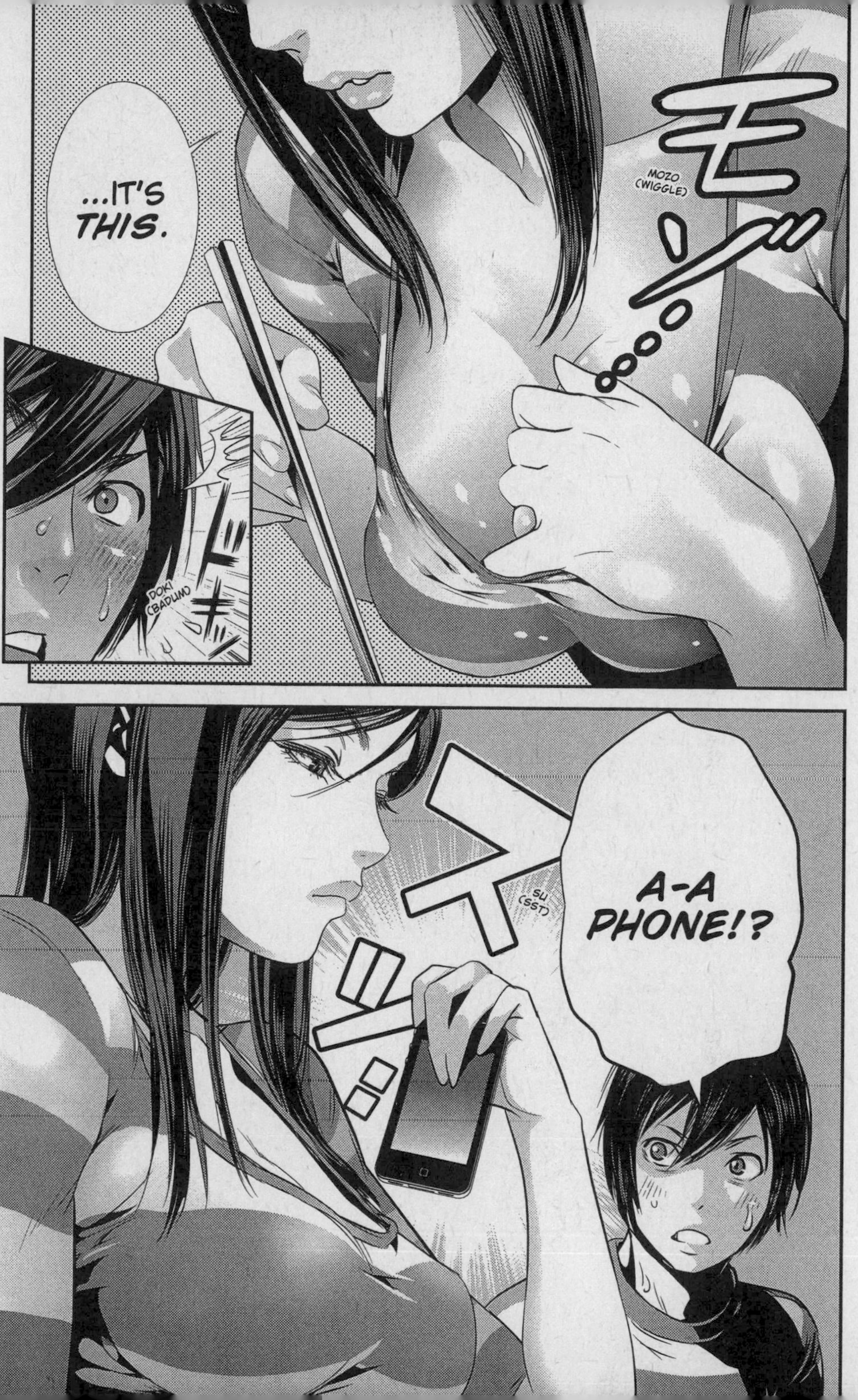
MOZO (WIGGLE)
...IT'S THIS.
DOKI (BADUMP)
A-A PHONE!?
SU (SST)

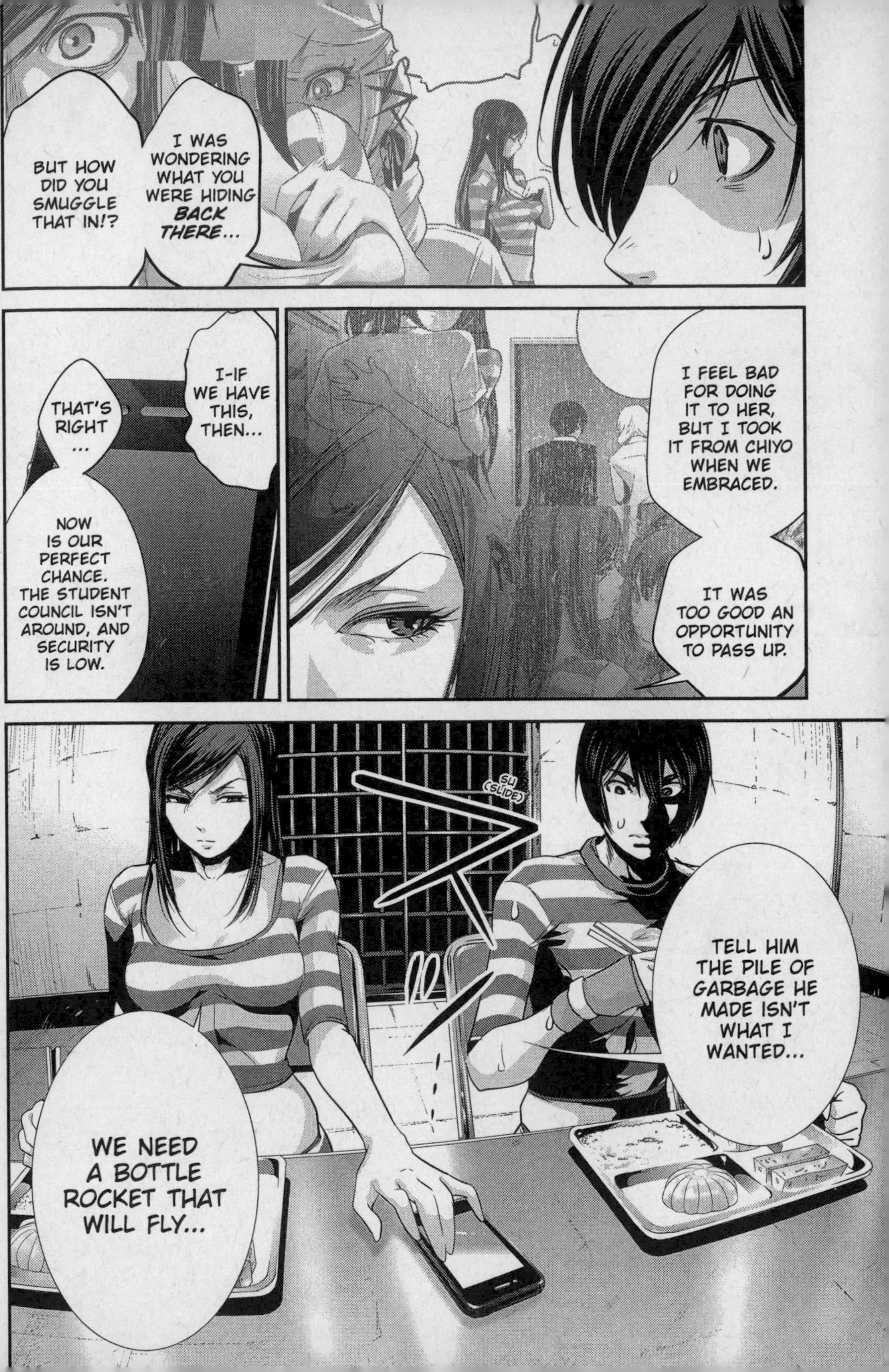
I WAS WONDERING WHAT YOU WERE HIDING *BACK THERE*...
BUT HOW DID YOU SMUGGLE THAT IN!?
I FEEL BAD FOR DOING IT TO HER, BUT I TOOK IT FROM CHIYO WHEN WE EMBRACED.
IT WAS TOO GOOD AN OPPORTUNITY TO PASS UP.
I-IF WE HAVE THIS, THEN...
THAT'S RIGHT...
NOW IS OUR PERFECT CHANCE. THE STUDENT COUNCIL ISN'T AROUND, AND SECURITY IS LOW.
SU (SLIDE)
TELL HIM THE PILE OF GARBAGE HE MADE ISN'T WHAT I WANTED...
WE NEED A BOTTLE ROCKET THAT WILL FLY...

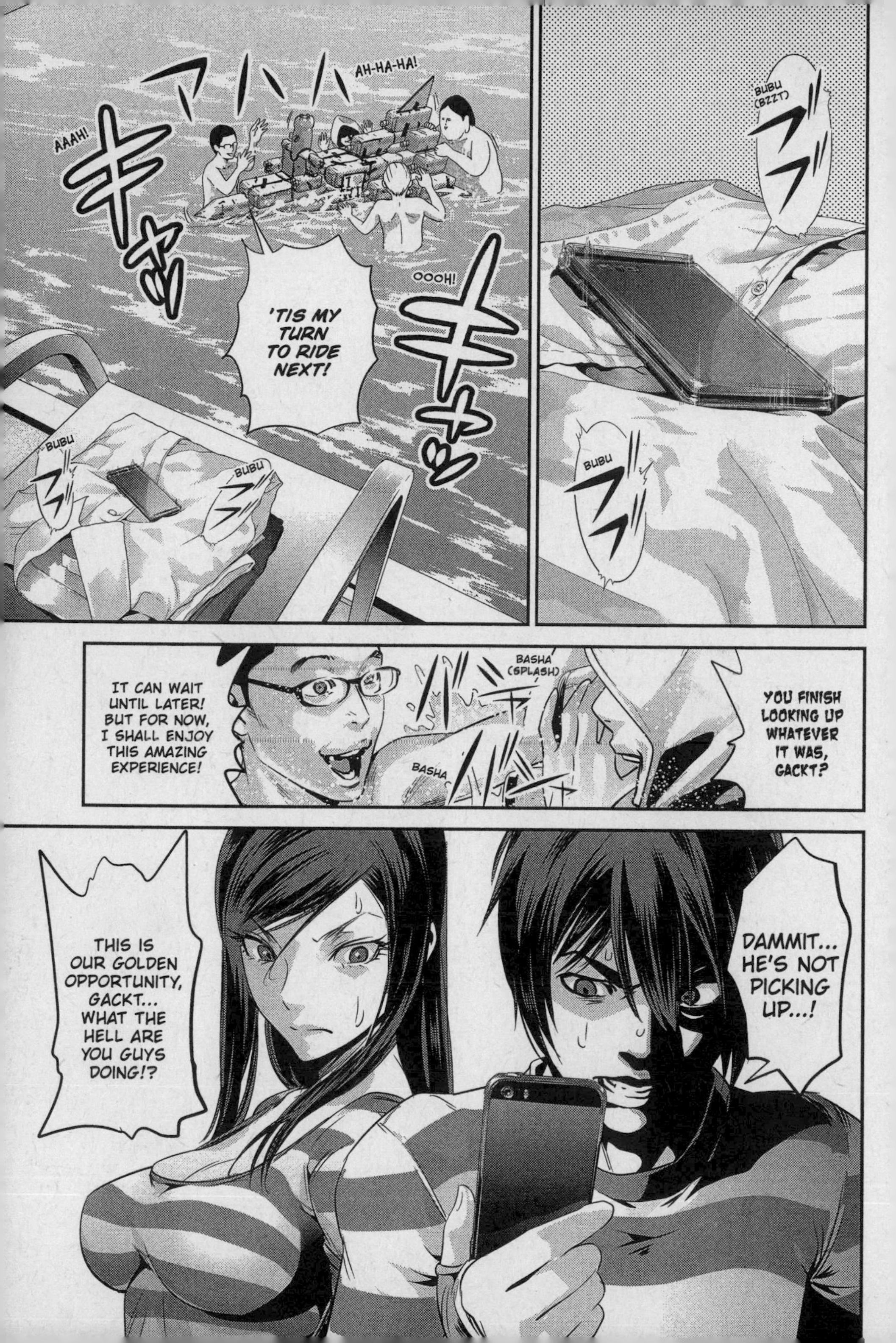
BUBU (BZZT)
BUBU
AH-HA-HA!
AAAH!
'TIS MY TURN TO RIDE NEXT!
OOOH!
BUBU
BUBU
YOU FINISH LOOKING UP WHATEVER IT WAS, GACKT?
BASHA (SPLASH)
BASHA
IT CAN WAIT UNTIL LATER! BUT FOR NOW, I SHALL ENJOY THIS AMAZING EXPERIENCE!
DAMMIT... HE'S NOT PICKING UP...!
THIS IS OUR GOLDEN OPPORTUNITY, GACKT... WHAT THE HELL ARE YOU GUYS DOING!?

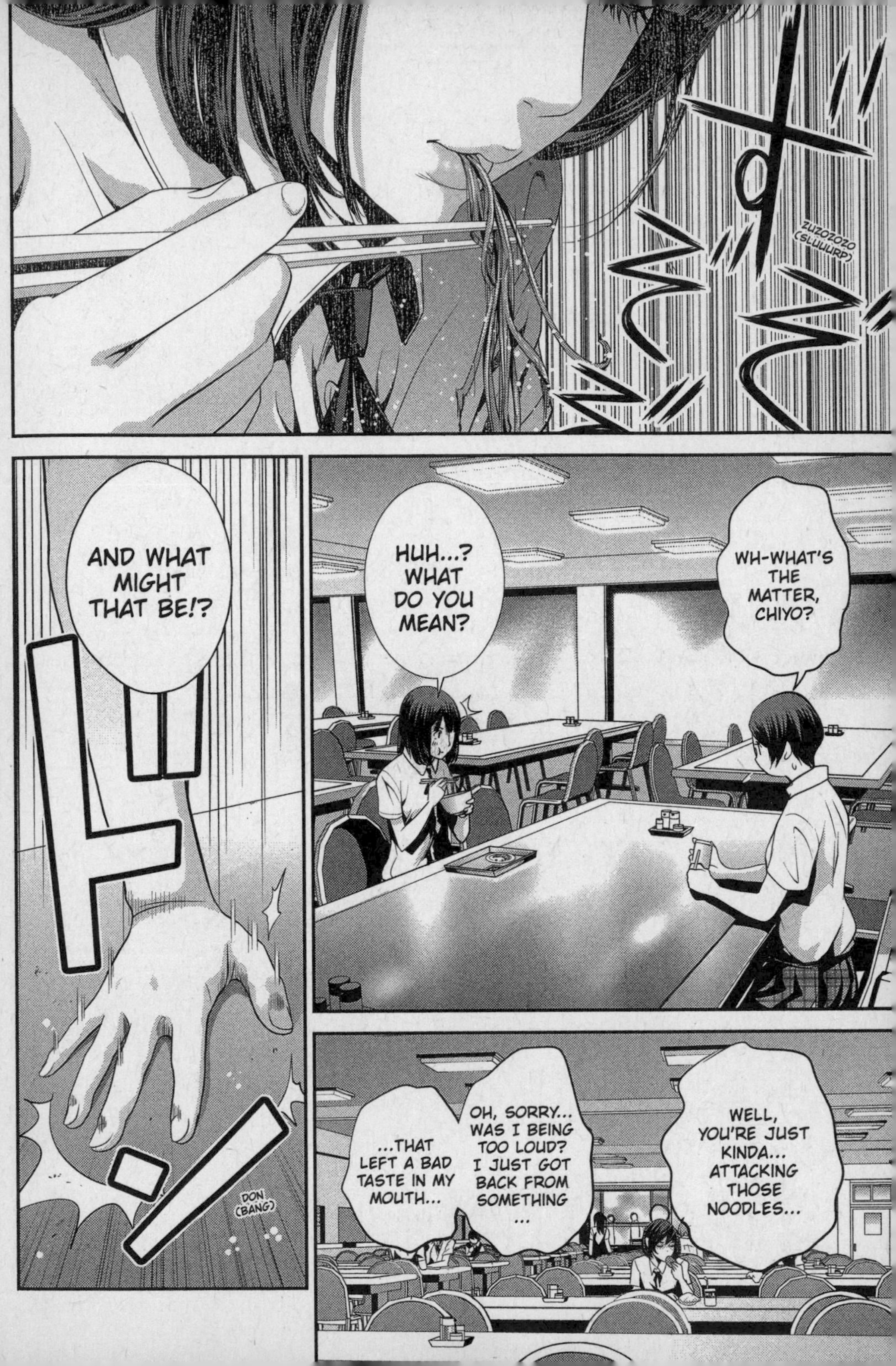
ZUZOZOZO (SLUUURP)
WH-WHAT'S THE MATTER, CHIYO?
HUH...? WHAT DO YOU MEAN?
WELL, YOU'RE JUST KINDA... ATTACKING THOSE NOODLES...
OH, SORRY... WAS I BEING TOO LOUD? I JUST GOT BACK FROM SOMETHING ...
...THAT LEFT A BAD TASTE IN MY MOUTH...
AND WHAT MIGHT THAT BE!?
DON (BANG)

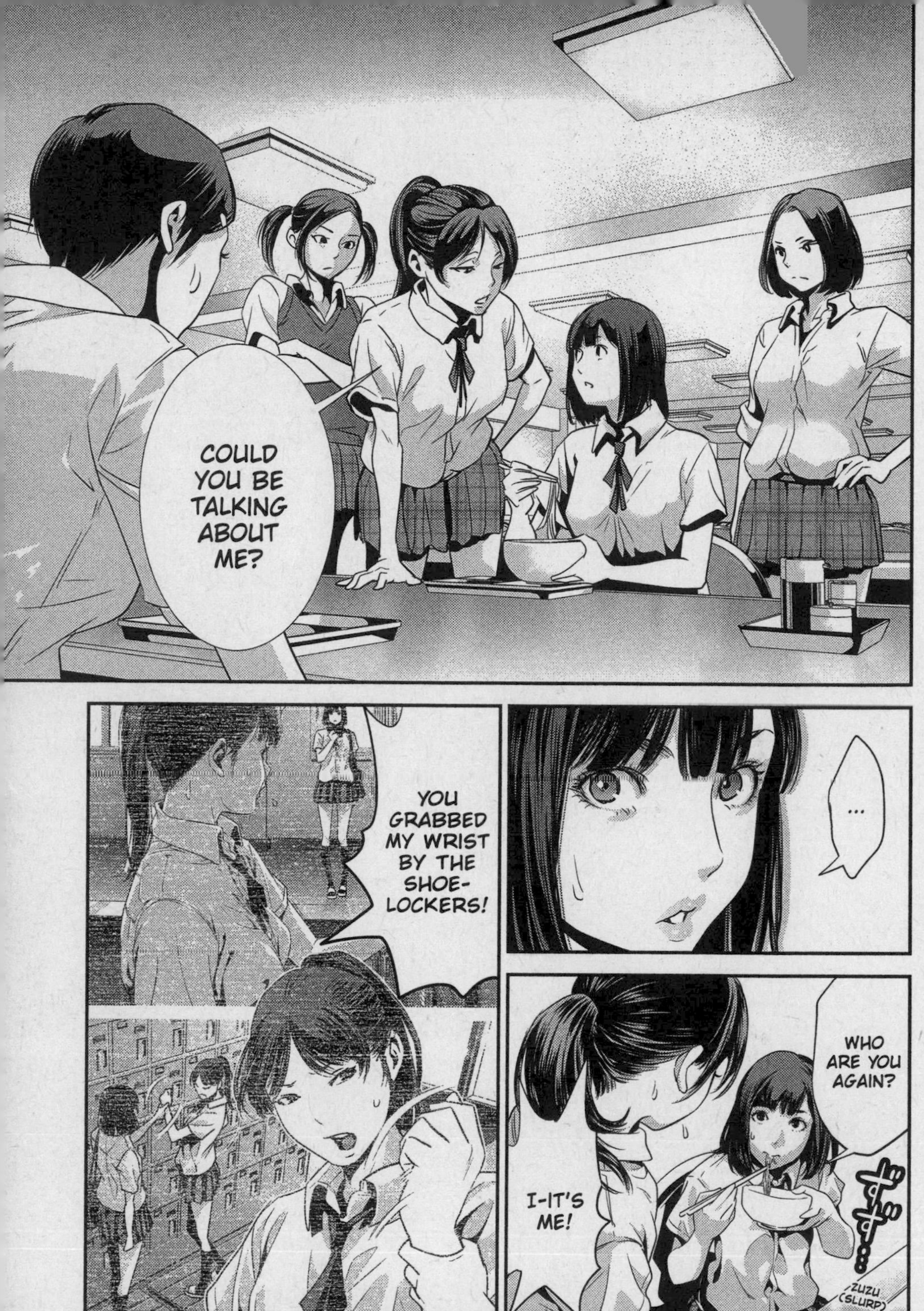
COULD YOU BE TALKING ABOUT ME?
...
YOU GRABBED MY WRIST BY THE SHOE-LOCKERS!
WHO ARE YOU AGAIN?
I-IT'S ME!
ZUZU (SLURP)

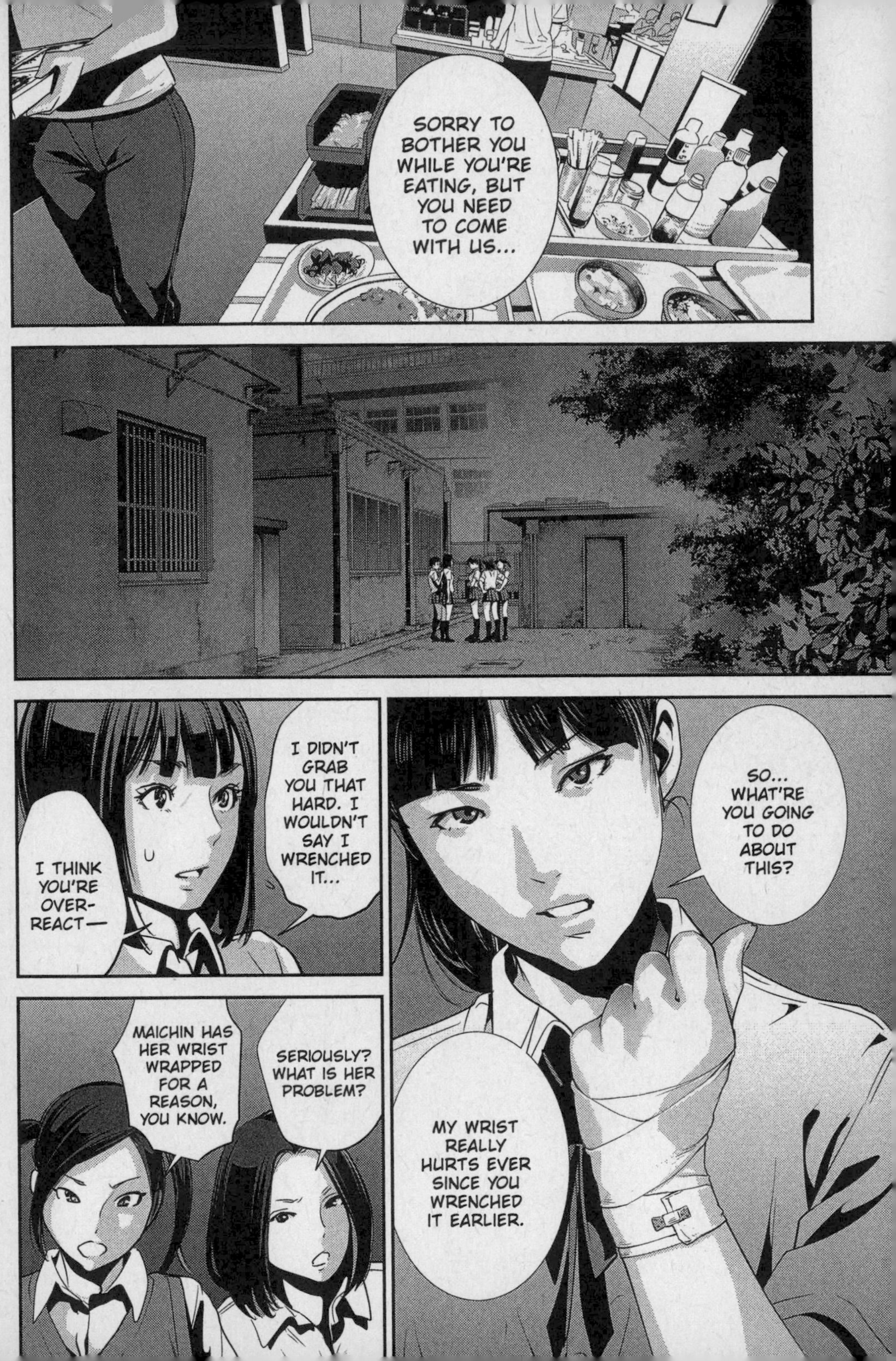
SORRY TO BOTHER YOU WHILE YOU'RE EATING, BUT YOU NEED TO COME WITH US...
SO... WHAT'RE YOU GOING TO DO ABOUT THIS?
MY WRIST REALLY HURTS EVER SINCE YOU WRENCHED IT EARLIER.
I DIDN'T GRAB YOU THAT HARD. I WOULDN'T SAY I WRENCHED IT...
I THINK YOU'RE OVER-REACT—
SERIOUSLY? WHAT IS HER PROBLEM?
MAICHIN HAS HER WRIST WRAPPED FOR A REASON, YOU KNOW.

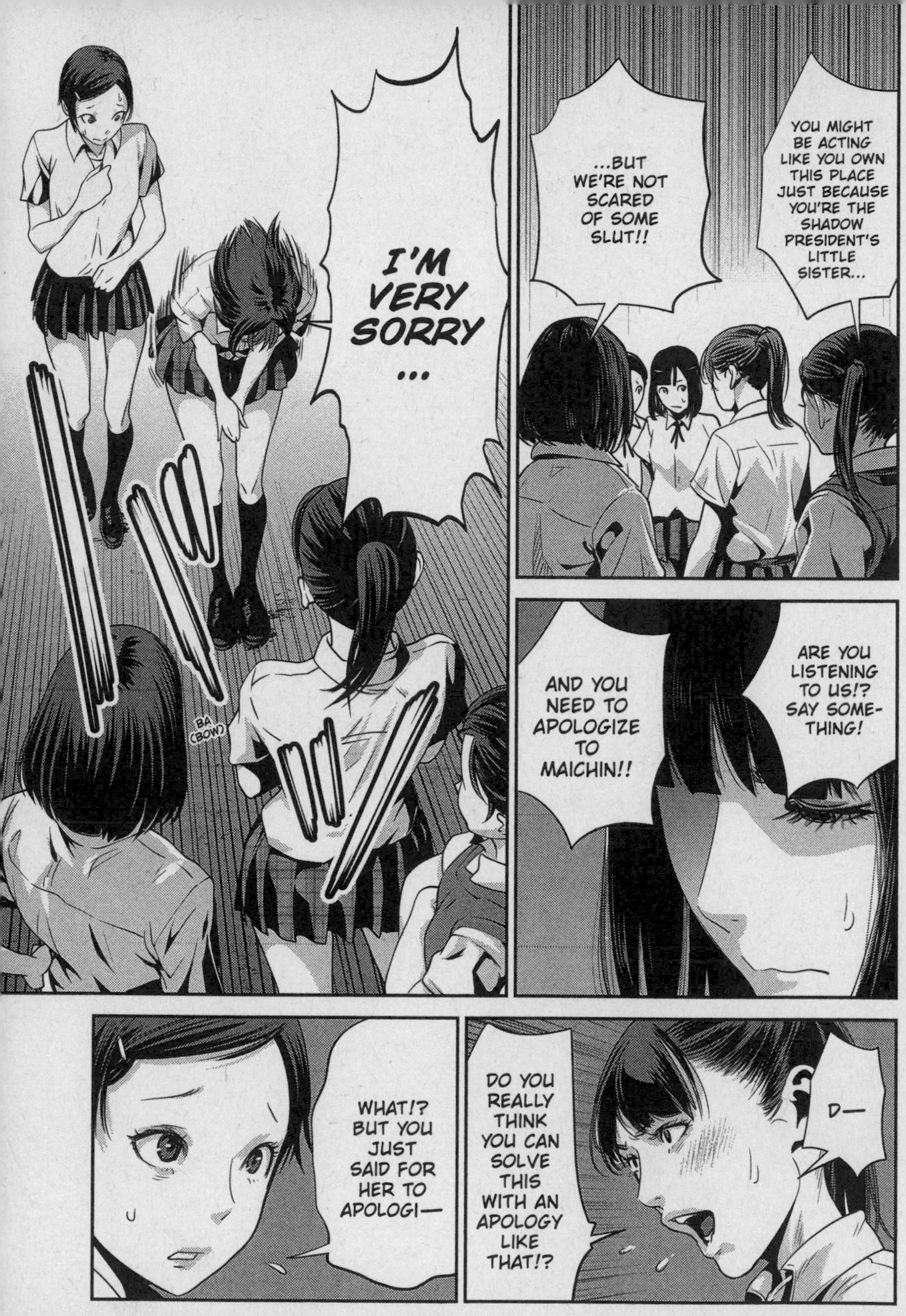
YOU MIGHT BE ACTING LIKE YOU OWN THIS PLACE JUST BECAUSE YOU'RE THE SHADOW PRESIDENT'S LITTLE SISTER...
...BUT WE'RE NOT SCARED OF SOME SLUT!!
I'M VERY SORRY ...
BA (BOW)
ARE YOU LISTENING TO US!? SAY SOME-THING!
AND YOU NEED TO APOLOGIZE TO MAICHIN!!
D—
DO YOU REALLY THINK YOU CAN SOLVE THIS WITH AN APOLOGY LIKE THAT!?
WHAT!? BUT YOU JUST SAID FOR HER TO APOLOGI—

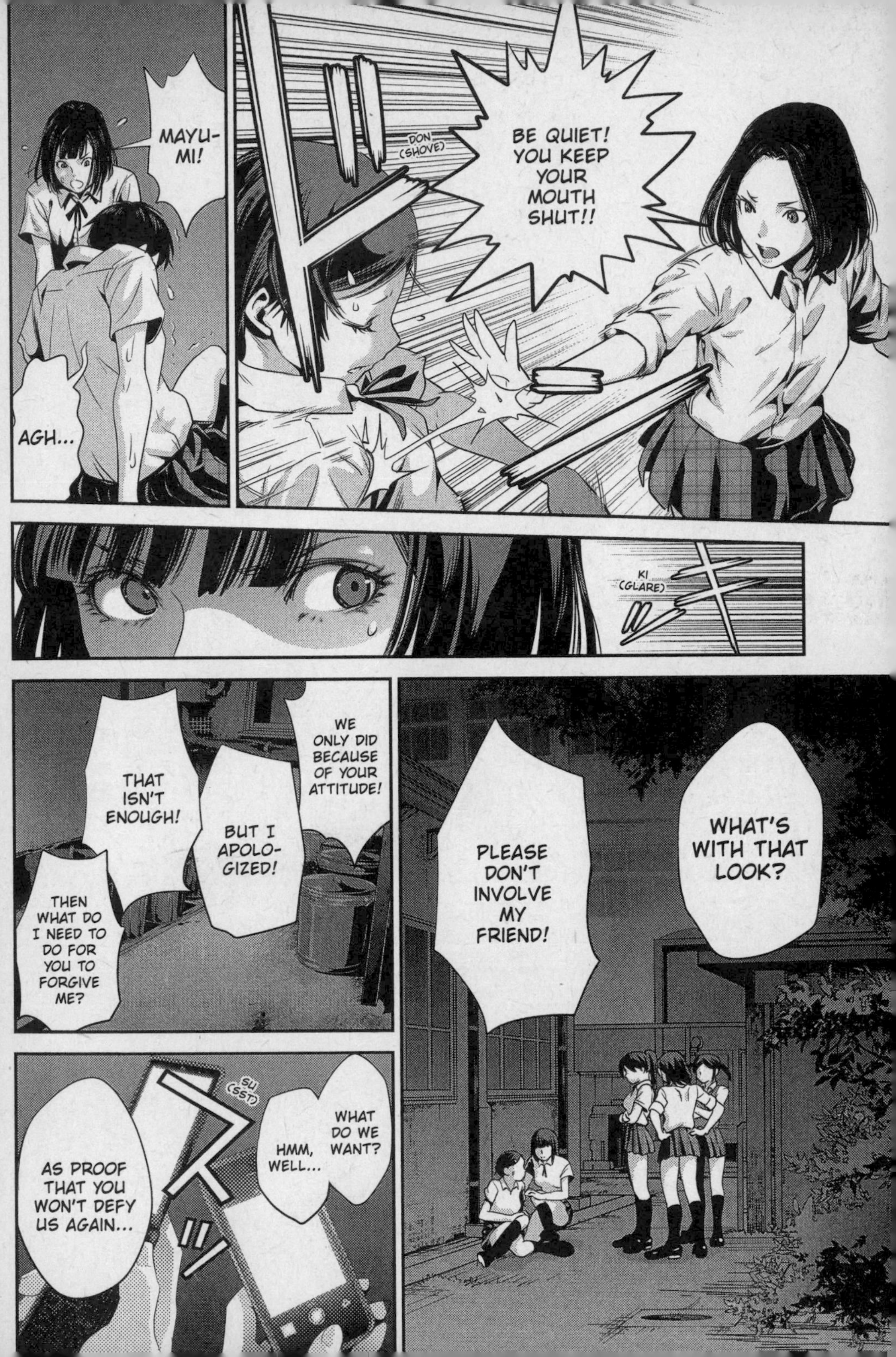

BE QUIET! YOU KEEP YOUR MOUTH SHUT!!
DON (SHOVE)
MAYU-MI!
AGH...
KI (GLARE)
WHAT'S WITH THAT LOOK?
PLEASE DON'T INVOLVE MY FRIEND!
WE ONLY DID BECAUSE OF YOUR ATTITUDE!
BUT I APOLOGIZED!
THAT ISN'T ENOUGH!
THEN WHAT DO I NEED TO DO FOR YOU TO FORGIVE ME?
WHAT DO WE WANT?
HMM, WELL...
SU (SST)
AS PROOF THAT YOU WON'T DEFY US AGAIN...

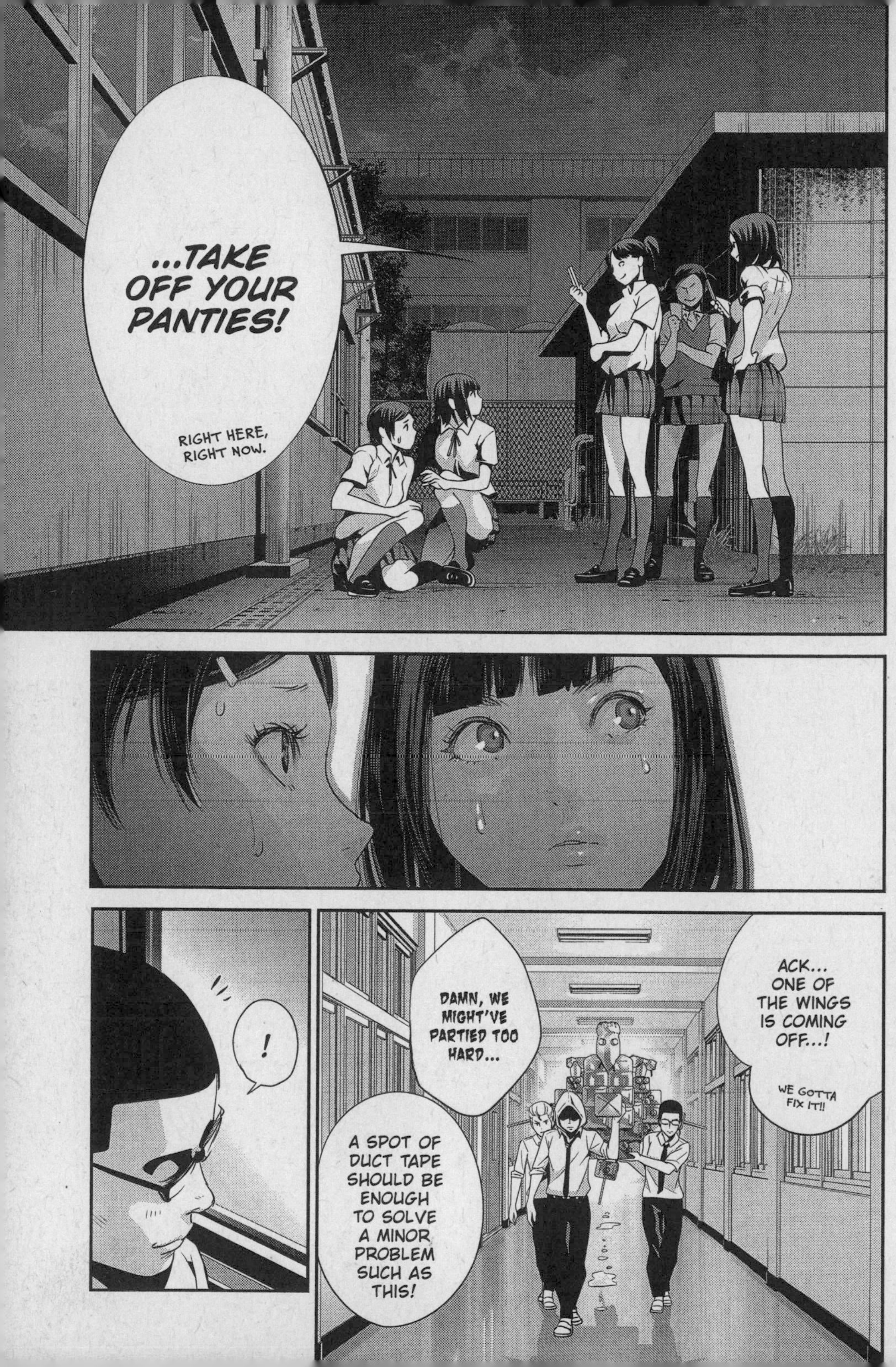
...TAKE OFF YOUR PANTIES!
RIGHT HERE, RIGHT NOW.
ACK... ONE OF THE WINGS IS COMING OFF...!
WE GOTTA FIX IT!!
DAMN, WE MIGHT'VE PARTIED TOO HARD...
A SPOT OF DUCT TAPE SHOULD BE ENOUGH TO SOLVE A MINOR PROBLEM SUCH AS THIS!
!

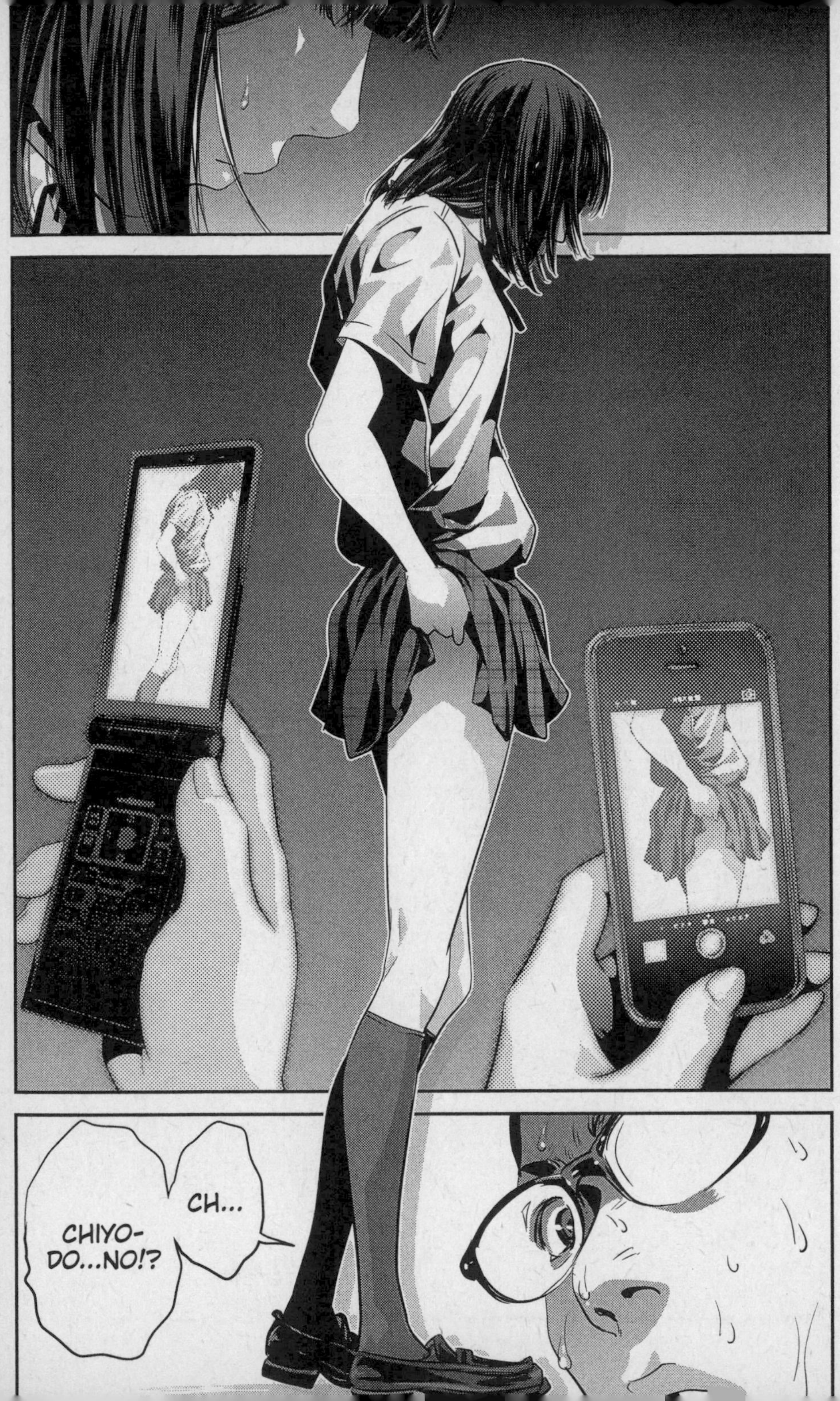
CH...
CHIYO-
DO...NO!?

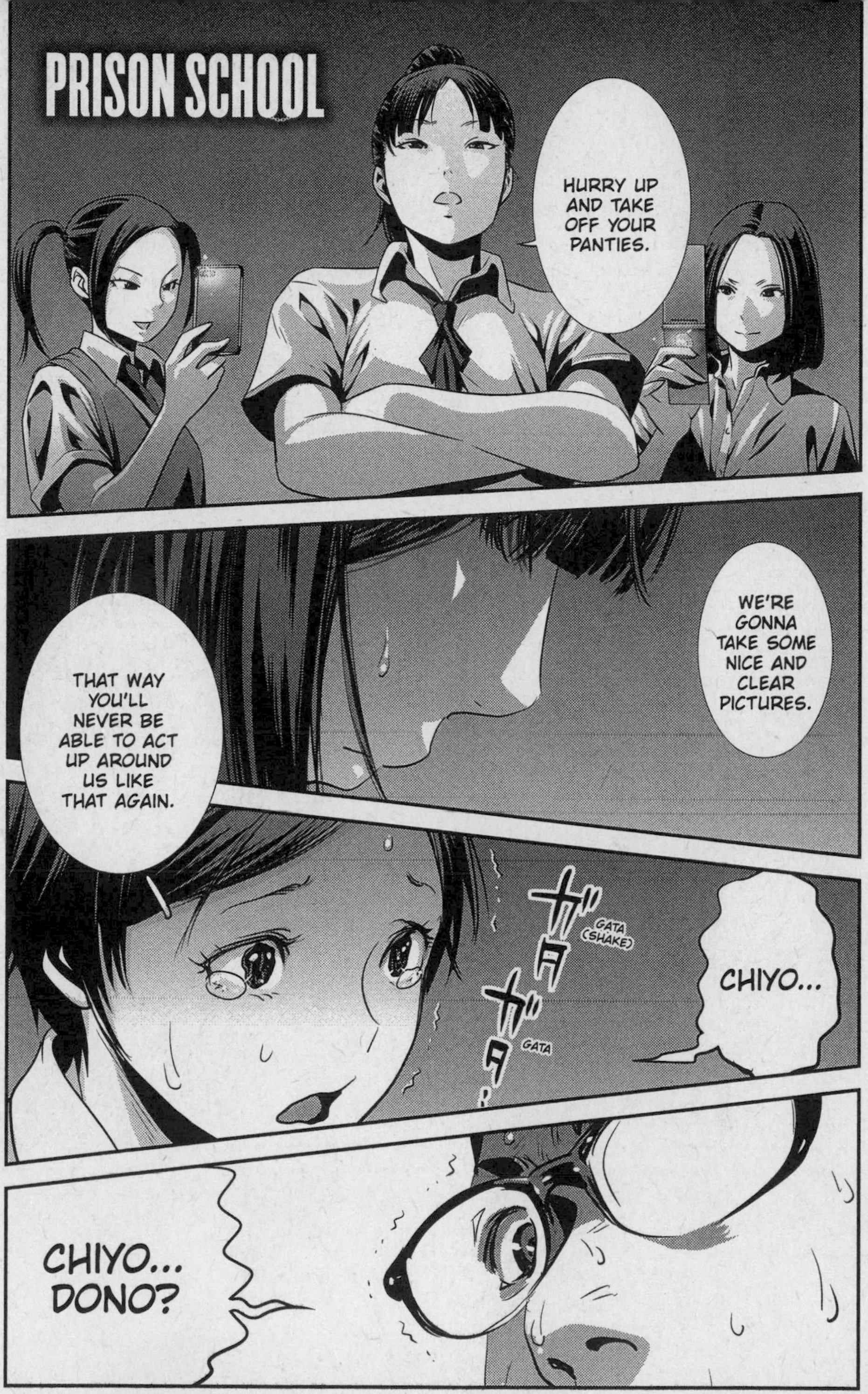
PRISON SCHOOL
HURRY UP AND TAKE OFF YOUR PANTIES.
WE'RE GONNA TAKE SOME NICE AND CLEAR PICTURES.
THAT WAY YOU'LL NEVER BE ABLE TO ACT UP AROUND US LIKE THAT AGAIN.
ガタ
GATA (SHAKE)
ガタ
GATA
CHIYO...
CHIYO... DONO?

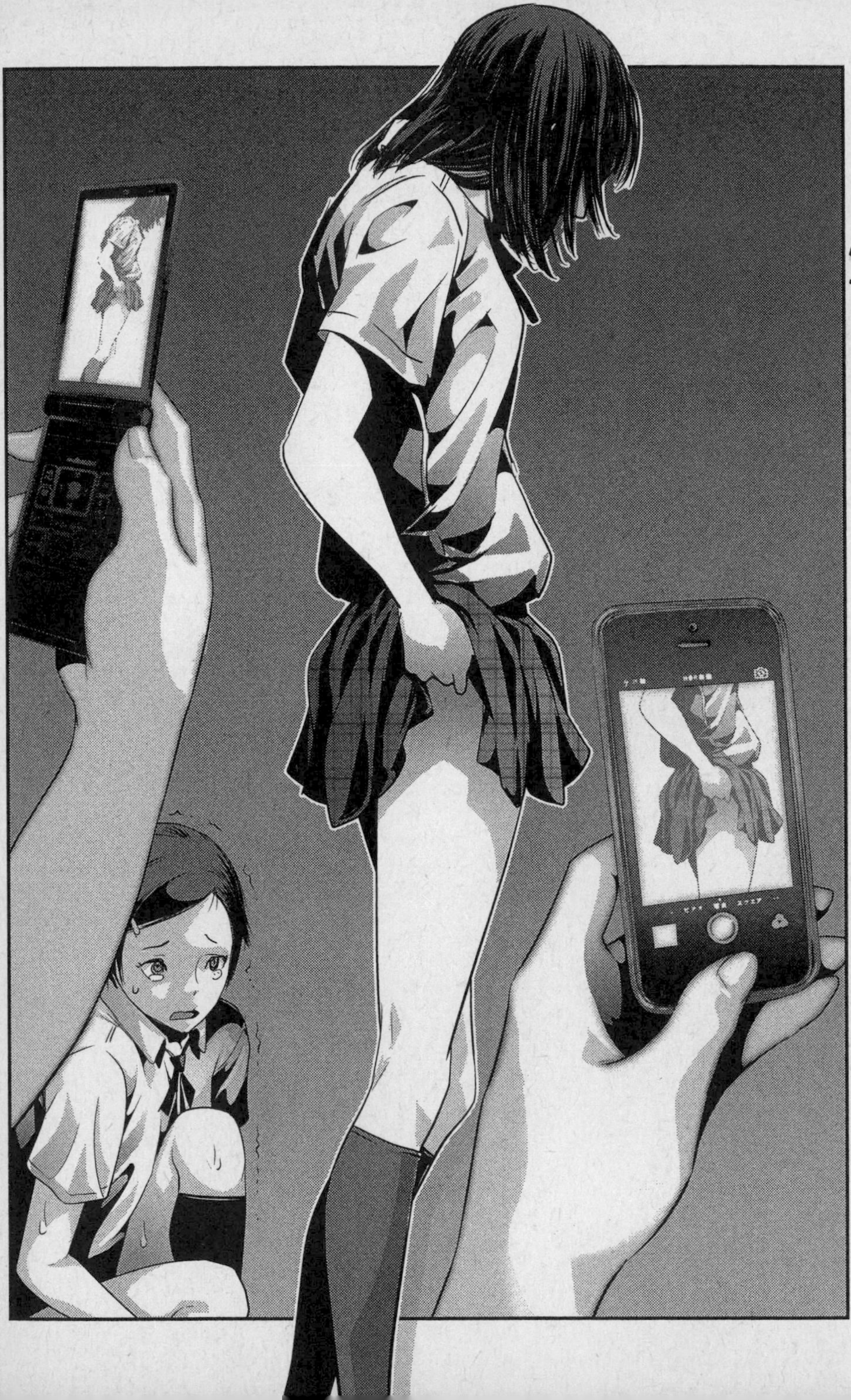

CHAPTER 134: KONSHIN

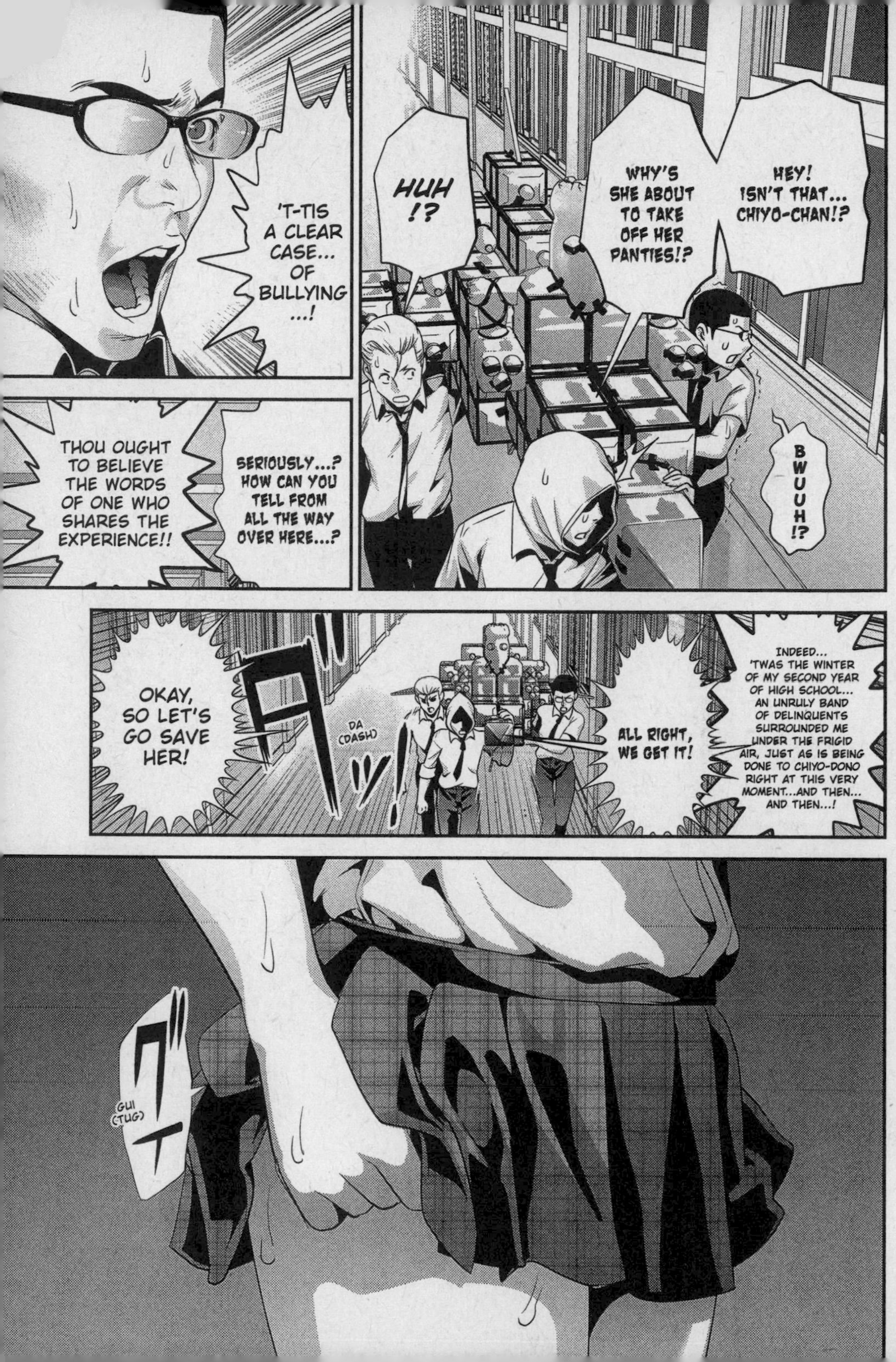
HEY! ISN'T THAT... CHIYO-CHAN!?
WHY'S SHE ABOUT TO TAKE OFF HER PANTIES!?
HUH!?
BWUUH!?
'T-TIS A CLEAR CASE... OF BULLYING ...!
SERIOUSLY...? HOW CAN YOU TELL FROM ALL THE WAY OVER HERE...?
THOU OUGHT TO BELIEVE THE WORDS OF ONE WHO SHARES THE EXPERIENCE!!
INDEED... 'TWAS THE WINTER OF MY SECOND YEAR OF HIGH SCHOOL... AN UNRULY BAND OF DELINQUENTS SURROUNDED ME UNDER THE FRIGID AIR, JUST AS IS BEING DONE TO CHIYO-DONO RIGHT AT THIS VERY MOMENT...AND THEN... AND THEN...!
ALL RIGHT, WE GET IT!
DA (DASH)
OKAY, SO LET'S GO SAVE HER!
GUI (TUG)

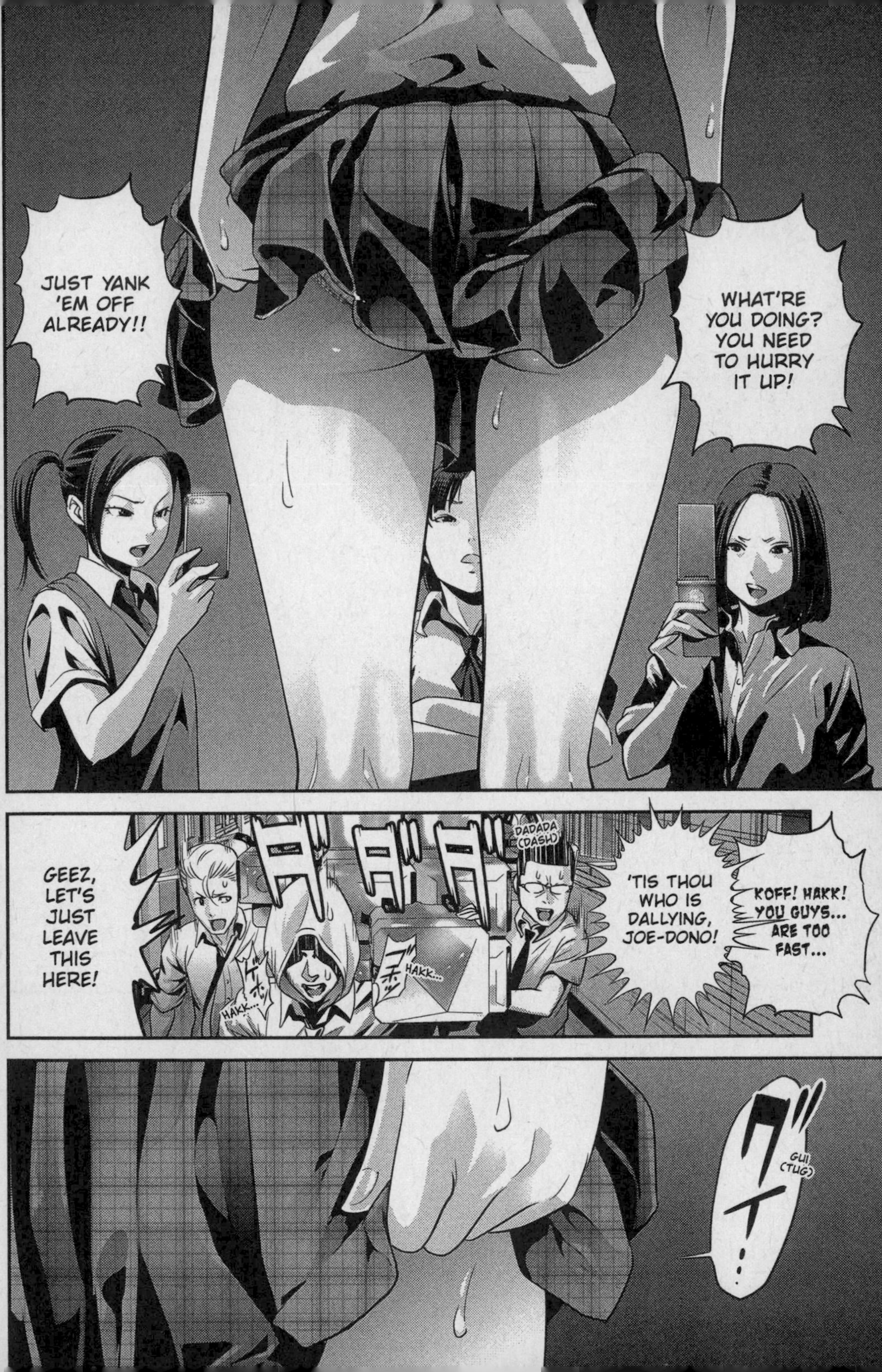
WHAT'RE YOU DOING? YOU NEED TO HURRY IT UP!
JUST YANK 'EM OFF ALREADY!!
KOFF! HAKK! YOU GUYS... ARE TOO FAST...
'TIS THOU WHO IS DALLYING, JOE-DONO!
DADADA (DASH)
HAKK...
HAKK...
GEEZ, LET'S JUST LEAVE THIS HERE!
GUI (TUG)

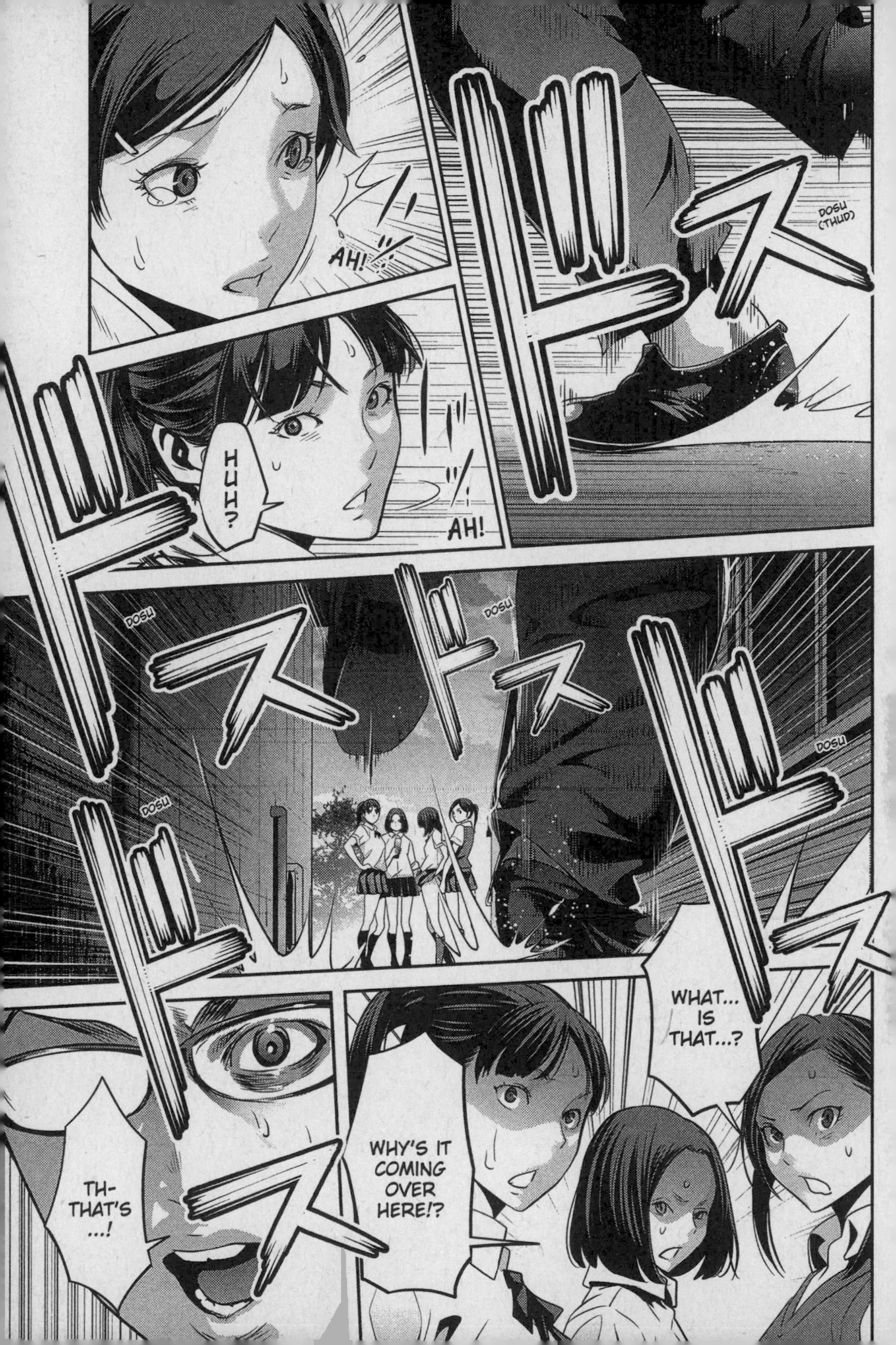
DOSU (THUD)
AH!
AH!
HUH?
DOSU
DOSU
DOSU
DOSU
WHAT... IS THAT...?
WHY'S IT COMING OVER HERE!?
TH-THAT'S ...!

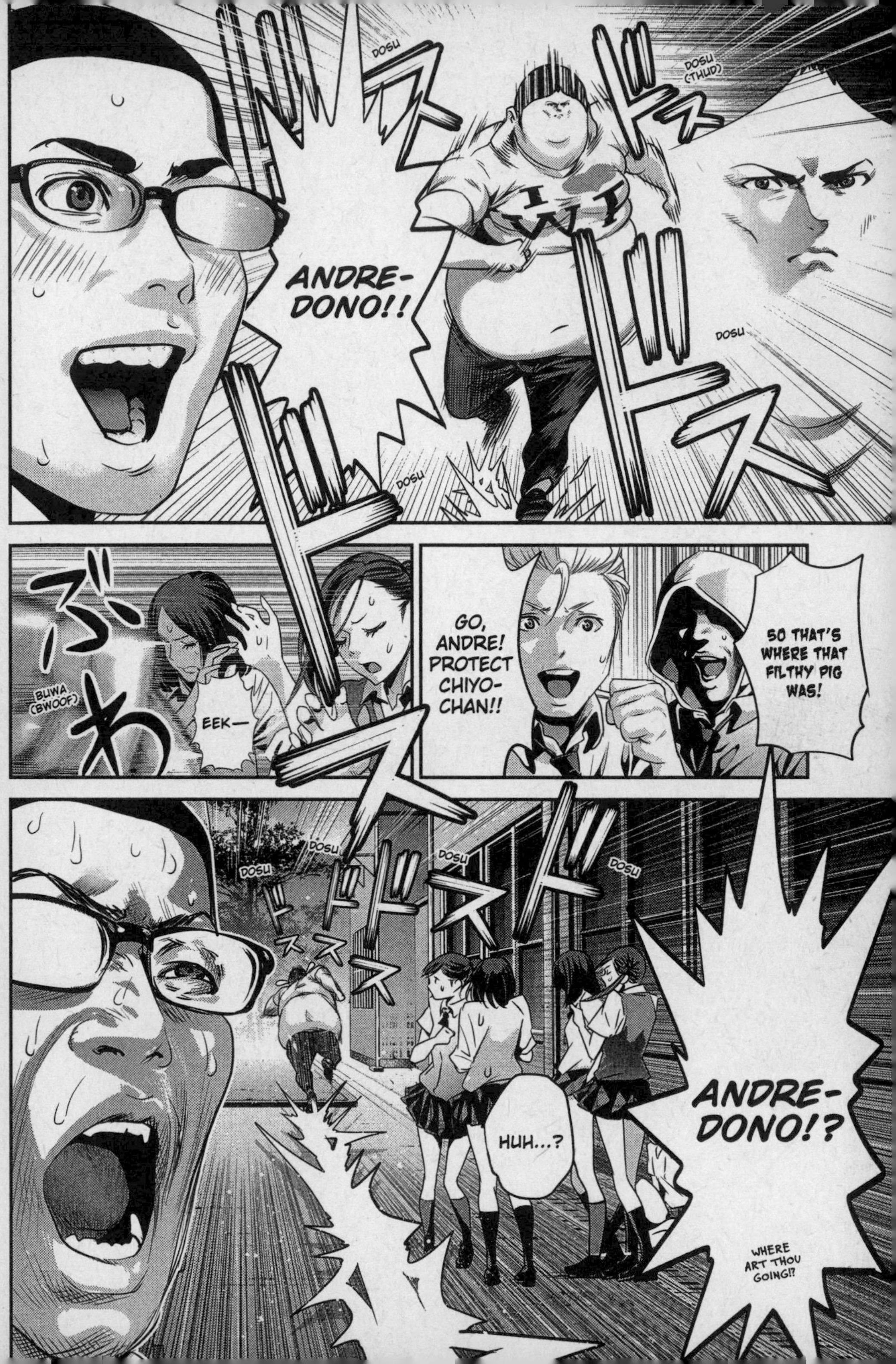
DOSU (THUD)
DOSU
ANDRE-DONO!!
DOSU
DOSU
SO THAT'S WHERE THAT FILTHY PIG WAS!
GO, ANDRE! PROTECT CHIYO-CHAN!!
EEK—
BUWA (BWOOF)
DOSU
DOSU
DOSU
DOSU
ANDRE-DONO!?
WHERE ART THOU GOING!?
HUH...?

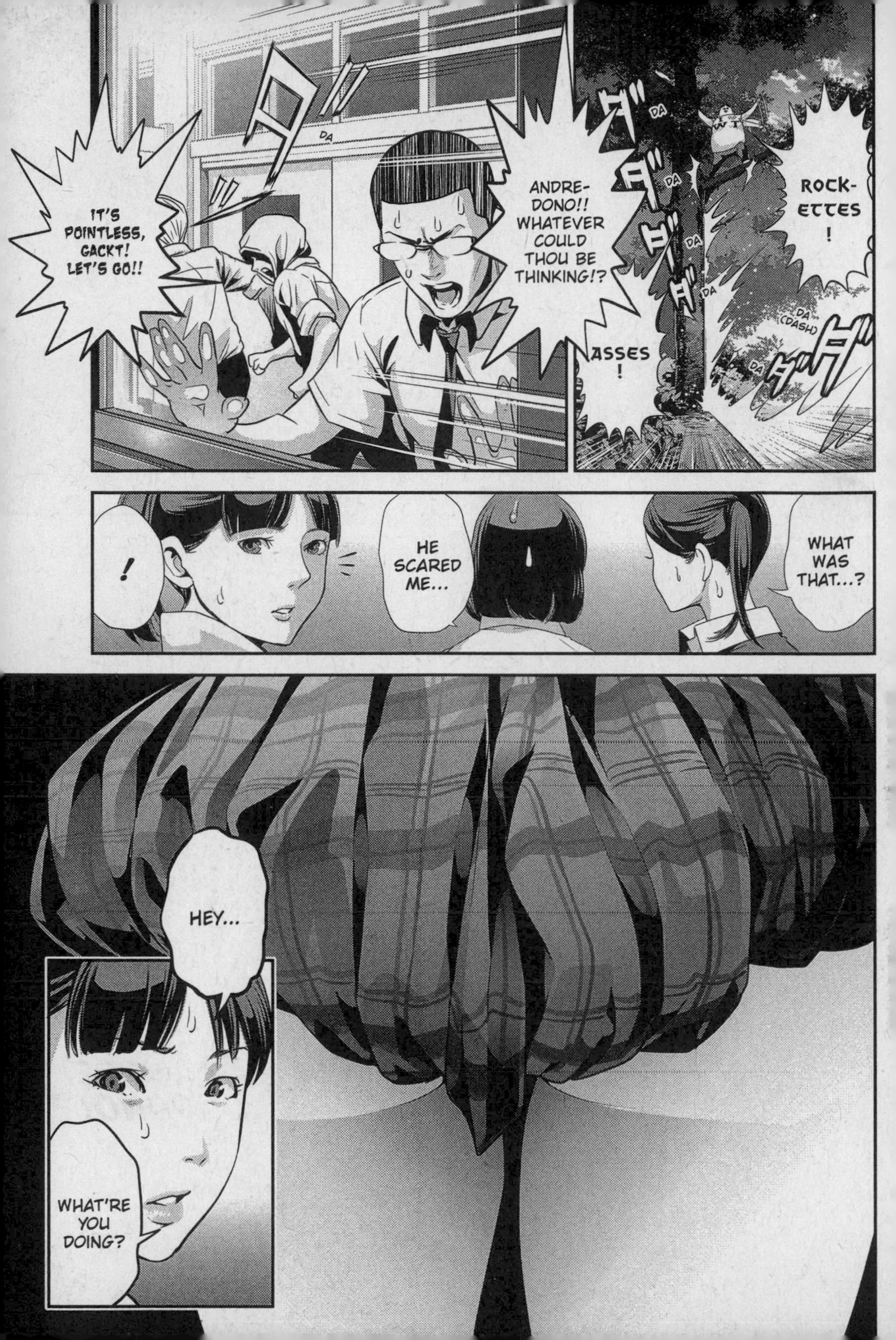
ROCK-ETTES!
ASSES!
DA
DA
DA
DA
DA (DASH)
DA
ANDRE-DONO!! WHATEVER COULD THOU BE THINKING!?
DA
IT'S POINTLESS, GACKT! LET'S GO!!
WHAT WAS THAT...?
HE SCARED ME...
!
HEY...
WHAT'RE YOU DOING?

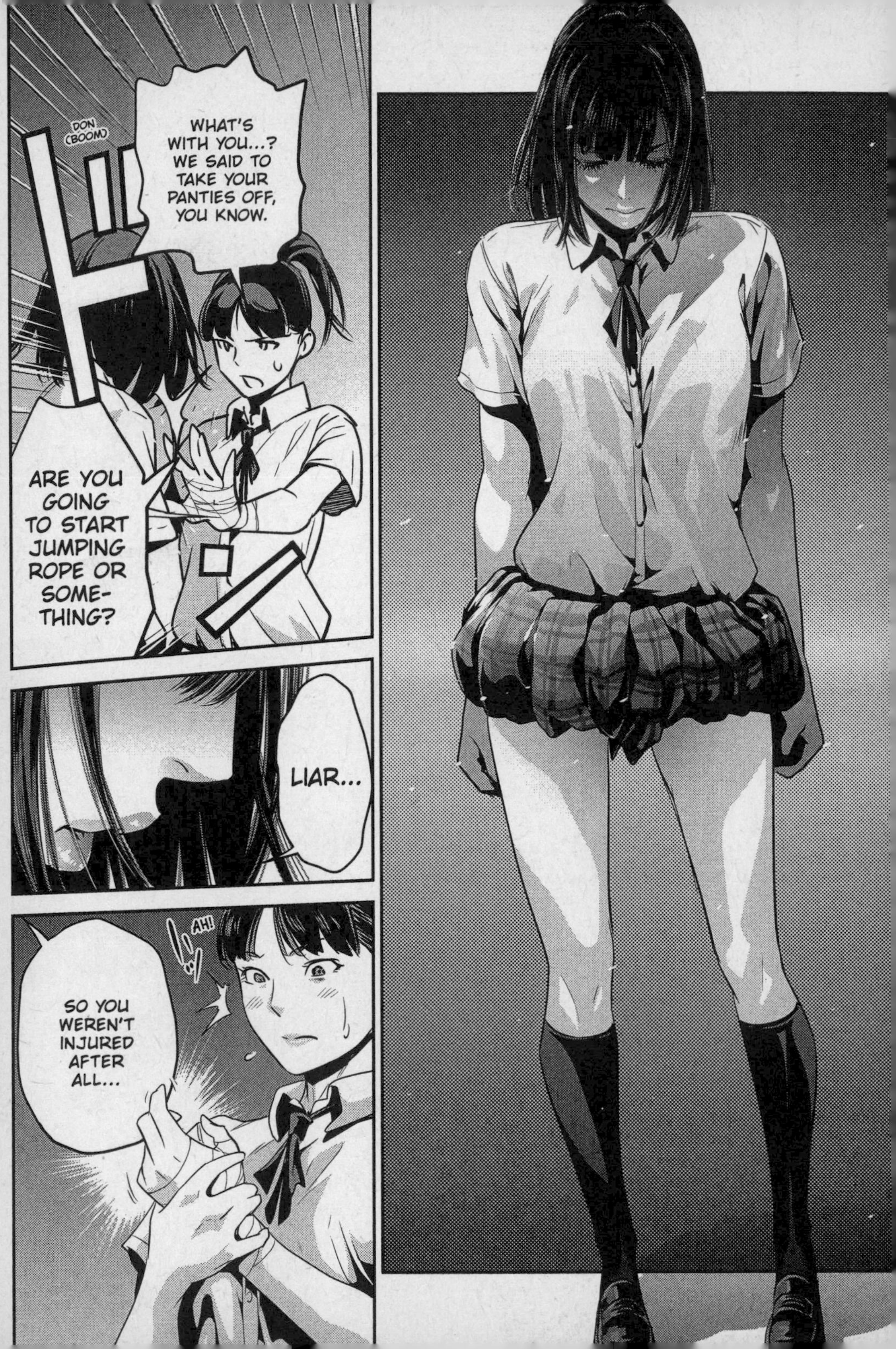
DON (BOOM)
WHAT'S WITH YOU...? WE SAID TO TAKE YOUR PANTIES OFF, YOU KNOW.
ARE YOU GOING TO START JUMPING ROPE OR SOME-THING?
LIAR...
AH!
SO YOU WEREN'T INJURED AFTER ALL...

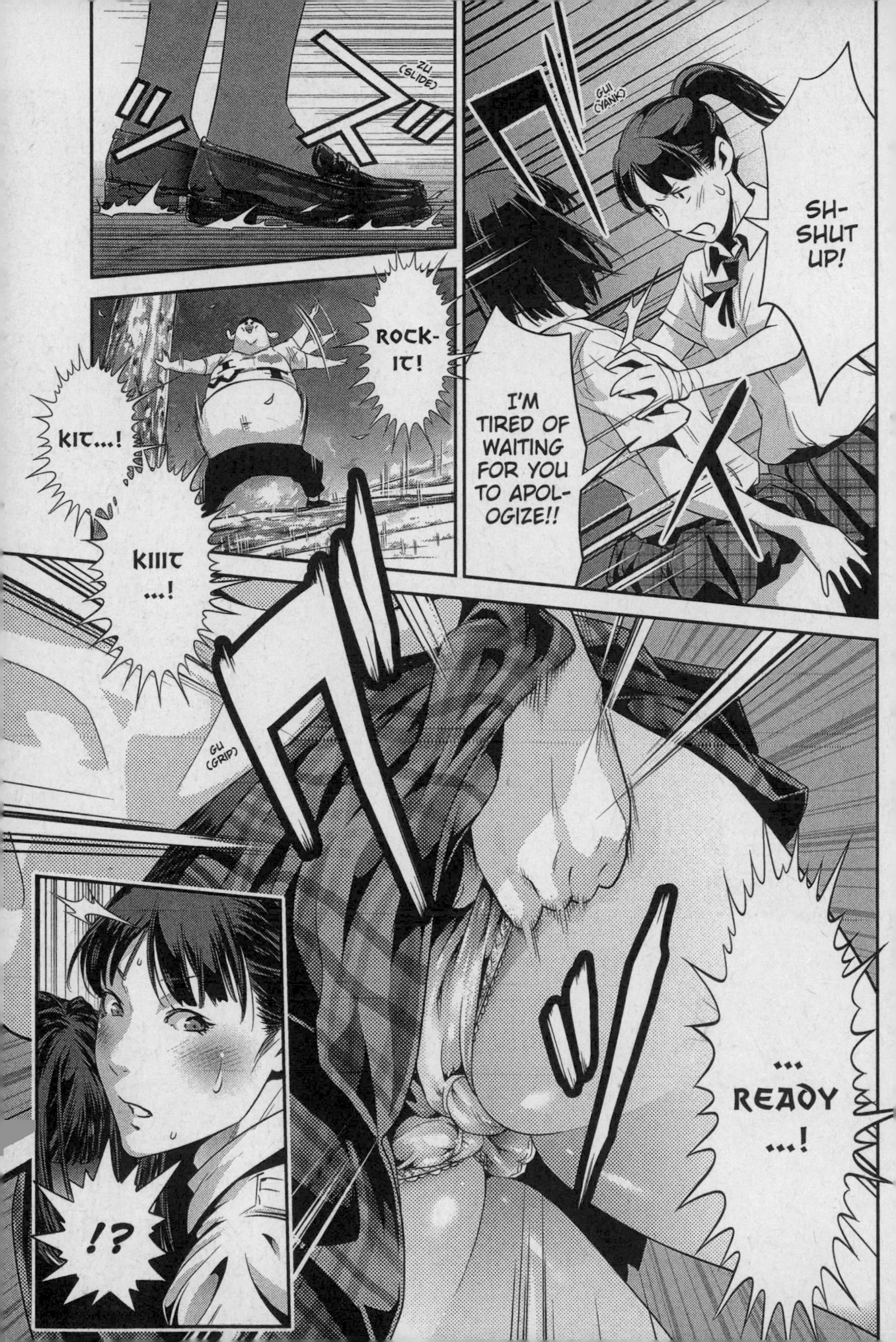
GUI (YANK)
SH-SHUT UP!
I'M TIRED OF WAITING FOR YOU TO APOLOGIZE!!
ZU (SLIDE)
ROCK-IT!
KIT...!
KIIIT ...!
GU (GRIP)
...READY ...!
!?

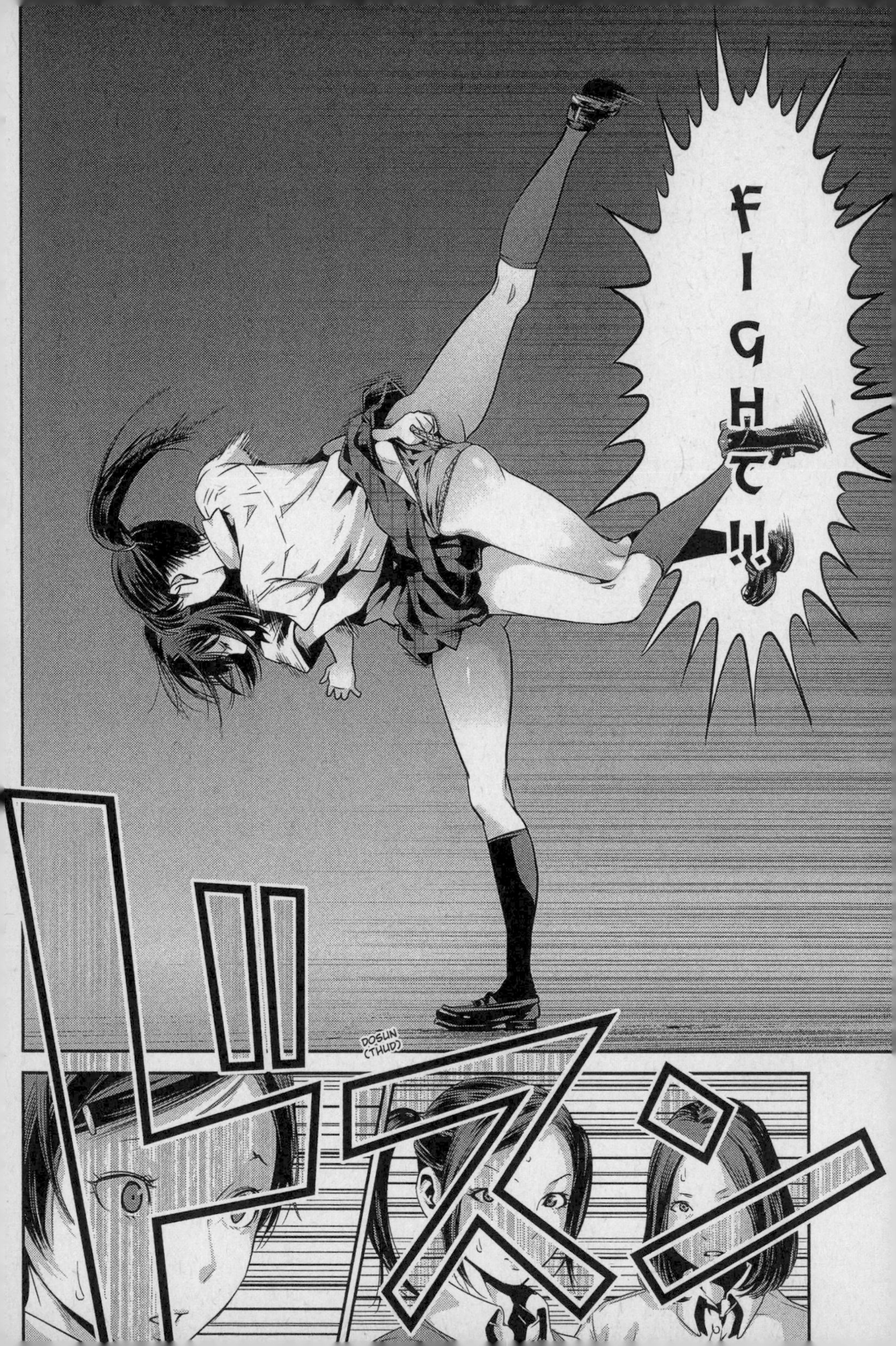
FIGHT!!
DOSUN (THUD)

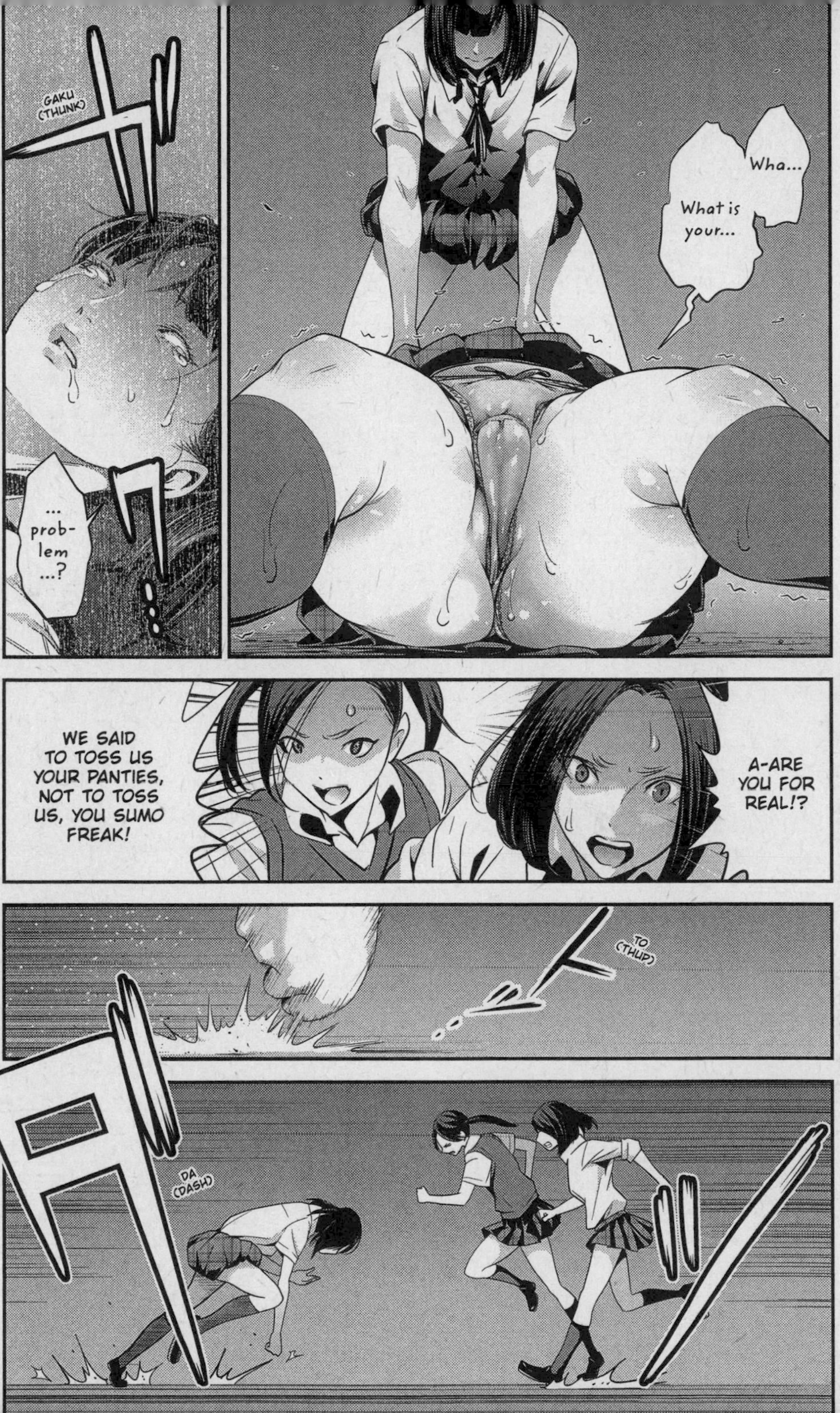
Wha...
What is your...
GAKU (THUNK)
...problem...?
A-ARE YOU FOR REAL!?
WE SAID TO TOSS US YOUR PANTIES, NOT TO TOSS US, YOU SUMO FREAK!
TO (THUP)
DA (DASH)

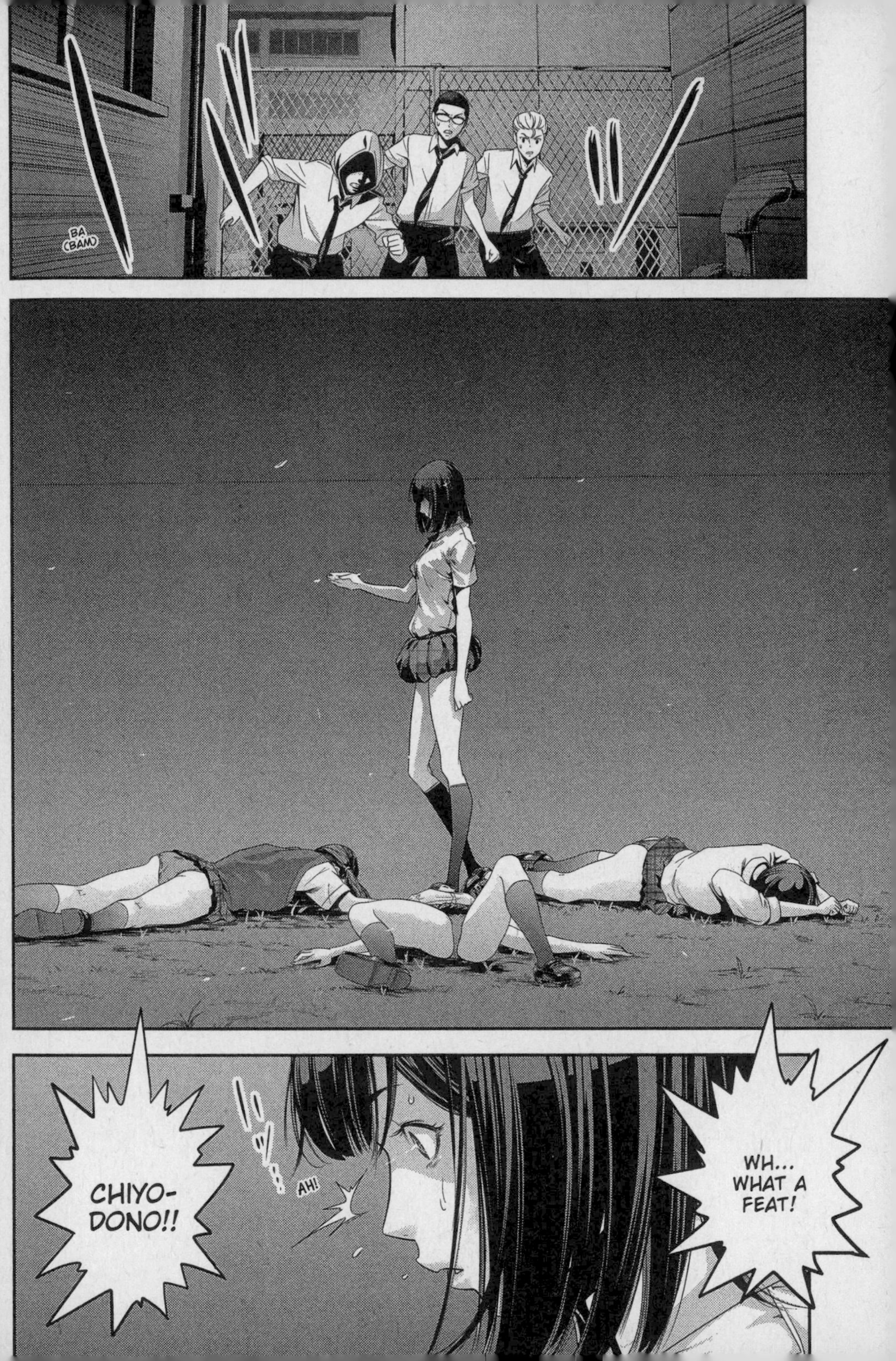
BA (BAM)
WH... WHAT A FEAT!
AH!
CHIYO-DONO!!

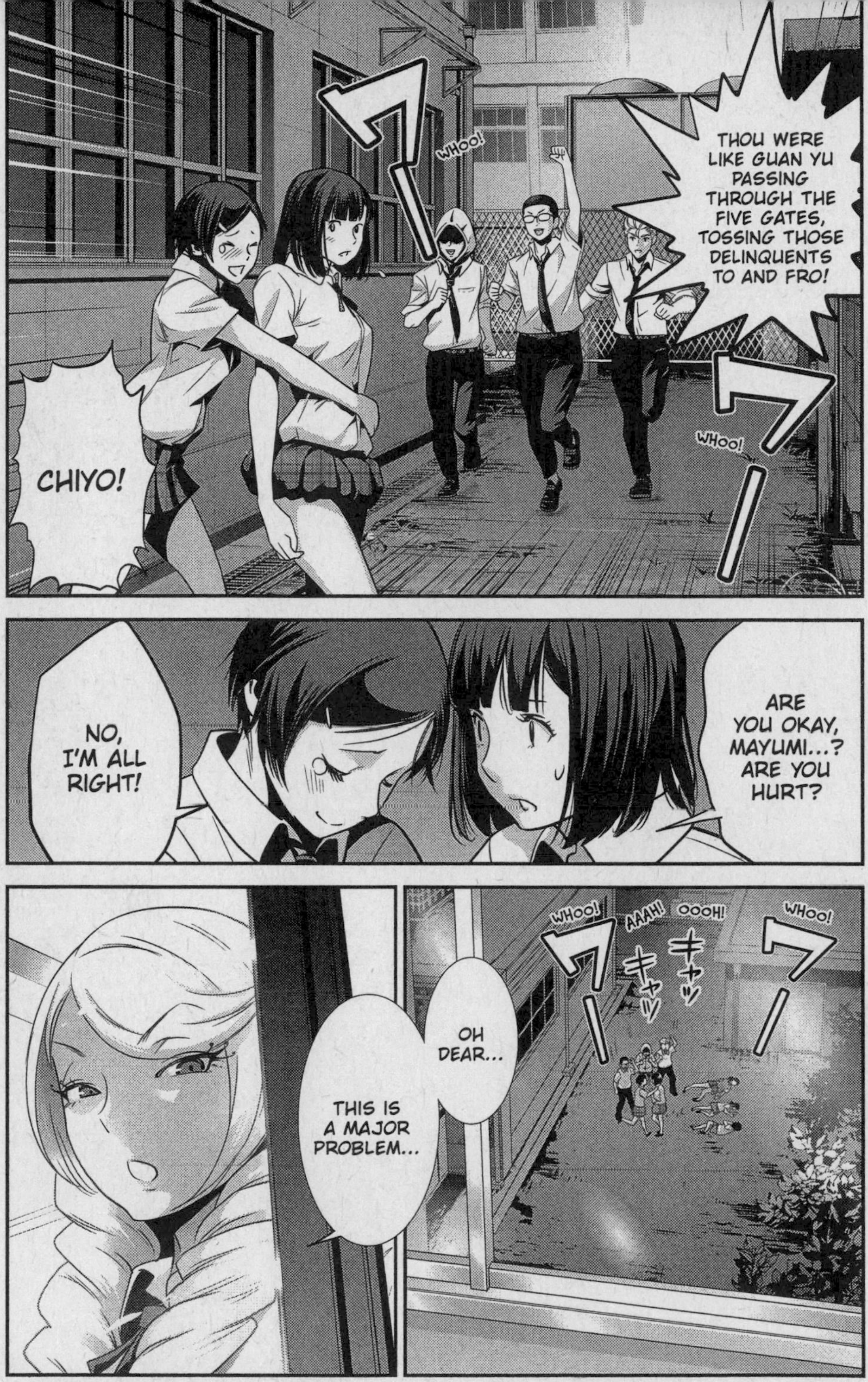
THOU WERE LIKE GUAN YU PASSING THROUGH THE FIVE GATES, TOSSING THOSE DELINQUENTS TO AND FRO!
WHOO!
WHOO!
CHIYO!
ARE YOU OKAY, MAYUMI...? ARE YOU HURT?
NO, I'M ALL RIGHT!
WHOO!
OOOH!
AAAH!
WHOO!
OH DEAR...
THIS IS A MAJOR PROBLEM...

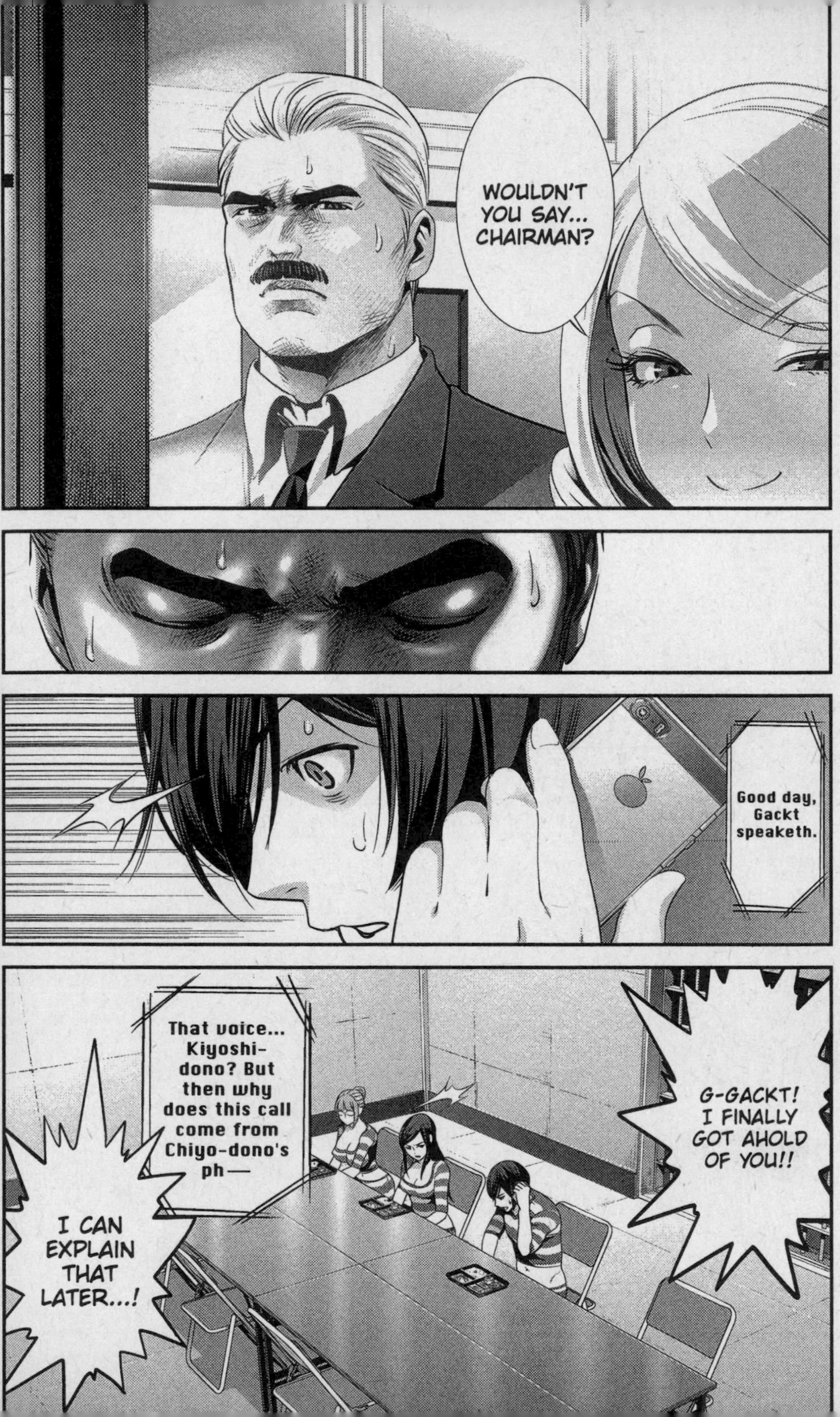
WOULDN'T YOU SAY... CHAIRMAN?
Good day, Gackt speaketh.
G-GACKT! I FINALLY GOT AHOLD OF YOU!!
That voice... Kiyoshi-dono? But then why does this call come from Chiyo-dono's ph—
I CAN EXPLAIN THAT LATER...!

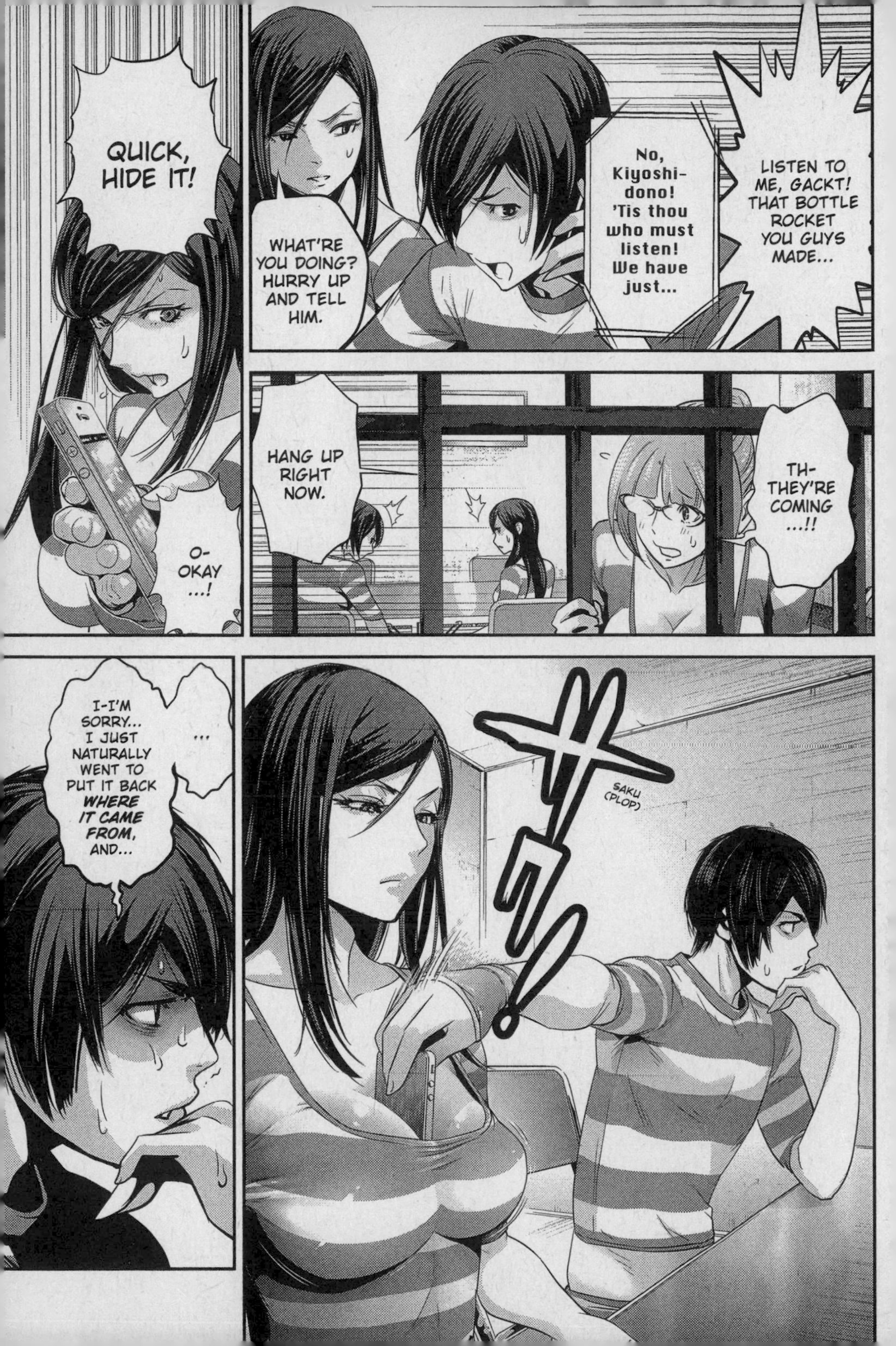
LISTEN TO ME, GACKT! THAT BOTTLE ROCKET YOU GUYS MADE...
No, Kiyoshi-dono! 'Tis thou who must listen! We have just...
WHAT'RE YOU DOING? HURRY UP AND TELL HIM.
QUICK, HIDE IT!
TH-THEY'RE COMING...!!
HANG UP RIGHT NOW.
O-OKAY...!
SAKU (PLOP)
...
I-I'M SORRY... I JUST NATURALLY WENT TO PUT IT BACK *WHERE IT CAME FROM*, AND...

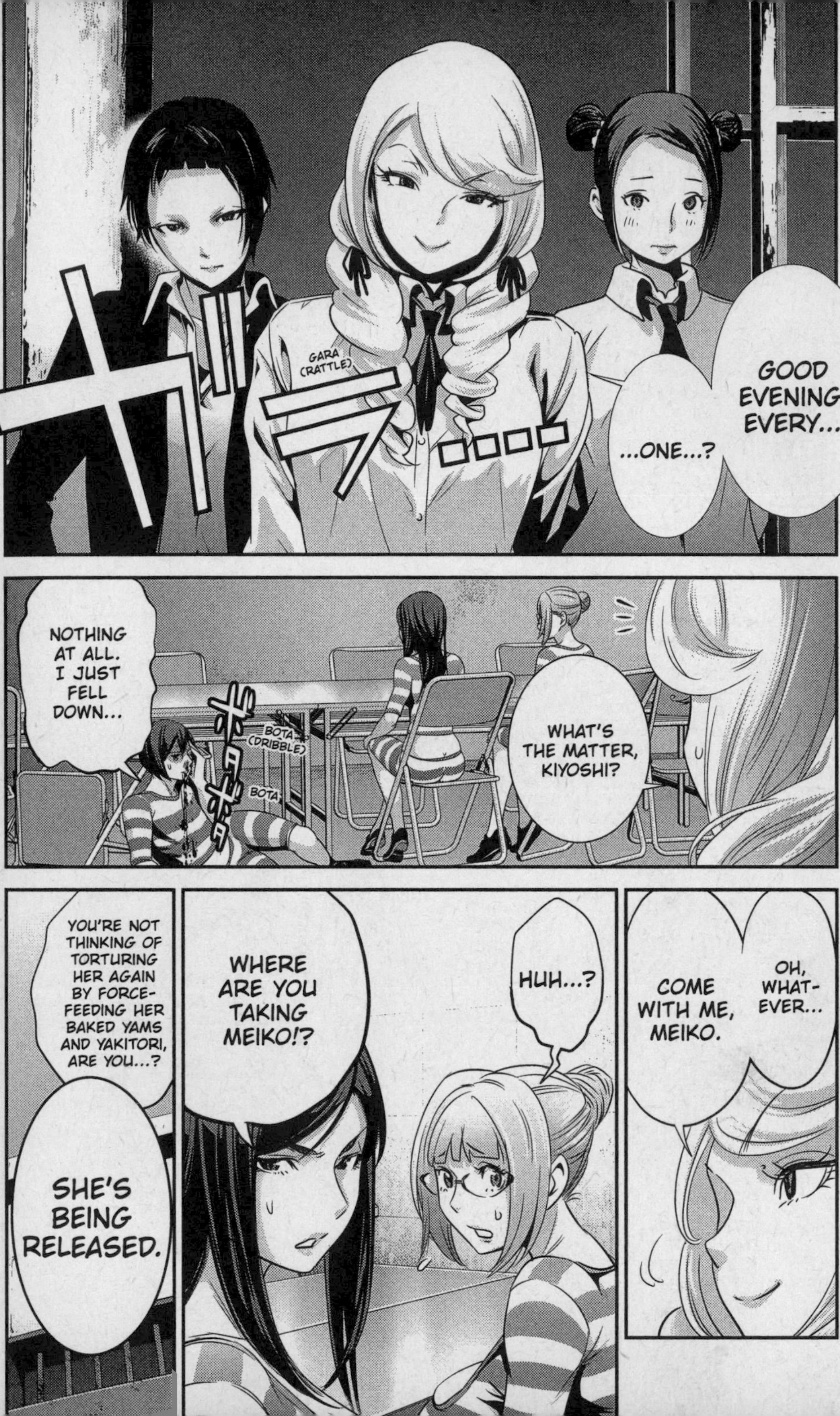
GARA (RATTLE)
GOOD EVENING, EVERY...
...ONE...?
WHAT'S THE MATTER, KIYOSHI?
BOTA (DRIBBLE)
BOTA
NOTHING AT ALL. I JUST FELL DOWN...
OH, WHAT-EVER...
COME WITH ME, MEIKO.
HUH...?
WHERE ARE YOU TAKING MEIKO!?
YOU'RE NOT THINKING OF TORTURING HER AGAIN BY FORCE-FEEDING HER BAKED YAMS AND YAKITORI, ARE YOU...?
SHE'S BEING RELEASED.

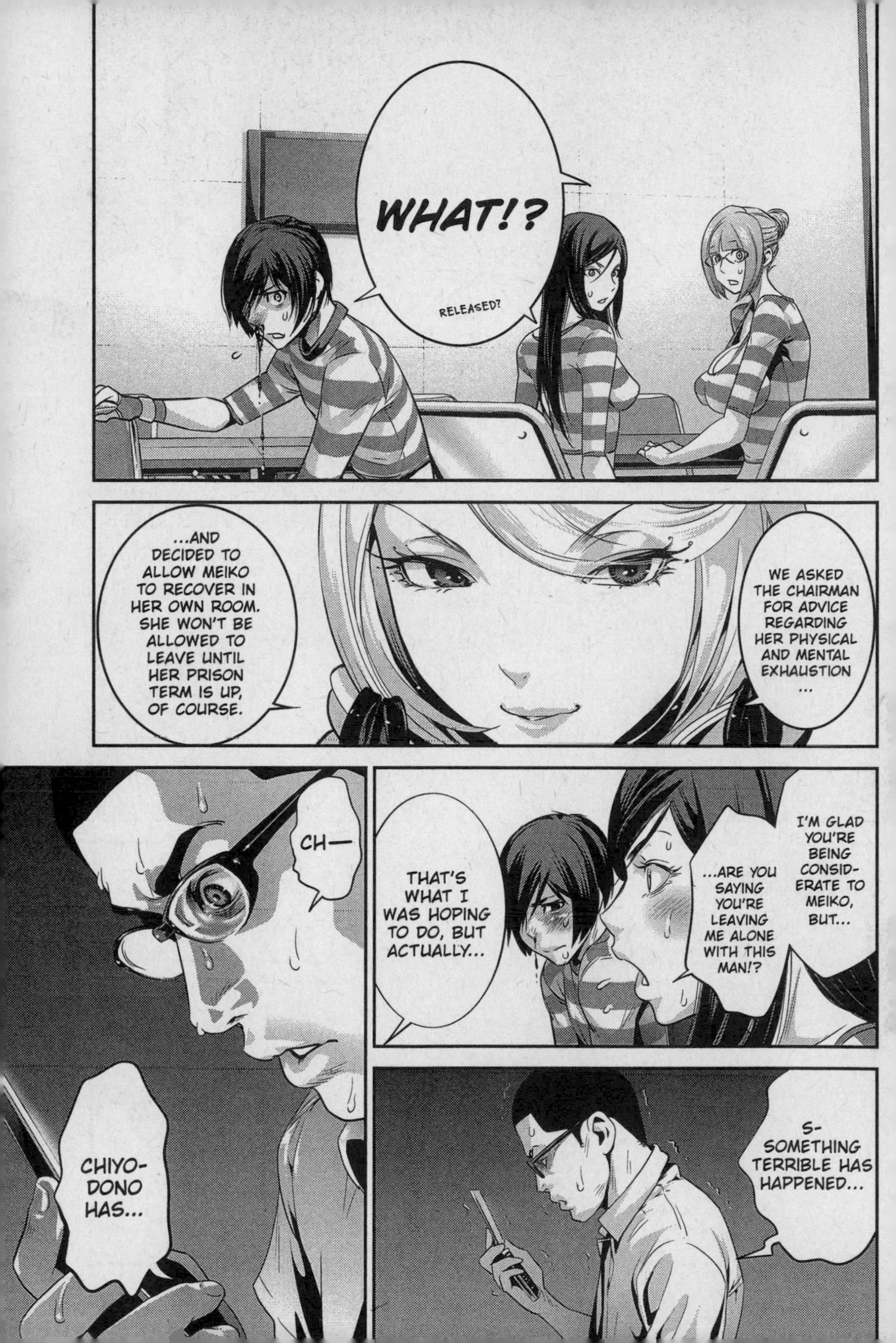
WHAT!?
RELEASED?
WE ASKED THE CHAIRMAN FOR ADVICE REGARDING HER PHYSICAL AND MENTAL EXHAUSTION ...
...AND DECIDED TO ALLOW MEIKO TO RECOVER IN HER OWN ROOM. SHE WON'T BE ALLOWED TO LEAVE UNTIL HER PRISON TERM IS UP, OF COURSE.
I'M GLAD YOU'RE BEING CONSID-ERATE TO MEIKO, BUT...
...ARE YOU SAYING YOU'RE LEAVING ME ALONE WITH THIS MAN!?
THAT'S WHAT I WAS HOPING TO DO, BUT ACTUALLY...
CH—
S-SOMETHING TERRIBLE HAS HAPPENED...
CHIYO-DONO HAS...

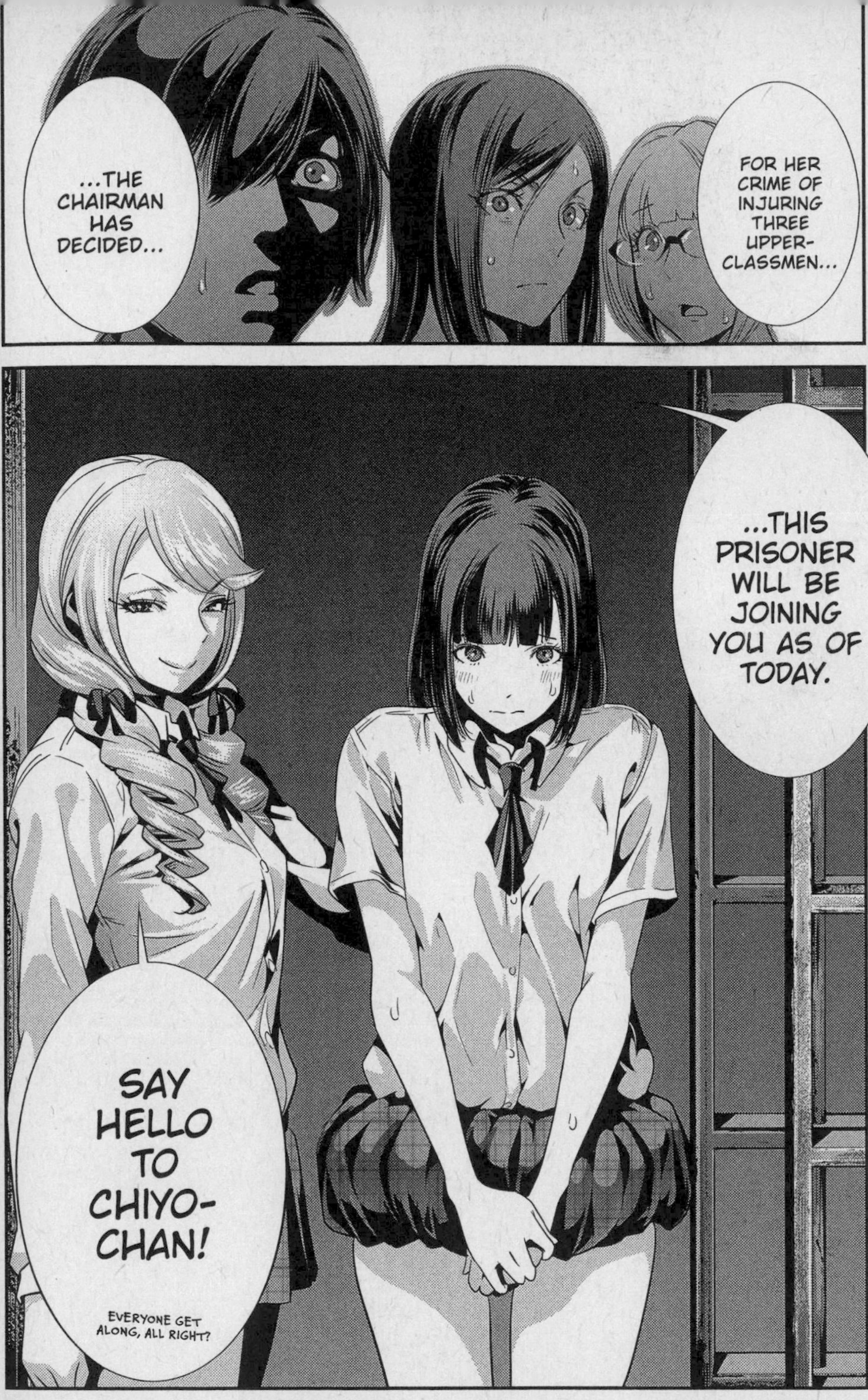
FOR HER CRIME OF INJURING THREE UPPER-CLASSMEN...
...THE CHAIRMAN HAS DECIDED...
...THIS PRISONER WILL BE JOINING YOU AS OF TODAY.
SAY HELLO TO CHIYO-CHAN!
EVERYONE GET ALONG, ALL RIGHT?

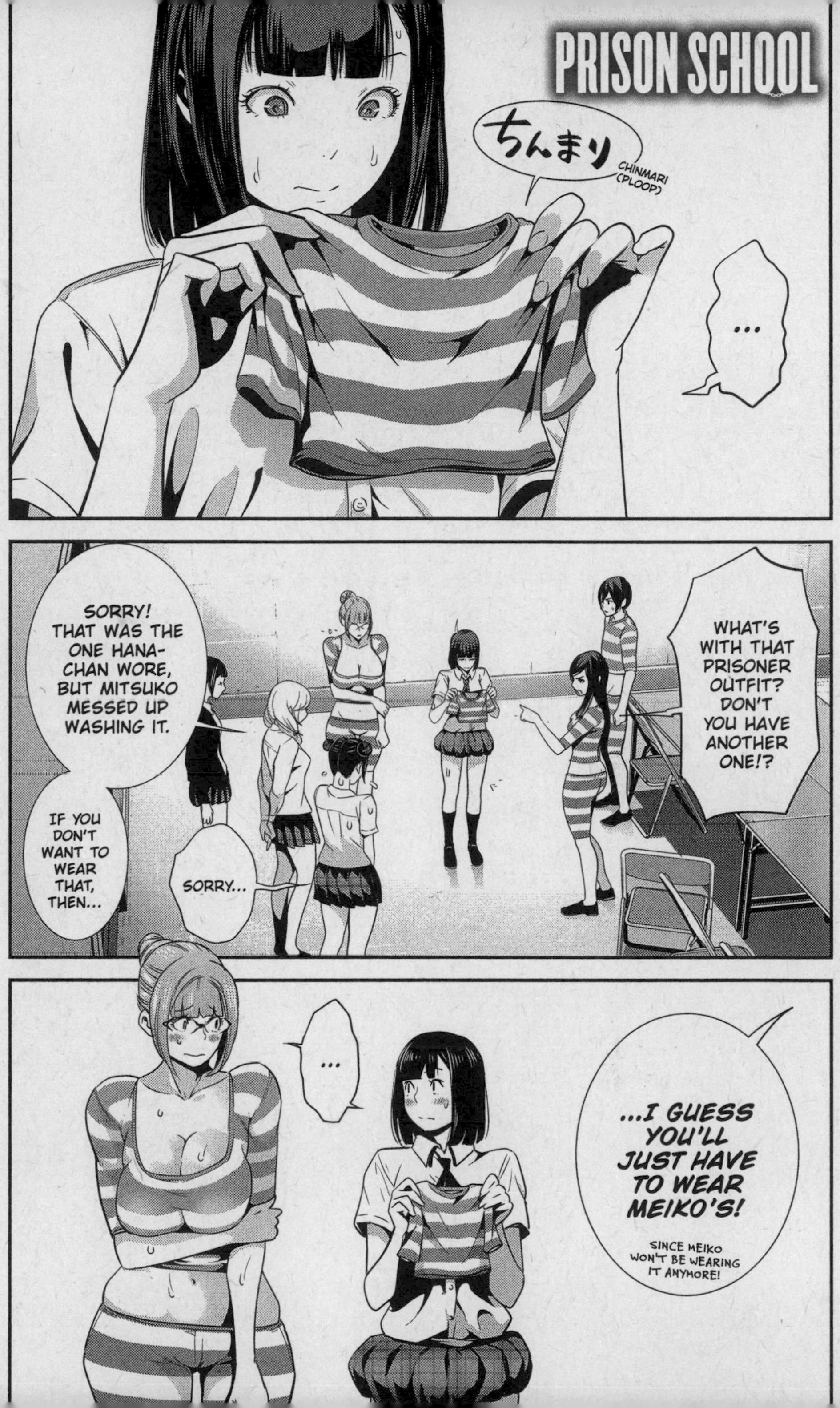
PRISON SCHOOL
...
ちんまり
CHINMARI (PLOOP)
WHAT'S WITH THAT PRISONER OUTFIT? DON'T YOU HAVE ANOTHER ONE!?
SORRY...
SORRY! THAT WAS THE ONE HANA-CHAN WORE, BUT MITSUKO MESSED UP WASHING IT.
IF YOU DON'T WANT TO WEAR THAT, THEN...
...I GUESS YOU'LL JUST HAVE TO WEAR MEIKO'S!
SINCE MEIKO WON'T BE WEARING IT ANYMORE!
...

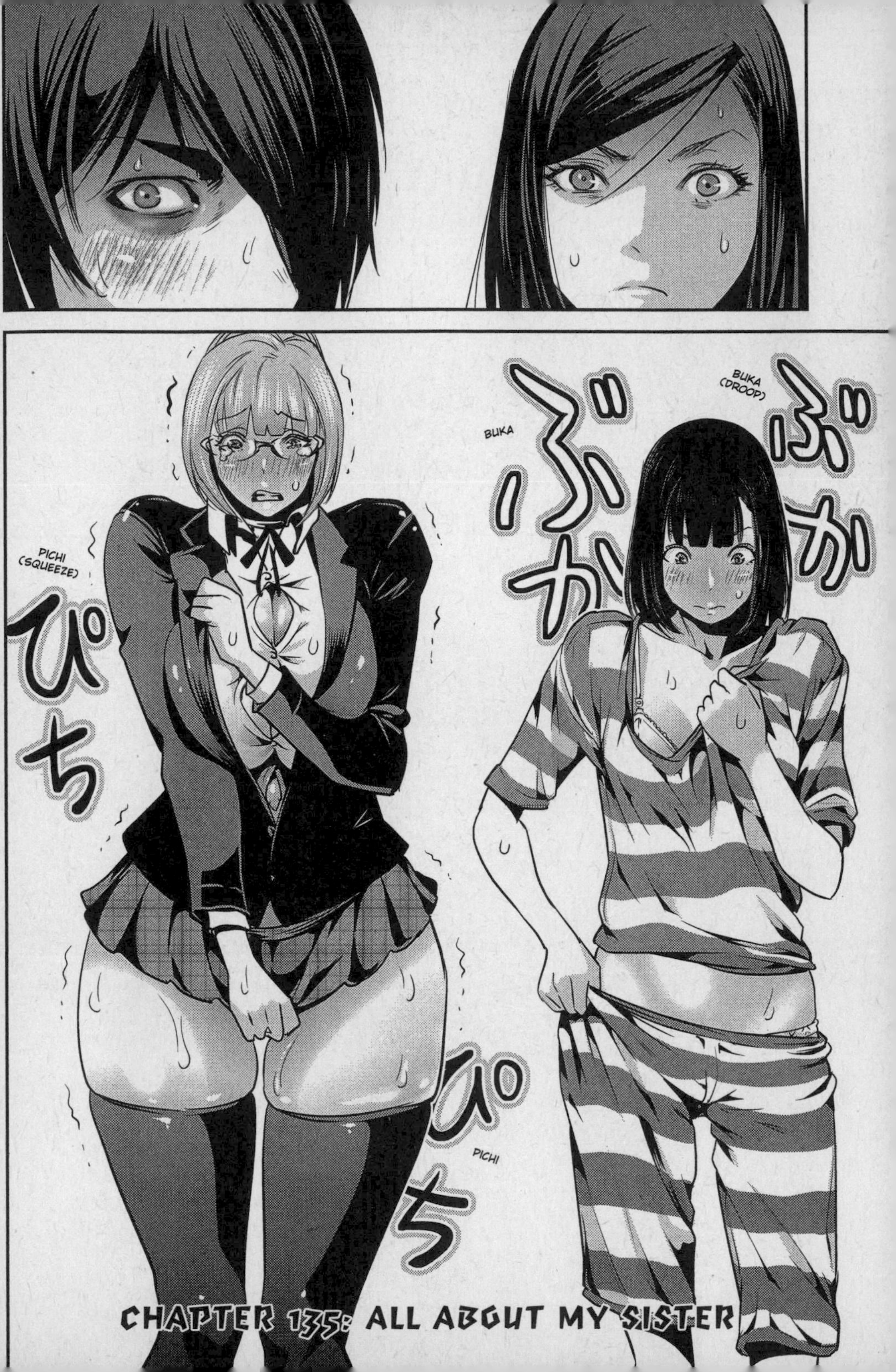
ぶか
BUKA (DROOP)
ぶか
BUKA
ぴち
PICHI (SQUEEZE)
ぴち
PICHI

CHAPTER 135: ALL ABOUT MY SISTER

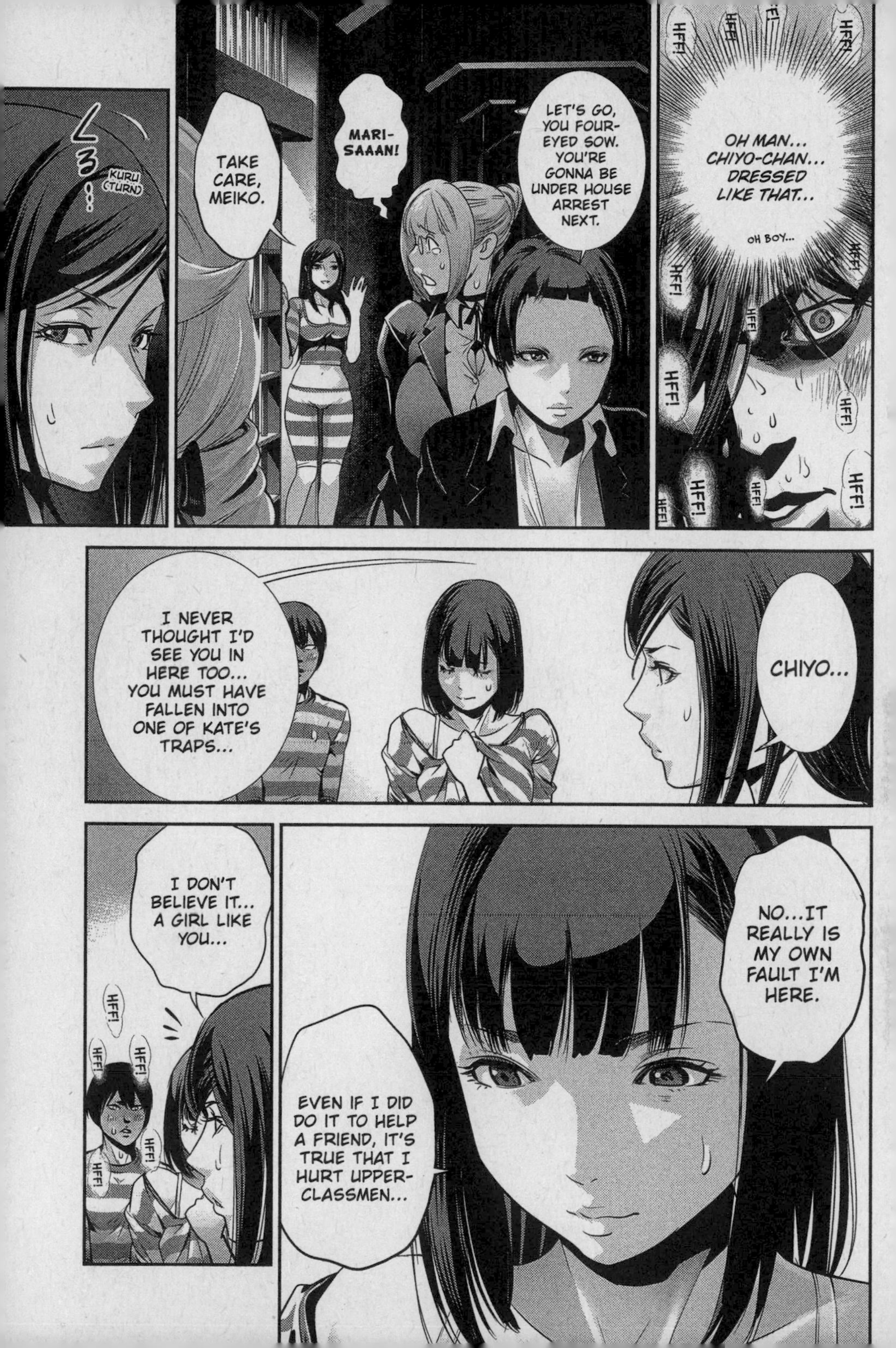
HFF!
HFF!
HFF!
OH MAN... CHIYO-CHAN... DRESSED LIKE THAT...
OH BOY...
HFF!
HFF!
HFF!
HFF!
HFF!
HFF!
HFF!
HFF!
LET'S GO, YOU FOUR-EYED SOW. YOU'RE GONNA BE UNDER HOUSE ARREST NEXT.
MARI-SAAAN!
TAKE CARE, MEIKO.
くる!! KURU (TURN)
CHIYO...
I NEVER THOUGHT I'D SEE YOU IN HERE TOO... YOU MUST HAVE FALLEN INTO ONE OF KATE'S TRAPS...
NO...IT REALLY IS MY OWN FAULT I'M HERE.
EVEN IF I DID DO IT TO HELP A FRIEND, IT'S TRUE THAT I HURT UPPER-CLASSMEN...
I DON'T BELIEVE IT... A GIRL LIKE YOU...
HFF!
HFF!
HFF!
HFF!
HFF!

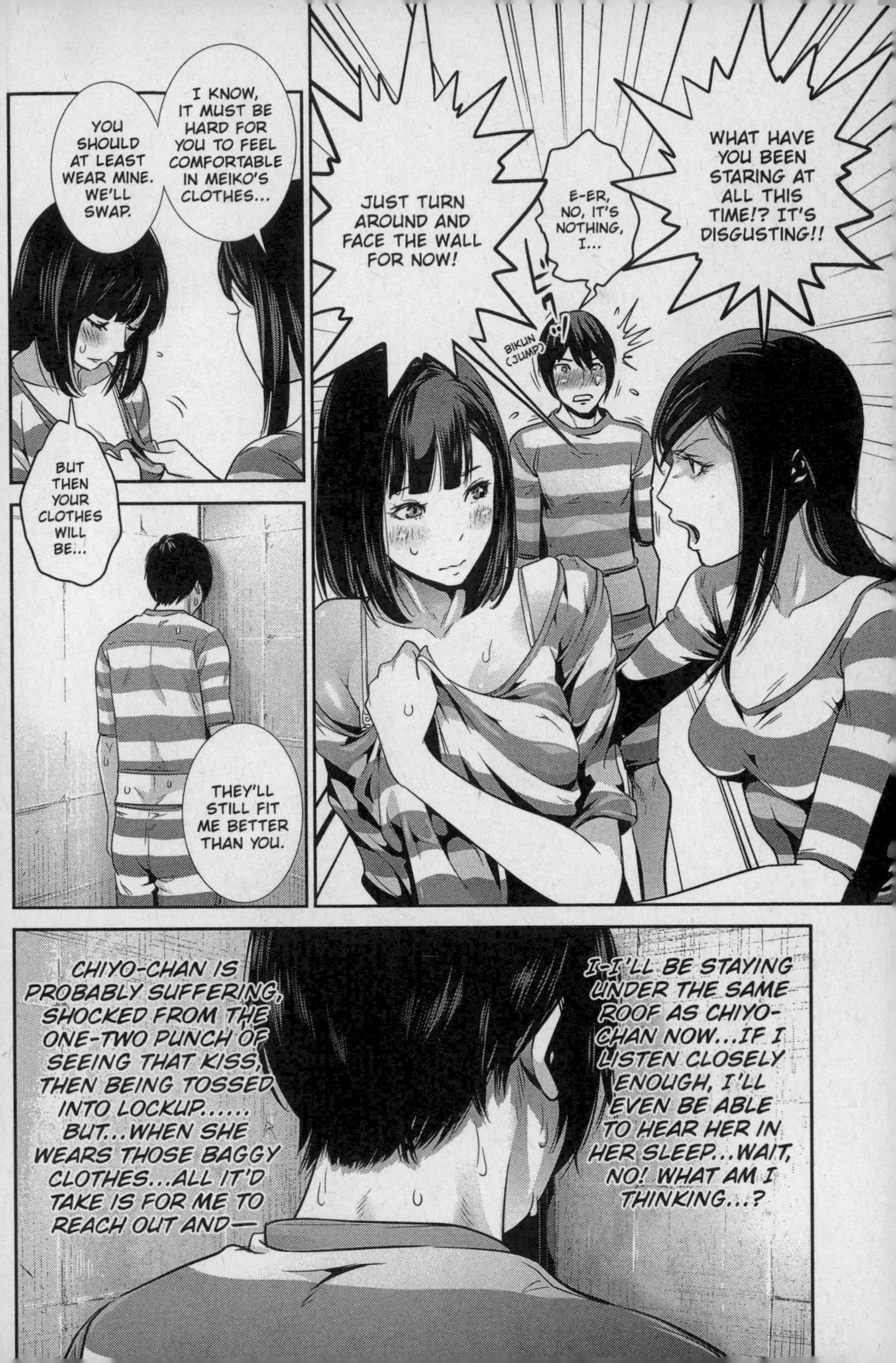
WHAT HAVE YOU BEEN STARING AT ALL THIS TIME!? IT'S DISGUSTING!!
E-ER, NO, IT'S NOTHING, I...
BIKUN (JUMP)
JUST TURN AROUND AND FACE THE WALL FOR NOW!
I KNOW, IT MUST BE HARD FOR YOU TO FEEL COMFORTABLE IN MEIKO'S CLOTHES...
YOU SHOULD AT LEAST WEAR MINE. WE'LL SWAP.
BUT THEN YOUR CLOTHES WILL BE...
THEY'LL STILL FIT ME BETTER THAN YOU.
I-I'LL BE STAYING UNDER THE SAME ROOF AS CHIYO-CHAN NOW...IF I LISTEN CLOSELY ENOUGH, I'LL EVEN BE ABLE TO HEAR HER IN HER SLEEP...WAIT, NO! WHAT AM I THINKING...?
CHIYO-CHAN IS PROBABLY SUFFERING, SHOCKED FROM THE ONE-TWO PUNCH OF SEEING THAT KISS, THEN BEING TOSSED INTO LOCKUP...... BUT...WHEN SHE WEARS THOSE BAGGY CLOTHES...ALL IT'D TAKE IS FOR ME TO REACH OUT AND—

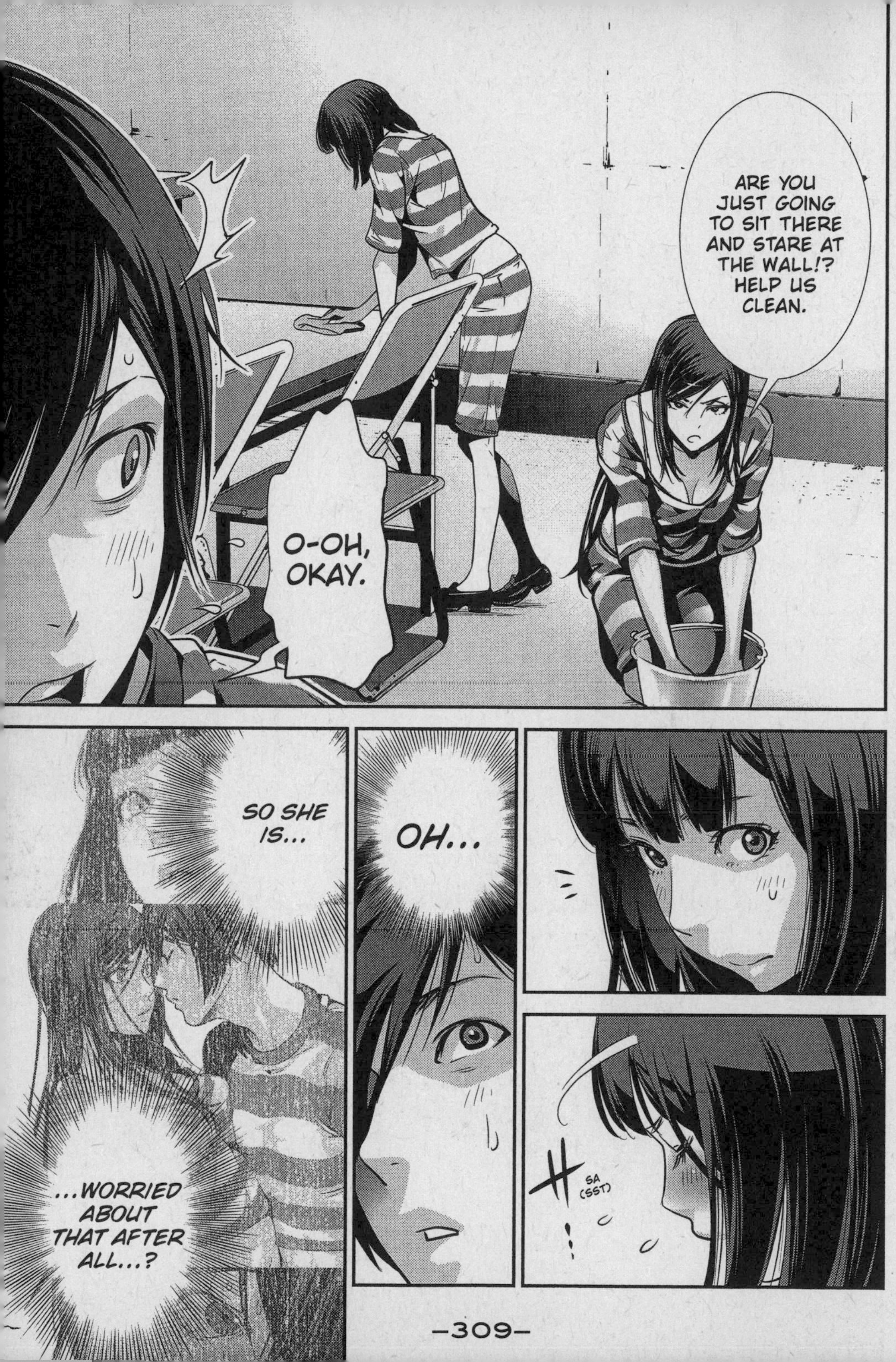
ARE YOU JUST GOING TO SIT THERE AND STARE AT THE WALL!? HELP US CLEAN.
O-OH, OKAY.
SA (SST)
OH...
SO SHE IS...
...WORRIED ABOUT THAT AFTER ALL...?

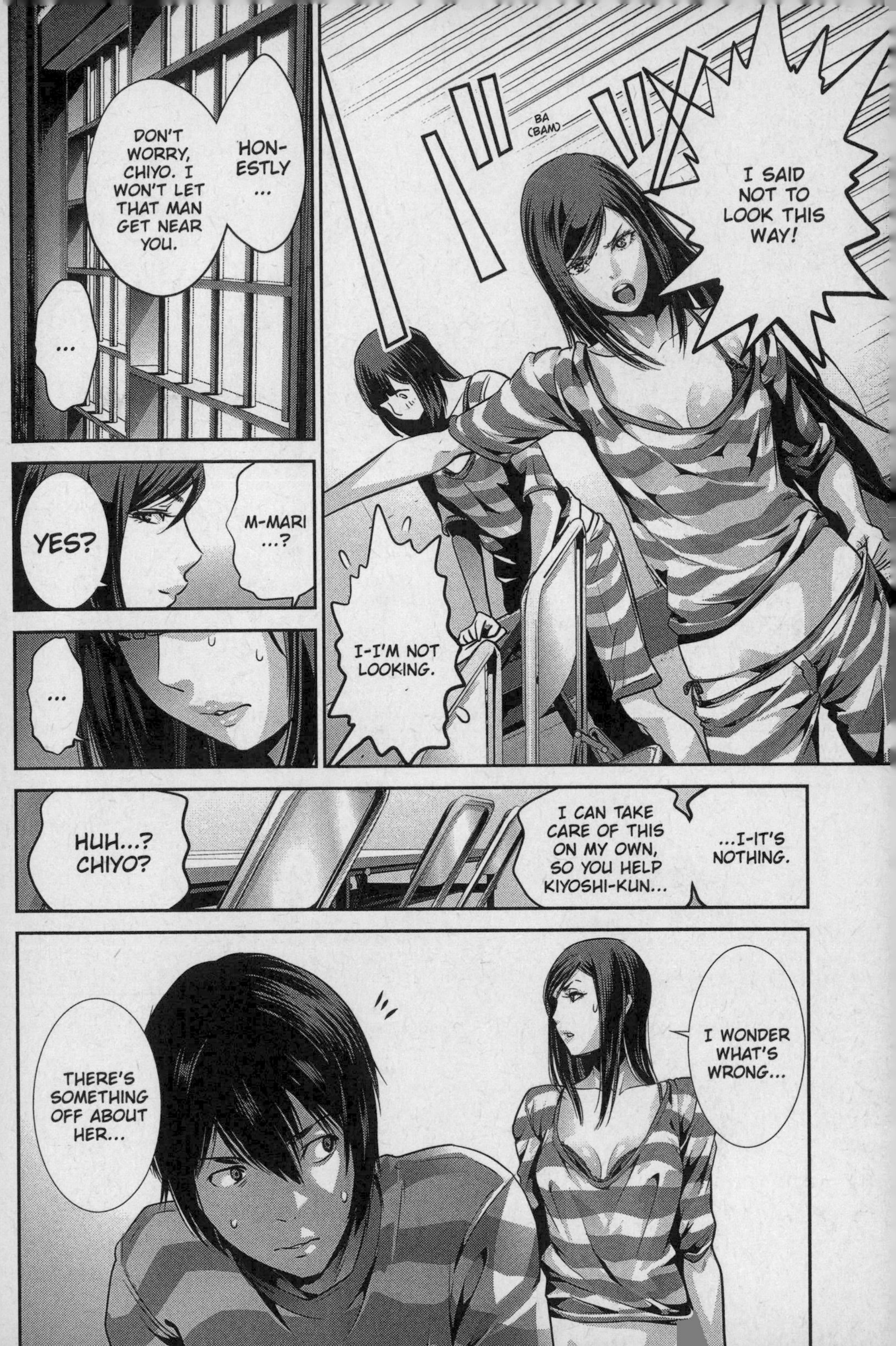
BA (BAM)
I SAID NOT TO LOOK THIS WAY!
I-I'M NOT LOOKING.
HON-ESTLY...
DON'T WORRY, CHIYO. I WON'T LET THAT MAN GET NEAR YOU.
...
M-MARI...?
YES?
...
...I-IT'S NOTHING.
I CAN TAKE CARE OF THIS ON MY OWN, SO YOU HELP KIYOSHI-KUN...
HUH...? CHIYO?
I WONDER WHAT'S WRONG...
THERE'S SOMETHING OFF ABOUT HER...

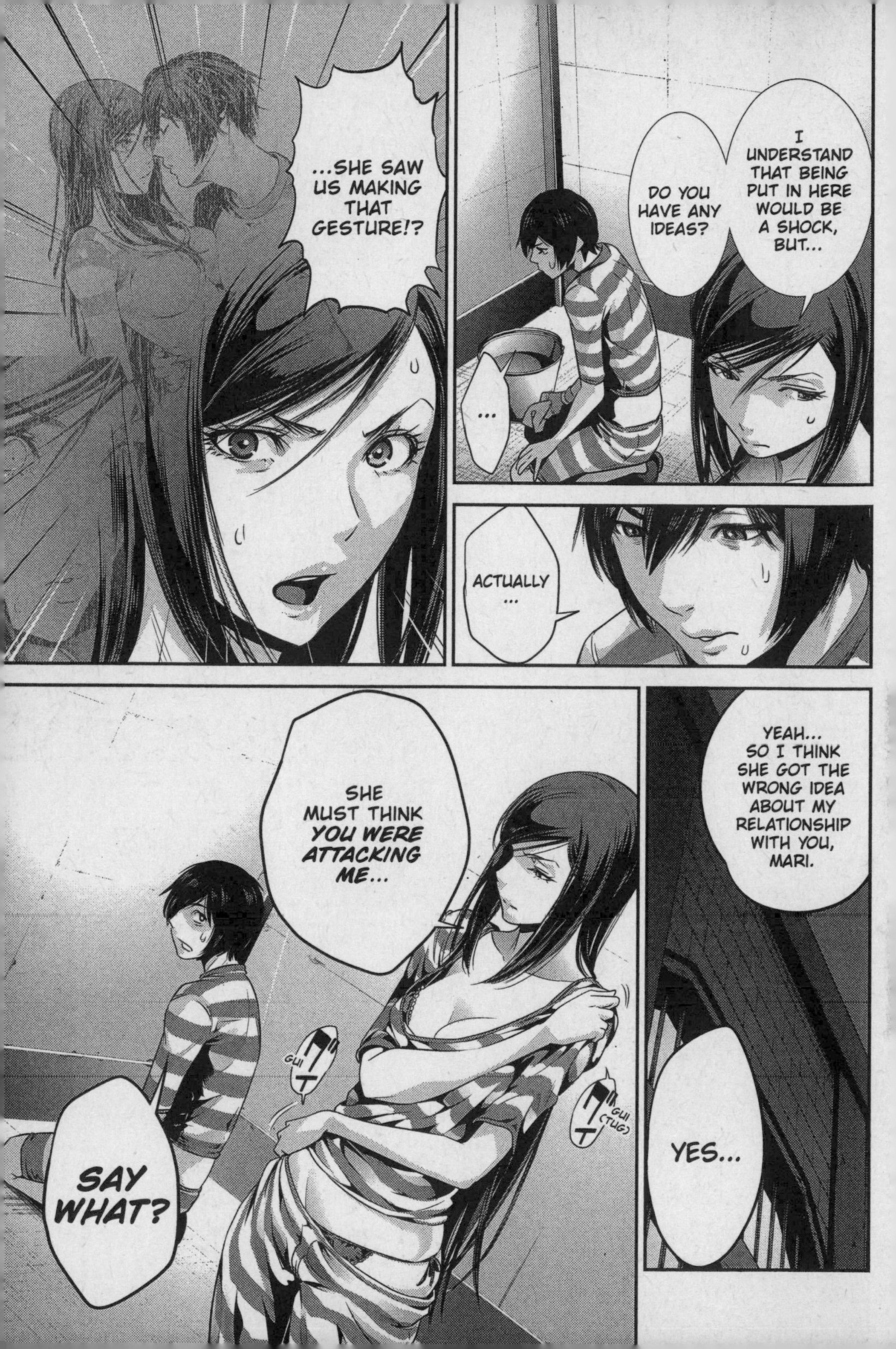
I UNDERSTAND THAT BEING PUT IN HERE WOULD BE A SHOCK, BUT...
DO YOU HAVE ANY IDEAS?
...
ACTUALLY ...
...SHE SAW US MAKING THAT GESTURE!?
YEAH... SO I THINK SHE GOT THE WRONG IDEA ABOUT MY RELATIONSHIP WITH YOU, MARI.
YES...
SHE MUST THINK *YOU WERE ATTACKING ME...*
GUI
GUI (TUG)
SAY WHAT?

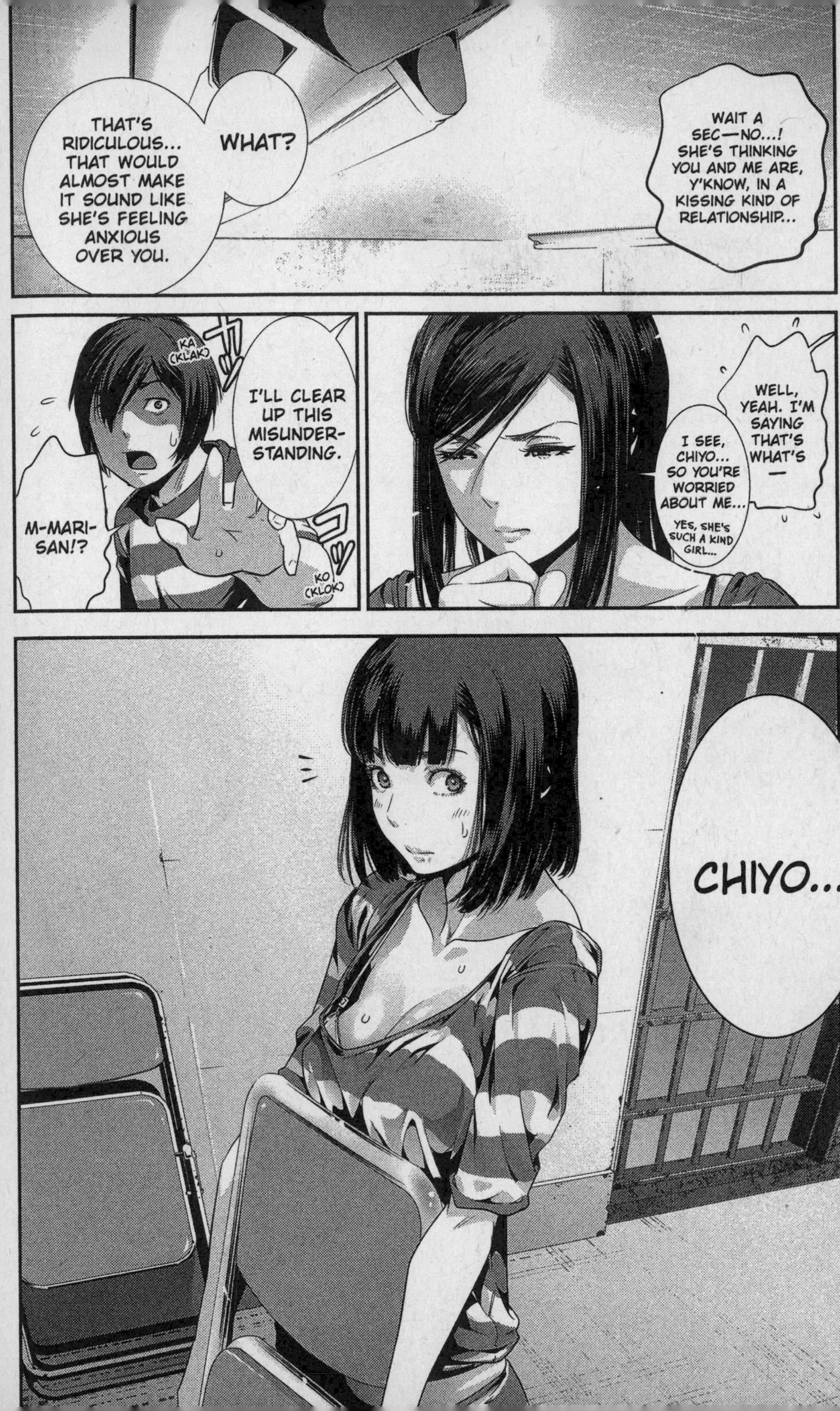
WAIT A SEC—NO...! SHE'S THINKING YOU AND ME ARE, Y'KNOW, IN A KISSING KIND OF RELATIONSHIP...
WHAT?
THAT'S RIDICULOUS... THAT WOULD ALMOST MAKE IT SOUND LIKE SHE'S FEELING ANXIOUS OVER YOU.
WELL, YEAH. I'M SAYING THAT'S WHAT'S —
I SEE, CHIYO... SO YOU'RE WORRIED ABOUT ME...
YES, SHE'S SUCH A KIND GIRL...
I'LL CLEAR UP THIS MISUNDER-STANDING.
KA (KLAK)
KO (KLOK)
M-MARI-SAN!?
CHIYO...

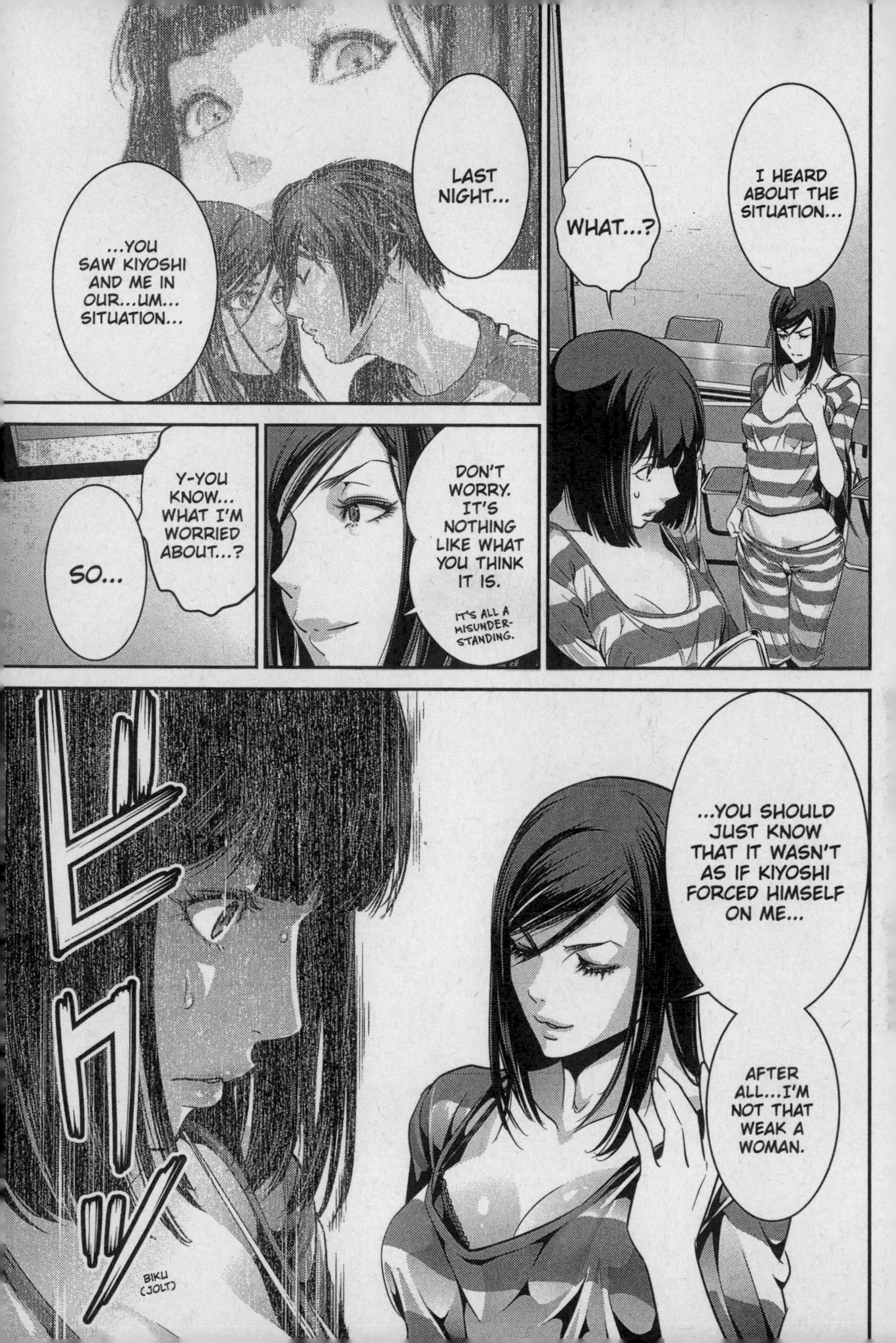
I HEARD ABOUT THE SITUATION...
WHAT...?
LAST NIGHT...
...YOU SAW KIYOSHI AND ME IN OUR...UM... SITUATION...
DON'T WORRY. IT'S NOTHING LIKE WHAT YOU THINK IT IS.
IT'S ALL A MISUNDERSTANDING.
Y-YOU KNOW... WHAT I'M WORRIED ABOUT...?
SO...
...YOU SHOULD JUST KNOW THAT IT WASN'T AS IF KIYOSHI FORCED HIMSELF ON ME...
AFTER ALL...I'M NOT THAT WEAK A WOMAN.
BIKU (JOLT)

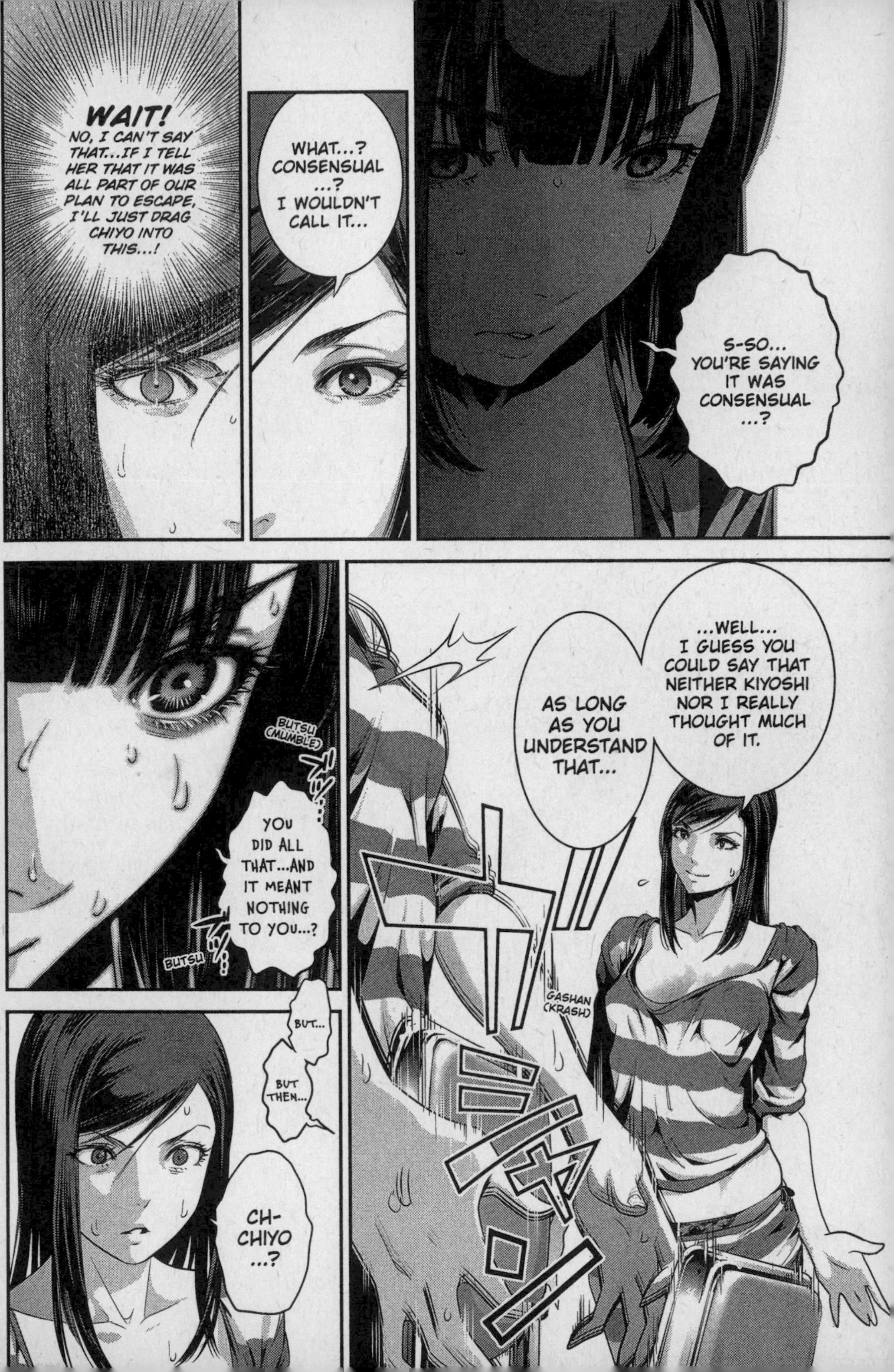
S-SO... YOU'RE SAYING IT WAS CONSENSUAL ...?
WHAT...? CONSENSUAL ...? I WOULDN'T CALL IT...
WAIT!
NO, I CAN'T SAY THAT...IF I TELL HER THAT IT WAS ALL PART OF OUR PLAN TO ESCAPE, I'LL JUST DRAG CHIYO INTO THIS...!
...WELL... I GUESS YOU COULD SAY THAT NEITHER KIYOSHI NOR I REALLY THOUGHT MUCH OF IT.
AS LONG AS YOU UNDERSTAND THAT...
GASHAN (KRASH)
BUTSU (MUMBLE)
YOU DID ALL THAT...AND IT MEANT NOTHING TO YOU...?
BUTSU
BUT...
BUT THEN...
CH-CHIYO ...?

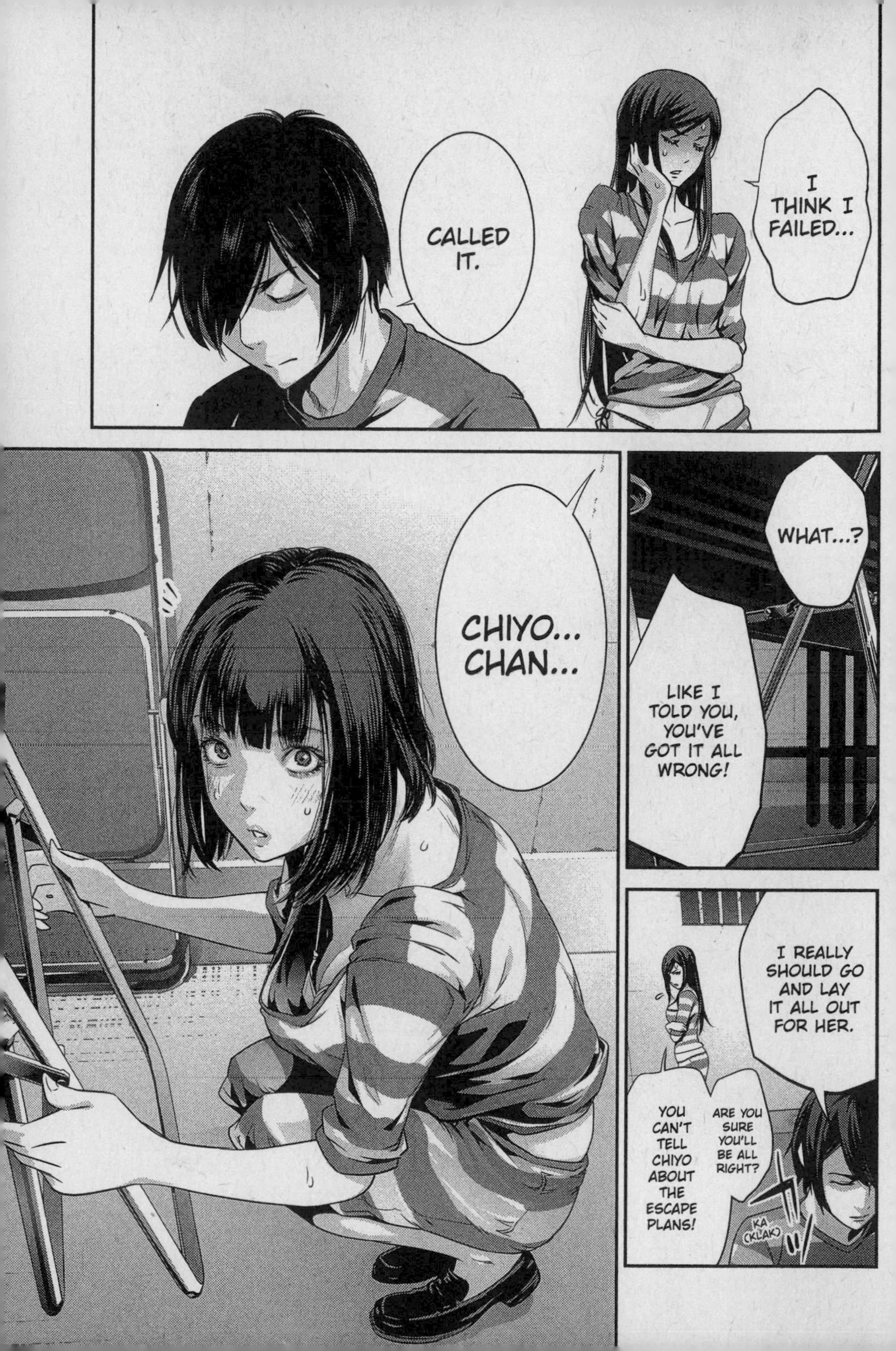
I THINK I FAILED...
CALLED IT.
WHAT...?
LIKE I TOLD YOU, YOU'VE GOT IT ALL WRONG!
CHIYO... CHAN...
I REALLY SHOULD GO AND LAY IT ALL OUT FOR HER.
ARE YOU SURE YOU'LL BE ALL RIGHT?
YOU CAN'T TELL CHIYO ABOUT THE ESCAPE PLANS!
KA (KLAK)

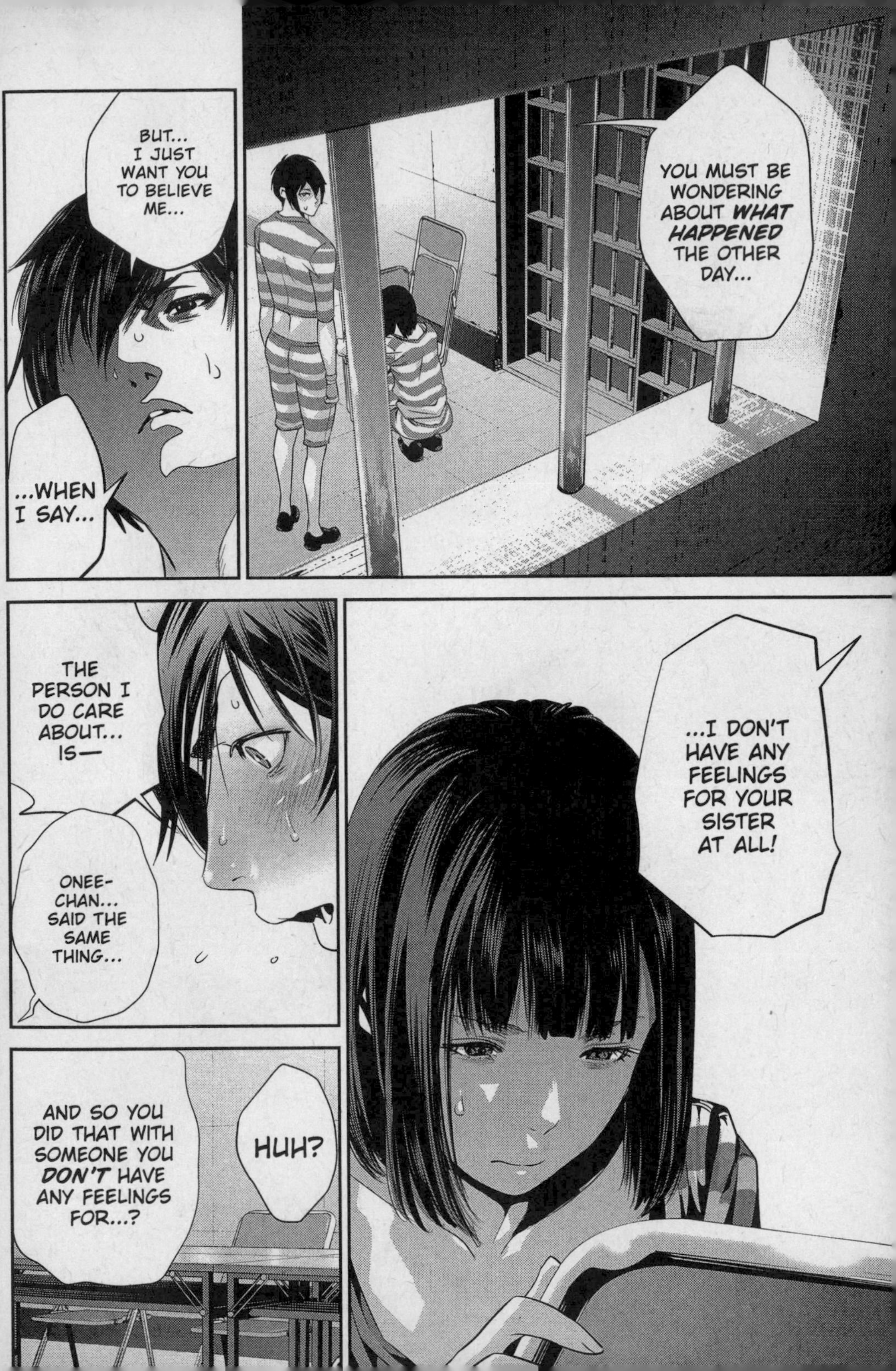
YOU MUST BE WONDERING ABOUT *WHAT HAPPENED* THE OTHER DAY...
BUT... I JUST WANT YOU TO BELIEVE ME...
...WHEN I SAY...
...I DON'T HAVE ANY FEELINGS FOR YOUR SISTER AT ALL!
THE PERSON I DO CARE ABOUT... IS—
ONEE-CHAN... SAID THE SAME THING...
HUH?
AND SO YOU DID THAT WITH SOMEONE YOU *DON'T* HAVE ANY FEELINGS FOR...?

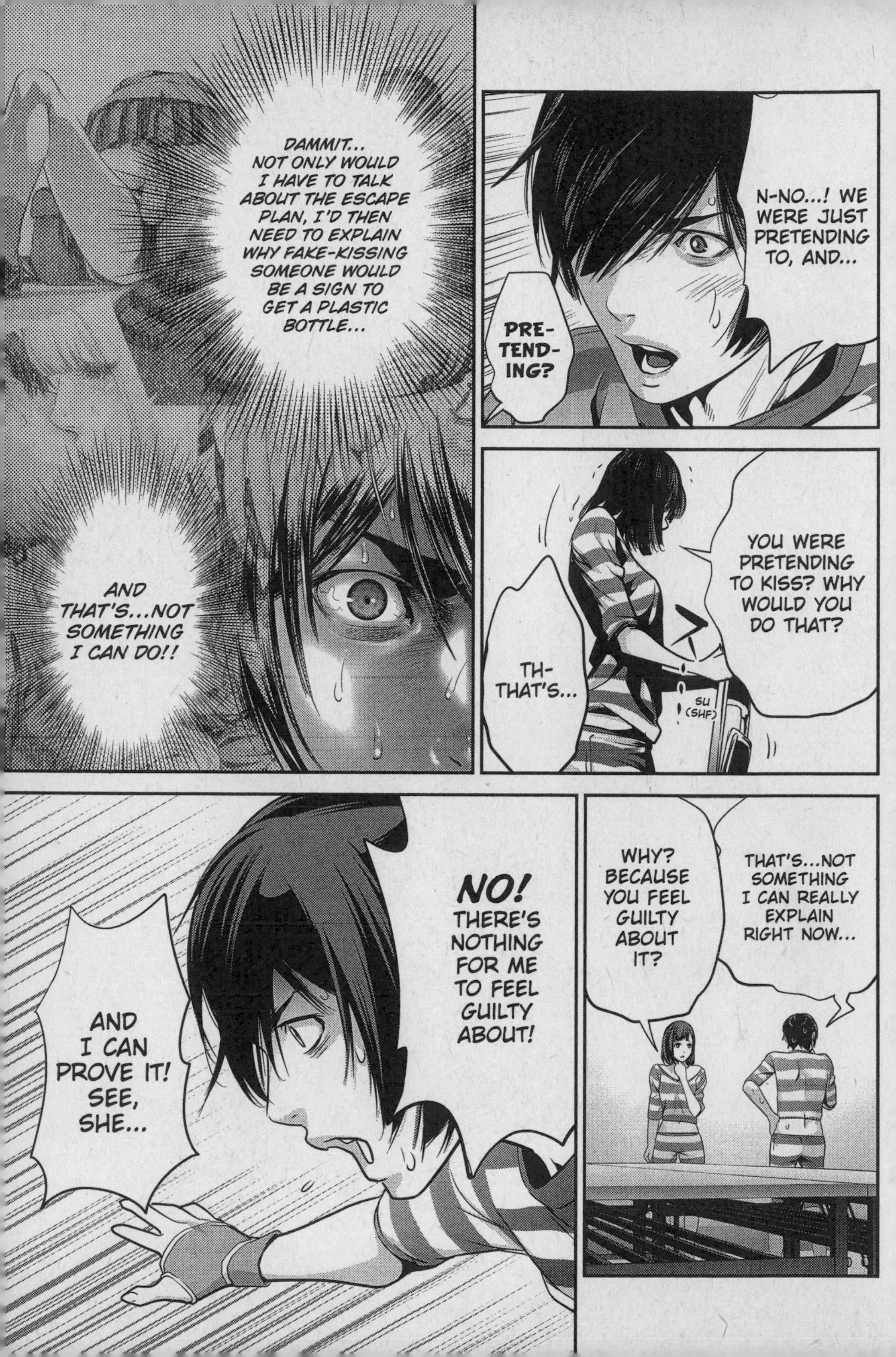

N-NO...! WE WERE JUST PRETENDING TO, AND...
PRE-TEND-ING?
YOU WERE PRETENDING TO KISS? WHY WOULD YOU DO THAT?
SU (SHF)
TH-THAT'S...
DAMMIT... NOT ONLY WOULD I HAVE TO TALK ABOUT THE ESCAPE PLAN, I'D THEN NEED TO EXPLAIN WHY FAKE-KISSING SOMEONE WOULD BE A SIGN TO GET A PLASTIC BOTTLE...
AND THAT'S...NOT SOMETHING I CAN DO!!
THAT'S...NOT SOMETHING I CAN REALLY EXPLAIN RIGHT NOW...
WHY? BECAUSE YOU FEEL GUILTY ABOUT IT?
NO! THERE'S NOTHING FOR ME TO FEEL GUILTY ABOUT!
AND I CAN PROVE IT! SEE, SHE...

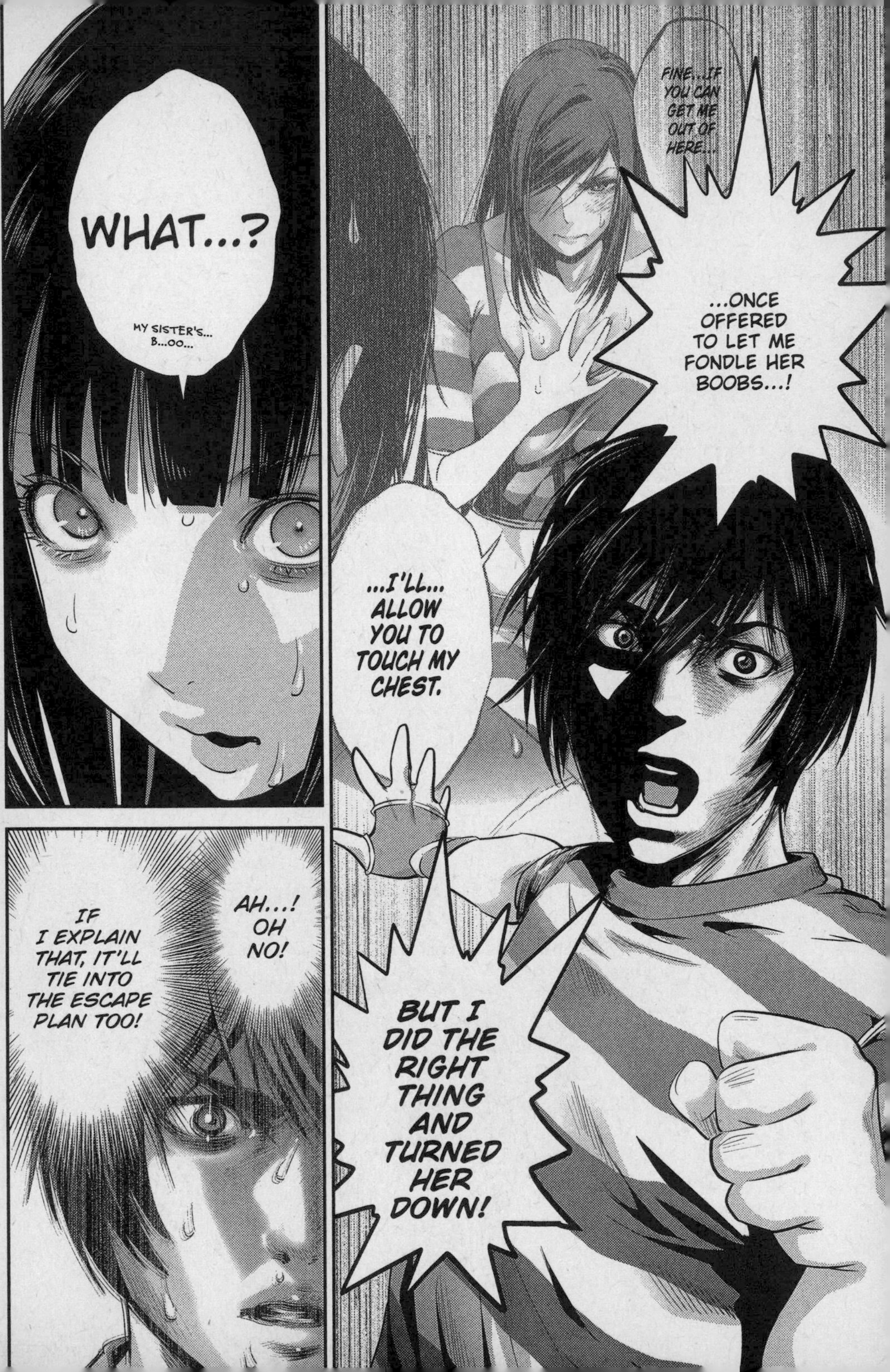
...ONCE OFFERED TO LET ME FONDLE HER BOOBS...!
FINE...IF YOU CAN GET ME OUT OF HERE...
...I'LL... ALLOW YOU TO TOUCH MY CHEST.
BUT I DID THE RIGHT THING AND TURNED HER DOWN!
WHAT...?
MY SISTER'S... B...OO...
AH...! OH NO!
IF I EXPLAIN THAT, IT'LL TIE INTO THE ESCAPE PLAN TOO!

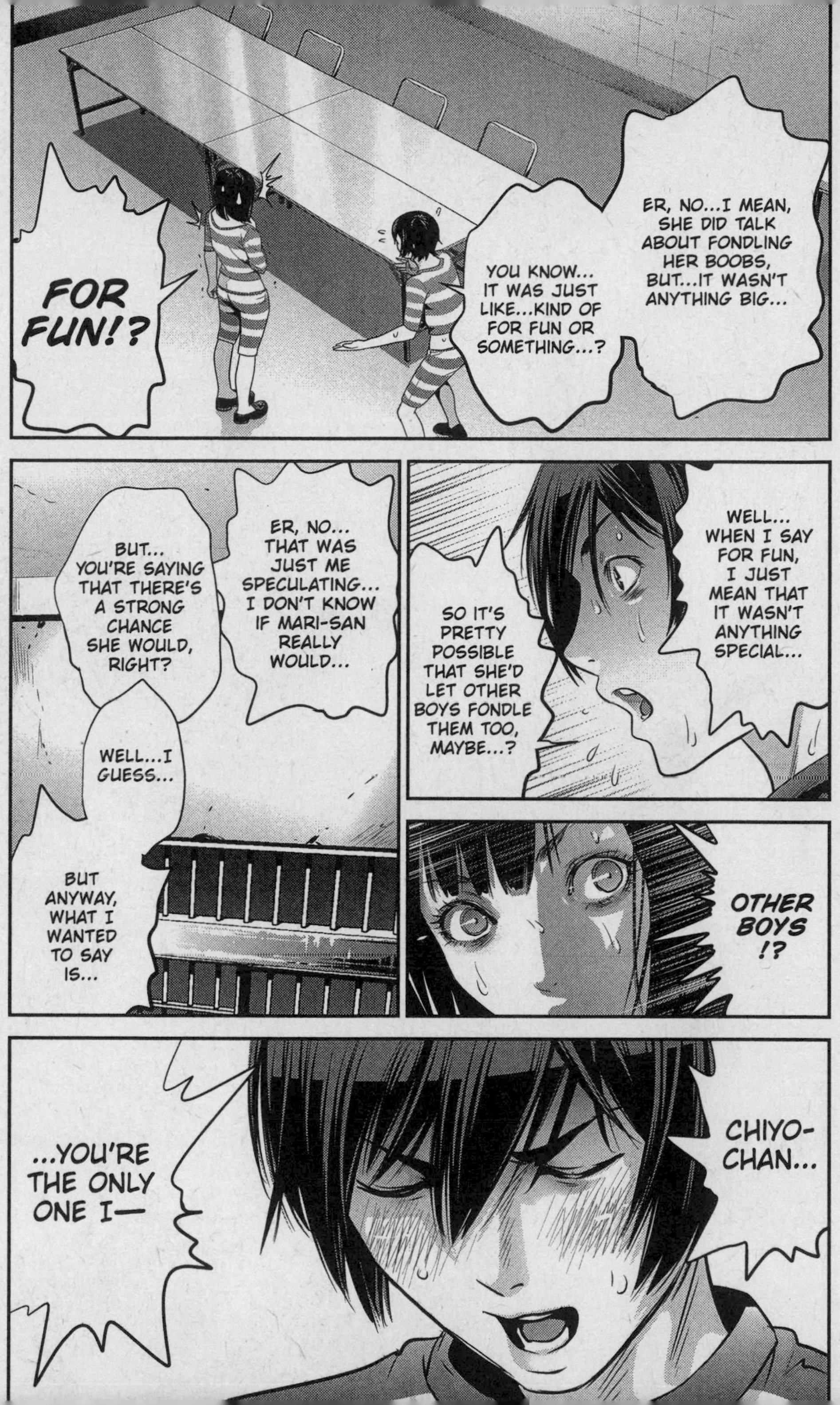
ER, NO...I MEAN, SHE DID TALK ABOUT FONDLING HER BOOBS, BUT...IT WASN'T ANYTHING BIG...
YOU KNOW... IT WAS JUST LIKE...KIND OF FOR FUN OR SOMETHING...?
FOR FUN!?
WELL... WHEN I SAY FOR FUN, I JUST MEAN THAT IT WASN'T ANYTHING SPECIAL...
SO IT'S PRETTY POSSIBLE THAT SHE'D LET OTHER BOYS FONDLE THEM TOO, MAYBE...?
OTHER BOYS !?
ER, NO... THAT WAS JUST ME SPECULATING... I DON'T KNOW IF MARI-SAN REALLY WOULD...
BUT... YOU'RE SAYING THAT THERE'S A STRONG CHANCE SHE WOULD, RIGHT?
WELL...I GUESS...
BUT ANYWAY, WHAT I WANTED TO SAY IS...
CHIYO-CHAN...
...YOU'RE THE ONLY ONE I—

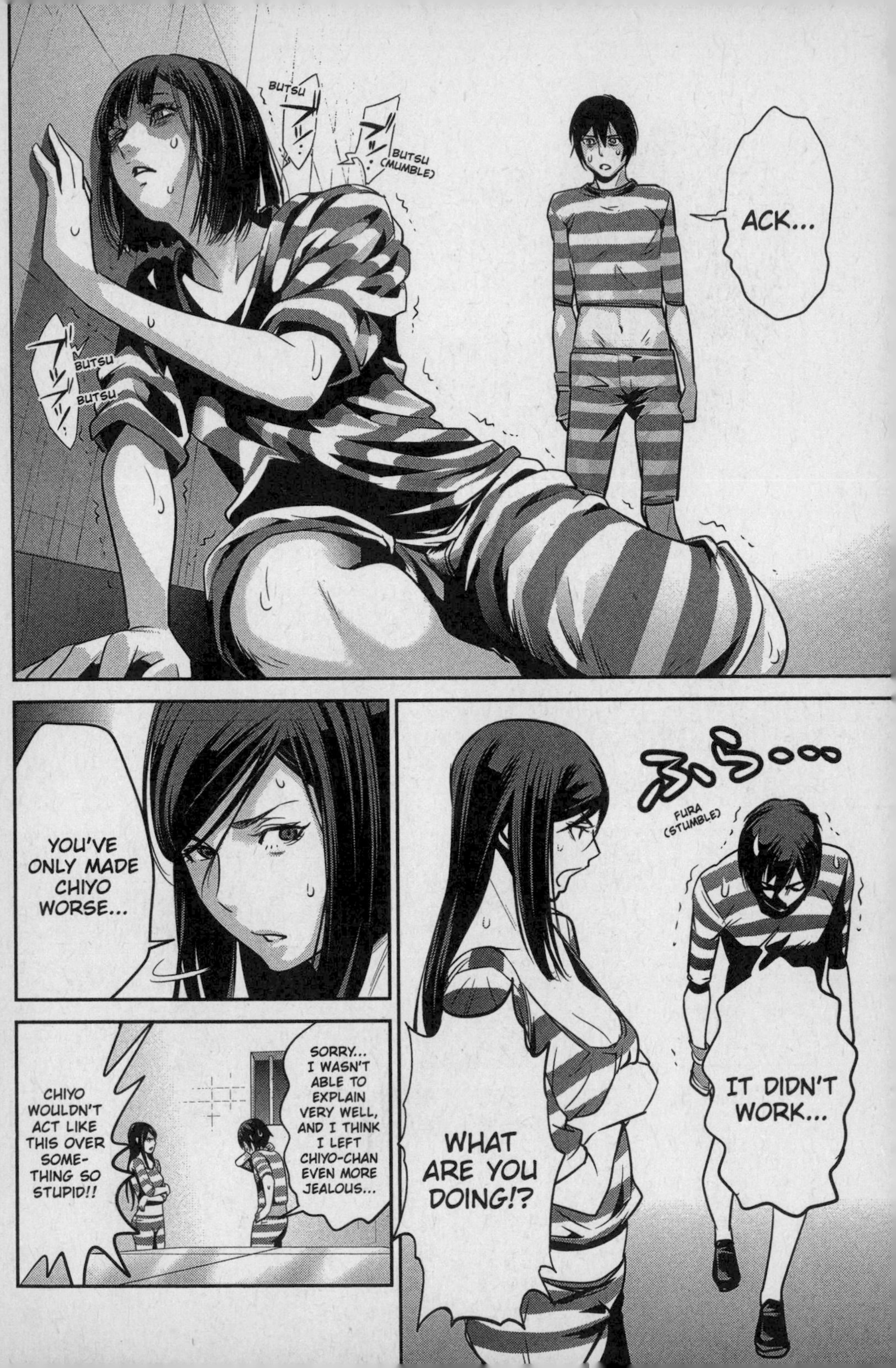
ACK...
BUTSU
BUTSU (MUMBLE)
BUTSU
BUTSU
ふら…
FURA (STUMBLE)
IT DIDN'T WORK...
WHAT ARE YOU DOING!?
YOU'VE ONLY MADE CHIYO WORSE...
SORRY... I WASN'T ABLE TO EXPLAIN VERY WELL, AND I THINK I LEFT CHIYO-CHAN EVEN MORE JEALOUS...
CHIYO WOULDN'T ACT LIKE THIS OVER SOME-THING SO STUPID!!

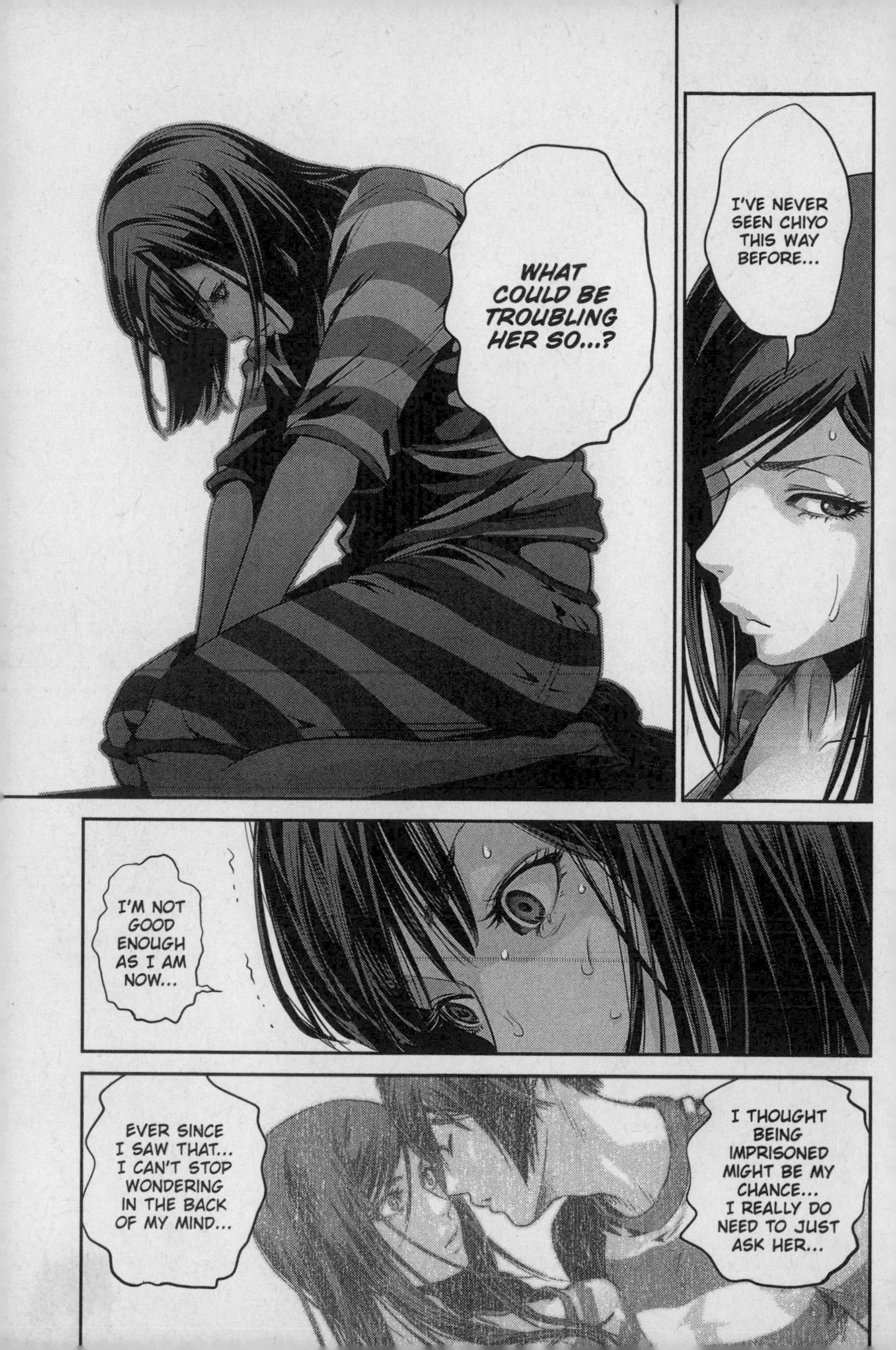
I'VE NEVER SEEN CHIYO THIS WAY BEFORE...
WHAT COULD BE TROUBLING HER SO...?
I'M NOT GOOD ENOUGH AS I AM NOW...
I THOUGHT BEING IMPRISONED MIGHT BE MY CHANCE... I REALLY DO NEED TO JUST ASK HER...
EVER SINCE I SAW THAT... I CAN'T STOP WONDERING IN THE BACK OF MY MIND...

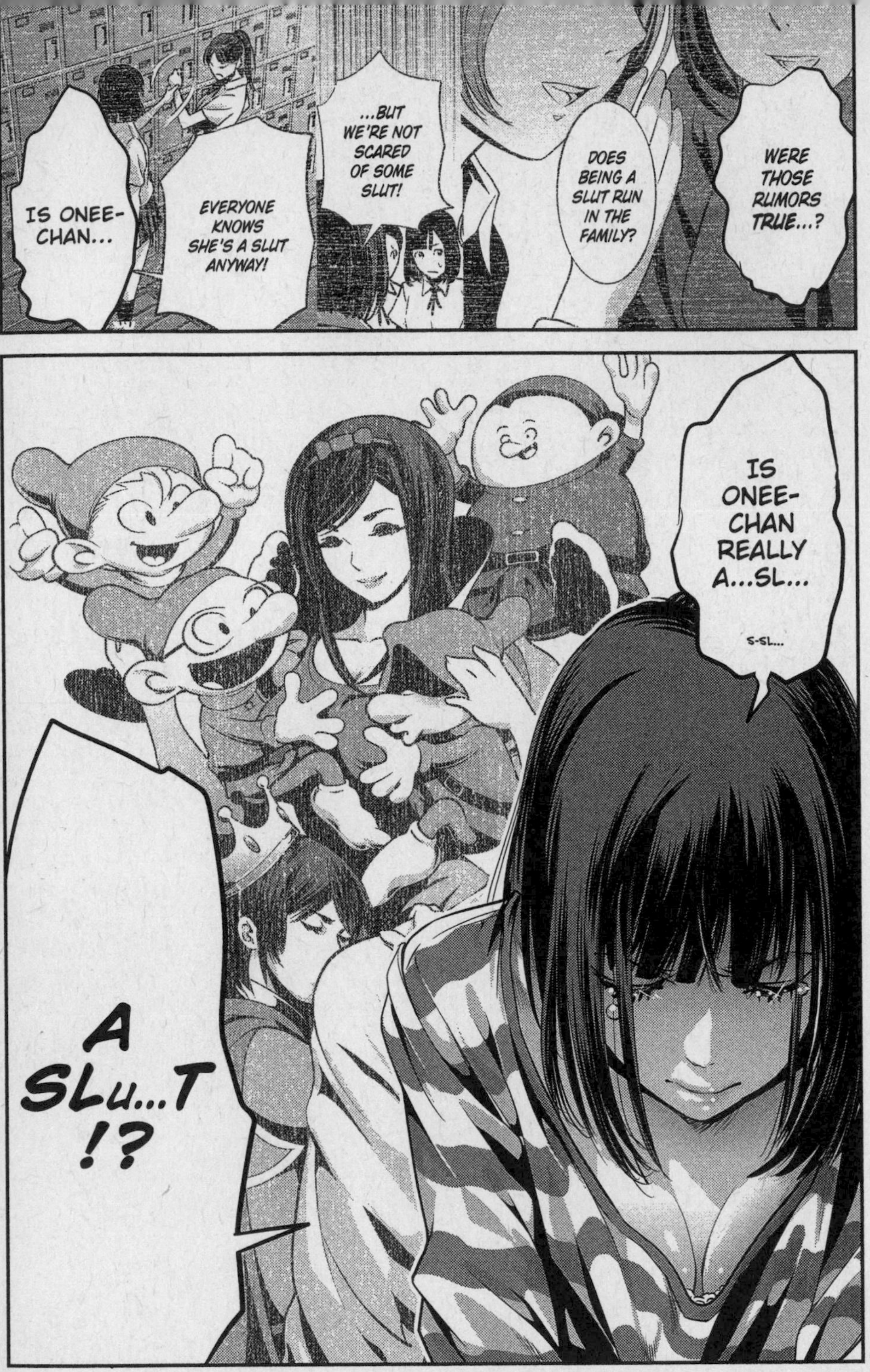
WERE THOSE RUMORS TRUE...?
DOES BEING A SLUT RUN IN THE FAMILY?
...BUT WE'RE NOT SCARED OF SOME SLUT!
EVERYONE KNOWS SHE'S A SLUT ANYWAY!
IS ONEE-CHAN...
IS ONEE-CHAN REALLY A...SL...
S-SL...
A SLu...T !?

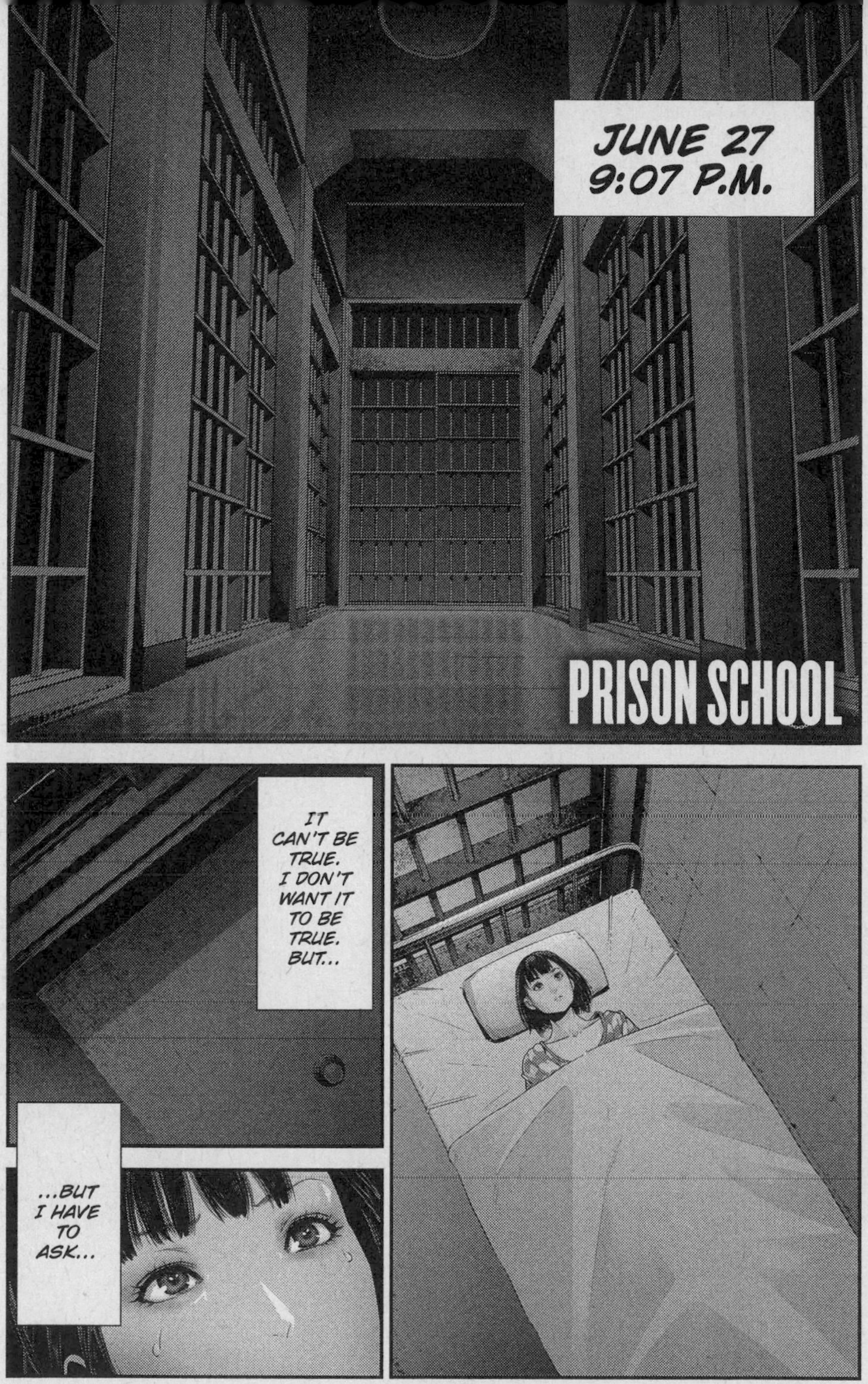
JUNE 27 9:07 P.M.
PRISON SCHOOL
IT CAN'T BE TRUE. I DON'T WANT IT TO BE TRUE. BUT...
...BUT I HAVE TO ASK...

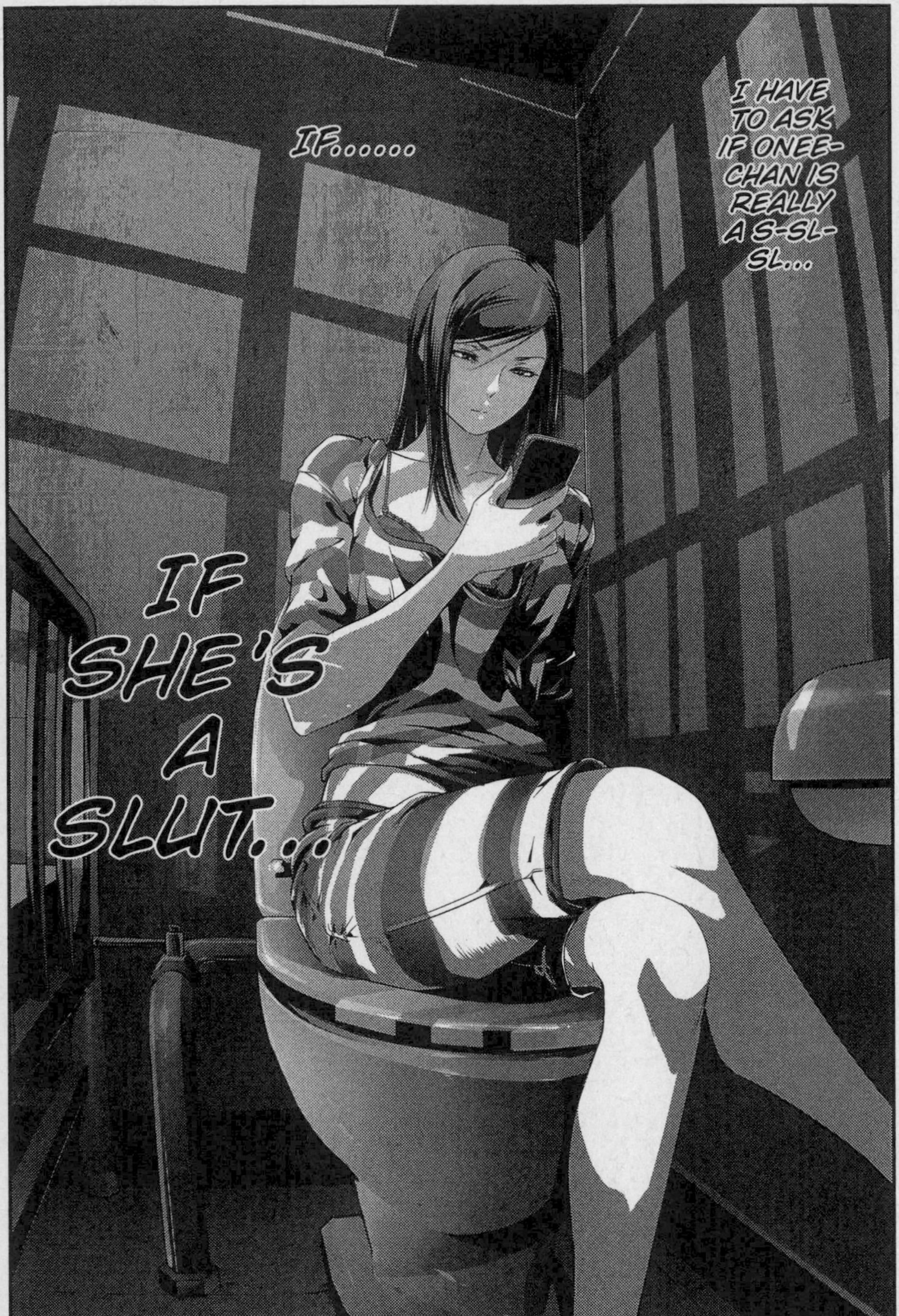
I HAVE TO ASK IF ONEE-CHAN IS REALLY A S-SL-SL...
IF......
IF SHE'S A SLUT...

CHAPTER 136: GOLDFINGER

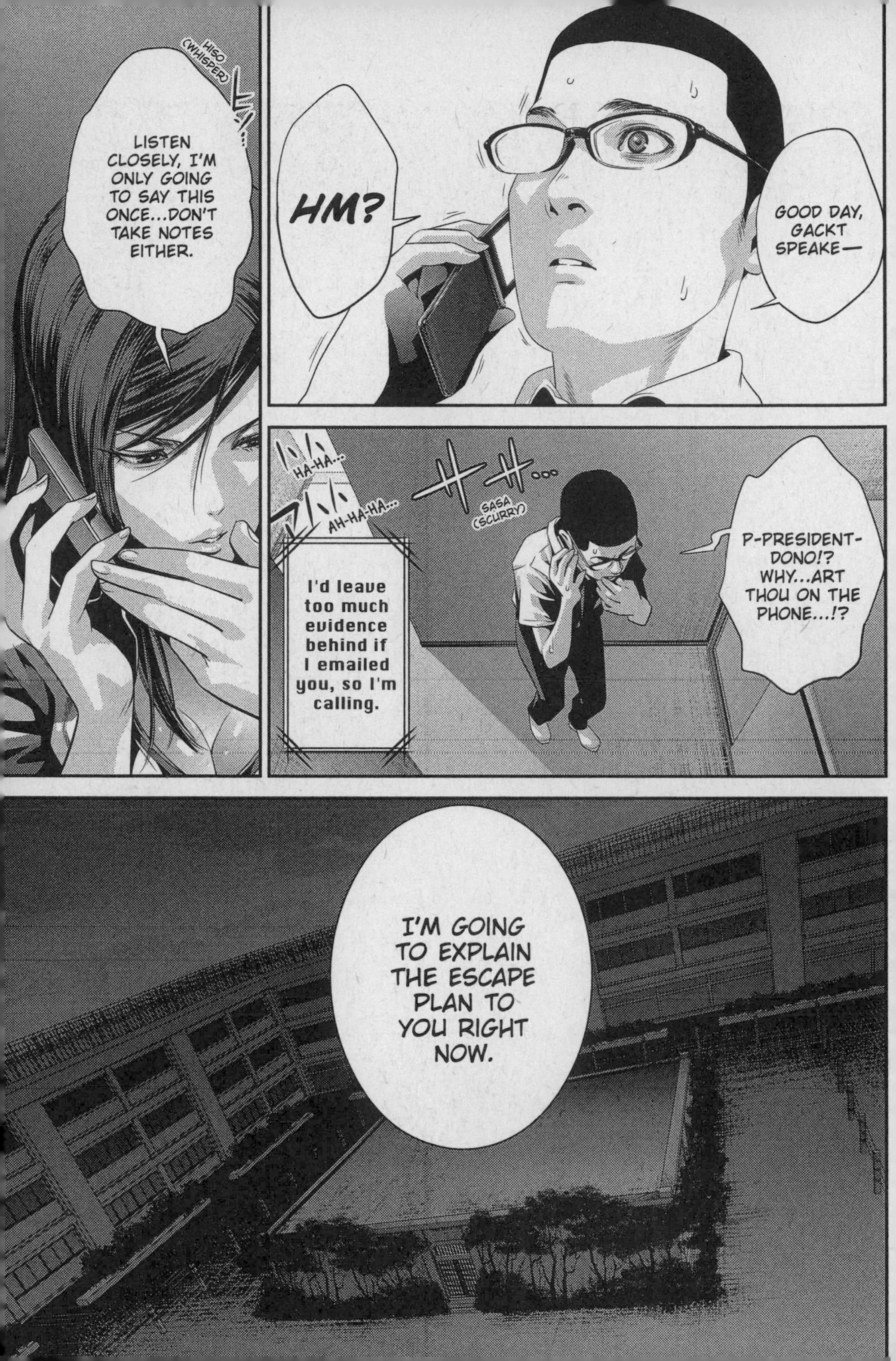
GOOD DAY, GACKT SPEAKE—
HM?
HISO (WHISPER)
LISTEN CLOSELY, I'M ONLY GOING TO SAY THIS ONCE...DON'T TAKE NOTES EITHER.
P-PRESIDENT-DONO!? WHY...ART THOU ON THE PHONE...!?
SASA (SCURRY)
HA-HA...
AH-HA-HA...
I'd leave too much evidence behind if I emailed you, so I'm calling.
I'M GOING TO EXPLAIN THE ESCAPE PLAN TO YOU RIGHT NOW.

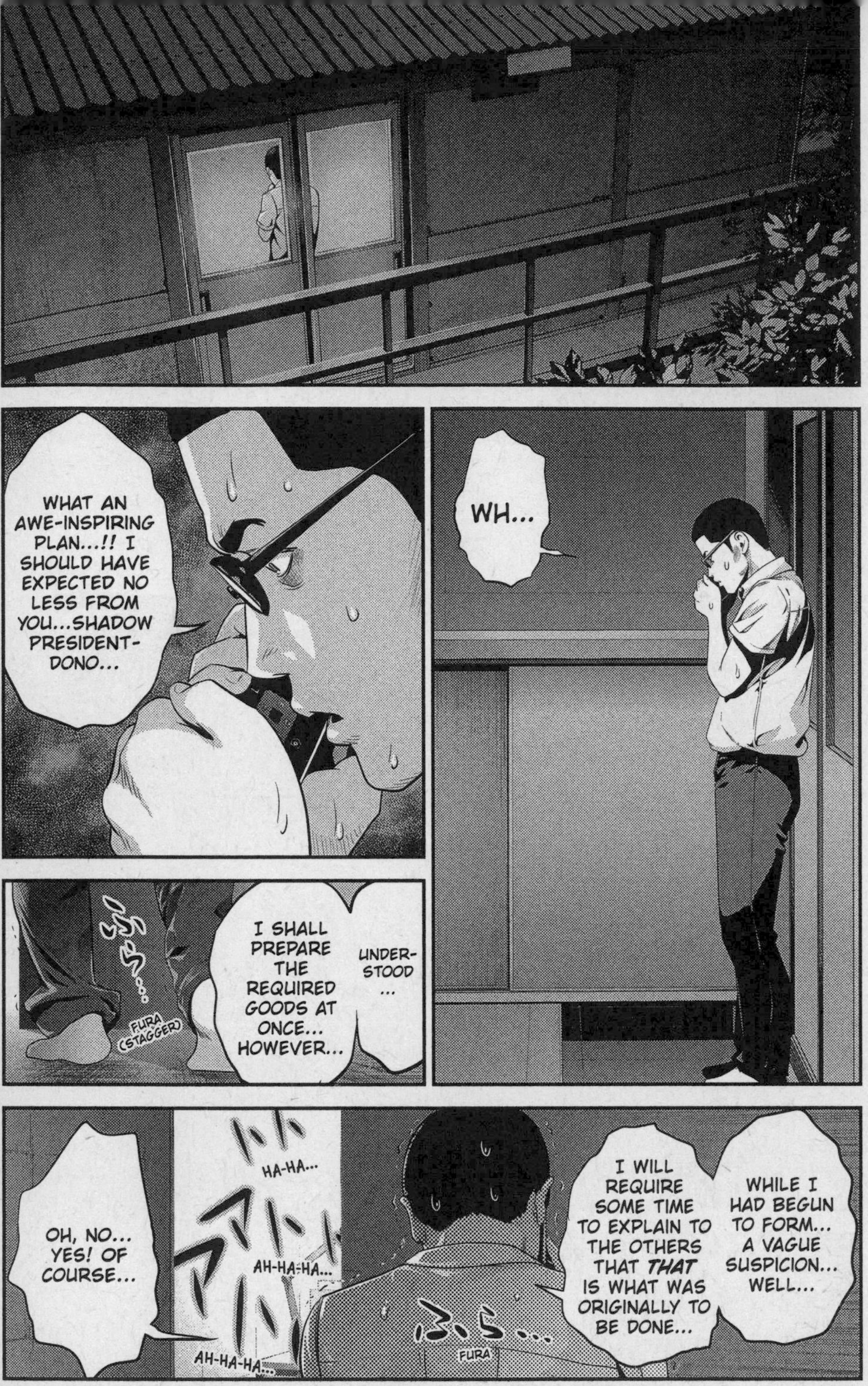
WH...
WHAT AN AWE-INSPIRING PLAN...!! I SHOULD HAVE EXPECTED NO LESS FROM YOU...SHADOW PRESIDENT-DONO...
UNDER-STOOD ...
I SHALL PREPARE THE REQUIRED GOODS AT ONCE... HOWEVER...
FURA (STAGGER)
WHILE I HAD BEGUN TO FORM... A VAGUE SUSPICION... WELL...
I WILL REQUIRE SOME TIME TO EXPLAIN TO THE OTHERS THAT *THAT* IS WHAT WAS ORIGINALLY TO BE DONE...
FURA
HA-HA...
AH-HA-HA...
AH-HA-HA...
OH, NO... YES! OF COURSE...

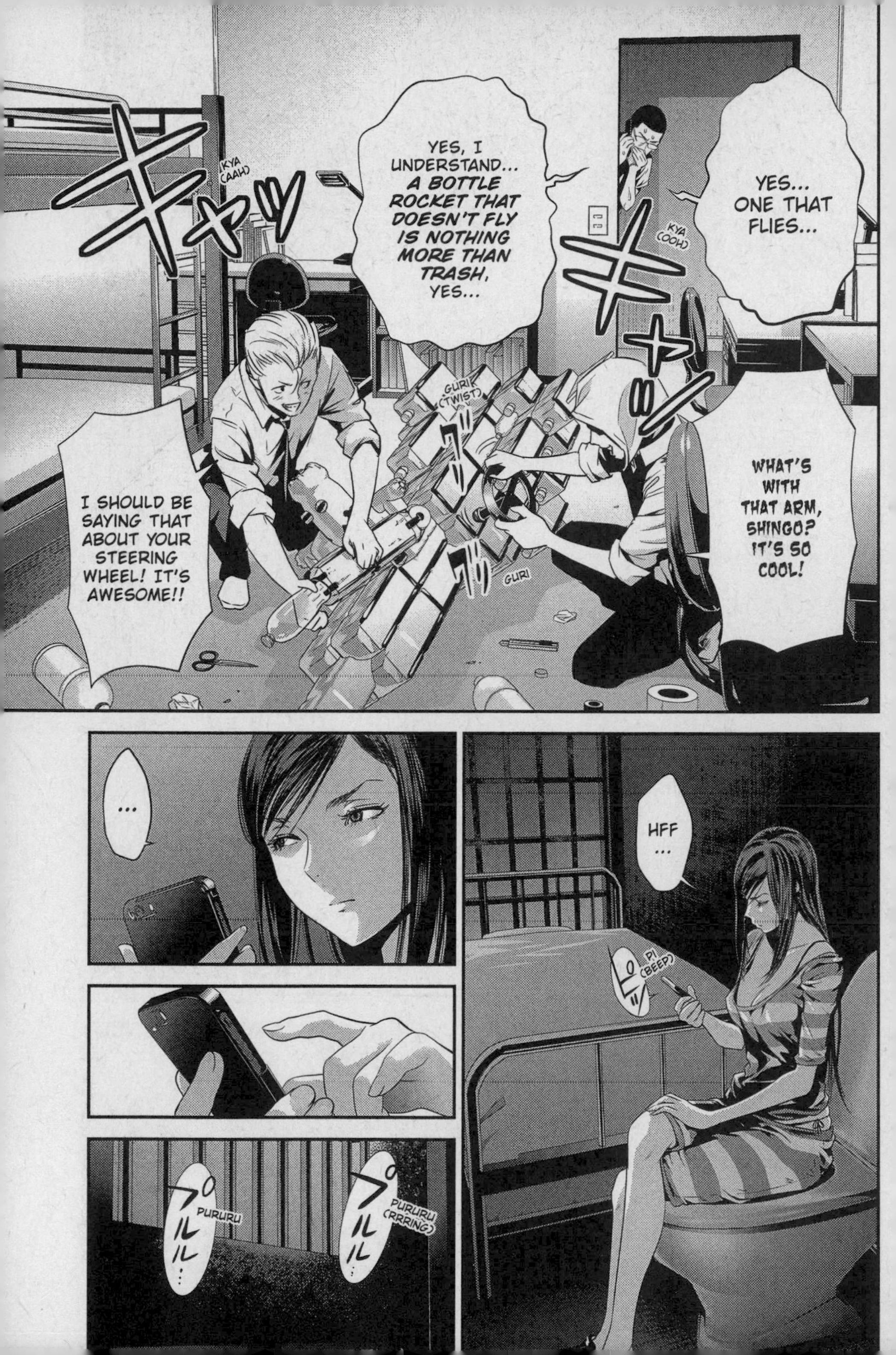
YES... ONE THAT FLIES...
KYA (OOH)
YES, I UNDERSTAND... A BOTTLE ROCKET THAT DOESN'T FLY IS NOTHING MORE THAN TRASH, YES...
KYA (AAH)
WHAT'S WITH THAT ARM, SHINGO? IT'S SO COOL!
GURI (TWIST)
GURI
I SHOULD BE SAYING THAT ABOUT YOUR STEERING WHEEL! IT'S AWESOME!!
HFF ...
PI (BEEP)
...
PURURU (RRRING)
PURURU

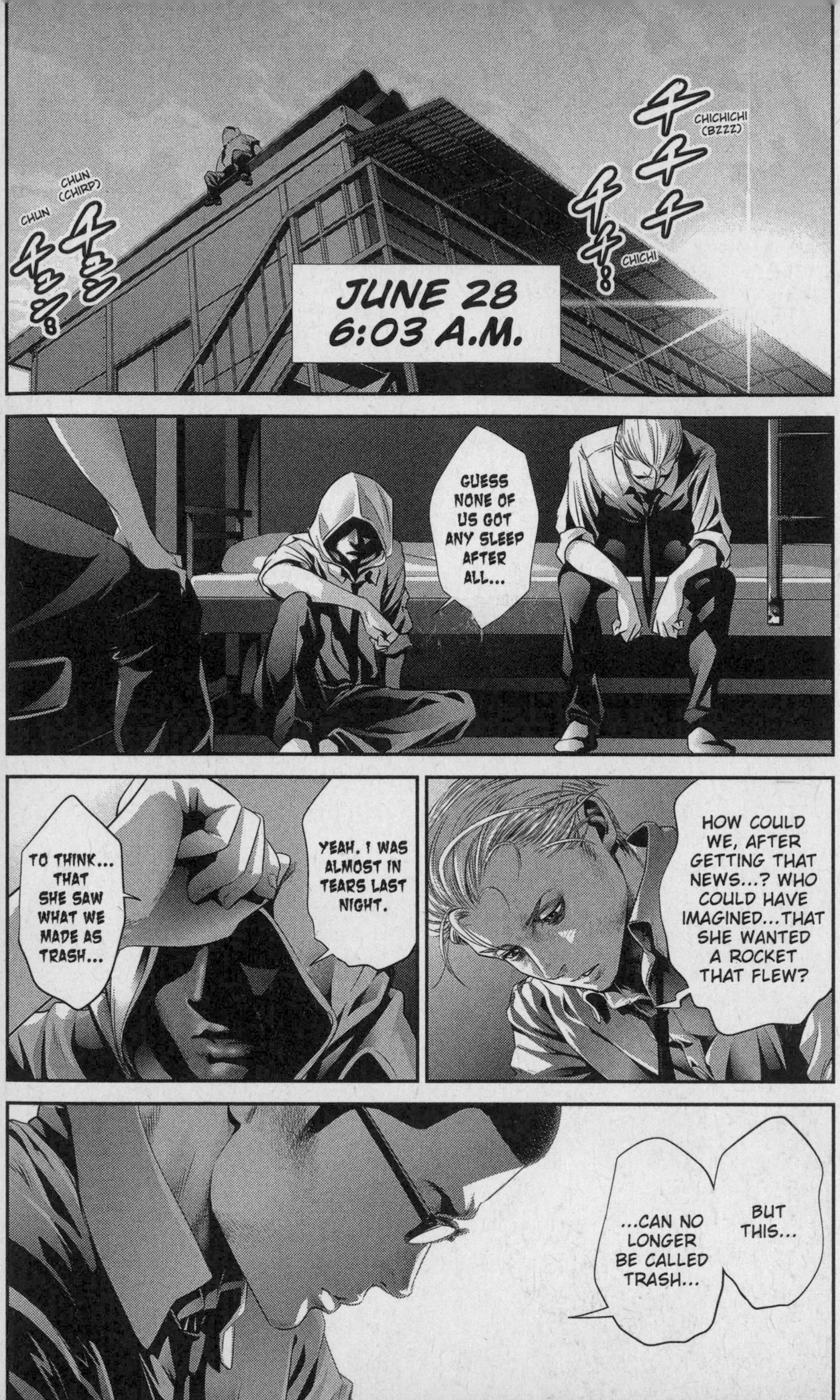
チチチ
CHICHICHI (BZZZ)
チチ
CHICHI
チュン
CHUN (CHIRP)
チュン
CHUN
JUNE 28
6:03 A.M.
GUESS NONE OF US GOT ANY SLEEP AFTER ALL...
YEAH. I WAS ALMOST IN TEARS LAST NIGHT.
TO THINK... THAT SHE SAW WHAT WE MADE AS TRASH...
HOW COULD WE, AFTER GETTING THAT NEWS...? WHO COULD HAVE IMAGINED...THAT SHE WANTED A ROCKET THAT FLEW?
BUT THIS...
...CAN NO LONGER BE CALLED TRASH...

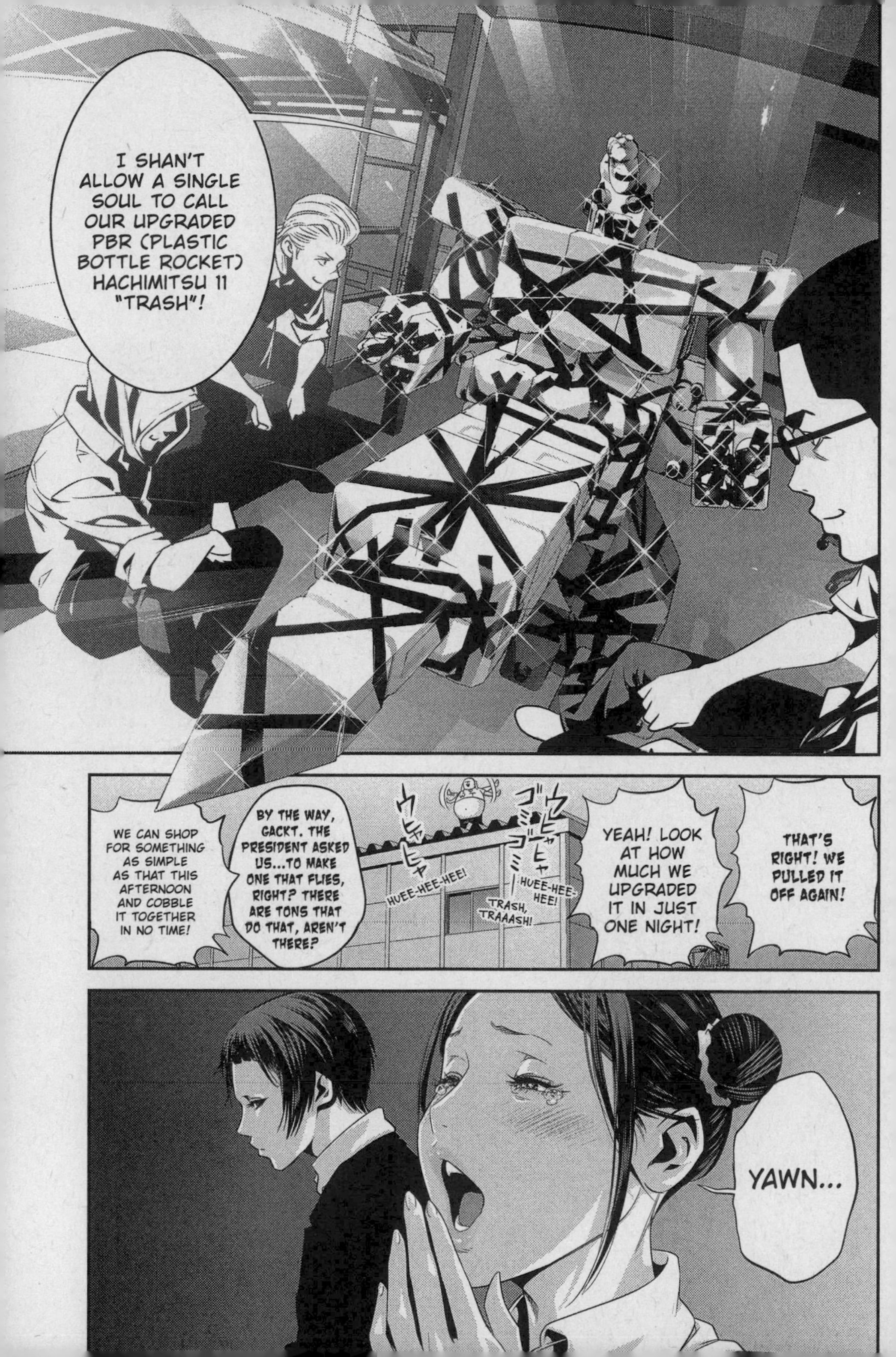

I SHAN'T ALLOW A SINGLE SOUL TO CALL OUR UPGRADED PBR (PLASTIC BOTTLE ROCKET) HACHIMITSU 11 "TRASH"!
THAT'S RIGHT! WE PULLED IT OFF AGAIN!
YEAH! LOOK AT HOW MUCH WE UPGRADED IT IN JUST ONE NIGHT!
HUEE-HEE-HEE!
TRASH, TRAAASH!
HUEE-HEE-HEE!
BY THE WAY, GACKT. THE PRESIDENT ASKED US...TO MAKE ONE THAT FLIES, RIGHT? THERE ARE TONS THAT DO THAT, AREN'T THERE?
WE CAN SHOP FOR SOMETHING AS SIMPLE AS THAT THIS AFTERNOON AND COBBLE IT TOGETHER IN NO TIME!
YAWN...

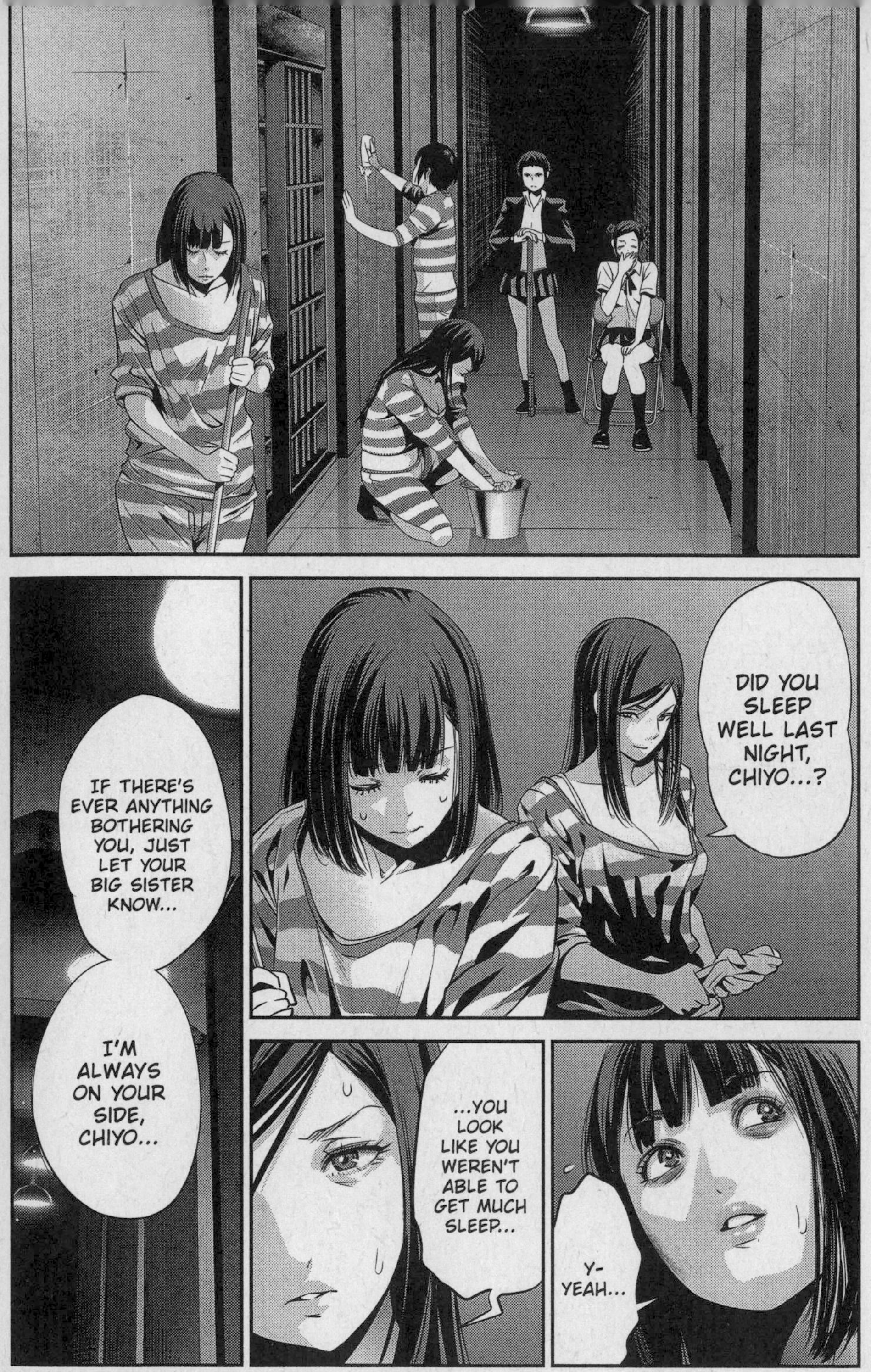
DID YOU SLEEP WELL LAST NIGHT, CHIYO...?
Y-YEAH...
...YOU LOOK LIKE YOU WEREN'T ABLE TO GET MUCH SLEEP...
IF THERE'S EVER ANYTHING BOTHERING YOU, JUST LET YOUR BIG SISTER KNOW...
I'M ALWAYS ON YOUR SIDE, CHIYO...

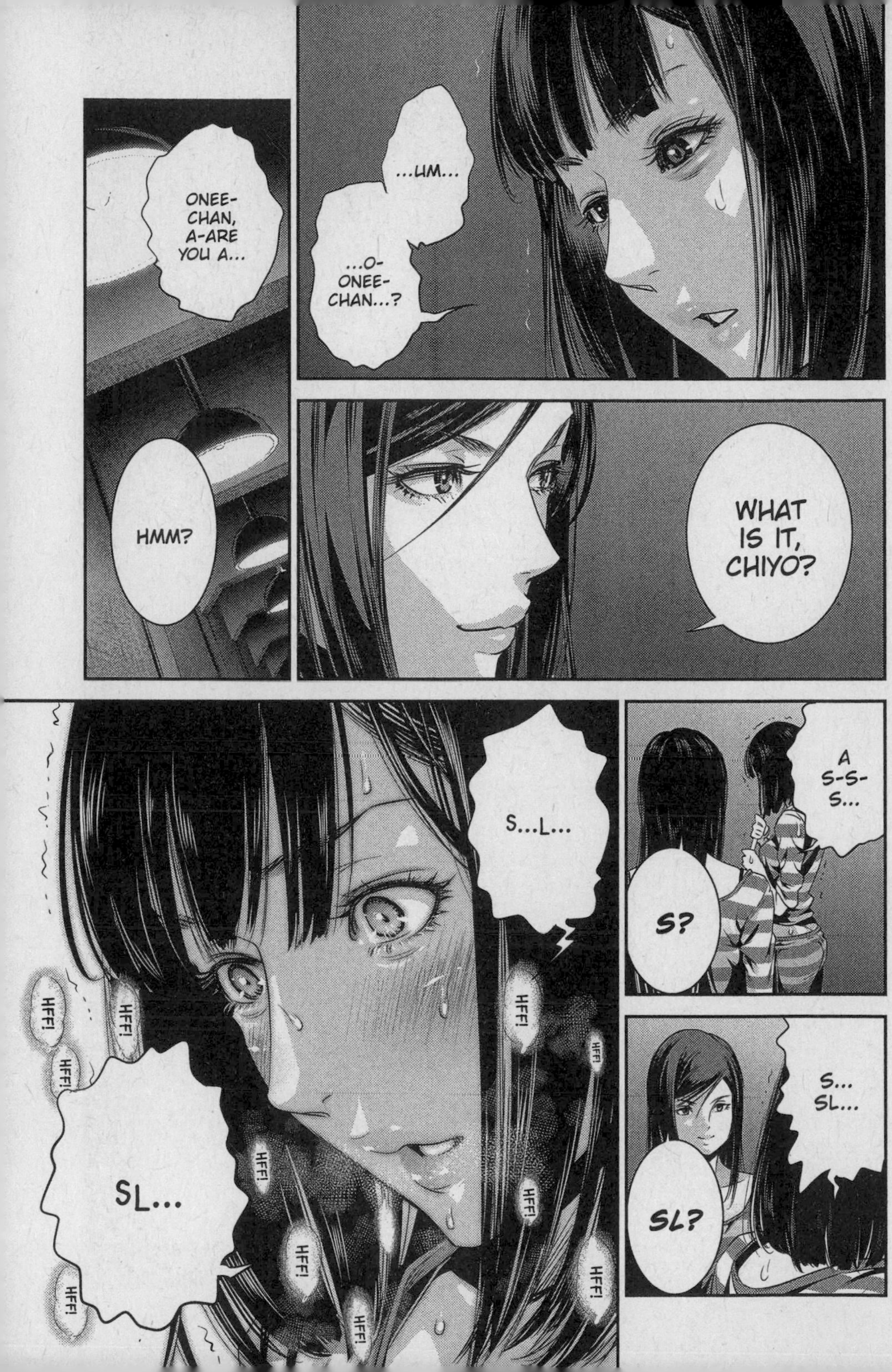
...UM...
...O-ONEE-CHAN...?
HMM?
WHAT IS IT, CHIYO?
ONEE-CHAN, A-ARE YOU A...
A S-S-S...
S?
S... SL...
SL?
S...L...
SL...
HFF! HFF! HFF! HFF! HFF! HFF! HFF! HFF! HFF! HFF!

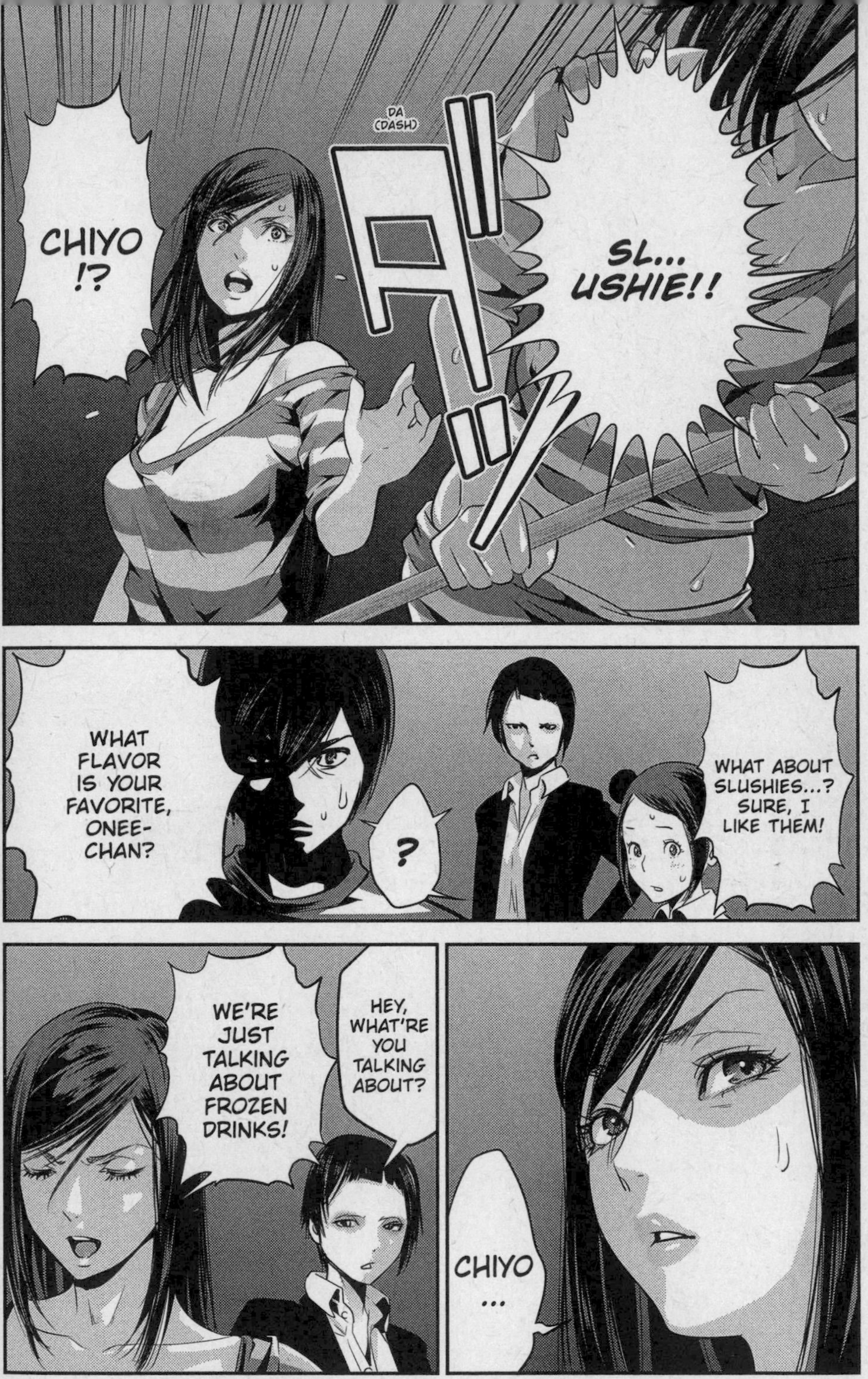
SL... USHIE!!
DA (DASH)
CHIYO !?
WHAT ABOUT SLUSHIES...? SURE, I LIKE THEM!
?
WHAT FLAVOR IS YOUR FAVORITE, ONEE-CHAN?
CHIYO ...
HEY, WHAT'RE YOU TALKING ABOUT?
WE'RE JUST TALKING ABOUT FROZEN DRINKS!

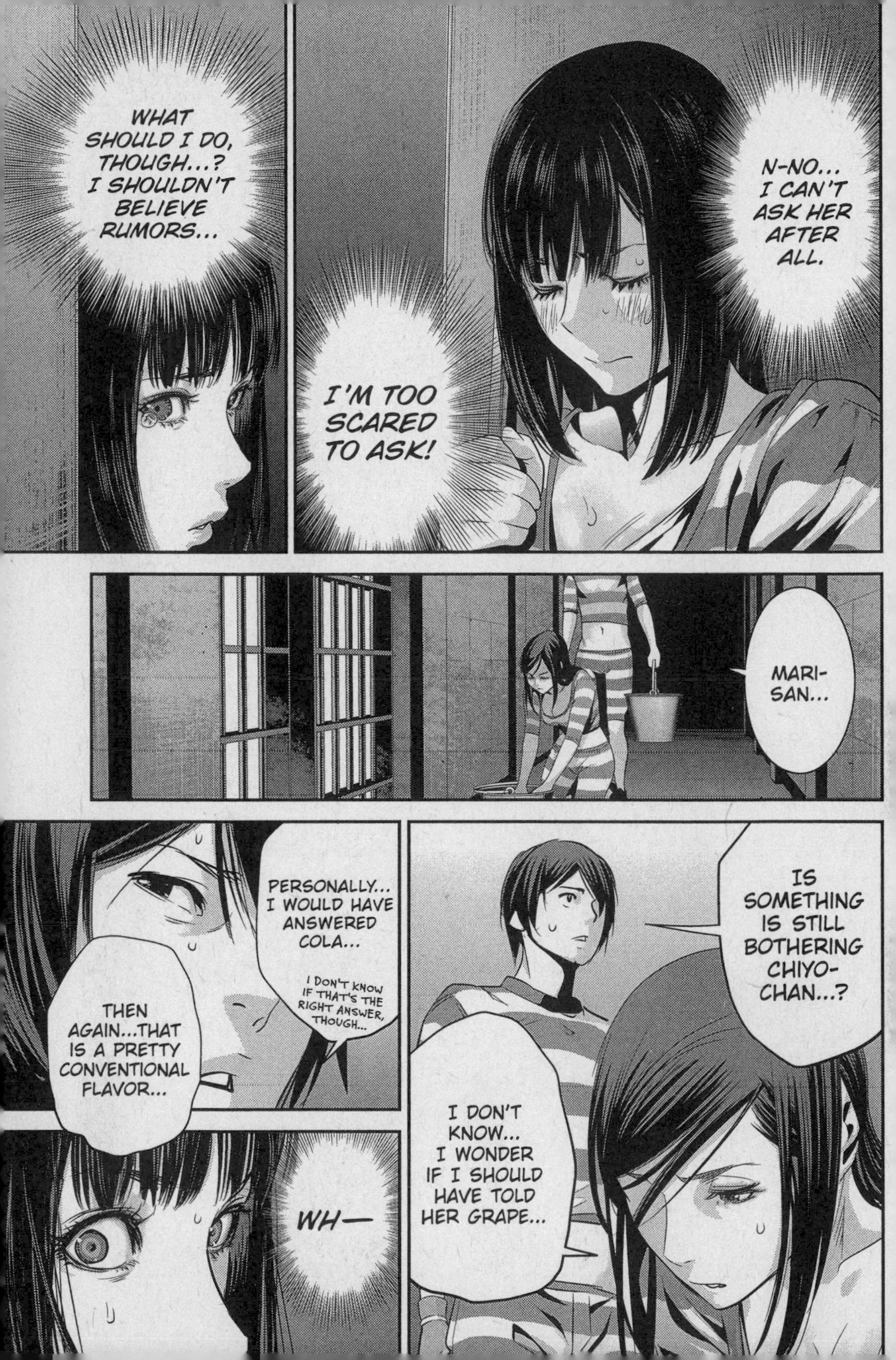
N-NO... I CAN'T ASK HER AFTER ALL.
I'M TOO SCARED TO ASK!
WHAT SHOULD I DO, THOUGH...? I SHOULDN'T BELIEVE RUMORS...
MARI-SAN...
IS SOMETHING IS STILL BOTHERING CHIYO-CHAN...?
I DON'T KNOW... I WONDER IF I SHOULD HAVE TOLD HER GRAPE...
PERSONALLY... I WOULD HAVE ANSWERED COLA...
I DON'T KNOW IF THAT'S THE RIGHT ANSWER, THOUGH...
THEN AGAIN...THAT IS A PRETTY CONVENTIONAL FLAVOR...
WH—

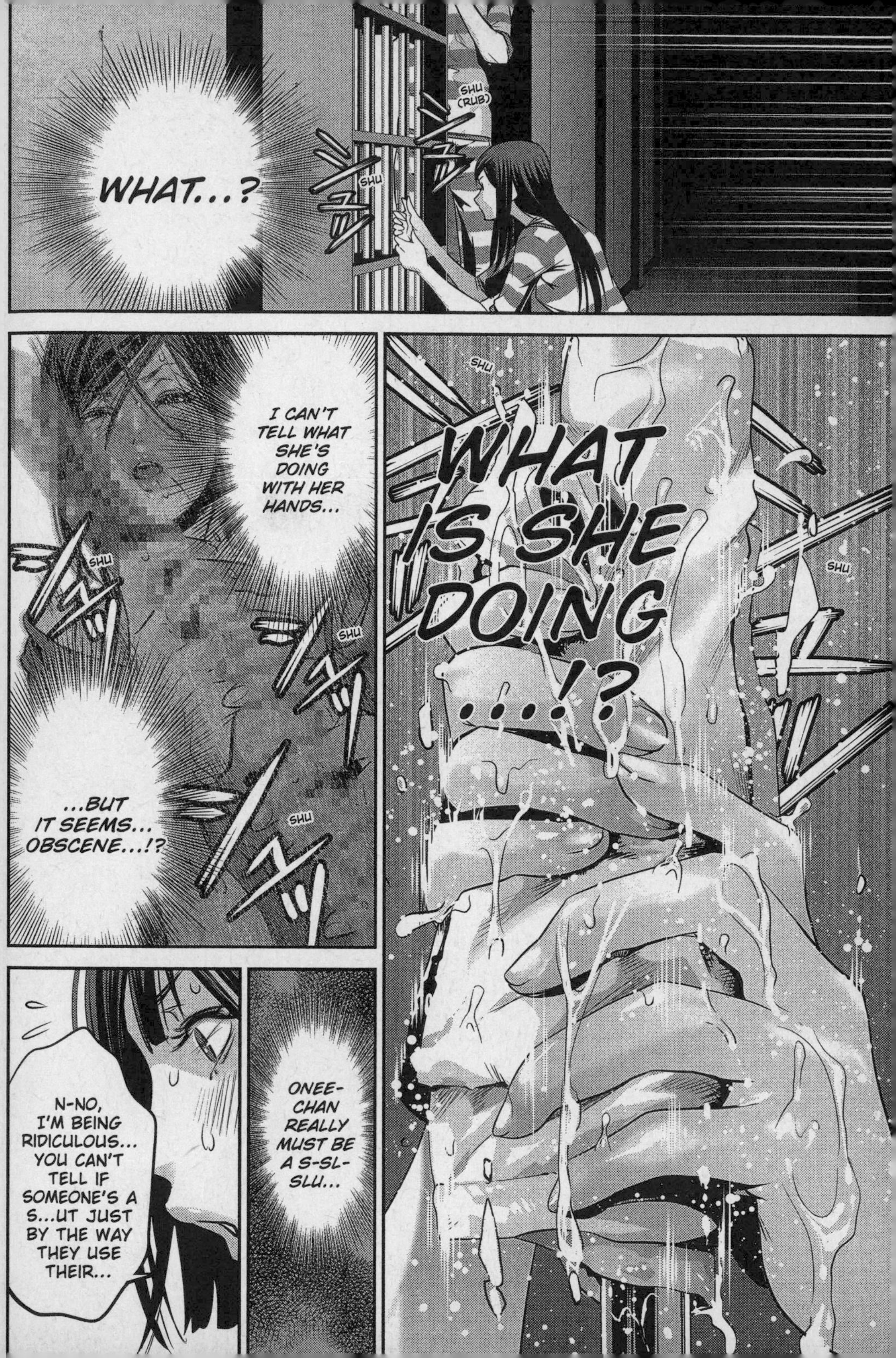
SHU (RUB)
SHU
WHAT...?
SHU
WHAT IS SHE DOING ...!?
SHU
SHU
I CAN'T TELL WHAT SHE'S DOING WITH HER HANDS...
SHU
SHU
...BUT IT SEEMS... OBSCENE...!?
SHU
ONEE-CHAN REALLY MUST BE A S-SL-SLU...
N-NO, I'M BEING RIDICULOUS... YOU CAN'T TELL IF SOMEONE'S A S...UT JUST BY THE WAY THEY USE THEIR...

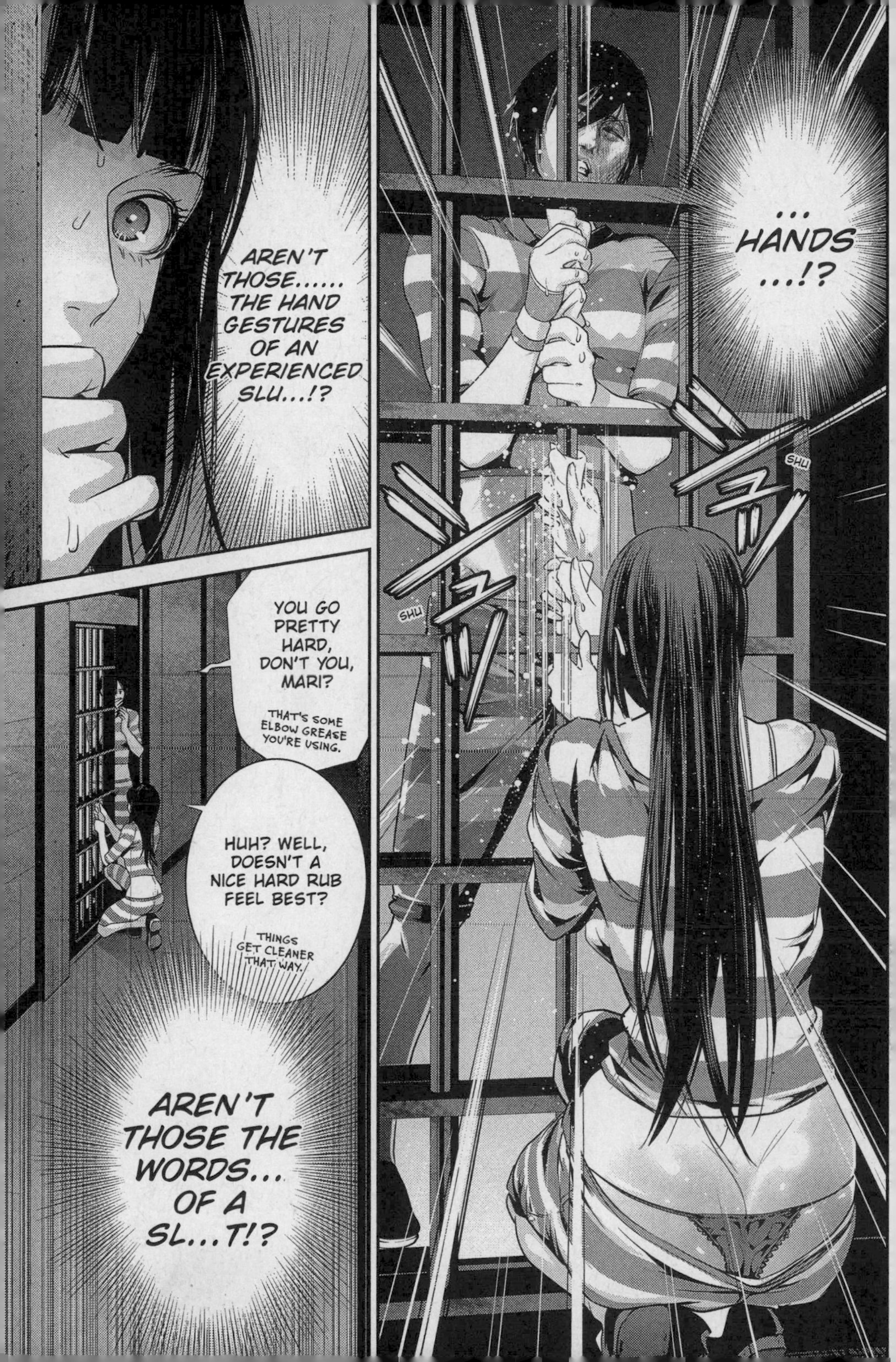

...HANDS ...!?
SHU
SHU
AREN'T THOSE...... THE HAND GESTURES OF AN EXPERIENCED SLU...!?
YOU GO PRETTY HARD, DON'T YOU, MARI?
THAT'S SOME ELBOW GREASE YOU'RE USING.
HUH? WELL, DOESN'T A NICE HARD RUB FEEL BEST?
THINGS GET CLEANER THAT WAY.
AREN'T THOSE THE WORDS... OF A SL...T!?

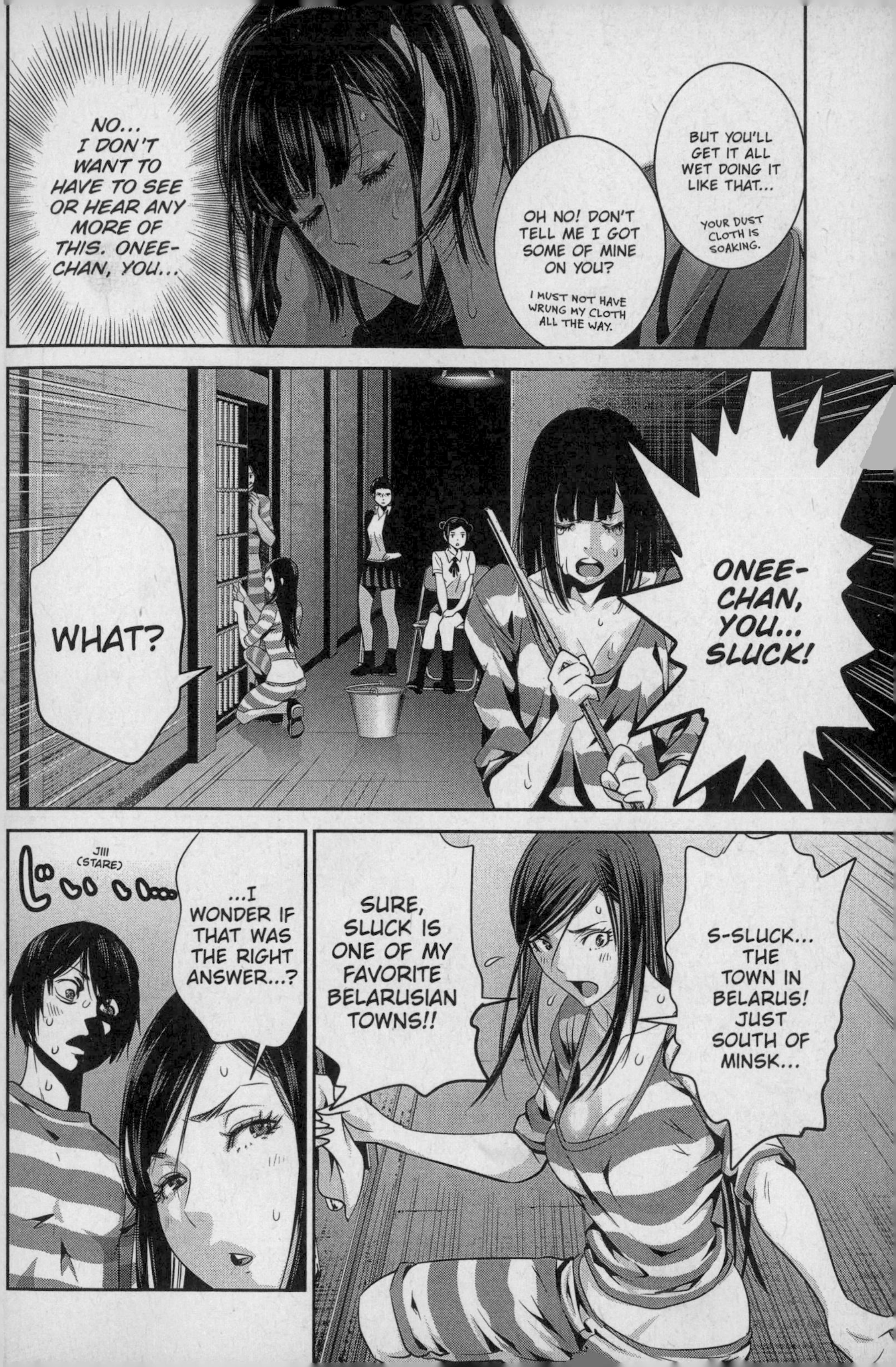
BUT YOU'LL GET IT ALL WET DOING IT LIKE THAT...
YOUR DUST CLOTH IS SOAKING.
OH NO! DON'T TELL ME I GOT SOME OF MINE ON YOU?
I MUST NOT HAVE WRUNG MY CLOTH ALL THE WAY.
NO... I DON'T WANT TO HAVE TO SEE OR HEAR ANY MORE OF THIS. ONEE-CHAN, YOU...
ONEE-CHAN, YOU... SLUCK!
WHAT?
S-SLUCK... THE TOWN IN BELARUS! JUST SOUTH OF MINSK...
SURE, SLUCK IS ONE OF MY FAVORITE BELARUSIAN TOWNS!!
...I WONDER IF THAT WAS THE RIGHT ANSWER...?
JIII (STARE)

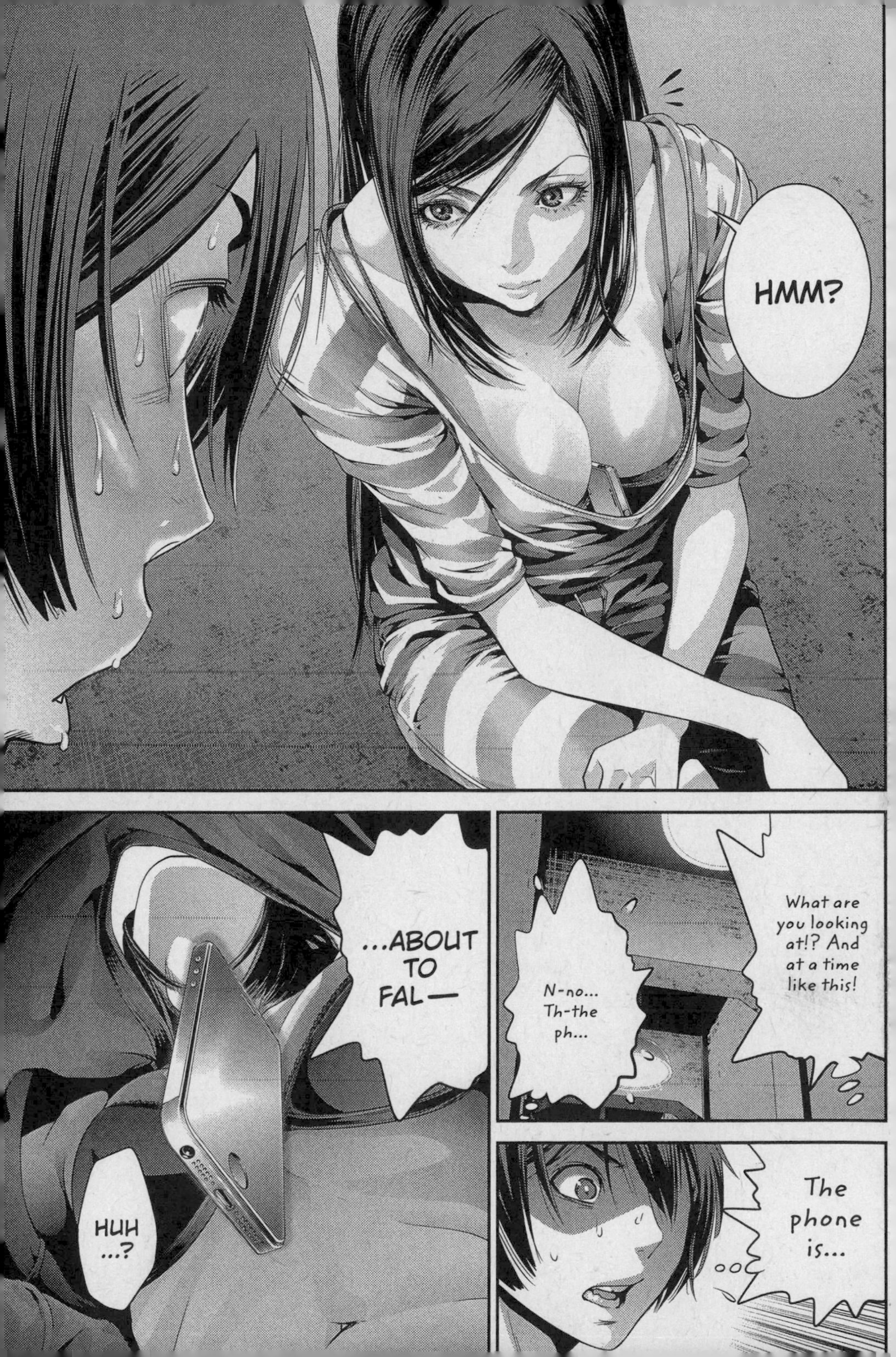
HMM?
What are you looking at!? And at a time like this!
N-no... Th-the ph...
The phone is...
...ABOUT TO FAL—
HUH ...?

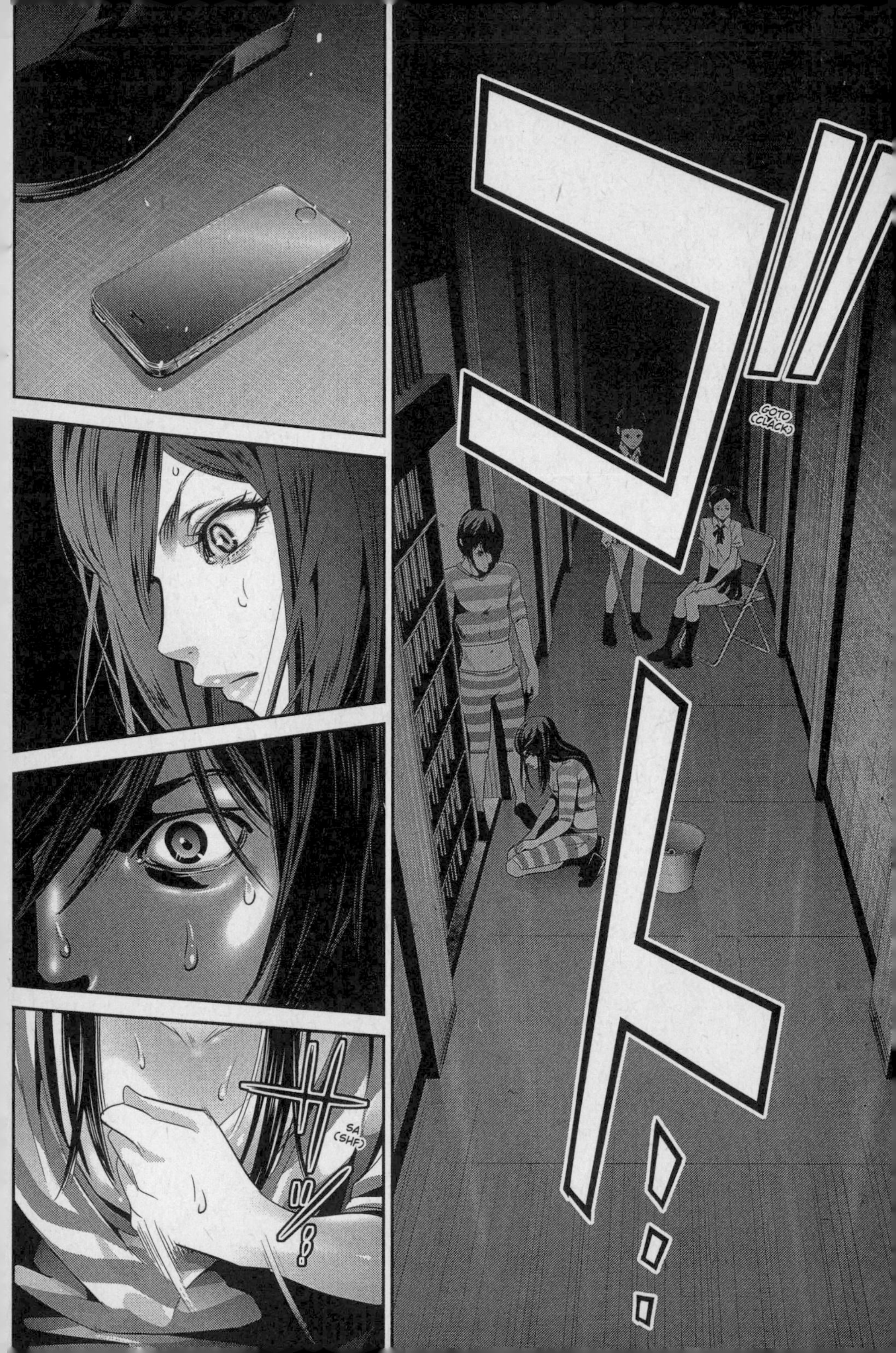
GOTO (CLACK)
SA (SHF)

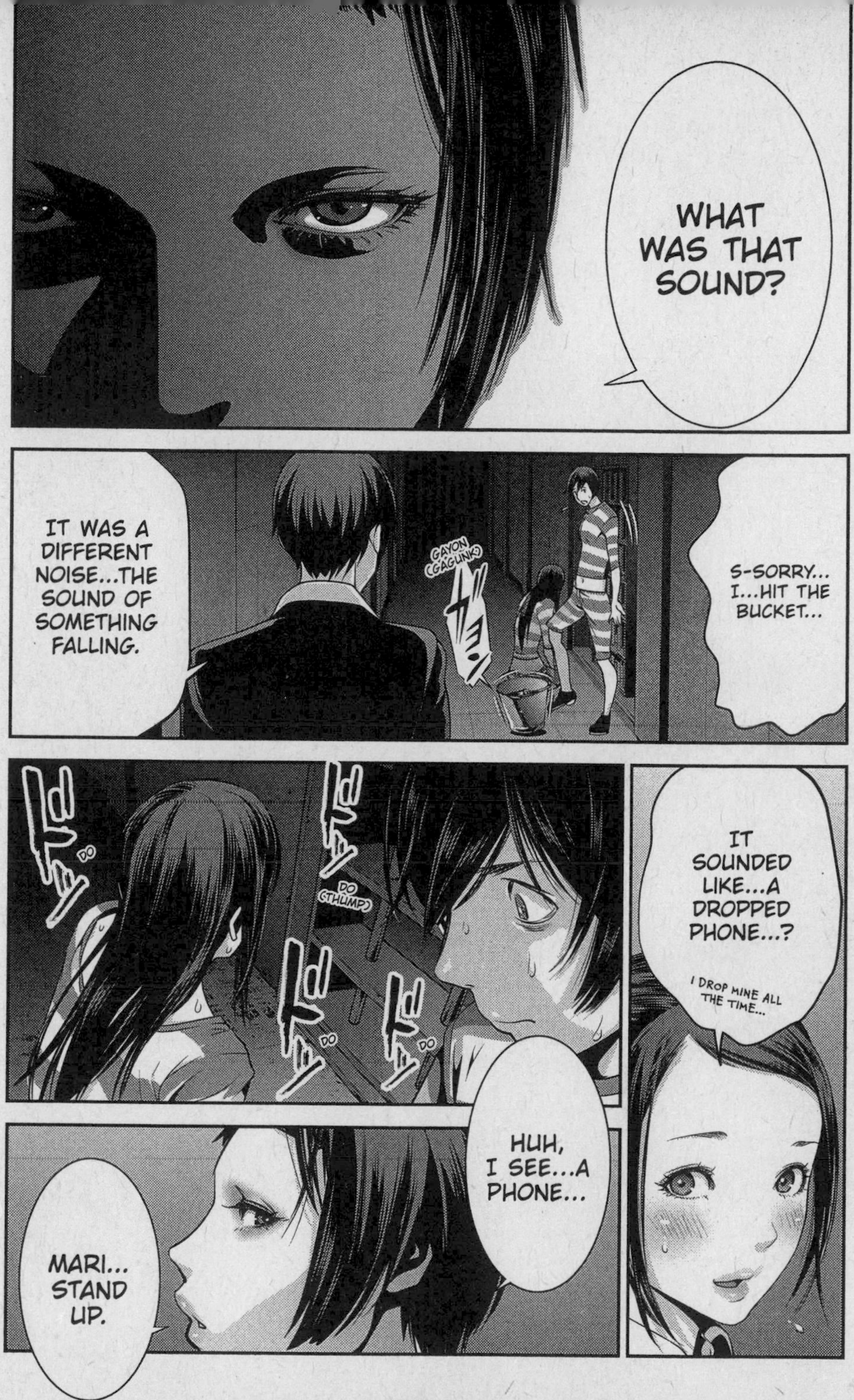
WHAT WAS THAT SOUND?
S-SORRY... I...HIT THE BUCKET...
GAYON (GAGUNK)
IT WAS A DIFFERENT NOISE...THE SOUND OF SOMETHING FALLING.
IT SOUNDED LIKE...A DROPPED PHONE...?
I DROP MINE ALL THE TIME...
DO
DO (THUMP)
DO
DO
HUH, I SEE...A PHONE...
MARI... STAND UP.

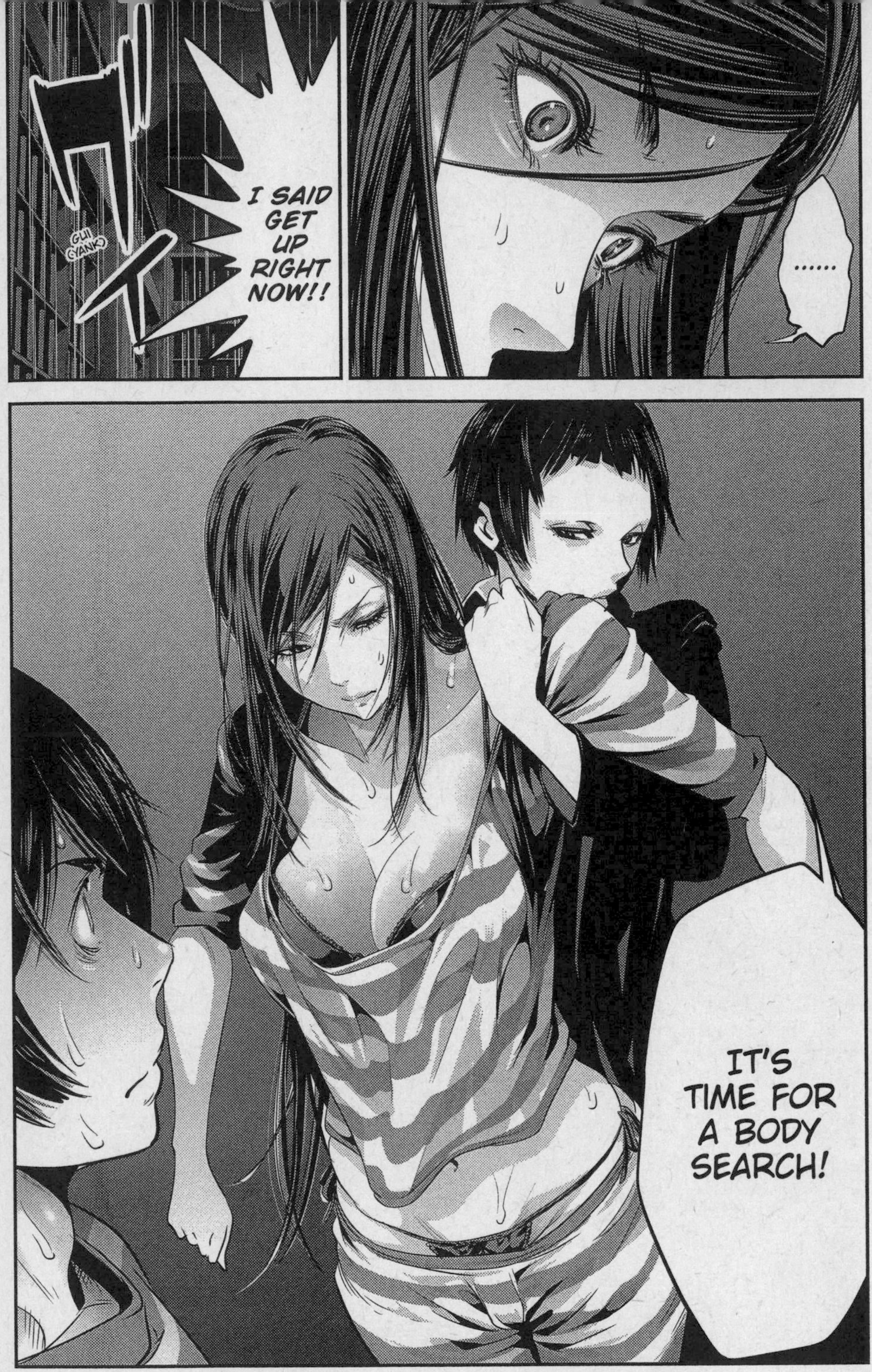
......
I SAID GET UP RIGHT NOW!!
GUI (YANK)
IT'S TIME FOR A BODY SEARCH!

CHAPTER 137: THE PRESTIGE

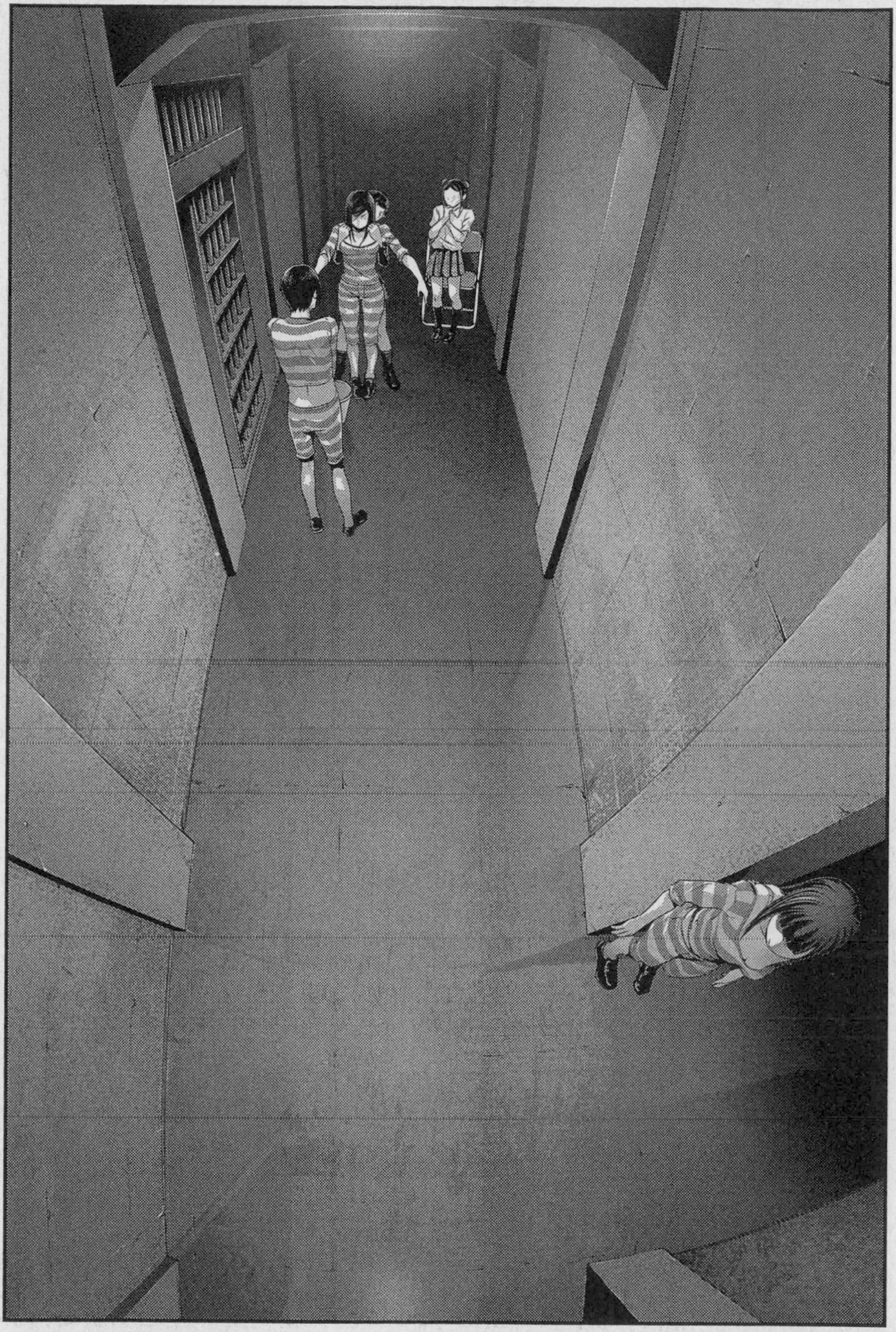

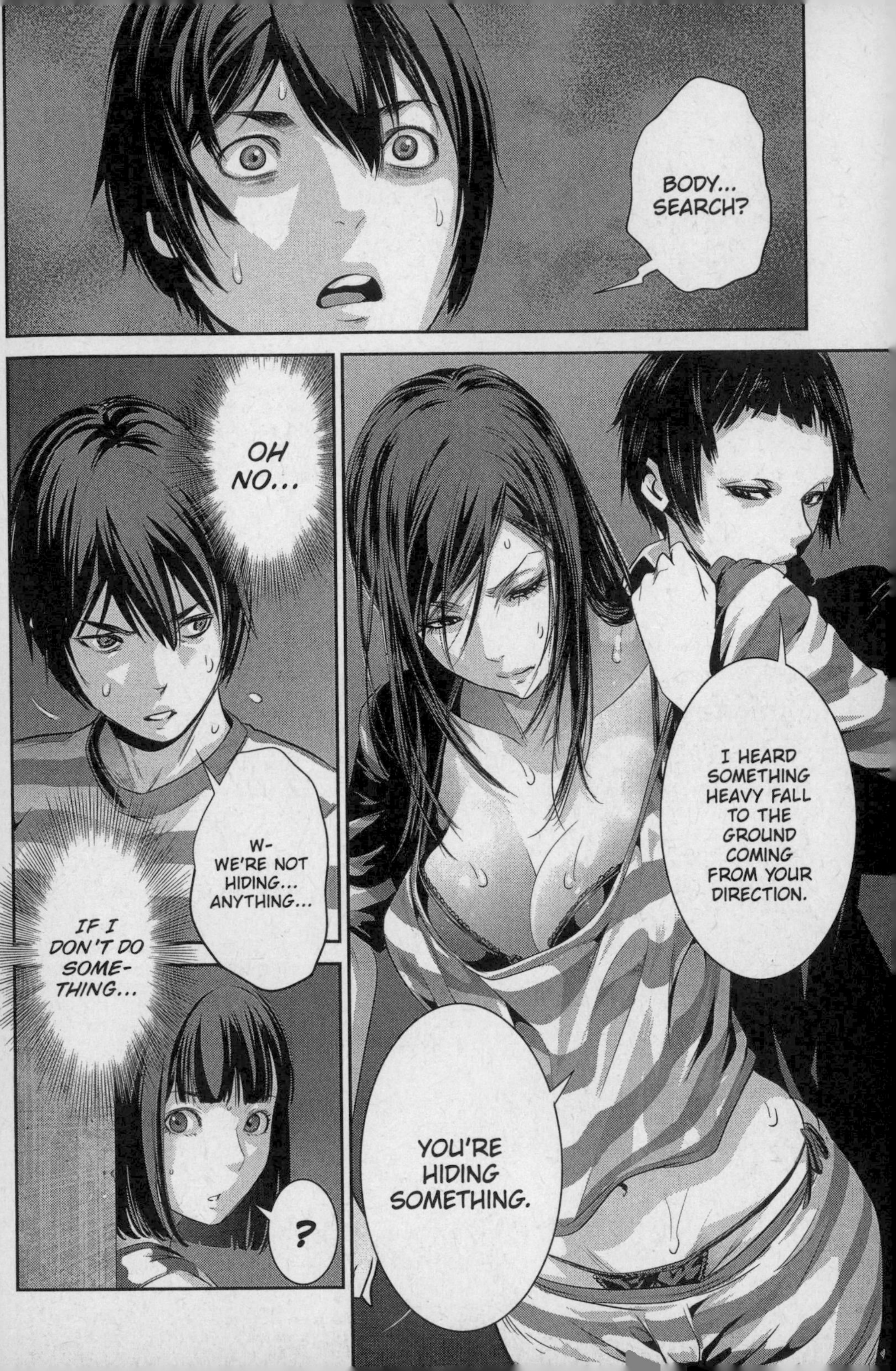
BODY... SEARCH?
I HEARD SOMETHING HEAVY FALL TO THE GROUND COMING FROM YOUR DIRECTION.
YOU'RE HIDING SOMETHING.
OH NO...
W- WE'RE NOT HIDING... ANYTHING...
IF I DON'T DO SOME-THING...
?

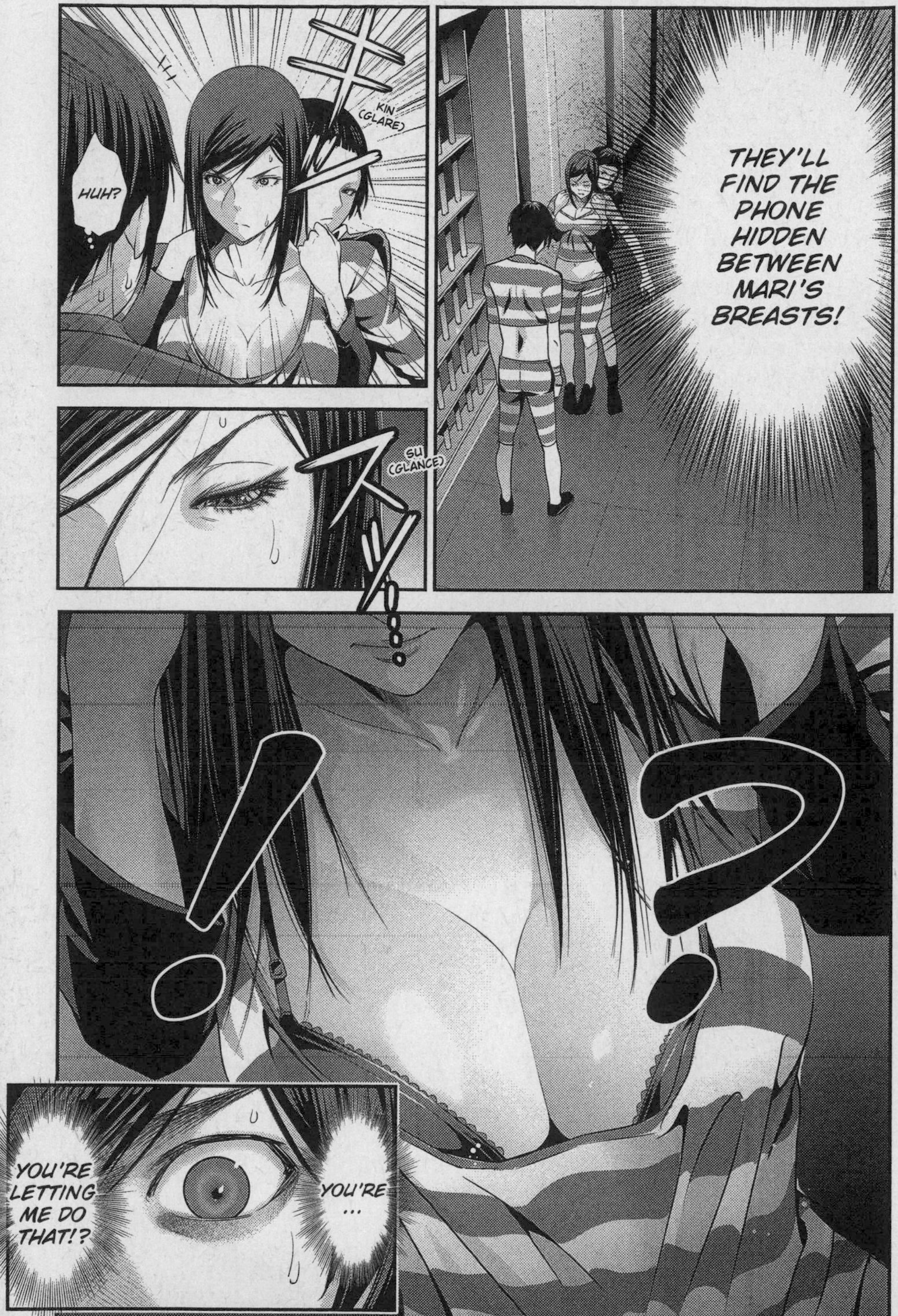

THEY'LL FIND THE PHONE HIDDEN BETWEEN MARI'S BREASTS!
KIN (GLARE)
HUH?
SU (GLANCE)
YOU'RE ...
YOU'RE LETTING ME DO THAT!?

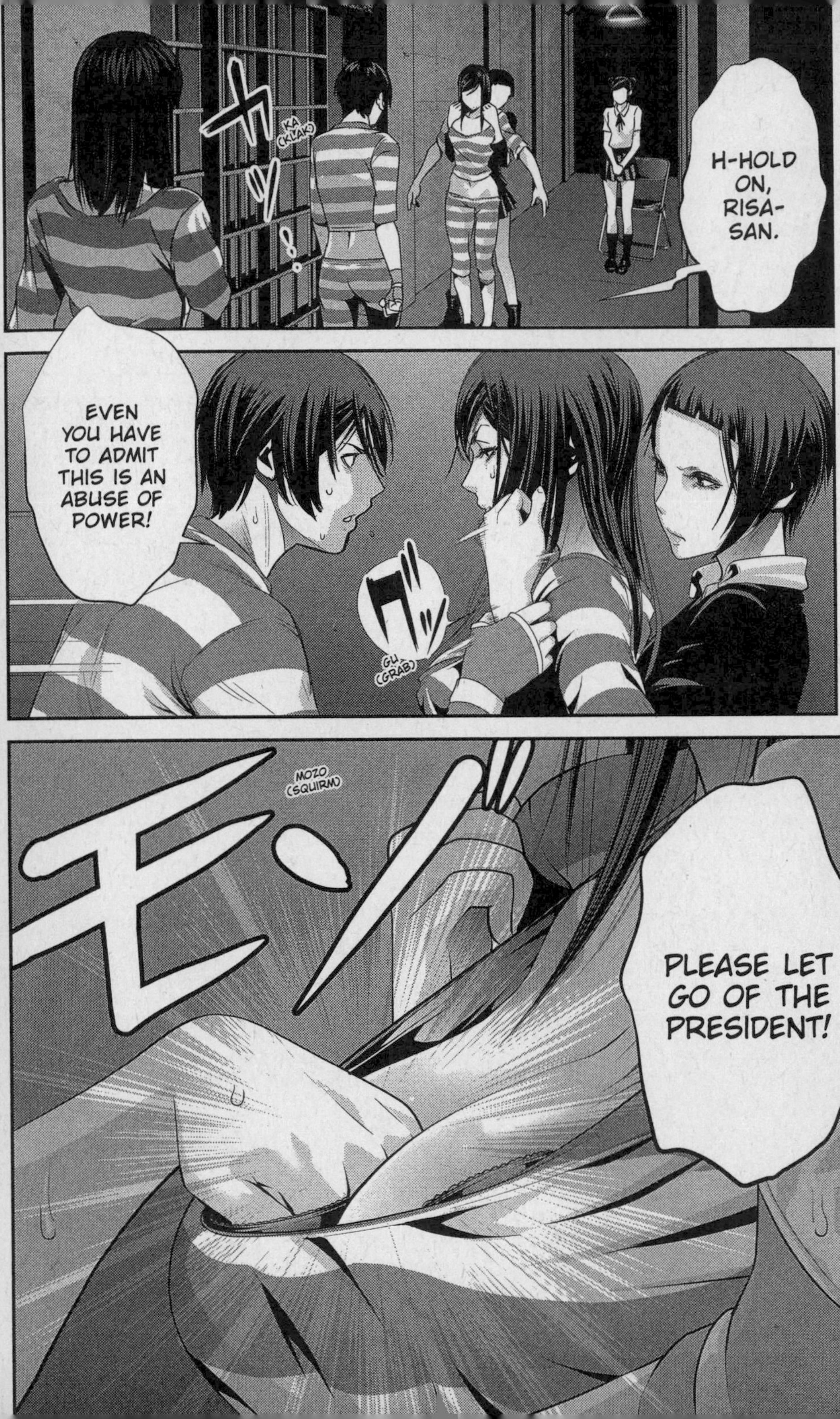
H-HOLD ON, RISA-SAN.
KA (KLAK)
EVEN YOU HAVE TO ADMIT THIS IS AN ABUSE OF POWER!
GU (GRAB)
MOZO (SQUIRM)
PLEASE LET GO OF THE PRESIDENT!

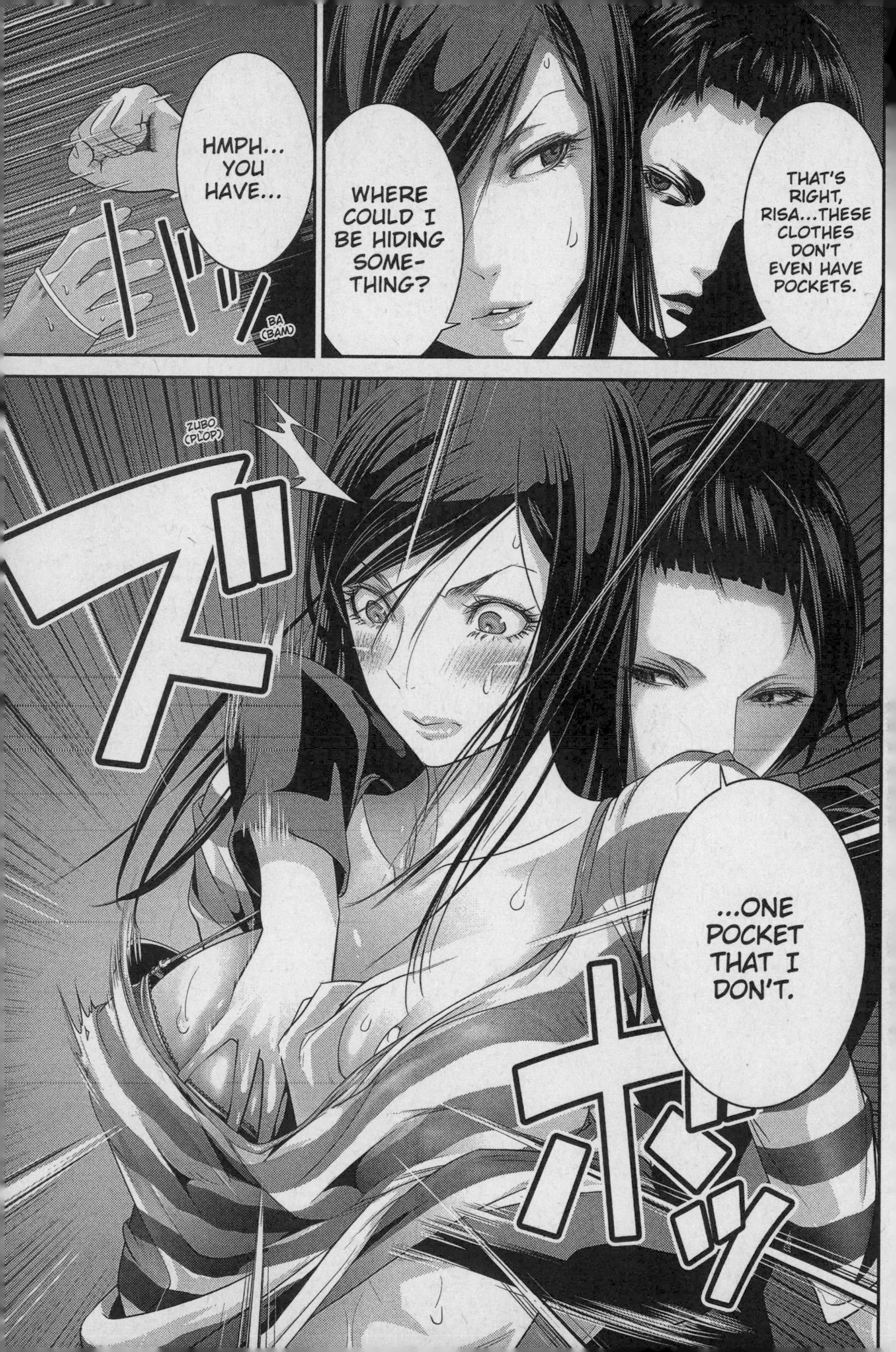

THAT'S RIGHT, RISA...THESE CLOTHES DON'T EVEN HAVE POCKETS.
WHERE COULD I BE HIDING SOMETHING?
HMPH... YOU HAVE...
BA (BAM)
ZUBO (PLOP)
...ONE POCKET THAT I DON'T.

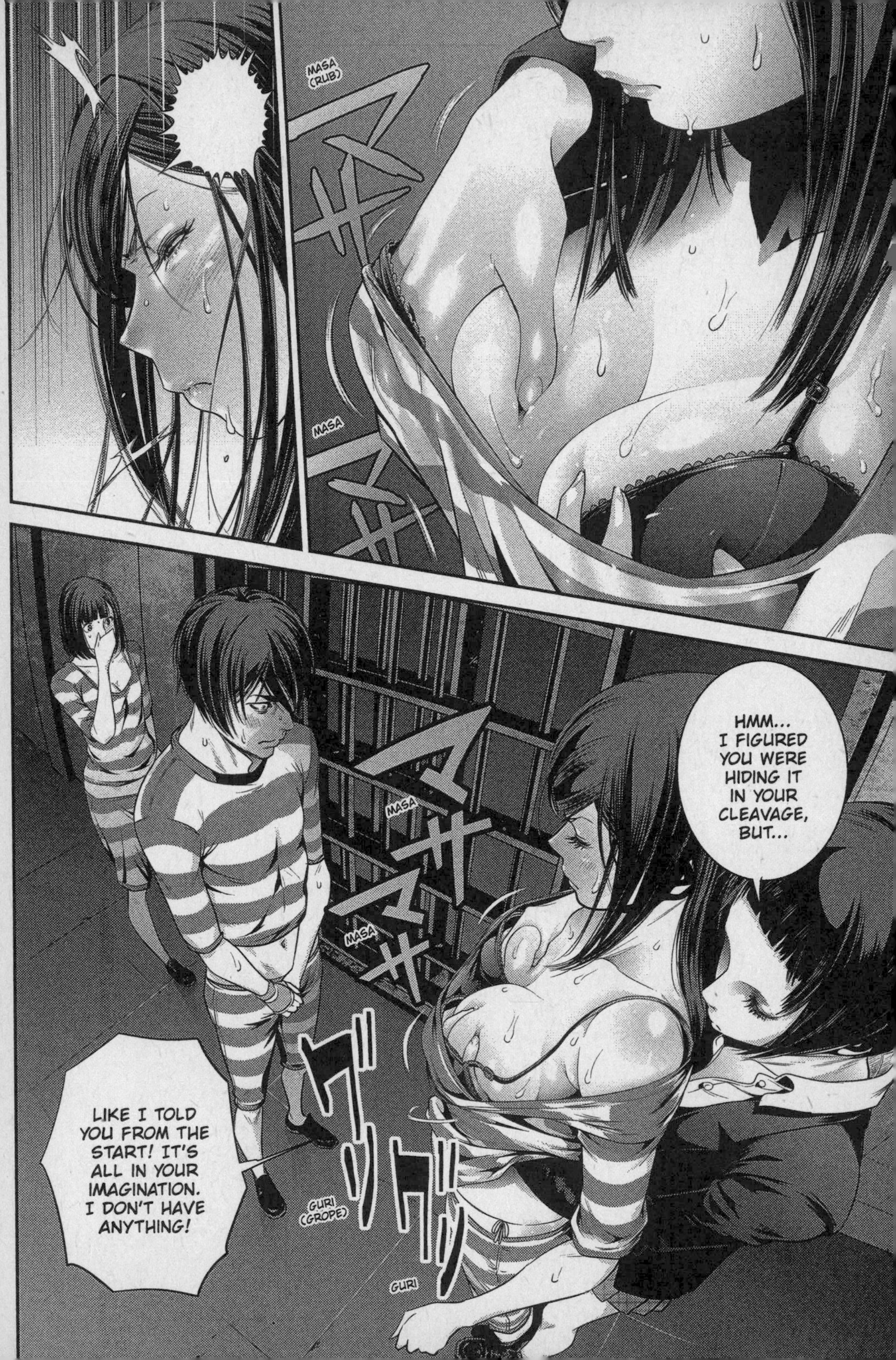
MASA (RUB)
MASA
HMM... I FIGURED YOU WERE HIDING IT IN YOUR CLEAVAGE, BUT...
MASA
MASA
GURI (GROPE)
GURI
LIKE I TOLD YOU FROM THE START! IT'S ALL IN YOUR IMAGINATION. I DON'T HAVE ANYTHING!

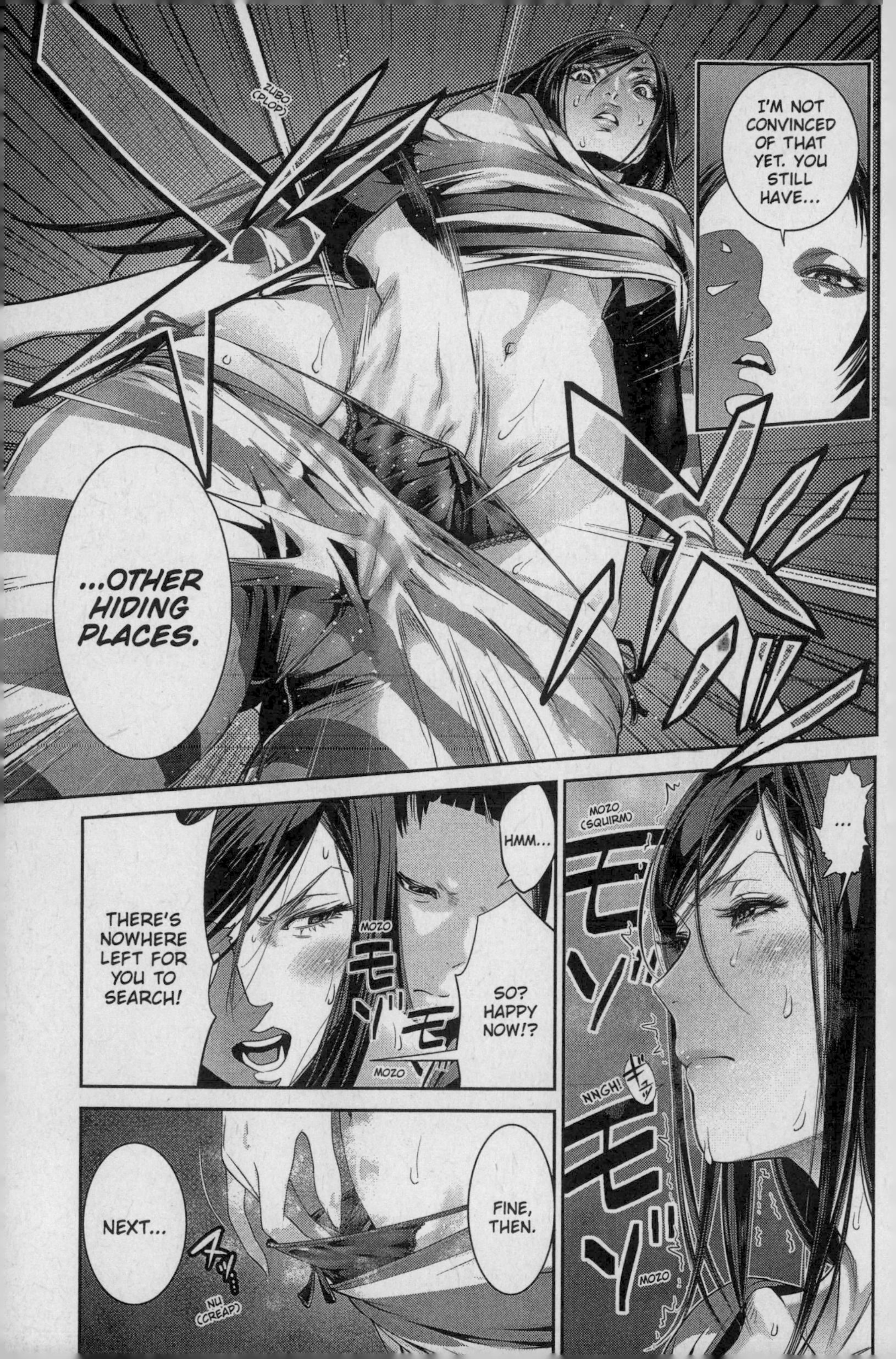
I'M NOT CONVINCED OF THAT YET. YOU STILL HAVE...
ZUBO (PLOP)
...OTHER HIDING PLACES.
MOZO (SQUIRM)
...
NNGH!
MOZO
HMM...
MOZO
SO? HAPPY NOW!?
THERE'S NOWHERE LEFT FOR YOU TO SEARCH!
MOZO
FINE, THEN.
NEXT...
NU (CREAP)

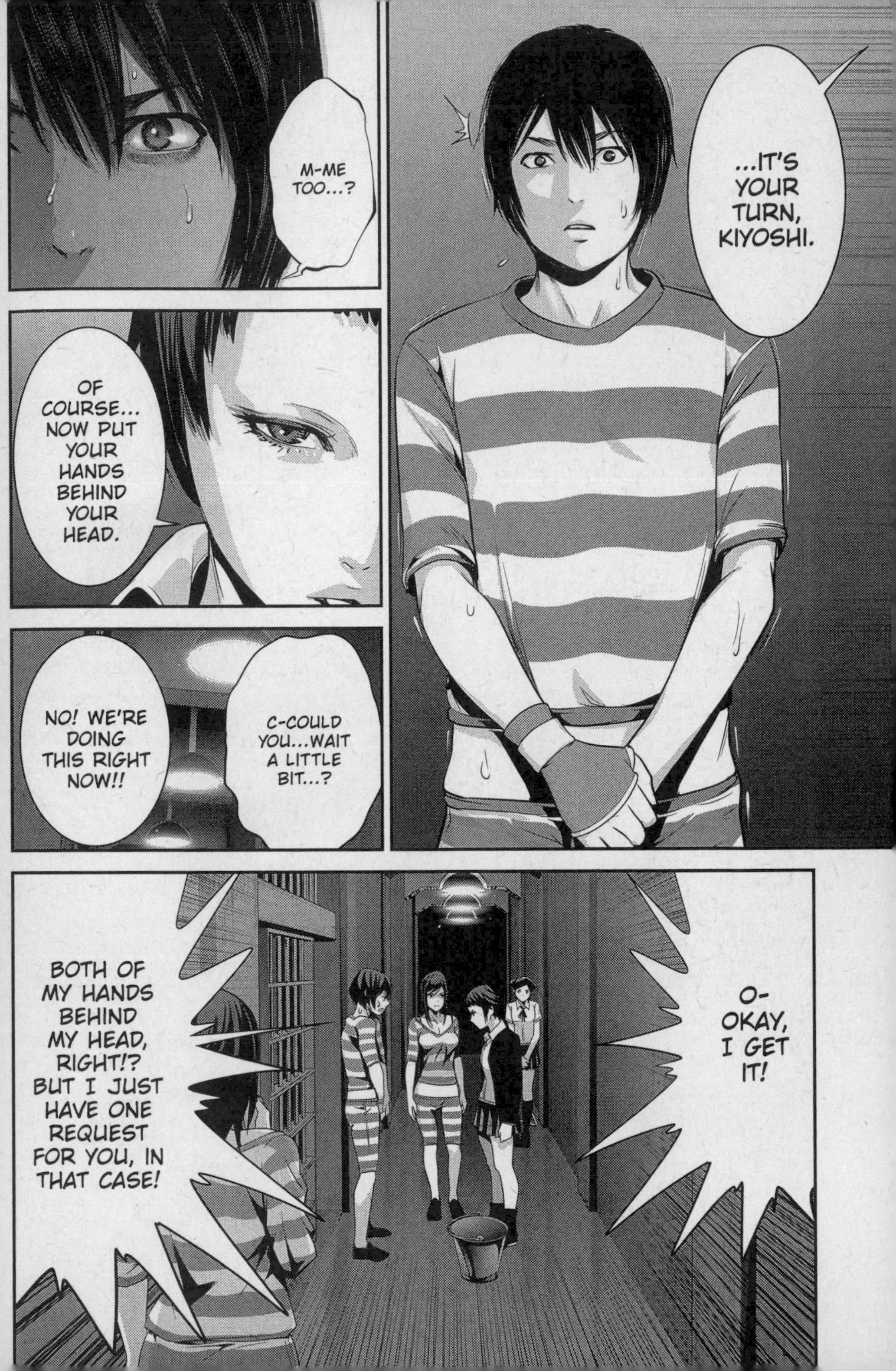
...IT'S YOUR TURN, KIYOSHI.
M-ME TOO...?
OF COURSE... NOW PUT YOUR HANDS BEHIND YOUR HEAD.
C-COULD YOU...WAIT A LITTLE BIT...?
NO! WE'RE DOING THIS RIGHT NOW!!
O-OKAY, I GET IT!
BOTH OF MY HANDS BEHIND MY HEAD, RIGHT!? BUT I JUST HAVE ONE REQUEST FOR YOU, IN THAT CASE!

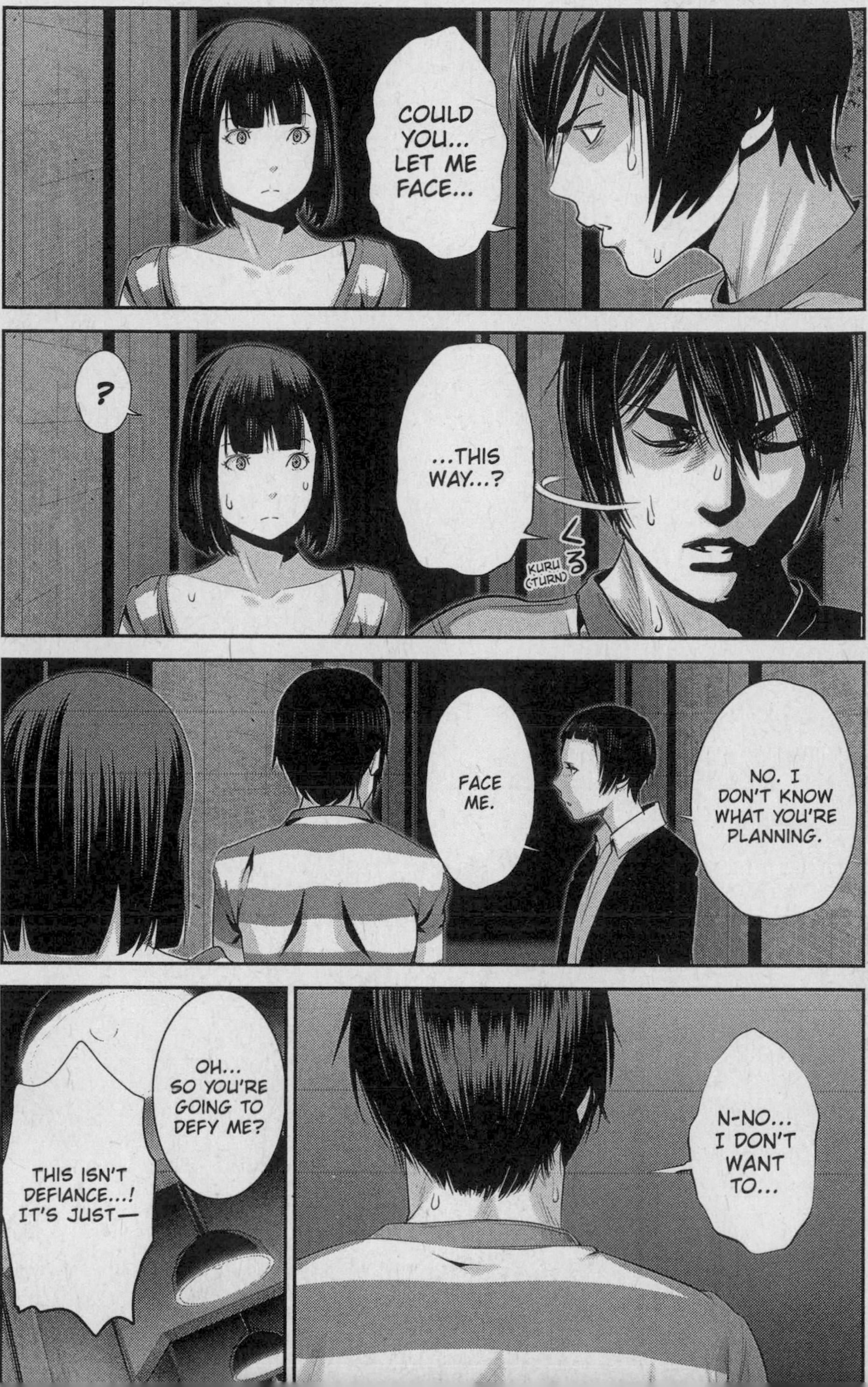

COULD YOU... LET ME FACE...
...THIS WAY...?
くる
KURU (TURN)
?
NO. I DON'T KNOW WHAT YOU'RE PLANNING.
FACE ME.
N-NO... I DON'T WANT TO...
OH... SO YOU'RE GOING TO DEFY ME?
THIS ISN'T DEFIANCE...! IT'S JUST—

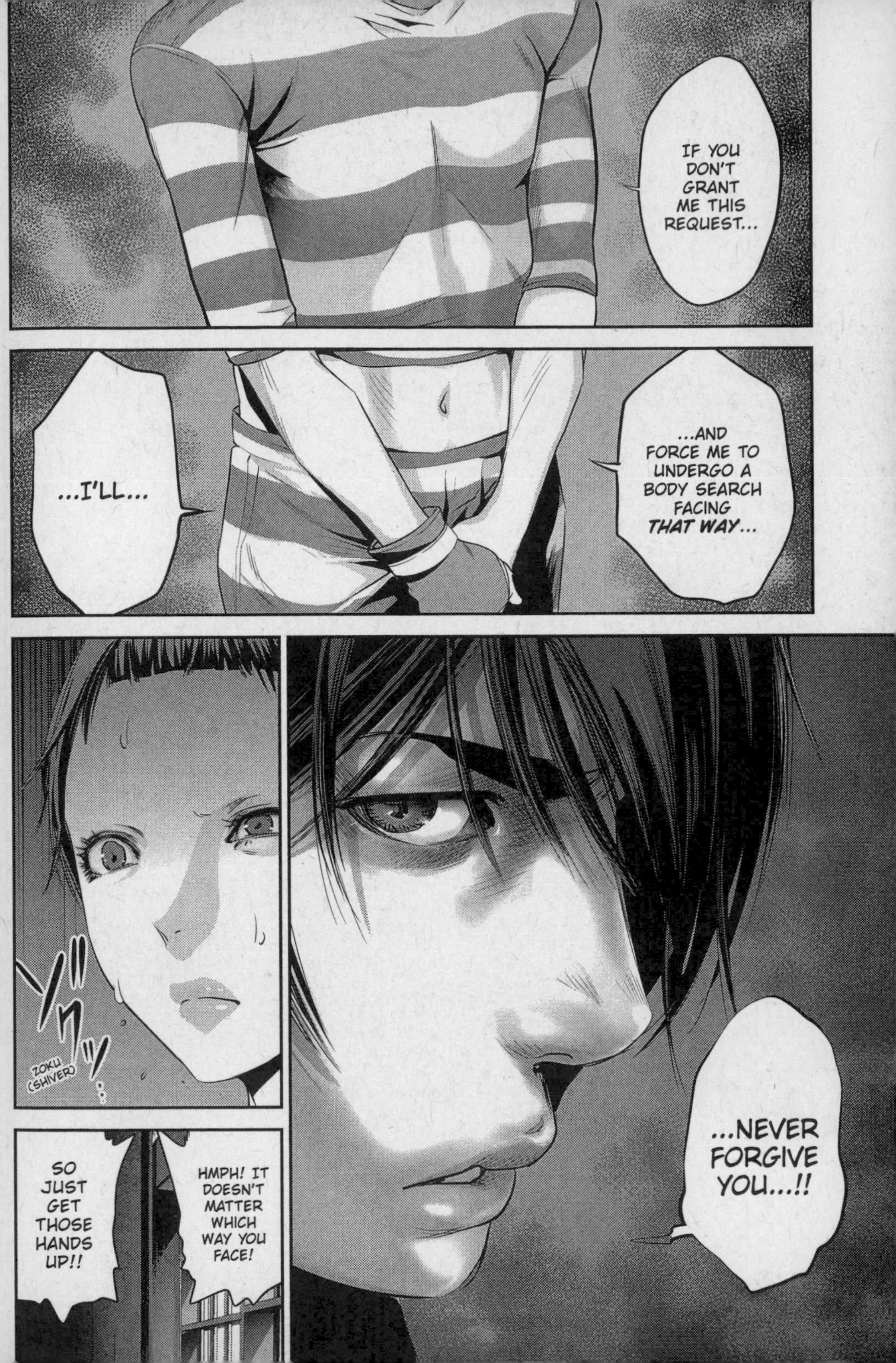
IF YOU DON'T GRANT ME THIS REQUEST...
...AND FORCE ME TO UNDERGO A BODY SEARCH FACING *THAT WAY*...
...I'LL...
...NEVER FORGIVE YOU...!!
ZOKU (SHIVER)
HMPH! IT DOESN'T MATTER WHICH WAY YOU FACE!
SO JUST GET THOSE HANDS UP!!

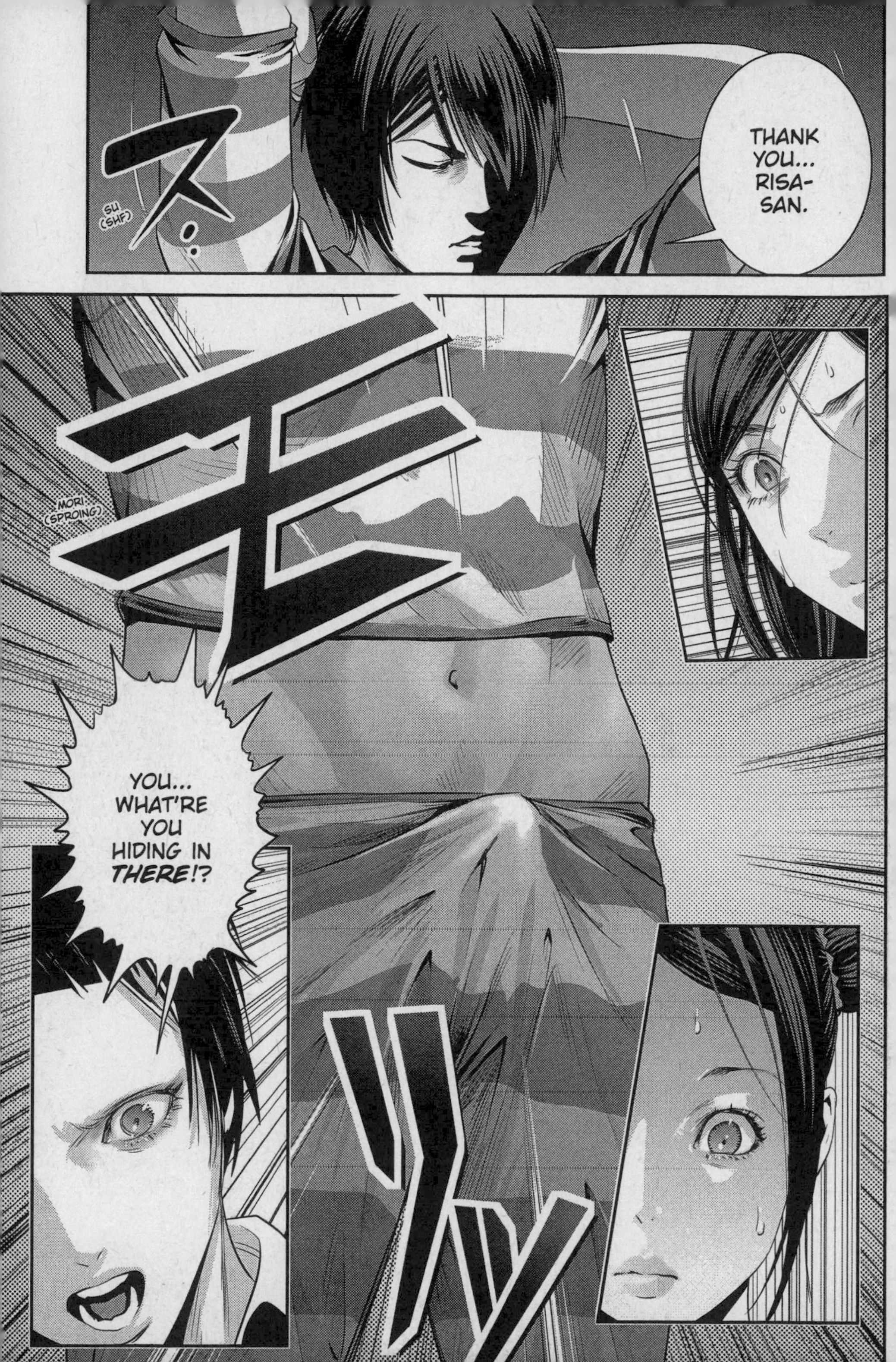
THANK YOU... RISA-SAN.
SU (SHF)
MORI (SPROING)
YOU... WHAT'RE YOU HIDING IN THERE!?

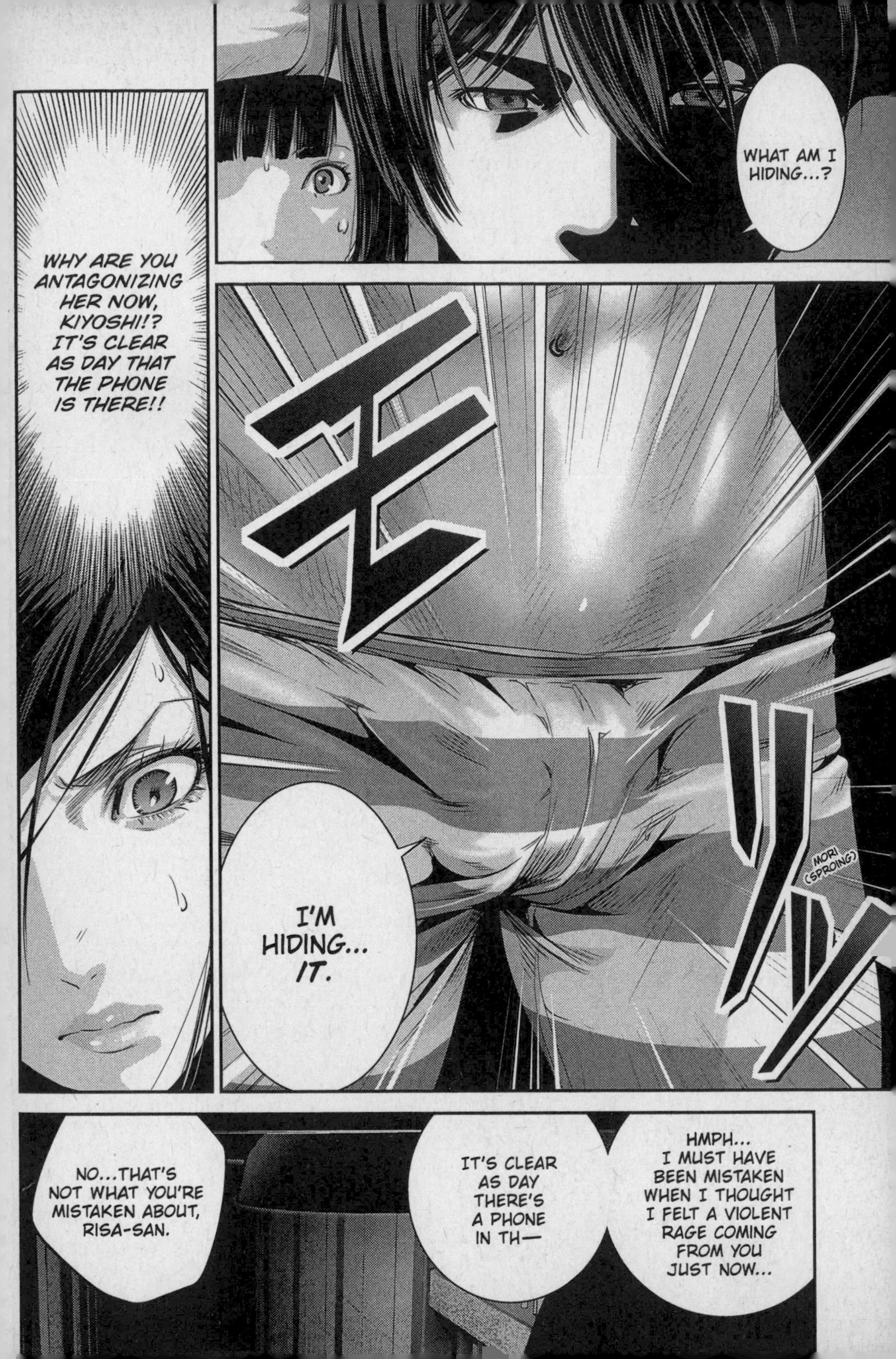
WHAT AM I HIDING...?
I'M HIDING... IT.
MORI (SPROING)
WHY ARE YOU ANTAGONIZING HER NOW, KIYOSHI!? IT'S CLEAR AS DAY THAT THE PHONE IS THERE!!
HMPH... I MUST HAVE BEEN MISTAKEN WHEN I THOUGHT I FELT A VIOLENT RAGE COMING FROM YOU JUST NOW...
IT'S CLEAR AS DAY THERE'S A PHONE IN TH—
NO...THAT'S NOT WHAT YOU'RE MISTAKEN ABOUT, RISA-SAN.

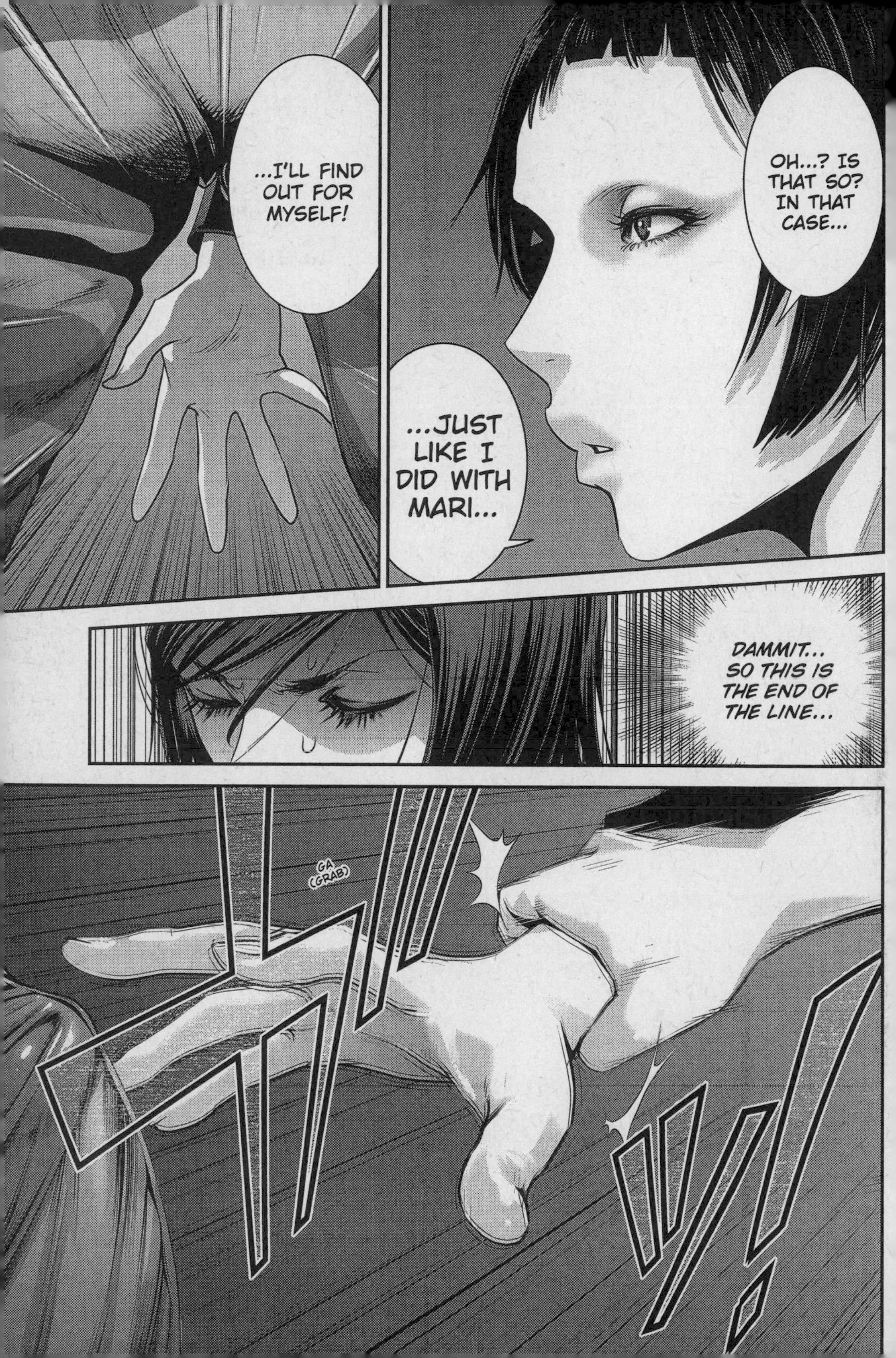
OH...? IS THAT SO? IN THAT CASE...
...JUST LIKE I DID WITH MARI...
...I'LL FIND OUT FOR MYSELF!
DAMMIT... SO THIS IS THE END OF THE LINE...
GA (GRAB)

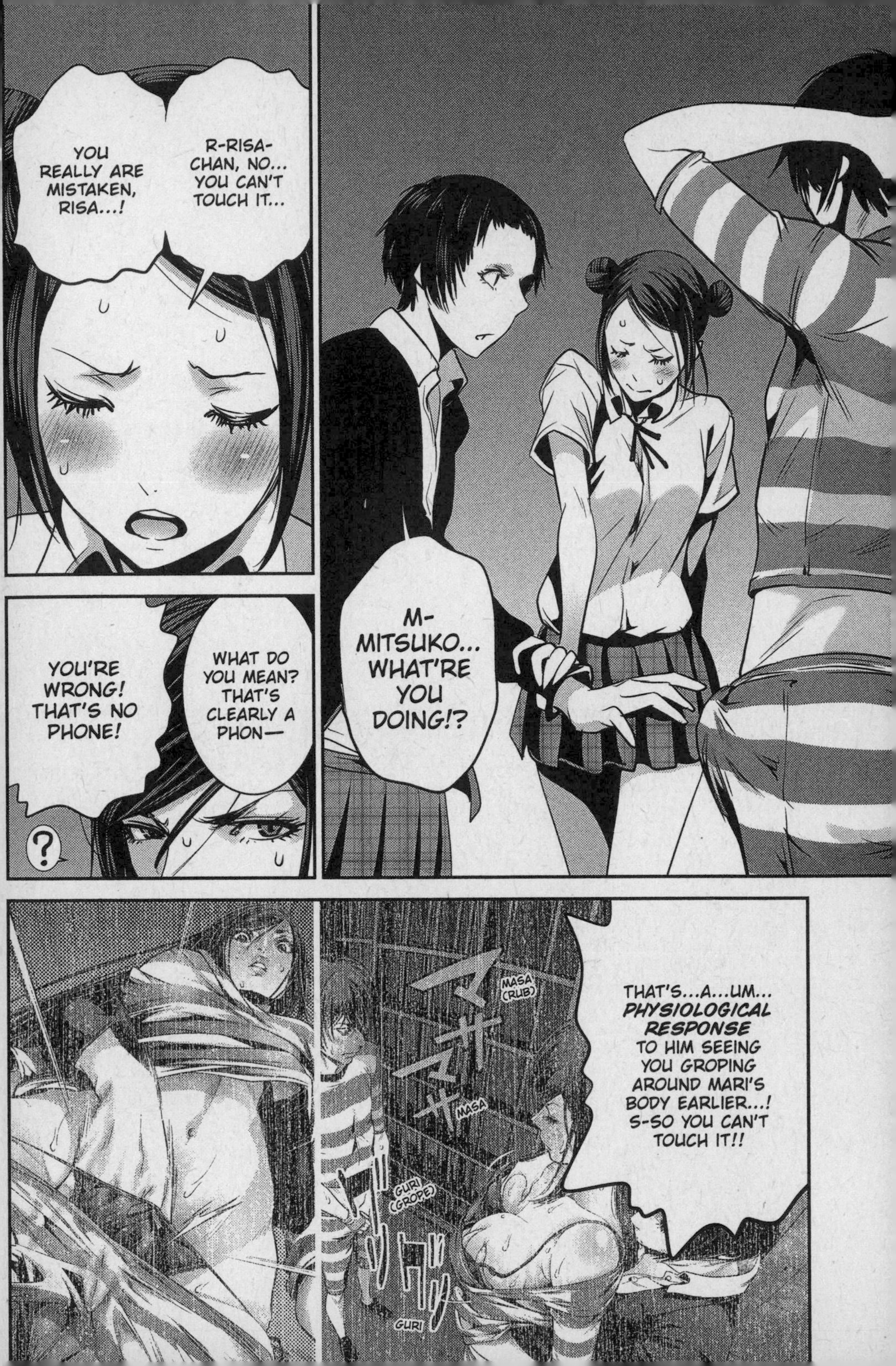
R-RISA-CHAN, NO... YOU CAN'T TOUCH IT...
YOU REALLY ARE MISTAKEN, RISA...!
M-MITSUKO... WHAT'RE YOU DOING!?
WHAT DO YOU MEAN? THAT'S CLEARLY A PHON—
YOU'RE WRONG! THAT'S NO PHONE!
?
THAT'S...A...UM... PHYSIOLOGICAL RESPONSE TO HIM SEEING YOU GROPING AROUND MARI'S BODY EARLIER...! S-SO YOU CAN'T TOUCH IT!!
MASA (RUB)
MASA
GURI (GROPE)
GURI

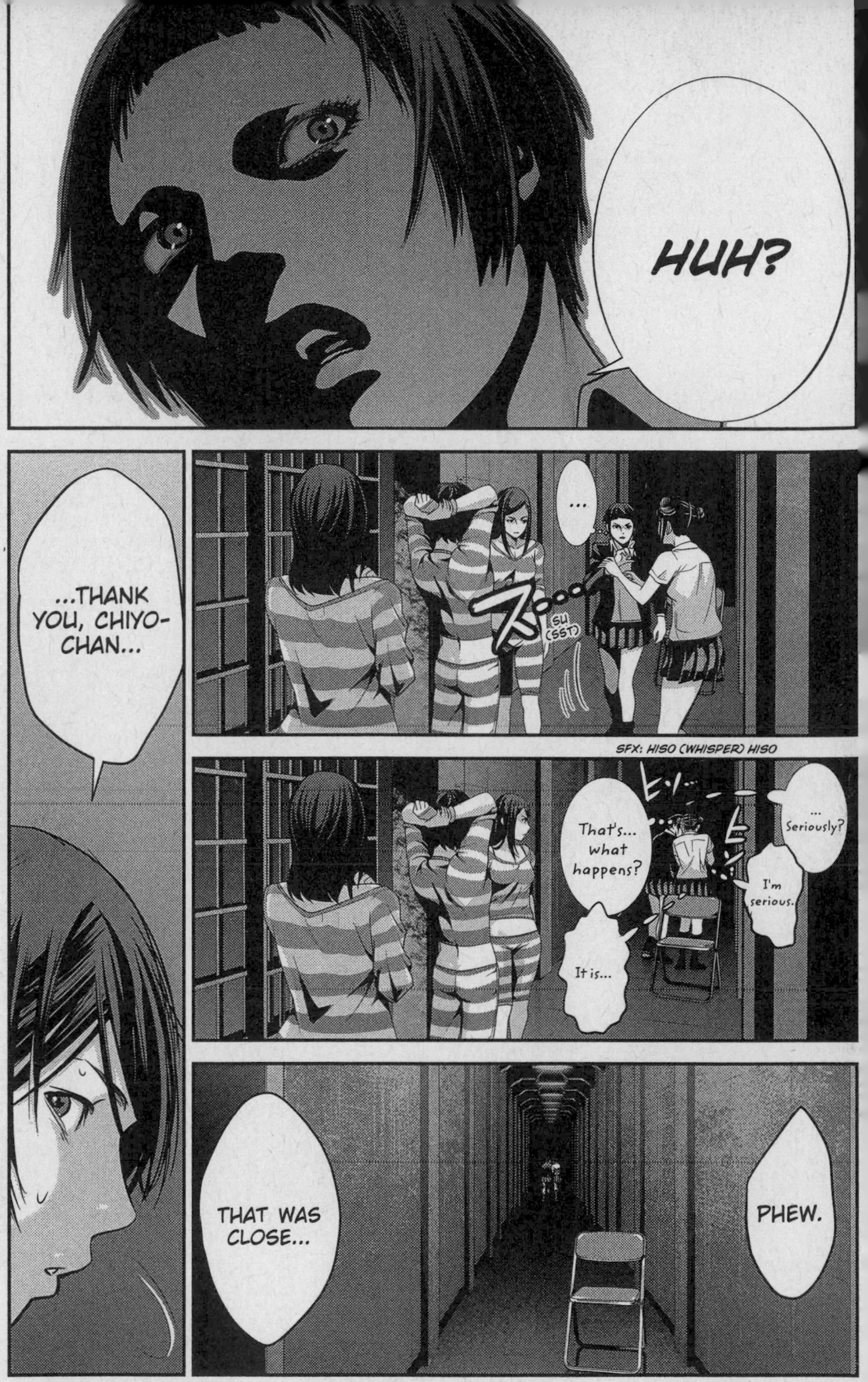
HUH?
...
SU (SST)
SFX: HISO (WHISPER) HISO
... Seriously?
I'm serious.
That's... what happens?
It is...
...THANK YOU, CHIYO-CHAN...
PHEW.
THAT WAS CLOSE...

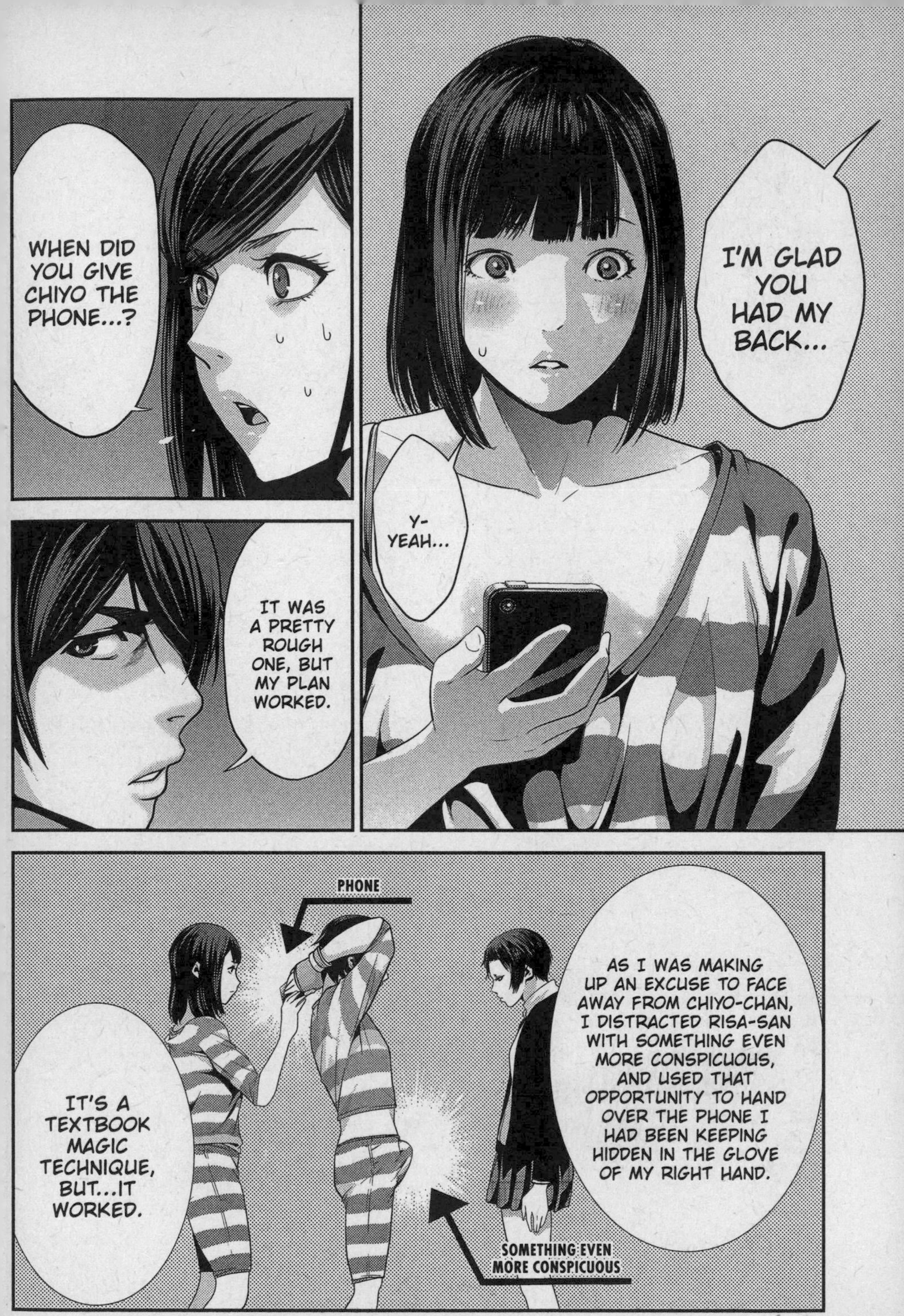
I'M GLAD YOU HAD MY BACK...
Y-YEAH...
WHEN DID YOU GIVE CHIYO THE PHONE...?
IT WAS A PRETTY ROUGH ONE, BUT MY PLAN WORKED.
AS I WAS MAKING UP AN EXCUSE TO FACE AWAY FROM CHIYO-CHAN, I DISTRACTED RISA-SAN WITH SOMETHING EVEN MORE CONSPICUOUS, AND USED THAT OPPORTUNITY TO HAND OVER THE PHONE I HAD BEEN KEEPING HIDDEN IN THE GLOVE OF MY RIGHT HAND.
PHONE
SOMETHING EVEN MORE CONSPICUOUS
IT'S A TEXTBOOK MAGIC TECHNIQUE, BUT...IT WORKED.

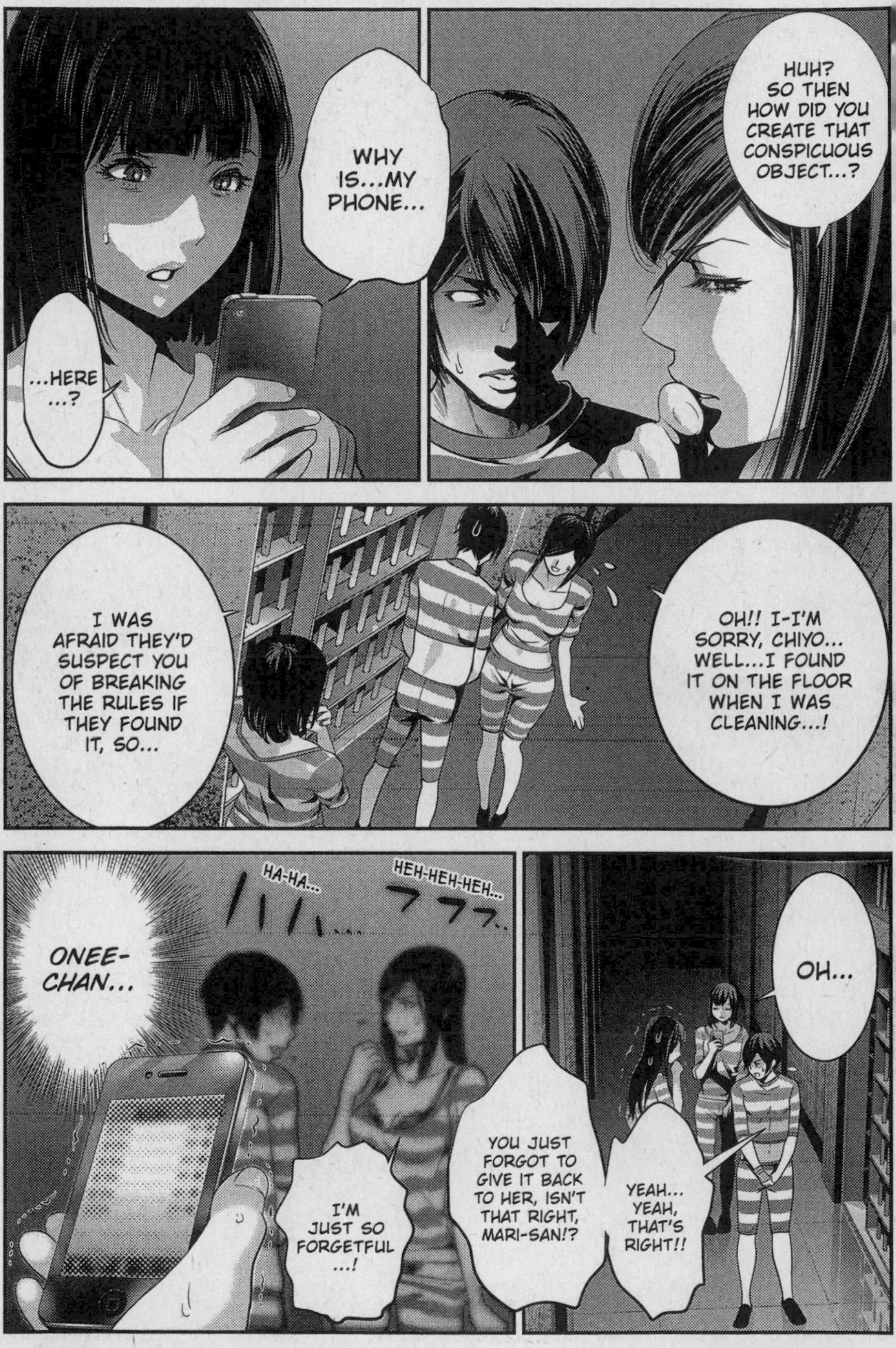
HUH? SO THEN HOW DID YOU CREATE THAT CONSPICUOUS OBJECT...?
WHY IS...MY PHONE...
...HERE ...?
OH!! I-I'M SORRY, CHIYO... WELL...I FOUND IT ON THE FLOOR WHEN I WAS CLEANING...!
I WAS AFRAID THEY'D SUSPECT YOU OF BREAKING THE RULES IF THEY FOUND IT, SO...
OH...
YEAH... YEAH, THAT'S RIGHT!!
YOU JUST FORGOT TO GIVE IT BACK TO HER, ISN'T THAT RIGHT, MARI-SAN!?
HEH-HEH-HEH...
HA-HA...
I'M JUST SO FORGETFUL ...!
ONEE-CHAN...

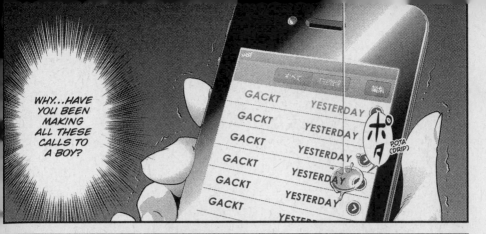

WHY...HAVE YOU BEEN MAKING ALL THESE CALLS TO A BOY?

GACKT YESTERDAY
GACKT YESTERDAY
GACKT YESTERDAY
GACKT YESTERDAY
GACKT YESTERDAY
GACKT YESTERDAY
YESTER

NOW I'M SURE OF IT...ONEE-CHAN...

HELLO? YOU WANT TO COME OVER FOR A GANG-BANG?

INDUBI-TABLY!

...IS A TOTAL SLUT...!

CHAPTER 138: WOMAN ON TOP

I'M SURE OF IT...

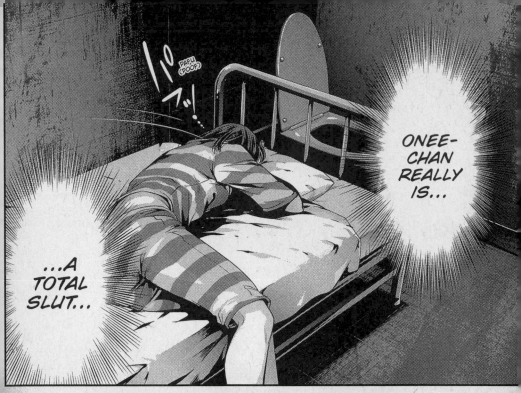

PAFU
(POOF)

ONEE-CHAN REALLY IS...

...A TOTAL SLUT...

ONEE-CHAN...

BUT...WHY WOULD SHE CHANGE!?

I DON'T GET IT...IT DOESN'T MAKE ANY SENSE...!

GYU
(SQUEEZE)

ONEE-CHAN...

SHE'S ALWAYS BEEN SO TALENTED. I LOOKED UP TO HER...

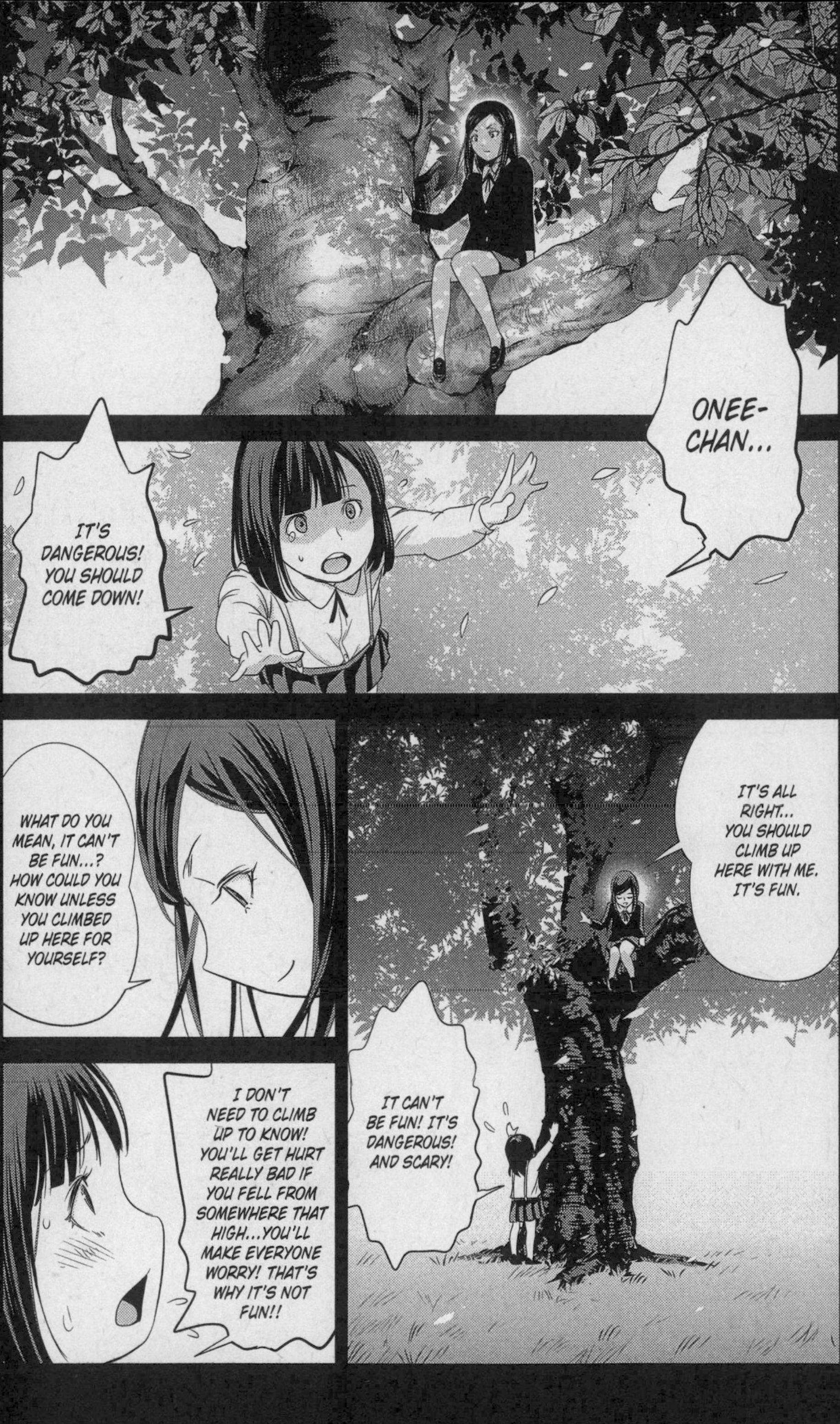
ONEE-CHAN...
IT'S DANGEROUS! YOU SHOULD COME DOWN!
IT'S ALL RIGHT... YOU SHOULD CLIMB UP HERE WITH ME. IT'S FUN.
IT CAN'T BE FUN! IT'S DANGEROUS! AND SCARY!
WHAT DO YOU MEAN, IT CAN'T BE FUN...? HOW COULD YOU KNOW UNLESS YOU CLIMBED UP HERE FOR YOURSELF?
I DON'T NEED TO CLIMB UP TO KNOW! YOU'LL GET HURT REALLY BAD IF YOU FELL FROM SOMEWHERE THAT HIGH...YOU'LL MAKE EVERYONE WORRY! THAT'S WHY IT'S NOT FUN!!

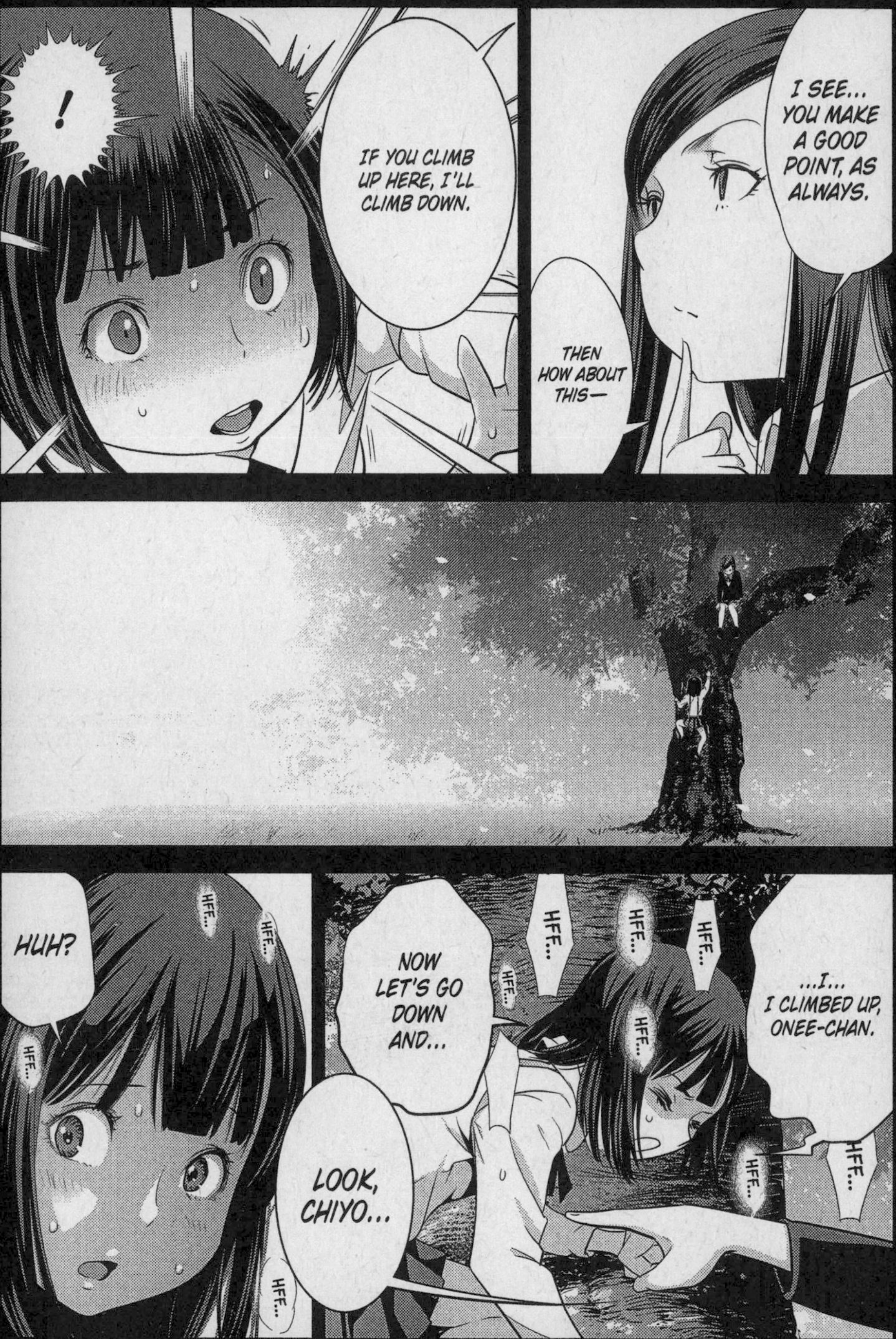
I SEE... YOU MAKE A GOOD POINT, AS ALWAYS.
THEN HOW ABOUT THIS—
!
IF YOU CLIMB UP HERE, I'LL CLIMB DOWN.
...I... I CLIMBED UP, ONEE-CHAN.
HFF...
HFF...
HFF...
HFF...
HFF...
NOW LET'S GO DOWN AND...
HFF...
LOOK, CHIYO...
HFF...
HUH?
HFF...
HFF...
HFF...

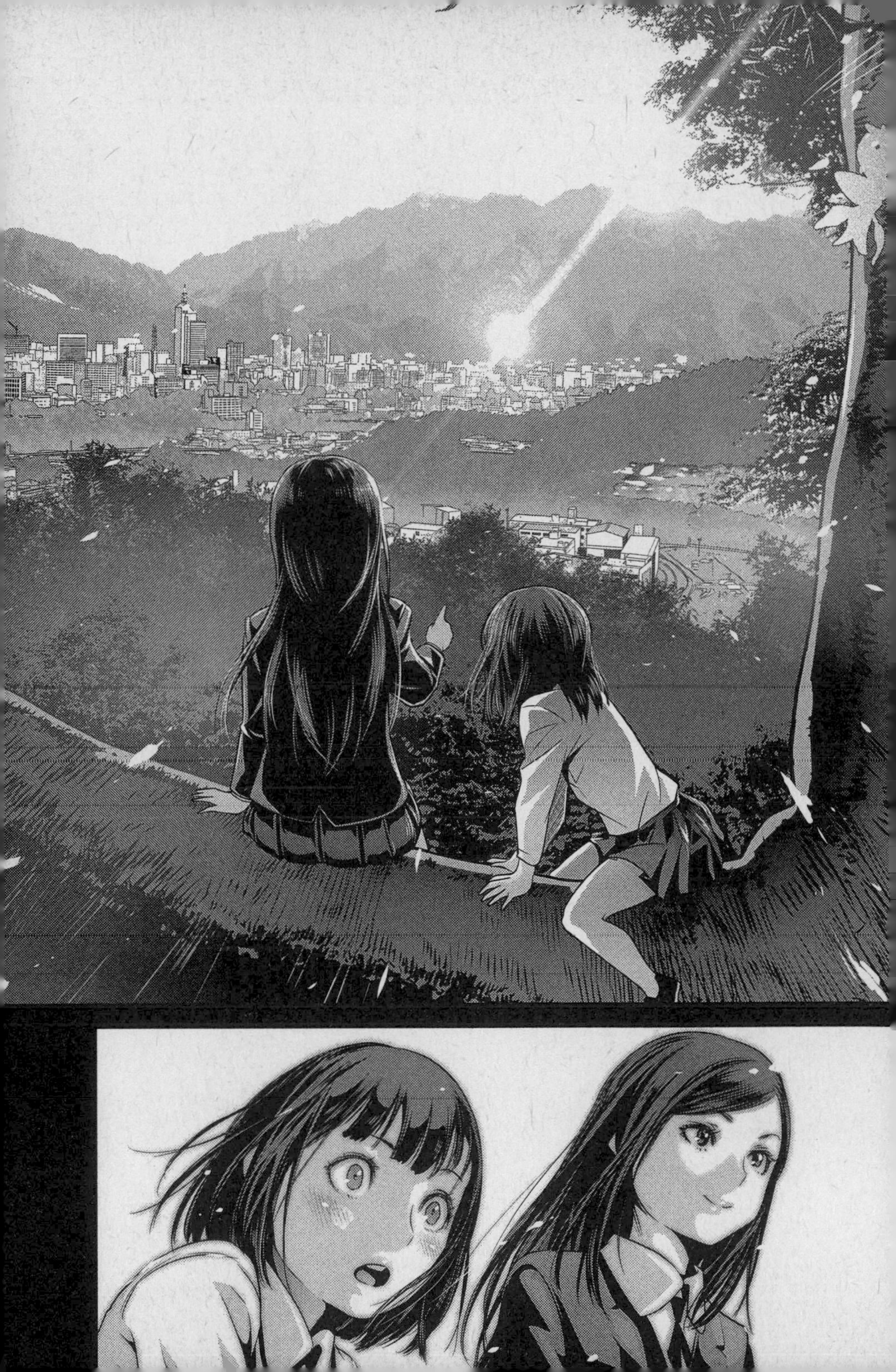

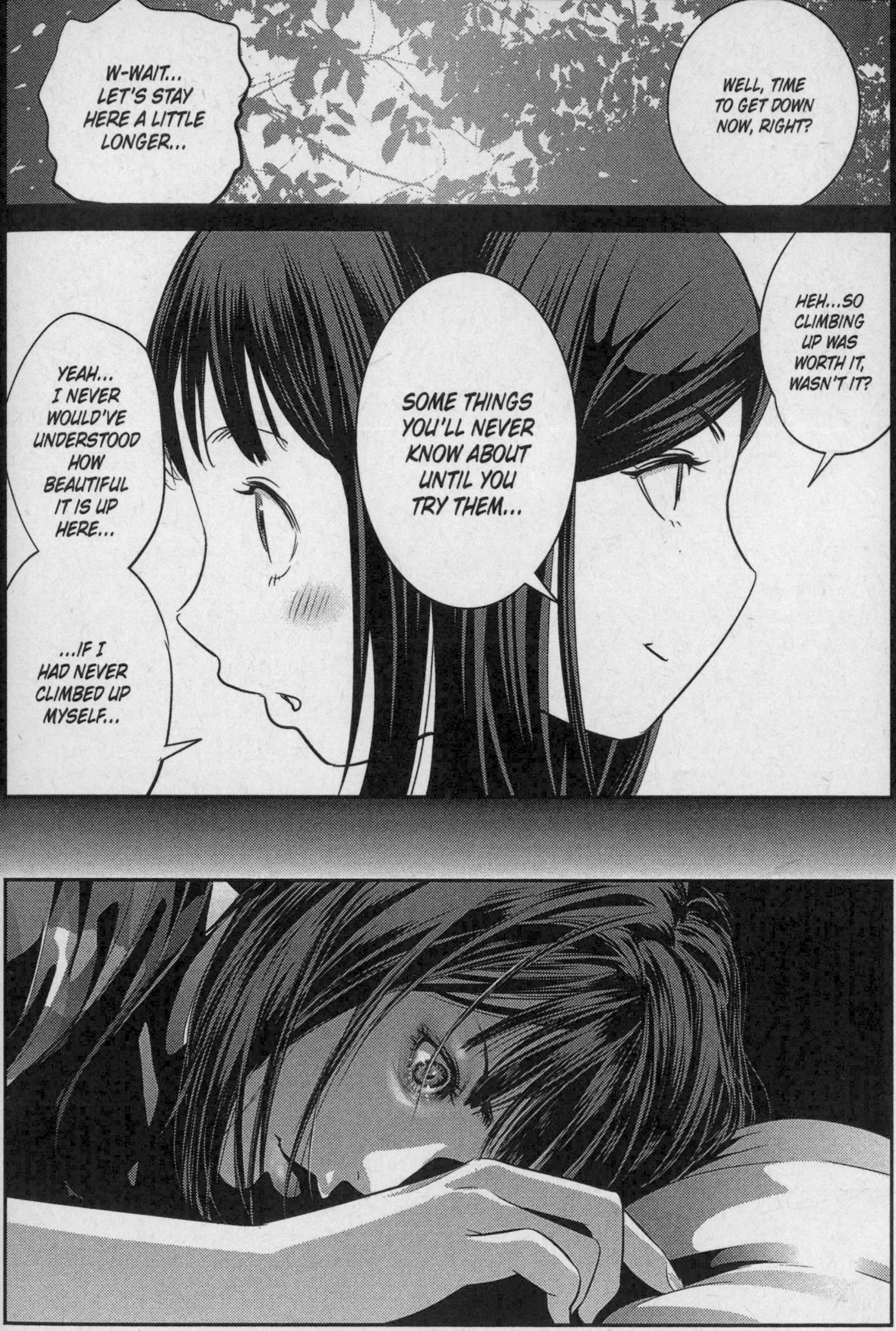
WELL, TIME TO GET DOWN NOW, RIGHT?
W-WAIT... LET'S STAY HERE A LITTLE LONGER...
HEH...SO CLIMBING UP WAS WORTH IT, WASN'T IT?
SOME THINGS YOU'LL NEVER KNOW ABOUT UNTIL YOU TRY THEM...
YEAH... I NEVER WOULD'VE UNDERSTOOD HOW BEAUTIFUL IT IS UP HERE...
...IF I HAD NEVER CLIMBED UP MYSELF...

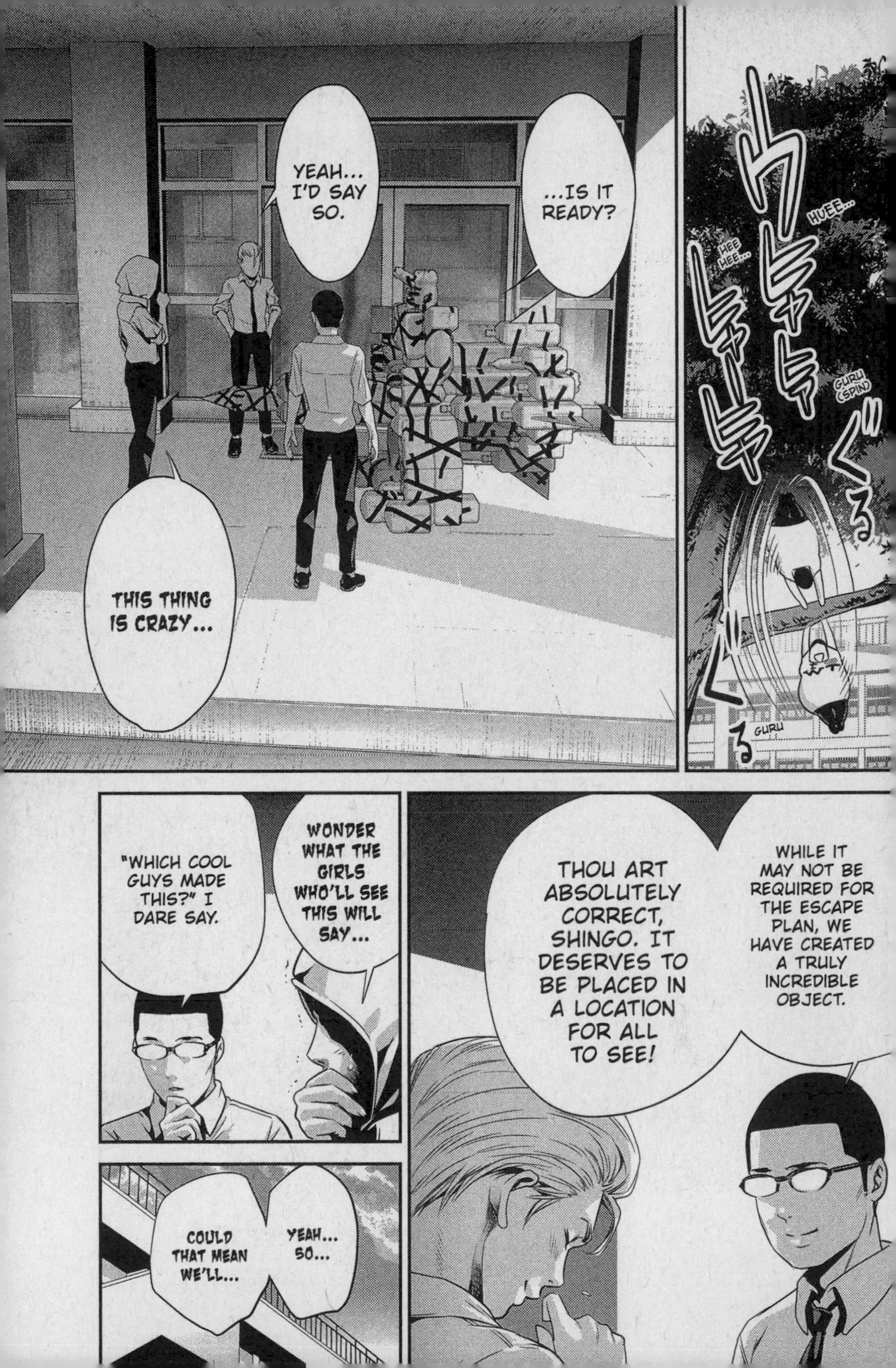
HUEE...
HEE HEE...
GURU (SPIN)
GURU
...IS IT READY?
YEAH... I'D SAY SO.
THIS THING IS CRAZY...
WHILE IT MAY NOT BE REQUIRED FOR THE ESCAPE PLAN, WE HAVE CREATED A TRULY INCREDIBLE OBJECT.
THOU ART ABSOLUTELY CORRECT, SHINGO. IT DESERVES TO BE PLACED IN A LOCATION FOR ALL TO SEE!
WONDER WHAT THE GIRLS WHO'LL SEE THIS WILL SAY...
"WHICH COOL GUYS MADE THIS?" I DARE SAY.
YEAH... SO...
COULD THAT MEAN WE'LL...

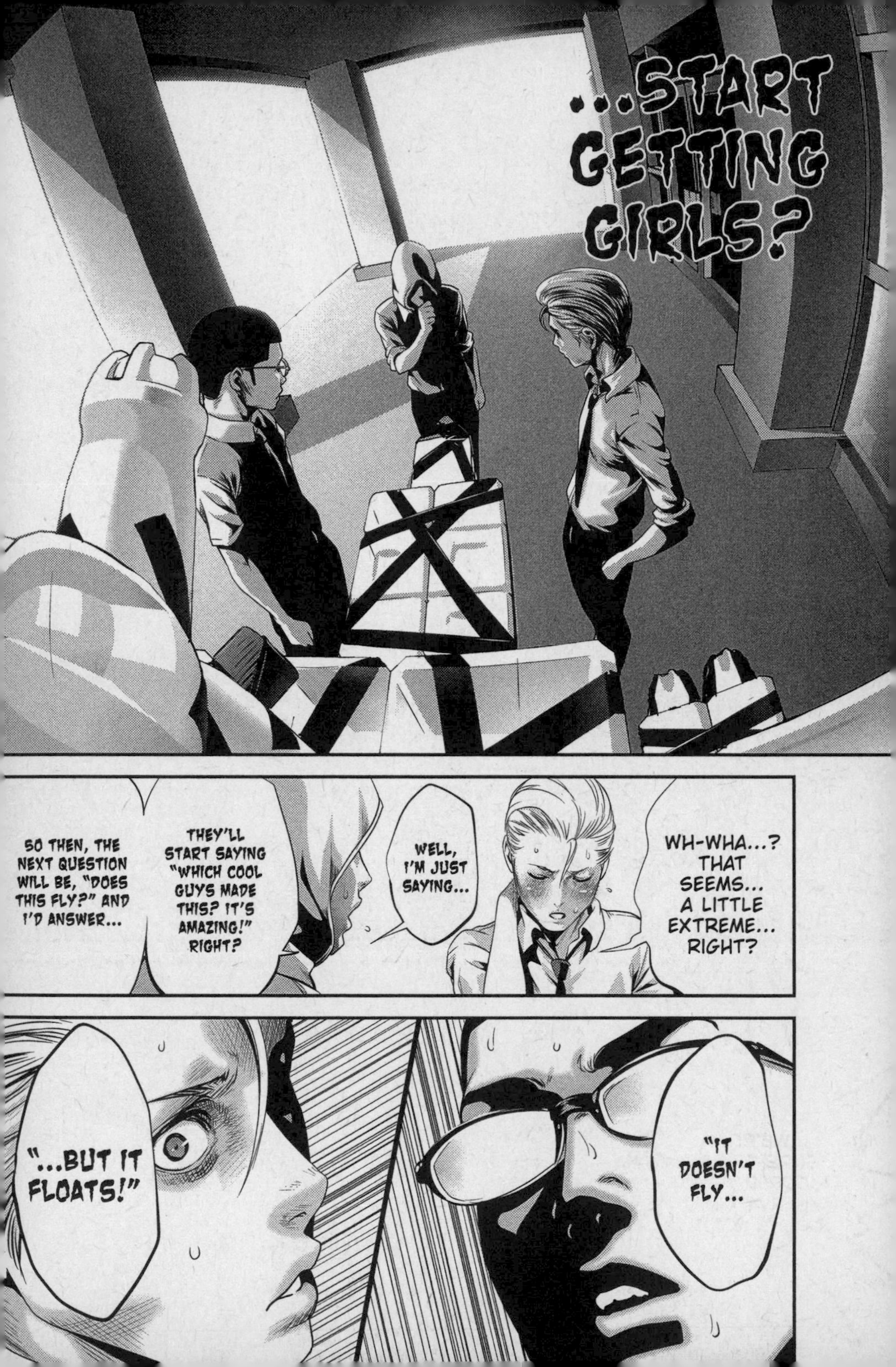
...START GETTING GIRLS?
WH-WHA...? THAT SEEMS... A LITTLE EXTREME... RIGHT?
WELL, I'M JUST SAYING...
THEY'LL START SAYING "WHICH COOL GUYS MADE THIS? IT'S AMAZING!" RIGHT?
SO THEN, THE NEXT QUESTION WILL BE, "DOES THIS FLY?" AND I'D ANSWER...
"IT DOESN'T FLY...
"...BUT IT FLOATS!"

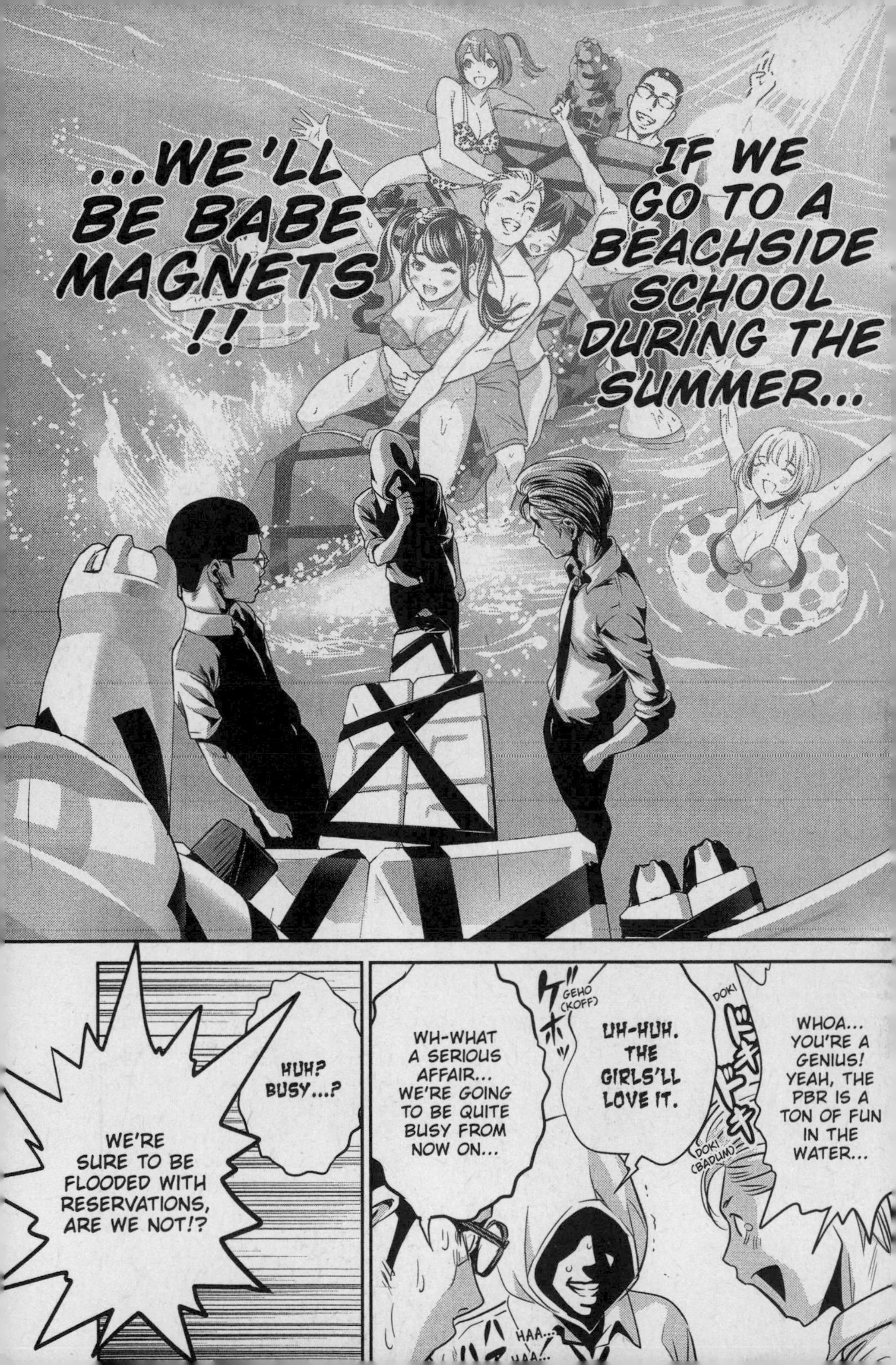
IF WE GO TO A BEACHSIDE SCHOOL DURING THE SUMMER...
...WE'LL BE BABE MAGNETS!!
WHOA... YOU'RE A GENIUS! YEAH, THE PBR IS A TON OF FUN IN THE WATER...
DOKI DOKI (BADUM)
UH-HUH. THE GIRLS'LL LOVE IT.
GEHO (KOFF)
WH-WHAT A SERIOUS AFFAIR... WE'RE GOING TO BE QUITE BUSY FROM NOW ON...
HAA... HAA...
HUH? BUSY...?
WE'RE SURE TO BE FLOODED WITH RESERVATIONS, ARE WE NOT!?

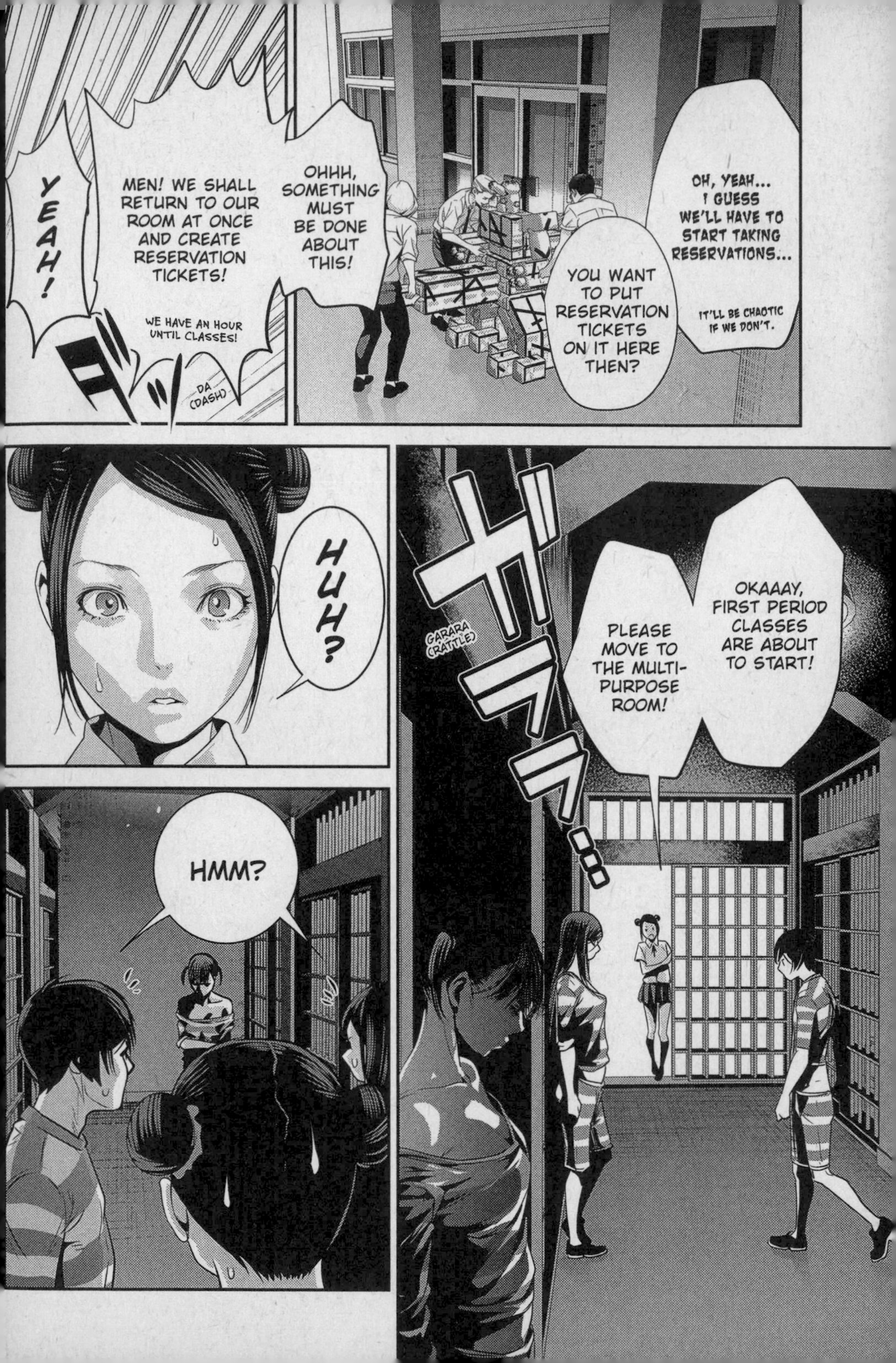
OH, YEAH... I GUESS WE'LL HAVE TO START TAKING RESERVATIONS...
IT'LL BE CHAOTIC IF WE DON'T.
YOU WANT TO PUT RESERVATION TICKETS ON IT HERE THEN?
OHHH, SOMETHING MUST BE DONE ABOUT THIS!
MEN! WE SHALL RETURN TO OUR ROOM AT ONCE AND CREATE RESERVATION TICKETS!
WE HAVE AN HOUR UNTIL CLASSES!
YEAH!
DA (DASH)
OKAAAY, FIRST PERIOD CLASSES ARE ABOUT TO START!
PLEASE MOVE TO THE MULTI-PURPOSE ROOM!
GARARA (RATTLE)
HUH?
HMM?

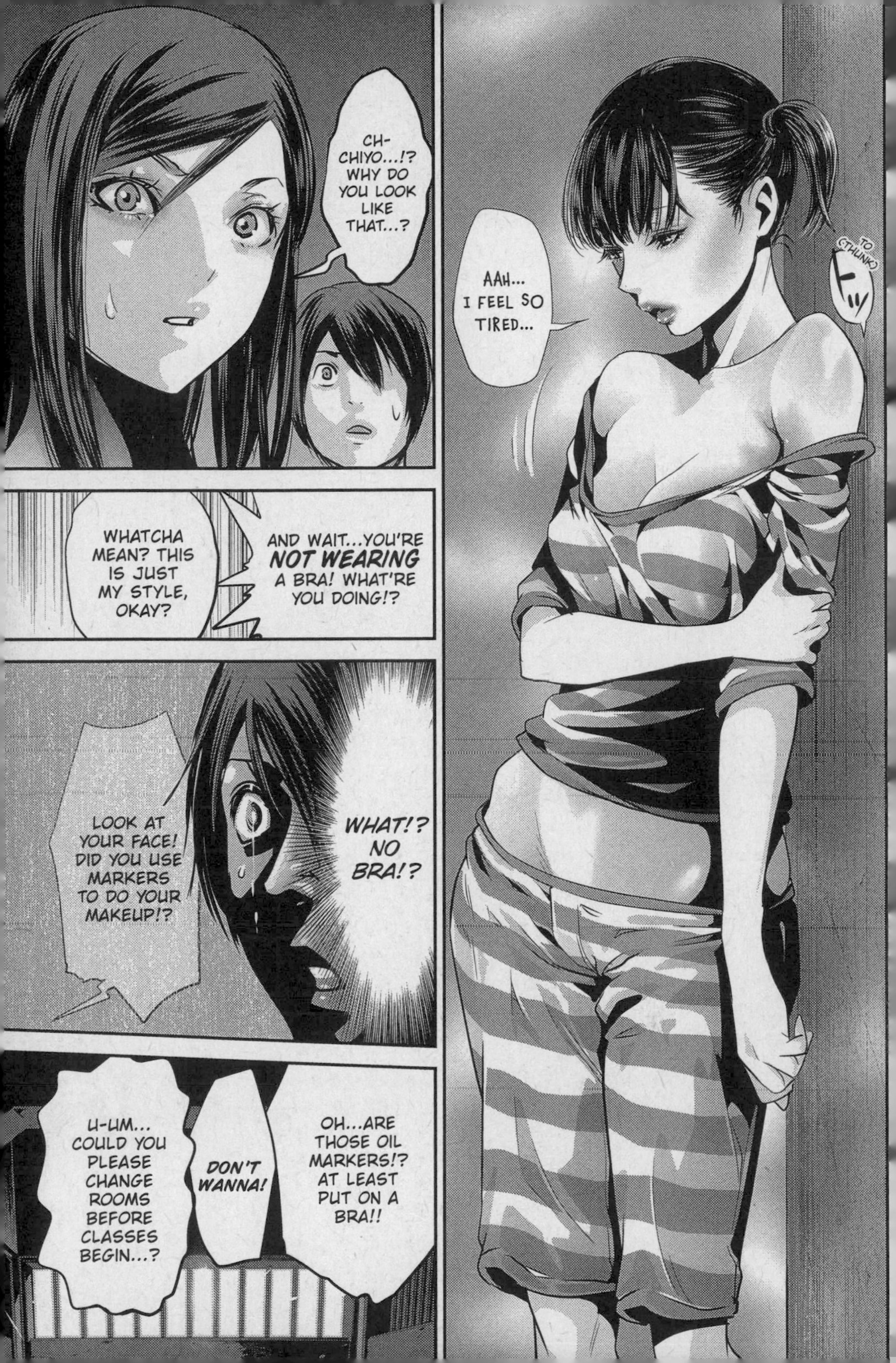
TO (THUNK)
AAH... I FEEL SO TIRED...
CH-CHIYO...!? WHY DO YOU LOOK LIKE THAT...?
AND WAIT...YOU'RE **NOT WEARING** A BRA! WHAT'RE YOU DOING!?
WHATCHA MEAN? THIS IS JUST MY STYLE, OKAY?
WHAT!? NO BRA!?
LOOK AT YOUR FACE! DID YOU USE MARKERS TO DO YOUR MAKEUP!?
OH...ARE THOSE OIL MARKERS!? AT LEAST PUT ON A BRA!!
DON'T WANNA!
U-UM... COULD YOU PLEASE CHANGE ROOMS BEFORE CLASSES BEGIN...?

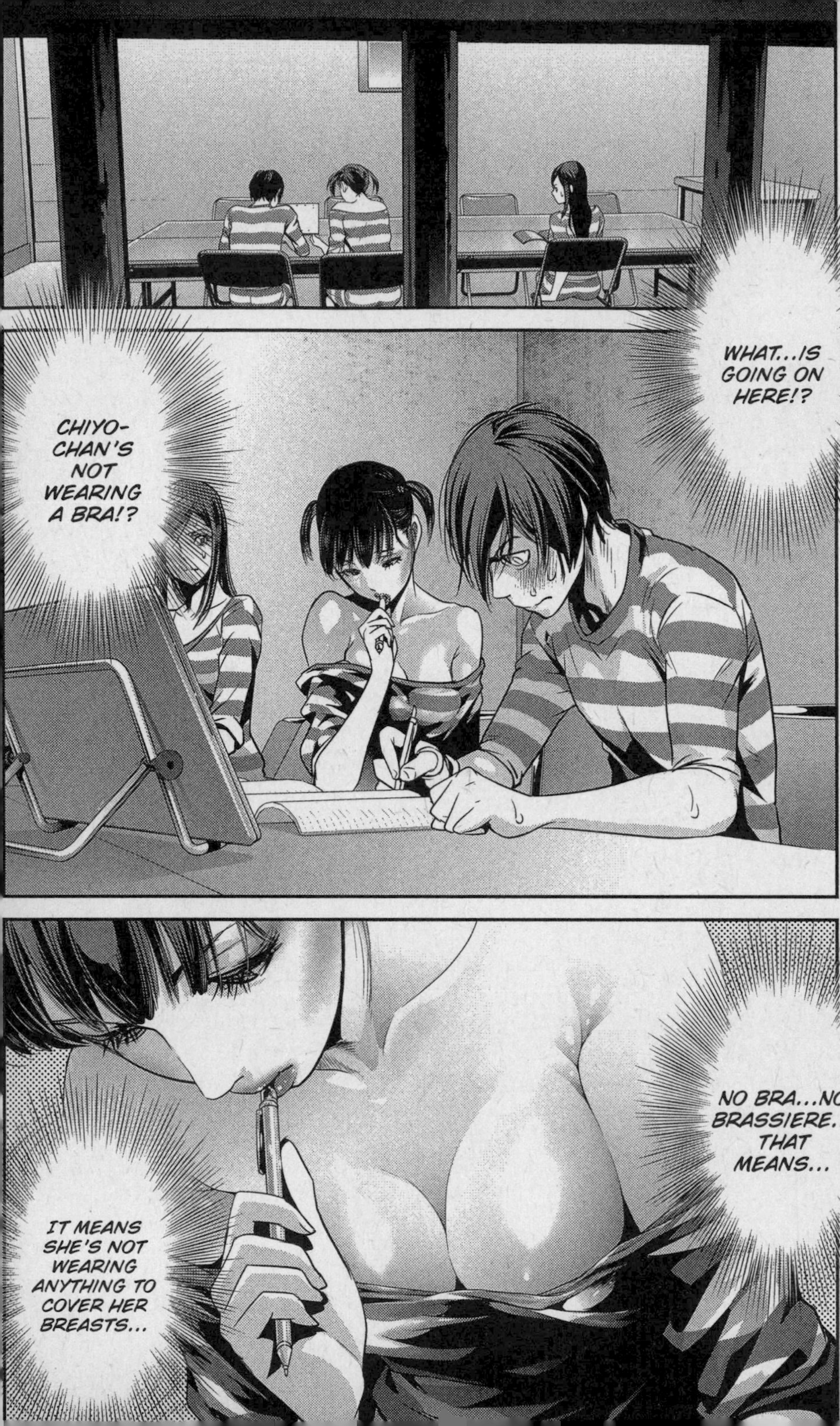
WHAT...IS GOING ON HERE!?
CHIYO-CHAN'S NOT WEARING A BRA!?
NO BRA...NO BRASSIERE... THAT MEANS...
IT MEANS SHE'S NOT WEARING ANYTHING TO COVER HER BREASTS...

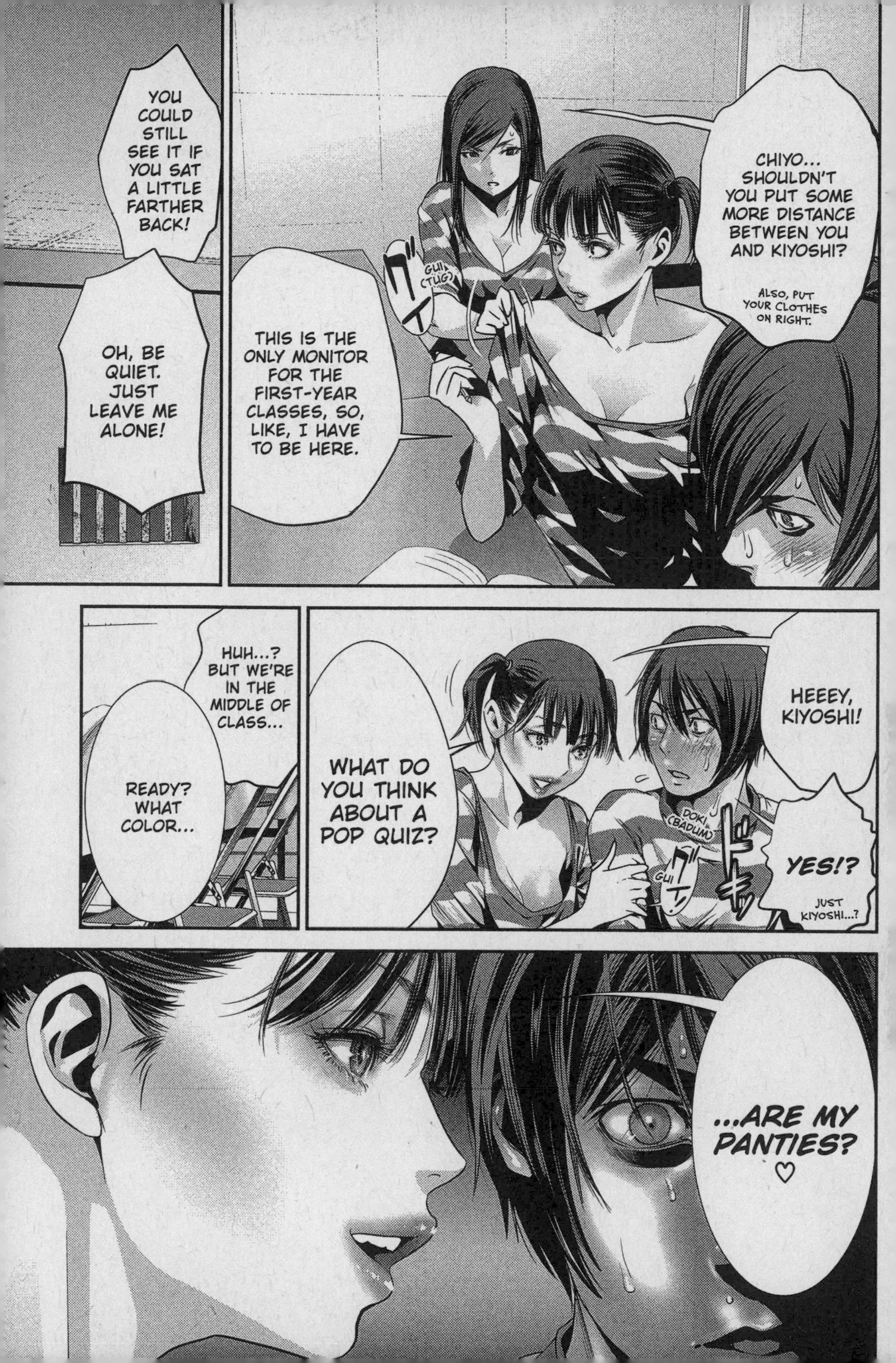
CHIYO... SHOULDN'T YOU PUT SOME MORE DISTANCE BETWEEN YOU AND KIYOSHI?
ALSO, PUT YOUR CLOTHES ON RIGHT.
GUI (TUG)
THIS IS THE ONLY MONITOR FOR THE FIRST-YEAR CLASSES, SO, LIKE, I HAVE TO BE HERE.
YOU COULD STILL SEE IT IF YOU SAT A LITTLE FARTHER BACK!
OH, BE QUIET. JUST LEAVE ME ALONE!
HEEEY, KIYOSHI!
YES!?
JUST KIYOSHI...?
DOKI (BADUM)
GUI
WHAT DO YOU THINK ABOUT A POP QUIZ?
HUH...? BUT WE'RE IN THE MIDDLE OF CLASS...
READY? WHAT COLOR...
...ARE MY PANTIES? ♡

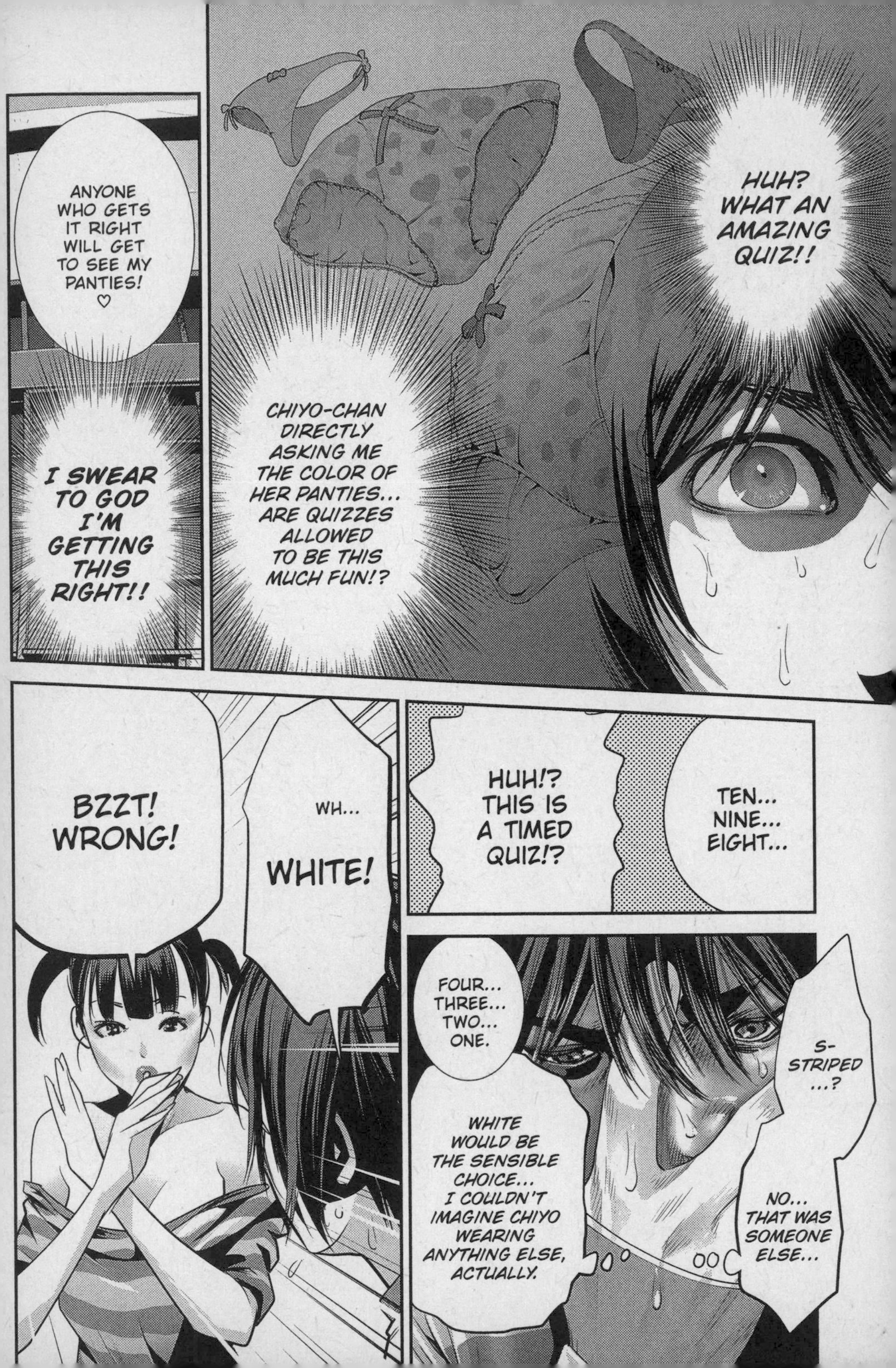
HUH? WHAT AN AMAZING QUIZ!!
CHIYO-CHAN DIRECTLY ASKING ME THE COLOR OF HER PANTIES... ARE QUIZZES ALLOWED TO BE THIS MUCH FUN!?
ANYONE WHO GETS IT RIGHT WILL GET TO SEE MY PANTIES! ♡
I SWEAR TO GOD I'M GETTING THIS RIGHT!!
TEN... NINE... EIGHT...
HUH!? THIS IS A TIMED QUIZ!?
FOUR... THREE... TWO... ONE.
S-STRIPED...?
NO... THAT WAS SOMEONE ELSE...
WHITE WOULD BE THE SENSIBLE CHOICE... I COULDN'T IMAGINE CHIYO WEARING ANYTHING ELSE, ACTUALLY.
WH...
WHITE!
BZZT! WRONG!

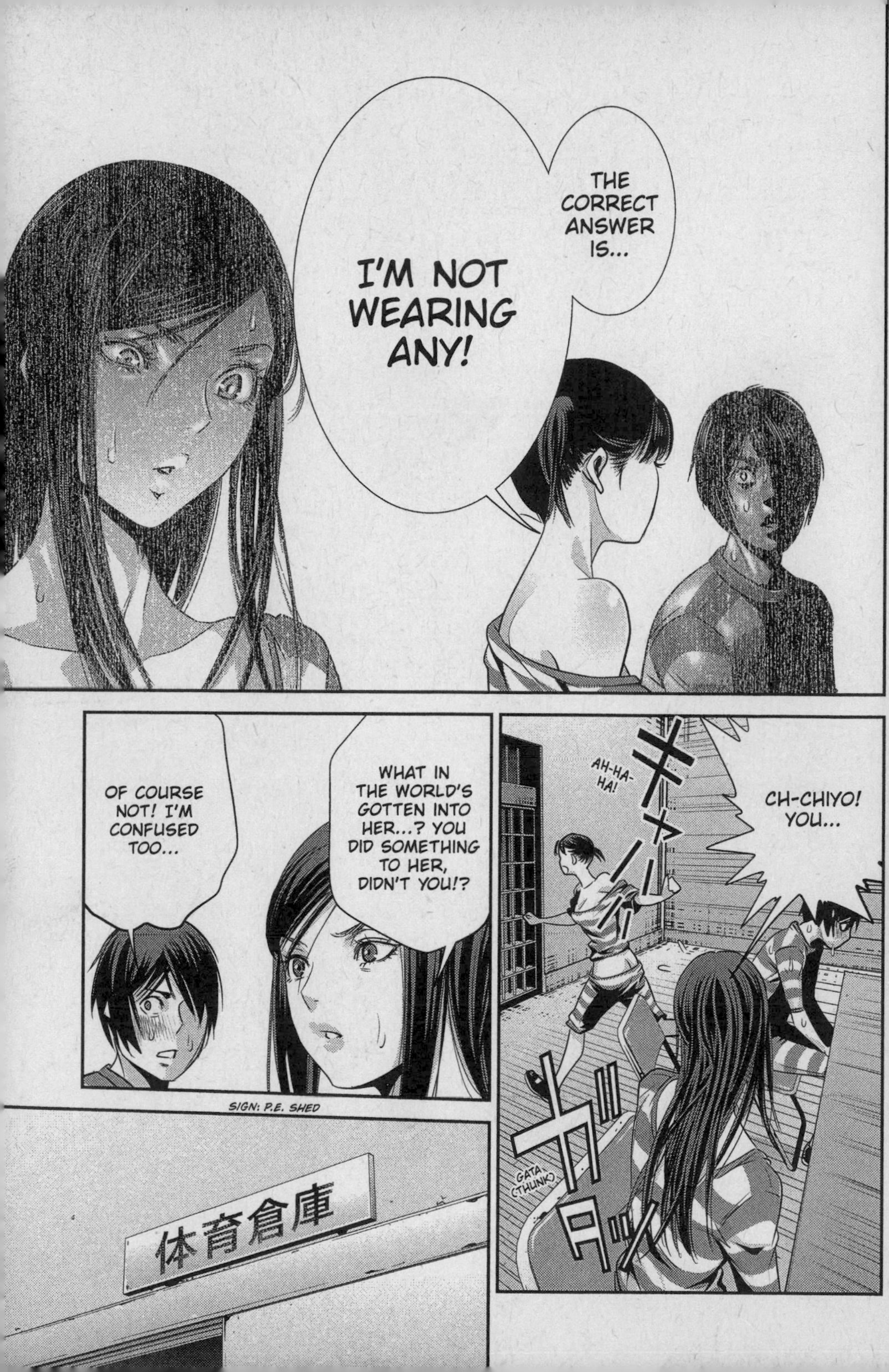
THE CORRECT ANSWER IS...
I'M NOT WEARING ANY!
CH-CHIYO! YOU...
AH-HA-HA!
GATA (THUNK)
WHAT IN THE WORLD'S GOTTEN INTO HER...? YOU DID SOMETHING TO HER, DIDN'T YOU!?
OF COURSE NOT! I'M CONFUSED TOO...
SIGN: P.E. SHED
体育倉庫

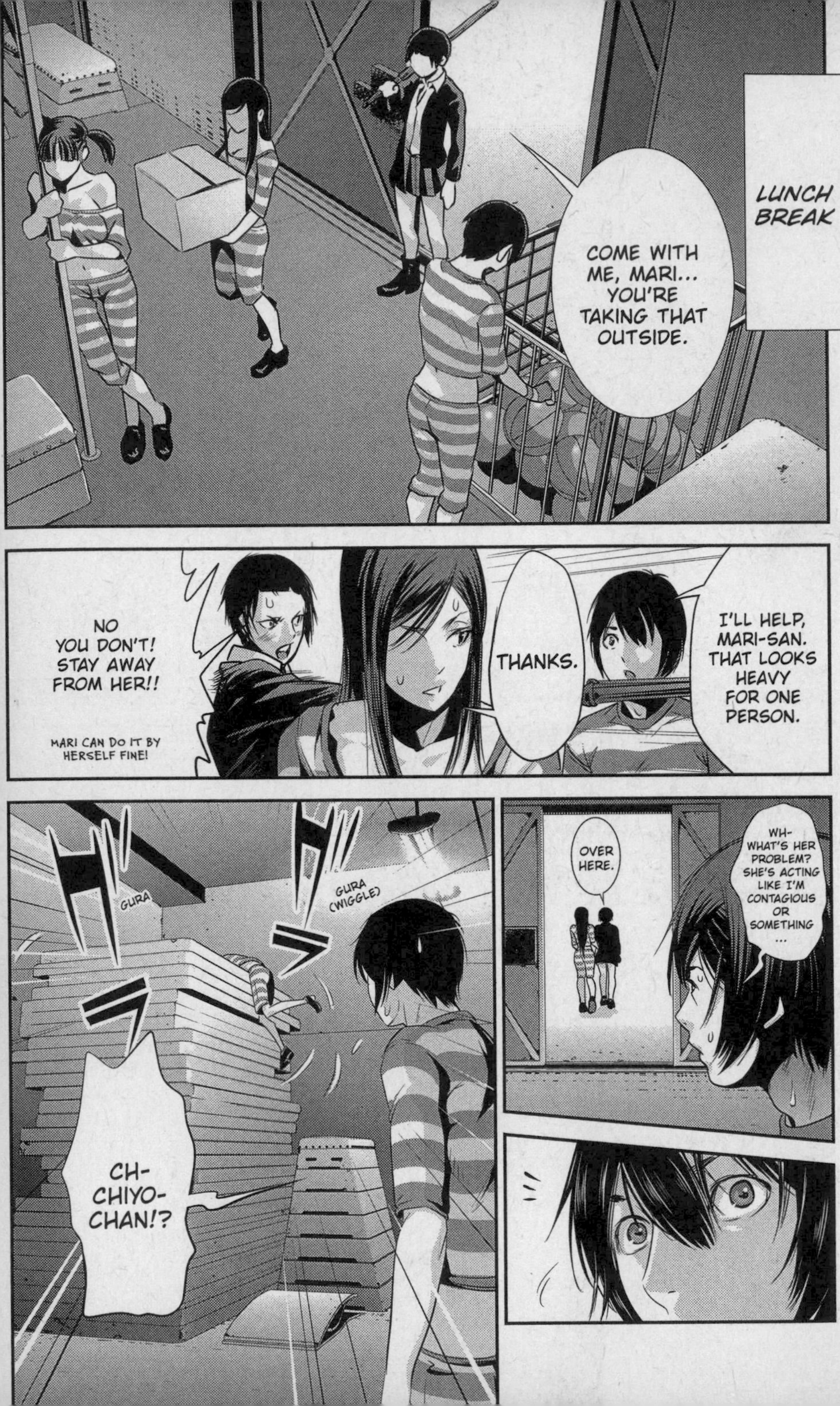
LUNCH BREAK
COME WITH ME, MARI... YOU'RE TAKING THAT OUTSIDE.
I'LL HELP, MARI-SAN. THAT LOOKS HEAVY FOR ONE PERSON.
THANKS.
NO YOU DON'T! STAY AWAY FROM HER!!
MARI CAN DO IT BY HERSELF FINE!
WH- WHAT'S HER PROBLEM? SHE'S ACTING LIKE I'M CONTAGIOUS OR SOMETHING ...
OVER HERE.
GURA (WIGGLE)
GURA
CH- CHIYO- CHAN!?

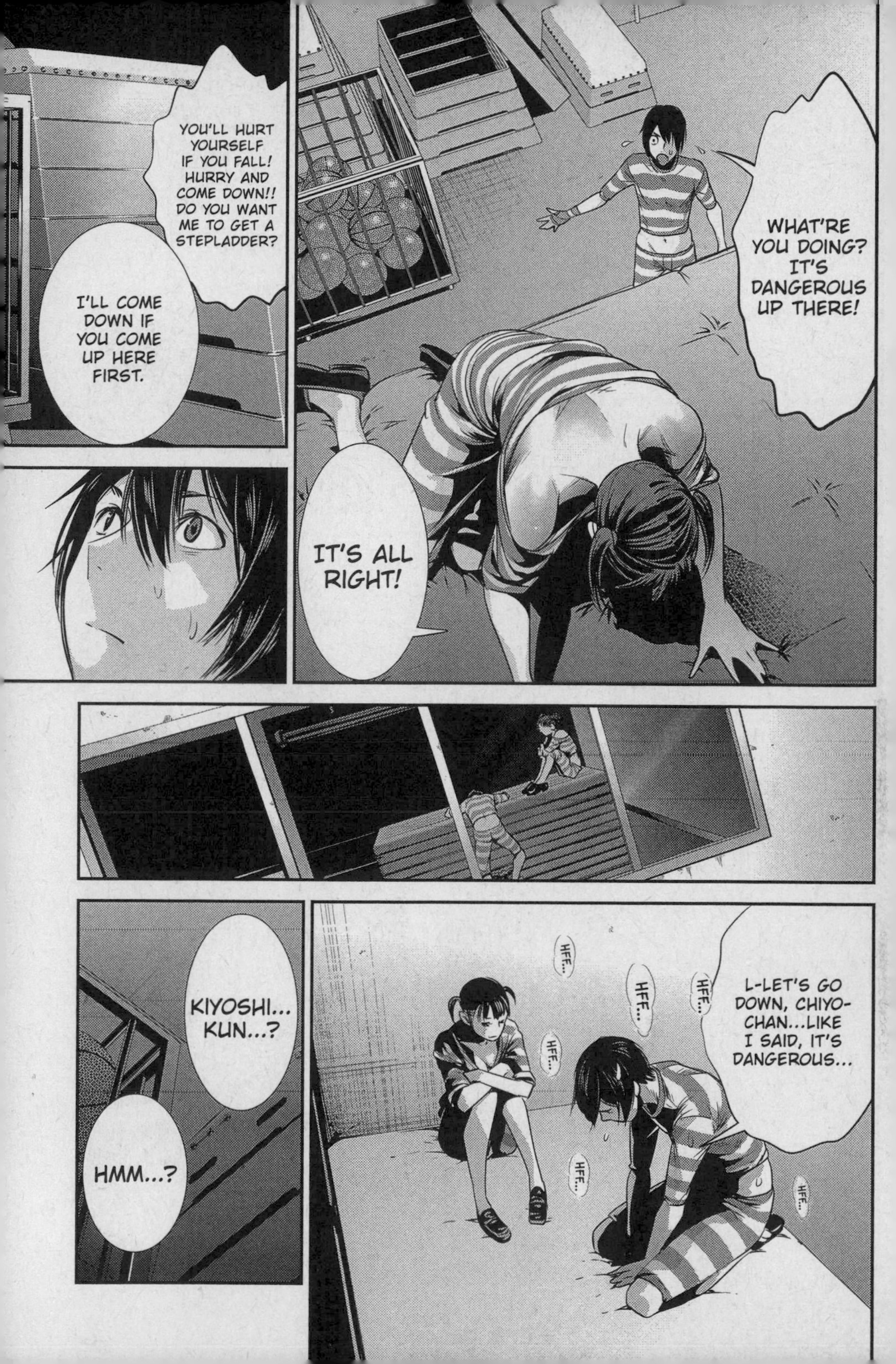
WHAT'RE YOU DOING? IT'S DANGEROUS UP THERE!
IT'S ALL RIGHT!
YOU'LL HURT YOURSELF IF YOU FALL! HURRY AND COME DOWN!! DO YOU WANT ME TO GET A STEPLADDER?
I'LL COME DOWN IF YOU COME UP HERE FIRST.
HFF...
HFF...
HFF...
HFF...
HFF...
HFF...
L-LET'S GO DOWN, CHIYO-CHAN...LIKE I SAID, IT'S DANGEROUS...
KIYOSHI... KUN...?
HMM...?

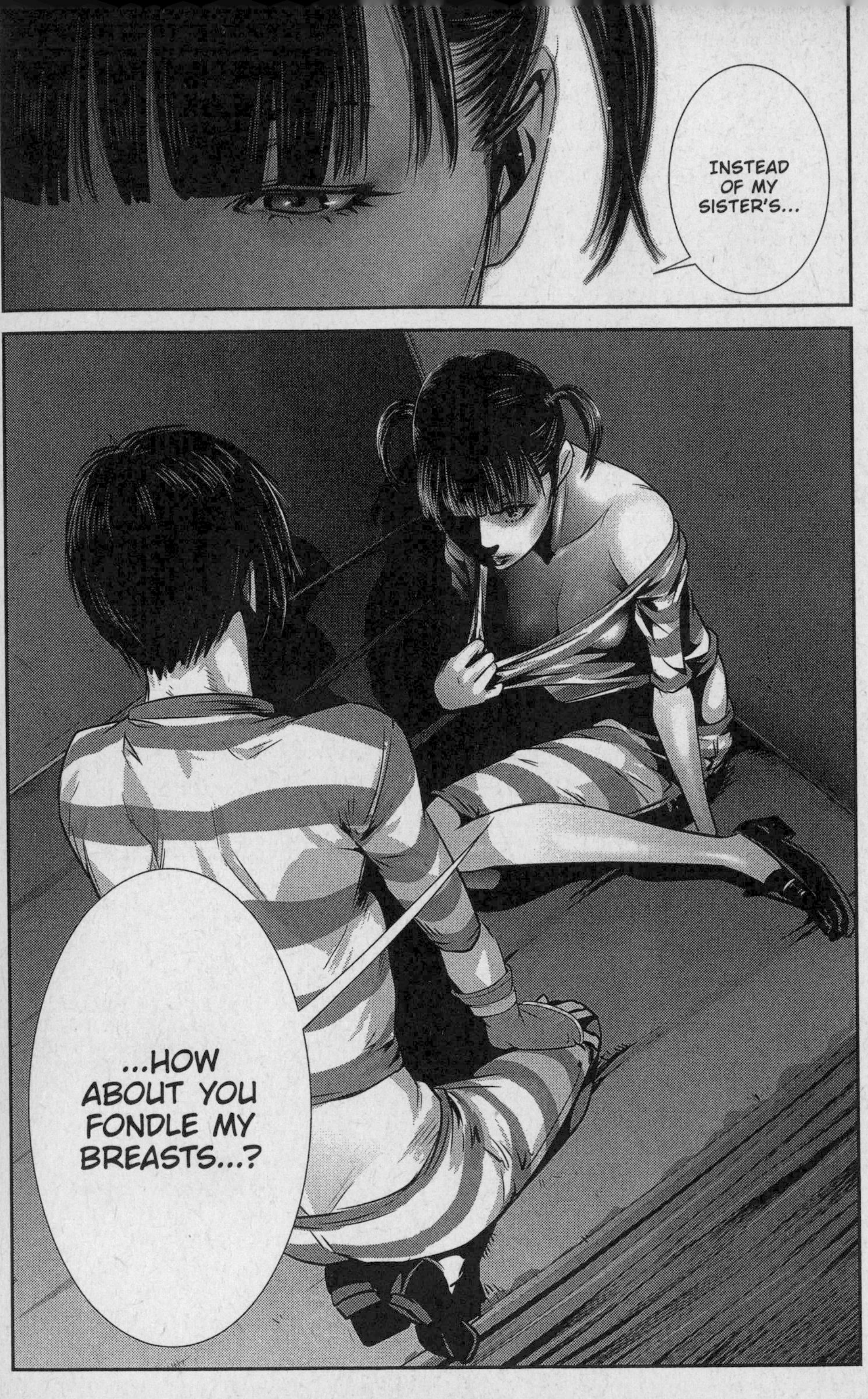
INSTEAD OF MY SISTER'S...
...HOW ABOUT YOU FONDLE MY BREASTS...?

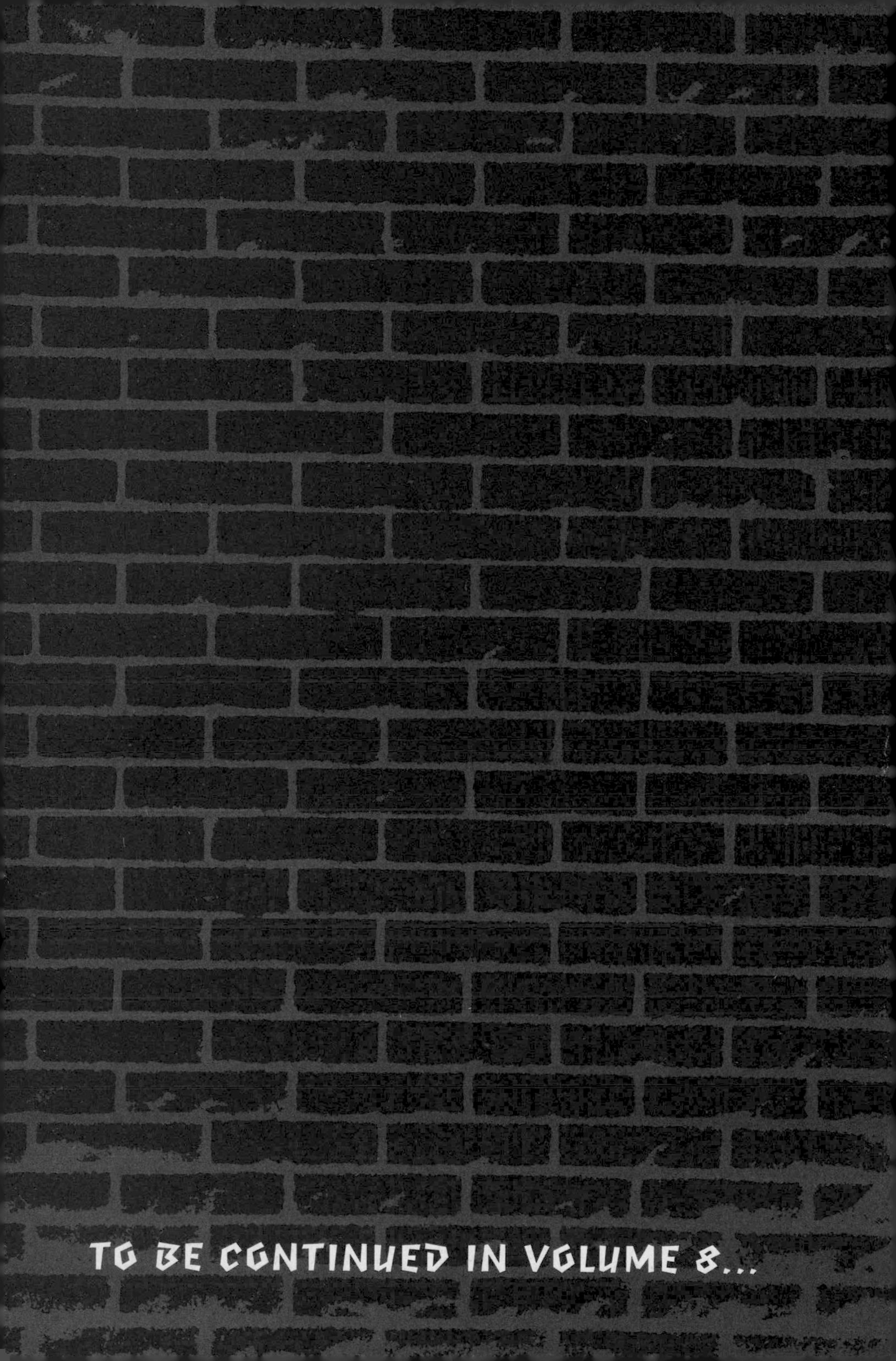
TO BE CONTINUED IN VOLUME 8...

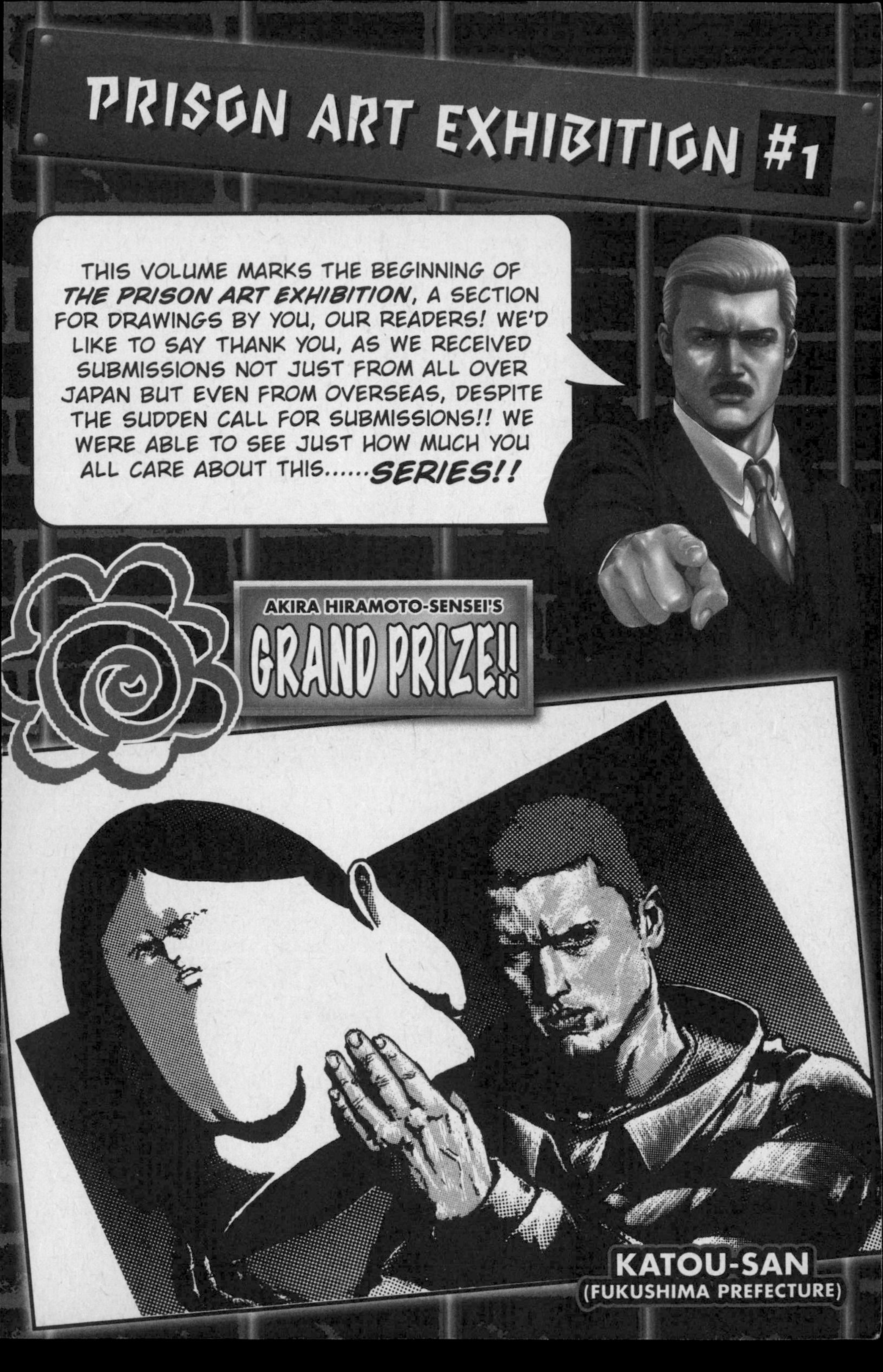
PRISON ART EXHIBITION #1
THIS VOLUME MARKS THE BEGINNING OF *THE PRISON ART EXHIBITION*, A SECTION FOR DRAWINGS BY YOU, OUR READERS! WE'D LIKE TO SAY THANK YOU, AS WE RECEIVED SUBMISSIONS NOT JUST FROM ALL OVER JAPAN BUT EVEN FROM OVERSEAS, DESPITE THE SUDDEN CALL FOR SUBMISSIONS!! WE WERE ABLE TO SEE JUST HOW MUCH YOU ALL CARE ABOUT THIS......*SERIES!!*
AKIRA HIRAMOTO-SENSEI'S
GRAND PRIZE!!
KATOU-SAN
(FUKUSHIMA PREFECTURE)

AKIRA HIRAMOTO-SENSEI

HIT ME RIGHT IN THE HEART PR...

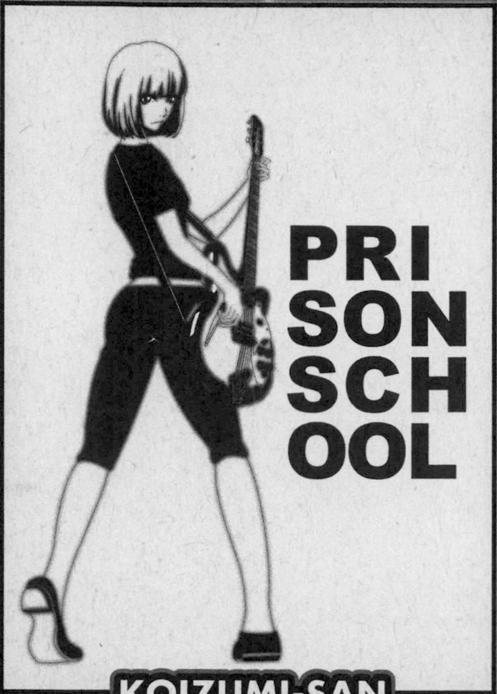
PRI
SON
SCH
OOL

KOIZUMI-SAN
(NAGANO PREFECTURE)

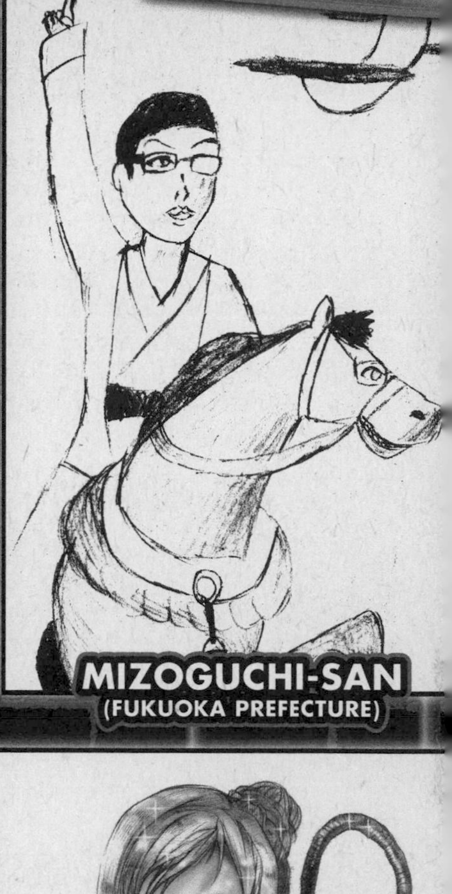

MIZOGUCHI-SAN
(FUKUOKA PREFECTURE)

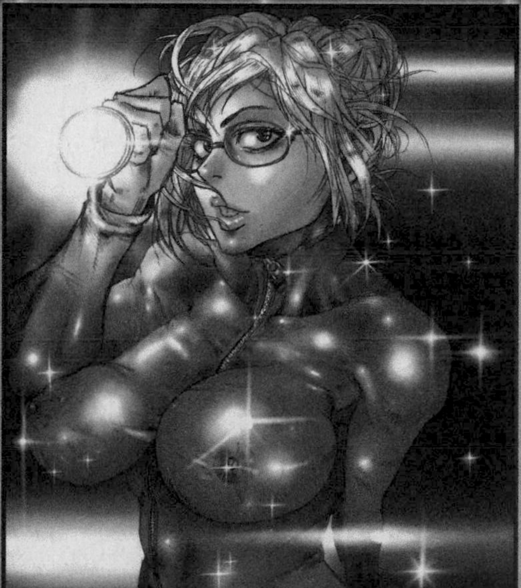

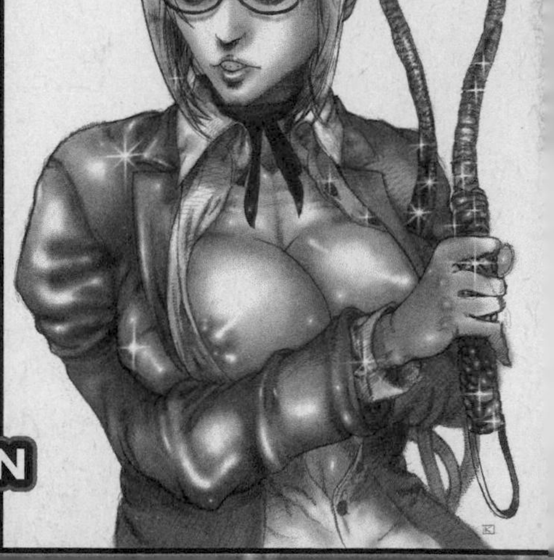

KARIM-SAN
(ITALY)

KUZUMOCHI-SAN
(HYOGO PREFECTURE)

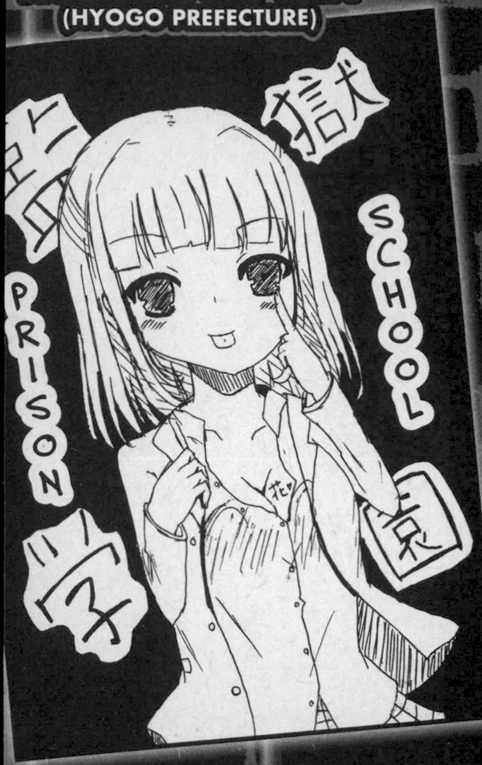
PRISON
SCHOOL

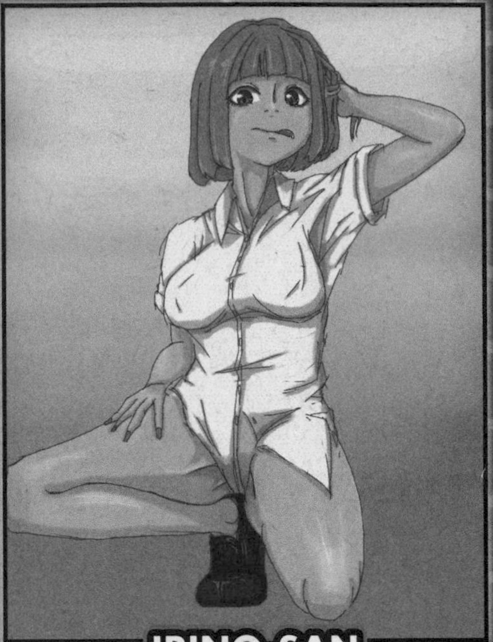

IRINO-SAN
(SAITAMA PREFECTURE)

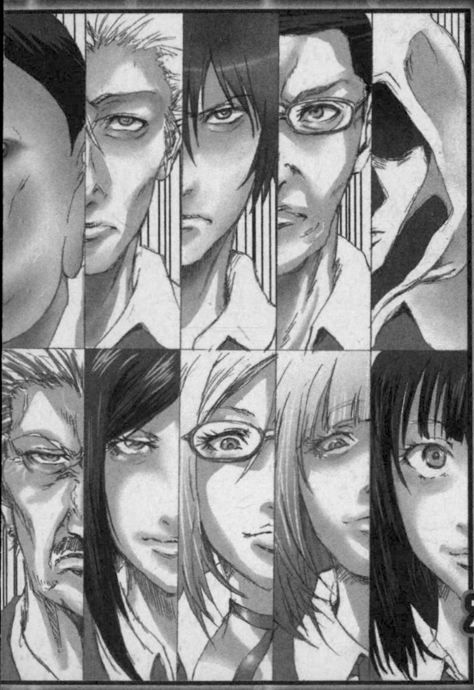

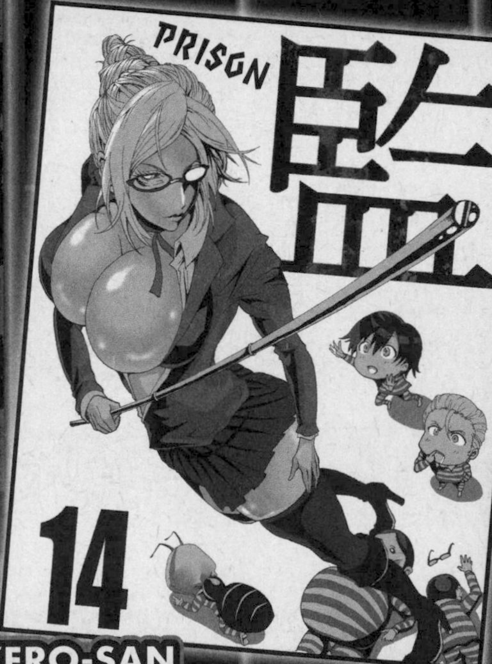
PRISON
監
14

ZERO-SAN
(KYOTO)

AKAITORI-SAN (AOMORI PREFECTURE)

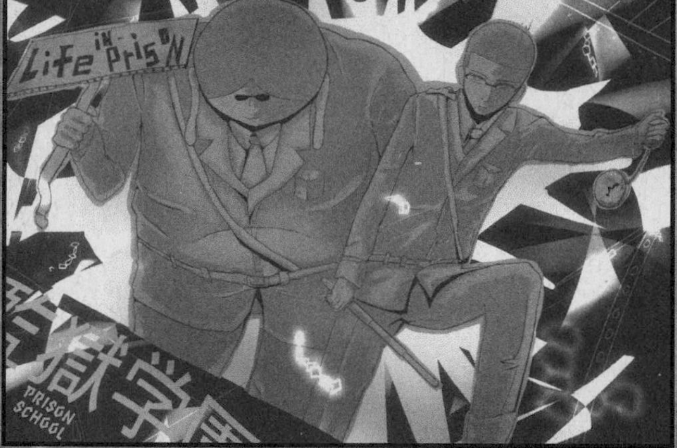

Life IN Prison
PRISON SCHOOL

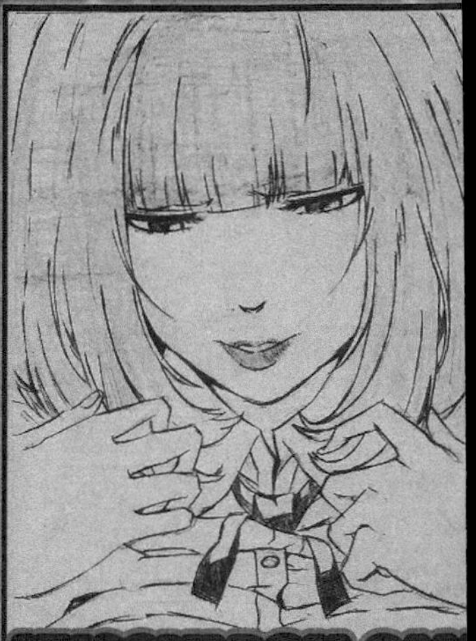

KUSOYAROU-SAN (OITA PREFECTURE)

YUU-SAN (FUKUSHIMA PREFECTURE)

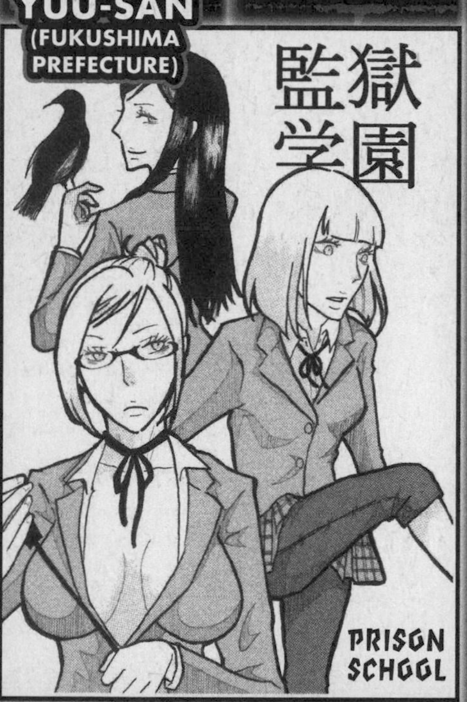

監獄学園
PRISON SCHOOL

TOKUDA-SAN (HIROSHIMA PREFECTURE)

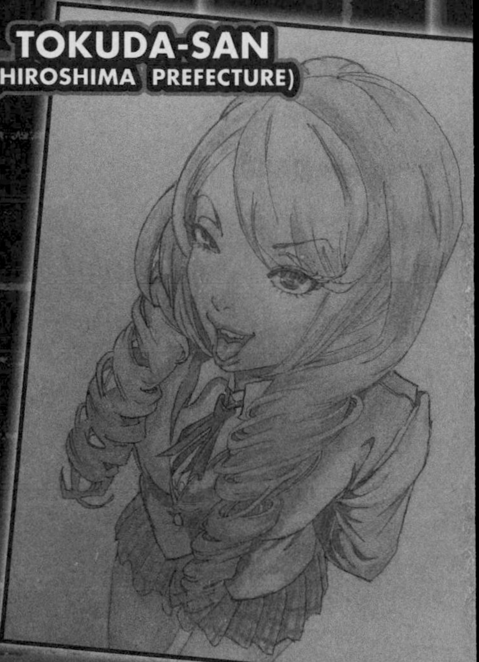

EVEN MORE ILLUSTRATIONS!

The Exhibition will be continuing in the next volume due to its popularity!!
We love seeing *Prison School* illustrations from all of our readers!!

*Note: This event was run during the Japanese publication of *Prison School*. If you'd still like to show your *Prison School* love, please send your submissions to:

yenpress@yenpress.com

※ Please include your name, location, and permission to reprint your artwork in your e-mail.
※ You must have proof of ID that you are 18 or older, or have a parent or legal guardian sign permission.
※ Please send a 3MB or smaller .jpg or .tif file.

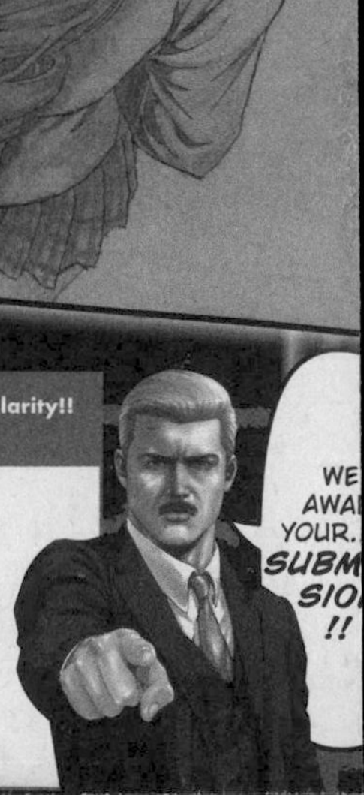

WE
AWA
YOUR
SUBM
SIO
!!

...BOOBS...BOOBS...!
...KIYOSHI-KUN...LET'S HURRY UP AND GET THIS OVER WITH...
...BEFORE MY SISTER AND THEM COME BACK, OKAY?
IT FEELS LIKE THERE'S MUCH TO BE DONE AS ESCAPE DAY DRAWS NEAR...
SAWA (TOUCH)
SAWA
SAWA
DO IT AS GRACE-FULLY...AS A GENTLEMAN WOULD...
AS IF I WERE HANDLING AN EXPENSIVE WORK OF FINE ART...
SAWA
SAWA
SAWA
SAWA
COMING OCTOBER 2017!!

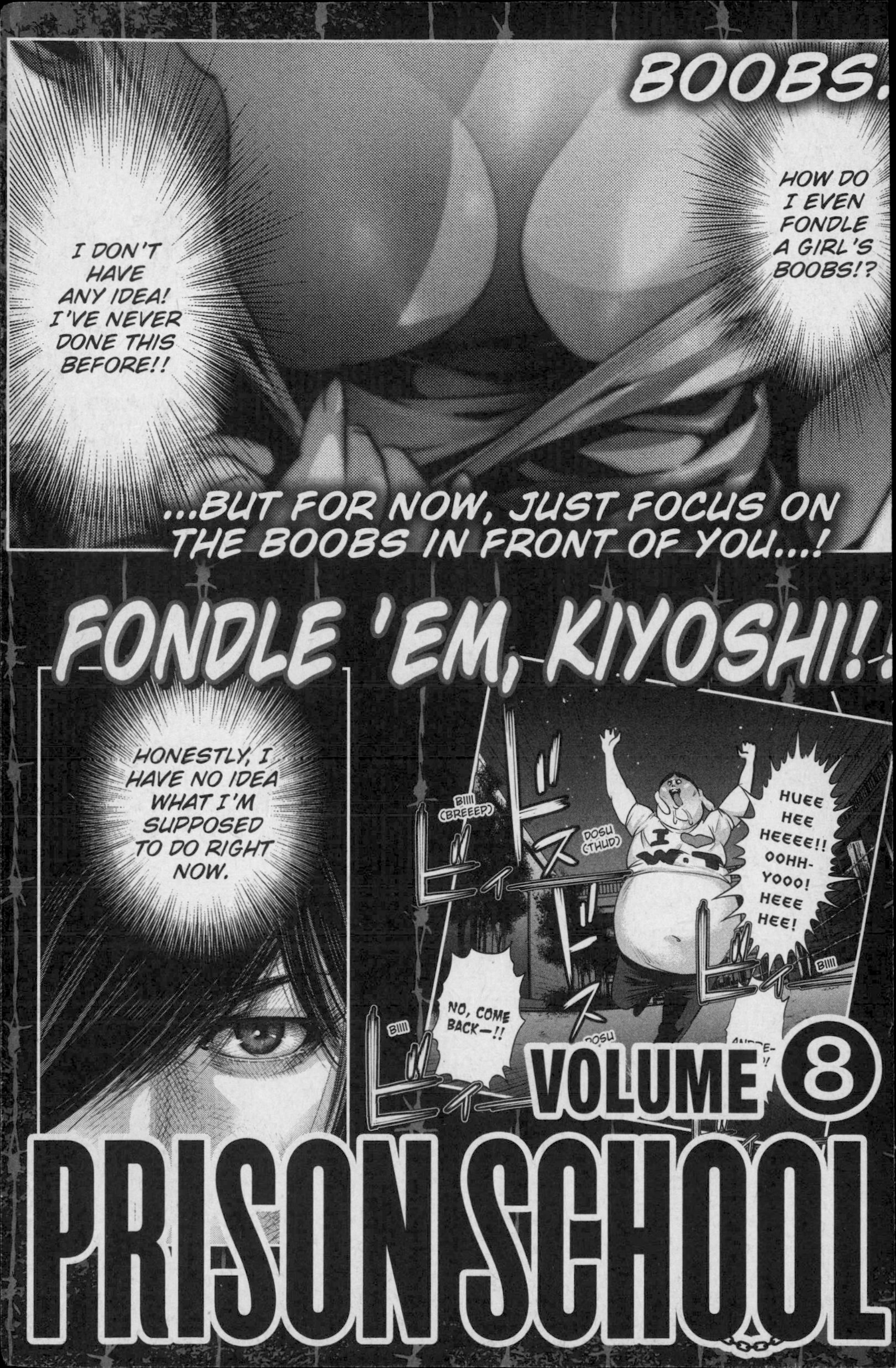
BOOBS.
HOW DO I EVEN FONDLE A GIRL'S BOOBS!?
I DON'T HAVE ANY IDEA! I'VE NEVER DONE THIS BEFORE!!
...BUT FOR NOW, JUST FOCUS ON THE BOOBS IN FRONT OF YOU...!
FONDLE 'EM, KIYOSHI!!
HUEE HEE HEEEE!! OOHH-YOOO! HEEE HEE!
DOSU (THUD)
BIIII (BREEEP)
BIIII
NO, COME BACK—!!
BIIII
HONESTLY, I HAVE NO IDEA WHAT I'M SUPPOSED TO DO RIGHT NOW.
VOLUME 8
PRISON SCHOOL

TRANSLATION NOTES

Common Honorifics

no honorific: Indicates familiarity or closeness; if used without permission or reason, addressing someone in this manner would constitute an insult.

-san: The Japanese equivalent of Mr./Mrs./Miss. If a situation calls for politeness, this is the fail-safe honorific.

-dono: Conveys an indication of respect for the addressee.

-kun: Used most often when referring to boys, this indicates affection or familiarity. Occasionally used by older men among their peers, but it may also be used by anyone referring to a person of lower standing.

-chan: An affectionate honorific indicating familiarity used mostly in reference to girls; also used in reference to cute persons or animals of either gender.

-senpai: A suffix used to address upperclassmen or more experienced coworkers.

PAGE 4
BL, or Boys Love, is a genre of fiction depicting homosexual relationships. Typically, BL is targeted toward female readers rather than gay men. It is also referred to as *yaoi*.

PAGE 78
Lu Bu is a powerful warrior from the Three Kingdoms period in China, famous for being nearly unrivaled in combat but lacking in intelligence otherwise. In *Romance of the Three Kingdoms*, his legendary strength and fighting ability are further embellished.

PAGE 159
In *Romance of the Three Kingdoms*, **Ma Su** is sentenced to death after a spectacular military blunder. However, since Kongming still has high respect for Ma Su at the time, it is a decision that tears at his heart. Gackt, turning against Anmitsu-sensei, has similar tearful underpinnings.

PAGE 190
Yakitori is skewered, grilled chicken meat. Crow yakitori would be highly unusual.

PAGE 230
Kiyoshi spells out **Rocket**—that is, *roketto* (ロケット)—using field day supplies. While Gackt is able to read the entire word, Andre is only able to see part of it—*keshi* (ケツ)—which leads to his cries of **"Asses! Asses!"**

PAGE 299
In *Romance of the Three Kingdoms*, **Guan Yu** has to pass through five gates and defeat six generals in order to make his escape from Cao Cao's territory.

PRISON SCHOOL

PRISON SCHOOL ❼

Akira Hiramoto

Translation: Ko Ransom

Lettering: D. Kim

This book is a work of fiction. Names, characters, places, and incidents are the product of the author's imagination or are used fictitiously. Any resemblance to actual events, locales, or persons, living or dead, is coincidental.

PRISON SCHOOL Vol. 13, 14
© 2014 Akira Hiramoto. All rights reserved.
First published in Japan in 2014 by Kodansha Ltd., Tokyo.
Publication rights for this English edition arranged through Kodansha Ltd., Tokyo.

English translation ©2017 by Yen Press, LLC

Yen Press
1290 Avenue of the Americas
New York, NY 10104

Visit us at yenpress.com
facebook.com/yenpress
twitter.com/yenpress
yenpress.tumblr.com
instagram.com/yenpress

First Yen Press Edition: June 2017

Yen Press is an imprint of Yen Press, LLC.
The Yen Press name and logo are trademarks of Yen Press, LLC.

The publisher is not responsible for websites (or their content) that are not owned by the publisher.

Library of Congress Control Number: 2015373915

ISBN: 978-0-316-34618-4

10 9 8 7 6 5 4 3 2

BVG

Printed in the United States of America